DATE DUE

DEMCO 38-296

HOTEL, RESTAURANT, AND TRAVEL LAW:

A PREVENTIVE APPROACH

Fifth Edition

Delmar Publishers is pleased to offer the following books on
HOSPITALITY, TRAVEL AND TOURISM

- **Catering & Convention Services**
  Ahmed Ismail

- **Conducting Tours, 2E**
  Marc Mancini

- **Destination: North America**
  Dawne M. Flammger

- **Dining Room and Banquet Management, 2E**
  Anthony Strianese

- **Domestic Ticketing and Airfare**
  Linda Hood

- **Geography of Travel & Toursim, 3E**
  Lloyd Hudman and Richard Jackson

- **Hospitality and Travel Marketing, 2E**
  Alastair Morrison

- **Hosting the Disabled: Crossing Communications Barriers Group Travel, 2E**
  Martha Sarbey deSouto

- **Hotel, Restaurant and Travel Law, 5E**
  Norman G. Cournoyer, Anthony G. Marshall and Karen L. Morris

- **Hotel Sales & Operations**
  Ahmed Ismail

- **International Air Fares Construction and Ticketing**
  Helle Sorensen

- **International Travel and Tourism**
  Helle Sorensen

- **Introduction to Corporate Travel**
  Annette Reiff

- **Learning Apollo: Basic and Advanced Training**
  Talula Austine Gunter

- **Marketing & Selling the Travel Product, 2E**
  James Burke and Barry Resnick

- **Math for Food Service, 3E**
  Robert Haines

- **Passport: An Introduction to Travel & Tourism, 2E**
  David Howell

- **Practical Food & Beverage Cost Control**
  Clement Ojugo

- **Practical Guide to Fares and Ticketing, 2E**
  Jeanne Semer-Purzycki

- **Sabre Reservations: Basic and Advanced Training**
  Gerald Capwell and Barry Resnick

- **Selling Destinations: Geography for the Travel Professional**
  Marc Mancini

- **Travel Agency Management**
  Gerald Fuller

- **Travel Perspectives: A Guide to Becoming a Travel Agent, 2E**
  Susan Rice and Ginger Todd

- **Welcome to Hospitality: An Introduction**
  Dr. Kye-Sung (Kaye) Chon and Dr. Ray Sparrowe

Delmar,
At Your Service!

Delmar Publishers
an International Thomson Publishing company I T P®

HOTEL, RESTAURANT, AND TRAVEL LAW:

A PREVENTIVE APPROACH

Fifth Edition

Norman G. Cournoyer
Anthony G. Marshall
Karen L. Morris

Delmar Publishers

an International Thomson Publishing company I(T)P®

Albany • Bonn • Boston • Cincinnati • Detroit • London • Madrid
Melbourne • Mexico City • New York • Pacific Grove • Paris • San Francisco
Singapore • Tokyo • Toronto • Washington

NOTICE TO THE READER

...cts described herein or perform any independent analysis in connection with any ...es not assume, and expressly disclaims, any obligation to obtain and include infor-...

...afety precautions that might be indicated by the activities described herein and to ...ontained herein, the reader willingly assumes all risks in connection with such in-...

The publisher makes no representation or warranties of any kind, including but not limited to, the warranties of fitness for particular purpose or merchantability, nor are any such representations implied with respect to the material set forth herein, and the publisher takes no responsibility with respect to such material. The publisher shall not be liable for any special, consequential, or exemplary damages resulting, in whole or part, from the readers' use of, or reliance upon, this material.

Cover Design: Charles Cummings Advertising/Art, Inc.

Delmar Staff
Publisher: Susan Simpfenderfer
Acquisitions Editor: Jeff Burnham
Acting Developmental Editor: Judy Roberts
Production Manager: Wendy Troeger
Production Editor: Elaine Scull
Marketing Manager: Katherine M. Hans

For more information, contact:
Delmar Publishers
3 Columbia Circle, Box 15015
Albany, New York 12212-5015

International Thomson Publishing Europe
Berkshire House
168–173 High Holborn
London, WC1V7AA
United Kingdom

Nelson ITP, Australia
102 Dodds Street
South Melbourne,
Victoria, 3205 Australia

Nelson Canada
1120 Birchmont Road
Scarborough, Ontario
M1K5G4, Canada

International Thomson Publishing France
Tour Maine-Montparnasse
33 Avenue du Maine
75755 Paris Cedex 15, France

International Thomson Editores
Seneca 53
Colonia Polanco
11560 Mexico D. F. Mexico

International Thomson Publishing GmbH
Königswinterer Strasse 418
53227 Bonn
Germany

International Thomson Publishing Asia
60 Albert Street
#15–01 Albert Complex
Singapore 189969

International Thomson Publishing—Japan
Hirakawa-cho Kyowa Building, 3F
2-2-1 Hirakawa-cho, Chiyoda-ku,
Tokyo 102, Japan

ITP Spain/Paraninfo
Calle Magallanes, 25
28015-Madrid, Espana

    4 5 6 7 8 9 10 XXX 03 02 01 00 99

Library of Congress Cataloging-in-Publication Data
Cournoyer, Norman G.
    Hotel, restaurant, and travel law : a preventive approach / Norman
G. Cournoyer, Karen L. Morris, Anthony G. Marshall. -- 5th ed.
        p.   cm.
    Includes bibliographical references and index.
    ISBN: 0-8273-7536-0
    1. Hotels--Law and legislation--United States. 2. Hospitality
industry--Law and legislation--United States. 3. Travel agents-
-Legal status, laws, etc.--United States. I. Morris, Karen, 1950-
. II. Marshall, Anthony G. III. Title.
KF951.C6 1997
343.73'07864794--dc21
                                        97-13961
                                        CIP
                                        AC

CONTENTS

CONTENTS

PREFACE

Hotel, Restaurant, and Travel Law: A Preventive Approach, Fifth Edition, focuses on *prevention* as the means to minimize the number of lawsuits a hospitality establishment experiences. While it it true that good hospitality management means satisfying patrons and guests, it also encompasses protecting the business from the kinds of accidents, attitudes and incidents that can lead to legal cases. Most lawsuits can be prevented if management and staff are properly trained to recognize potential pitfalls and to guard against them. Throughout the five editions of this book one of the authors' primary objectives has always been to arm future industry personnel with the legal knowledge needed to prevent lawsuits against their companies.

Revised for Clarity and Critical Thinking

This fifth edition has been revised and updated to make this complex subject more approachable and understandable for students. We think this edition is a better tool for the development of critical thinking skills in managers—skills needed to adapt to the contemporary legal environment which includes new laws and regulations, high expectations by patrons, and many legal rights of employees. For example, this edition includes the following:

- **A new chapter** on casinos presents students with the law applicable to this fast-expanding addition to the hospitality industry.
- **The text** presents plain-English explanations of essential legal concepts. Also, each chapter includes many subtopics. The effect of both is to enable students to easily read and comprehend the material.
- **Case questions** engage readers at the end of most case examples, drawing together practices and principles.
- **End-of-chapter questions** expand review and discussion and add the challenge of applying legal principles to business situations.

Training Intelligent Management

This book is not intended to train students to be lawyers. Its goal is to enable managers to understand the law as it relates to the hospitality industry, to appreciate how a legal case proceeds in the courts, and to engage their lawyers more intelligently. It is important that managers recognize the legal ramifications of the policy and practices of their businesses and be able to apply legal principles to everyday operations. Without this knowledge and ability, avoidable accidents and illegal conduct will go unabated resulting in unfortunate and preventable lawsuits.

The book gives managers a base of expertise on which to build and includes the following:

- **Clearly defined legal terms** help students understand the important principles when they are first introduced, and to apply them to the cases we present and the law they are learning.
- **"Preventive Law Tips for Managers"** recast the main points of each chapter as review and practical advice.

Profiting from Real-World Experience

Above all, this book provides its readers with the opportunity to profit from the experience of others through the careful study of real lawsuits that resulted from mistakes of hotel and restaurant managers working in the field.

- **Case examples** detail recent legal situations and the reasoning of the courts. The examples present principles, facts, reasoning, and in-text case questions concisely to focus students on the most important lessons from each case.
- **Updated coverage** strengthens understanding of employment law, the Americans With Disabilities Act, sexual discrimination, other civil rights issues, negligence, dram shop liability and casino operations.

Organization

The fifth edition of *Hotel, Restaurant, and Travel Law* is organized in four units:

Unit 1, **Legal Fundamentals for the Hospitality Industry**, presents the sources and principles of hospitality law, basic court procedures, civil rights issues, and contract law.

Unit 2, **Negligence**, presents the legal principles relevant to this topic and many cases that help define the scope of obligations and liability.

Unit 3, **Relationships with Guests and Other Patrons**, explores the special obligations that hospitality businesses have to their different publics, and the obligations individuals owe those businesses, as well.

Unit 4, **Special Topics**, addresses food and alcohol liability, travel agent relationships, employment issues, franchising, copyright and trademarks, licensing, and casino law.

Supplementary Materials

The *Instructor's Guide* contains answers to the end-of-chapter questions, answers to in-text case questions, case briefs, and transparency masters.

Acknowledgments

The authors wish to express their appreciation to the reviewers who enhanced the quality of this book:

Christina M. Blanchet
Bay State College
Boston, Massachusetts

Erna Marquis
Johnson and Wales University
Providence, Rhode Island

Al Martin*
Johnson and Wales University
Providence, Rhode Island

G. Michael Harris, Jr.
Bethune-Cookman College
Daytona Beach, Florida

Jeanie Harris-Farace
Long Beach City College
Long Beach, California

Tomas Skartes
Grand Valley State University
Grand Rapids, Michigan

Peter Wilmarth
Madison Area Technical College
Madison, Wisconsin

*A special thanks goes to Professor Al Martin who provided research assistance for this edition and prepared the Instructors Guide.

Norman G. Cournoyer
Anthony G. Marshall
Karen L. Morris

ABOUT THE AUTHORS

Norman G. Cournoyer is a lawyer and Professor Emeritus at University of Massachussets, Amherst. A nationally recognized expert in hospitality law, zoning for service industries, labor management, computer applications, and econometrics for hospitality management, he has ten years experience owning and operating hotels and restaurants.

A widely published writer, Dr. Cournoyer has authored several texts, references, and directories for the hospitality disciplines. He has contributed scholarly journals and has published numerous studies for the Massachussets Department of Commerce and Development.

Dr. Cournoyer is currently president of Applied Econometrics and has served as consultant to Hilton Corporation, Sheraton Corporation, the U.S. Army, and Canadian National Marine Services, Inc.

Dr. Cournoyer holds a Juris Doctorate from American University, and an MBA in financial accounting and a Ph.D. in econometrics from the University of Massachussetts. He resides in Amherst.

Anthony G. Marshall, Dean of the School of Hospitality Management at Florida International University in Miami, Florida, is a nationally recognized expert in Risk Management and Hospitality Law. He is well known by members of the hospitality industry through his speaking engagements and journal publications.

Dr. Marshall serves as a board member of the Commission Scolaire of the Centre International de Glion, Switzerland; a board member of the Greater Miami Convention & Visitors Bureau and vice chair of the Board of Trustees of the Educational Institute of the American Hotel and Motel Association. He is the recipient of the American Hotel and Motel Association's "Lamp of Knowledge" award.

Dr. Marshall authors the column "At Your Risk" (21 issues per year) in *Hotel and Motel Management* magazine. He is publisher and editorial board member of the *Florida International University Hospitality Review*; and a member of the editorial board of the *International Journal of Hospitality Management*.

He earned a Juris Doctorate from the College of Law at Syracuse University and a Bachelor of Science in Hotel Administration from the University of New Hampshire.

Dr. Marshall resides on Key Biscayne, Florida.

Karen L. Morris is a lawyer, judge, and Professor of Law at Monroe Community College, in Rochester, New York where she teaches courses including Hospitality Law, Business Law, Constitutional Law, Criminal Law and Law 101. As a town judge she presides over criminal and civil cases, including lawsuits brought by and against hotels and restaurants.

She has published an instructional software program and a case study book, as well as articles in various publications on topics of interest to the hospitality industry.

Dr. Morris is the legal advisor to the New York State Restaurant Association, Rochester Chapter, and a past president of the Greater Rochester Association for Women Attorneys. She has also served as president of Alternatives for Battered Women, Inc., an organization that operates a shelter and administers support services. Her favorite volunteer activity is being a Big Sister in the Big Brother program.

Before becoming a professor, Dr. Morris was in-house counsel for a corporation that operates department stores throughout the United States, and thereafter a criminal prosecutor.

She has a Juris Doctor degree from St. John's University and a Masters of Law (LL.M.) in Trade Regulation from New York University.

TABLE OF CASES

UNIT I

Legal Fundamentals for the Hospitality Industry

CHAPTER 1

Introduction to Contemporary Hospitality Law

CHAPTER OUTLINE

Introduction

What is Law?

Sources of Law

Principles of Hospitality Law

Attributes of Law

INTRODUCTION

You are about to embark on an exciting study. Law is a unique and contemporary discipline with applications to our everyday lives. You will sometimes applaud a court's decision and at other times you will be perplexed at the outcome. But above all you will be fascinated, engaged, and sometimes surprised as you study hotel, restaurant, and travel law.

This chapter will introduce you to basic principles of law including its sources, some of its attributes, and important definitions. The chapter will also teach you how to read a case.

What is Law?

Law has many definitions. They include a body of rules to which people must conform their conduct; a form of social control; and a set of rules used by the courts in deciding disputes. The common denominator is that **law** consists of rules enforceable in court requiring people to meet certain standards of conduct.

Principles of Hospitality Law

Hospitality law covers a wide range of law applied primarily to restaurants, places that offer lodging to the public (referred to collectively as either hotels or inns), travel agents, and airlines. Much of this body of law also applies to recreational facilities such as health clubs, theaters, night clubs, and sports facilities, to mention only a few.

Balancing Rights and Duties

As you study hospitality law you will notice that the various lawmaking branches of government try to balance the interests of travelers with those of business proprietors. We will study in depth the legal rights and duties of the hotel guest and restaurant patron, as well as those of the innkeeper and restaurateur. While these rights and obligations are quite complex, at the basic level the hotel or restaurant owner must provide patrons a safe place in which to lodge or eat, and the customer must act within acceptable bounds and pay for the services received. Similarly, the duty of the travel agent is to provide travel services, and the responsibility of the traveler is to pay. Often the interests of the service providers and patrons conflict. As is its function, the law provides an organized set of rules to resolve these conflicts.

History of Hospitality Law

The history of hospitality law is not a proud one. It is based on a very low opinion of innkeepers. In fourteenth- and fifteenth-century England, innkeepers were believed to associate with robbers and even to help the robbers steal from the guests. To counteract innkeepers' supposed illegal activities, laws pertaining to inns and taverns were stringent and usually favored the guests.

A quotation from a book entitled, *The Inns of the Middle Ages* by W. C. Firebaugh, illustrates that strict laws were necessary to protect guests:

> *"[I]n the eyes of the law, the innkeeper, the pander and others of like standing were on the same footing. . . . In past ages, the tavern and innkeeper have been guide, philosopher, and friend to all the evil reprobates in his neighborhood."*

Today, innkeepers are in a different league from their fifteenth-century counterparts and enjoy a respectable reputation.

Another factor that contributed to the harshness of hospitality laws in prior times was the limited number of inns and therefore the relative monopoly enjoyed by the innkeeper. When competition is virtually nonexistent, unscrupulous businesspeople may take advantage of the situation. The law was the guest's primary protection. Today, of course, inns are no longer few and far apart. On the contrary, competition is keen.

Sources of Law

Our law comes from four main sources: the Constitution; statutes; common law (case law), and administrative law. The following material explains each of these sources.

Constitutional Law

The law embodied in the United States constitution is called **constitutional law**. It prescribes the organization of the federal government, including the executive, legislative, and judicial branches, and defines the powers of the federal government. As you will recall from early American history, the states were suspicious of the federal government. Having just overthrown England, the states wanted significant limitations on the authority granted to the federal government. As a result, its authority is limited to the delegated powers. **Delegated powers** are those powers expressly allocated to the federal government in the Constitution. All other authority was left to the states. Examples of delegated powers include the right to develop a system of money and the right to regulate interstate commerce. **Interstate commerce** is business affecting more than one state, as opposed to business done between two parties in the same state.

The process by which the federal government as well as other units of government adopt laws is called the **legislative process**. The Constitution defines the method by which **Congress**, the primary lawmaking body of the federal government, adopts laws. The legislative process is described in greater detail in Chapter 2.

The Constitution establishes important rights such as equal protection of the laws, freedom of speech, and freedom of religion. We will study more about civil rights in Chapter 3.

The Constitution also authorizes the federal government to enter treaties with other countries. Some of these treaties affect travel to foreign countries. We will study one of them in Chapter 13. Another treaty addresses international protection of a copyright, which is the exclusive right to reproduce certain types of works such as art work, literary works, and musical compositions. We will study this treaty in Chapter 15.

Statutory Law

The second source of our law is statutory law. **Statutory law** is law promulgated via the legislative process and generally agreed to by the executive (president, governor, mayor). A **legislature** is a lawmaking body whose members are elected to office by the citizenry. The elected members of the legislature are called **legislators**. We elect legislators at the federal level (members of the House of Representatives and Senators), the state level (state legislators) and the local level (county legislators, and city or town councilmembers). When a federal or state legislature adopts a law it is called a **statute**. When a local legislature adopts a law it is often called an **ordinance**.

Common Law

The third source of our law is **common law**, the legal rules that evolved not from statutes but rather from decisions of judges and customs and practices. Historically, it was called common law because it was intended to be common or uniform for the entire English kingdom. These customs and practices obtained their authority from the test of time. Common law was modified gradually as habits were modified, and as new inventions created new wants and conveniences and new modes of doing business.

Precedents.   A feature of a common law system that distinguishes it from other legal systems is its reliance on case decisions. A **case decision** is an interpretation of the law applied by a judge to a set of facts in a given case. The case decision becomes a **precedent**, that is, a basis for deciding future cases. If another judge at some later time is deciding a case with a similar issue (set of facts and law), the judge should consult the precedent for help in deciding the case. Absent a good reason not to follow precedent, the judge will likely decide the later case consistent with the earlier case. This process of following earlier cases is called "**stare decisis**" which is Latin for "the matter stands decided".

The purpose of stare decisis is to give some uniformity to the law. Since judges are expected to follow precedent, you can anticipate that the case law you study today will continue in effect until a court decides that a good reason exists to change it. Sometimes circumstances suggest that a decision made earlier is no longer appropriate. Perhaps the judge made a bad decision in the first case, or societal forces have changed suggesting a different outcome would be more in tune with the times. Under these circumstances a judge is not bound by stare decisis to follow the prior judge's decision. Rather, the judge can decide the case differently and may even adopt the opposite position. The new decision then becomes the precedent for subsequent judges addressing the same issue.

For example, the United States Constitution provides that we all have the right to equal protection under the law. What does that mean? In 1896 the highest court in our country, the United States Supreme Court, determined that racial segregation was consistent with the constitutional mandate of equal protection; facilities could be separate provided they were substantially equal. The case was *Plessy v. Ferguson*, 163 U.S. 537 (1896). Applying the doctrine of stare decisis, other courts throughout the country followed that ruling whenever segregation issues arose. Almost sixty years later, in *Brown v. Board of Education*, 347 U.S. 483 (1954), the Supreme Court reversed *Plessy* and held the exact opposite, the separate-but-equal doctrine, at least in connection with public schools, is inconsistent with the equal protection clause of the Constitution. The case was the legal death knell of segregation in other public facilities as well. Why did the court not follow precedent? It explained in its decision that circumstances and knowledge developed since *Plessy* had established that separate-but-equal worked to deprive black people of the range and quality of opportunities available to whites, and was thus inherently unequal. Therefore, the precedent was no longer acceptable.

In cases where judges are confronted with issues that have not been previously resolved, they will use their best judgment to determine the case after considering the facts, relevant social factors, other cases that may not be directly on point but analogous, and any other factors that may be helpful. Thereafter, that decision will be a precedent for future cases.

The common law has survived because, when coupled with stare decisis, it provides consistency to our law and yet its foundations are sufficiently flexible to develop and adapt to changes over time, including social and technological advances.

Relationship between Statutes and Common Law.   To some extent statutes and common law are intertwined. Sometimes statutes are ambiguously worded. If such a statute is relevant in a lawsuit, the judge in the case will have to interpret the law, that is, determine its meaning. The judge's decision in that case will become precedent for future cases.

For example, a statute in New York makes it a felony to cause physical injury to someone while using a dangerous instrument. The term "dangerous instrument" is defined as an article which, under the circumstances in which it is used, is readily capable of causing death or serious physical injury. In a recent case a defendant caused injury to his victim by beating him with a cane. The judge had to determine whether a cane was a dangerous instrument. Consistent with stare decisis, the judge first researched to determine if any other cases with the same issue had been previously decided. If so, the judge would have considered following that prior decision. No prior decision existed. Therefore, the judge analyzed all the facts and circumstances, reviewed the statute defining a dangerous instrument, and determined that the cane qualified. This decision will be precedent for the next case that presents the same issue.

Sometimes statutes are adopted to modify the common law. For example, common law imposed absolute liability on innkeepers for all goods of guests. If a guest's property was stolen while the guest was at the inn, the innkeeper was almost always liable. Massachusetts was the first state to change the common law rule by statute. That state's legislature passed a statute in 1850 that limited the liability of innkeepers for lost property. New York followed in 1853, and all states now have such a statute. We will study these laws in Chapter 9.

Administrative Law

The fourth source of law is administrative law. **Administrative law** refers to laws that define the powers, limitations, and procedures of administrative agencies.

An **administrative agency** is a governmental subdivision charged with administering legislation that applies to a particular industry. Administrative agencies have many names, including departments, commissions, bureaus, councils, groups, services, divisions, and agencies. Agencies exist at all levels of government, but generally they are part of the executive branch. Examples of administrative agencies include the following:

- The Federal Communications Commission, which oversees the communications/broadcasting industry;
- The Food and Drug Administration, which oversees food and pharmaceutical businesses; and
- The Consumer Product Safety Commission, which polices the safety of consumer products.

Some agencies are authorized to adopt laws relevant to the industry they administer. For example, the Occupational Safety and Health Administration not only investigates and enforces statutes addressing safety in the workplace, but also passes laws on the topic. Laws adopted by administrative agencies are called **regulations** to distinguish them from laws passed by legislators. Unlike legislators, the people who govern administrative agencies are not elected. Rather, they are appointed by elected officials.

Attributes of Law

Law is a dynamic discipline, always changing to adjust to societal transformations yet also striving to remain constant enough not to disrupt the legal order that has developed. Law can be both an exciting and difficult field to study. It is not a discipline with clear-cut rules whose application to factual situations is easy and obvious. Reasonable people can disagree on how and whether a particular rule of law applies in a given case. Confusion may result from the fact that different judges have decided seemingly similar cases differently. Sometimes the law on a particular topic may be unclear because it is in a developing stage, for example, when the law relating to new technological advances has not yet been crystallized. The law is further complicated by the fact that it can vary from state to state. Because of these challenges, the study of law can be difficult but rewarding.

The Role of the Judge

The role of the judge in our legal system is very significant. As we have seen, the judge both "makes" the law in cases where no precedent or statute exists, and interprets the law in cases where a statute applies. We will see that some judges also review decisions of other judges. The words "judge" and "court" are frequently used interchangeably.

Civil and Criminal Law

There are numerous classifications of law. One classification is civil and another is criminal. The differences are as follows.

1. In civil law a wrong usually is done to an individual. In criminal law the wrong is considered to be done against society at large and involves violation of a criminal statute.

2. The objective of a civil lawsuit is compensation for an injury. The objective of a criminal case is punishment of the wrongdoer.

3. The party who commences the lawsuit in a civil case is the injured person. The title of the case, which will normally be in italics throughout this book, includes that person's name. Thus the title of a civil case involving injury to the female coauthor of this textbook caused by one Mindy Sanders would be *Karen Morris v. Mindy Sanders*. The party who undertakes a criminal case is society-at-large, usually referred to as "The State," "The People of the State of . . .," or "The Commonwealth of . . ." Thus, a Massachusetts criminal case might be titled *The Commonwealth of Massachusetts v. John Doe*.

4. In a civil case the person who is suing hires and pays for his/her own lawyer. In a criminal case, society (e.g., The People of the State of Idaho) is represented by a lawyer paid by the government. The title frequently used for that attorney is district attorney and/or prosecutor.

Examples of Civil Law

The following are examples of civil law.

Contracts.   A **contract** is an agreement between two or more parties that is enforceable in court. If one person fails to abide by the agreement, the other can sue in court for breach of contract. Unlike statutes, which are laws made by legislatures, and unlike common law, which is law made by judges, contracts represent "law" made by individuals. Businesses in the hospitality industry enter numerous contracts on a regular basis including contracts with patrons and contracts with suppliers. We will study more about contracts in Chapter 4.

Torts.   A tort is a violation of a legal duty by one person causing injury to another. (Breaches of contractual duties, however, are not considered torts.) Included among the various torts are the following:

- **Negligence**, which means breach of a legal duty to act reasonably. For example, a hotel is negligent if it fails to fix a broken railing on steps. We will study negligence in Chapters 5, 6 and 7.

- **Trademark Infringement**, which means use of another company's business name or logo without permission. For example, a restaurant infringes a trademark if it adopts as its name the same name used by another restaurant in the same vicinity without the other restaurant's approval. We will study this tort in Chapter 15.

- **Fraud**, which is an intentional untruthful statement made to induce reliance by another person. For example, if a resort represents in its advertising that it has a golf course and it does not, this is fraud. We will revisit this tort in a number of contexts throughout the book.

Remedies in Civil Cases

The remedy sought by the injured party in a civil case is **damages**, meaning reimbursement for injuries. Different types of damages include compensatory and punitive. **Compensatory damages** include out-of-pocket expenses, such as medical bills, lost wages, and certain other losses for which a monetary amount is determined by a jury or, in a nonjury case, the judge. Such losses can include pain and suffering, meaning physical distress or mental anguish; loss of enjoyment of life, meaning inability by the plaintiff to continue to engage in those activities that brought joy or fulfillment before the injury; loss of consortium, meaning loss of the companionship and sexual relations of a spouse; and loss of services, meaning loss of the aid, assistance, and companionship of another person such as a parent.

Punitive damages, also called exemplary damages, refers to money over and above compensatory damages. Punitive damages are awarded to a plaintiff not for reimbursement of a loss but rather to punish or make an example of the defendant. They are awarded only in cases where the defendant's wrongful acts are aggravated by violence, malice, fraud, or similar wrong.

Examples of Crimes

Included among the many types of crimes are the following:

Theft of services, which is the use of services, such as a hotel room, with the intent of avoiding payment. We will study theft of services in Chapter 10.

Assault, which is intentionally causing physical injury to another person. We will read in Chapter 7 about the unfortunate circumstance of assaults occurring in hotel rooms where security is lax.

Rape, which is forceful sexual intercourse against the victim's will. As with assault, we will study in Chapter 7 about rapes occurring in hotel rooms.

Penalties and Remedies in Criminal Cases

The possible penalties for the commission of a crime include community service, fines, probation, jail, and, in some states, death. **Probation** is a system whereby criminal offenders remain out of jail but are supervised by a probation officer. What punishment will be applied in a given case is determined in part by statute and in part by the judge. The applicable statute will provide a range of sentences available to the judge. For example, in New York, the range of sentences for petit larceny (stealing merchandise valued at $1,000 or less) includes a jail sentence up to one year, a fine up to $1000, probation for up to three years, and unlimited community service. The judge must decide in each case what sentence within the range is appropriate for the particular defendant. The sentence will vary depending upon the facts of the particular case, the background and circumstances of the perpetrator, and the impact of the crime on the victim.

How to Read a Case

Judges' decisions are customarily written and recorded in books. These written decisions are called **cases**, and the books in which they are published are called **case books**. These cases are part of the common law. You will read many cases in your study of hotel and restaurant law. Although at first they may seem hard to understand, you will soon develop the skill necessary to read them with a high level of comprehension. To understand a case you should attempt to identify four elements as you read it: (1) the facts; (2) the issue; (3) the judge's decision; and (4) the reasoning supporting the decision. The facts are those circumstances that give rise to the lawsuit. The issue is the legal question that the parties have asked the judge to resolve. The decision is the judge's response to the issue. The reasoning is the basis and rationale for the decision.

After reading the case consider its implications vis-a-vis stare decisis; the implication of the decision informs hospitality managers how the law may be applied to their own situations. The application of legal principles to a wider population—not just the parties to a case—establishes the innkeeper's ability to predict how the law will be applied and therefore to prevent legal disputes before they arise. By understanding the implications of cases, the manager/owner can modify company and personnel policies to conform to the law.

The following is a case example. As you read it, write down the four elements as you come to them. Then compare your findings with the analysis that follows the case.

CASE EXAMPLE 1–1

Cooper Hotel Services, Inc. v. MacFarland
662 So.2d 710 (Florida, 1995)

In May, 1993, MacFarland sued Cooper Hotel for injuries she sustained when she slipped and fell in a bathtub while a guest at a Holiday Inn owned by Cooper Hotel. At trial, MacFarland testified that on the date in question, she turned on the shower in her hotel room bathtub and stepped into it . . . She explained that as she turned to wash the back of her body, she fell. She described the tub on that occasion as being "as slick as anything [she had] ever felt." Later in the proceeding, MacFarland introduced evidence showing that Cooper Hotel installed smooth-bottomed bathtub units in its Holiday Inn, though its own specifications for the hotel called for textured-bottomed tubs.

Cooper Hotel now argues that the evidence adduced at trial failed to establish that it breached a duty of care it owed to MacFarland. For that reason, Cooper Hotel contends MacFarland failed to prove her case of negligence . . .

[To be successful in this lawsuit] the plaintiff must show that the defendant failed to maintain its property in a reasonably safe condition, . . . Negligence however may not be inferred from the mere happening of an accident alone. . . .

In the instant case, the undisputed facts are that MacFarland fell and was injured in her hotel room bathtub; that Cooper Hotel's specifications for the construction of the hotel called for textured-bottomed tubs; and that inquiries made by hotel architects as to tubs that would meet specifications resulted in the installation of smooth-bottomed tubs.

The record shows that in response to the architects' inquiries, the manufacturer in fact recommended the smooth-bottomed tubs at issue, contending that the materials out of which they were made met all nonslip and other safety requirements, yet had the additional benefit of being easy to clean. The manufacturer also indicated that such units were the bathtubs of choice of several major hotel chains with the same safety concerns as Cooper Hotel. The evidence further showed that more than 300,000 showers had been taken without incident in the bathtubs at the Holiday Inn involved herein; that MacFarland, herself, had previously showered in safety in such tubs upon an earlier stay at the same Holiday Inn; and that the only two other reported incidents bearing any remote connection with the bathtubs on the same Holiday Inn premises were dissimilar to the one at bar.

It is undisputed that Cooper Hotel, as an innkeeper, is required to use ordinary care to keep its premises in a reasonably safe condition so that its guests may use them in the ordinary and reasonable way without danger. It is common knowledge, however, that a small amount of water in the bottom of a bathtub creates a slippery condition.

In the instant case, the record is devoid of evidence—expert or otherwise—to establish that Cooper Hotel breached its duty of care to MacFarland. MacFarland made no showing that Cooper Hotel failed to make diligent inquiries to secure proper tubs for the hotel establishment; that the smooth-bottomed tubs installed failed to meet the nonslip specifications required; that smooth-bottomed tubs do not or cannot offer the same nonslip performance as textured tubs regardless of the materials they are made of; that Cooper Hotel failed to properly maintain the tub in which MacFarland fell; that the tub was, otherwise, unreasonably dangerous; or that Cooper Hotel failed to warn MacFarland of a concealed peril of which it knew or should have known.

To the contrary, MacFarland showed only that she safely stepped into the tub while the water was running, and fell upon turning around. Viewed in the light most favorable to her, such evidence shows only that at some point during the course of her shower, the tub became slippery. The evidence, however, does not establish why.

Based on the foregoing, MacFarland failed to establish a prima facie case of negligence. We therefore conclude, as a matter of law, that a verdict should have been directed in favor of Cooper Hotel. . . .

Now the analysis of the four elements. The important **facts** are that MacFarland fell while using the shower; the hotel had installed smooth-bottom bathtub units; they were recommended to the hotel's architect by the manufacturer as satisfying all nonslip and safety requirements; while 300,000 showers had been taken in the hotel's tubs, no one else had been injured in a manner similar to plaintiff. The **issue** is—Did the hotel's choice of a floor for the bathtub units constitute negligence (carelessness)? The **decision** was no, the hotel was not negligent. The **reasoning** for that conclusion is that the plaintiff presented no evidence to suggest the hotel had failed to act reasonably. Instead, it inquired about appropriate bathtub flooring; plaintiff submitted no evidence to suggest that the hotel did not investigate the problem, or that the tubs were dangerous, or that the hotel maintained them in a dangerous condition. Therefore, there was no basis from which to conclude that the hotel was negligent. The implications of the decision is if a hotel owners/managers can demonstrate they acted in a reasonable manner to safeguard their guests, the plaintiff in a lawsuit may be unable to prove the hotel was negligent. The plaintiff will therefore lose the case.

Terms to Know

The following terms are defined in the glossary and appear regularly throughout the book. Familiarity with them will enhance your understanding of the course material.

Appeal	**Injunction**
Appellant	**Innkeepers, hoteliers, hotelkeepers**
Appellee	**Liability**
Defendant	**Patron**
Duty	**Plaintiff**
Guest	**Preventive law**
Guest room	**Restaurateur**
Hospitality law	**Transient**
Hotel, inn, motel	

Summary

Law is at once an exciting and challenging study.

Hospitality law is impacted by the history of innkeepers.

Our law comes from four sources—the Constitution, statutes, common law, and administrative law. In deciding cases, the rule of stare decisis encourages judges to decide cases with reference to precedents.

Numerous classifications of law exist, including civil and criminal. Civil law involves wrongs against individuals whereas criminal law involves wrongs against society.

When reading legal cases, the four main elements to identify are the facts, the issue, the decision, and the reasoning. The student should also consider the implications of the case.

Review Questions

1. How is law defined?
2. In what country did common law originate?
3. What is a precedent and how is it related to stare decisis?
4. Define tort and name two.
5. According to common law, who was liable when a guest's property was stolen from a room at an inn?
6. What changes have been made to the common law concerning liability to a hotel when guests' property is stolen?
7. What is the difference between common law and statutory law?
8. Name several differences between civil and criminal law.

9. Under what circumstances can a judge deviate from stare decisis?

10. What are the differences among the following: statutes, ordinances, and regulations?

11. When reading a case, what are the four elements to look for?

Discussion Questions

1. Why did the lack of competition among inns contribute to the development of laws that favored guests rather than innkeepers?

2. In what way does stare decisis enhance the stability of the law?

3. In what way is the common law able to adapt to changes in society?

4. If no precedent exists in a case, what factors will the judge use to decide it?

5. What is the difference between a plaintiff and an appellant?

Application Questions

1. Natalie, who is married with two children, was injured at a hotel due to its negligence. She broke her leg and suffered a back injury. As a result she was bedridden for five weeks, missed work during that time, and experienced considerable pain. What type(s) of damages should she be able to collect from the hotel?

2. The defendant in a criminal case has been found guilty of stealing several lounge chairs from a hotel. The lounge chairs were returned to the hotel unharmed. The applicable statute authorizes the judge to sentence the defendant to a maximum of one year in jail, fine him up to $1,000, and/or place him on probation for one year. The defendant is 23 years old and is unemployed. He had one prior conviction for stealing a pack of cigarettes from a grocery store. The sentence on that prior charge was a $100 fine. If you were the judge, what might be an appropriate sentence in this case? Why?

3. A criminal statute renders illegal touching without consent the "intimate body parts" of another person. Intimate body parts is defined as "sexual or other intimate body parts" of a person. Susan is a guest at a hotel that has a nightclub which arranged group seating for those interested. Susan participated in the group seating. While she was watching the nightclub act, a stranger sitting next to her began rubbing her knee and lower thigh. She brought criminal charges against him; he denied that the knee and lower thigh were intimate body parts. What is the issue in this case? If a precedent exists, what effect will that have on the decision? What do you think the decision will be? Why?

CHAPTER 2

Legal Procedures: Journey of a Case Through the Courts

INTRODUCTION

Conflicts can be resolved in a variety of ways. Some will grow into lawsuits and be heard in court. Others will be settled either before or after a lawsuit is begun. (In settling a case, the injured party may compromise and accept less than he originally sought.) Still other cases are resolved through alternative dispute resolution methods whereby a person other than a judge listens to both parties' positions and then either makes a determination concerning the merits of the case or assists the parties to develop a mutually acceptable resolution.

When a claim is asserted against a hospitality establishment, or if the establishment has a claim against an individual or a business, a decision must be made on how to proceed. A **claim** is a demand for a remedy, usually money, to compensate for a perceived wrong. Should the claim be settled? Should it be pursued in court? Is some form of alternate dispute resolution the best option? In answering these questions the owner or manager of the establishment must consider the merits of the claim, the cost in both time and money required to pursue the case, and the effect of the decision on future, similar cases. The costs include attorney's fees (which may be hundreds of dollars an hour), court fees (charged for the services of the court), expert witness fees, and the time of employees to oversee the case, work with the lawyer, and testify. These expenses are minimized if the case is settled early. Another factor that may impact the decision on how to handle a case is the wishes of the insurance company of the party being sued. Sometimes a hotel or restaurant's insurance coverage will allow the insurance company to determine whether to settle the case or pursue it.

The decision on how to proceed with the claim will vary from case to case as the relevant factors are weighed. A very small percentage of cases go to trial. Most cases are settled earlier in the proceedings due in large part to the costs involved. The decision on how to proceed with the claim may be the most important strategic decision in the entire case.

This chapter will acquaint you with fundamental legal procedure and describe what takes place throughout the various stages of a claim that is pursued in court. It will also explain different methods of alternate dispute resolution.

The Parties and Proof

Although the procedure for pursuing a legal case through the courts varies from state to state, certain practices are common. The **parties** to a lawsuit are the individuals in conflict, also referred to as **litigants**. A party may be a person, a business, or a governmental body. The **plaintiff** is the party who initiates the lawsuit. The plaintiff usually has suffered an injury or loss, and believes the defendant is responsible. The **defendant** is the party that the plaintiff has sued.

To be successful in the lawsuit plaintiff must prove that: (a) defendant violated the law; (b) plaintiff suffered an injury or loss; and (c) the cause of plaintiff's injury or loss was defendant's violation of the law.

The system of justice employed in the United States is an adversary system. It rests on the premise that when a lawsuit develops between two people, it will best be resolved if each party to the dispute vigorously pursues its side of the case against the other.

Commencing the Lawsuit

The lawsuit is begun by serving or filing a complaint and a summons.

The Complaint

The **complaint** is a document issued by the plaintiff which contains **allegations**, that is, unproven statements of the charges or claims against the defendant. The complaint informs the defendant of the basis for plaintiff's claims. Depending on the law of the state where the case is pursued, lawsuits are commenced by either filing the complaint with the appropriate court, and/or serving the complaint on the defendant. A complaint consists of three parts: (1) a statement showing the jurisdiction of the court; (2) details about why the plaintiff is suing the defendant; and (3) a claim for relief. Figure 2–1 shows a sample complaint.

SUPREME COURT OF ALBANY COUNTY
STATE OF NEW YORK

Nancy Lauter,
Plaintiff,
vs.
Randshire Hotel, Inc.   **COMPLAINT**
Defendants.

Plaintiff, complaining of the Defendant, alleges as follows:

1. Plaintiff lives in Detroit, Michigan.
2. Defendant operates a 120-room hotel located in Albany, New York.
3. On June 14, 199X, plaintiff was a guest in defendant's hotel. While plaintiff was walking through the hotel lobby carrying an expensive vase she had bought in a nearby antique shop, the heel of her shoe caught in a hole in the lobby rug. Plaintiff lost her footing and fell.
4. Defendant was negligent in permitting a hole to exist in the lobby rug.
5. As a result of the fall and due to defendant's negligence, plaintiff suffered serious physical injuries and the vase was broken. Plaintiff paid $29,000 in hospital and doctor bills for her injuries; she lost $13,000 in wages; and the vase was worth $3,500.

WHEREFORE, Plaintiff demands judgment in the amount of $45,000 with interest and costs and disbursements plus any additional relief as to the court may seem just and equitable.

DATED: September 12, 199X

By _____
Patricia Bordon, Esq.
Attorney for Plaintiff
25 Main Street West
Albany, New York 12204
518-555-1606

Figure 2–1 A complaint is a formal document that details allegations by the plaintiff against the defendant. Those allegations form the basis for the lawsuit.

Statement of Jurisdiction. **Jurisdiction** is the authority of a court to hear a case. Jurisdiction is determined by the legislature. No single court has the power to decide all kinds of cases. For example, the United States Bankruptcy Courts have the power to decide cases involving bankruptcy. If a catering patron with a large outstanding bill petitions the court for bankruptcy protection, the Bankruptcy Court will hear and decide the case. The same court does not have authority to hear such cases as contract disputes between a hotel and its employees, or claims that a restaurant supplier sold unhealthy food to a restaurant which was ultimately provided to a guest who became ill as a consequence of eating it. The statement of jurisdiction in the complaint must set forth facts that demonstrate that the court designated by plaintiff has the authority to decide the particular case.

Each state, as well as the District of Columbia and Puerto Rico, has its own system or network of courts, as does the federal government. Federal Courts have jurisdiction to hear two types of cases: (a) Lawsuits that involve the United States Constitution, a federal treaty, or a federal law—called collectively, federal questions; and (b) lawsuits that involve diversity of citizenship—that is, the plaintiff and defendant are from different states, or one is from a different country, and the amount of money in controversy exceeds $50,000. All other types of cases are heard in state court. See Figure 2–2 for an illustration of a typical state court system, and Figure 2–3 for an illustration of the federal court system.

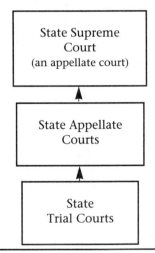

Matters of note:
1. Trial courts are called "courts of original jurisdiction" because they are the first courts to hear and decide a case. Examples of trial courts are city and town courts, county courts, family courts, and surrogate's courts.
2. A case that has been decided by a state supreme court can seek review by the United States Supreme Court, the highest court in the country.

Figure 2–2 State court systems include courts of original jurisdiction and courts of appeal. This diagram reflects the system adopted in most states, but not all states.

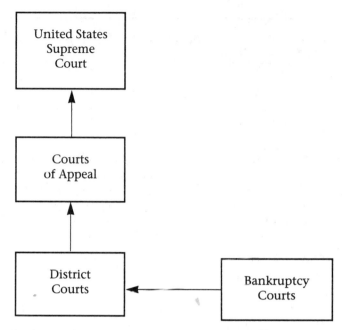

Figure 2–3   Federal courts hear two categories of cases: those dealing with federal questions and those involving diversity of citizenship and a minimum of $50,000 in controversy.

The Basis for the Claim.   The complaint must explain to the defendant and the court the facts on which the plaintiff's case is based. The complaint contains allegations—that is, unproven statements—detailing the occurrence which plaintiff alleges results in liability on the defendant.

The Claim for Relief.   The complaint must tell the court what the plaintiff wants the court to do, for example, award money.

In many states, once the complaint has been prepared, it must be filed with the clerk of the court. In this way, the court receives notice that a dispute exists. Once that is done, the adverse party must be notified that a suit has been filed so that a defense may be prepared. Notice is given by serving the complaint on the defendant. Most states specify the manner in which service must be made. In some states the complaint is served on the defendant before it is filed with the court.

The Summons

A summons is a document ordering the defendant to appear and defend the allegations made against him. It is served with the complaint. Among other things, it informs the defendant of the time within which he or she must respond to the complaint and the consequences of a failure to do so. A sample summons is provided in Figure 2–4.

SUPREME COURT OF ALBANY COUNTY
STATE OF NEW YORK

Nancy Lauter,
    Plaintiff,
       vs.
Randshire Hotel, Inc.,   **SUMMONS**
    Defendants.

YOU ARE HEREBY SUMMONED and required to appear in the Supreme Court of Albany County located at 1000 Ridge Road, in the City of Albany, County of Albany, State of New York, by serving an Answer to the annexed Complaint upon Plaintiff's attorney at the address stated below, within thirty days after service of this Summons and Complaint is complete. Upon your failure to so answer, judgment will be taken against you for the relief demanded in the annexed Complaint, together with the cost of this action.

DATED: September 12, 199X

                      By _____
                      Patricia Bordon, Esq.
                      Attorney for Plaintiff
                      25 Main Street West
                      Albany, New York 12204
                      518-555-1606

Figure 2–4   The summons is delivered to the defendant with the complaint. This is called "service of process."

Service of Process

Delivery of the summons and complaint to the defendant is known as **service of process**. The summons and complaint are known as "process". In most states these documents are filed with the court after which a specially appointed agent of the court serves them on the defendant. In other states they are served on the defendant before they are filed with the court. If the documents are properly served and the defendant fails to timely respond, the defendant loses the case by default. In such circumstances, plaintiff is entitled to a default judgment, that is, a court order summarily declaring plaintiff the winner of the lawsuit due to defendant's failure to defend.

Responses to the Complaint

After being served with the complaint, a nondefaulting defendant must do one of two things in response: either file motions addressed to some defect in the complaint; or, if defendant concludes that no defects exist, file an answer to the complaint.

Preliminary Motions.   A **motion** is a request to a judge for relief made while a lawsuit is ongoing. For example, motions may consist of a request for an extension of time, a request to clarify the allegations in the complaint, or a request that the suit be dismissed because the court lacks jurisdiction. Motions are usually made in writing.

After a motion has been filed with the court, attorneys for both the plaintiff and defendant appear at a hearing and argue their respective sides. The judge then either grants or denies the motion. The case proceeds in accordance with the ruling. For example, if the defendant makes a successful motion to dismiss because the court lacks jurisdiction, the case ends. Plaintiff may, however, file the case again in another court that does have jurisdiction. If the defendant makes a successful motion for clarification of the complaint, the case will continue but plaintiff will have to supplement the complaint with explanatory information.

The Answer.   If the case is not dismissed on motion, the defendant must serve an answer on the plaintiff and the court. The answer states the defendant's response to the allegations in the complaint, and presents facts defendant wishes to bring to the court's attention. Thus the answer serves the following purposes: it admits or denies the allegations made by the plaintiff in the complaint; it sets forth any defenses the defendant may have to the plaintiff's claim; and it states any claims the defendant may have against the plaintiff, that is, a counterclaim. A sample answer is provided in Figure 2–5.

SUPREME COURT OF ALBANY COUNTY
STATE OF NEW YORK

            Nancy Lauter,
              Plaintiff,
                 vs.
    Randshire Hotel, Inc.   **ANSWER**
              Defendants.

The Defendant, answering the Complaint:

1. Denies knowledge and information sufficient to form a belief as to the allegations contained in paragraph 1.
2. Admits the allegations contained in paragraph 2.
3. Concerning paragraph 3, admits that Plaintiff was a guest in Defendant's hotel on June 14, 199X; and denies each and every other allegation contained therein.
4. Denies each and every allegation contained in paragraph 4.

WHEREFORE, Defendant demands judgment dismissing the complaint against it.

DATED: October 8, 199X

                                        By _____
                                        Mark Fuller, Esq.
                                        Attorney for Defendant
                                        423 Monroe Street
                                        Albany, New York 12210
                                        518-555-4591

Figure 2–5   The answer is the defendant's response to the complaint.

Responses to the Answer

Motions Directed to the Answer.   After the defendant files an answer, the plaintiff is entitled to make motions relating to it. For example, plaintiff may move for a more definite statement if the answer is vague, or move to strike all or parts of defendant's answer because the information is redundant or immaterial.

Reply.   If the answer contains a counterclaim, plaintiff must issue a **reply**, which is a document much like an answer. It states the plaintiff's response to the allegations in the counterclaim.

Summary Judgment

The complaint, the answer, and the reply are known as **pleadings**. Once the pleadings have been filed and all motions relating to the pleadings have been made and ruled on by the judge, either party may make a motion for judgment on the pleadings. Such a motion, called a motion for summary judgment, asks the judge to decide the case in favor of the moving party without the need for a trial. This motion asserts that the opposing party's pleading has not raised any genuine issue in the case.

Pretrial Procedure

Once the pleadings have been filed and perhaps clarified through use of the various motions, the parameters of the legal dispute become apparent. Both parties know the general framework of the opponent's position. To win a lawsuit, a party must convince a jury that her version of the facts is the more probable one. So the second stage of the suit is devoted to the collection of facts and evidence with which to convince the jury.

Discovery

If justice is to be done, all facts and evidence must be equally available to both parties. The law does not permit one party to hoard evidence and surprise the adversary at trial when it may be too late to prepare a response. Rather, the law facilitates each side's obtaining evidence and information available to the other. This is done through the process of **discovery**—that is, the process by which each side obtains evidence known to the other side.

Discovery usually occurs after the filing of the complaint and answer and before the trial. Discovery may take one or more of several forms, such as: (a) written or oral questions (interrogatories and depositions, respectively) posed by one party to the other party or to a witness; (b) inspection of physical evidence that may be relevant to a case, such as a hotel elevator that malfunctioned; (c) review of documents or other evidence held by the adverse party or by a potential witness; and (d) if the mental or physical condition of one of the parties is in issue, a physical or mental examination of the party concerned.

A plaintiff or defendant who proceeds to trial without undertaking discovery forfeits a valuable opportunity to obtain information about the other party's case and is at a significant disadvantage.

Pretrial Conference

After discovery is completed, the judge and the opposing lawyers meet to prepare for the trial. The judge normally utilizes this opportunity to encourage the parties to reach a **settlement**, that is, a resolution of a dispute without a trial. Usually, when a settlement is reached, the plaintiff agrees to accept less than the amount sought in the complaint and the defendant agrees to pay part of the plaintiff's claim.

Although the parties may settle a case at any time, the period following discovery is particularly advantageous. Through discovery the parties have learned the strengths and weaknesses of their position and that of their adversary's and can realistically assess the chances of success at trial. A weak case will often prompt a party to seek a settlement. If the parties do not settle, the case proceeds to trial.

The Trial

After the preliminaries of serving the pleadings and gathering evidence, the attorneys present the case to an impartial tribunal—a judge or jury. This tribunal must weigh the evidence and render a verdict as required by the evidence and the law. This process whereby the parties present evidence and the judge or jury decides the issues is called a trial.

Just as rules regulate the pretrial process, rules regulate the trial's progress. These laws are designed to resolve the conflict in an orderly fashion.

The following trial procedure is generally followed in the states.

A. Selection of the jury

B. Opening statements

C. Plaintiff's case-in-chief

D. Defendant's case-in-chief

E. Plaintiff's case in rebuttal

F. Summation

G. Judge's charge to the jury

H. Jury's deliberations

I. The verdict

J. The judgment

Types of Trials—Jury and Bench

A case may be tried by a jury (called a jury trial) or by the judge (called a bench trial), depending on the wishes of the parties.

In a criminal case—one in which the state charges a defendant with a violation of the state's criminal law—the determination of whether or not to have a jury is made exclusively by the defendant. In a civil (noncriminal) case, if either the plaintiff or the defendant wants a jury, the case will be tried by a jury. Only if neither party desires a jury will the case be tried by a judge without a jury. Factors a party might consider when deciding whether to choose a jury trial include:

1. *Will my case benefit from emotional appeals?* For example, a child who became a paraplegic as a result of a dive in a hotel pool will evoke sympathy. Conventional wisdom suggests a jury is more apt to be swayed by emotional appeals than a judge because jurors are inexperienced in lawsuits whereas judges are exposed daily to difficult cases. A judge is therefore arguably more likely to be objective in evaluating the case.

2. *Will I be presenting technical evidence?* For example, the proof in an embezzlement case against a restaurant manager may include analysis of many checks and financial records. The proof in a case involving injuries caused by a faulty hotel escalator may require extensive evidence about the mechanical aspects of equipment. Jurors may be inexperienced listeners and tune out technical testimony. An experienced judge has a lot of opportunity to perfect listening skills.

3. *Is there anything about the case that may evoke distaste in a jury for me or my position?* For example, a defendant charged with a gruesome murder in a restaurant parking lot may choose a bench trial on the theory that a jury will likely develop animosity towards him when the testimony is presented.

Jury Selection

If the case is to be tried before a jury, the trial begins with the examination of prospective jurors, a process called **voir dire**. Prior to the date set for trial, people are randomly selected as potential trial jurors from the jury pool. The pool consists of registered voters, utility subscribers, licensed operators of motor vehicles, registered owners of motor vehicles, state and local taxpayers, recent high school graduates, and persons who have volunteered to serve as jurors, and other state-specific categories. Those selected are notified that they are to appear at the courthouse on a given day. The trial jurors are chosen from this group.

Most judges start the voir dire by asking jurors general questions, such as whether they know or are acquainted with either the plaintiff or defendant, their attorneys, or the judge. Jurors who answer affirmatively may be dismissed. When the judge has concluded general questioning, the attorneys ask more detailed questions.

Individual jurors may be challenged by either attorney for cause when, among other reasons, a juror expresses an inability to render an impartial verdict because of prior knowledge of the facts in the case, bias, or some other reason. If the judge agrees that the juror is ineligible for cause, the juror will be dismissed.

The attorneys also can make a limited number of peremptory challenges—that is, dismissal of potential jurors without a specific cause.

Opening Statements

An **opening statement** is a presentation to the jury outlining the proof each lawyer expects to present during the trial. Each lawyer has an opportunity to make an opening statement before any evidence is presented. The opening statement is the first exposure the jury has to the specific facts of the case.

The Case-in-Chief

After the opening statements, the plaintiff presents its evidence. Testimony is presented one witness at a time through a process of direct examination and cross-examination. The party who calls a witness questions that person first. This is called direct examination. The purpose of direct examination is to elicit pertinent information to help prove the party's claim. Next, opposing counsel questions the same witness, called cross-examination. The purpose of cross-examination is to discredit the witness. Once cross-examination is concluded, the party who called the witness may ask additional questions, called redirect examination, after which the opposing party will have an opportunity to recross.

After plaintiff has called all its witnesses, the defendant presents its case-in-chief in the same manner as the plaintiff.

The Plaintiff's Rebuttal Case

When the defendant has concluded its case, the plaintiff can present evidence in rebuttal. Suppose, for example, the plaintiff has sued a hotel for injuries sustained when the elevator malfunctioned and claims the hotel failed to inspect it properly. The hotel defends the case by introducing into evidence inspection records that indicate the elevator had been inspected and serviced at frequent intervals. The plaintiff, in its rebuttal case, may present evidence showing that the inspection records had been altered and, in fact, the elevator had not been inspected for a long period of time.

Summation

After the cases-in-chief and the plaintiff's rebuttal, the attorneys summarize the case, called summations or closing statements. Summations allow the attorneys to review for the jury the contentions of their respective sides and to demonstrate how the evidence supports these contentions. In many states, the plaintiff proceeds first, followed by the defendant and concluded by the plaintiff, who gets a last opportunity to respond to defendant's closing argument. In other states, the defendant gives a summation first, followed by the plaintiff.

Charging the Jury

After the summations, the judge informs the jury of the law that is applicable to the case. For example, in a case that involves a question of negligence, the judge will instruct the jury on the law of negligence and will explain what that term means. The judge will inform the jury that unless they find from the evidence presented in court that the defendant was negligent within the legal meaning of that word, they cannot return a verdict for the plaintiff. In effect, the judge gives the jury a short course on the principles of law applicable to the case.

Jury Deliberations

Once the jury has heard the evidence and the applicable law, it retires to a jury room to consider the evidence. The jury first makes findings of fact. Despite contradictory evidence, the jury must determine what happened in the case. For example, a jury may be called upon to determine whether or not the food served at a restaurant caused the plaintiff's illness. As fact finder, the jury has a large degree of discretion in deciding what evidence to believe and what evidence not to believe. When the jury has decided what actually happened, it considers whether, based on the law as told to them by the judge, the defendant has violated the law. For example, if the food served at the restaurant did cause plaintiff's injuries, does the law impose liability on the restaurant under the circumstances? Thus we may identify two separate processes that take place during jury deliberations: (1) determination of the facts; and (2) determination of how the law applies to the facts in the given case.

The Verdict

The verdict is the jury's decision in a case. In most states, to have a verdict, the jury must reach a unanimous decision that the defendant is either liable or not liable. In some states agreement by most but not all the jurors is sufficient for a verdict. If less than the necessary number of jurors are in agreement the jury is "hung," the judge will declare a mistrial, and the plaintiff can begin again with a new jury.

The Judgment

A judgment is the official decision of a judge about the rights and claims of each side in a lawsuit. A verdict is not binding on the losing party until the court has entered judgment on the verdict. Basically, this means that the attorney for the losing party will have a chance to attack the verdict after it is issued by the jury and before the judge issues a judgment. The attorney may pursue any one or more of the following procedures after the verdict and before the judgment.

1. Ask that the jury be polled to ensure that the necessary number of jurors were in agreement.
2. Ask for judgment notwithstanding the verdict, that is, an order from the judge reversing the jury's decision.
3. Ask for a new trial on the grounds of an erroneous ruling of the judge during the trial, a prejudicial statement improperly heard by the jury, or improper charge by the judge.
4. Ask for a remittitur—a claim that the amount of money awarded by the jury was unreasonable.

If the trial judge denies these motions, a judgment on the verdict is entered.

Appeal

Grounds for Appeal

An **appeal** is a complaint made by a litigant to a superior court that a trial judge committed an error, and a request that the superior court correct the error. Appellate courts have the authority to review the handling and decision of a case tried in a lower court. Many events at a trial occur rapidly. The decisions a judge makes during trial must, by necessity, be made without much time for deliberation. For this reason, mistakes will be made from time to time. These mistakes may entitle a party to an appellate court review of the proceedings of the trial. Appeals occur in a calm and reflective environment removed from the passions and speed of the trial.

Appellate Courts

An appellate court is very different from a trial court. In appellate courts there are no juries. Whereas a trial court consists of one judge, an appellate court consists of three to nine judges. To reverse the results of a trial, the vote of a majority is necessary. To appeal, the attorneys first submit **briefs**, or written arguments. Briefs attempt to convince the court that the trial judge was right or wrong, depending on the position of the party submitting a particular brief. Sometime after submission of the briefs, the case will be scheduled for oral argument, at which time the attorneys argue their positions in person before the court, and the judges have the opportunity to ask questions. The court will thereafter issue its decision in a written opinion justifying its conclusions.

The appellate court can do any of the following: affirm the decision of the lower court, in which case the judgment stands; reverse the decision of the lower court and order a new trial; or order the case to be dismissed altogether.

Normally, each party has a right to appeal to at least one appellate court. However, the right to an appeal to the highest appellate court—the state supreme court in most state court systems, or the U.S. Supreme Court in the federal court system—is restricted. The party seeking to appeal must demonstrate that his case falls into one of the limited categories for which appeal to the highest appellate court is permitted by law. Even if this can be demonstrated, the highest appellate court may still, in many cases, refuse review in its own discretion. For example, the U.S. Supreme Court hears only about one out of every fifteen cases seeking that court's review.

Alternative Dispute Resolution

The cost to pursue or defend a lawsuit can be very high, including attorney's fees, court costs, witness fees, and the parties' time away from work. In civil cases, a number of alternatives to trial exist, called collectively Alternative

Dispute Resolution (ADR). They are usually less formal, quicker, and less expensive than a trial. More and more, litigants are choosing ADR and some courts are even requiring it.

Methods of ADR include arbitration, mediation, and summary trials. **Arbitration** is a process in which a dispute is submitted for resolution to an **arbitrator**, an objective third party who may or may not be a lawyer. An informal hearing is held at which evidence is presented. After the hearing is completed the arbitrator will decide who should win the case. The parties pay a fee for the services of the arbitrator.

Mediation is a process in which a **mediator** facilitates discussion and negotiations between the parties to the dispute in an informal setting. Unlike an arbitrator, the mediator does not impose a decision. Rather, the mediator assists the parties in reaching a settlement of their dispute. The parties pay a fee for the services of the mediator.

Summary jury trials are used in federal courts. The parties present their arguments to a jury without using witnesses. The jury renders a nonbinding decision and the law requires the parties to negotiate their dispute after the jury rules. Since no witnesses are used, the process is much faster than a trial. If the negotiations do not result in a settlement, either side can demand a trial.

The high cost of trials in both money and time suggest the trend toward ADR will continue to grow.

Interpreting a Case Citation

Throughout the book you will see case citations. A **citation** is a reference to a legal authority such as a court decision, a statute, or a treatise. A case citation will appear as follows: 88 N.Y.2d 99 (1996). Each part of the citation provides important information to aid the reader in locating the case. The middle section refers to a set of books that contains case decisions written by judges. In the referenced citation, "N.Y.2d" refers to the second series of a set containing cases from the highest court in New York.

Books in sets are numbered sequentially. The first number in the citation identifies the volume within the set in which the case is located. The second number identifies the page within the volume on which the cited case begins.

In the citation 88 N.Y.2d 99 (1996), the cited case begins on page 99 of the 88th volume in the New York Second set of books in the library.

The date in parenthesis identifies the year in which the case was decided. Thus, in this example, the case was decided in 1996.

As another example, consider the following federal court of appeals citation: 76 F.3d 320 (3rd Cir., 1996). The case begins on page 320 of the 76th volume of the set of books entitled, *Federal Reporters, 3rd series.* "3rd Cir." means Third Circuit, which is the geographical location of the country in which the court is located. The United States is divided into twelve circuits for purposes of distinguishing federal district courts. To assist your understanding of the material, throughout this book the authors will include in Federal Reporter citations the state in which the case originated rather than the circuit.

Summary

Claims can be resolved by lawsuits, settlement, and alternative dispute resolution. Which method to pursue in a given circumstance is an important question that should be decided only after careful review of the case.

The stages of a lawsuit include the pleadings, pretrial procedures, the trial and appeals. The purpose of the pleadings is to identify the factual issues in the case. The purpose of pretrial procedures is to eliminate surprises at trial. The objective of the trial is to determine the facts of the case and how the law applies to the facts. The reason for an appeal is to provide an opportunity to correct an erroneous ruling.

The specific steps in a lawsuit are as follows:

COMMENCING THE LAWSUIT
    The Complaint
        Statement of jurisdiction
        The basis for the claim
        The claim for relief
    The Summons
    Service of process
    Responses to the complaint
        Preliminary motions
        Answer
    Response to the answer
        Motions directed to the answer
        Reply
    Summary judgment motion
PRETRIAL PROCEDURE
    Discovery
    Pretrial conference
THE TRIAL
    Selection of the jury
    Opening statements
    The cases-in-chief
    Plaintiff's rebuttal
    Summations
    Charge to the jury
    Jury deliberations
    The verdict
    The judgment
APPEAL

Alternative dispute resolution methods include arbitration, mediation and summary trials. These options are quicker and less expensive than lawsuits.

Preventive Law Tips for Managers

If You Are the Plaintiff

- *Avoid Needless Motions—Be Sure the Allegations in Your Complaint Are Clear and the Court Has Jurisdiction.* Motions delay the trial and may be costly, both in attorney's fees and court costs. Avoid motions seeking a clearer statement in the complaint of the basis for the lawsuit by including in the original complaint adequate detail to inform the defendant of the grounds for the case. Similarly, the court identified in the complaint should be one that has jurisdiction of the case. If not, the defendant will make a motion for dismissal and it will be granted. Ask your lawyer to verify that the complaint is sufficiently detailed and the case is brought in the proper court.

- *Avoid a Summary Judgment—Be Sure the Allegations in Your Complaint Amount to A Legal Wrong.* If your claims against the defendant do not constitute a violation of law, the defendant will make a motion for summary judgment and it will be granted. The lawsuit will be over almost before it started. You will have incurred numerous expenses for naught— lawyer's fees, court fees, and service of process fees. To avoid this distasteful outcome, always discuss with your lawyer whether your case is properly grounded in law.

If You Are the Defendant

- *Avoid a Default Judgment!* A default judgment means you lose automatically, without the opportunity for a trial. This results from the defendant's failure to respond to the complaint. Immediately upon receipt of a complaint, you should contact your lawyer. With your lawyer, prepare and serve an answer to the complaint within the allotted time period, thereby avoiding the default judgment.

Concerns for Both Plaintiffs and Defendants

- *Avoid Needless Motions—Be Sure the Allegations in Your Answer are Clear.* Avoid costly motions seeking a clearer statement of the information in the pleadings by including in the original answer adequate and intelligible detail, thereby enabling the other party to understand the contents.

- *Avoid Unnecessary Court and Trial Costs—Consider Alternative Dispute Resolution.* Not every dispute should result in a lawsuit. Court cases are expensive in time and money. In appropriate situations, much time and money can be saved by pursuing alternative dispute resolution such as arbitration. Determinants include the type of case involved, the amount of money in issue, and whether the dispute is a factual or legal one.

Consider whether your case is better pursued in a more efficient forum than a court.

- *Avoid Surprises At Trial—Undertake the Necessary Discovery.* Do not over-look the importance of the discovery phase of the lawsuit. Discovery proceedings provide the means to obtain much information about your opponent's case. If you do not take advantage of these procedures, you may be surprised at trial with evidence you did not expect. In such circumstance your opportunity to locate evidence with which to rebut the surprise testimony will be greatly handicapped by lack of time. Prepare ahead and avoid the unexpected.

- *Avoid an Unnecessary Trial—Settle if Appropriate.* In many cases settlement is an appropriate resolution. After discovery is complete, the parties should have a good idea of the strengths and weaknesses of their respective cases and thus the likelihood of success. With the resulting bargaining power that the information gives, you should make an earnest effort to resolve the case without the considerable expense of trial.

Review Questions

1. How is a lawsuit begun?
2. What is jurisdiction?
3. What is contained in a complaint?
4. What is a counterclaim?
5. What happens if the defendant does not respond to the complaint?
6. What is the name given to the procedure for examination of prospective jurors?
7. What does the judge do when charging a jury?
8. What is a motion? Name two types of motions that might be made during a trial.
9. What is an appellate court?
10. Name two differences between a trial and an appellate court hearing.

Discussion Questions

1. What role do the pleadings play in a lawsuit?
2. What role does discovery play in a lawsuit?
3. Why, in the case of a hung jury, is the prosecutor entitled to retry the case?
4. Why do most states require that the jury be unanimous for a verdict?
5. Why do different courts have different types of jurisdiction?

Application Questions

1. Assume that you live in California and are on vacation, travelling by car from California to Texas. You are injured in a motel room when the bed on which you are sleeping collapses, causing you to fall to the floor. You suffer substantial back and leg injuries, requiring many medical treatments and causing you to miss work for fifteen weeks. Your doctor bills total $16,000, and your lost wages are $9,000. You intend to sue the owner of the Texas motel. Can you bring your case in federal court? Why or why not?

2. If you were the defendant in the following cases, would you opt for a jury trial or a bench trial? Why?

   a. A 12 year old guest at a hotel broke her spine and became a quadriplegic as a result of a dive she took into a hotel pool. Plaintiff claims the hotel was at fault for not maintaining the water in the pool at required levels.

   b. A guest in a hotel is suing the hotel because a receptionist assaulted her. The receptionist admits to the assault but claims that the guest was intoxicated at the time and threatening to hit the receptionist because he would not disclose the room number of another guest.

   c. Matt, a state senator, is charged with bribery. The legislature is debating a bill that would reduce the drinking age from 21 to 19. Matt is accused of accepting money from several bars and restaurants in exchange for his promise to vote for the bill.

3. What information would you try to obtain through discovery in the following cases? What methods of discovery would you use to obtain that information?

   a. A child was riding on the ferris wheel at an amusement park. Something malfunctioned and the seat in which the child was riding dropped 60 feet with the child in it. The fall killed the child. Assume you are the child's parent and you are considering a lawsuit against the amusement park.

   b. Inez is a guest at a hotel. She returns to the hotel after an evening out. While she is walking to her hotel room she trips in the lobby. She claims to have suffered two broken ribs, a painful injury to her back and a broken ankle. She further claims the hotel is at fault and sues for $1,000,000. Assume you are the vice-president of the hotel responsible to oversee legal cases.

CHAPTER 3

Civil Rights and Hospitality Businesses

INTRODUCTION

According to common law, a hotel with a vacancy cannot refuse accommodations to a guest desiring to stay at the inn. (A few exceptions are discussed in Chapter 10, Rights of Innkeepers.) Because travelers need rooms in which to stay while they are away from home, hotel accommodations are viewed by the law as quasi-public, creating a duty on the part of innkeepers to accept all transients who come seeking accommodations.

Until the 1960s, this common law rule was largely ignored in southern hotels which regularly practiced discrimination, particularly against blacks. Most wronged guests were discouraged from bringing lawsuits by the expense involved.

This common law rule did not apply to restaurants. Before the advent of civil rights laws (statutes that prohibit discrimination), a restaurant owner could refuse any person, including blacks and other minorities, without violating the law. Many restaurant proprietors did discriminate.

In the aftermath of the Civil War, Congress enacted a series of civil rights acts intending to implement the constitutional mandate of equal protection of the laws. Relevant to hospitality law is section 1981 of the Civil Rights Act of 1866 which reads as follows:

> *"All persons within the jurisdiction of the United States shall have the same right in every State and Territory to make and enforce contracts, . . . and to the full and equal benefit of all laws . . . as is enjoyed by white citizens . . .".*

These early civil rights acts were seldom invoked prior to the passage of an additional Civil Rights Act a century later. As a result of hotels, restaurants and others withholding services to blacks, numerous confrontations including protest marches, sit-ins, and demonstrations occurred in the 1950s and 1960s. Many turned violent. It was not a proud time in the history of hospitality law.

The Civil Rights Act of 1964

Against this backdrop Congress passed the historic Civil Rights Act of 1964 (hereafter "the Act").[1] **Civil Rights** are the personal rights that derive primarily from the Constitution, such as free speech, freedom of contract, privacy, and due process, to mention just a few. The act outlaws discrimination on the basis of race, color, religion, and national origin in most hotels, restaurants, and places of entertainment. **Discrimination** means failing to treat all people equally. The general intent and overriding purpose of the Act was to end discrimination in hospitality facilities open to the public, thereby eliminating the unfairness and humiliation of racial discrimination as well as the difficulty and inconvenience discrimination created for blacks who wish to dine out. The Act set the stage for eventual desegregation and a new social order. It was the death knell of Jim Crow, the name given to the unequal treatment of blacks in education, social circumstances, and transportation sanctioned by either law or tradition. No longer could hotel owners refuse to provide rooms to blacks. No longer could a restaurant provide sit-down services for whites and restrict blacks to take-out service. No longer could restaurants set aside a particular room and shepherd all black customers to it, separated from the white customers.

---

[1]42 U.S.C. Section 2000a et seq.

As far reaching as the Act is, it left some gaps. For example, it does not cover discrimination based on gender, marital status, or disability. Bars are not expressly covered, nor are stores or schools. To remedy these omissions, most states have passed their own laws extending protection to groups and facilities not otherwise covered by the Act. Discrimination based on disability is now prohibited by the Americans With Disabilities Act, a federal law which became effective in 1992.

This chapter will discuss: (a) what the 1964 Civil Rights Act covers; (b) what state statutes cover; (c) the Americans With Disabilities Act; (d) exceptions to civil rights laws (permissible discrimination); and (e) implications of these statutes for service industry managers.

Scope of the Act

The Act outlaws discrimination based on any of four factors: 1) race; 2) color; 3) religion; and 4) national origin. To be illegal under the Act, the discrimination must occur in one of four types of establishments and then only if the establishment is engaged in interstate commerce. The four places covered by the Act are: 1) lodging facilities for transients; 2) dining facilities; 3) places of entertainment; and 4) gasoline stations. **Interstate commerce** means business transactions between people or companies from two or more states and will be explored in more detail later in this chapter.

To achieve the goal of ending discrimination, courts construed the Act broadly to include within its reach the maximum number of incidents of discrimination. A single act of illegal discrimination violates the Act; a pattern of discriminatory conduct is not required. *Hughes v. Marc's Big Boy*, 479 F.Supp. 834 (Wisc., 1979). The following is a discussion of each of the four areas where the Act prohibits discrimination.

Lodging for Transients

The Act defines overnight accommodations covered by it as, "any inn, hotel, motel, or other establishment which provides lodging to transient guests." Court decisions have determined that the following establishments are included: places that rent rooms not only by the night but also weekly; YMCAs; trailer parks that rent to short-term guests; and cottages at beach resorts.

Dining Facilities

The dining facilities covered by the Act are "any restaurant, cafeteria, lunchroom, lunch counter, soda fountain, or other facility principally engaged in selling food for consumption on the premises . . . if its operation affects [interstate] commerce." Court decisions have determined that the following establishments are included: drive-in restaurants, retail store lunch counters, sandwich shops, lunch counters at golf courses, food facilities at hospitals, and like establishments.

Places of Entertainment

The Act prohibits discrimination in "any motion picture house, theater, concert hall, sports arena, stadium or other place of exhibition or entertainment" that "affects commerce." Such an establishment affects commerce if it regularly presents movies, performances, exhibits, athletic teams, or other sources of entertainment that are imported from other states. The catch-all phrase "places of entertainment" includes both establishments that present shows for viewing by an audience, such as an auditorium staging a rock concert, and establishments that provide recreational or other activities in which patrons actively participate, such as bowling alleys.

According to case law, a youth football association that used equipment manufactured outside the state was a covered place of entertainment, and a theater group that imported travelling shows qualified. Golf courses that purchase from out of state carts, pro shop inventory, rental equipment, or related items likewise would qualify.

Jurisdiction Through Interstate Commerce

Why must a hospitality business affect interstate commerce to be covered by the Act? As we discussed in Chapter 1, when our country was formed, the states were very jealous of a strong central government. They had the bad taste of England's autocratic rule in mind when they crafted the Constitution, so they reserved much lawmaking authority to the states. The only powers given to the federal government were specifically listed in the Constitution. These powers are called the "delegated powers." Congress, the legislative body of the federal government, can only pass laws that address delegated powers. One of these areas of authority designated for Congress is **interstate commerce**, that is, business done between people or companies from two or more states. Thus, Congress can pass laws dealing with interstate commerce; it does not have the authority to outlaw discrimination in establishments that are purely local. Those establishments are governed by state or local law.

Serving Interstate Travelers.   Normally, food establishments do not inquire whether their patrons are residents of the state or from another state. The courts have devised certain rules to determine whether a restaurant services interstate travelers. A dining facility located near a federal highway will be deemed to serve interstate travelers. A coffee shop in a hotel is likewise assumed to serve interstate travellers since most of a hotel's guests are travellers and it is likely that some will be from out of state. If it advertises in a magazine delivered to hotels and motels for distribution to guests, and advertises on the radio, the restaurant qualifies because the magazine and radio advertisements reach out-of-state readers and listeners. In one case a restaurant in Puerto Rico argued that it was not engaged in interstate commerce noting that it was not located at an airport or on an interstate highway. However, the restaurant was located in a primary tourist area near several large hotels. The court held that the restaurant's location was sufficient evidence that it serves interstate travelers. *Bermudex Zeonon v. Restaurant Compostela, Inc.*, 790 F.Supp. 41 (USDC, Puerto Rico, 1992).

Using Food Moved In Interstate Commerce.   A dining facility that does not serve interstate travelers will nonetheless be covered if a substantial portion of the food it serves was imported from another state. Although the statute does not provide a test for determining "substantial," precedents provide guidelines. Cases have held that, where ingredients in three of four items sold by a snack bar (hot dogs, hamburgers, milk and soft drinks) were from out of state, the "substantial portion" test was satisfied. *Daniel v. Paul*, 395 U.S. 298, 23 L.Ed.2d 318, 89 S.Ct. 1697 (1969). In another case the requirement was met where 46 percent of an establishment's purchases was meat bought from a local supplier who purchased it from outside the state. *Katzenbach v. McClung*, 379 U.S. 294, 13 L.Ed.2d 290, 85 S.Ct. 377 (1964). Also qualifying as substantial was a snack bar at a beach club that purchased syrup used in Coca-Cola beverages from outside the state. Many of the purchases at the snack bar were for cold drinks, and Coca-Cola was the most popular. *United States v. Landowne Swim Club*, 894 F.2d 83 (3rd Cir., 1990).

Relief

The Act provides several kinds of relief for people who have been discriminated against illegally. The possibilities include:

1. *Injunctive relief*, that is, a court order that requires a party to refrain from doing a particular act. In Civil Rights Act cases, an injunction usually orders the offending person or business to stop discriminating. It is a preventive measure that guards against future injuries rather than affording a remedy for past injuries.

2. *Reasonable attorney's fees* charged by the attorney for a successful plaintiff. This is unusual in the law; in most lawsuits the parties pay for their own attorneys. Even a successful plaintiff is normally not entitled to collect attorney's fees from the defendant. The policy reason for allowing attorney's fees in cases involving civil rights violations is the legislature's recognition of the importance of eradicating discrimination. By eliminating attorney's fees as a deterrent for bringing a civil rights lawsuit, victims of discrimination are more likely to pursue the wrongdoer.

Enforcing the Act

Facilities that had discriminated before the passage of the Act did not embrace the new law. Many sought to challenge the Act's legality. Indeed, the constitutionality of the Act was tested immediately after its passage in two landmark cases involving recalcitrant proprietors who resisted the law. (A **landmark** decision sets an important precedent sometimes marking a turning point in the interpretation of law.)

Establishing Jurisdiction

The first landmark case challenging the Act involved a hotel and the second, a restaurant. In the first case, plaintiff, a corporation that owned and operated a 216-room motel in Atlanta, Georgia, did not rent rooms to blacks before the passage of the Act. When charged with violating the Act, plaintiff claimed he was not engaged in interstate commerce and therefore application of the Act to its business exceeded congressional power. The suit was filed in an effort to perpetuate that policy and invalidate the Civil Rights Act. The evidence established that plaintiff solicited guests from outside the state of Georgia through various national advertising media and also maintained over fifty billboards and highway signs within the state. The motel accepted convention trade from outside Georgia, and approximately 75 percent of registered guests were from out of state.

The court upheld the application of the Act to plaintiff as constitutional, pointing out that the evidence proved the motel served interstate travelers. *Heart of Atlanta Motel, Inc. v. United States*, 379 U.S. 241, 13 L.Ed.2d 258, 85 S.Ct. 348 (1964).

In the second test case of the Act's constitutionality, a family-owned restaurant in Birmingham, Alabama—Ollie's Barbecue—catered to a family and business trade, with only take-out service available for blacks. The restaurant purchased much of its meat, as well as other products, from out of state. The restaurant denied that it was engaged in interstate commerce. The court upheld the application of the statute to the restaurant, concluding that Congress acted within its power to protect and foster commerce by extending the coverage of the Civil Rights Act to restaurants that serve either interstate travelers or food purchased from out of state. *Katzenbach v. McClung*, 379 U.S. 294, 13 L.Ed.2d 290, 85 S.Ct. 377 (1964).

The hotel and restaurant involved in these cases both argued that if they were required to serve blacks they would lose a substantial amount of business from whites who did not wish to dine with blacks or stay in a hotel that accommodated them. The district (lower) courts accepted this argument and barred government officials from enforcing the Civil Rights Act against the businesses involved in the two cases. The United States Supreme Court, which granted certiorari in both cases and heard the appeals, rejected loss of business as a justification to avoid the mandates of the Act. The high court noted that enforcement of the Act would increase business by expanding the potential clientele. Interstate commerce would likewise be expanded. Said the court, referencing testimony in Congress in support of the Act prior to its passage,

> *A comparison of per capita spending by Negroes in restaurants, theatres, and like establishments indicated less spending, after discounting income differences, in areas where discrimination is widely practiced. . . . This diminutive spending springing from a refusal to serve Negroes and their total loss as customers has . . . a close connection to interstate commerce. The fewer customers a restaurant enjoys the less food it sells and consequently the less it buys. . . . Moreover there was an impressive array of testimony that discrimination in restaurants had a direct and highly restrictive effect upon interstate travel by Negroes. This resulted, it was said, because discriminatory practices pre-*

vent Negroes from buying prepared food served on the premises while on a trip, except in isolated and unkempt restaurants, and under most unsatisfactory and often unpleasant conditions. This obviously discourages travel and obstructs interstate commerce for one can hardly travel without eating. Likewise, it was said, that discrimination deterred professional, as well as skilled, people from moving into areas where such practices occurred, and thereby caused industry to be reluctant to establish there.

Enforcement Regardless of Violator's Motive

In recent times, too, the Act continues to be vigorously enforced. In a 1988 case, several blacks claimed to have been discriminated against by the admission policies of a local, well-attended restaurant and nightclub called the Glass Menagerie. The plaintiffs claimed they were kept waiting in line outside the nightclub while white people were admitted ahead of them. Their protests to employees were ignored. Two former doormen testified they had been instructed to discourage black customers from coming to the restaurant and nightclub because the owner believed they did not spend as much money as white customers, they bothered white female patrons, and they were not big tippers. The court, finding that this constituted discrimination, stated,

The court would like to believe that these discriminatory acts occurred through shortsightedness rather than malice. The court is optimistic that voluntary corrective action will be promptly taken to eliminate all vestiges of discrimination at the Glass Menagerie. Even so, however, and even though the discrimination was sporadic, compelling public interests require the immediate issuance of injunctive relief [a court order prohibiting any further discrimination]." U.S. v. Glass Menagerie, Inc., 702 F.Supp. 139, 142 (E.D. Ky., 1988).

Racial Discrimination

Refusing to permit anyone to enter an establishment because of race constitutes a violation of the Act. In a 1996 settlement of a Louisiana case, a Louisiana nightclub owner admitted the club discriminated against blacks. The case arose when a white woman, out for the evening with two friends—one black and one white, walked to the entrance of the nightclub to see if it was open. Meanwhile, her two friends waited in the car. When the bouncer advised her the bar was open, she and her friends parked the car and sought entry. They were then advised they would not be admitted because the club was hosting a private party. The white woman later that evening returned to the club alone and was admitted. After she reported the incident to law enforcement, the government sent two pairs of FBI agents, one white couple and one black couple, to the nightclub. The latter was denied entry while the former was admitted.

In a settlement, the bar owner agreed to stop violating the Civil Rights Act of 1964, train employees in civil rights law requirements, and advertise openly that the bar is open to all races. Said a prosecutor involved with the case, "Over three decades ago, Congress spoke for all decent Americans by making it illegal to exclude people from [restaurants and bars] because of their skin color . . . America must have zero tolerance for racial discrimination." 1996 WL 66969 (1966).

In *O'Connor v. 11 West 30th Street Restaurant Corp. d/b/a/ Apkujungdong Restaurant*, 1995 WL 354904 (SDNY, 1995), a Korean restaurant refused to seat and serve plaintiff, "a male of European descent". When O'Connor sought service, he was advised by the restaurant host that the restaurant was a private club and since O'Connor was not a member he could not enter. O'Connor returned a month later with "another white male" and was again refused service. Thereafter on two occasions of which plaintiff was aware, Korean males who were non-members were seated and served at the restaurant. On other occasions, two white males and an African-American woman sought service and were denied because they were not members.

In response to plaintiff's lawsuit claiming a violation of various civil rights laws, the restaurant argued that only members of a racial minority are protected and therefore, plaintiff who was white could not sue. The court rejected this claim, holding that "A white person, just as a nonwhite," is protected by the statutes. The restaurant's motion to dismiss plaintiff's case was denied.

Case law also teaches that the Civil Rights Acts do not remedy all perceived wrongs. Instead, it protects only against discriminatory denial of the right to enter a covered facility and receive service. While the right to enter and receive service are important rights, indignities other than exclusion are not covered.

In one such case, plaintiff, a black male, entered a Burger King and ordered breakfast. He was the first in line. Several white men entered the line behind plaintiff. The employee serving the food stopped waiting on plaintiff and attended to the others. When plaintiff complained to the assistant manager, he left his office and prepared plaintiff's order. Upon receiving his order, the plaintiff paid and left. In this action, plaintiff claims the delay in his service was the result of racial discrimination.

The court dismissed plaintiff's case stating, "In the instant case, plaintiff was not denied admittance or service—his service was merely slow. While inconvenient, frustrating, and all too common, the mere fact of slow service in a fast-food restaurant does not, in the eyes of this Court, rise to the level of violating one's civil rights." *Robertson v. Burger King., Inc.*, 848 F.Supp. 78 (E.D.La., 1994).

In another case plaintiff, a black patron of a dance bar, claimed the bar's owner discriminated against blacks by discontinuing rap music and playing rock and roll music to induce black patrons to leave. Employees of the restaurant testified that the manager would tell the disc jockeys that it was "too dark in here" when it was thought there were too many blacks in the bar. In response, the disc jockeys allegedly began playing "hard rock and roll" music which was not the favored music of blacks. The court dismissed the case noting that the manager did not refuse plaintiff admittance to the bar or service while he was there. Said the court, "A bar's music selection cannot be grounds to find that it engages in discriminatory conduct." *Sterns v. Baur's Opera House, Inc.*, 778 F.Supp. 375 (C.D. Ill., 1992).

Religious Discrimination

Similar to racial discrimination, a successful case of religious discrimination requires a showing that service was refused. Where service is offered but a requested accommodation of one's religious practices is refused for good reason, the Act has not been violated.

In *Boyle v. Jerome Country Club*, 883 F.Supp. 1422 (D. Idaho, 1995), plaintiff was a tournament golfer and member of the Church of Jesus Christ of Latter-day Saints. Due to religious beliefs, plaintiff did not play golf on Sunday. The club's tournaments were customarily played on Saturday and Sunday. When the club refused to accommodate his request for an alternate playing schedule, he sued, claiming a violation of the Act. The club claimed that to provide plaintiff an alternate schedule would create complications and expense, making the administration of the tournament more difficult. Among the problems would be increased workload of the tournament marshals and umpires, delay of the public's access to the course, and possible disruption of the practice of the lowest scoring golfers playing at the end of the tournament which serves economic purposes.

The court dismissed plaintiff's action noting that the club had "legitimate business reasons, completely unrelated to religious considerations, for scheduling its final round of play on Sunday." Id. at p. 1430. Further, "It is undisputed that the Club has never refused to permit Plaintiff to enter a tournament or to play a round of golf." at p. 1425.

Broad Enforcement Through the Unitary Rule

The Act covers only lodging facilities, dining facilities, places of entertainment, and gasoline stations. Other businesses, such as stores, barber shops and beauty parlors, transportation facilities, bars, and colleges, are not covered. However, if a food counter is physically located within the premises, such as a snack bar in a store or a food car on a train, the food facility and the store or train are *both* covered. Similarly, a barber shop, which is not covered by the Act, will be covered if located within a hotel. This principle is known as the **unitary rule**, which means that where a covered facility is located within a noncovered business, both the covered and noncovered business are subject to the Act.

A bar or lounge, while normally not subject to the Act, is governed by the Act if it provides entertainment and if it is engaged in interstate commerce. A Florida bar that provided its customers with the use of a piano, juke box, and television set manufactured outside the state was bound by the Act. *United States v. Deetjen*, 356 F.Supp. 688 (Fla., 1973).

Exempt Establishments

The Act excludes from its coverage certain establishments, including bed-and-breakfast operations and private clubs. These businesses are not barred by the Act from discriminating.

"Mrs. Murphy's Boarding House"

The Act exempts tourist homes, known today as bed-and-breakfasts, with five or fewer rooms and occupied by the proprietor. A specific provision of the statute creates this exception and is referred to as the "Mrs. Murphy's boarding house clause."

Private Clubs

The ban on discrimination in the Act does not apply to "private clubs or other establishments not in fact open to the public." The Act does not clearly define what constitutes a private club, so the courts must interpret the statute when the issue arises. It usually arises when a club claiming to be private excludes someone on the basis of race, color, religion or national origin and that person challenges the legality of the exclusion. In considering whether a club is private, the courts consider one or more of the following tests:

1. Is the club sufficiently selective in choosing its members? A private club usually has a limited number of members. The more selective the club is, the more likely it will qualify as a private club.

2. Are new members sought discretely? If the club publicly advertises for members it most likely is not a private club.

3. Does the club have clearly designated criteria for choosing members? A private club typically has specific traits it seeks to perpetuate in its members. The more specific the criteria, the more likely the club will qualify as private.

4. Do members govern and control the club's operations? A private club is usually owned and governed by members. If the "club" is simply a business operated for profit, it will not qualify as a private club.

5. To what extent are club facilities available for use by nonmembers? The more access by nonmembers, the less likely it is to be a private club.

6. Is the primary purpose of the club social or business? If the primary purpose is business, it likely will not be a private club.

The following two case examples illustrate private clubs.

A bridge club was found to be private in *Baptiste v. Cavendish Club, Inc.*, 670 F.Supp. 108 (N.Y., 1987), for the following reasons,

> [T]he club is dedicated to the promotion of bridge and other games of skill. . . . Club facilities are open only to members and their guests, . . . Prospective members must be sponsored by a current member and seconded by another member. They are subject to evaluation of their ethical reputation at the bridge table, their skill and knowledge of the game, their standards of dress and deportment, and their ability to meet their financial commitment to the Club. Members are admitted only if they are approved by the Board of Directors.

Similarly, in *Moose Lodge v. Irvis*, 407 U.S. 163, 92 S. Ct. 1965 (1972), a black man was refused service by Moose Lodge, a local branch of the national fraternal organization. He sued claiming illegal discrimination. The court held the club was private for the following reasons,

> Moose Lodge is a private club . . . It is a local chapter of a national fraternal organization having well-defined requirements for membership. It conducts all of its activities

in a building that is owned by it. It is not publicly funded. Only members and guests are permitted in any lodge of the order; one may become a guest only by invitation of a member or upon invitation of the house committee.

Clubs that Qualify as Private

Many clubs have sought exemption from application of the Act on the basis of being a private club. The issue in many discrimination cases is whether the defendant club is, in fact, private.

Assailing "Private-in-Name-Only" Clubs

If a club claimed by its members to be private is really a place of public entertainment, it will be subject to the restrictions of the Civil Rights Act, as the following case shows. The case also illustrates the unfortunate practice, following passage of the Civil Rights Act, of groups forming "quickie" private clubs in an attempt to avoid serving blacks and other minorities.

CASE EXAMPLE 3–1

Daniel v. Paul
89 S.Ct. 1697 (1969)

Petitioners, Negro residents of Little Rock, Arkansas, brought this class action to enjoin respondent from denying them admission to a recreational facility called Lake Nixon Club owned and operated by respondent, Euell Paul, and his wife. The complaint alleged that Lake Nixon Club was a "public accommodation" subject to . . . the Civil Rights Act of 1964, . . . and that respondent violated the act in refusing petitioners admission solely on racial grounds. After trial, the District Court, although finding that respondent had refused petitioners admission solely because they were Negroes, dismissed the complaint on the ground that Lake Nixon Club was not within any of the [enumerated] "public accommodations" covered by the 1964 Act. . . .

Lake Nixon Club, located 12 miles west of Little Rock, is a 232-acre amusement area with swimming, boating, sun bathing, picnicking, miniature golf, dancing facilities, and a snack bar. The Pauls purchased the Lake Nixon site in 1962 and subsequently operated this amusement business there in a racially segregated manner.

. . . [T]he Civil Rights Act of 1964 enacted a sweeping prohibition of discrimination or segregation on the ground of race, color, religion, or national origin at places of public accommodation whose operations affect commerce. This prohibition does not extend to discrimination or segregation at private clubs. But, as both courts below properly found, Lake Nixon is not a private club. It is simply a business operated for a profit with none of the attributes of self-government and member-ownership traditionally associated with private clubs. It is true that following enactment of the Civil Rights Act of 1964, the Pauls began to refer to the establishment as a private club. They even began to require patrons to pay a 25-cent "membership" fee, which gains a purchaser a "membership" card entitling him to enter the Club's premises for an entire season and, on payment of specified additional fees, to use the swimming, boating, and miniature golf facilities. But this "membership" device seems no more than a subterfuge designed to avoid coverage of the 1964 Act. White persons are routinely provided "membership" cards, and some 100,000 whites visit the establishment each season. Negroes, on the other hand, are uniformly denied "membership" cards, and thus admission, because of the Pauls' fear that integration would "ruin" the "business". The conclusion of the courts below that Lake Nixon is not a private club is plainly correct—indeed, respondent does not challenge that conclusion here.

We, therefore, turn to the question whether Lake Nixon Club is "a place of public accommodation" as defined by . . . the 1964 Act, and, if so, whether its operations "affect commerce" within the meaning of . . . that Act.

Petitioners argue first that Lake Nixon's snack bar is a covered public accommodation . . . and that as such it brings the entire establishment within the coverage. . . . Clearly, the snack bar is "principally engaged in selling food for consumption on the premises." Thus, it is a covered public accommodation if "it serves or offers to serve interstate travelers or a substantial portion of the food which it serves. . .has moved in commerce." We find that the snack bar is a covered public accommodation under either of these standards.

The Pauls advertise the Lake Nixon Club in a monthly magazine called "Little Rock Today," which is distributed to guests at Little Rock hotels, motels, and restaurants, to acquaint them with available tourist attractions in the area. Regular advertisements for Lake Nixon were also broadcast over two area radio stations. In addition, Lake Nixon has advertised in the "Little Rock Air Force Base," a monthly newspaper. This choice of advertising media leaves no doubt that the Pauls were seeking broad-based patronage from an audience which they knew to include interstate travelers. Thus, the Lake Nixon Club unquestionably offered to serve out-of-state visitors to the Little Rock area. And it would be unrealistic to assume that none of the 100,000 patrons actually served by the Club each season was an interstate traveler. Since the Lake Nixon Club offered to serve and served out-of-state persons, and since the Club's snack bar was established to serve all patrons of the entire facility, we must conclude that the snack bar offered to serve and served out-of-state persons.

The record also demonstrates that a "substantial portion of the food" served by the Lake Nixon Club snack bar has moved in interstate commerce. The snack bar serves a limited fare—hot dogs and hamburgers on buns, soft drinks, and milk. The District Court took judicial notice of the fact that the "principal ingredients going into the bread were produced and processed in other States" and that "certain ingredients [of the soft drinks] were probably obtained . . . from out-of-State sources.". . . Thus, at the very least, three of the four food items sold at the snack bar contain ingredients originating outside of the State. There can be no serious doubt that a "substantial portion of the food" served at the snack bar has moved in interstate commerce.

The snack bar's status as a covered establishment automatically brings the entire Lake Nixon facility within the gambit of . . . [the] Civil Rights Act of 1964.

Petitioners also argue that the Lake Nixon Club is a covered public accommodation under [other provisions of the statute.] . . . These sections proscribe discrimination by "any motion picture house, theater, concert hall, sports arena, stadium or other place of exhibition or entertainment" which "customarily presents films, performances, athletic teams, exhibitions, or other sources of entertainment which move in commerce." Under any accepted definition of "entertainment," the Lake Nixon Club would surely qualify as a "place of entertainment." And indeed it advertises itself as such. Respondent argues, however, that . . . "place of entertainment" refers only to establishments where patrons are entertained as spectators or listeners rather than those where entertainment takes the form of direct participation in some sport or activity. We find no support in the legislative history for respondent's reading of the statute. The few indications of legislative intent are to the contrary. . . .

The remaining question is whether the operations of the Lake Nixon Club "affect commerce." . . . We conclude that they do. Lake Nixon's customary "sources of entertainment. . . move in commerce." The Club leases 15 paddle boats on a royalty basis from an Oklahoma company. Another boat was purchased from the same company. The Club's juke box was manufactured outside Arkansas and plays records manufactured outside the State. The legislative history indicates that mechanical sources of entertainment such as these were considered by Congress to be "sources of entertainment" within the meaning of [the Act.]

Ruling of the Court: Reversed.

CASE QUESTIONS

1. Summarize the two separate grounds the court used to determine that Lake Nixon was a place of public accommodation and thus covered by the Act.

2. Can you think of any business within the hospitality/entertainment industry that is not covered by the Civil Rights Act?

Scrutinizing Admission Policies

Many cases involve clubs that claim to have sufficiently selective admission policies to qualify as a private club. The court in these cases will carefully review those policies to determine if in fact they are adequately selective.

In a Virginia case, a golf club was accused of violating the Civil Rights Act by ejecting a foursome because one golfer, who was invited to the club by a member, was black. The club defended on the ground that it was a private club and so could discriminate on the basis of race. The club's requirements for membership included a $750 initiation fee, the signature of two members on a written application, and approval of the application by the club's board of directors. The club adopted a membership ceiling of 450. The club did not routinely investigate the background and character of its applicants, nor did it measure applicants against any moral, religious or social standards. The evidence presented indicated that only four white applicants had been rejected in the previous 15 years. The court ruled that these admission procedures, while "official and formal," were not sufficiently selective to render the club private.

Said the court, "If only four white applicants have been denied membership [in the last fifteen years], the club cannot fairly be described as truly selective about its members." *Brown v. Loudoun Golf & Country Club, Inc.*, 573 F.Supp. 399, 403 (E.D.Va., 1983).

Another case raised the issue whether the Lions Club, a service organization with a worldwide membership of 313,000, was a private club. The application process for new members was as follows: they had to be sponsored by a current member; they were required to complete an application form; the club was supposed to investigate applicants' backgrounds thoroughly, but customarily no investigation was done; the board of directors then voted on the applicants; if approved by a majority of the board, applicants are asked to join. No proposed member had been rejected in eighteen years. Noting that the screening process for new applicants was "cursory and operates to allow vast numbers of members," the court rejected the club's claim that it was private. *Rogers v. International Association of Lions Clubs*, 636 F.Supp. 1476 (E.D. Mich., 1986).

A similar case involved the Jaycees, another service organization. The local chapter in question had 430 members. The club did not use any criteria for judging applicants for membership. New members were routinely admitted with no background inquiry. The court denied the club's claim that it was a private club, stating, "[T]he local chapters of the Jaycees are neither small nor selective." *Roberts v. United States Jaycees*, 468 U.S. 609, 82 L.Ed.2d 462 (1984). For a similar holding, see also *Kiwanis International v. Ridgewood Kiwanis Club*, 627 F.Supp. 1381 (D.N.J., 1986).

The following case illustrates the application of the private club rules to a swimming club.

CASE EXAMPLE 3–2

U.S. v. Lansdowne Swim Club,
894 F.2d 83 (3rd Cir., 1990)

The Lansdowne Swim Club (LSC), . . . a nonprofit corporation, is the only group swimming facility in the Borough of Lansdowne, Pennsylvania. Since its founding in 1957, LSC has granted 1400 full family memberships. Every white applicant has been admitted, although two as limited members only. In that time, however, LSC has had only one nonwhite member.

The uncontroverted experiences of the following Lansdowne residents are significant. In 1976, the Allisons wrote to LSC requesting an application but LSC did not respond. Dr. Allison is black; his three children are part-black. In 1977, the Allisons twice again wrote for an application but LSC did not respond. The following year, the Allisons repeated the procedure with similar results. In 1983, the Allisons filed a timely application and otherwise qualified for membership but were rejected. The following year, the Ryans filed a timely application and otherwise qualified for membership. Nonetheless, they were rejected. Two of the Ryans' adopted children are black. The Ryans then complained to the media and picketed LSC, joined by the Allisons. In 1986, the Iverys, who are black, filed a timely application and otherwise qualified for membership. Nonetheless, they were rejected (as were the Ryans and Allisons who had again applied).

The United States alleges that LSC is a place of public accommodation . . . which has engaged in a pattern or practice of discrimination by refusing membership to blacks because of their race or color, in violation of [the Civil Rights Act]. . . .

LSC's first argument is that it is a private club. Under [the Civil Rights Act], "a private club or other establishment not in fact open to the public" is exempt from the statute. . . . LSC has the burden of proving it is a private club. . . . Although the statute does not define "private club", cases construing the provision do offer some guidance. The district court distilled eight factors from the case law as relevant to this determination, three of which it found dispositive of LSC's public nature: the genuine selectivity of its membership process, its history, and use of its facilities by nonmembers. LSC disputes these findings.

First, the court concluded that LSC's membership process was not genuinely selective. Essential to this conclusion was the court's finding that "LSC possesses no objective criteria or standards for admission." The court identified four "criteria" for admission to LSC: being interviewed, completing an application, submitting two letters of recommendation and tendering payment of fees. We agree, and LSC apparently concedes, that these criteria were not genuinely selective. Nonetheless, LSC challenges the court's failure to consider membership approval a criterion for admission. . . . [A] formal procedure requiring nothing more than membership approval is insufficient to show genuine selectivity. . . . In addition, LSC stipulated that the only information given to the members prior to the membership vote is the applicants' names, addresses, their children's names and ages, and the recommenders' identities. In such a situation, the court was correct to conclude that LSC "provides no information to voting members that is useful in making an informed decision as to whether the applicant and his or her family would be compatible with the existing members." Therefore, even if membership approval were considered a fifth criterion, it would not make the process any more genuinely selective in this case.

The district court also found the yields of the membership process indicative of lack of selectivity. Since 1958, LSC has granted full memberships to at least 1400 families while denying them to only two non-black families. LSC contends that emphasizing the few instances of non-black applicant rejection "misconstru[es] the significance of selectivity. The crucial question should be whether the members exercised their right to be selective rather than the statistical results of the exercise of that right.". . . [F]ormal membership requirements have little meaning when in fact the club does not follow a selective membership policy. . . . We find the evidence of lack of selectivity convincing.

CASE QUESTION

1. What would the club need to do differently to qualify as a private club?

Extending Civil Rights Protection

The Act represented a major step forward in this country's attempt to eliminate discrimination. As we have seen, however, the classes of people protected and the types of facilities covered are limited. Other federal, state and local laws help to fill the gaps.

Application of Civil Rights Laws to Some Private Clubs

A trend is developing among some cities to bring even legitimate private clubs under coverage of local anti-discrimination laws. A case in point involves New York City, which amended its Human Rights Law in 1984 to prohibit discrimination in certain private clubs. The amendment covers clubs with "more than four hundred members [that] provide regular meal service and regularly receive payment for dues, fees, use of space, facilities, services, meals or beverages directly or indirectly from or on behalf of nonmembers for the furtherance of trade or business." The reason the amendment was adopted was that business deals and valuable business contacts are often made at such private clubs thereby placing women and minorities, who are the classes usually excluded, at a professional disadvantage. An association of 125 private clubs unsuccessfully challenged the amendment; the court upheld its validity. Thus, even private clubs in New York City are barred from discriminating against women and minority group members if the clubs fall within specifications of the amendment. *New York State Club Assn. v. New York City*, 487 U.S. 1, 101 L.Ed.2d 1, 108 S.Ct. 2225 (1988).

State Civil Rights Laws

Virtually every state has a civil rights law that, in part, duplicates the Act, and in part, expands its coverage. The differences are as follows:

Coverage. The state laws include within their coverage businesses that are purely in*tra*state in nature, that is, not involved in in*ter*state commerce. Remember, the Civil Rights Act of 1964 applies only to businesses engaged in interstate commerce.

Covered Facilities.   The Act applies only to lodging facilities, dining facilities, gasoline stations and "places of entertainment." Most state laws include most "places of public accommodation" which is defined broadly to include, in addition to the Act's coverage, bars, stores, clinics, hospitals, barber and beauty shops, libraries, schools, colleges, public halls, public elevators, and public institutions for the care of neglected or delinquent children, garages, and public transportation.

Protected Classes.   The protected classes of the Act are limited to race, color, religion, and national origin. The state statutes customarily expand the categories of protected classes and frequently include gender, marital status, and disability. Some statutes and local government ordinances outlaw discrimination on the basis of sexual orientation.

Advertisements.   Many state statutes prohibit advertisements that contain statements or suggestions, express or implied, that accommodations will be denied because of a protected characteristic, such as race, religion, or sex.

The issue arose in a 1974 New York State case in which female plaintiffs objected to the name and exterior sign of a bar because it implied women would not be served. The objectionable name was "Silent Women Tavern" and the exterior sign depicted a headless woman. The owner conceded that the sign and name were intended to attract male patrons. The court refused to require the bar to remove the sign or change its name, and said,

> *The law does not prohibit appealing by signs or trade name to one sex or another. Rather, the prohibition is against displaying notice or advertisement to the effect that any of the facilities or privileges will be refused or withheld from or denied a person on account of sex. . . . There is nothing about the name or the exterior sign, in the form used here, that would suggest that women would be refused the use of the facilities.* Rosenberg v. State Human Rights Appeal Board, 45 A.D.2d 929, 357 N.Y.S.2d 325 (4th Dept., 1974).

Remedies.   Under the federal Act, remedies include injunctive relief and attorney's fees. Under state laws, customary remedies include jail and fines.

The Americans With Disabilities Act

The Americans With Disabilities Act, (hereinafter "Disabilities Act"),[1] a federal law passed by Congress in 1991, is a far-reaching commitment to rights of

---

[1]42U.S.C. Section 12101

the disabled. Its purpose is "(1) to provide a clear and comprehensive national mandate for the elimination of discrimination against individuals with disabilities; and (2) to provide clear, strong, consistent, and enforcible standards addressing discrimination against individuals with disabilities."

The Disabilities Act states that no individual shall be discriminated against on the basis of disability in the full and equal enjoyment of the "goods, services, facilities, privileges, advantages and accommodations" (hereinafter "goods, services and facilities") in any place of public accommodation. As defined by the Disabilities Act, places of public accommodation include places of lodging, establishments serving food or drink, and places of entertainment and recreation, to name only some.

The Disabilities Act does not apply to private clubs, which are defined in the same manner as under the Civil Rights of 1964.

Modifying Rules to Accommodate the Disabled.   It is illegal discrimination for a place of public accommodation to deny a person on the basis of a disability the opportunity to participate in or benefit from the goods, services, or facilities offered by it. Thus, a resort offering an exercise class cannot exclude from the class a person in a wheelchair on the ground that the disabled person cannot do all the exercises.

A goal of the Act is to ensure that goods, services, and facilities are provided to disabled persons in the most integrated setting possible. Thus, the resort could not require the wheelchair-bound patron to attend a special exercise class for the disabled. Similarly, a restaurant cannot place all wheelchair accessible tables in an isolated corner of the dining room. Instead, they must be placed throughout the dining area.

The Disabilities Act is violated if requirements are placed on people with disabilities that are not imposed on others. For example, a restaurant that requires patrons in wheelchairs to be chaperoned by a companion but seats single, able-bodied customers violates the Disabilities Act.

Where the policies or practices of a place of public accommodation have the effect of discriminating against people with disabilities, the place of public accommodation must modify its policies or practices unless the modification would fundamentally alter the nature of the goods or services provided. For example, a place of public accommodation may have a rule prohibiting pets but must modify that rule by permitting entrance to a service dog. Similarly, a bar may have a rule requiring a customer ordering a drink to present a driver's license as proof of age. The Disabilities Act requires that the bar, to accommodate persons with disabilities that prevent them from driving, modify the rule to accept an alternative form of identification.

Providing Auxiliary Aides and Alternative Services.   The Disabilities Act requires places of public accommodation to provide auxiliary aides and services for disabled individuals where it is necessary to accommodate them, unless such aides or services would fundamentally alter the nature of the goods or services offered, or would result in an undue burden. For example, while a restaurant is not required to provide braille menus for blind patrons, it will be required to provide someone to read the non-braille menu to the visually-impaired diner.

Structural Modifications for Existing Buildings.   The Disabilities Act contains requirements concerning accessibility of facilities. Structural obstacles often preclude access by disabled persons to places of public accommodation. For example, a second floor reachable only by steps is not available to a person in a wheelchair. Blind persons may be unable to use an elevator because they cannot determine which button to push. The requirements to remove obstacles vary depending on whether the inaccessible building is an existing one, an existing one that is being altered, or a new one under construction.

For existing buildings, the Disabilities Act requires places of public accommodation to undertake removal of barriers that is "readily achievable". **Readily achievable** is defined as easily accomplishable without much difficulty or expense. Examples of barrier removal that the Disabilities Act considers readily achievable include:

- ramping of a few steps (such as those to a sunken area of a dining room in a restaurant),
- lowering of telephones,
- adding raised letters and braille markings on elevator control buttons,
- adding flashing alarm lights,
- adding grab bars where only routine reinforcement of the wall is required, and
- similar modest corrections.

In restaurants, generally all dining areas must be made accessible. Tables may need to be rearranged to permit wheelchair passage. Where removal of a barrier is readily achievable, failure to remove it constitutes illegal discrimination. If, however, the removal of the barrier is not readily achievable, its continued presence does not violate the Disabilities Act. For example, installation of an elevator for access to a second floor would be quite costly and not required for existing buildings by the Disabilities Act.

If removal of a physical barrier is not readily achievable, the obligation to accommodate disabled persons is not eliminated. Instead, the Act requires the place of public accommodation to make its goods or services available through alternate methods, provided the alternate method is readily achievable. For example, it may not be readily achievable for a bar to alter the placement of stools around the bar counter even though the stools are not accessible to wheelchair-bound persons. To accommodate these patrons the restaurant may need to modify a rule barring customers from sitting at tables unless they intend to order food and instead, permit disabled persons to order just drinks from a table.

Structural Requirements During Construction.   Newly built facilities and those being altered must be constructed in such a way that they can be approached, entered, and utilized easily and conveniently by people with disabilities. New construction and alterations must comply with ADA Accessibility Guidelines. These guidelines contain technical standards for most aspects of a facility. If, however, the cost to make the new or altered building accessible would be disproportionate to the overall alteration or construction in terms of cost and scope, alternative methods should be sought. Alterations and new construction are not required by the Disabilities Act; the barrier removal required in these circumstances applies only when the establishment elects to make alterations or undertake new construction. The requirement of barrier removal imposed when making alterations is not triggered by minor repairs such as painting or wallpapering. More extensive modifications are required.

For a new hotel, the Disabilities Act requires the following: all doors and doorways must be designed to allow passage by a wheelchair; bathrooms need to be sufficiently wide to allow use by people in wheelchairs; a percentage of each class of hotel room must be fully accessible, including grab bars in the bathroom and at the toilet; accessible counters in the bathrooms; audio loops in meeting areas; emergency flashing lights or alarms; braille or raised letter words and numbers on elevators and signs; and handrails on stairs and ramps.

If a person with a disability needing a fully accessible room makes a reservation without informing the hotel of the need for such a room and, when the person arrives, a fully accessible room is not available, the hotel has not violated the Disabilities Act. While the hotel must make an effort to afford disabled persons accessible rooms, it can rent those rooms to nondisabled persons if other rooms are not available and a disabled person has not sought reservations.

Transportation and Telecommunication.   The Disability Act also requires that facilities offering transportation must attempt to make their facilities accessible to the disabled. A hotel that provides a hospitality van must remove transportation barriers to the extent removal is readily achievable.

The Disabilities Act also requires that companies offering telephone service provide telecommunication devices for the deaf which will permit a hearing-impaired person to communicate with anyone in this country who has a telephone.

Legal Action to Address Noncompliance.   Two types of lawsuits can be brought under the Act for noncompliance. One is a private suit by individuals and the other is a lawsuit by the Department of Justice. A private lawsuit can be brought by a disabled person who is subjected to discrimination on the basis of disability or who has reason to believe that he is about to be subjected to discrimination, for example, a hotel is being planned but the specifications are not in compliance with the Disabilities Act. Remedies for a private lawsuit include an injunction against further discrimination, a court order requiring alteration of facilities to comply with the Disabilities Act, and a court order requiring an auxiliary aide or service be provided, or a policy be modified, or an alternate method of barrier removal be undertaken. Compensatory and punitive damages are not recoverable.

The second type of lawsuit can be brought only by the United States Attorney General, the chief law enforcement officer of the country. This type of action is pursued against a violator where a pattern or practice of discrimination exists or where the discrimination raises an issue of general public importance, as where the discrimination impacts many people. In addition to the remedies available in a private action, a court in a case brought by the Attorney General may award monetary damages, including out-of-pocket expenses and damages for pain and suffering. Punitive damages cannot be awarded, although a court may assess a civil penalty not exceeding $50,000 for first violation and not exceeding $100,000 for any subsequent violation.

Just as the *Heart of Atlanta Motel* and *Ollie's Barbecue* unsuccessfully challenged the enforceability of the Civil Rights Act of 1964, a franchisee of the International House of Pancakes (hereinafter "Pancake House") lost a challenge to the constitutionality of the Disabilities Act in *Pinnock v. International House of Pancakes Franchisee*, 844 F. Supp. 574 (S.D.Cal., 1993). The court rejected the Pancake House's claim it was not engaged in interstate commerce because the restaurant was located within two miles of two interstate highways, and three hotels were within walking distance of the restaurant. The court likewise rejected Pancake House's claim that the term "readily achievable", used as the standard for determining when a modification must be made, was too vague to guide those bound by the act. The court noted that the statute lists examples of what qualifies as readily achievable—including rearranging tables and chairs, installing small ramps, and installing grab bars in the restrooms. Further, federal regulations explaining the statute clarify the term.

Pancake House also claimed that the term "most integrated setting appropriate", used by the statute to describe the goal for accommodating disabled patrons, was too vague to be enforceable. The court noted that the statute contains two pages of examples and explanations, and thus was sufficiently clear. An example of a violation referenced by the court is requiring people with mental disabilities to eat in the back room of the restaurant.

Thus, like the Civil Rights Act of 1964, the Disabilities Act withstood constitutional challenge early in its history.

In the following case several restaurant patrons with asthma or lupus claimed a violation of the Act by restaurant policies that permit smoking in the building.

CASE EXAMPLE 3–3

**Staron v. McDonald's Corp.
and Burger King Corp.
51 F.3d 353 (2nd Cir., 1995)**

These actions are brought by three children with asthma and a woman with lupus against two popular fast-food restaurant chains: McDonald's Corporation ("McDonald's") and Burger King Corporation ("Burger King"). Plaintiffs claim that

defendants' policies of permitting smoking in their restaurants violates the Americans With Disabilities Act (the "ADA" or "Act"). Plaintiffs appeal judgments granting defendants' motions to dismiss plaintiffs' claims. . . .

For the reasons stated below, we reverse the judgements and remand the cases [send them back to the court of original jurisdiction] for further proceedings.

Background

The facts alleged in plaintiffs' complaints are rather straightforward. During one week in February, 1993, each plaintiff entered both a McDonald's and a Burger King restaurant in Connecticut. Each plaintiff found the air in each restaurant to be full of tobacco smoke, and because of his or her condition, was unable to enter the restaurant without experiencing breathing problems. Each plaintiff has also encountered similar difficulties at other times in other restaurants owned by McDonald's and Burger King.

After registering complaints with the defendants . . . without satisfactory results, plaintiffs filed separate suits against McDonald's and Burger King on March 30, 1993. Their complaints alleged that the defendants' policies of permitting smoking in their restaurants constituted discrimination under the Act. Each complaint requested . . . an injunction to prohibit defendants from maintaining any policy which interfered with plaintiffs' rights under the Act, 'and more specifically to require [defendants and their franchisees] to establish a policy of prohibiting smoking in all of the facilities they own, lease or operate." . . .

Discussion

Because we find that plaintiffs' complaints do on their face state a cognizable claim against the defendants under the Americans with Disabilities Act, we reverse the district court's orders of dismissal.

The ADA was promulgated "to provide a clear and comprehensive national mandate for the elimination of discrimination against individuals with disabilities" as well as to establish "clear, strong, consistent, enforceable standards" for scrutinizing such discrimination.

"Discrimination" includes the failure of an owner, operator, lessee, or lessor of public accommodations to make reasonable modifications in policies, practices or procedures, when such modifications are necessary to afford such goods, services [or] facilities . . . to individuals with disabilities, unless the entity can demonstrate that making such modifications would fundamentally alter the nature of such goods, services, [or] facilities. . . .

[D]efendants do not dispute that the [Act] applies to them as owners and operators of public accommodations. They also concede at this point that plaintiffs qualify as individuals with disabilities under the ADA. . . . The principal contention of McDonald's and Burger King on appeal, is that a total ban on smoking does not constitute a "reasonable modification" under the ADA.

The ADA and cases interpreting it do not articulate a precise test for determining whether a particular modification is "reasonable" . . . [A predecessor statute] stated that "accommodation is not reasonable if it either imposes 'undue financial and administrative burdens' . . . or requires 'a fundamental alteration in the nature of the [business].'"

Although neither the ADA nor the courts have defined the precise contours of the test for reasonableness, it is clear that the determination of whether a particular modification is "reasonable" involves a fact-specific, case-by-case inquiry that considers, among other factors, the effectiveness of the modification in light of the nature of the disability in question and the cost to the organization that would implement it.

. . . [I]n the case before us a fact-specific inquiry was required. None has occurred. The [judge in the court of original jurisdiction] concluded that plaintiff's request for a ban on smoking in all of defendants' restaurants was unreasonable as a matter of law. . . .

It is plain to us that Congress did not intend to isolate the effects of smoking from the protections of the ADA. In fact, language of the Act expressly permits a total ban on smoking if a court finds it appropriate under the ADA. We therefore reject any argument by defendants to the contrary . . . "The determination as to whether allergies to cigarette smoke . . . are disabilities covered by the regulation must be made using the same case-by-case analysis that is applied to all other physical or mental impairments. We see no reason why, under the appropriate circumstances, a ban on smoking could not be a reasonable accommodation. . . .

To be sure, the few courts that have addressed the question of reasonable modification for a smoke-sensitive disability have found a total ban unnecessary. Yet these courts only reached this conclusion after making a factual determination that existing accommodations were sufficient. . . .

Plaintiffs in this case are entitled to an opportunity to prove that a ban on smoking is a reasonable modification to permit them access to defendants' restaurants. Given that McDonald's has voluntarily banned smoking in all corporate-owned restaurants, the factfinder may conclude that such a ban would fully accommodate plaintiffs' disabilities but impose little or no cost on the defendants. Plaintiffs have alleged that, regardless of the different structural arrangements in various restaurants, the environment in each establishment visited by the plaintiffs contained too much smoke to allow them use of the facilities on an equal basis as other nondisabled patrons. These allegations belie the [lower court] judge's assumption that no-smoking areas offer a sufficient accommodation to plaintiffs. . . .

If plaintiffs should fail in their quest for an outright ban on smoking, they may still be able to demonstrate after discovery that modifications short of an outright ban, such as partitions or ventilation systems, are both "reasonable' and "necessary," and plaintiffs should be allowed the opportunity to do so.

Defendants raise another objection. . . . They contend that plaintiffs' request for a smoking ban is unreasonable because it applies to all of defendants' restaurants "regardless of whether these four plaintiffs have ever visited, will visit, might visit, or never will visit" the many McDonald's and Burger King restaurants across the country. This objection pertains to the permissible scope of injunctive relieve in this case . . . doubts about the scope do not justify dismissal of the complaints where plaintiffs have alleged cognizable claims at least with respect to the restaurants they expect to visit.

We therefore reverse the judgments of the district court and remand for proceedings consistent with this opinion.

CASE QUESTIONS

1. Explain the differences between the decision of the court of original jurisdiction and the decision of the appeals court.

2. What factors in this case suggest that a total ban on smoking in defendants' restaurants would be a reasonable modification? What factors suggest such a ban would be unreasonable?

Language Discrimination

The following case involves discrimination against Spanish-speaking bar patrons, which is discrimination based on national origin. As we have seen, discrimination on that basis is outlawed by the Act. However, since the Act does not cover bars, the court could not rely on the Act to stop the tavern from discriminating. Instead, the court creatively used different federal laws that grant all citizens of the United State equal rights to enter contracts and purchase property. The proprietor in this case violated those laws by limiting the rights of the Spanish speaking patrons to purchase beer.

CASE EXAMPLE 3–4

Hernandez v. Erlenbusch
368 F.Supp. 752 (Oregon, 1973)

. . . At trial, a preponderance of the evidence showed the following: The setting for both cases is the same—a community of approximately 8,500 persons in which more than 2,000 Mexican-Americans have been living for at least the last four years. The plaintiffs in these cases are all U.S. citizens, most of them native born. Some two years ago, the defendants, owners of the Taffrail Tavern ("Tavern"), issued these orders to their bartenders:

"You are instructed to observe the following. . . .

"11. Do not allow a foreign language to be used at the bar, if it interferes with the regular trade. If there should be a chance of a problem, ask the 'Problem' people to move to a table and turn the juke box up. (Use house money)."

The rationale for this policy, as explained by its formulators and enforcers, is that the tavern has many Anglo and Chicano patrons, with attendant friction between the two groups caused by the dislike by some of the local white populace of the "foreigners" in their midst. According to the Erlenbusches, the tavern's owners, the language rule as carried out by them and their employees served everyone's interests by accommodating both Anglo and Chicano customers and ensuring peaceful continuance of the tavern business. The complaints concerning Spanish spoken at the bar allegedly stem from fear on the part of the white clientele that the Chicanos are talking about them. It was in this atmosphere ridden with mistrust and apprehension that the following incidents occurred:

On August 23, 1972, Gilberto Hernandez and Abel and Alfredo Maldonado went to the tavern where defendant Krausnick, the bartender, served them beer. While drinking, the three men began conversing in Spanish, their native tongue. Anglo customers, who were also sitting at the bar, were "irritated" and complained to Krausnick. She advised the Chicanos that if they persisted in speaking Spanish, they would have to go to a booth or leave the premises.

Hernandez and the Maldonados took issue with these orders and an argument ensued. Krausnick poured out their remaining beer and refused to refund any money. The police were called, the plaintiffs left peacefully.

Two days later, the scene was reenacted with different plaintiffs and an additional three antagonists. Krausnick "pulled" the beers of Gonzalez, Perez and Vasquez who were then followed out of the tavern and assaulted by defendants Salisbury, Dunn, and Clary, three Anglo regular customers. Clary was subsequently tried and convicted in state court for battering Gonzalez over the right eye with a fire extinguisher. (Gonzales was the only plaintiff who was physically struck.)

Defendant Krausnick testified that she agreed with and willingly enforced "Rule 11." Clary, Dunn, and Salisbury concurred, saying they knew of the rule and wholeheartedly endorsed it. John Erlenbusch testified he adopted the policy simply to avoid trouble and to preserve his license.

Conclusions of Law

. . . In examining the practical effect of the tavern's policy against the speaking of foreign languages at the bar, it is obvious that it amounts to patent racial discrimination against Mexican-Americans who constitute about one-fourth of the tavern's trade, regardless of an occasional visit by a customer able to speak another language. The rule's results are what count; the intent of the framers in these circumstances is irrelevant. . . . In the instant case, Rule 11, as intended and applied, deprives Spanish-speaking persons of their rights to buy, drink and enjoy what the tavern has to offer on an equal footing with English-speaking consumers.

Plaintiffs' rights . . . to the full and equal benefit of all laws and proceedings for the security of person and property as is enjoyed by white citizens have been violated. Likewise, plaintiffs have been denied their . . . guarantee that [a]ll citizens of the United States shall have the same right . . . to . . . purchase . . . personal property. The "property" involved in the "contract" here is a bottle of beer instead of a job, a house, or a ticket to a recreational activity, but the principle is the same as that involved in the lunch counter and bus cases of the 1960s. Just as the Constitution forbids banishing blacks to the back of the bus so as not to arouse the racial animosity of the preferred white passengers, it also forbids ordering Spanish-speaking patrons to the "back booth or out" to avoid antagonizing English-speaking beer-drinkers.

The lame justification that a discriminatory policy helps preserve the peace is as unacceptable in barrooms as it was in buses. Catering to prejudice out of fear of provoking greater prejudice only perpetuates racism. Courts faithful to the Fourteenth Amendment will not permit, either by camouflage or cavalier treatment, equal protection so to be profaned.

CASE QUESTION

1. What can the Erlenbusches do legally to address the friction between the Anglo and Chicano patrons?

Sex Discrimination

Another type of discrimination not outlawed by the Civil Rights Act of 1964 was discrimination based on sex. In a 1969 case, a woman was refused service at a bar operated by a hotel. She was forced to leave although she was sitting quietly and not disturbing other patrons. She sued the bar challenging its discriminatory policy. The court reiterated that the Civil Rights Act of 1964 did not cover sex discrimination and dismissed the case, suggesting that the plaintiff address her complaint to Congress, which has the authority to change the law, and not to the courts. *DeCrow v. Hotel Syracuse Corp.*, 288 F.Supp. 530 (N.Y., 1968).

Although the Civil Rights Act does not protect women, under some circumstances they can obtain redress for discrimination in places of public accommodation through the Fourteenth Amendment to the Constitution. That amendment states, "[N]or shall any *state* . . . deny to any person within its jurisdiction the equal protection of the *laws*." (emphasis added). The operative word is "state", meaning the government. The amendment does not prohibit private discrimination, it only prohibits unequal treatment by the state. How does a place of public accommodation qualify as the state? It qualifies only if it serves the public and is subject to considerable supervision and control by the government. Is a bar or restaurant with a liquor license issued by the state subject to the necessary degree of state supervision and control to qualify as an instrumentality of the state and therefore bound by the Fourteenth Amendment prohibition against unequal protection of the laws?

That question was answered in the affirmative in *Seidenberg v. McSorley's Old Ale House, Inc.*, 308 F.Supp. 1253 (N.Y., 1969). Two female members of the National Organization of Women (NOW) entered the defendant establishment, a bar primarily engaged in serving alcoholic and nonalcoholic beverages. They were told by the bartender that the establishment did not serve women and that it had consistently adhered to this practice throughout its 114 years of existence. The two women sued the bar claiming illegal discrimination on the basis of the Act and the Fourteenth Amendment. The court denied their Civil Rights Act claim, noting that Congress did not outlaw discrimination based on sex. The Court did however find that the bar's refusal to serve women may violate the Fourteenth Amendment, noting that a liquor licensee is restricted by state law in who it can sell alcohol to and when it can sell, and the licensee is subject to inspection of its premises by the State Liquor Authority, which can suspend or revoke the license. The court held this may be sufficient supervision and control to qualify the bar as an instrumentality of the state.

Supplementing the Constitution, virtually all states now have state statutes that prohibit discrimination in "places of public accommodation" based on sex. The term "place of public accommodation" under state law usually covers more establishments than does the federal Act. It includes almost every place open to the public including, for example, stores and schools.

In a case involving the New York statute, the plaintiff sought a court order barring owners of a tavern that refused to serve women at the bar during certain hours from continuing that practice. The court granted plaintiff's request and ordered the bar to cease and desist its discriminatory practice. *Rosenberg v. State Human Rights Appeal Board*, 357 N.Y.S.2d 325 (1974).

In another case involving Michigan's civil rights statute, the court barred the Lion's Club, an all-male service organization, from denying women membership. The club had refused to accept a woman who met all membership requirements except sex. *Rogers v. International Association of Lions Club*, 636 F.Supp. 1476 (E.D. Mich., 1986).

The right of a golf club to refuse to grant membership to women was at issue in *Warfield v. Peninsula Golf & Country Club*, 896 P2d 776 (Cal., 1995). Plaintiff wife and her husband had a family membership at defendant golf club. When they divorced, plaintiff was awarded the couple's membership. A rule of the club provided that family memberships "shall be issued only in the name of adult male persons, . . . "and shall not be approved for females or minors." The rule further provided that where a family membership was awarded to the wife in a divorce and the husband failed to purchase it from the wife, the board of directors of the country club could terminate the membership.

The board cancelled plaintiff's membership accordingly and plaintiff sued based on gender discrimination. The club claimed it was a private club and so was not bound by the California state statute that prohibited discrimination by "business establishments" based on sex.

The court rejected the golf club's argument that it was a private club and held for the plaintiff wife. Pivotal to the decision was the significant use of club facilities by nonmembers. While as a general rule the club's facilities were open only to members, notable exceptions existed. These included the following: the golf and tennis pro shops were open to the public; nonmembers were permitted to take paid lessons from the professinals and use the club's facilities during the lessons; nonmembers could use the club to host an event such as a golf or tennis tournament, wedding reception, special luncheon or dinner, provided it was "sponsored" by a member, but charges incurred for the event were often billed directly to the nonmember; nonmembers, while at the club for any of the stated purposes, were entitled to use the dining room and bars.

Noting the significant direct and indirect financial benefit that inures to the benefit of the club from transactions with nonmembers, the court held the golf club was not a private club and thus was bound by the mandates of the California state civil rights act preventing discrimination on the basis of gender.

In another case, male bar patrons challenged a "ladies drink free" promotion that defendant bar sponsored weekly. On Wednesday nights, defendant featured "Men's Night Out" which offered reduced drink prices and free darts for the gents. On other nights of the week, promotions were offered to all patrons. The Wisconsin state statute in issue prohibited a place of public accommodation from giving preferential treatment because of sex. The court held that ladies' night promotions gave preferential treatment to women on the sole basis of gender and, therefore, violated the law. Said the court, "Our interpretation of [the law] does not prohibit [defendant bar] from offering a wide array of promotions in the form of reduced or no prices for food, drinks and entertainment. It prohibits only those promotions that base price differentials on the categories specified in the statute [which include sex]." *Novak v. Madison Motel Associates*, 188 Wis.2d 407, 418–419; 525 N.W.2d 123, 127 (Crt. Appls, Wis., 1994)

One of the bar's arguments was that, since it gave men promotional benefits on another night, it was not discriminating. The court responded, "Preferential treatment to men on other nights does not correct the violation." Id, at p. 419, 128.

Rights of Proprietors

Discrimination against certain categories of people is not prohibited by law. For example, no law offers protection against discrimination in places of public accommodation to people who are barefoot, dressed in jeans, or of a particular age. Thus, for example, a restaurant's policy of refusing to serve anyone in jeans is legal even though it discriminates against people in jeans. Another unprotected class is nonsmokers. In *King v. Hofer*, 49 Cal. rptr.2d 719 (1996), a regular patron of the defendant restaurant experienced respiratory distress from smoke emanating from the smoking area in the restaurant. The patron wrote a letter of complaint to the city manager and phoned the restaurant owner expressing his displeasure. The owner advised the patron that if he did not like smoke, he should dine elsewhere,. The owner further stated that the patron was no longer welcome in the restaurant and would not be served in the future. The patron sued the restaurant claiming discrimination. The court held for the restaurant noting that the patron's complaint was based on discrimination for being a nonsmoker. Said the court, "A local ordinance allows smoking [in a restaurant] confined to one area. . . . Should the patron insist on smoke-free air, employees may have no choice but to ask him or her to leave . . . nonsmokers are not a protected class" under the civil rights act.

An interesting case involved a casino's ejection of a patron who was a counter, that is, someone who keeps track in blackjack of what cards have been played. When certain cards which tilt the odds in favor of the player remain to be played, the counter bets the house limits and frequently wins, to the chagrin of the casino.

The expelled counter challenged the casino's right to evict him. The court held the counter was not protected by the Civil Rights Act because his exclusion was not based on race, color, religion, or national origin. *Uston v. Airport Casino, Inc.*, 564 F.2d 1216 (Cal., 1977). The counter also claimed that the casino violated the common law duty of an innkeeper to accommodate all seeking service. As you no doubt anticipate, the court rejected this argument because the relationship of the casino to the counter was not one of innkeeper and guest.

The common law obligation of innkeepers to provide accommodations to all who seek them remains in effect. However, even this rule has exceptions that allow an innkeeper to refuse accommodations to a guest who is unable to prove ability to pay, a guest who is disorderly, or who has a contagious disease. These exceptions and others will be discussed in Chapter 10.

Permissible to Remove a Disorderly Person

Removal of a patron who is acting disorderly does not violate the civil rights laws. Although the unruly diner may be a member of a protected minority, ejection based on conduct does not violate the Act. The following case, involving a McDonald's restaurant, illustrates this point. As you read the case, note how the customer sought to prove racial discrimination and the reasons why the court rejected that proof.

CASE EXAMPLE 3–5

Alexis v. McDonald's Restaurants of Massachusetts, Inc.
67 F.3d 341 (1st Cir., 1995)

At approximately 10:00 p.m. on July 20, 1990, in Framingham, Massachusetts, Alexis and her family, who are African Americans, entered a McDonald's restaurant, proceeded to the service counter, placed their order, and paid in advance. When the food was placed before them at the service counter, it became apparent that Alfredo Pascacio, whose native tongue is Spanish, had mistaken their order. During the ensuing exchange between Alexis and Pascacio, defendant-appellee Donna Domina, the "swing manager," intervened on behalf of Pascacio, which prompted Alexis to say: "[You] take care of the people in front of you. He's taking care of me, and we're sorting this out." Domina nonetheless persisted for several more minutes.

Ultimately, Domina said to Alexis, "I don't have to listen to you." Alexis replied, "[Y]ou're damn right you don't have to listen to me. I was not speaking to you. I was speaking to him." Domina then instructed Pascacio: "just put their stuff in a bag and get them out of here." Turning to Alexis, Domina retorted: "You're not eating here. If you [do] we're going to call the cops." Alexis responded: "Well you do what you have to do because we plan to eat here." Notwithstanding

Domina's instructions, Pascacio placed the food order on a service tray, without bagging it. The entire incident at the service counter had lasted approximately ten minutes.

After the Alexis family went into the dining area, Sherry Toham, a managerial employee, summoned defendant Michael Leporati into the restaurant. Leporati, a uniformed off-duty police sergeant, had been patrolling on foot outside the restaurant by prearrangement with the Town of Framingham, but had witnessed no part of the earlier exchange among Alexis, Pascacio, and Domina.

Upon entering the restaurant, Leporati was informed by Domina that Alexis had been yelling, creating a "scene" and an "unwarranted disturbance" over a mistaken food order, and directing abusive remarks at Pascacio. Domina informed Leporati that Alexis had argued loudly with her and another employee; that she "just wasn't stopping"; and that Alexis was still in the dining area though Domina had "asked her to leave." Finally, Domina told Leporati, "I would like her to leave."

Without further inquiry into the "disturbance" allegedly caused by Alexis, Leporati proceeded to the dining area where Alexis and her family were seated, and informed the entire Alexis family that the manager wanted them to leave and that they would have to do so. Alexis immediately asked why, denied causing any disturbance, and claimed a right to finish eating in the restaurant. When she urged Leporati to ask other restaurant customers whether there had been a disturbance, Leporati simply reiterated that the family would have to leave. . . .

Approximately ten minutes later, Officer William Fuer arrived, and Alexis was told by Leporati that she was being placed under arrest. . . .

Alexis eventually was charged with criminal trespass, a misdemeanor. Following her acquittal by a jury, Alexis and her family filed the present action . . . asserting civil rights claims under 42 USC Section 1981. . . . The district court granted summary judgment for the defendants. . . .

Alexis presses her section 1981 claim against Domina and McDonald's on the theory that her race-based exclusion from the dining area violated her right to make and enforce contracts. [Presumably the contract to which Alexis was referring was the contract to purchase food from McDonald's.]. . .

Alexis submitted deposition testimony of six witnesses—the five Alexis family members and Karen Stauffer, an eyewitness to the events—each of whom opined, in effect, that had Alexis been a "rich white woman," she would not have been treated in the same manner. The court found that the proffered testimony was "not supported by sufficient factual undergirding" to permit a reasonable inference that either Domina or McDonald's discriminated against Alexis on the basis of her race. . . . The six deponents based their inferences of racial animus on their personal observations that Domina reacted "angrily" toward Alexis and with a "negative tone in her voice," was "unfriendly," "uncooperative," "high strung," "impolite," "impatient," and had "no reason" to eject Alexis. Although these observations may be entirely compatible with a race-based animus, there simply is no foundation for an inference that Domina harbored a racial animus toward Alexis or anyone else, absent some probative evidence that Domina's petulance stemmed from something other than a race-neutral reaction to the stressful encounter plainly evidenced in the record, including Alexis's persistence (however justified). . . .

As Alexis points to no competent evidence that Domina and McDonald's intentionally discriminated against her on account of her race, the district court correctly ruled that this section 1981 claim [should be dismissed]. Disputes generally arise out of mutual misunderstanding, misinterpretation, and overreaction, and without more, such disputes do not give rise to an inference of discrimination. Accordingly, the summary judgment entered in favor of Domina and McDonald's must be affirmed. . . .

CASE QUESTIONS

1. On what basis did the court find that the restaurant was not liable for discrimination?

Discrimination

Age is a classification not protected in places of public accommodation by the Act or most state civil rights laws. Thus, it is normally not illegal to treat varying age groups differently in such places. For example, a large discount department store, concerned about the high rate of shoplifting in the CD and tape department, barred school-age youths in the store after 3:30 P.M. on weekdays unless accompanied by an adult. Again, although this amounts to treatment of young people differently from others, discrimination on the basis of age is not illegal. Similarly, a skating rink that wishes to promote a Saturday evening session as an event for teens can exclude from the rink people who are younger or older.

An interesting case involved a discount on a city's fee for use of municipal tennis courts offered to adults over 60 and young people under age 18. The plaintiff did not qualify for either discount and claimed the reduced cost constituted discrimination based on age. The state involved, Arizona, unlike many states, had a statute that prohibited discrimination in places of public accommodation based on age. The court nonetheless rejected plaintiff's claim noting, "[S]enior citizens are entitled to retire at some point in their lives. Further, that upon retirement, income diminishes and encouraging and enabling citizens to enjoy life and the benefits of society as they reach an elderly age is a favored public policy." *Kahn v. Thompson*, 916 P.2d 1124 (Ariz., 1995).

While discrimination on the basis of age in places of public accommodation is generally permissible, discrimination on the basis of age in employment decisions is restricted, as we will discuss in Chapter 14.

Reasonable Rules of an Establishment

The management of a service establishment, like any other business enterprise, must have rules to maintain order and express the philosophy of its management. Often these rules result in different treatment of different groups. To pass muster, the rules must be reasonable and must not result in discrimination against protected classes.

In the following case, the management of a restaurant had a rule that excluded any person who was barefoot. A woman, ejected from the restaurant because she had removed her shoes, challenged the legality of the rule.

CASE EXAMPLE 3–6

Feldt v. Marriott Corporation
322 A.2d 913 (D.C., 1974)

[Appellant], about 26 years of age, and her male escort had attended a dance at a fraternity house and after leaving the dance went to a Junior Hot Shoppe, owned and operated by appellee. They went through a cafeteria line, selected, and paid for some food and then sat at a table and began to eat. The manager of the shop approached the table and told appellant she would have to leave because she was not wearing shoes. [Appellant left her shoes in her escort's automobile parked near the entrance.] No sign to that effect was posted, but the manager said it was the company's policy to serve no one who was not wearing shoes. She replied she would leave as soon a she finished eating. The manager did not offer to refund her money, and she asked for no refund. [There was testimony that the manager offered to get a bag so she could take the food—a hamburger and french fries—with her.] He continued to insist that she leave, and she continued to insist she would leave only when she had finished eating. The argument continued and she finally said to the manager: "Will you, please, go to hell." He walked outside and returned with a police officer. The manager again asked her to leave, and the officer told her she would be violating the unlawful entry statute if she refused to leave after the manager had asked her to leave. She replied she would leave when she had finished eating. The officer took her arm and said unless she left he would arrest her. She arose and walked to the door and then, observing the officer behind her, began struggling with him and hit him.

Appellant was then placed in a patrol wagon, taken to a precinct station, and later taken to the Women's Detention Center. Hours later she was released on her personal recognizance and told to appear in court the next day. When she appeared in court, she was told the charge against her would be dropped and she was free to leave.

It is clear that appellant entered the premises lawfully, but it is also clear that under our unlawful entry statute . . . one who lawfully enters may be guilty of a misdemeanor by refusing to leave after being ordered to do so by the person lawfully in charge of the premises. Our question is whether the police officer was justified in arresting appellant when she, in his presence, refused to leave after being ordered to do so by the manager.

At common law, a restaurant owner had the right to arbitrarily refuse service to any guest.

Absent constitutional or statutory rights, the common law still controls in this jurisdiction. This is not a case of racial discrimination or violation of civil rights. We do have a statute making it unlawful for a restaurant to refuse service to "any quiet and orderly person" or to exclude anyone on account of race or color; but, as we have said, there was no racial discrimination here and we do not think the requirement to serve any quiet or orderly person prevents a restaurant from having reasonable requirements as to the dress of its customers, such as a requirement that all male customers wear coats and ties, or, as here, that all customers wear shoes. Had the restaurant manager observed that appellant was not wearing shoes when she first entered the restaurant, he could have properly and lawfully refused to serve her and requested her to leave. Our question narrows down to whether the fact that the restaurant had served appellant food and received payment for it prevented the restaurant from ordering appellant to leave when her shoeless condition was observed.

The status of a customer in a restaurant, as far as we can ascertain, has never been precisely declared. It is not the same as a guest at an inn. . . .

The nearest analogy we have found in the reported cases to the one here is that of a patron of a theater, racetrack, or other place of public entertainment, who, after having purchased a ticket, is ordered to leave. It has been generally held that such a patron has only a personal license, which may be revoked at any time, leaving him only with a breach of contract claim [against the proprietor].

We think that is the applicable rule here. When appellant was ordered to leave, her license to be on the premises was revoked, whether legally or illegally, and she had no right to remain. Her remedy, if any, was a civil action for breach of contract. . . .

Our conclusion is that when appellant, in the presence of the police officer, refused to leave on the demand of the restaurant manager, the officer was justified in arresting her for violation of the unlawful entry statute. . . .

Ejection of Objectionable Persons

Patrons who do not leave the premises after being requested to leave, or those who enter the premises despite a warning not to enter may be guilty of criminal trespass. Even if the patrons enter the premises lawfully, they may be guilty of trespass if they fail to obey a lawful order by the owner to leave. To commit this crime patrons must first be informed they are on the premises against the owner's will. What should hoteliers and restaurateurs do if an individual they have asked to leave refuses to go? The best response is to call the police to handle the matter. Ideally, a confrontation like the one described in *Feldt v. Marriott Corp.* will be avoided. The rights of the proprietor in this situation will be discussed at more length in Chapter 10.

Summary

Sadly, discrimination was a practice quite prevalent in the hospitality industry before the passage of the Civil Rights Act of 1964. Today, many laws prohibit discrimination. The common law prohibits innkeepers from refusing accommodations to anyone who seeks them, unless certain exceptions apply. The Civil Rights Act of 1964 prevents hotels, restaurants, gas stations, and places of entertainment engaged in interstate commerce from discriminating on the basis of race, color, religion, or national origin. State Civil Rights laws fill in the gaps by preventing discrimination within the state in a large class of facilities on the grounds of not just race, color, religion, and national origin, but also sex, marital status, and disability. The Americans With Disabilities Act prohibits discrimination on the basis of disability and requires various accommodations for disabled patrons.

We have seen in this chapter how the law can be used as a tool to discourage unacceptable conduct and encourage action viewed by lawmakers as necessary for the well-being of our country and states.

Preventive Law Tips for Managers

- *Do Not Refuse a Hotel Room to Anyone Who Shows Ability to Pay.* The common law requires that hotels provide rooms for everyone requesting accommodations. Failure to provide a room to a would-be guest with the financial means to pay can result in liability.

- *Do Not Refuse a Hotel Room to Anyone Based on Membership in a Protected Class.* Failure to provide a room based on race, color, religion, or nationality violates the Civil Rights Act of 1964 and can result in an injunction and judgment for attorney's fees in favor of the plaintiff. Refusal to provide a room based on sex, marital status, or disability may violate a state civil rights law and subject the innkeeper to criminal penalties. If the hotel is located in a locality that forbids discrimination based on sexual orientation, refusal to provide a room to someone who is homosexual will result in liability. In addition to the legal penalties, discrimination contradicts the basic principle of equal opportunity and treatment on which our country was founded, and violates a basic tenet of the hospitality industry to treat customers well and make them feel comfortable.

- *Do Not Refuse Restaurant Services to Someone on the Ground of Race, Color, Religion, or Nationality.* The Civil Rights Act of 1964 outlaws discrimination on these grounds.

- *Do Not Refuse Restaurant Services to Someone on the Grounds of Sex, Marital Status, or Disability.* State civil rights laws customarily outlaw discrimination on these grounds, and the federal Americans with Disabilities Act outlaws discrimination against disabled persons. Failure to abide by these laws can result in civil and criminal liability. Also, local ordinances may prohibit discrimination on the basis of sexual orientation. These types of discrimination can be as hurtful to the guest and damaging to the hospitality industry as discrimination based on race, color, religion, and nationality.

- *Do Not Refuse Access to Places of Entertainment on the Grounds of Race, Color, Religion, or Nationality.* The Act prohibits discrimination in places of entertainment based on race, color, religion, or nationality. The word "Entertainment" as used by the Act includes enterprises such as movie theaters that offer entertainment presentations to a viewing audience, as well as places where the patron actively participates in the activity such as a ranch offering horseback riding.

- *Do Not Refuse Access to Places of Entertainment on the Grounds of Sex, Marital Status, or Disability.* State civil rights laws customarily outlaw discrimination on these grounds, and the federal Americans With Disabilities Act outlaws discrimination against disabled persons. Violation of these laws can result in civil and criminal liability. Also, local ordinances may prohibit discrimination on the basis of sexual orientation.

- *If Covered by the Americans With Disabilities Act, Eliminate Barriers to Accessibility if the Removal is Readily Achievable.* Places of public accommodation are required to remove hindrances that can be eliminated easily and without a lot of expense. Barrier removal that would be costly or difficult to achieve is not required. If new construction or alterations are undertaken, more extensive obstacle removal will be required. However, accessibility is not required where the cost to remove barriers is out of proportion with the cost or scope of the alteration or construction project.

- *A Private Club Wishing to Retain That Status Should Limit Membership, Develop Clear Selection Criteria, Ensure that Control and Ownership of the Club Rests with Members, and Refrain from Widely Advertising for Members.* The courts have developed rules to determine what clubs are private— and therefore not bound by the Act—and which clubs are not. Unless the rules are followed closely, a club will not be deemed private.

Review Questions

1. According to the common law, to whom can a hotel refuse to provide accommodations?
2. Why did Congress pass the Civil Rights Act of 1964?
3. Who is protected by the Civil Rights Act of 1964?
4. What facilities are covered by the Act?
5. What is interstate commerce and why is it relevant to the Act?
6. What remedies are available to a plaintiff suing for a violation of the Act?
7. Name three types of businesses not covered by the Act.
8. Identify three differences between the Act and state civil rights laws.
9. In addition to prohibiting the denial of a room or services to certain persons, what conduct is outlawed by state civil rights laws?
10. Identify three tests used by the courts to determine whether or not a club is private.
11. What is a restaurant required to do under the Americans With Disabilities Act to remove barriers to accessibility?
12. Can a restaurant require that all wheelchair-bound customers eat in the same area of the restaurant?

Discussion Questions

1. Many localities have laws that require restaurants to seat smokers in an area separate from nonsmokers. Do these laws require restaurants to discriminate illegally? Why or why not?
2. Why do you think Congress did not include sex as a protected class in the Act?
3. Why is a successful plaintiff in most lawsuits unable to collect attorney's fees from the defendant, but a successful plaintiff suing under the Act can?
4. Identify three laws that impact a hotel's ability to refuse a room to a would-be guest. How do they differ from each other?
5. Why do you think the Act outlaws even single acts of discrimination rather than requiring a pattern of discriminatory conduct?
6. A train station has a snack bar located in it. What additional information would you need to know to determine if the train station is covered by the Act? Why would you need that additional information?

7. Why do you think Congress omitted many bed-and-breakfast operations from the Act (the "Mrs. Murphy's Boarding House" clause)?

8. If you were devising an expansion of the civil rights laws, would you include any additional protected classes? Who and why?

9. What distinguishes the establishments covered by the Americans With Disabilities Act and those covered by the Civil Rights Act of 1964?

Application Questions

1. Devise an operating plan for a private club that would pass muster if challenged.

2. A community college, serving primarily residents of the local county, has a candy shop on campus. Of twenty varieties of candies it sells, only one ingredient of one variety was purchased from out of state. Is the college governed by the Act? Why or why not?

3. Identify whether the following is illegal discrimination and explain your reasoning:

   a. A restaurant refuses to serve anyone who is Swiss.

   b. A restaurant refuses to serve someone who arrives for dinner two minutes before the kitchen closes.

   c. A restaurant refuses to serve a person in a wheelchair with a service dog because the restaurant does not allow pets in the dining area.

   d. A hotel refuses to provide a room to a couple because they are not married.

   e. A movie theater refuses to sell a ticket to someone who is carrying a weapon.

   f. A private club refuses to admit someone who is Protestant.

   g. A hotel refuses to provide a room to a person who is deaf because he is unable to provide proof of ability to pay.

CHAPTER 4

Contract Law and the Hospitality Industry

CHAPTER OUTLINE

INTRODUCTION

A **contract** is an agreement between two or more parties that is enforceable in court. Examples of contracts include the following:

- A hotel agrees to buy new furniture for its lobby and in exchange agrees to pay a specified price for it;

- A guest agrees to rent a room for next weekend and pay the agreed rate. In exchange, the hotel agrees to reserve it for the guest and not rent it to anyone else;

- An association agrees to hold its annual convention at a hotel and pay the specified costs. In exchange, the hotel agrees to provide rooms, banquet facilities, food, and related services.

A contract can be in writing and signed, or it can be oral. It can even be implied, which means it can come into existence without a word ever being written or spoken. For example, on your way to an 8:00 A.M. class you stop at the cleaners with a pair of slacks. You are in a hurry to get to class, and the attendant is in the back of the store reading the morning paper. He hears you enter and looks up. You put the slacks on the counter and waive. He waives back and resumes reading. The two of you have not exchanged a word yet a contract exists obligating the cleaning company to clean your slacks and for you to pay the going rate.

The Elements of a Contract

Regardless of whether the contract is written, oral or implied, certain essential elements must exist for the contract to be **valid**, meaning enforceable in court. These elements are: contractual capacity, mutuality, legality, consideration, proper form, and genuine assent.

Capacity to Contract

For a valid contract, the parties must have legal **capacity to contract**, that is, the ability to both understand the terms of the contract and appreciate that failure to perform its terms can lead to legal liability, including a lawsuit. According to the law, the following groups of people lack sufficient judgment or mental ability to appreciate fully the nature of a contractual commitment and thus do not have the capacity to contract: minors (people under age 18 in some states, under 19 or 21 in others); very intoxicated persons; and the mentally incompetent. Their contracts are voidable.

A **voidable contract** is one that may be canceled at the option of one party (in this case, the person with the disability). This right to cancel (also called the right to "avoid" or "disaffirm") applies while the disability exists and for a reasonable time after it disappears, that is, after the minor reaches 18, the very intoxicated person becomes sober, or the incompetent person becomes competent. Thus, a 17 year old who purchases a car can return it if she changes her mind about the purchase. She can do so anytime before she turns eighteen and for a reasonable period of time thereafter. Depending on the state, she will receive a refund of all or some of the price she paid. The reasonable time allowed after removal of the disability is to permit the previously incapacitated person to rethink the appropriateness of a contract with the benefit of new-found capacity.

Certain exceptions and modifications exist to the right to cancel, the most significant being contracts for the purchase of necessities. A minor who enters a contract for necessities can disaffirm the contract but remains liable for the reasonable value of the necessities he received. Necessities include food, shelter, and clothing, and, depending on the minor's circumstances, possibly other items as well. Thus, a minor who decides after enjoying a full meal at a restaurant that he wants to avoid the contract will be liable to the restaurant for the reasonable value of the meal. The main reason for this rule is concern for the well-being of the minor. If minors could avoid payment for necessities, sellers would be reluctant to contract with even those minors who are in need of the basics.

Mutuality: Offer and Acceptance

Mutuality means that all parties to the contract are interested in its terms and intend to enter an agreement to which they will be legally bound. Mutuality is sometimes called a "meeting of the minds". Mutuality is established by one party making an offer and the other party accepting.

An **offer** is a proposal to do or give something of value in exchange for something else. For example, "We have a room we can give you for the night for $65," or, "We can cater your dinner party for fifteen people with the menu you requested for $25 per person." An **offeror** is the person who makes an offer; an **offeree** is the person to whom the offer is made.

The Offer Must be Definite.   The terms of an offer must be definite. If the terms are vague, a contract may not result either because the lack of clarity may evidence a lack of commitment to enter a contract or because the terms are too indefinite to obligate the parties to do anything sufficiently specific. For example, the following statements are too general and vague to constitute offers: "The rooms in this hotel range from $42–$95 a night"; "We cater parties of all sizes". Rather than offers, these statements constitute what the law calls **invitations to negotiate** which means they open discussions that may or may not lead to an offer.

Responses to an Offer.   When an offer is made, the offeree has two options: accept the offer or reject it. An **acceptance** is an expression of agreement by the offeree to the terms of the offer. If the offeree accepts the offer, mutuality is achieved. If the other essential elements needed for a contract are present, an enforceable contract will exist. If, however, the offeree rejects the offer, the parties have not mutually agreed upon the terms of a contract and so no contract exists.

Sometimes the offeree is interested in the offer but wants to change a few terms. In such case the offeree makes a **counteroffer**, a response to an offer that modifies one or more of its provisions. A counteroffer is not an acceptance. Rather, the counteroffer is treated as a new offer. The original offeror then has the option of accepting the counteroffer, rejecting it, or making another counteroffer. For example, a hotel makes an offer to an association to host its annual three-day conference—including guest rooms, meeting rooms and meals—for $465 per person based on a specified minimum number of reservations. The organization likes the location and layout of the hotel but thinks the price is high. It responds by saying it will hold its conference at the hotel if the hotel lowers its price to $425 per person. This is a counteroffer and no contract exists unless the hotel accepts the counteroffer, or unless the hotel makes another counteroffer that is accepted by the association.

Legality

To be enforceable a contract must have a legal objective. If what the parties obligate themselves to do is illegal, the contract is not just voidable but rather void. A **void contract** is one which is unenforceable in court. For example, we will study in Chapter 15 that it is illegal for competing hotels to agree among themselves to charge the same amount for rooms, and for competing restaurants to agree to charge the same price for meals. This is called price-fixing and violates antitrust laws. If one hotel to such a contract deviates from the agreed price and the other hotels attempt to sue for the first hotel's failure to abide by the contract, the court will summarily dismiss the case without hearing the merits. The reason: contract is void due to its illegal nature.

Consideration

For an agreement to be binding and enforceable in court there must be consideration. The word "consideration" used in this legal sense means something quite different from the definition of consideration in normal parlance. In connection with contracts, **consideration** means something of value exchanged for something else of value. For example, a guest in a hotel gives the innkeeper money and receives in return the right to occupy a room. The consideration for the guest's payment is the right to occupy the room; the consideration for the hotel's providing the room is the guest's money.

Another way to understand consideration is to recognize it as the phenomenon that distinguishes a contract from a gift. A gift transaction is one-sided; one person gives something to the other and receives nothing in return. With a contract, each person gives something and each also receives something in exchange. That which is received is the consideration.

Consideration can take one of three forms:

1. a tangible item or a promise to give such an item (such as food, money, etc.);
2. performance or a promise to perform (such as cleaning a swimming pool, working as a front desk clerk, waiting on tables, etc.); and
3. forbearance or a promise to forbear.

Forbearance means refraining from doing something you have a legal right to do. For example, if you are injured while at a restaurant, you might promise to forbear from suing the restaurant for your injuries if the owner agrees to pay you a satisfactory sum of money.

Parties to a contract can exchange one form of consideration for the same form of consideration, such as when a restaurant patron buys dinner. The customer gives money (something tangible) and the restaurant gives food (something tangible). The parties can also mix two forms of consideration in the same contract such as when an employee contracts to work for a hotel. The employee gives services (a performance) and the hotel gives money (a tangible item). Sometimes the terms of the contract may express such uncertainty about performance that what may appear to be a promise of performance is in fact illusory. Such uncertainty often results where one party places conditions on its promise to perform. An illusory promise does not constitute consideration and will not give rise to a contract. In the following case, the court found that an association scheduling its annual convention did not, in fact, agree to rent any rooms from the plaintiff hotel.

CASE EXAMPLE 4–1

Lederman Enterprises, Inc. v. Allied Social Science Associates
709 P.2d 1 (Colo. App., 1985)

The defendant, Allied Social Science Association (ASSA) . . . an unincorporated group of associations which meet together annually, contacted the Denver Convention and Visitors' Bureau in 1975 when ASSA was considering holding its 1980 convention in Denver. The Visitors' Bureau wrote to several Denver hotels, including The Regency, asking that the hotels commit to hold open a block of rooms in order to attract the ASSA convention to Denver. The Regency responded to the Visitors' Bureau, indicating it would hold 375 rooms open. This information was conveyed by the Bureau to ASSA.

Thereafter, ASSA and The Regency corresponded and, on March 19, 1980, the parties signed a document prepared by The Regency, entitled "Regency Inn-Meeting/Convention Contract." In May of 1980, ASSA mailed preregistration forms to its members informing them of the different Denver hotels available, and requesting the members to list their preferences. When the forms were returned by the members to ASSA, they were forwarded to the Visitors' Bureau which then assigned members of ASSA to the hotels in accordance with the preferences of the members.

Few of the 2,500 members who registered for the convention listed The Regency on their preference list, and none selected it as their first choice. Therefore, the Visitors' Bureau did not assign any members to The Regency. On July 21, 1980, realizing that no members would be making reservations at the Regency, the convention coordinator for ASSA wrote to the Regency stating that: "There is no need to continue to hold rooms for us. . . ."

The Regency filed suit against ASSA and its convention coordinator. . . .

We agree with ASSA that The Regency's form "contract" entitled "Regency Inn-Meeting/ Convention Contract" did not, as a matter of law, constitute a reservation of rooms by ASSA. . . .

The "contract" between the parties specified that reservation cards had to be returned by August 4, 1980, and then stated:

The Regency's cut-off policy calls for all unreserved rooms within your block to be released for sale 30 days prior to arrival. All reservations received thereafter will be accepted on a space available basis only. Should you wish to guarantee any unreserved rooms past the cut-off date, please advise us in writing . . . [Payment of] one night's deposit with each guest room reservation [is requested]. All reservations and agreements are made upon, and are subject to the rules and regulations of the Regency, and the following conditions: . . .

We require a non-refundable deposit of first night's room rate with reservation, unless your organization guarantees payment for any "no shows" in your group.

The gist of this "contract" is that, for an ASSA member to make a reservation at The Regency, a reservation card had to be used and had to be returned to the reservation manager of The Regency by August 4, 1980, accompanied by a deposit. To say that the document itself made reservations [which is what the Regency asserts in this breach of contract case] would make meaningless the need to return reservation cards.

Other provisions in the "contract" are also inconsistent with an interpretation that it constituted a reservation of rooms at The Regency. The several references to "unreserved rooms" within the block of rooms held by The Regency would be rendered meaningless by so holding. The provision that "all unreserved rooms within your block . . . [will] be released 30 days prior to arrival" demonstrates that the rooms within the block had not been reserved merely by ASSA's agreement to the contract's terms.

In our view, the "contract" merely imposed upon The Regency the obligation to make available, under certain conditions, a number of rooms to ASSA; it did not obligate ASSA to reserve any rooms. ASSA's only obligation was to mention The Regency as one of the hotels where members could obtain rooms. Only if further steps were taken by the members would rooms actually be reserved.

There being no reservation of rooms under the "contract" . . . [ASSA did not breach the contract and therefore is not liable to The Regency].

CASE QUESTION

1. How might the wording of the Regency's "contract" have been changed so as to obligate ASSA to rent rooms from The Regency?

Proper Form

Is an oral contract enforceable? The general rule is yes, it is enforceable. It may, however, be difficult to prove. For example, Mrs. Gordon called the Townhouse Hotel and made a reservation for next weekend. In contract terms, she agreed to pay for a room in consideration of the hotel agreeing to reserve one for her use and making it available to her on the specified dates. Neither the hotel nor Mrs. Gordon reduced the contract to writing. Nevertheless, the contract is valid and enforceable. If, when Mrs. Gordon arrives at the hotel, the reservation clerk acknowledges Mrs. Gordon's reservation but apologetically informs her that the hotel has no available rooms and will not be able to accommodate her, the hotel will be liable to Mrs. Gordon for breach of contract; the fact that the contract was not in writing is of no consequence.

Now assume a different set of facts. Mrs. Gordon arrives at the hotel and requests her room. The hotel not only has no room for her but denies ever making a reservation in her name. Despite Mrs. Gordon's protests, the hotel holds firm to its position. In this situation Mrs. Gordon will have a difficult task proving the hotel agreed to reserve a room for her. As this scenario indicates, a good practice is to put all contracts in writing and thereby avoid the "proof problem." But, assuming you can prove an oral contract, it is enforceable.

Contracts That Must Be in Writing: The Statute of Frauds.   The rule that oral contracts are enforceable is a general rule; several exceptions exist. Certain types of contracts are not enforceable unless they are in writing. For these contracts *only*, oral agreements are *not* enforceable. The primary law that requires a writing for these contracts is called the **Statute of Frauds**. The name derives from the statute's objective of preventing someone from perpetrating a fraud by claiming a contract exists when in fact none does. It might better be named the "Statute to Prevent Frauds."

The types of contracts within the Statute of Frauds that must be in writing to be enforceable include the following:

- Contracts for the purchase and sale of real property (land and buildings). For example, a contract to purchase a hotel.

- Contracts that cannot be completed within a year from when they are made. For example, a restaurant manager's employment contract for two years.

- Contracts made in consideration of marriage. For example, "I will give you a boat if you marry me." Better get that promise in writing!

- Contracts to pay another person's debt if that person fails to pay. For example, a hotel guest, when registering, presents the credit card of a small out-of-town company as the means for payment of the hotel bill. The hotel may require that the guest agree to pay the hotel bill if the company fails to do so. This commitment by the guest must be in writing to be enforceable.

In addition to the Statute of Frauds, other laws sometimes impose a writing requirement on contracts. One of these laws mandates a writing for contracts for the sale of goods (moveable, tangible objects, not services) in excess of $500. An example is a contract between a hotel and a furniture store for the purchase of a $1200 couch for the hotel lobby.

The required writing need not be a formal contract. Notes, a letter, or memorandum are sufficient. The writing can be on one piece of paper or pieced together from several. Generally, the writing should specify the essential terms of the agreement. At minimum, to be enforceable, the writing must identify the contractual obligation of the party who is the defendant in a lawsuit to enforce the contract and that person's signature. Initials will suffice in lieu of a full signature.

Parol Evidence Rule.   Often in the course of negotiating a contract, many tentative terms are added and dropped before the final agreement is reached. If the final agreement is reduced to writing, the parties usually intend the writing to be the complete documentation of their agreement. Any terms not included in the writing are viewed by the law as purposely abandoned by the parties.

However, one party may later claim that one of the terms abandoned in the negotiation process was intended by the parties to survive the writing. Such a claim will likely be barred by the parol evidence rule. **Parol** means oral. The **parol evidence rule** prevents the parties from successfully modifying the written agreement with evidence of oral agreements made prior to signing the writing. The purpose of this rule is to protect written contracts from modifications by alleged *prior* oral agreements. For example, assume you are negotiating to purchase a motel. In the rear of the property is an unsightly storage shed. You ask the seller to remove it and she agrees. Thereafter you prepare a written contract containing the terms of your purchase agreement, and it is signed by you and the seller. The writing does not mention the seller's agreement to remove the shed. You want it removed and remind the seller of the agreement but she refuses. In this case the parol evidence rule supports the seller. She need not remove the shed. Since the agreement about the shed was reached prior to signing the contract, and since the promise to remove the shed was not included in the writing, the parol evidence rule bars the buyer from enforcing the seller's commitment to remove the shed. Be sure to include in your written contracts all of the terms of your aggreement!

The parol evidence rule does not apply to statements made *after* a contract is signed. Therefore, evidence can be introduced of agreements made after parties sign a contract even if those agreements vary or modify the written agreement.

Genuine Assent

Another requirement for a valid contract is genuine assent: the parties must genuinely agree to the contract terms. If, for example, one party enters a contract not because he truly consents to its terms but because he was subjected to duress (threats of harm if he did not sign), the contract is voidable and can be disaffirmed by the party who was threatened.

Fraud and Misrepresentation.   A person who enters a contract due to fraud or innocent misrepresentation can avoid the contract. **Fraud** is an intentionally untruthful statement made for the purpose of misleading someone, usually for the other's gain. For example, you make a reservation at a hotel because the reservation clerk, under pressure to increase sales, informed you that the hotel is air conditioned. The clerk knows that the hotel is not. When you arrive in the heat of the summer you discover the hotel is not air conditioned. You have been defrauded and can cancel the reservation contract. **Innocent misrepresentation** is an untruthful statement that the speaker believes is accurate. For example, you arrive at a hotel on a hot summer day and find the temperature in the lobby uncomfortably warm. You ask the manager if the air conditioning is working properly. The repair person had worked on it that afternoon and informed the manager that it was now working correctly. Based on that statement, the manager, believing the air conditioner is working properly, tells you that it is. Relying on the manager's statement, you contract for a room. In fact, the air conditioner is not working, as you discover a short time later when the temperature fails to cool. The manager made an innocent mistake; you can cancel your contract for the room and go elsewhere. The law allows the buyer to avoid the contract in both cases of fraud and innocent misrepresentation because in both circumstances, the buyer has been misled.

Mistakes.   Parties to a contract may make various types of mistakes in the process of negotiating and agreeing to the contract. Some of those mistakes have legal significance and others do not. Mistakes made by a buyer as to value or quality of a good being purchased will not affect the validity of the contract. For example, the manager of a restaurant purchases a desk for the receptionist, believing it is an antique made from expensive wood. The manager's belief in this regard is based on her own judgment of the desk and not on any representations made by the seller. Later the manager learns that the desk is an imitation of an antique and worth significantly less than the amount paid. The manager in this case has made a mistake in judgment as to the value or quality of the good. The contract is not affected by this mistake; the manager cannot cancel the contract. The manager should have investigated the value of the desk more thoroughly before completing the purchase.

Mistakes as to facts, as opposed to value or quality, may affect the validity of the contract. Two types of factual mistakes exist—unilateral and mutual. A **unilateral mistake** is an error made by only one party to the contract as to the terms or performance expected. A **mutual mistake** is one made by both parties.

Generally, a unilateral mistake is not a basis to avoid a contract. Thus, when one party only makes a mistake as to a fact involved with the contract, that party cannot cancel the contract on the basis of the mistake. For example, in *Freeman v. Kiamesha Concord Inc.*, 351 N.Y.S.2d 541 (1974), a guest at a resort hotel misread an advertisement concerning the Memorial Day weekend entertainment and so believed that a popular entertainer would be performing for three nights during the weekend rather than just one. Upon learning the truth he sought to cancel part of his three-day reservation. The court held that his mistake was a factual one and it was unilateral. The mistake, therefore, did not support a cancellation of his reservation. Although he departed the resort before the end of the three day weekend, he remained obligated to pay his hotel bill for the full three days.

Unlike unilateral mistakes, mutual mistakes involving an important fact will enable either party to avoid the contract. For example, Theresa owns two hotels. She contracts to sell one of them to Jeff. Theresa thinks she is selling the hotel on East Main Street. Jeff thinks he is purchasing the one on Dewey Street. The parties in this example made a mutual mistake as to an important fact, the identity of the hotel. Since the parties never had a meeting of the minds, either can avoid the contract.

Trade Usage

It is important for contracting parties to state the terms of their agreement clearly and without ambiguity. If the terms are vague or confusing, the parties may end up in court disputing the meaning. Careful drafting can avoid such lawsuits. Unfortunately for the parties in the following case, the language in their contract left room for argument as to the meaning. Time and money thus had to be invested in a lawsuit.

CASE EXAMPLE 4–2

Lire, Inc. v. Bob's Pizza Inn Restaurants, Inc.
541 N.W.2d 432 (N.D., 1995)

In 1989 Lire, Inc. purchased Bob's Pizza Inn Restaurant in Rugby, North Dakota, from the Schmidts for $400,000. A July 3, 1989, "offer to purchase" said: "Seller to agree to a noncompetition agreement for the selling of Italian type foods for a period of 5 years and within a radius of 60 miles of Rugby." The Schmidts accepted the offer on July 10, 1989. No other documents to the transaction mentioned a noncompetition agreement.

In May 1993 the Schmidts opened Bob's Pizza Inn Restaurant and Lounge in Rugby. Lire sued the Schmidts for breach of contract, seeking damages and injunctive relief. The Schmidts contended the language in the offer to purchase did not create an enforceable noncompetition agreement. [The Schmidts argued that the statement in the offer— "seller to agree"— anticipated a noncompetition agreement in the future which never was entered into]. . . .

The dispositive issue in this appeal is the interpretation of the parties' written contract, specifically the noncompetition language. . . .

Contracts are construed to give effect to the mutual intention of the parties at the time of contracting. . . . Unless used by the parties in a technical sense, words in a contract are construed in their ordinary and popular sense, rather than according to their strict legal meaning. . . .

To create an enforceable contract, there must be a mutual intent to create a legal obligation. . . .

The phrase "seller to agree" was part of a July 3, 1989 written offer to purchase, which was accepted by the Schmidts on July 10, 1989. The remaining noncompetition language was definite and certain as to its terms—"a noncompetition agreement for the selling of Italian type foods for a period of 5 years and within a radius of 60 miles of Rugby." Those terms completely describe the type of business restriction, the duration of the restriction, and the geographic limitation for the restriction. . . . When this noncompetition language is read as a whole and as part of a subsequently accepted offer to purchase, we believe the ordinary and popular understanding of the phrase "seller to agree" objectively evidences the parties' mutual intent to create an enforceable noncompetition agreement at the time of the Schmidts' acceptance. We conclude the written noncompetition language is unambiguous and creates an enforceable noncompetition agreement for Rugby.

Because the parties' written contract unambiguously created an enforceable noncompetition agreement in Rugby, Lire was entitled to judgment. . . .

CASE QUESTION

1. How might the parties have drafted the noncompetition clause to avoid the ambiguity that led to this lawsuit?

When contract terms are ambiguous the court can use "trade usage" to clarify the ambiguity. **Trade usage** means practices or modes of dealing generally adhered to in a particular industry, such that an expectation arises that they will be honored in a given transaction. For example, in *Frigaliment Importing Co., Ltd. v. B. N. S. International Sales Corp.*, 190 F. Supp. 116 (N.Y., 1960), the contracting parties were unable to agree on the meaning of the word "chicken." Their contract required the seller to deliver a specified quantity of chicken to the buyer. Seller delivered stewing chickens, the least expensive poultry. Buyer objected, claiming the word "chicken" as used in the contract required a higher grade of chicken. The dispute ended up in court. Experts in the poultry field testified that various grades of chicken exist, and that each is identified by a different name except for the lowest grade which is called simply "chicken." The court thus determined the seller had fulfilled its contractual obligation by delivering the bottom-of-the-line stewing chickens.

The following case provides another example of the application of trade usage as an aid to interpretation of a contract.

CASE EXAMPLE 4–3

Pennyrile Tours, Inc. v. Country Inns, USA, Inc.
559 F.Supp. 15 (Tenn., 1982)

. . . In December 1981 the defendant, Country Inns, mailed a brochure to the plaintiff, Pennyrile Tours, advertising that defendant [hotel which was under construction] was accepting reservations. . . .

Subsequent to receipt of the brochure, plaintiff orally contracted for various group room reservations with the defendant by telephone and was required to pay advance deposits totalling $10,720. Defendant represented that its facilities would be completed well before May 1982, the opening day of the 1982 World's Fair. At this time there was no discussion between the parties of a cancellation policy. Plaintiff's first reservations were for May 16 and May 17, 1982.

Subsequent to the telephone conversation between the parties, plaintiff received written confirmation of room reservations on the dates requested at each of defendant's three locations. Subsequent to the receipt of confirmation of room reservations, the plaintiff mailed checks at various times which totalled $10,720 to the defendant as deposits for room reservations.

The Court is convinced from the testimony that there is an industry-wide custom and standard used in the motel business for a refund of reservation deposits. [According to this custom,] a refund is made if reservations are canceled at least 30 days prior to the reserved dates.

On or about March 27, 1982, representatives of plaintiff inspected the facilities advertised by the defendant. The facilities were not near completion as of that date, as the defendant had previously represented they would be. . . .

On or about April 16, 1982, plaintiff's representatives returned to Knoxville to again inspect defendant's facilities. The facilities remained far from completion and serious doubts were raised as to whether the facilities would ever be completed. . . . [T]he plaintiff, by letter dated April 18, 1982, canceled its reservations with the defendant and demanded full refund of all deposits.

By letter dated April 23, 1982, the defendant refused to refund any deposits made by the plaintiff because of company policy. Mrs. Miller, representative of plaintiff, testified that she never received the company policy until she canceled the reservations. She says that the letter of April 23, 1982, was the first knowledge that she had of any cancellation policy contrary to the industry-wide standard. . . .

The plaintiff has not received any refund of the deposits in the amount of $10,720 from the defendant.

The parties agree that they had a valid oral contract. Defendant promised to provide motel accommodations in exchange for plaintiff's promise to pay for the accommodations. The Court has found that the parties did not discuss the terms for cancellation of the contract and that there was no written provision relating to refunds of deposits. We must therefore look to the intention of the parties for the fair and reasonable construction [of the contract] under the circumstances. . . .

[U]sages of trade may be considered in determining the intentions of the parties . . . . A usage of trade is defined as:

any practice or method of dealing having such regularity of observance in a place, vocation or trade as to justify an expectation that it will be observed with respect to the transaction in question.

The practice of refunding deposits if reservations are canceled thirty days prior to the scheduled arrival date is a regular method of dealing in the tourist business. Exceptions to the usual practice are made known during initial negotiations between the parties. Plaintiff relied on defendant's silence and the customary practice in this case. . . .

Accordingly, it is ORDERED [that defendant must return plaintiff's deposit and] that judgment be entered in favor of plaintiff in the amount of $10,720.

CASE QUESTIONS

1. Why did the Court apply the industry-wide cancellation practice to the contract between Pennyrile Tours and Country Inns?

2. What could Country Inns have done to avoid the application of the industry practice to its contract with Pennyrile?

The previous cases underscore the importance of careful drafting of a contract. The terms should be clear and the parties' intentions obvious. If language used in a contract is susceptible to more than one meaning, the result may be an expensive and timely lawsuit which could have been avoided simply by more careful wording.

Breach of Contract

Failure to perform as required by a contract constitutes **breach of contract**, a civil wrong, not a criminal one. The nonbreaching party may be entitled to a remedy including damages or specific performance.

Compensatory Damages

The breaching party may be required to pay compensatory damages to the other contracting party (the nonbreaching party). **Compensatory damages** refers to the sum of money necessary to cover loss incurred by the nonbreaching party as a result of the breach. Stated differently, the nonbreaching party is entitled to the "benefit of the bargain," meaning the breaching party must put the nonbreaching party in the position it would have been in had the contract been fully performed. The nonbreaching party is generally not entitled to pain and suffering, that is, compensation for physical pain, mental anguish, stress, or other similar injury resulting from breach of contract. Pain and suffering as an element of damages is limited to negligence and other torts.

Requirement of Foreseeability.   A plaintiff seeking to collect damages for breach of contract must prove that the damages were foreseeable to the breaching party. If the latter could not anticipate the loss, the plaintiff will not be awarded compensation for the loss.

Requirement of Reasonable Certainty.   The plaintiff in a breach of contract case must prove to a reasonable certainty that she suffered a loss as a result of the breach. Some states also require that the plaintiff prove the amount of the loss to a reasonable certainty. For example, a resort hotel hired an unknown singer to perform in the nightclub. Due to low reservations the hotel canceled the show. Unknown to the hotel, the singer had arranged for a talent scout to attend. When the hotel breached the contract, the singer sued for loss of income that might have resulted from the presence of the talent scout had the scout liked the performance and agreed to promote the singer. The singer will lose for two reasons: inability to prove reasonable certainty of the fact or amount of damages; and inability to prove the hotel could have foreseen those damages.

In the following case the issue arose as to proof of damages to a reasonable certainty.

CASE EXAMPLE 4–4

**Cardinal Consulting Company
v. Circo Resorts, Inc.
297 N.W.2d 260 (Minn. 1980)**

Cardinal Consulting was established by William O'Neill and Wayne Haas in August 1974 to operate one-stop charter tours to Las Vegas and other holiday areas. . . . The defendant was Circo Resorts, a Nevada corporation that operates the Circus Circus Hotel in Las Vegas. Jay Valentine was the sales manager for Circus Circus Hotel and had made the original contract with Cardinal Consulting.

Valentine verbally agreed that Circus Circus would set aside fifty rooms at a price of $16 per night for Cardinal, and if rooms had to be canceled later, it would pose no problem because that period was traditionally slow in Las Vegas.

In November 1975, the management of Circus Circus was reorganized under the leadership of Mel Larson, . . . In an attempt to make the operation of the hotel more efficient and to ensure that all rooms were full, Larson decided to draft formal contracts to govern Circus Circus's relations with all tour operators using its facilities. . . .

On December 10, 1975, Valentine called Cardinal from Las Vegas to set up a meeting in Minneapolis for December 13. Haas told Valentine then and on December 13 that Cardinal was canceling the first three tours. Valentine then told him to put it in writing, which he did in his letter of December 16.

At their meeting, Valentine presented Haas with the proposed written contract between Cardinal and Circus Circus, which Haas refused to sign because it did not represent their agreement. Although Valentine agreed to take it back and get it redrafted, Larson refused to alter the contract and took the position that without the signature of O'Neill and Haas, there was no agreement.

On January 5, 1976, Cardinal received a letter from Circus Circus canceling the rooms that had been reserved by Cardinal for the entire 1976 season. O'Neill and Haas immediately called Las Vegas, and Larson told them that since they had refused to sign the agreement, they had no rooms. . . .

After Circo's cancellation, O'Neill and Haas attempted to salvage their tour package. They contacted numerous Las Vegas hotels, and, finally, . . .

they learned that the Marina Hotel, which had just opened, still had rooms available . . . they were able to salvage eight tours that operated at 100 percent capacity, although not back-to-back. [Therefore] they had to use the money they would have earned from these tours to cover the charges of bringing back empty planes, [and so] Cardinal never made a profit.

The disastrous nature of the 1976 season ruined Cardinal Consulting Company, although in subsequent years the one-stop charter business from the Upper Midwest to Las Vegas flourished. . . .

Circo contends that Cardinal's claim for lost profits should have been dismissed because Cardinal was not an established business and could not prove its lost profits with the requisite degree of certainty to support recovery. It attacks [Cardinal's claimed right to damages] on [the following] grounds: (1) that Cardinal did not prove the fact of lost profits because it could show no past or future profitability; (2) that Cardinal did not prove causation because other factors, such as its undercapitalization and lack of advertising, more plausibly explained its failure; . . .

The general rule is that damages in the form of lost profits may be recovered where they are shown to be the natural and probable consequences of the act or omission complained of and their amount is shown with a reasonable degree of certainty and exactness. . . . This rule does not call for absolute certainty.

The controlling principle is that speculative, remote, or conjectural damages are not recoverable. . . . Although the law recognizes that it is more difficult to prove loss of prospective profits to a new business than to an established one, the law does not hold that it may not be done. . . . Uncertainty as to the fact of whether any damages were sustained at all is fatal to recovery, but uncertainty as to the amount is not. . . .

We agree with Circo that the evidence relating to lost profits that was presented by Cardinal lacks precision. Nevertheless, we cannot say that it was unreasonable for the jury to award lost profits to Cardinal, given the unusual circumstances of this particular enterprise and the devastating effect of Circo's breach.

Although Cardinal was able to demonstrate no past or future profitability, one of several substitutes was available in the evidence presented at trial. Haas and O'Neill were portrayed as persons with extensive experience in arranging tours who were also familiar with Las Vegas. They entered the one-stop charter market early with packages that others, such as retail agencies or social clubs, would be selling for them. Moreover, the market they chose was a fertile one. Las Vegas was very popular with the people from the Upper Midwest, and the small cities on which they were concentrating offered an untapped source of tour participants. . . . [T]hey were planning to operate their tours during the peak tourist period. . . . This same market and time period have been extremely profitable for those travel agencies who began one-stop charter packages the following year. . . .

Similarly, the evidence, although weak, supports the inference that, were it not for the cancellation by Circo, Cardinal would have been able to fill all its flights except the first three. . . . Cardinal sold out the eight trips it actually ran, which could not have been accomplished but for the energy and skill of Haas and O'Neill, and the significant unmet demand for a travel service of this kind. That they were able to do so well on such short notice is persuasive to us, particularly because the substituted hotel, being new, lacked the appeal that the better known and advertised Circus Circus Hotel would have had for prospective customers. . . . As the wrongdoer, Circo should not be permitted to evade its liability just because its wrongful cancellation involved a new business rather than an established one. . . .

Moreover, although Cardinal's capital was limited, the business depended more on the character and personality of the entrepreneurs than on the amount available either for investment or advertising. . . .

Ruling of the Court: [Cardinal is entitled to collect lost profits from Circus.]

CASE QUESTIONS

1. Why is reasonable certainty as to damages a prerequisite for a non-breaching party to collect damages?

2. Why did Cardinal have difficulty proving its damages to a reasonable certainty?

Duty to Mitigate.   A plaintiff seeking to collect damages for breach of contract must prove that it attempted to mitigate its loss. **Mitigate** means to reduce, to lessen. If the plaintiff takes no steps to contain the damages and instead ignores the possibility of reducing them, plaintiff will not be able to recover any of its loss from the breaching defendant. The reason for this rule is the law's objective to avoid economic waste, that is, an unnecessary loss. Assume a hotel has a contract with a snowplower to plow the hotel's driveway. Following a big storm the plower does not plow and the hotel is unable to contact her. If the hotel takes no steps to locate another plower, guests might cancel reservations because they are unable to drive into the hotel's parking lot. The hotel may be able to avoid the loss of income that will result from canceled reservations by locating another plower to do the job. If the hotel does not attempt to mitigate its loss, it will not be able to collect its lost profits from the plower. If the hotel makes a good faith effort to hire a substitute but is unable to find someone available to plow, the original plower will be liable for the hotel's lost profits.

Punitive Damages

As we have learned, punitive damages means a sum of money awarded to a plaintiff in excess of compensatory damages, the purpose of which is to punish the defendant. Punitive damages are awarded only if the defendant's actions are wanton or malicious. This type of damage is not often awarded in a breach of contract case.

Specific Performance

Another remedy for breach of contract is **specific performance**, which is a court order requiring the defendant to perform the act promised in the contract. Specific performance is applicable only to contracts involving the sale of unique, one-of-a-kind items such as a particular restaurant or a famous painting. If the seller fails to execute the sale, the buyer can sue for specific performance.

Contracting for a Room

As with all contracts, a contract for a room between an innkeeper and a guest must satisfy the essential elements—contractual capacity, mutuality, legality, consideration, proper form, and genuine consent.

Most contracts for hotel rooms begin with an invitation to negotiate from a would-be guest who inquires as to room availability and price. An offer is often thereafter made by the hotel or guest. If it is accepted, the necessary mutuality exits.

As we have seen, if the hotel and guest are savvy they will put their agreement in writing. Misunderstandings as to dates, duration of stay, and special needs of the guest are thereby avoided.

The agreement for one or more rooms between the hotel and guest can take many forms, including:

- *Walk-in:* A guest without a reservation requests and receives accommodations.
- *Confirmed reservation:* The hotel has agreed, usually in writing, to the guest's reservation request.
- *Guaranteed reservation:* The guest promises to pay for the room, even if the guest never takes possession of it.
- *Prepaid reservation:* Payment of the first day's charge is made by a guest to either the hotel, a travel agency, or through a computer network.
- *Blanket reservation:* A block of rooms is held for a particular group, with individual members of the group requesting individual room assignments from that block.

Overbooking and Breach of Reservation Contract

The hotel reservation, once made and confirmed, is valid and binds the hotel to provide accommodations. Nonetheless, hotels sometimes overbook, that is, they confirm more reservations than the number of rooms they have available. Experience proves that a certain percentage of confirmed guests will not use their reservations. Hotels that overbook "play the odds," that is, they overbook by a number approximately equal to the number of confirmed reservations who, based on the hotel's experience, are expected not to show. If the numbers work out, everyone with a reservation who comes to the hotel will have a room. However, if the expected no-shows do appear, the hotel will not be able to accommodate everyone. For those the hotel cannot accommodate, the hotel will be in breach of contract and liable for damages.

In *Brown v. Hilton Hotels Corporation*, 211 S.E.2d 125 (Ga., 1974), the hotel failed to honor plaintiffs' confirmed reservation. Plaintiffs were unable to find other accommodations and so were forced to fly home. The plaintiffs sought and received damages for breach of contract.

Damages Allowed for Overbooking

The would-be guest who is denied a room because the hotel has overbooked is entitled to collect compensatory damages. This would include payment of travel expenses associated with seeking and finding alternate lodging, telephone calls necessitated by the move, and other costs incurred in a particular case. The overbooked hotel should assist the guest in finding a room at a second hotel. This was done by the hotel in the following case and may have saved it from liability for punitive damages.

CASE EXAMPLE 4–5

Dold v. Outrigger Hotel
501 P.2d 368 (Ha., 1972)

[The issue before the court was whether plaintiff was entitled to punitive damages.] . . . Upon arrival at the Outrigger on February 18, 1968, the plaintiffs were refused accommodations and were transferred by the Outrigger to another hotel of lesser quality because the Outrigger lacked available space. On February 19 and 20, the plaintiffs again demanded that the defendants honor their reservations, but they were again refused.

Though the exact nature of the plaintiffs' reservations is in dispute, the defendants claim that since the plaintiffs made no cash deposit, their reservations were not "confirmed" and, for that reason, the defendants justifiably dishonored the reservations. Plaintiffs contend that the reservations were "confirmed," as the American Express Company had guaranteed to Outrigger a first night's payment in the event that the plaintiffs did not show up. Further, the plaintiffs claim that this guarantee was in fact the same thing as a cash deposit. Thus, plaintiffs argue that the defendants were under a duty to honor the confirmed reservations. . . .

An examination of the record . . . shows the following: . . .

3. In lieu of a cash deposit, the Outrigger accepted American Express Company's guarantee that it would pay the first night's deposit for the plaintiffs.

4. On February 18, 1968, the Outrigger referred twenty-nine parties holding reservations at the Outrigger to the Pagoda Hotel, which deemed these referrals "overflows."

5. On February 18, 1968, the Outrigger had sixteen guests who stayed beyond their scheduled date of departure.

6. From February 15 to 17 and 19 to 22, 1968, the Outrigger also had more reservations than it could accommodate. Plaintiff's exhibits . . . indicate the number of overflows and referrals . . . made by the Outrigger to the Pagoda Hotel on the following dates:

February	15	20	referrals
"	16	20	"
"	17	32	"
"	19	44	"
"	20	9	"
"	21	9	"
"	22	20	"

7. Evidence was adduced that the Outrigger made a profit from its referrals to the Pagoda Hotel. Upon advance payment for the rooms to American Express, who in turn paid Outrigger, the plaintiffs were issued coupons representing the prepayment for the accommodations at the Outrigger. On the referral by the Outrigger, the Pagoda Hotel's practice was to accept the coupons [from the guests in full payment of the room] and bill the Outrigger for the actual cost of the rooms provided [which was less than the Outrigger's rate]. The difference between the coupon's value and the actual value of the accommodations was retained by the Outrigger.

The plaintiffs prevented a profit from being made by the Outrigger by refusing to use the coupons and paying in cash for the less expensive accommodations.

May Plaintiffs Recover Punitive Damages for Breach of Contract? The question of whether punitive damages are properly recoverable in an action for breach of contract has not been resolved in this jurisdiction. . . .

We are of the opinion that the facts of this case do not warrant punitive damages. . . . It has long been recognized that an innkeeper, holding himself out to the public to provide hotel accommodations, is obligated, in the absence of reasonable grounds for refusal, to provide accommodations to all persons upon proper request. . . . However, where the innkeeper's accommodations had been exhausted, the innkeeper could justly refuse to receive an applicant. . . .

We are not aware of any jurisdiction that renders an innkeeper liable on his common law duty to accommodate under the circumstances of this case. Consequently, plaintiffs are not entitled to . . . punitive damages. . . .

The following case includes factual material about the scope and causes of overbooking. The reader should not conclude from the court's decision that a hotel can overbook with virtual impunity. Not all courts are as sympathetic to the hotel as the court in this case seems to have been. As you read this case, take note of the following: 1) the different types of losses suffered by the plaintiff; and 2) which types of damages plaintiff was able to recover for and which not.

CASE EXAMPLE 4–6

Vern Wells et al. v. Holiday Inns, Inc.
522 F.Supp. 1023 (W.D. Mo. 1981)

This case arose out of the events which occurred when the individual plaintiffs, Vernon Lee Wells and Robert K. Hughes, traveled to San Francisco, California in July of 1976 for a convention of the National Office Machine Dealers Association (NOMDA). At that time, Wells [and Hughes were co-owners] of the corporate plaintiff, Central Office Machines. Wells planned the trip as both a business undertaking relating to the convention and as a vacation, taking his wife and son with him. The Wells family, Hughes and another co-owner of the corporation had reservations at defendant's Union Square Holiday Inn for three nights commencing July 15, 1976.

The reservations were made through the NOMDA travel coordinator in Bridgeport, Connecticut, to whom the check to cover the entire travel package cost was sent. . . . Although the check to cover costs included the hotel, reservation confir-

mation slips sent to plaintiff's by the Housing Bureau . . . indicated that no deposit had been received and that the confirmation would not be held after 6:00 P.M. unless the hotel is notified of late arrival. The Holiday Inn also sent its own confirmation slip to plaintiffs, which did not specifically indicate whether a deposit had been received but did state that these were "6 P.M. only" reservations.

On July 15, 1976, after a flight delay of approximately an hour, the plaintiffs' party arrived in the lobby of the Union Square Holiday Inn at around 3:00 in the afternoon to find a crowd waiting to check in to the hotel. After a considerable wait, and inquiries with various hotel personnel, plaintiffs were informed that no rooms were available for that night and that arrangements would be made with another hotel for one night. They were referred to the Jack Tarr Hotel, and vouchers for taxi fares to the Jack Tarr and for the return trip to the Holiday Inn were provided. Plaintiff Hughes used the vouchers but plaintiff Wells did not. Hughes returned and stayed at the Holiday Inn on

July 16; Wells did not, but remained at the Jack Tarr that night and moved to the Hyatt Regency for the night of July 17, 1976.

The Inn Operations Manual of defendant contains provisions for procedures for defendant's personnel to follow in the event reservations are dishonored. These include arranging substitute accommodations and paying the difference in cost if that of the substitute is higher, providing taxi fare, and other incidental expenses necessitated by the change, such as the cost of telephone calls to notify family members of a change. Such procedures appear to have been followed in plaintiffs' case. Plaintiffs received a refund of all payment made to the NOMDA convention group which was to have been applied to lodging at Holiday Inn for the nights when it was not actually used, a total of $268.40. Because Hughes and the other business associate went to Las Vegas for the last scheduled night of the San Francisco trip, plaintiffs paid, overall, $41.95 less than the amount which had been anticipated by them as payment for lodging prior to the trip. Plaintiff Wells was required to pay $16.00 for parking when he removed his rental car from the Holiday Inn garage which he would not have been charged had he been registered at the Holiday Inn, and testimony indicated that some taxi fares expended would not have been necessary if the plaintiffs had stayed at Holiday Inn.[1]

Plaintiffs contend that the dishonoring of the reservations by Holiday Inn gives rise to a claim for fraud or misrepresentation and for breach of contract. They seek actual damages in very substantial amounts, asserting (1) business losses from failure to acquire equipment at the convention for which they had a ready market, and, as to Wells (2) the triggering of a series of excruciating cluster headaches which continued for approximately two months. Punitive damages are sought under the fraud claims.

Absent a showing that defendant knowingly or willfully misrepresented a material fact to plaintiffs or intended not to reserve a room, there is no fraud. The failure to perform a contract cannot be transmuted into fraud or misrepresentation absent that intent. Although there may be a duty to disclose *material* facts, concealment of a remote possibility of nonperformance does not seem to be considered deceitful at common law.

A promissory statement may of course be deceitful if the promisor actually had no intention of performing. In addition, the promisor impliedly represents that he "knows of nothing which will make the fulfillment of his promise impossible or improbable." But one asserting fraud has generally been put to a difficult test of showing that the promisor "knew that the possibilities (of performance) were so remote . . . as to render (it) almost certainly unable to perform its obligations." Even if the Court were to assume some liberalization of this rule, to protect persons subject to major unexpected barriers to performance, the "concealment" herein does not rise to that level.

Expert testimony indicated that overbooking to some extent is a recognized and accepted practice within the hotel industry. The day that plaintiffs were refused their rooms there was a dishonor rate at that Holiday Inn of almost four percent (4%). However, the hotel's average dishonor rate was much lower, or about half the national average of one-half of one percent. Moreover, the dishonor rate is not completely attributable to the practice of overbooking, but also is affected by such unknowns as unexpected "stay-overs." . . . The evidence before the Court indicates that the [Federal Trade Commission] has considered but has not been persuaded to adopt such regulations dealing with hotel and motel overbooking, or requiring notice to the public of such a practice.

The fraud claim is also deficient in that . . . failure to disclose the practice on the confirmation slip cannot be reasonably said to be material to one's decision to make or not make reservations at a hotel. . . . The gist of the message [on the confirmation slip] was simply that Holiday Inns had received the request for the room and intended contractually to provide hotel space on that night, and the message was accurate.

Further, the television commercials aired by defendant, which plaintiffs testified they viewed and took into account before making the reservations, add nothing to the claim for fraud or misrepresentation. The most pertinent commercial, on the general

---

[1]The additional fares total $22.00 as to Wells and $4.00 as to Hughes for a trip to Chinatown (within walking distance of the Holiday Inn).

theme "The Best Surprise Is No Surprise" depicts a traveler being rejected at the front desk of another hotel or motel by a desk clerk who denies receipt of a reservation. The message most obviously derived from the scene is that Holiday Inns are comparatively reliable in their reservation practices. There is no evidence in this case to the contrary. The reservation system described by the witnesses, particularly the "Holidex," appears to be generally efficient. The overbooking practice of Holiday Inns is fairly conservative compared with the general industry, and any slight exaggeration of the extent of reliability contained in the commercial falls within the category of mere "puffing" [an expression of opinion not made as a statement of fact and not legally binding as a promise or warranty] which is not actionable.

As a general rule, the measure of damages for breach of contract is that "compensation should be equal to the injuries subject to the condition that the damages be confined to those naturally and approximately resulting from the breach and be not uncertain or speculative." [R]ecovery for breach of contract [is limited] to those damages which could reasonably be supposed to have been within the contemplation of the parties at the time they entered into the contract. The rule generally precludes such special, consequential damages as lost profits from transactions not known to the party charged with breach, in addition to barring recovery for disappointment, mental distress, and similar claims, because such items are not normally predictable by the party breaking a contract. . . .

In the alternative, if damages beyond those allowed under the above-stated principles were to be considered, the Court finds that plaintiffs have failed in their proof of causation. Proof as to lost business opportunities is not adequate to support an assessment of damages with reasonable certainty. A claim for loss of anticipated profits of a commercial business may be too remote, speculative and too dependent upon changes of circumstances to warrant judgment for recovery. The Court is satisfied that a considerable amount of business is conducted at the trade show in question, and that plaintiffs had a ready market in Kansas City for various items of business equipment. However, the proof is not satisfactory as to the critical nature of the room reservation at the Holiday Inn-Union Square to acquisition

of the necessary items, or that the lost room reservation seriously impeded the business activities. . . Plaintiff Hughes and the third co-owner lost no appreciable time in attempting to locate desirable equipment. Plaintiff Wells appears to have been more interested in litigating than in buying. He voluntarily took time off to confer with a lawyer about the prospects of litigation. . . .

The Court must also be skeptical of the theory that plaintiffs could not reasonably have located suitable equipment except at the convention. Trade shows are doubtless the most convenient times to negotiate sales agreements, but it is likely that any solid prospects would have been followed up before or after the convention closed, and no showing was made why acquisitions could not be made from Kansas City after the convention, in time to satisfy the needs of the potential purchasers. The purchasers waited months and even years before buying substitute equipment. The frustrations of the trip are thus not shown to have foreclosed the market. Skepticism as to the critical nature of the NOMDA convention is increased by Wells' failure to attend the shows in 1977, 1978, or 1980.

The Court does not discount the very serious nature of Mr. Wells' problem of cluster headaches. The evidence is convincing that he suffered intermittent excruciating pain, so severe that it caused him to pace the floor at night, occasionally rolling weeping on the floor or making other attempts to block the pain, such as striking his head against the wall. Cluster headaches were shown (as the name indicates) to occur in series, the onset of which has been observed in Mr. Wells' case to be closely associated with stress, such as business pressures or overwork. . . . Shortly after midnight on Friday night, July 16, Wells experienced the first in what became a new cluster of headaches. . . . [T]he Court concludes that this is not recoverable under present legal standards.

It is accordingly hereby

ORDERED that judgment shall be entered in favor of plaintiff Vernon L. Wells and against defendant in the amount of Thirty-eight dollars ($38). . . . It is further

ORDERED that judgment shall be entered in favor of plaintiff Robert K. Hughes and against defendant in the amount of Four dollars ($4). . . .

CASE QUESTIONS

1. Why was Wells able to collect for the cab fares to Chinatown but not for the business losses from failure to acquire the desired equipment at the convention?

2. Why did the court refuse to award damages for Wells' cluster headaches?

3. The court referenced a reservation system utilized by Holiday Inns. What impact did this system have on the outcome of the case?

4. How did the court distinguish the acts of the hotel from fraud?

Damage to Goodwill

If the plaintiff in an overbooking case is not an individual but rather a tour operator, it may suffer tour cancellations and loss of future business as a result of a hotel not honoring reservations. The tour operator thus may have substantial damages for loss of goodwill. **Goodwill** is a favorable reputation producing an expectation of future business. In the next case loss of goodwill was an element of plaintiff's damages for which the defendant, a hotel that overbooked, paid a significant amount of money.

CASE EXAMPLE 4–7

Rainbow Travel Services, Inc. v. Hilton Hotels, Corp.
896 F.2d 1233 (10th Cir., 1990)

. . . [P]laintiff Rainbow Travel Service [Rainbow] won a jury verdict against the defendants for breach of contract and fraud. . . . The Fontainebleu Hilton is a deluxe resort hotel in Miami Beach, Florida. The hotel is operated by the defendant Hilton Hotels, Inc. ("Hilton"), a Delaware corporation, on behalf of the hotel's owner, defendant Hotelerama Associates, Ltd., a Florida limited partnership. Plaintiff Rainbow is a travel agency with its principal place of business in Oklahoma City, Oklahoma. . . .

In the spring of 1986, Rainbow began organizing several tour packages for Oklahoma football fans who wanted to attend a University of Oklahoma versus University of Miami football game. The game was scheduled for September 26, 1986, in Miami, Florida. Rainbow initially con-tacted the Fontainebleu concerning the possibility of reserving hotel rooms for Rainbow's groups. After telephone calls and correspondence between the parties, the Fontainebleu sent Rainbow two contracts which called for the hotel to reserve one hundred and five rooms for Rainbow on the weekend of September 27, 1986. The second of these contracts, which is at issue in this case, provided that forty-five rooms were to be reserved for Rainbow on September 26, 1986. Rainbow executed the agreements and returned them to the Fontainebleu. In June of 1986, the Fontainebleu confirmed Rainbow's reservation by mail and requested prepayment for one night for Rainbow's groups. In response, Rainbow sent a partial payment of over $6,000. The Fontainebleu sent another confirmation in August and requested the remainder of the payment. The payments were made by checks drawn on Rainbow's account in Oklahoma.

Rainbow's president, A.J. Musgrove, went to Miami on September 24, 1986, to make sure that all arrangements had been made for his groups' stay at the Fontainebleu. One group from Rainbow arrived on September 25 and was accommodated as planned. Musgrove met with the hotel's tour representative, Livia Cohen, on September 24, twice on September 25, and again on the morning of September 26. Ms. Cohen assured Mr. Musgrove that everything was fine and that all of the reserved rooms would be available. When the Rainbow group arrived at the hotel on the afternoon of September 26, however, they were told by Hilton representatives that no rooms were available at the Fontainebleu. Hilton made arrangements for the group to stay at the Seacoast Towers, a hotel/apartment complex located about ten blocks away from the Fontainebleu. Rainbow subsequently filed this action. . . .

The jury found that Rainbow had sustained $37,500 in damages to its good will. Rainbow's primary witness on this issue was its president, A.J. Musgrove, who testified that he was familiar with the value of Rainbow's goodwill from his history with the company and from reviewing Rainbow's financial statements. Mr. Musgrove estimated that the incident at the Fontainebleu damaged Rainbow's goodwill in the amount of $250,000. His opinion was based in part on his observation that when customers are dissatisfied they tell others about it, meaning that a bad incident such as this one has a "rippling effect" on a business' reputation. He indicated that this is particularly true for the travel agency because it relies heavily on its reputation in the community. Additionally, Rainbow presented the testimony of witnesses who had traveled to Miami on the Rainbow tour. These witnesses stated that they were dissatisfied with Rainbow because of the hotel incident and stated they probably would not choose Rainbow again as a travel agent.

Viewing this evidence in the light most favorable to the plaintiff, we find that there was substantial evidence reasonably tending to support the jury's verdict. . . . Appellants argue nonetheless that the amount of damages to goodwill was so uncertain as to be speculative. The rule in Oklahoma, however, is that the prohibition against recovery of damages because the loss is uncertain or too speculative in nature applies to the fact of damages, not to the amount.

Rainbow presented evidence that Hilton accepted reservations for more rooms than were available on September 26, 1986. Hilton admitted that its policy was to book the Fontainebleu up to one hundred and fifteen per cent of its capacity, but argued that it did so based on a historic fifteen per cent "no-show" rate for guests with reservations. Hilton insisted that this policy allowed the hotel to honor almost all of its reservations. Although Hilton showed that an exceedingly high percentage of reservations were in fact honored over the course of the year, Rainbow presented evidence showing that on fifty per cent of those occasions when the hotel was operating at capacity the hotel had to dishonor reservations. Additionally, Rainbow presented evidence tending to show that Hilton was aware of a substantial likelihood that Rainbow's reservation might be dishonored. Rainbow showed that Hilton knew at least one month in advance that a large number of rooms would be closed for maintenance during September of 1986. . . . Additionally, Rainbow showed that on the date in question Hilton gave a block of rooms to a group from the University of Oklahoma even though the group had not reserved the rooms. Despite these factors, and pursuant to Hilton policy, Rainbow was not informed of the practice of overbooking and was not told there was a possibility that "guaranteed" reservations might be dishonored. Instead, Hilton assured Rainbow that the rooms would be available.

Hilton argued strenuously . . . that the overbooking situation was due to factors beyond its control, such as guests extending their stay at the Fontainebleu and rooms being out of order for repairs. These explanations may have sounded rather hollow to the jury, however, in light of a portion of the Fontainebleu's policy manual which read:

Overbooked
We never tell a guest we "overbooked." If an overbook situation arises, it is due to the fact that something occurred that the hotel could not prevent.
Examples:
1. Scheduled departures do not vacate their rooms.
2. Engineering problems with a room (pipe

busted, thus water leaks, air conditioning, heating out of commission, broken glass, etc.) Always remain calm and as pleasant as possible.

In addition to the foregoing, the record contains much circumstantial evidence showing that Hilton had knowledge of a likelihood of dishonoring reservations at the time in question. The Fontainebleu was extremely busy during the week of Rainbow's visit. On September 22 and 23 for instance, the hotel was completely sold out and the Fontainebleu had to dishonor reservations. Although there were some vacant rooms on September 24 and 25, the number of vacancies was very few. Also, the "no-show" rate for reservations was much less during this period than the fifteen per cent annual average used by Hilton. Although Hilton's agent indicated to Mr. Musgrove on the morning of September 26 that his rooms would be available, the Night Clerk Summary for September 25 indicated that the hotel would be short of rooms even if fifteen per cent of the reservations for the 26th failed to show.

Some of the testimony at trial raised questions about the candor of Hilton's explanation concerning its treatment of Rainbow's reservations. Hilton said that it only became aware of a shortage of rooms after Mr. Musgrove had gone to the airport to pick up his group, yet when the group arrived back at the hotel they had already been assigned specific rooms at the Seacoast Towers. Hilton explained that the shortage of rooms was caused by guests not checking out on the 26th, but the decision to move Rainbow was made well before checkout time on that date. . . . [W]e find substantial evidence in the record that Hilton was aware of having overbooked the hotel to such an extent as to create a substantial likelihood that Rainbow's reservation would be dishonored. Despite this, Hilton repeatedly told Rainbow that its rooms would be available and did not tell Rainbow that the group might be "bumped." Based on this and all of the evidence in the record before us, we find that a reasonable juror could find by clear and convincing evidence that Hilton recklessly made statements without knowledge of their truth, that Hilton did so with the intention that plaintiff rely on them, and that plaintiff relied on the statements to its detriment. . . .

[The hotel] objected to the admission into evidence of letters from some of Rainbow's dissatisfied customers. On appeal, Hilton argues that the letters were irrelevant and unfairly prejudicial. The letters were clearly relevant to the issue of goodwill, however, as Rainbow was entitled to present evidence of damage to its reputation. . . .

[The hotel] also argues that the court erred by allowing one of plaintiff's witnesses to testify as to statements made by a bus driver in Miami. The driver was apparently employed by the Fontainebleu to drive a shuttle bus back and forth between the Seacoast Towers and the Fontainebleu Hilton. The driver told Rainbow's customers that his job was to transport guests who had been bumped from the Fontainebleu and to try to keep them happy. Rainbow's customers concluded from their conversations with the driver that being bumped from the Fontainebleu was quite common. Hilton objected to this testimony on the grounds that a bus driver was not qualified to make statements concerning the Fontainebleu's reservation practices. . . . The driver's statements were all related to the scope of his employment with the hotel [and therefore were admissible].

Damages for Breach of Contract

Appellants contend that the jury's award of $5,493.10 for breach of contract was not supported by the evidence. We have examined the record in detail and we agree with appellant that this figure is not supported by the record. There was little evidence presented as to damages from the breach of the contract. Rainbow did not seek damages for lost profits from the Miami trip. Indeed, the evidence was that the travel agency realized its expected profit from the trip. Rainbow only suffered out of pocket expenses of $796 from the breach.[2] [Other footnotes omitted.] Aside from these expenses, however, Rainbow sought to recover $8,740, which was the amount paid by Rainbow's clients to Rainbow for the Miami trip (excluding airfare). A.J.

---

[2]These expenses consisted of a payment of $768 to one of Rainbow's clients and a miscellaneous payment of $28. The client demanded a refund in Miami upon finding out that the group would not be accommodated at the Fontainebleu.

Musgrove testified that he would like to repay his customers since they did not get the rooms that Rainbow promised they would get. Hilton argued that this was an improper attempt to recover on behalf of Rainbow's clients. Rainbow's response was to argue that this was a necessary expense to help repair Rainbow's goodwill. . . .

[I]t was improper to allow Rainbow to recover an amount to pay back to its customers. Clearly, Rainbow had no right to recover on behalf of its clients. . . . Awarding Rainbow both the full extent of injury to its goodwill, however, *and* the means to repair that damage amounts to a double recovery. Mr. Musgrove's opinion that Rainbow had suffered damage to its goodwill did not take into account the effect of giving refunds to its customers for the Miami trip. In fact, Rainbow's argument that its goodwill had been injured relied heavily on the fact that its customers had not been paid back. . . . Rainbow cannot have it both ways. It cannot recover the full extent of damage to its good will while seeking additional money that it claims is necessary to repair the injury to goodwill. In view of this fact, there is simply no evidence to support the jury's award of $5,493.10 for breach of contract. [Plaintiffs were entitled to recover $37,500 as compensatory damages for injury to its reputation.]

CASE QUESTIONS

1. Why is the potential for damages great when a hotel dishonors the reservations of a tour group?
2. How can a hotel damage its own goodwill by overbooking?

Breach By a Guest

Sometimes the party who fails to perform in a hotel reservation case is not the hotel but rather the guest, as where the latter cancels the reservation. The hotel may have a cancellation policy that permits the guest to cancel without liability until a specified number of days prior to the date of the reservation. If such a policy is not applicable, a guest who cancels a reservation may be liable for damages for breach of contract. In such a case the same legal rules apply to the hotel as applied to the guest when the hotel breached: the hotel must attempt to mitigate the loss by renting the room to another guest. If the hotel is unable to relet the room, it is entitled to collect compensatory damages from the guest. Commonly the appropriate amount of compensatory damages is the agreed price for the room.

The next case illustrates a situation where the guest breached the contract. The hotel was entitled to damages.

CASE EXAMPLE 4–8

Freeman v. Kiamesha Concord, Inc.
351 N.Y.S.2d 541 (1974)

. . . Plaintiff, a lawyer, has commenced this action against the defendant, the operator of the Concord Hotel (Concord), one of the most opulent of the resort hotels in the Catskill Mountains resort area, to recover the . . . rate for a day charged and not refunded after he and his wife checked out before the commencement of the third day of a reserved three-day Memorial Day weekend. . . .

The testimony adduced at trial reveals that in early May 1973, after seeing an advertisement in the New York Times indicating that Joel Gray would perform at the [Concord] during the forthcoming Memorial Day weekend, plaintiff contacted a travel agent and solicited a reservation for his wife and himself at the hotel. In response, he received an offer of a reservation for a "three-night minimum stay" that contained a request for a $20 deposit. He forwarded the money confirming the reservation, which was deposited by the defendant.

While driving to the hotel, the plaintiff observed a billboard, located about twenty miles from his destination, that indicated that Joel Gray would perform at the Concord only on the Sunday of the holiday weekend. The plaintiff was disturbed because he had understood the advertisement to mean that the entertainer would be performing on each day of the weekend. He checked into the hotel, notwithstanding this disconcerting information, claiming that he did not wish to turn back and ruin a long-anticipated weekend vacation. The plaintiff later discovered that two subsequent New York Times advertisements, not seen by him before checking in, specified that Gray would perform on the Sunday of that weekend [only].

After staying at the hotel for two days, the plaintiff advised the management that he wished to check out because of his dissatisfaction with the entertainment. He claims to have told them that he had made his reservation in reliance upon what he understood to be a representation in the advertisement to the effect that Joel Gray would perform throughout the holiday weekend. The management suggested that since Gray was to perform that evening, he should remain. The plaintiff refused and again asserted his claim that the advertisement constituted a misrepresentation. The defendant insisted upon full payment for the entire three-day guaranteed weekend in accordance with the reservation. Plaintiff then told the defendant's employees that he was an attorney, and that they had no right to charge him for the third day of the reserved period if he checked out. . . . The plaintiff was finally offered a one-day credit for a future stay if he made full payment. He refused, paid the full charges under protest, and advised the defendant of his intention to sue them. . . . This is that action.

I find that the advertisement relied upon by the plaintiff did not contain a false representation. It announced that Joel Gray would perform at the hotel during the Memorial Day weekend. Gray did actually appear during that weekend. . . .

The advertisement contained no false statement. It neither represented nor suggested that Gray would perform throughout the holiday weekend. The defendant cannot be found liable because the plaintiff misunderstood its advertisement. . . .

It must be noted at the outset that the plaintiff checked into the defendant's hotel pursuant to a valid, enforceable contract for a three-day stay. The solicitation of a reservation, the making of a reservation by the transmittal of a deposit, and the acceptance of the deposit constituted a binding contract in accordance with traditional contract principles of offer and acceptance. Unquestionably the defendant would have been liable to the plaintiff had it not had an accommodation for plaintiff upon his arrival. The plaintiff is equally bound under the contract for the agreed minimum period.

The testimony reveals that the defendant was ready, willing, and able to provide all of the services contracted for, but that plaintiff refused to accept them for the third day of the three-day contract period. These services included lodging, meals, and the use of the defendant's recreational and entertainment facilities. . . .

Hotels such as the one operated by the defendant have developed techniques to provide full utilization of their facilities during periods of peak demand. One such method is the guaranteed minimum one week or weekend stay that has gained widespread public acceptance. Almost all of these enterprises have offered their facilities for minimum guaranteed periods during certain times of the year by contracting with willing guests who also seek to fully utilize their available vacation time. These minimum period agreements have become essential to the economic survival and well-being of the recreational hotel industry. The public is generally aware of the necessity for them to do so and accepts the practice. . . .

A hotel such as the defendant's services thousands of guests at a single time. The maintenance of its facilities entails a continuing large overhead expenditure. It must have some means to legitimately ensure itself the income that its guests have contracted to pay for the use of its facilities. The minimum period reservation contract is such a device. The rooms are contracted for in advance and are held available while other potential guests are turned away. A guest who terminates his contractual obligations prior to the expiration of the contract period will usually deprive the hotel of anticipated income if that guest cannot be held financially accountable upon his contract. At that point, replacement income is virtually impossible. . . .

The defendant has contracted to supply the plaintiff with a room, three meals a day, and access to the use of its varied sports, recreational, or entertainment facilities. As long as these are available to the plaintiff, the defendant has fulfilled its contractual commitment. . . .

Ruling of the Court: Judgment is accordingly awarded to the defendant. . . .

CASE QUESTIONS

1. What is the meaning of the court's statement in the third-to-last paragraph, "At that point, replacement income is virtually impossible"?
2. Would the decision have been different if the hotel could have rented the room to someone else? Why?
3. Why could plaintiff not avoid the contract based on his mistake concerning when Joe Gray would perform?

If the hotel is able to relet the room for the same or higher price than the breaching guest had contracted to pay, the hotel cannot collect the agreed price for the room from the breaching guest, nor can it retain any deposit the guest might have made. Otherwise the hotel would recover twice and profit from the breach, neither of which is permitted. The hotel in the following case tried unsuccessfully to retain an advance payment.

CASE EXAMPLE 4–9

2625 Building Corp. (Mariott Hotel)
v. Deutsch
385 N.E.2d 1189 (Ind., 1979)

. . . [O]n December 7, 1972, Deutsch, a resident of Connecticut, made reservations by telephone for six rooms at the Mariott for the 1973 "500" Mile Race weekend (May 27, 28, 29). Mariott requested advance payment for the rooms. Deutsch complied with Mariott's demand and paid by check in the amount of $1,008 in full for the reserved rooms. At the end of March, or the beginning of April, 1973, Deutsch, by telephone, canceled the reservations and requested the return of his advance payment. Mariott refused his demand. Deutsch did not use the rooms and later brought action against Mariott to recover the $1,008 advance payment, alleging the above facts and, in addition, that Mariott had relet the rooms and was not harmed by the cancellation. . .

The Mariott cites *Freeman v. Kiamesha Concord, Inc.* in support of its proposition that it had a right to refuse to refund $1,008 to Deutsch when he canceled his reservations. However, we find the facts in the case at hand to be clearly distinguishable. In Freeman the guest had checked into the hotel pursuant to the contract, whereas in this case Deutsch had not. Moreover, *Freeman* involved a "last minute" checkout prior to the end of the contract period, whereas Deutsch gave the Mariott approximately two months' advance notice of his cancellation.

We do not disagree with the reasoning in *Freeman* as applied to the facts therein, and such reasoning is certainly applicable in "last minute" cancellation cases, especially at resort-type hotels. Thus, we recognize there may be instances when a guest's cancellation of reservations would not justify a refund of an advance payment. . . . [T]he making and acceptance of the reservation in this case constituted a binding contract. Upon Deutsch's breach, Mariott was entitled to actual damages in accordance with traditional contract principles. . . .

The evidence in the record reveals that Deutsch made reservations, tendered full payment for the use of the rooms in advance, and approximately two months prior to Marriott's time for performance, canceled the reservations and demanded refund, which demand was refused. In addition, we take judicial notice that the Indianapolis "500" Mile Race has the largest attendance of any single, one-day, arena-type sporting event in the world. The influx of dedicated racing fans to the Indianapolis metropolitan area in order to witness this spectacle of racing is legend. Attendant with this influx is the overwhelming demand for, and shortage of, hotel accommodations.

Therefore, we find that the facts of this case justified the trial court's conclusion that assessing Deutsch for the full amount of his room payments would cause him to suffer a loss that was wholly disproportionate to any injury sustained by Mariott. Since Mariott sustained no damage, [it is not entitled to retain any of plaintiff's money].

CASE QUESTIONS

1. Do you agree with the distinction made by the court between this case and *Freeman v. Kiamesha Concord, Inc.*? Why?

The Tort of Intentional Interference with Contractual Relations

Contracts can also give rise to the tort of intentional interference with contractual relations. A **tort** is noncriminal conduct done by one person that injures another. To commit the tort of intentional interference with contractual relations, three elements are necessary:

1. a valid contract must exist between two parties;
2. a third party must be aware of the existence of the contract; and
3. the third party must intentionally cause or induce one of the contracting parties to break the contract and do business instead with the third party.

The third party inducing the breach will be liable in damages to the contracting party who did not breach.

For example, if a particular cola company has a two-year contract to be the exclusive supplier of soda for a fast-food chain, and a competing cola company induces the chain to break the contract and purchase its beverage instead, the competing company has committed the tort; the original cola company can sue it for damages.

The following case vividly illustrates the tort of intentional interference with contractual relations.

CASE EXAMPLE 4–10

Melo-Tone Vending, Inc. v. Sherry, Inc.
656 N.E.2d 312 (1995)

. . . Melo-Tone Vending, Inc., the plaintiff (Melo-Tone), is in the business of installing coin-operated vending machines (e.g., cigarette machines, jukeboxes, games, amusements, and pay telephones) in locations such as barrooms and restaurants. Among its accounts was Bentley's Steak House, an establishment owned by Sherry, Inc. (Sherry). . . . On June 22, 1989, Melo-Tone and Sherry entered a contract under which Melo-Tone was to install at Bentley's a jukebox and two pool tables, in addition to a cigarette machine already in place. Sherry was to receive a "commission" of 22.75% on each package of cigarettes sold and 50% of the net yield from the jukebox and pool tables. For a term of eight years (i.e., until June 21, 1997), Melo-Tone would have the "sole and exclusive right" to operate vending machines in . . . Sherry's premises. Melo-Tone identified its machines by large green labels, bearing its name and telephone number, that were placed on the fronts of the machines.

Business between Melo-Tone and Sherry was uneventful until January, 1992, when Sherry was approached on behalf of James Indelicato, propri-etor of Park Square Vending (Park Square), with a proposition about making Bentley's over into a sports bar, for which—not incidentally—Park Square's machines would replace Melo-Tone's. Sherry . . . gave the word to Park Square's advance man that there was a small matter of a contract with Melo-Tone, but that did not derail the sports bar project. Late in January or early in February 1992 Melo-Tone's principal officer, Jack D. Kerner, got wind that Park Square was going to install an air hockey game at Bentley's. Kerner called Park Square and mailed to Park Square a copy of his "exclusive" contract with Sherry. Nevertheless, on February 11, 1992, Park Square moved its air hockey game machine onto the Sherry premises.

By letter dated February 18, 1992, Melo-Tone's lawyer informed Park Square that it had exclusive rights to place vending machines at Sherry's establishment and demanded immediate removal of Park Square's air hockey machine. Park Square instead added two pool tables and a cigarette machine, as well as some other machines, at Sherry's place of business. Space was a problem that Park Square solved by furnishing funds to Sherry to move Melo-Tone's machines out. On March 6, 1992, Melo-Tone brought an action against Indelicato [for wrongful interference with contractual relations], and Sherry [for breach of contract] . . .

As to the defendant Sherry, the plaintiff Melo-Tone stipulated dismissal well before trial. There had been a reconciliation; Melo-Tone was back in and Park Square was out. Melo-Tone's [claim for wrongful interference with contractual relations] was tried to a jury. The jury returned a verdict that the defendant Indelicato had intentionally interfered with the contractual relationship between Melo-Tone and Sherry; . . . The jury set the damages at $21,000 . . . Indelicato has appealed, raising multiple issues, among them, that intentional interference with contractual relations had not been proved because there was no evidence of an exclusive contract or of an improper purpose. . . .

To make out a case of intentional interference with a contract, a plaintiff must prove that: 1) he had a contract with a third party; 2) the defendant knowingly induced the third party to break that contract; 3) the defendant's interference, in addition to being intentional, was improper in motive or means; and 4) the plaintiff was harmed by the defendant's actions. . . .

[T]there was more than sufficient evidence to permit the jury to find that: 1) Sherry had entered into an eight-year contract with Melo-Tone to have Melo-Tone operate vending machines on Sherry's premises; 2) Indelicato had induced Sherry to get vending machines from him and to push Melo-Tone's out the door; and 3) Melo-Tone lost profits while its machines were excluded from Sherry's place. . . .

Indelicato argues that his motives were competitive and financial, not to harm Melo-Tone, and that his conduct was not improper. . . . For competition and for the rough and tumble of the world of commerce, there is tolerance even though the fall-out of that rough and tumble is damage to one of the competitors.

It is one thing to lure a customer away from someone with whom it has been doing business by means of better product, service, or prices, but quite another to abet the repudiation of solemn contractual obligations of which the party interfering is well aware. Indelicato not only knew Melo-Tone's contract with Sherry still had five years to run, but also received a copy of it. Indelicato went beyond inducing Sherry to commit a breach of contract, itself sufficient to make out the tort; he abetted the breach by paying to have his competitor's machines unlawfully moved from Sherry's premises. . . . The means were improper and spoke eloquently to Indelicato's purpose, although it is enough to prove either improper means or motive.

CASE QUESTIONS

1. Could Melo-Tone have sued Indelicato for breach of contract? Why or why not?

2. In what way could Indelicato legally compete with Melo-Tone for Sherry's business?

Catering and Convention Contracts

Restaurants and hotels should exercise great care when entering a catering contract to ensure the parties are in agreement on all the terms. Mistakes made at banquets and other catered affairs can cause very unhappy customers.

Given the many details involved when planning a catered event, there is virtually no excuse for not having a written contract. The items that should be included in the writing are identified in Figure 4-1.

CATERING CONTRACTS

The following subjects should be addressed in a catering contract:

1. Names and addresses of the restaurant and the customer;
2. The date of the affair;
3. The location at which the food will be served (the customer's home, a specific room in the restaurant, etc.). If in the restaurant, the time limit on use of the room, if any.
4. The shape and arrangement of the tables;
5. The type of dishes to be used—paper plates, china or other types;
6. If the food is to be served away from the restaurant, what kitchen/cooking facilities will be available for the restaurant staff and when they will be available;
7. If the location is away from the restaurant, whose dishes will be used—the restaurant's or the customer's;
8. The type of service ordered (buffet or sit-down);
9. The menu in its entirety;
10. If hors d'oeuvres are ordered, whether they will be served on a table or carried;
11. Whether the restaurant will provide liquor, and if so, what types of liquor? Will the bar be open (guests pay no fee for drinks) or cash (guests pay for their own drinks)?
12. Will the restaurant provide bartenders, and if so, how many?
13. Decorations, color scheme, and theme;
14. Arrangements for a head table, if applicable;
15. Whether the restaurant will provide a musician or other entertainer;
16. The number of people expected; a minimum guaranteed number, if applicable; when the final count must be relayed to the caterer;
17. Price; amount of deposit; when payment is due; policy on gratuities;
18. Circumstances under which the price might be adjusted, for example, an increase in the costs of food, beverage or labor between when the contract was entered and the date of the affair;
19. Equipment to be provided by caterer;
20. Attire of servers;
21. Parking arrangements (e.g., will valet services be provided);
22. Circumstances under which the caterer will be excused from performance, such as labor troubles, accidents, restrictions on food or beverage, or other causes beyond the caterer's control;
23. Cancellation policy, including any penalties that will be charged; and
24. Any other terms relevant to the particular event.

Figure 4–1   Recommended subjects for a catering contract

Leaving undecided or unclear any of these terms can result in a displeased patron, lost opportunity for repeat business, and a lawsuit for breach of contract. By putting the agreement in writing and including in it the parties' understandings on all terms, the restaurant is protected against unjustified complaints from the customer. If, for example, the customer complains that no ham is included on the cold cut trays and the restaurant can point to a contract provision that lists the meats to be included and ham is not among them, the customer cannot reasonably continue to complain. The written contract goes a long way to ensuring a successful event, goodwill with the patron, and avoidance of litigation.

Another type of contract that requires much planning and involves many details is a convention contract, that is, a contract between an organization planning a conference and the hotel at which the conference will be held. Typically, conventions held at hotels are annual gatherings of an organization's members who come from a wide geographical area. The organization might be a professional association such as accountants, or a group whose common denominator is religion, athletics, or a hobby, to mention but a few.

The services offered to conventioneers by a hotel are many and varied. They can include, in addition to rooms, food, banquet facilities, recreational facilities, entertainment, meeting rooms, equipment such as overhead projectors, and tourist information about the area. The particular services to be provided at a given convention are subject to agreement between the association and the hotel. Some conventions are elaborate affairs while others are low-cost operations. The hotel and the organization sponsoring the convention must discuss what services the organization desires and can afford, and what services the hotel is willing and able to provide. Customarily a representative from the organization will negotiate with the hotel on these matters. When they agree on the services and price, they have a contract.

The parties should prepare a written contract embodying their agreement. The terms in the contract should be specific and unambiguous to avoid disputes later. For example, a member of the organization who registered late and was unable to reserve a room in the main convention hotel might complain that it failed to reserve an adequate number of rooms for the organization's members. The hotel can avoid an argument if it can refer the person to a provision in the organization's contract that specifies the number of rooms to be reserved, assuming the hotel reserved the number required by the contract.

A thorough contract will contribute greatly to a smooth flow of events during the convention. The written contract should include the terms identified in Figure 4–2.

Summary

By using contracts, a hotel or restaurant can create legally binding obligations. To be enforceable a contract must satisfy the following essential elements: contractual capacity, mutuality, legally, consideration, proper form and genuine assent.

Failure to perform a contractual obligation constitutes breach of contract. Overbooking by a hotel resulting in cancellation of reservations constitutes breach of contract, as does cancellation by a guest.

The following subjects should be addressed in a convention contract:
 1. The name and address of the hotel, organization and person(s) authorized to act on behalf of the organization;
 2. The dates of the convention;
 3. The number of guest rooms the hotel will reserve for the organization's members;
 4. The type of rooms (luxury, medium-priced, budget);
 5. The location of the rooms (main building, wing, etc.);
 6. The deadline for convention-goers to make reservations;
 7. The method for convention-goers to reserve rooms;
 8. Check-in and check-out procedures;
 9. The number of meals to be provided by the hotel;
10. All the applicable terms identified in Figure 4-1 for catering contracts;
11. Number and location of meeting and exhibit rooms;
12. The arrangement of tables and/or chairs in meeting rooms;
13. The type of equipment to be provided in meeting rooms (e.g., overhead projector);
14. Cancellation deadline and procedures;
15. Restrictions on posting signs and announcements;
16. Any other special services to be provided by the hotel such as food for coffee breaks, a hospitality suite, complimentary rooms, or entertainment; and
17. Any other terms relevant to the particular event.

Figure 4–2   Recommended subjects for a convention contract

A party who breaches a valid contract will be liable to compensate the nonbreaching party for its resulting loss. The nonbreaching party must be able to prove the damages to a reasonable certainty and must mitigate damages, if possible.

While most oral contracts are enforceable, they may be difficult to prove. Whenever possible, contracts should be reduced to writing. This is particularly important for catering and convention contracts because of the many details involved. Well-written contracts will help achieve and maintain good relationships with guests and patrons, and avoid lawsuits.

Preventive Law Tips for Managers

- *Be Sure Your Contracts Contain the Six Essential Elements.* To be enforceable, a contract must have six essential elements: legality, proper form, contractual capacity, mutuality, consideration, and genuine assent. If even one is missing, the enforceability of the contract is in jeopardy.

- *Do Not Enter An Illegal Contract.* Contracts that are illegal are unenforceable. If you enter an illegal contract and perform your part of the transaction, and the other party refuses to perform its obligation, you will not be able to sue for damages or to enforce the contract. Assume your business generates toxic wastes. The law requires specific procedures be followed for their disposal. To save money, you contract with a company to dispose of those wastes illegally. You pay the company but it fails to discard the wastes. You will not be able to sue to get your money back. Because you were a party to an illegal contract, the courts will not come to your aid.

- *For Contracts Covered by the Statute of Frauds, Be Sure to Generate a Writing Signed by the Other Contracting Party.* Contracts covered by the Statute of Frauds are unenforceable without a writing. The writing must be signed by the party who is the defendant in the lawsuit, which means your concern is to get the other party's signature. Without the signed writing, you will not be able to pursue a breach of contract case. Contracts required to be in writing include: contracts for the purchase and sale of real estate; contracts that cannot be completed within one year from when they are made; contracts made in consideration of marriage; contracts to pay another's debts; and contracts for the sale of goods $500 or more.

- *Reduce All Your Contracts to Writing Even If They Are Not Covered by the Statute of Frauds.* A party can easily prove the existence and terms of a written contract. The writing indisputably establishes the terms. An oral contract is difficult to prove. The only evidence is your word and that of the other contracting party. In a disagreement, you lack documentation to prove the truthfulness of your position. If the dispute goes to court, a judge or jury will determine which of the two of you is telling the truth. The process is cumbersome, and the wrong person could win. A written contract avoids these problems and facilitates easy resolution of contract disputes.

- *Include in Written Contracts All the Terms Agreed Upon.* A written contract should contain the entire agreement between the parties. The parol evidence rule prevents parties from modifying a written contract with evidence of additional terms agreed upon by the parties but not included in the writing. Failure to include a term in the writing will result in that term being unenforceable. Review your contracts carefully before signing them to ensure they are complete.

- *Use Clear and Unambiguous Language in Your Contracts. Know the Meaning of the Contract Terms.* When contract terms are unclear and a dispute results, their meaning may be determined by reference to trade usage. The application of trade usage may or may not result in terms the parties intended when they entered the contract. It is best to use clear language. Also, before working in a field you should familiarize yourself with the industry jargon. Use of terms with double meanings—one from normal parlance and the other from industry usage—can produce unexpected and unwanted results.

- *Keep Good Records of Information That Might Be Helpful in Proving the Amount of Damages Suffered from Breach of a Contract.* To recover damages for breach of contract, the nonbreaching party must prove the amount of the loss to a reasonable certainty. Maintaining good records of such matters as sales figures, occupancy rates, and cost of supplies . . . can enhance your ability to prove a loss.

- *Mitigate Damages Resulting from Breach of Contract.* To collect damages for breach of contract, the nonbreaching party must mitigate its loss. Failing to attempt to reduce the loss may negate the right to obtain damages for the breach. Whenever someone breaches a contract with you, consider what you might reasonably do to avoid or reduce the loss, and do it.

- *If You Have Overbooked and Cannot Accommodate Would-be Guests with Reservations, Assist in Locating Alternate Accommodations, and Be Sure Your Staff is Courteous.* If you are unable to provide accommodations to a guest with reservations, you are in breach of contract. To assist the customer and defuse a lawsuit be as helpful to the would-be guest as possible. At a minimum, help arrange alternate accommodations, pay for transportation to the second hotel, if the second room costs more, pay the difference, and pay for phone calls necessitated by the move, such as calls by the guest to home or office to inform relatives or colleagues of the new location. Additional courtesies may be in order including a gift certificate for a complimentary room at a later time. Keep good records to establish the cause for the overbooking.

- *If Requiring a Minimum Stay at the Hotel, Be Sure Your Contract with the Guest Clearly States the Number of Days Required.* If your hotel is offering a special rate or event requiring a minimum stay, you will want to collect for the full period of the minimum stay even in the event a guest departs early. To preclude the guests from arguing that they were unaware of the minimum stay and therefore should not have to pay, the contract should clearly state the minimum number of days required and the liability of guests to pay for those days even if they leave before the end of the minimum period.

- *Draft Detailed Contracts for Catering Engagements.* Catering contracts involve numerous details, many of which are very important to your customer, the host of the event. To avoid misunderstandings and mix-ups, reduce the agreement and all the details to writing.

- *Draft Detailed Contracts for Convention Agreements.* Convention contracts also involve many details and an ongoing relationship during a lengthy period while the convention progresses from planning to execution. To avoid disputes and unnecessary ill will, document all decisions and agreements relating to every aspect of the convention. Failure to do so will likely lead to dissatisfaction with the hotel's service jeopardizing future business opportunities with the organization. An avoidable lawsuit might also result.

Review Questions

1. What are the six essential elements of a contract?
2. What categories of people lack contractual capacity?
3. What is meant by mutuality?
4. What is the legal effect of an illegal contract?
5. Name three types of contracts that are unenforceable unless they are in writing.
6. Which of the following types of damages will a plaintiff in a breach of contract case be able to recover?
   a. Lost profits.
   b. Pain and suffering.
   c. Punitive.
7. If a guest cancels her reservation with a hotel, how can the hotel mitigate its loss?
8. If a plaintiff in a breach of contract case is unable to determine the amount of its loss, is it entitled to recover any damages?
9. List five items that should be included in a catering contract.
10. List five items that should be included in a convention contract. Do not include any of the five items you listed in response to question 9.

Discussion Questions

1. Identify whether each of the following is an offer or an invitation to negotiate.
   a. Three pounds of fresh shrimp will cost $23.50.
   b. I will play the piano at your restaurant from 5:30 until 9:00 P.M. every night during October for $50 a night.
   c. I have gourmet ice cream for sale.
   d. I am thinking about selling my motel.
   e. Private swimming lessons are available at the hotel pool for $25 per half hour.
2. Why, in a breach of contract case, must the amount of the plaintiff's damages be proven to a reasonable certainty?

3. If a contract term is ambiguous, how will a court decide its meaning? How can parties to a contract avoid ambiguity?

4. Which of the following contracts must be in writing to be enforceable?

   a. A contract to hire a banquet manager for three years.

   b. A promise made by a casino patron to cover the betting debts of his friend.

   c. A contract to hire a musical trio to play for three weekends at a restaurant for a total fee of $1200.

   d. A contract to purchase three acres of land on which the buyer intends to build a restaurant.

5. Why does the law require a nonbreaching party to mitigate damages?

6. Why, as a practical matter, should all contracts be put in writing?

Application Questions

1. In a telephone conversation with a sales representative of a linen company, the manager of a hotel ordered $1000 worth of sheets. Following the conversation he wrote a memo to file documenting the agreement, initialed it and sent a copy to the sales representative. A dispute arose between the parties and the linen company sued the hotel. Does the parol evidence rule bar the lawsuit? Why or why not?

2. Laurie is planning a reception for her parents' fiftieth wedding anniversary. She and her parents keep kosher, which means they follow dietary laws prescribed in the Jewish religion. She decided to hold the anniversary party at the Westside Party House because the manager, under pressure to increase sales, told Laurie the Party House serves kosher food. Laurie later discovers that the Party House does not serve kosher food. If she cancels her contract with the Party House and holds the party elsewhere, will she be liable to the Party House for breach of contract? Why or why not?

3. A restaurant ordered 20 cases of champagne for New Year's Eve. Delivery was due on December 29, but the seller failed to deliver. As a result the restaurant was unable to offer its New Year's Eve patrons a midnight champagne toast. The hotel sued the seller for breach of contract, claiming lost profits from the midnight toast and from future parties the angry patrons would be discouraged from hosting at the restaurant. Discuss the restaurant's chances for success in this lawsuit.

UNIT II

Negligence

CHAPTER TITLES

CHAPTER 5

Principles of Negligence

INTRODUCTION

Guests at a hotel or restaurant can injure themselves in many ways. One might trip in the dining room. Another might suffer burns from scalding water in a shower. Yet another might drown in the pool. This chapter answers the question, When is the hotel or restaurant liable for guests' injuries? Stated differently, must the hospitality facility compensate patrons for injuries they suffer while at the restaurant or hotel?

The answer to the question depends on whether the establishment violated a legal duty. The hotel or restaurant is not an insurer of guests' safety. This means the hotel is not liable for all injuries that occur while on the premises. With few exceptions, the hotel or restaurant will only be liable when it does something wrong, that is, commits a tort. The term **tort** refers to many types of noncriminal wrongful conduct done by one person and injuring another, but not to breaches of contract. If the guest who tripped in the dining room did so because the heel on her shoe broke due to shoddy workmanship, the restaurant did not do anything wrong and therefore will not be liable. Similarly, if the scalding water in the shower occurred because the guest carelessly left the knob turned to hot, the hotel will not be obligated to compensate the guest. If, however, the patron tripped on a hole in the dining room rug, or the hot water resulted from a defective plumbing system, the restaurant or hotel may indeed be liable to the guest.

Negligence

As we said in Chapter 1, **negligence** is the breach of a legal duty to act reasonably that is the direct (or proximate) cause of injury to another. In nonlegal language, negligence is carelessness that causes harm. Assume the hole in the rug had been there for two weeks. Failure to fix the hole is careless; the restaurant could anticipate that someone would be injured by it. As a result, the restaurant will be liable for the customer's injury.

Assume the hotel had received several complaints about excessively hot water during the week before the accident, yet the hotel had not called a plumber or taken any steps to fix the problem. Failure to investigate and correct the water problem was careless; the hotel could anticipate that someone would be injured. As a result the hotel will be liable to the guest.

The law requires that people and businesses act reasonably in attempting to prevent injuries. When someone acts unreasonably or carelessly, that person is negligent. A reasonable restaurant employee, seeing a hole in the dining room rug, would repair it to avoid an accident. A reasonable hotel employee who had been alerted to hot water problems in the hotel would investigate and correct the problem. Failure to make the necessary repairs in these examples constitutes negligence.

If the cause of a hotel guest's injury was the carelessness of an employee, the hotel will be liable to the guest. Managers and employees of restaurants and hotels should strive to act reasonably in the way they perform their duties in order to avoid liability for negligence. The cases in this chapter and in Chapters 6 and 7 will illustrate some of the countless injuries that can occur at a restaurant or hotel and result in liability. By reading these cases, managers will appreciate situations that can cause injuries and will cultivate a keener eye with which to survey the hotel or restaurant to ensure they are in suitable condition for customers and guests.

Elements of a Negligence Case

A plaintiff suing in negligence must prove four elements; failure to prove any one of them is fatal to plaintiff's case. The four elements are: (1) the existence of a duty to act reasonably owed by the defendant to the plaintiff; (2) a breach of that duty; (3) injury to plaintiff; and (4) proximate cause. This last element means the breach of duty must be the direct cause of the injury and no intervening cause exists. Let us examine each element individually.

Existence of a Duty to Act Reasonably.   Surprisingly, we do not owe to everyone the duty to act reasonably. We owe the duty only to those people who would foreseeably be injured by our actions. A restaurant can foresee that if the leg of a chair is broken, a patron will sit on the chair and fall. Therefore the restaurant owes a duty to its guests to repair the chair. If a restaurant or hotel cannot foresee a particular type of injury it does not owe a duty to protect patrons against that injury even though someone is in fact injured. In the following case, the court concluded that the inn could not have foreseen that a bee would sting a diner causing serious injury. Therefore, no duty existed to warn patrons of the presence of bees.

CASE EXAMPLE 5–1

**Febesh v. Elcejay Inn Corp. d/b/a/ Fox Hollow Inn
157 A.D.2d 102, 555 N.Y.S.2d 46
(1st Dep't., 1990)**

On August 24, 1985, plaintiffs Joseph and Shirley Febesh attended a 50th anniversary party catered by and held at Fox Hollow Inn ("the Inn"), owned by defendant Elcejay Inn Corp. . . . Approximately one and one-half to two hours after arriving at the party, Joseph Febesh was on an outdoor patio of the Inn which was surrounded by shrubbery and trees, and on which hors d'oeuvres and drinks were being served, when he was stung by a bee or a yellow jacket. It is undisputed that the sting resulted in anaphylactic shock and cardiac arrest, which in turn, rendered Febesh a permanent quadriplegic.

Introduced into evidence were numerous photographs taken by various partygoers. We have seen these photographs, which show a clean, neatly maintained patio and bar area with guests both eating and drinking. Notably, the photographs do not show bees or yellow jackets on or near the tables, bar, food, or surrounding shrubbery, all of which the court below correctly noted appeared to have been maintained in a sanitary condition. Testimony was received that the area was sprayed for bees and other insects at least once a day and that, while bees had been occasionally observed on the premises, this was the first reported incident of a bee or yellow jacket stinging someone at the Inn in some 20 years.

Neither before nor after the incident herein was a nest or hive discovered. While there had been some complaints as to the presence of "a

few" or "some" or even "many" bees at the party, a former employee of the Inn, who testified on behalf of plaintiffs, noted that on the day in question there were only "a few bees, somewhere in the area of ten." The record is devoid of evidence tending to prove that there was a "swarm" of bees or yellow jackets at the Inn.

The central area of dispute in the case at bar is the duty owed by the Inn towards plaintiff. Of course, for a plaintiff to establish a cause of action sounding in negligence, he must meet the initial burden of showing (1) the existence of a duty flowing from defendant to plaintiff; (2) a breach of this duty; (3) a reasonably close causal connection between the contact and the resulting injury; and (4) actual loss, harm or damage. . . . Where the plaintiff fails to introduce evidence legally sufficient to support each and every one of these essential elements, the jury cannot properly find that the defendant has been negligent. . . . Here, the duty owed by the Inn was that of exercising reasonable ordinary care, including maintaining the premises in a reasonably safe and suitable condition and warning partygoers of any hidden or concealed perils known or reasonably discoverable by the Inn; however, this Court is aware that even after the exercise of reasonable care, some risk may well continue to exist. . . .

[W]e find . . . that the presence of ten or even more bees was insufficient to impose upon defendant a duty, the breach of which would impose liability. . . . We are, in particular, mindful of the lack of prior incidents of this sort at the Inn; the fact that plaintiff was not attacked by a swarm of bees or yellow jackets, but rather by one such insect; the absence of a nest or hive; and the generally sanitary conditions of the Inn. We also note that plaintiff, who was one of over 50 partygoers, was not stopped from going indoors. . . .

[T]he only rational conclusion to be reached was one in favor of defendant.

CASE QUESTION

1. What changes in the facts might have resulted in the inn being liable?

In another case, a bridesmaid was injured at the wedding reception when several party-goers, participating in a "wheelbarrow race" (where one person walks on his hands and his partner runs and steers from behind by holding the legs of the first person) ran into plaintiff from behind. She sued the restaurant at which the reception was held, claiming it had not adequately protected her safety. The court, noting that the race was "spontaneous and inappropriate", found the restaurant could not have anticipated the race and thus owed no duty to protect plaintiff from it. *Lee v. Durow's Restaurant, Inc.,* 656 N.Y.S.2d 321 (App Div, 2nd Dept, 1997)

Similarly, the owner of an amusement park has no duty to protect patrons against unforeseeable and unexpected assaults. Thus, where a patron who had just exited the roller coaster was attacked spontaneously and unexpectedly, the park was not liable for failing to prevent the assault. *Scotti v. W.M. Amusements,* 266 A.D.2d 522, 640 N.Y.S.2d 617 (2nd Dep't., 1996).

Breach of Duty.   For a defendant to be liable for negligence, the defendant must not only owe a duty to the plaintiff to act reasonably, but must also breach that duty. A restaurant owes a duty to its customers not to serve rancid food because customers will foreseeably become ill. If it serves unhealthy food, the restaurant breaches that duty.

Determining if the defendant acted reasonably is not always easy. The law provides a standard to help judge whether a defendant's actions were or were not within the bounds of the law. While the standard is difficult to apply in some cases, it is a helpful guide. The standard is a mythical "reasonable person of ordinary prudence." The issue in each case is whether the defendant acted like a reasonable person of ordinary prudence would have acted under similar circumstances.

Sometimes this imaginary person is described not only as "reasonable" but also "prudent" and as "a person of average prudence," or even as "a person of ordinary sense using ordinary care and skill." All these phrases mean much the same. This reasonable person does not have bad days; he is always up to standard, a personification of a community ideal of reasonable behavior. And what constitutes reasonable behavior in a given situation is determined by a jury or, in a bench trial, by the judge.

If the defendant in a lawsuit has not breached a duty it is not liable. The plaintiff has the burden of proving defendant's wrongdoing. As illustrated in the following case, if the plaintiff is unable to prove that the defendant breached a duty, plaintiff will not be able to recover.

CASE EXAMPLE 5–2

Thomas v. Grand Hyatt Hotel
749 F.Supp. 313 (D.C., 1990)

. . . Plaintiff brings this action alleging negligence on the part of the defendant in connection with a slip-and-fall incident on September 26, 1987, at the Grand Hyatt Hotel. On that date, plaintiff was modeling clothes for Woodward & Lothrop, which had leased space from the defendant for a fashion show. While plaintiff was exiting the stage, she slipped and fell, injuring her left foot and ankle. . . .

In this case, the burden is on the plaintiff to prove that the defendant was negligent "either in creating a dangerous condition or in allowing one to continue without correction and that this negligence was the proximate cause of the injuries.". . .

To make out a . . . case of liability predicated upon the existence of a dangerous condition it is necessary to show that the party against whom negligence is claimed had actual notice of the dangerous condition or that the condition had existed for such length of time that, in the exercise of reasonable care, its existence should have become known and corrected.

. . . In fact, plaintiff concedes that she "must show there was a substance . . . on the floor, how it came to be on [the] floor, and that defendant was aware of the substance."

In this case, however, plaintiff does not know what caused her to slip, let alone whether defendant was aware of a dangerous condition that caused her to slip. She can only say that it was something "liquidy." She then offers deposition testimony that there was a dishwasher room which opened into the hallway used by the models, and that employees of the defendant washed dishes during the fashion show, using the hallway itself when putting the dishes to be washed on carts. Also, [another model] claims that there was water in the hallway from melted ice.

Although plaintiff believes that something on her shoe caused her fall, she does not know if she stepped in water or any other substance in the hallway. Nor did anyone else see her do so. Moreover, she did not pay attention to whether there was any water or other substance on the stage or on the stairs and did not show anyone a substance on her shoe. She is simply assuming that the cause of her fall was a substance picked up in the hallway leading from the dressing room to the stage. However, plaintiff did not slip in the hallway; in fact, she did not slip until after she had gone up the stairs leading to the stage, walked down the runway and back, and was approaching the stairs to exit. Thus, it is hard to believe that she would have slipped on a substance from the hallway only after making a full trip down the runway and back. Based on these facts, the jury could only find negligence through speculation, and "[s]peculation is not the province of the jury." . . .

Thus, the Court concludes that defendant is entitled to . . . judgment in its favor.

CASE QUESTIONS

1. What more would plaintiff need to prove in order to establish that defendant breached a duty?

2. What is meant by "deposition testimony" as used in the fifth paragraph?

Proximate Cause.   **Proximate cause** of an injury refers to its direct and immediate cause. The requirement of proximate cause means that the injury must have been caused by the breach of duty; in other words, there must be a cause-and-effect relationship between the injury and the unreasonable conduct. The connection also must be direct or immediate, so that a reasonable person could foresee the potential danger of the careless act.

Events independent of and occurring after the alleged negligence may be the direct cause of the injury. Such an event is called an intervening or superseding occurrence and has the effect of breaking the chain of liability. In the following case the connection between the alleged negligence and the plaintiff's injury was not sufficiently direct or immediate as to give rise to liability.

CASE EXAMPLE 5–3

**Smith v. West Rochelle Travel Agency, Inc.
656 N.Y.S.2d 340 (2nd Dept 1997)**

. . . The plaintiffs commenced an action against all the parties who had any connection with a 1993 spring break vacation trip to the Bahamas in which their 17-year-old son, Thomas Smith, Jr. (hereinafter the decedent), participated. . . . During the vacation, the decedent purchased a ticket for a "booze cruise", a sunset cruise in international waters where alcoholic beverages were sold to anyone, regardless of their age. The decedent voluntarily leapt overboard and was killed when he came in contact with the cruise vessel's propellers. The evidence indicated that the vessel was not owned or operated by the defendant . . . Wyndham Hotel Co., Ltd.

The parents sued Wyndham, the hotel at which the decedent was registered, arguing that since the groundhandler promoted the "booze cruise" on the hotel premises during an "orientation party" at which alcoholic beverages were served, the hotel bore some liability for facilitating the sale of tickets to the cruise. . . .

[T]he court correctly determined that, as a matter of law, the decedent's action of voluntarily jumping off a moving vessel in open waters was a superseding event which severed whatever causal connection there may have been between the occurrence of the accident and Wyndham's alleged negligence three days earlier in permitting alcohol to be served on its premises during the orientation party. . . .

In another case, a valet parking attendant at a nightclub negligently facilitated the theft of a patron's car. Later the same night a police officer observed the stolen car and attempted to stop it. The thief fled, first in the car and then on foot. The officer fell and was injured as he apprehended the thief. His lawsuit against the nightclub was dismissed because its negligence was not the direct cause of the injury. "The conduct of the thief was an intervening cause which the defendant was not bound to anticipate and guard against." *Poskos v. Lombardo's of Randolph, Inc.*, 423 Mass. 637, 638, 670 N.E.2d 383, 384 (Mass., 1997).

In *Messina v. Sheraton Corporation of America*, 291 So.2d 829 (La., 1974), the plaintiff was the promoter of a boxing match that was to feature one Beau Jaynes. The night before the fight, Jaynes injured his hand in his room at a Sheraton Hotel when a venetian blind collapsed as he was adjusting it. The boxing commission canceled the fight and the promoter sued the Sheraton to recover his lost revenue. The court said that while Jaynes might have a good lawsuit against the hotel, the promoter did not. It is a basic principle of tort law that a wrongdoer is responsible only for the direct and proximate injuries resulting from its acts. When a third person such as a boxing promoter suffers damage because of a contractual obligation of the injured party, such damage is too remote and indirect to hold the wrongdoer liable.

Injury.   To win a lawsuit, a plaintiff must have suffered injury as a result of defendant's breach of duty. The injury might be bodily harm (the legal term for this is "personal injury") such as a broken arm or a head injury. The injury could also be property damage such as a dented car, or emotional or monetary loss.

Summary of the Elements of Negligence

Remember, before a hotel or restaurant will be liable to a plaintiff for negligence, all four elements must be present: 1) the existence of a duty; (2) breach of that duty; (3) proximate cause; and (4) injury. If any element is missing the hotel or restaurant is not liable.

Legal Status of Plaintiff

The duty of care owed by a hotel or restaurant for the safety of its patrons depends, in many states, on the legal status of the person injured. He may be an invitee, a licensee, or a trespasser. The greatest degree of care is owed to an invitee, the next greatest to a licensee, and the least amount to a trespasser.

Duty Owed to Invitees

In the hospitality industry an **invitee** is someone who comes to an establishment for the purpose for which the business is open to the public, or for a purpose directly or indirectly connected with that business. For a hotel, invitees include guests and visitors of guests. For a restaurant, diners are invitees. For a bar, patrons are invitees. For all three, employees are invitees, as is a delivery person delivering some item necessary for the business.

The hotel or restaurant owes a duty to its invitees to reasonably inspect the premises for dangerous conditions and to exercise reasonable care to eliminate them. Liability may result if and only if the business: (a) knows, or by the exercise of reasonable care would discover, a dangerous condition that presents an unreasonable risk of harm to the invitees; and (b) should expect that invitees will not discover or realize the danger, or will fail to protect themselves against it; and (c) fails to exercise reasonable care to protect its invitees against the danger. The necessary reasonable care (lack of negligence) encompasses both repair of and warning about the dangerous condition.

Assume that on a rainy night the floor in the entrance to a restaurant is wet and slippery. A patron entering the restaurant falls and is injured. Is the food establishment liable? The customer is an invitee, so the restaurant owes the duty to make a reasonable effort to discover the condition and eliminate it by mopping frequently, or at the very least, to warn of its presence. Failure to do so will result in liability for the restaurant.

Active Vigilance Required.   Note that ignorance on the part of the restaurant of the presence of the water on the floor and resulting slipperiness normally will not relieve the restaurant of liability. The restaurant has a duty to inspect for and discover the wetness, and then to protect guests from resulting risks. The following case illustrates this point.

CASE EXAMPLE 5–4

Montes v. Betcher
480 F.2d 1129 (8th Cir., 1973)

On the warm Sunday afternoon of July 13, 1968, 35 year old Fernando Montes, a citizen of Nebraska, took a running dive off a short dock which served the Appellants' resort, one of the many enhancing Minnesota's beautiful lakes. He surfaced with a severely lacerated scalp and a vertebral fracture. Shortly after the incident, a jagged piece of concrete was recovered from the lake floor in the general area where plaintiff had entered the water. The concrete piece resembled the homemade boat anchors constructed by Appellants to use in the boats which frequented the boat dock.

Plaintiff, Montes, a proficient swimmer and diver, claims that he executed a flat, "racing" dive because he knew he was plunging into shallow water. The water depth was variously described to be from 27 inches to waist level. Montes testified, however, that his ultimate purpose was to grab the ankles of a friend who was standing in the water 15 feet from the end of the dock, a purpose which would require either a deep dive or a subsequent submergence.

Montes was very familiar with the swimming area, and had executed dives from the boat dock on numerous previous occasions. Never before had he encountered rocks or blocks in the water. He admitted to having imbibed two or three drinks on the afternoon of the accident.

The Appellants, Mr. and Mrs. Betcher, citizens of Minnesota, had owned the resort since 1963. They charged $10 per day for cabin accommodations. Although the area surrounding the boat dock was perennially in use by Appellants' swimmer-patrons and although Mr. Betcher had seen swimmers jump off the boat dock, he testified that he had never made any special attempt to inspect the lake bottom for debris nor had he ever "raked" the shoreline lake bottom. Never had he erected signs warning of the dangers of diving in the shallow water or the possible presence of debris in the swimming area. Never had he placed floats in the water to discourage the intrusion of boats into the swimming and diving area; in fact there was no segregation whatsoever of swimming waters from boating waters. . . .

Appellants . . . first contend that a riparian owner [an owner of waterfront property] is not responsible for the safe maintenance of property beyond the . . . line . . . that marks the boundary between Appellants' shoreline land and submerged land which belongs to the state. But even if Appellants are held responsible for the maintenance of submerged lands, Appellants contend, that responsibility extends only to the remedy of dangerous conditions known to Appellants or of which they could have acquired knowledge had they . . . exercised reasonable care. Since there was no evidence that Appellants knew of the presence of the cement block nor that it had been there long enough to mandate . . . constructive knowledge, Appellants contend [they breached no duty]. . . .

[This argument was properly rejected.] . . . A resort owner who avails himself of the advantages of riparian ownership for resort purposes owes to his patrons a duty of reasonable care which includes "active vigilance" in their protection from foreseeable risks. . . .

The jury was perfectly justified in determining that Appellants had violated this duty in any one or more of three respects: (1) their failure to warn of the dangers of diving off the boat dock; (2) their failure to periodically "rake" the swimming-diving area in search of dangerous obstructions; and (3) their failure to segregate swimming areas from boating areas.

This case clearly establishes that, for a resort to satisfy its obligation to an invitee, it is not enough to correct dangerous conditions of which it is aware. The business must, in addition, regularly inspect the premises to locate and identify dangerous conditions, and correct them as well. If the hotel fails to inspect, it will be liable for injuries caused by conditions that an inspection would have revealed.

Duty Owed to Licensees

A **licensee** is someone who has been given permission by the owner or occupier of a facility to enter or remain on the property, but his presence does not further defendant's business. An example of a licensee is a waitress or front desk clerk who, on a day off, goes to the place of employment to pick up a pay check. At that time the employee is not furthering the employer's business interests but nonetheless is on the premises with the employer's consent.

Similarly, a former employee who enters the premises for purposes of meeting with a current employee is a licensee. *Mutual Life Insurance Co. v. Churchwell*, 221 Ga. App. 312, 471 S.E.2d 267 (Ga., 1996).

Different states define the duty owned to licensees differently. In a majority of the states, the duty owed is twofold: (1) refrain from willfully or wantonly injuring the licensee or acting in a manner to increase peril; and (2) warn of any latent dangers on the premises of which the property owner has knowledge.

In some states, the duty owed to licensees is merely to refrain from willful or wanton injury.

Note that, for the invitee, the hotel or restaurant must inspect for dangerous conditions and either repair them or warn the invitee about them. For the licensee the duty is less. The hotel or restaurant can dispense with the inspection. According to the majority rule, the hotel or restaurant's only duty is to warn of those dangers about which it knows. Thus, the hotel or restaurant must disclose known defects but need not make any effort to determine what defects exist. Had the plaintiff in *Montes v. Betcher*, p. 112, been a licensee rather than an invitee, the resort would have satisfied its obligation and the plaintiff would have lost.

In states where the minority rule applies, the hospitality facility does not even owe a duty to disclose and warn of known dangers.

The following case explores the circumstances under which a visitor of a hotel guest qualifies as an invitee and when he is treated as a licensee.

CASE EXAMPLE 5–5

Steinberg v. Irwin Operating Co.
90 So.2d 460 (Fla., 1956)

. . . Appellant, Essie Steinberg, accompanied two friends to the Cadillac Hotel operated by appellee. The purpose of the mission was to enable one of the friends to deliver a message to a registered guest at the hotel. Inquiry at the desk revealed that the registered guest was not in. Thereupon, Mrs. Steinberg and her friends decided to explore various lounges and other rooms adjacent to the lobby. This was done for their own diversion. They first went into a "TV Room." They didn't like the program then showing. They then apparently attempted to enter an adjoining "Movie Room." This room was dark except for the light cast by the movie screen and projector. The floor level of the "Movie Room" was four inches lower than the floor level of the "TV Room." Claiming that she did not see the difference in level, Mrs. Steinberg fell and suffered injuries. She filed a complaint seeking compensation for damages resulting from the alleged negligence of appellee. The alleged negligence was the difference in the floor level. . . .

Appellant contends that at the time of the alleged injury, Mrs. Steinberg was an invitee of the hotel. They seek recovery on the theory that the hotel was obligated to furnish its invitees with reasonably safe premises.

Appellee contends that Mrs. Steinberg was merely a licensee. They assert that the only duty owed to her was to refrain from willfully or wantonly injuring her.

There is no doubt that a registered guest of a hotel is a business invitee and is entitled to receive the degree of care applicable to invitees. We are of the view that one entering a hotel to communicate with a registered guest is entitled to receive and enjoy the same degree of care. This rule is subject to the limitations hereafter expressed. . . . [B]y the very nature of the business, the operator of the hotel is bound to anticipate that a registered guest is apt to have business and social callers. The invitation to such callers arises by operation of law out of the relationship between the hotel and its registered guests. The operator of the hotel should provide reasonably safe ways of ingress and egress for those legally entering and leaving the place pursuant to the implied invitation implicit in the relationship between hotel operator and registered guests.

However, this implied invitation is not without its limits. The invitation to enter the hotel to visit a guest is circumscribed by the rule that it extends only to appropriate usage of the means of ingress and egress, such as the lobby, elevator, hallways, and room area rented to the guest.

It would be stretching the doctrine of implied invitation beyond justifiable limits to hold that such invitation extends to all of the private or semi-public rooms of the hotel. When the visitor crosses the boundaries of the invitation, he ceases to be an invitee. His status then changes to that of a licensee or even a trespasser. He is entitled to the status of an invitee only to the extent justified by the implied invitation.

In this case, it is perfectly clear that Mrs. Steinberg enjoyed the status of an implied invitee when she entered the hotel lobby. This status continued so long as she used the facilities of the hotel reasonably included within the invitation. When, for her own pleasure and convenience, she crossed the bounds of the invitation on her own initiative, sought entertainment in the "TV Room," and later in the "Movie Room," she became at most a licensee. While she was in this status, the hotel owed to her only the duty to refrain from willfully or wantonly injuring her. The record is clear that there was no willful or wanton injury.

Ruling of the court: The judgment [for the hotel operator] is affirmed.

CASE QUESTIONS

1. What change of facts would be necessary to make Mrs. Steinberg an invitee at the time of her injury?
2. If Mrs. Steinberg was an invitee, what duty would the hotel have owed to her?

A Tennessee court dealt with the issue of a guest's visitor's status in the case of *Kandrach v. Chrisman*, 473 S.W.2d 193 (Tenn., 1971). A young man drowned while he was visiting his fiance, who was a guest at the defendant's motel. Neither could swim. They entered the motel pool together at a time when no one else was in it. He was either walking or standing in the water when he suddenly started to struggle and sank beneath the surface.

The case hinged on whether the deceased was an invitee. A sign at the end of the pool read, "Motel Guests Only." The lower court held that the visitor ceased to be an invitee upon entering the pool and that the motel from that time on owed him only the duty owed to a trespasser. The appellate court reversed, saying that a visitor of a hotel guest is in fact an invitee of the hotel provided the visitor has not exceeded the bounds of the invitation to visit extended by the guest. In this case the visitor was invited by the guest to join her in the pool. Thus the hotel owed the deceased a duty to exercise reasonable care in the maintenance of the pool. Contrast this situation to the case where the hotel guest invites a visitor to lunch and when the meal is through bids him farewell. On his own initiative and unaccompanied by the hotel guest, he utilizes the pool. While in the pool this visitor is beyond the parameters of the invitation to visit extended by the hotel/guest and therefore is not an invitee of the hotel.

Duty Owed to Trespassers

The least duty is owed to a **trespasser**, a person who enters a place without permission of the owner or occupier. If an employee who has been fired and ordered not to return to the hotel nonetheless enters the premises, he is a trespasser. Someone who enters a restaurant after it is closed for the night without the owner's permission is a trespasser. A landowner or possessor does not owe a duty to safeguard a trespasser from injury due to conditions on the land. Some states impose a duty not to willfully or randomly injure a trespasser, and other states impose this duty only when the trespasser's presence is known or reasonably foreseeable. A trespasser's presence would be known or foreseeable where, for example, neighborhood children regularly use for snowmobiling vacant land located adjacent to, and owned by, a hotel and the hotel is aware of this use.

The following case illustrates the application of the rule for trespassers.

CASE EXAMPLE 5–6

David Hanson v. Hyatt Corp.
196 Ill.3d 618, 554 N.E.2d 394 (1990)

[P]laintiff was not a registered guest at defendant's hotel. He entered the pool area sometime after 9:30 P.M. through a gap/hole in a fence surrounding the pool. It was dark, and the lights around the pool area were off. . . .

[H]e dove into Hyatt's pool and sustained injuries which rendered him a quadriplegic; he was 19 years old at the time of the accident. . . .

Hanson argues that he properly alleged the element of duty . . . based upon Hyatt's "implied invitation" to him to enter upon its premises "for the purpose of inspection and use of its restaurant, gift shop, meeting rooms, lobbies, and swimming pool," as a licensee or invitee. The implied invitation concerning his use of Hyatt's swimming pool is specifically based on the allegation that the pool "was not fully enclosed and was open to access by the public at large." . . .

Hanson was required to allege facts to support

a relationship which imposed a duty on Hyatt to protect him from his injury. . . .

A [business operator] has a duty to exercise reasonable care for the safety of an invitee. The duty owed to a licensee or trespasser is not to wilfully and wantonly injure him and to use ordinary care to avoid injuring him after he is discovered in a place of danger.

Hanson . . . appears to define an implied invitation as a failure by Hyatt to take reasonable steps to secure access to the pool area, presumably by closing up a hole in the fence through which he entered on the date of the accident . . . We find this argument without merit. . . . [T]o be upon premises by an implied invitation means that the person is there for a purpose connected with the business in which the owner of the premises is engaged. Here, Hanson simply failed to allege facts to support a position that he was using Hyatt's swimming pool for a reason connected with Hyatt's business . . . Plaintiff is a trespasser. Judgment for the hotel.]

In another case, a plaintiff was hungry late one night and left his house to walk to Hardee's Restaurant. He took a shortcut through a parking lot of a then-closed Burger King. After arriving at Hardee's he discovered he had forgotten his wallet. On this return trip he decided to check if there was any food in the Burger King dumpster. The dumpster was shielded on three sides by brick walls which were close to eight feet tall, and on the fourth by a set of wooden hinged gates. In an attempt to enter the dumpster area, plaintiff jumped upon one of the brick walls which then collapsed, severely injuring him. Unknown to plaintiff, the wall had been damaged a month earlier by a trash truck and had not been repaired. Employees had been alerted not to touch the wall. Plaintiff sued Burger King which argued that plaintiff was a trespasser and, therefore, Burger King owed him no duty to keep the wall safe. Agreeing with Burger King, the court stated, "[A] trespasser . . . assumes the risk of injury from the condition of the premises. . . . While a possessor of land may not intentionally set booby traps with the design of causing injury, the possessor owes no duty to adult trespassers for conditions on the premises." *Cochran v. Burger King Corp.*, 937 S.W.2d 358 (Mo. Crt. App., 1996).

Minority Position

Some states have abolished the distinction between licensees, invitees and trespassers and the duties owed to each. Instead, in those states, the occupier of land owes a duty of care to all three. However, the standard of reasonable care may vary with the circumstances of the visitor's entry on the premises.

No Special Duty Owed to Others

What about people who do not qualify as invitee, licensee or trespasser? In most cases, no duty is owed. In the following case, the innkeeper had no relationship with the injured party and, therefore, owed no duty of care.

CASE EXAMPLE 5-7

Callender v. MCO Properties, 885 P.2d 123 (Ariz., 1994)

. . . On March 26, 1988, appellant John Scott Callender was boating with friends on Lake Havasu. . . . They steered the boat toward the beach at the Crazy Horse Campground. Two women occupants of the boat got out to retrieve an inflatable raft they had left at the beach. The young women attempted to row the raft out into the water. When Callender saw that they were having difficulty, he dived from the boat into the water to assist them. During the dive, however, he struck his head on the bottom of the lake, broke his neck, and was rendered a quadriplegic.

At the time of Callender's accident, the State of Arizona owned the land along the Lake Havasu shore where the Crazy Horse Campground was located. The federal government owned and controlled the lake itself. . . . Appellees Ray and Marie Totah . . . operated the Crazy Horse Campground. Callender filed a civil action . . . alleging that the defendants failed to adequately warn that it was unsafe to dive in the water near the Crazy Horse Campground. . . . In response, the Totahs pointed out that Callender's accident occurred between twenty and fifty feet offshore from the campground premises, Callender had not been a guest of the campground, nor had he ever been on the premises nor docked at the campground. Finally, they argued that the lake's waters and subsurface were owned by the United States Department of the Interior and that Crazy Horse had no leasehold or other legal interest in those waters. The Totahs thus argued that they had no duty to Callender.

Callender argued in response that because the Totahs reasonably could foresee that patrons of the campground and nonpatrons in the company of patrons would approach the Crazy Horse beach by boat and might dive from the boats, the Totahs had a duty to act reasonably to warn people of the risk of diving. . . .

The campground was a business enterprise. A business invitee "is a person who is invited to enter or remain on the land for a purpose directly or indirectly connected with business dealings with the possessor of the land." . . . Callender was not an invitee of the Totahs. He did not enter the campground before the accident nor did he use any of the campground services or its dock. He was not attempting to enter the campground at the time of the injury. There simply was no relationship between Callender and the campground that would have imposed a duty of care on the Totahs for his benefit. . . .

The trial court correctly granted summary judgment for the Totahs after finding they had no duty to warn Callender of the dangers of diving in waters offshore from the campground. We therefore affirm the trial court judgment in favor of the Totahs.

CASE QUESTION

1. How would the liability of the Totahs for the accident have been different if Callender had been a camper at the campground, and if he had been within the campground beach area at the time of his diving accident? Why would the liability have been different?

In another case a motel owner rented a room to the owner of a used car lot located next door. In the middle of the night, the motel owner was awakened by noises from two unauthorized men on the used car lot. The motel owner called the used car lot owner and informed him of the intruders. The used car lot owner shot at the intruders from the motel room. One intruder was killed; the other wounded. The intruders sued the motel owner, among others. The motel owner contested liability. Since the intruders were not guests of the motel or otherwise connected with it, the court found no duty was owed and entered judgment for the motel. *Fedie v. Travelodge Intern, Inc.*, 782 P.2d 739 (Ariz., 1989).

No Duty Owed on Property Not Owned or Maintained by the Hospitality Facility

A hotel or restaurant is generally not liable for injuries that occur to patrons on property not owned or maintained by it, even if the property is near the hotel or restaurant's facility. Thus, a restaurant was not liable to diners who were assaulted in a parking lot located behind the restaurant but not owned or maintained by it. The court specifically noted that the restaurant did not pave, snowplow, clear, or patrol the area where the assault occurred. *Mankowski v. Denny's, Inc.*, 1997 WL 525083 (Oh., 1997).

Negligence Doctrines Generally Favoring the Plaintiff

Numerous legal doctrines are associated with negligence. In any negligence case one or more of these doctrines may apply and affect the outcome. Some favor the plaintiff by making the plaintiff's case easier to prove. Others benefit the defendant. We will examine first those that benefit the plaintiff, and then those that favor the defendant.

Res Ipsa Loquitur

In many negligence cases the plaintiff has difficulty proving the necessary elements. Evidence to prove defendant negligent does not always exist even though the facts of the case may strongly suggest defendant was negligent. The legal doctrine of res ipsa loquitur aids the plaintiff in such a case. It applies in cases where the circumstances suggest the defendant was negligent, but no proof of specific acts of negligence exists. In such cases the doctrine of **res ipsa loquitur**, which means "the thing speaks for itself," frees the plaintiff from the burden of proving the specific breach of duty committed by the defendant.

In the classic example of a res ipsa case, plaintiff is walking by a flour factory when, for an unexplained reason, a barrel of flour falls out of a window and injures plaintiff. Because he was not inside the factory at the time of the incident plaintiff cannot prove why the barrel fell from the window. Yet the occurrence is such that it would not have happened without negligence on the part of someone inside the factory. In such a case the doctrine of res ipsa loquitur creates an inference that defendant was negligent, and allows the plaintiff to proceed with the lawsuit without having to prove through witnesses or otherwise the specific way in which the defendant was negligent.

To use the doctrine, plaintiff must prove the following three elements:

1. Plaintiff's injury was caused by an accident that would not normally have happened without negligence;

2. The thing causing the injury (in this case, the barrel of flour) was within the exclusive control of the defendant; and

3. Plaintiff did not provoke the accident. For example, if plaintiff had been throwing rocks up to the window from which the flour fell and the rocks had dislodged the barrel of flour causing it to fall, plaintiff would not be able to use res ipsa loquitur.

Where the doctrine applies, the defendant does not automatically lose. Rather, the defendant has an opportunity to rebut the inference that it was negligent. If the defendant can prove that the cause of the accident was some factor other than its own negligence the defendant will not be liable.

The res ipsa loquitur doctrine has been applied in hotel and restaurant cases. In one such case the plaintiffs were sleeping in a double bed in a room in the defendant's hotel when plaster fell from the ceiling and injured them. Plaintiffs sued the hotel but were unable to prove exactly how the hotel was negligent. The court held that the doctrine of res ipsa loquitur applied because ceilings do not normally fall and the maintenance of the ceiling was under the exclusive control of the hotel. *McCleod v. Nel-Co Corp.*, 112 N.E.2d 501 (Ill., 1953).

The following case involves an accident that normally would not have happened without negligence. The grocery store's malfunctioning automatic door is similar to those used by many hotels and restaurants.

CASE EXAMPLE 5–8

Trefney v. National Super Markets, Inc.
803 S.W.2d 119 (Mo. App., 1990)

[O]n March 27, 1985, plaintiff was a customer at a store owned and operated by National. After grocery shopping, she was leaving the store by way of an automatic door which was controlled by a "Vision Pulse" stick and which swung outward. When she was only partly through the door, it swung backward, striking her in the chest and knocking her to the ground. As a result of the fall, she sustained serious injury.

The morning of the accident, the assistant manager of the store had unlocked the door and had checked to see if it opened. He had not, however, tested the operation of the door by walking completely through it. After the accident, that same assistant manager walked through the door to see if it was working. When it worked properly, he kept the door in service. He notified Schultz Door Company (Schultz), the company with whom National had a service agreement, of the problem with the door. Schultz found that the activation side of the Vision Pulse stick was inoperable; and, two days after the accident, replaced the Vision Pulse stick and the "end caps" on the door. . . .

The sole issue . . . is whether the evidence supported submission of plaintiff's claim under [res ipsa loquitur].

Res ipsa loquitur is a doctrine based upon circumstantial evidence. The doctrine permits a jury to infer negligence without proof of specific negligent conduct on the part of the defendant. In Missouri, we apply the doctrine and, thus, permit the inference when (1) the incident resulting in injury is of the kind which ordinarily does not occur without someone's negligence; (2) the incident is caused by an instrumentality under the control of the defendant; and (3) the defendant has superior knowledge about the cause of the incident. . . .

National asserts that plaintiff did not prove the first element of the doctrine, that the incident was not of the kind which ordinarily does not occur in the absence of negligence. National argues that other factors could have caused the door to mal-

function; namely, normal wear and tear, damage by a shopping cart, defective parts, or merely an electronic glitch.

To prove the first element, . . . [t]he plaintiff need not conclusively exclude all other possible explanations. It is enough that the facts proved reasonably permit the conclusion that negligence is the more probable explanation.

In the instant action, the evidence and the reasonable inferences drawn therefrom were that, on the day of the accident, National's assistant store manager had failed to test the automatic door adequately by doing a complete walk through. Schultz's records indicated that the Vision Pulse stick was inoperable. Within two days of the accident, Schultz repaired the door by replacing the Vision Pulse stick and the end caps of the door. . . . The trier of fact could reasonably conclude that the closing of the automatic door on plaintiff was the type of sudden, unusual malfunction which would not normally occur in absence of National's negligence. . . . There was substantial evidence to establish the first element essential for the application of res ipsa loquitur.

National also contends that plaintiff failed to show the second element of res ipsa loquitur, that the incident was caused by an instrumentality under defendant's control. . . .

In the present case, plaintiff's evidence was that, at the time of the accident, the automatic door was located in a store which was owned and operated by National. A National employee was responsible for unlocking the door, turning it on, checking to see if it worked, and reporting any malfunction to Schultz. After the accident, pursuant to the maintenance agreement with Schultz, National reported the door's malfunction. The trier of fact could reasonably conclude that National had control over the automatic door at the time of the accident. There was substantial evidence to establish the second element for the application of res ipsa loquitur. . . .

[Plaintiff was entitled to use res ipsa.]

CASE QUESTIONS

1. What was the basis for the court's decision that the type of accident involved in this case does not normally occur absent someone's negligence?

2. Could the plaintiff in the previous case, *Thomas v. Grand Hyatt Hotel*, p. 109, have used res ipsa loquitur? Why or why not?

Children and the Reasonable Person Test

Children do not comprehend dangers obvious to more mature persons. Instead they act impulsively. Nor are children able to weigh cause and effect accurately. This impacts the duty imposed by law *on* young people as well as the duty owed by adults *to* children. The law excuses a young child from negligent acts; a person injured by a young child's acts is not entitled to compensation. Similarly, the duty owed by adults to act reasonably is usually greater when young children are involved. Unlike the adult, children cannot be expected to recognize risks and take appropriate precautions.

In the following case the court discusses the impact on a hotel's liability of the injured guest being a "child of tender years".

CASE EXAMPLE 5–9

Baker v. Dallas Hotel Co.
73 F.2d 825 (Tex., 1934)

Mr. and Mrs. Robert F. Baker sued the Dallas Hotel Company, owners and operators of a hotel in Dallas, Texas, under the Texas death statute . . . for the death of their infant son, Bobby, who fell from a window of the twelfth story of the hotel. On the evidence, the judge held that no actionable negligence appeared on the part of the defendant and that there was contributory negligence on the part of the plaintiffs and directed a verdict for the hotel company. Mr. and Mrs. Baker appeal, and assign as the sole error the refusal to permit the jury to pass upon the issues of negligence.

The evidence shows without substantial conflict that the Bakers, having with them the child two years and five months old, registered as guests of the hotel and were assigned to a room with adjoining bath on Wednesday. At about nine o'clock the next Saturday morning, Mrs. Baker had just bathed the child and left him playing with his blocks on the floor near the center of the room while she was washing something in the adjoining bathroom. Mr. Baker was in bed, awake, but with his back toward the window a few feet away. The sash was raised, but the opening was covered by a wire window screen that they knew was there, but had never examined. The windowsill was about the height of Bobby's face. In front of it was a radiator that did not extend the whole length of the sill, but left a space on each side. The cut-off valve of the radiator was under one of these spaces, and Bobby could have stepped upon this valve and climbed into the window. Neither Mr. nor Mrs. Baker knew he was near the window until, after a short absence, she returned from the bathroom and saw him sitting sidewise on the windowsill with his head pressed against the screen, and before she could reach him the screen opened outwards and he fell below and was killed.

An examination of the screen showed that it was hinged at the top and was intended to be secured from opening outwards by two spring plungers of metal, one on each side near the bottom of the screen frame that passed through the frame into holes in the wooden window facing. The screen was old, and the springs had become weak, and the window facing had grooves worn by the ends of the plungers from each hole outwards so that the plungers got but little hold in the facing. A slight pushing on the screen was found by experiment sufficient to open it. The hotel company had employees whose duty it was to inspect windows and screens. This screen had not been reported as out of order to the superintendent, but he did not know whether it had been reported to the housekeeper or carpenter. There were heavy iron grills outside of some of the windows of the hotel, but none on this window.

[S]ince the parents here sue for their own [loss], they may be defeated by their own contributory negligence. . . .

The diligence of counsel has produced no case relating to the liability of an innkeeper for an injury to a child guest due to a defective window screen. An innkeeper is not an insurer of the safety of his guests, but owes to them ordinary care to see that the premises assigned to them are reasonably safe for their use and occupancy. . . .

When a child of tender years is accepted as a guest, the inexperience and the natural tendencies of such a child become a part of the situation and must be considered by the innkeeper. We do not mean that the innkeeper becomes the nurse of the child, or assumes its control when accompanied by its parents, but only that he is bound to consider whether his premises, though safe enough for an adult, present any reasonably avoidable dangers to the child guest. The control and general responsibility for the child accompanied by a parent or nurse is with the latter, who are also bound to exercise ordinary care to keep the child from harm. As has been stated, when parents are complaining of the negligence of the innkeeper their own negligence that contributes to the injury is a good defense to their suit. [The state involved in this lawsuit followed the contributory negligence rule which prohibits recovery by individuals whose own negligence contributed in any way to their injuries. See the discussion on contributory negligence later in this chapter.] Negligence is not attributable as such to a child of two and a half years. . . . The conduct of such a child being natural, spontaneous and instinctive is like that of an animal and is similarly to be anticipated and guarded against by those charged with any duty in respect to the child.

What then should this innkeeper and these parents have anticipated that this child might do, and what have they respectively done or failed to do that was negligent? There is no statutory requirement respecting hotel windows or window screens. . . . There is no course of decisions establishing any rule applicable specially to children and hotel windows. The only available standard of care is the conduct of the ideal person of ordinary prudence, to be judged by the jury as a question of fact. A jury should consider whether the defects attributed to this screen were known to the innkeeper or had existed for such time that he is to be charged with knowledge of them, whether he should in due prudence have anticipated that a child of this age would be attracted towards the window, and would climb to see what was outside, and might be led to lean against the insecure screen and be endangered; and whether another room, or at least a warning about the insecurity of this screen, was due.

On the other hand, the jury ought also to inquire whether the parents should not have anticipated the same danger and kept better watch over the child or have tested the screen, and whether they themselves were contributorily negligent if the innkeeper was negligent. The innkeeper and the parents perhaps ought equally to have anticipated the danger of a child trying to get into the window, but the duty of inspecting the screen is not the same. The responsibility for the premises is primarily on the innkeeper, and the guest may generally assume that they are safe. But it is argued that the screens are there to keep insects out and not to keep children in, and there is no duty on the innkeeper to have them safe for the latter purpose, and parents have no right to rely on them for such purpose. . . . But yet if the screen to all appearances, and as screens are usually found, would serve to protect the child, the false appearance of an insecurely fastened screen might easily mislead the parent or even inspire confidence in a child to lean against it. . . . Though there was no original duty to have any screen in the window for the purpose of keeping the child in, the jury might conclude that prudence would as respects this child have required that it be as securely fastened as screens customarily are, lest it prove a deception and a trap.

We agree with the trial judge that the failure to have protecting grills at the windows is not negligence. Their absence was apparent, and no law and no custom requires them. But on the issues of negligence in the innkeeper touching the condition of the screen, and in the parents touching their conduct, we are of the opinion that jury questions exist. Children have often fallen through insecurely fastened window sashes and screens so that the jury might conclude that such a thing is reasonably to be anticipated by those under duty to guard against danger. . . . The duty of parents to watch over their infant child is to be viewed in the light of all the demands made at the time upon them, and the circumstances usually make negligence on their part a question for the jury. [The case was remanded for trial.]

CASE QUESTIONS

1. If you were on the jury, would you find the hotel negligent? Why or why not?
2. If you were on the jury, would you find the parents negligent? Why or why not?

The following case, involving a child walking into a glass panel, restates that the innkeeper's duty to a child is greater than that owed to an adult. Further, in the previous case, we saw that contributory negligence by the deceased child's parents can defeat their right to recovery. In this case we learn that even if children under the age of seven are negligent in a way that contributes to their injuries, they may nonetheless recover for their injuries when someone else is also negligent. As previously stated, the law excludes young children from consequences of their own negligence.

CASE EXAMPLE 5–10

Waugh v. Duke Corporation
248 F.Supp. 626 (N.C., 1966)

The Court finds as a fact that the defendant, The Duke Corporation, was negligent in that it failed to take proper measures to warn Emily Waugh of the existence of the floor to ceiling glass panels which constituted the major portion of the east wall of room 58 of the defendant's motel, and in that it failed to construct guards around such or place anything around or on the glass to give notice that a panel existed, and failed to give verbal warning to Emily Waugh and such negligence was the proximate cause of the child's injury. . . .

The duty of an innkeeper to a guest who is an infant is a greater duty than that owing to his adult guests and he is bound to consider whether his premises, although safe enough for an adult, present any reasonably avoidable dangers to his infant guest. . . .

This Court has found as a fact that the glass panels in the Duke Motor Lodge were installed in the usual manner, according to the customs of the trade and are similar to glass of the type and thickness employed in other motels of recent vintage, however, the mere fact that there has been compliance with the general standards of the trade and general usages of the business is not itself conclusive on the issue of negligence.

This Court has also found as a fact that the defendant motel was not negligent in utilizing the type of glass, i.e., crystal plate of the thickness which it employed in the panels. The negligence of the defendant therefore consists of something other than its employment of defective or unsafe material in the construction of its motel and that negligence, the Court finds, consists of the failure of the defendant to warn Emily Waugh of the potential danger of the glass panels adjacent to the east door of the room or to place on said panels some marking, device or some guard in front thereof which would prevent a child from inadvertently walking thereinto.

It is impossible to reconcile the cases cited in the briefs submitted by the plaintiff and defendant. On seemingly almost identical facts courts have reached opposite conclusions in the various jurisdictions. . . .

Circumstances alter the application of the rule to cases. What is reasonable care to one class of invitees might fall short as to another. Those who invite children, who have not arrived at the age of discretion, to go upon their premises are required to exercise a relatively higher degree of care for their safety than to adults. That degree of care is commensurate with the attending facts and circumstances of each case. . . .

It takes more indication of danger to alert a child than to alert an adult. "Children are necessarily lacking in the knowledge of physical causes and effects. . . . They must be expected to act upon childish instincts and impulses, and must be presumed to have less ability to take care of themselves than adults have." . . .

In the present case, there was a finding that prior to the injury complained of, individuals had collided with panels in various parts of the motel. Such prior accidents should have been indicative to the defendant that the conditions of transparency, light and shadow were such that others would be likely to collide therewith to their injury, unsuspecting the existence of such panels and, . . . while adults can be expected to employ discretion and care to recognize and avoid the panels, such cannot reasonably be expected of a child of tender years coming upon a panel in the defendants' motel for the first time.

An innkeeper is required to give warning of such hidden perils. . . . His duty to give such warning is increased when infant guests are present. . . .

The defendant . . . has raised the issue of contributory negligence. Emily Waugh was not seven years of age at the date of the accident and in this state it is conclusively presumed that a child under the age of seven years is incapable of contributory negligence.

The defendant therefore by its failure to warn its infant guest of the hidden danger of the glass panel or to place thereon such markings as would indicate the presence of the glass to Emily Waugh or failed to construct guards around the panels was negligent and such negligence was the proximate cause of the injury complained thereof.

Emily Waugh is, therefore, entitled to recover . . . for her injuries. . . .

CASE QUESTION

1. What indication of danger did the motel have, and how should it have protected its child guests?

While a proprietor of a hospitality facility owes an enhanced duty to protect the safety of children, some young people may have a duty to act reasonably to protect themselves from harm. The existence and extent of that duty depends on the age and circumstances of the child, and the relevant facts. The following case discusses these issues in relation to a ten-year-old boy who was injured in a restaurant.

CASE EXAMPLE 5–11

Frelow v. St. Paul Fire & Marine Insurance Co., 631 So.2d 632 (La., 1994).

On December 30, 1990, a Sunday afternoon at about 2:00 P.M., James Papillion, ten years old, was having lunch at Western Sizzlin Steakhouse in Lake Charles with his mother, brothers, and sisters. James had just been to the salad bar with his mother and sister and was carrying his salad plate back to his family's table. His sister was right behind him. James's mother, Carolyn Frelow, had already returned to the table.

James and his sister chose the most direct route between the tables back to their own table, a fairly straight path. This route took them past a recently vacated booth which was being cleaned by Michael Bruce, a busboy. On the other side of the aisle was an occupied table. As James proceeded to pass this point, at a fast walk, he tripped over Bruce's foot, which was sticking into the aisle as he leaned into the booth he was cleaning. James reeled and hit his back on the corner of a table, then fell onto the floor face down. His salad plate fell on the back of his head. . . . His mother had previously admonished James for running in the restaurant, before they had gone to the salad bar. . . .

Carolyn Frelow, James's mother, testified at trial that James complained of headaches and a backache for a week after the accident. Carolyn gave him Tylenol® for the headaches. Then, the following Sunday, James developed a severe headache during church which caused him to break into a cold sweat. . . . [He was treated by a chiropractor for three months,] at which time he was asymptomatic.

The trial judge found James Paillion was negligent for walking too fast and Bruce was negligent for obstructing James's path after he saw James approaching. The court apportioned 40 percent fault to James and 60 percent to Bruce [See the discussion on comparative negligence later in this chapter.]. . . .

An owner of a business who permits the public to enter his establishment has a duty to exercise reasonable care to protect them. This duty extends to keeping the premises safe from unreasonable risks of harm or warning persons of known dangers. When the presence of small children is expected, the duty increases. . . .

[W]e find that Bruce did have a duty to Western Sizzlin customers to use reasonable care not to obstruct the aisles so that customers could travel freely between the food service stations and the tables. A reasonable man would realize that he may trip someone if he extends his leg into an aisle in a self-service restaurant. . . .

A patron is charged with using reasonable care for his own safety and must see and avoid obvious hazards. However, a child is not held to the same standard of care as that of an adult; rather, the test is whether the child, considering his age, background, and inherent intelligence, indulged in gross disregard of his own safety in the face of known, understood, and perceived danger.

It is well settled that a child of nine or ten years of age may be capable of negligence. However, in determining the negligence of a child, the actions of the child must be judged by his maturity and capacity to evaluate circumstances. The degree of caution expected of a nine- or ten-year-old boy varies with the circumstances of each case.

In the case before us, an apparently normal, average ten-year-old boy was carrying a plate of salad through a restaurant to the table where his family was sitting. The testimony of all eye witnesses, including Michael Bruce, the busboy, was that James was walking fast, but not running.

The defendants would have us assess 100 percent fault to James for walking too fast, for not watching where he was going, and for not taking a different route to his table. However, we are discussing a ten-year-old boy who was trying to carry a plate of salad from the salad bar to his table without spilling it. We do not believe that a ten-year-old child generally has sufficient experience to discern the best possible route by which to negotiate a crowded self-service restaurant while carrying a plate of food;

many adults find this difficult. The route he did take led directly to his family's table. The trial judge found this was a reasonable route and we agree.

However, we do not believe that the danger inherent in walking too fast in a self-service restaurant while carrying a plate of food is beyond the understanding of a normal ten-year-old boy. Moreover, James had already been admonished by his mother not to run in the restaurant. The trial judge found that James's conduct was negligent. We cannot say the trial judge was clearly wrong.

CASE QUESTION

1. What is the standard of care an adult must exercise for his own safety? How does that differ from the standard of care a child is expected to exercise?

Reasonable Accommodations for Children

A hotel must anticipate dangers and use reasonable care to protect against them when furnishing a room that will be occupied by children. In *Seelbach, Inc., v. Cadick*, 405 S.W.2d 745 (Ky., 1966), the court upheld a jury award of $56,000 to an eight-month-old infant who fell from an adult bed against hot radiator pipes in a hotel room where no baby crib was furnished. The hotel had at least one crib available when the family arrived at the hotel but the clerk did not offer or give it to the plaintiffs. The court ruled that the jury could properly hold a hotel negligent for failing to provide a baby bed while maintaining exposed hot radiator pipes in the hotel room. The court said that a hotel owes its guests a "duty to provide articles of furniture that may be used by them in the ordinary and reasonable way without danger." The negligence in the facts of this case was not in the exposed pipe in the room; the question rather was whether the hotel was negligent in not providing a bed suitable for the infant given the existence of the exposed pipe. The appeals court upheld the jury's determination that the hotel was negligent.

Attractive Nuisance Doctrine

This doctrine is an outgrowth of youngsters' limited capability to detect danger and protect themselves from risk. An **attractive nuisance** is a potentially dangerous object or condition of exceptional interest to young people, such as a swimming pool, a large empty box, or a snow pile suitable for sliding accumulated by a plow. If an attractive nuisance exists on the property, the owner or occupier is required to exercise reasonable care to protect a child from associated risks. Thus, a hotel with a pool would be well advised to install a tall, locked fence to prevent children from using the pool when it is closed or unattended. A restaurant that purchased a new refrigerator should discard the box only after removing all tacks and other sharp items, and flattening it.

The elements of an attractive nuisance are the following:

1. A condition exists that is attractive to children and is likely to cause them injury;

2. The owner or occupier of the land knows or should know of the condition; and

3. Due to the child's immaturity, he does not appreciate the danger.

In such case the owner or occupier must take reasonable steps to eliminate the danger.

The case of *Aleanese v. Edwardsville Mobile Home Village, Inc.*, 529 P.2d 163 (Kan., 1974), is illustrative. Donald, a minor, lived with his family in the Edwardsville Mobile Home Village, a project with an area of 120 acres and containing 146 trailers. The owner of the village had assured residents that playgrounds and play equipment would be provided for the children, but these assurances had not been fulfilled at the time of Donald's accident. Workers employed by the owner knew that the children played in the neighboring ditch. There was no fence or warning signs, nor did the law require a fence or posting. A ditch caved in while Donald was playing in it, and he was killed. His father sued the owner to recover for Donald's wrongful death. The court, holding the ditch constituted an attractive nuisance, said,

> *The propensity of small boys to dig caves, to dig plain holes in the ground, has ancient roots. . . . We think it may be said as a matter of plain, common knowledge that the condition prevailing in defendant's ditch would prove . . . an irresistible invitation to boys of tender years to give vent to the principal urge to dig caves, unaware of latent dangers. In other words, we have little reluctance in saying that the canyon might reasonably have been expected to attract and lure young boys who might not sense the odor of hazards.*

The owner's negligence in failing to provide a fence to keep youngsters out or otherwise restrict access resulted in liability for Donald's death.

Some states have abolished the concept of attractive nuisance in circumstances where the risk should be obvious to the child. These states hold that certain risks are so obvious even children are expected to exercise caution when confronting them, relieving the property owner from liability.

In *Logan v. Old Enterprise Farms, Ltd.*, 564 N.E.2d 778 (Ill., 1990), the fifteen-year-old plaintiff was playing on a swing attached to a tree by owners of a farm. The swing became stuck in the branches and, attempting to fix it, he climbed a ladder that had been provided to him by the owners of the farm. After kicking the swing loose, and on his descent, he fell backward, resulting in an injury that left him a quadriplegic. The court stated that Illinois had replaced the attractive nuisance doctrine with a standard imposing liability only where the dangerous condition leading to the injury would not reasonably be "fully understood and appreciated by the child." The court dismissed plaintiff's case noting that he was fifteen, that the risk of falling from the tree was an obvious danger, and that plaintiff could reasonably be expected to understand and appreciate that risk.

Recovery was also denied to a ten year old who fell while walking or jumping on large pipes which extended approximately 12 to 15 inches above the ground. Noting that a child might think it fun to jump from one to another, the court said, "The risk involved in doing so was simple and obvious. Indeed the challenge offered by the risk of falling is probably what provided the fun. There is no suggestion of any surprising danger, such as instability of the pipes, or unusual slipperiness." *Schilz v. Walter Kassuba, Inc.*, 134 N.W.2d 453 (Wis., 1965).

In *Daniels v. Byington*, 707 P.2d 476 (Id., 1985), a six-year-old boy fell four feet to the ground from the deck of a stationary boat used as a playhouse on the defendants' property. His parents sued the property owners to recover for the lad's broken arm. The court held for the defendants on the ground that the fall was not caused by a hidden defect in the boat, and the danger of falling should have been apparent to the boy. Said the court,

> *From the time they are born all children realize the danger of falling and instinctively clutch at something when they feel that danger is near. While the instinct to climb is practically universal, and it is carried on in a venturesome spirit, a consciousness of the risk of falling is always present.*

Negligence Per Se Doctrine

Negligence per se describes an act that violates a law or ordinance designed to protect the safety of the public. Under the majority view, such acts are treated as negligence without any further proof of breach of duty. When applicable, this doctrine is of great help to the plaintiff because he does not have to prove that defendant failed to act as a reasonable person. Instead, the only facts the plaintiff needs to prove are the existence of the law or ordinance, defendant's violation of it, the extent of the injury, and proximate cause between the violation and the injury.

Under the minority view, noncompliance with the safety law or ordinance is not conclusive on the issue of defendant's breach of duty but is some evidence of such a breach. In some states such noncompliance is prima facie evidence of negligence, which means it alone is sufficient evidence if unrebutted to support a judgment for plaintiff.

The reasoning supporting the negligence per se doctrine is that the proprietor of an establishment has a duty always to comply with legal mandates designed to protect patrons. This legal duty applies even when the owner is unaware of the existence of the safety laws. Innkeepers and restaurateurs must therefore stay current on both new laws applicable to their business and changes in existing laws. Sources of this information include trade journals and presentations at trade association meetings. In addition, a business can request a lawyer to perform a legal audit in which the attorney will examine the business and its compliance with applicable laws, and advise the owner of any deficiencies.

The following case illustrates the application of the majority view of negligence per se in a case against a hotel that was woefully deficient in its compliance with safety laws relating to swimming pools.

CASE EXAMPLE 5–12

First Overseas Investment Corp. v. Cotton
491 So.2d 293 (Fla., 1986)

. . . Cleophus Cotton and his wife were guests at the Monte Carlo Hotel (hotel). Mr. Cotton went swimming in the shallow end of the hotel pool. The pool water was extremely cloudy as the pool attendant had that morning dumped a bucketful of soda ash into it to "sweeten" the PH. The pool attendant testified that the pool's soda ash feeder was inoperable, hence his practice of dumping the soda ash directly into the pool. Expert testimony was offered that soda ash should never be dumped directly into a pool and that a bucketful was ten to twelve times more than is needed. Soda ash increases turbidity [muddiness, thickness, darkness] and makes the water cloudy until completely filtered. The pool attendant testified that he had no training in first aid or in the use of lifesaving apparatus. He further testified that the pool's filtration system was inoperable. The pool did not have lifesaving apparatus such as a shepherd's hook, an elevated lifeguard's chair, or first aid equipment.

Michael Wolfe testified that he observed Mr. Cotton swimming in the shallow end of the pool. Mr. Wolfe turned away from the pool for about 60 seconds and when he looked back, Mr. Cotton was gone. Mr. Wolfe went to the side of the pool and looked for Mr. Cotton, but did not see him. He asked another hotel guest, Daniel Jones, if he had seen Mr. Cotton. Mr. Jones indicated that he had not seen him. Mr. Wolfe told the pool attendant that he thought Mr. Cotton was in the pool. The pool attendant and Mr. Wolfe stood at the edge of the pool and looked for Mr. Cotton, but still did not see him. Subsequently, Mr. Wolfe and Mr. Jones began swimming the length of the pool at the bottom, looking for Mr. Cotton. They testified that they did not find Mr. Cotton on the bottom until they were practically on top of him. They then brought him up to the side of the pool. Mr. Jones ran down the beach to get a lifeguard. A lifeguard was located by Mr. Jones. The lifeguard attempted to resuscitate Mr. Cotton, but his efforts were unsuccessful, as were the efforts of a fire rescue squad which arrived at the scene shortly after the lifeguard.

Mr. Wolfe testified that twelve to twenty minutes elapsed between the time he first started looking for Mr. Cotton and the time resuscitation efforts were first made. According to expert testimony, there was a high probability of Mr. Cotton's survival if he had been rescued within four to five minutes after disappearing. It was plaintiff's contention that Mr. Cotton would have been rescued within four to five minutes and would not have drowned if the hotel had complied with the following Florida Department of Health and Rehabilitative Services (HRS) rules:

Rule 10D-5.66(3)

All items of equipment designed for recirculation, filtration, disinfection, and pool water treatment, shall be kept in service at all times and shall be properly maintained to perform the functions of the units and protect the swimming pool water from contamination.

Rule 10D-5.68(6)

Clearness—At all times the pool water shall be sufficiently clear so that the main drain or drains are clearly defined when viewed from the pool deck.

Rule 10D-5.81(1)

All owners, managers, and/or other attendants

in charge of a public swimming pool shall be responsible for supervision and safety of the pool. The attendant, if provided, shall be in full charge of bathing, shall have authority to enforce all rules, and shall be trained in first aid and the use of lifesaving apparatus.

Rule 10D-5.81(2)

Lifesaving apparatus—All swimming pools shall be provided with a shepherd's hook securely attached to a one piece pole not less than sixteen (16) feet in length, and at least one (1) eighteen (18) inch diameter lifesaving ring with sufficient rope attached to reach all parts of the pool from the pool deck. Lifesaving apparatus shall be mounted in a conspicuous place and be readily available for use. Pools greater than fifty (50) feet in length shall have multiple units with at least one (1) shepherd's hook and one (1) lifesaving ring located along each of the longer sides of the pool.

Rule 10D-5.81(3)

Lifesaving chairs—One elevated lifeguard chair . . . platform shall be provided for pools having over two thousand (2,000) square feet up to four thousand (4,000) square feet of pool water surface area. One additional lifeguard chair or platform shall be provided for each two thousand (2,000) square feet, or major fraction thereof, of pool water surface area above four thousand (4,000) square feet. The lifeguard chair(s) or platform(s) shall be located to allow a clear and unobstructed view of the pool bottom in the area of surveillance.

Rule 10D-5.81(6)

First aid equipment and materials—Each pool shall have available first aid equipment and materials sufficient for use in connection with injuries which may occur in the pool or on the pool deck.

Plaintiff contended that Mr. Cotton would not have drowned if the pool's filtration system had been operating properly; the water in the pool had been clear; an elevated lifeguard chair had been in place affording a clear and unobstructed view of the pool; there had been lifesaving apparatus and first aid equipment available and the pool attendant had been trained in the use of lifesaving apparatus and first aid. . . .

The well established rule is that it is "negligence per se" for a defendant to violate a statute which establishes a duty to protect a particular class of persons from a particular type of injury. This applies to violations of HRS rules as well. . . . We find that all of the HRS rules at issue obligated the hotel to protect a particular class of persons (guests using the pool), from a particular type of harm (drowning). All of the rules were designed to ensure a clear view of swimmers in distress and/or the capability of saving them from drowning. . . .

[Judgment for plaintiff.]

CASE QUESTIONS

1. What class of persons were the pool maintenance laws designed to protect? Why do these people need protection?

2. How did the plaintiff prove proximate cause in this case?

For a restaurant or hotel to be liable on a per se theory, it is not enough that the establishment violated the law. In addition, the violation must be the proximate cause of the plaintiff's injury. If it is not, the hotel or restaurant will not be liable.

A 1991 New York case involved a residential hotel which provided long-term occupancy to tenants rather than temporary rooms to guests. A law required the hotel to provide an intercom device enabling communication between the occupant of each apartment and visitors outside the locked front door. The defendant hotel failed to provide the intercom system. The plaintiff, a resident in the hotel, was injured in two assaults perpetrated by two other residents. The first assault occurred in the first floor stairwell, and the second in the lobby. The assault victim sued the hotel, claiming negligence per se. The court dismissed the case, holding that the violation of the statute by the hotel was not the proximate cause of plaintiff's injuries. Since plaintiff was not in his room at the time of the attacks, he would not have been able to use the intercom system to solicit help even if the intercom system had been installed. Stated differently, even if the hotel had supplied intercoms, they would not have saved plaintiff from the attacks. *Simms v. St. Nicholas Ave. Hotel Co.*, N.Y.L.J., Nov. 21, 1991, p. 27, Col. 1.

The same point is illustrated in *Truett v. Morgan*, 266 S.E.2d 557 (Ga., 1980). Sanders and Truett, both guests at a hotel, had an altercation. Shortly after the fight Sanders went to Truett's room and knocked on the door. When Truett opened it, Sanders shot him. Contrary to law, the door opened outward instead of inward. Truett sued the hotel, claiming it was negligent per se. The court rejected the claim because no connection existed between the direction in which the door opened and the injury.

Obligations Beyond Regulation

Suppose a hotel fully complies with a statute but the requirements of the law are inadequate to protect the guests. Can that hotel be found negligent for failing to do more than the law requires? The answer is yes. The hotel has a duty to exercise reasonable care to protect guests from injury. If satisfying the law falls short of reasonable care, the hotel must do more than what the statute requires. In the following case the hotel's compliance with the law did not protect it from liability for guests' injuries.

CASE EXAMPLE 5–13

Miller v. Warren
390 S.E.2d 207 (W. Va., 1990)

The plaintiffs, David Miller, Linda Grapes, and Joshua Grapes . . . [o]n April 1983, . . . checked into Room 8 of the Flagg Motel . . . which was operated by the defendant, Barbara Warren, and Leonard Frantz. Ms. Warren had owned the motel since 1973. The plaintiffs had been driving for several hours, and they fell asleep shortly after entering their room in the early afternoon. In the late afternoon, Ms. Grapes awoke to hear her son cry-

ing. Smoke filled the motel room. Ms. Grapes woke Mr. Miller. Mr. Miller tried the room door, but it was too hot to open. At that time, the motel clerk saw smoke coming from Room 8 and used his pass-key to open the room door. The guests crawled to safety. Mr. Miller, Ms. Grapes and Joshua sustained serious burns in the fire.

On 12 October 1983, the plaintiffs filed their complaint . . . alleging that their injuries were the result of the defendant's negligence. . . . The plaintiffs' theory was that the fire was caused by the defendant's placing the bed in the room too close to the baseboard heater. Expert witnesses for the plaintiffs and the defendant agreed that the fire started in the area between the heater and the bed. The plaintiffs' expert opined that the heater caused the fire, and the defendant's expert opined that the cause was instead a burning cigarette dropped by the plaintiffs. Furthermore, the plaintiffs argued, the absence of a smoke alarm at least aggravated their injuries. . . .

The plaintiffs argue that the jury was improperly instructed on the defendant's standard of care. The parties agree that the motel was in compliance with the local fire code, which did not require a smoke detector in each room. The judge's instructions indicated that the appropriate standard of due care in the matter of a smoke detector is met if the motel complies with the fire code. . . .

Failure to comply with a fire code or similar regulation constitutes . . . negligence, if an injury proximately flows from the non-compliance and the injury is of the sort the regulation was intended to prevent. . . . On the other hand, the converse, that compliance with a regulation is *per se* the exercise of due care, is not the law. Compliance with a regulation does not constitute due care *per se*. Compliance with the appropriate regulations is competent evidence of due care, but not *conclusive* evidence of due care. If the defendants knew or should have known of some risk that would be prevented by reasonable measures not required by the regulation, they were negligent if they did not take such measures. It is settled law that a statute or regulation merely sets a floor of due care. . . . Circumstances may require greater care, if a defendant knows or should know of other risks not contemplated by the regulation.

CASE QUESTIONS

1. What did the court mean when it stated, "A statute or regulation merely sets a floor of due care"?
2. What greater care might the defendant have exercised?

This case holds that if a hotel can prevent a risk by reasonable precautions, the hotel must do so, even when those safety measures are not required by statute. How does an innkeeper or restaurateur know what is required to satisfy the due care obligation if compliance with statutory mandates are not enough? The level of care required will be determined in part on standards followed in the industry as well as technological advances. Proprietors must stay abreast of new products and techniques, and should always be asking, "What new can I be doing to enhance the safety of my patrons?"

Strict or Absolute Liability

Normally defendants are not liable unless they do something wrong. If a patron trips and falls in a restaurant solely because he is intoxicated, the restaurant will not be liable for any injuries sustained in the fall. Since the restaurant was not negligent it did not breach any duty owed to the customer.

One exception does exist. If applicable, a defendant will be liable even though it violated no duty and did nothing wrong. That exception is sometimes called strict liability and sometimes absolute liability. **Strict liability** imposes liability from an ultrahazardous activity upon those who engage in it. Such activities might include keeping wild animals or using explosives. This doctrine imposes liability for resulting injuries even if the defendant took every precaution and was not negligent. The principle supporting this rule is that the ultrahazardous activity could be outlawed because of the danger it creates. In lieu of outlawing the activity, the law imposes liability for the activity on the party who engages in it, without regard for fault.

Suppose Jake purchases an old office building in the downtown section of a sizeable city intending to destroy the building with dynamite and build a ten story luxury hotel. He plans the dynamiting for a Sunday morning when very few people are downtown. He constructs a tall barricade-like fence around the building to prevent people from entering the site and to protect against any debris hitting a passerby. Nonetheless, following the explosion, a piece of the building is propelled over the fence and hits a pedestrian. Under normal negligence rules Jake would not be liable; he satisfied the duty to exercise reasonable care to prevent injury. But under strict liability, freedom from negligence is not a defense. Therefore he will be liable to the injured passerby.

Strict Products Liability

In recent times the doctrine of strict liability has been extended significantly to sellers of defective products. This application of strict liability is called **strict products liability** and, like strict liability, imposes liability on the seller of a defective product without regard to negligence. A product is defective for this purpose if it is designed or manufactured improperly or if it contains inadequate warnings of dangers it presents. For example, suppose a chef buys a toaster for a restaurant. When he plugs it in and turns it on it explodes, causing injury. The store that sold the toaster is strictly liable; the chef does not have to prove negligence. Liability in these circumstances is a matter of social policy and based on the theory that the manufacturer can best bear the cost of injury because it can spread the cost throughout society by purchasing insurance and increasing the price of its goods to pay for it.

Restaurants and hotels can both benefit and be hurt by strict products liability. If they buy products that are defective and incur a loss as a result, they can sue the seller without the need to prove negligence. Thus, where a Hunan restaurant sustained significant damage from a fire because the fire suppression system it had purchased malfunctioned and failed to extinguish the fire, the manufacturer of the system may be liable in strict products liability. *Chiang v. Pyro Chemical, Inc.*, 1997 WL 330622 (Conn., 1997).

Restaurants and hotels can also be sued in strict products liability if they sell defective products, such as rancid tuna salad in the dining room or an exploding hair dryer from the gift shop. If the product was defective when it was sold to the hospitality facility, the restaurant or hotel can sue the manufacturer when the hotel or restaurant is sued by a customer or guest.

Respondeat Superior

Hotels and restaurants employ many people. In general, a employer is liable for the acts of its employees done in furtherance of their jobs. Thus, employers are liable to their customers, guests and other invitees for the negligence of their employees. If a bellhop negligently drops a heavy suitcase on a guest's foot, the innkeeper will be liable for the resulting injuries. If a waiter carelessly spills hot coffee on a customer causing burns, the restaurant will be liable.

This liability of the employer for the acts of its employees is called **respondeat superior** which means "let the master (employer) answer". The doctrine is founded on the theory that an employee is an agent of the employer; whenever an employee is performing the duties of the job he is acting on behalf of the employer. The law in effect renders acts of the employee those of the employer. Stated differently, the employer is vicariously (through a substitute) liable for the employee's wrongful conduct.

Several explanations exist for this doctrine. It encourages employers to exercise caution in the selection of employees and encourages employers to train their employees well. This should have the desirable effect of limiting the number of injuries occurring from employee wrongdoing. Another rationale for the doctrine is that it increases the injured party's chances of receiving compensation because the employer usually has more resources than does the employee.

An employer is not liable for every negligent act of its employee. It is not liable for negligent acts committed by the employee at home or school during nonwork time. The employer is liable only if the employee's negligent act occurred within the scope of his employment, which means in furtherance of duties owed to his employer and the employer is or could be exercising some control, directly or indirectly, over the employee's work.

In the following case the negligence clearly occurred while the employee was acting within the scope of his employment.

CASE EXAMPLE 5–14

Scott v. Salerno and GNOC, Corp., d/b/a/ Bally's Grand Hotel & Casino, 297 N.J. Super. 437, 688 A.2d 614 (N.J., 1997)

On June 14, 1993, Salerno, while operating an automobile owned by Pauline N. Marchese (Marchese), was involved in an accident with an automobile owned and operated by plaintiff Denise Rae Bishop Scott (Scott) in Atlantic City, New Jersey. At the time of the accident, Salerno was valet parking automobiles for Bally's as an employee. . . .

Bally's was legally responsible for the acts or omissions of Salerno. . . . Marchese gave Bally's permission to park her automobile. At the time of the accident, the automobile was being driven by Salerno, as agent for Bally's, for the very purpose for which it was given to Bally's. Bally's was responsible for the acts of Salerno. . . .

Whether an employee is acting within the scope of his employment is not always obvious. The term "scope of employment" is often interpreted broadly. The employment duties of a Burger King supervisory employee included resolving customer disputes. While talking with a woman who was dissatisfied with her order and wanted a refund, the customer accused the employee of attacking her son in school. In response, the employee became angry and swung his fists into a stack of trays which rebounded and hit the customer in the face. She sued for her resulting injuries. Burger King claimed that, since the comments that triggered the employee's anger were related to an incident at school and not at work, the episode occurred outside the scope of employment and therefore Burger King should not be liable. The court held the fact that the employee's action may have been mingled with personal motives and the fact that the offending comments were unrelated to the restaurant does not necessarily take the incident out of the scope of the employer's business. A jury trial was ordered to determine whether the actions were within the scope of employment. *Reynolds v. L&L Management, Inc.*, 492 S.E.2d 347 (Ga., 1997).

As you read the following case, consider whether you think the employee was acting in furtherance of his job at the time of the accident. The case presents an interesting twist: the facts involved damage caused to a hotel by a guest, and the hotel seeks to hold the guest's employer liable based on respondeat superior. Also, this case involves two matters discussed in Chapter 2—judgment notwithstanding the verdict and precedents. Note how the court handles the judgment N.O.V. and the conflicting precedents.

CASE EXAMPLE 5-15

Edgewater Motels, Inc. v. Gatzke
277 N.W.2d 11 (Minn., 1979)

. . . The fire in question broke out on August 24, 1973, in a room at the Edgewater Motel in Duluth, Minnesota, occupied by Arlen Gatzke. In July 1973, Gatzke, a 31-year Walgreen employee and then district manager, spent approximately three weeks in Duluth supervising the opening of a new Walgreen's restaurant. During that time, he stayed at the Edgewater Motel at Walgreen's expense. On about August 17, 1973, Gatzke returned to Duluth to supervise the opening of another Walgreen-owned restaurant. Again, he lived at the Edgewater at the company's expense. . . . In addition to working at the restaurant, Gatzke remained on call 24 hours per day to handle problems arising in other Walgreen restaurants located in his district. Gatzke thought of himself as a "24 hour a day

man." He received calls from other Walgreen restaurants in his district when problems arose. . . .

[On the night in question Gatzke and a district manager went to a bar for drinks.]

Between 1:15 and 1:30 A.M. Gatzke and Hubbard left the Bellows and walked back to the Edgewater. [Gatzke] . . . then "probably" sat down at a desk to fill out his expense account because "that was [his] habit from travelling so much.". . . It took Gatzke no more than five minutes to fill out the expense form.

While Gatzke completed the expense account he "probably" smoked a cigarette. The record indicates that Gatzke smoked about two packages of cigarettes per day. A maid testified that the ash trays in Gatzke's room would generally be full of cigarette butts and ashes when she cleaned the room. She noticed at times that the plastic wastebasket next to the desk contained cigarette butts.

After filling out the expense account Gatzke went to bed, and soon thereafter a fire broke out. Gatzke escaped from the burning room, but the fire spread rapidly and caused extensive damage to the motel. The amount of damages was stipulated by the parties at $330,360.

One of the plaintiff's expert witnesses, Dr. Ordean Anderson, a fire reconstruction specialist, testified that the fire started in, or next to, the plastic wastebasket located to the side of the desk in Gatzke's room. He also stated that the fire was caused by a burning cigarette or match. After the fire, the plastic wastebasket was a melted "blob." . . .

The jury found that Gatzke's negligence was a direct cause of 60 percent of the damages sustained by Edgewater. The jury also determined that Gatzke's negligent act occurred within the scope of his employment with Walgreen's. Plaintiff was found to be negligent [apparently for providing a plastic wastebasket] and such negligence was determined to be responsible for 40 percent of the fire damage sustained by Edgewater. . . .

The question raised here is whether the facts of this case reasonably support the imposition of vicarious liability on Walgreen's for the conceded negligent act of its employee.

It is well settled that for an employer to be held vicariously liable for an employee's negligent conduct the employee's wrongful act must be committed within the scope of his employment. . . .

To support a finding that an employee's negligent act occurred within his scope of employment, it must be shown that his conduct was, to some degree, in furtherance of the interests of his employer. . . . Other factors to be considered in the scope of employment determination are whether the conduct is of the kind that the employee is authorized to perform. . . . [E]ach case must be decided on its own individual facts. . . .

A number of courts which have dealt with the instant issue have ruled that the act of smoking, even when done simultaneously with work-related activity, is not within the employee's scope of employment because it is a matter personal to the employee which is not done in furtherance of the employer's interests. . . .

Other courts which have considered the question have reasoned that the smoking of a cigarette, if done while engaged in the business of the employer, is within an employee's scope of employment because it is a minor deviation from the employee's work-related activities, and thus merely an act done incidental to general employment. . . .

The question of whether smoking can be within an employee's scope of employment is a close one, but after careful consideration of the issue we are persuaded by the reasoning of the courts which hold that smoking can be an act within an employee's scope of employment. . . .

Thus, we must next determine whether Gatzke was otherwise in the scope of his employment at the time of his negligent act. . . .

The record, however, contains a reasonable basis from which a jury could find that Gatzke was involved in serving his employer's interests at the time he was at the bar. Gatzke testified that, while at the Bellows, he discussed the operation of the newly-opened Walgreen's restaurant with Hubbard. . . .

But more importantly, there is evidence from which a jury could reasonably find that Gatzke resumed his employment activities after he returned to his motel room and filled out his expense account. . . .

In light of the above, we hold that it was reasonable for the jury to find that Gatzke was acting within the scope of his employment when he completed his expense account. Accordingly, we set aside the trial court's grant of judgment for Walgreen's and reinstate the jury's determination that Gatzke was working within the scope of his employment at the time of his negligent act.

While an employer is liable for the acts of its employees committed in the scope of employment, a company may not be liable for the acts of independent contractors it hires to do various jobs. An **independent contractor** is someone who contracts to do one or more specific projects for someone else and maintains control of the method for doing the work. In *Robinson v. Jiffy Executive Limousine Co.*, 4 F.3d 237 (3rd Cir., 1993), a casino called a limousine service to transport a patron. While en route to the patron's destination, the limousine driver caused a car accident which resulted in serious injuries to the patron. The patron sued the casino for his damages. The court determined that the limousine service was an independent contractor and therefore the casino was not liable.

Determining whether a worker is an employee or independent contractor is often not easy. While there exists no definitive rule for determining the status of a worker, additional factors to consider are provided by the Restatement Second of Agency, a compilation of recommended rules of agency law. Those additional factors include: who as between the employer and worker supplies the tools and the place of work (if by the employer, the worker is more likely to be considered an employee); the length of time for which a person is hired (the longer the engagement, the more likely the worker will be considered an employee); the method of payment—whether by time or by the job (if by time, the more likely the worker will be considered an employee); whether or not the work being performed is part of the regular business of the employer (if so, the more likely the worker will be considered an employee); and the intentions and beliefs of the parties concerning their relationship.

A nightclub was sued by a patron who was injured when a member of the band playing that night broke a beer bottle in the customer's face. The case was dismissed because the band member was an independent contractor and therefore the bar was not liable for his actions. *Stevens v. Spec, Inc.*, 224 A.D.2d 811, 637 N.Y.S.2d 979 (3rd Dep't., 1996).

In another case the issue arose whether a driver for a service that delivered food from participating restaurants to customers' homes was an employee or independent contractor. A woman was injured when the driver struck her as she was crossing a street. She argued that the driver was an employee, seeking to hold the delivery service liable for her injuries based on respondeat superior. The delivery service argued that the driver was an independent contractor. The court determined the driver to be an independent contractor for the following reasons: his contract stated he was in independent contractor; he paid all his own income taxes; he determined his own work schedule and could work as many or as few hours as he wanted; and if he did not show up for work he was not reprimanded or terminated. *McKelvey v. Manley*, 1997 WL 528001 (Del., 1997).

Nondelegable Duties

An exception exists to the general rule that an employer is not liable for the acts of an independent contractor. Normally, the duty imposed on a hospitality facility to keep the premises reasonably safe for guests is **nondelegable**, meaning it cannot be transferred (or delegated) to another. For policy reasons, the employer is not permitted to avoid liability on the ground that the independent contractor failed to properly perform the work. The rule is intended to motivate the hotel or restaurant to monitor carefully the work of the independent contractors it hires. Thus, a hotel may be liable to a guest who slips and falls on the sidewalk due to failure of a snow removal service, which had been hired by the hotel, to sufficiently clear the snow. *Wood v. Chalet Susse International*, 1995 WL 317058 (Conn., 1995). Similarly, a hotel that hires an independent contracting service to provide security for its premises remains liable to a guest who was criminally attacked where the security service was negligent in the performance of its duties. *Security Services Corp. v. Ramada Inn., Inc.*, 665 So.2d 268 (Fl., 1996).

Where liability is imposed due to a nondelegable duty, the responsible hotel or restaurant may be able to seek compensation from the negligent independent contractor.

If a plaintiff, although injured on work performed by an independent contractor at a hospitality facility, is unable to establish that the contractor performed the work negligently, the hotel or restaurant will not be liable. For example, when a plaintiff at Bally's Grand Hotel was injured on an escalator repaired by an independent contractor but was unable to establish the cause of her injury or that the repair work was done negligently, the hotel was not liable to the guest. *Jimenez v. Bally's Grand Hotel and Casino*, 670 A.2d 24 (N.J., 1996).

Duty to Aid a Person in Distress

If someone in need calls out to you for help, are you legally obligated to offer assistance? If you fail to respond, will you be liable for resulting injuries to the person in trouble? The answer to both questions is generally no. The law does not impose a legal penalty on individuals for refusing to rescue someone in trouble. Indeed, courts have denied damage claims in the following situations:

- A man who watched while a young woman drowned, even though he could easily have gone to her aid; and

- A man who failed to warn a neighbor's child he saw hammering on a tube of gunpowder.

In each case, the moral duty was plain enough, but the courts agreed that moral duties are a matter of conscience and not of law.

If a person does come to the aid of another the law imposes a duty on the rescuer to exercise reasonable care. While no liability would have resulted had the rescuer chosen to do nothing, liability will result if a rescue attempt is done improperly.

Assume you are at a resort hotel with an ice skating rink. While you are skating a man has a heart attack. You are distressed by the incident and attempt to help him. You do not know CPR (a medically-recognized method of stimulating the heart in an emergency) and you are unsure what to do. You do something that makes his situation worse. Had you continued to skate and not assisted him, you would not be liable for your inaction because you had no legal duty to lend aid. However, since you attempted to help but lacked the necessary knowledge and skills, you may be liable for the man's resulting injuries.

An application of these principles is found in a case involving Gimbels Department Store. A shopper fainted on the floor of the store. Store personnel moved her to the ladies room and there mishandled her injuries. She sued the store for negligence. The court stated that the store management owed no duty to come to her rescue "even if death resulted." However, by removing her to the ladies room the store precluded other potential rescuers from coming to her aid and so owed her a duty to act reasonably in caring for her. *Zelenko v. Gimbel Bros.*, 287 N.Y.Supp. 134 (1935).

Duty to Invitees in Danger

The law in some states requires hotels and restaurants to lend a hand under certain circumstances. These include situations where the injury was caused by something under the defendant's control, and lack of care would aggravate the injury. For example, in one case a bar customer fell down an open stairway and died. His wife alleged that the bar operator and employees failed to obtain medical assistance for the deceased for over an hour after they became aware of his fall. The bar denied that it owed any duty to help the customer and asked the court to dismiss the case. Refusing to do so, the court agreed that, while at common law there is no general duty to aid a person who is in peril,

> under some circumstances, moral and humanitarian considerations may require one to render assistance to another who has been injured, even though the injury was not due to negligence on his part and may have been caused by the negligence of the injured person. Failure to render assistance in such a situation may constitute actionable negligence if the injury is aggravated through lack of due care . . . There may be a legal obligation [on one who invites others to his premises] to take positive or affirmative steps to effect the rescue of a person who is helpless and in a situation of peril . . . or when the injury resulted from use of an instrumentality under the control of the defendant. Palace Bar, Inc. v. Fearnot, 376 N.E.2d 1159 (Ind., 1978).

Thus, a business open to the public owes a duty to its patrons to aid them if in danger while on the premises. In the following case, this duty was breached.

CASE EXAMPLE 5–16

Starling v. Fisherman's Pier, Inc., 401 So.2d 1136 (Fl., 1981)

. . . The complaint charged a corporation, which operated a commercial fishing pier, with negligence for failure to safeguard a passed-out drunk customer who was left lying near the ocean on the pier, by himself, in the early hours of the morning, and who rolled over into the water and drowned.

The above facts involve gross conduct on the part of the man who drowned, perhaps exacerbated by the fact that his consumption of the alcoholic beverage, which he brought with him to the

pier, was in violation of a municipal ordinance. . . . The question here presented is: when an invitee comes upon the commercial premises of another and passes out cold on the floor, whether through illness, injury, or drunkenness, can the owner or operator of the premises ignore the inert figure lying in a dangerous place or does that owner or operator have an affirmative duty to make at least some minimal steps to safeguard the inert figure? We believe the owner or operator does have such a duty. . . .

The pier operator cites us to [a legal encyclopedia] for the proposition that there is "no general duty to come to the assistance of a person who is so ill or intoxicated as to be unable to look out for himself." However, that section appears to be concerning itself with the level of duty owed by a chance bystander or neighbor, and there is no discussion on whether the quoted statement would apply to a customer found on commercial premises. . . .

A proprietor simply cannot ignore and step over an unconscious customer lying in a dangerous place upon his premises, and he must take some minimal steps to safeguard any customer upon his premises from extreme danger, even though the customer has allowed himself to be exposed to that danger in the first place. . . .

The complaint thus stated a cause of action and should not have been dismissed.

In the following case a hotel became aware of a guest in danger. The hotel thus had a duty to aid the guest to remove the hazard. Like the pier in the previous case, the hotel's reaction was insufficient to satisfy its duty and liability resulted.

CASE EXAMPLE 5–17

Boles v. La Quinta Motor Inns
680 F.2d 1077 (Tex., 1982)

This suit was brought by Jackie Bernice Boles against La Quinta Motor Inns for personal injuries sustained while she was a guest at La Quinta Motor Hotel in Laredo, Texas. On October 14, 1977, Mrs. Boles was raped while she was a guest at the motel. As she opened the door to her motel room one evening, an attacker pushed her inside and raped her. The rapist bound and gagged her and left, threatening to return and kill her. Alone in the pitch-dark room, Mrs. Boles managed to kick the telephone receiver off the hook, and, while still bound, she managed to contact the motel front desk. Mrs. Boles identified herself to the desk clerk and told her that she had been raped and robbed and that she thought the rapist would come back and kill her. There was a long period of silence. After a while someone came to the telephone and asked her who she was. She identified herself once again and asked for help. She further testified that she talked to a woman on two separate occasions and a man on one occasion before anyone made an attempt to call the police. After a lengthy pause a woman came on the line and stated that she had called the police. Mrs. Bole then asked if someone was going to help her and was told by the desk clerk, "No, we won't be coming down." The clerk then said, "Mrs. Boles, we have called the police.

Would you hang up the telephone?" Mrs. Boles replied, screaming, "I don't even know where the phone is. How can I hang it up?" The desk clerk replied sarcastically, "Well, Mrs. Boles, if you don't know where the telephone is, how did you call us?"

The clerk then called the relief managers, Mr. and Mrs. Hill, both of whom proceeded to Mrs. Boles' room and waited outside. They and the manager, Mrs. Walding, were waiting outside Mrs. Boles' room when the police arrived. Mrs. Boles was therefore left in her dark room for about 20 to 25 minutes. She testified that she was terrified the entire time, thinking that her attacker would return. She was unaware that several people were listening to her screams just outside her room, as none of these persons tried to soothe her fears.

Mrs. Boles brought this diversity suit against La Quinta, alleging: (1) that the motel was negligent in failing to maintain a safe, well-lit corridor and (2) that the motel employees were negligent in the manner in which they responded to her call for help. In answer to special interrogatories, the jury found that although La Quinta was negligent in not maintaining a safe corridor, this negligence was not the legal cause of the rape. However, the jury found in plaintiff's favor on her second claim—that the hotel employees were unreasonably dilatory in coming to her aid and that this delay contributed to her physical and psychic injuries. The jury found that the negligence of the employees was the legal cause of the damages and awarded $35,000 from the date of the attack to the date of trial and $43,000 for future damages. The district court rendered judgment and denied defendant's motion for judgment notwithstanding the verdict. . . .

Under Texas law, a duty of ordinary care is owed by a hotel to its guests. . . . [A]n innkeeper can be held liable for the manner in which he responds to a guest's peril. . . . It is also clear that under Texas law a restaurant or motel owner owes his invitees the duty of reasonable care to protect them from assaults by third persons while on the premises.

La Quinta argues, however, that the duty of ordinary care is discharged by promptly notifying the police. . . . La Quinta argues that a reasonably prudent person would not have gone to Mrs. Boles' room and that La Quinta employees were motivated by reasonable fears for their own personal safety in refusing to do so. The problem is that there is no evidence that the hotel employees ever feared that the rapist was still in Mrs. Boles' room. In fact, the desk clerk testified that she told Mrs. Boles that she would not go to her room because she had to attend to her front desk duties, and Mrs. Boles testified that she informed the desk clerk that the rapist had left and that she was afraid that he would return. . . . The fact that three hotel employees stood outside of Mrs. Boles' room listening to her screams and moans without even calling to reassure her, combined with the callous manner in which she was treated by the desk clerk, is adequate evidence to support a finding that the motel did not use ordinary care in protecting Mrs. Boles.

La Quinta further urges that it should not be held liable because Mrs. Boles' injuries were not foreseeable to the employees. Mrs. Boles testified that the delay in getting anyone to come to her room aggravated both her physical injuries (the chafing caused by the bindings) as well as her mental anguish. La Quinta argues that its employees were not required to anticipate these "improbable" consequences. This argument is not convincing. The motel employees knew that Mrs. Boles was alone, bound in her room, fearing for her life. A reasonably prudent person would have anticipated mental anxiety and possible bodily injury resulting from the delay. . . .

A reading of the testimony of Dr. Freedman, the psychiatrist who treated Mrs. Boles, establishes that she suffered two traumatic events—one occurring during the time of the rape and the second occurring after the rape and during the time she was waiting to be rescued. Dr. Freedman was also asked to make a distinction between a case where a woman was raped and promptly rescued and a case such as the instant one where there was a 20-minute delay in the rescue of the victim. Dr. Freedman expressed the opinion that the person suffering the time delay in being rescued would sustain a greater impact and more injury and symptoms. He also was of the opinion that her problems would be more significant and more intense. He further stated that the longer a person is in a situation of stress, the more problems she would have later. . . .

Since there was sufficient evidence for the jury to find that the employees of La Quinta were negligent in responding to Mrs. Boles, and because the psychiatrist testified that she sustained injuries from this tortious conduct, future damages are rightly recoverable.

CASE QUESTION

1. What should the hotel have done in this case to avoid liability?

Limitation on Duty to Invitees.   If the guest who is in danger is being cared for by others who appear competent to render the necessary assistance, the hotel does not have a duty to offer aid. The following case illustrates this point.

CASE EXAMPLE 5–18

**Fish v. Paul, d/b/a Horseshoe Motel
574 A.2d 1365 (Me., 1990)**

Gretchen Fish, individually and as personal representative of the estate of her son, Mark Colvin . . . argues that [defendant motel owners] are liable for their failure to help Colvin, a guest who became ill at their motel. . . .

The plaintiff alleges the following: On August 13, 1987, Colvin, who was 18 at the time, travelled with two companions, Steven Fahsel and Frederick Wood, from Bangor to Old Orchard Beach to attend a concert. After the concert, the three rented a room in Saco at the Horseshoe Motel, owned by the Pauls. During the night the three drank a substantial quantity of alcohol. The next morning an employee of the motel saw Fahsel and Wood carrying Colvin, who was semiconscious, to a waiting car. After placing Colvin in the rear seat, Fahsel and Wood started back toward Bangor. On I-95 near Etna, the car overheated and stopped. A police offi-

cer stopped and called an ambulance for Colvin, but he was pronounced dead on arrival at St. Joseph's Hospital in Bangor. The complaint sought compensatory damages. . . .

We have recognized the general duty of a business proprietor to exercise reasonable care to prevent injury to business invitees. . . . We also recognize that in certain circumstances the relationship between a guest and an innkeeper may give rise to a duty to render aid in case of illness or injury. . . . [H]owever, . . . the innkeeper "is not required to give any aid to one who is in the hands of apparently competent persons who have taken charge of him, or whose friends are present and apparently in a position to give him all necessary assistance." The defendants contend that . . . the presence of Colvin's friends already rendering aid relives the motel of any obligation to do so. . . . We find the defendants' argument persuasive. . . . We conclude that the facts alleged are not sufficient to state a claim against the [motel owners].

Statutory Protection for Good Samaritans.   While requiring rescuers to act reasonably, the law also recognizes that the conditions available to the rescuer in an emergency may be far from ideal and often even crude. For example, roadside treatment immediately following a car accident involves conditions drastically different from the sterile environment of an operating room. The law affords the rescuer protection from liability resulting from these less-than-ideal conditions. This is accomplished through Good Samaritan Statutes, which are laws that protect a person who reacts in an emergency situation by trying to help a sick or injured person or someone in peril. According to these statutes, the rescuer will not be liable for any injuries caused in the attempt to render assistance if the means used were reasonable in relation to the emergency conditions at the time. Many such statutes further provide that the rescuer is not liable for ordinary negligence but only for gross negligence (excessive negligence). The purpose of these statutes is to induce voluntary aid to persons in danger by removing the rescuer's fear of potential liability.

A related principle called the **rescue doctrine** benefits a rescuer who is injured while administering aid. It provides that a person who negligently creates a peril and thereby endangers another person is liable for injuries to a rescuer who comes forward to offer assistance. The leeway given to a rescuer to take risky lifesaving measures in an emergency situation is illustrated in the following case.

CASE EXAMPLE 5–19

Altamuro v. Milner Hotel, Inc.
540 F.Supp. 870 (Pa., 1982)

Plaintiff's case against the defendant, Milner Hotel, is based principally on the "rescue doctrine", which provides that when [a] person is exposed to peril of life or limb by the negligence of another, the latter [the negligent person] will be liable in damages for injuries received by a third person in a reasonable effort to rescue the one so imperiled.

Perhaps the most quoted articulation of this doctrine was that by then New York Court of Appeals Justice Cardozo:

Danger invites rescue. The cry of distress is the summons to relief. The law does not ignore these reactions of the mind in tracing conduct to its consequences. It recognizes them as normal. It places their effects within the range of the natural and probable. The wrong that imperils life is a wrong to the imperiled victim; it is a wrong also to his rescuer. The state that leaves an opening in a bridge is liable to the child that falls into the stream, but liable also to the parent who plunges to its aid. . . . The risk of rescue, if only it be not wanton, is born of the occasion. . . . The wrongdoer may not have foreseen the coming of the deliverer. He is accountable as if he had. . . .

Twenty-one years earlier, the Pennsylvania Supreme Court stated: . . .

One who imperils his own life for the sake of rescuing another from imminent danger is not chargeable, as a matter of law, with contributory negligence; and, if the life of the rescued person was endangered by the defendant's negligence, the rescuer may recover from the defendant for the injuries which he suffered in consequence of his intervention.

In applying the rescue doctrine, I must first determine the negligence . . . of the Milner Hotel.

Under Pennsylvania law, a hotel keeper, while not an insurer or guarantor of the safety of his guests, must nonetheless exercise ordinary or reasonable care to keep them from injury. The plaintiff's decedent died in a fire at defendant's hotel while he was a guest there. . . .

Here, the fire at The Milner Hotel on October 11, 1978 originated in the defective television set in Room 706. The defective condition of the television was known to the Hotel through its employee, Jennings, who nevertheless left the set plugged in, unattended and with the power switch in the "on" position. I have no difficulty in concluding that, under these circumstances and given the substantial risk of fire resulting from a short-circuited or otherwise faulty television set, Jennings' conduct clearly amounted to negligence and that his negligence was a substantial factor in placing the lives of the Hotel guests in peril. The very least a reasonably prudent person would have done would have been to disconnect the power source by turning the set off or removing the plug. Of course, Jennings' negligence is imputed to his employer under the doctrine of respondeat superior.

That a fire in a ten-story hotel presents an imminent danger to the residents cannot be gainsaid. The Hotel employees, the police and firemen as well as Altamuro recognized the need for immediate action. The prompt action taken by them at considerable risk to themselves was undoubtedly responsible for preventing a catastrophic loss of life. . . .

Defendant Hotel argues that since Altamuro's death occurred after the firemen ordered all civilians out of the Hotel and because it can be inferred from the evidence that the deceased heard the command by his conduct in immediately leaving the Hotel, then his final rescue effort was so unreasonable as to preclude recovery by [his estate]. The test, . . . is whether the rescuer "acted with due regard for his own safety, or so rashly and imprudently" as to bar recovery. [In another case] the court stated that "where another is in great and imminent danger, he who attempts a rescue may be warranted, by surrounding circumstances, in exposing his limbs or life to a very high degree of danger. In such a case, he should not be charged with the consequences of errors of judgments resulting from the excitement and confusion of the moment. . . . [E]rrors of judgment are to be weighed in view of the excitement and confusion of the moment in determining whether the rescuer acted without rashness or imprudence." Thus the standard of care for a rescuer is not to act rashly or imprudently. . . .

Altamuro did not act rashly, imprudently or so unreasonably as to constitute negligence on his part under the rescue doctrine.

There is no dispute that during the initial phase of the fire, Altamuro busied himself warning guests at the Hotel of the fire, and later he assisted Officer Markowski in helping people out of the building. The last time Altamuro was seen alive was when he left the Hotel after the firemen ordered all civilians out of the building. There was no evidence as to how Altamuro got back into the building. What prompted his return can only be surmised but, having been successful in two prior missions to the upper floors of the Hotel, I am not convinced that it was unreasonable for him to conclude that he could successfully complete another mission without unduly imperiling his own safety even though he disobeyed the order of the firemen by returning to the building. . . .

I therefore conclude that the plaintiff sustained the following damages . . . (1) Funeral expenses: $2,001; (2) Loss of deceased's earnings which would have gone to the benefit of his wife and children: $334,372; and (3) Value of non-monetary or intangible services which the deceased would have provided to his wife and children: $50,000.

Plaintiff is entitled to judgment in her favor and against defendant, The Milner Hotel, Inc., in the amount of $396,373.

Rule in Choking Situations.   A classic emergency at a restaurant occurs when a piece of food becomes lodged in a person's airway, blocking off all air to the lungs. Such a situation presents a grave condition because there is very little time to act. A person with a blocked airway will be unconscious in about a minute, will suffer irreversible brain damage in about four to five minutes, and will die usually within the next couple of minutes. These situations occur with significant frequency so as to be recognized as a real problem in the restaurant industry.

At least for the present, it appears that the law throughout the country does not *require* a restaurant to aid a choking patron. Instead, a restaurant whose employees do not come to the patron's aid will be free from liability for its apparent indifference to suffering and death. If a restaurant comes to the aid of a choking patron but does so negligently, the restaurant will be liable in many states.

To encourage restaurants to attempt to save the afflicted person's life, some states have enacted statutes to protect actors in such situations. A typical law requires that every restaurant and cafeteria in the state display prominently a poster showing the proper first aid procedures to use in assisting a person who has a blocked airway and is choking. This procedure is termed the Heimlich Maneuver and is a relatively simple method of first aid which requires no instruments or medical knowledge. The legislation does not require anyone to act; no duty exists upon restaurateurs or their employees to render any assistance to the choking victim. If restaurant owners, their employees, or patrons assist the choking person in accordance with the instructions on the poster, they will not be liable to the injured party except for gross negligence. If the rescuer deviates from the poster's directions, liability may result. The statutes also provide that the restaurant cannot be held liable for injuries or death of the choke victim if the poster is not displayed.

The following case illustrates an application of the relevant California law.

CASE EXAMPLE 5–20

Breaux v. Gino's Inc.
200 Cal. Rptr. 260 (Cal., 1984)

The undisputed facts are that the decedent choked while eating at a restaurant owned and operated by respondent. An assistant manager of the restaurant called for an ambulance as soon as he became aware that decedent was in distress. No one attempted to give first aid to decedent, who was alive when the ambulance arrived.

It is also undisputed that respondent complied with the provisions of [the applicable law] by posting in an appropriate place the state-approved first aid instructions for removal of food which may become stuck in a person's throat.

[The restaurant argues] that it met its duty, as a matter of law, when it promptly summoned an ambulance. We conclude that respondent's contention is correct. . . .

In [the applicable law], the Legislature has established standards for restaurants' actions with respect to patrons who have food stuck in their throats. That section provides: ". . . Nothing in this section shall impose any obligation on any person to remove, assist in removing, or attempt to remove food which has become stuck in another person's throat. . . ." We hold that this statute establishes as a matter of law that a restaurant meets its legal duty to a patron in distress when it summons medical assistance within a reasonable time. Accordingly, respondent met its duty to decedent by summoning an ambulance promptly. . . .

The facts in *Drew v. LeJay's Sportsmen's Cafe, Inc.*, 806 P.2d 301 (Wyoming, 1991) are similar to those in *Breaux v. Gino's, Inc.* except that restaurant personnel were slower to summon an ambulance. Citing *Breaux*, the court held that the restaurant owed its choking customer a duty to summon medical assistance within a reasonable time, but that it did not owe a duty to provide medical training to its food service personnel or medical rescue services to its customers. The court in *Drew* explained its decision as follows:

"We are concerned that a specific requirement of first aid, rather than aid in the form of a timely call for professional medical assistance, would place undue burdens on food servers and other business-invitors. . . . Courses in first aid techniques require both time and money. Annual recertification classes are required in CPR and the Heimlich maneuver. Because employee turnover in the food service industry is high, continual training efforts might be required to provide a staff capable of providing first aid. This duty would apply to every food server, regardless of size. . . . Ms. Zuber of the Wyoming Heart Association, testified that lay persons receiving CPR training are advised that they may exercise their own discretion in choosing to administer CPR in any given situation. Clearly a business-invitor's employees remain lay persons and cannot be compelled to perform first aid against their better judgment. It would not be appropriate to either remove the employee's discretion or hold the employer liable if it is exercised. The only per-

*sons expected to perform rescue techniques regardless of circumstances are the profes-
sional medical responders called for just that purpose. Whether that call is made within
a reasonable time is the appropriate factual issue for jury consideration.*

If a diner is choking due to fault of the restaurant, the duty to render aid is
greater and requires the establishment to exercise reasonable care to rescue the
person in distress. Said the court in *Parra v. Tarasco, Inc.*, 595 N.E.2d 1186 (Ill.,
1992), involving a diner who choked and died on a piece of food that became
lodged in his throat and prevented him from breathing, "The [cause of the choking in this case] differs substantially from . . . tort cases where a restaurant patron
suffers injuries due to foreign substances in the food, or food poisoning. [In
those cases the restaurateur owes a duty to use reasonable care to rescue the customer from danger.] Instead, in a case such as the present one, where a restaurant patron chokes on food, the cause of the injury is wholly idiopathic, i.e., it is
of an internal, personal origin [and the only duty owed is to take steps to obtain
medical care, such as calling an ambulance]."

Negligence Doctrines Generally Favoring Defendants

The following doctrines benefit the defendant by shifting some or all of the
responsibility for an injury to the plaintiff.

Contributory Negligence and Comparative Negligence

In some situations where a plaintiff is injured, not only is the defendant negligent but the plaintiff is as well. For example, assume that a plaintiff who trips
on a hole in a restaurant's rug was wearing a high-heeled shoe she knew had a
loose heel. The plaintiff fell due to both the loose heel and the hole. What effect
does the plaintiff's negligence in wearing the shoe have on the lawsuit against
the restaurant? Does the restaurant's duty to keep the premises reasonably safe
give plaintiff immunity from the consequences of her own inattention?

The impact on the lawsuit of plaintiff's negligence depends on the applicable
state's law. Each state follows either the rule of contributory negligence or the
rule of comparative negligence.

Contributory Negligence.   According to the rule of contributory negligence,
if plaintiff's negligence contributed to the injury, plaintiff cannot successfully
sue a negligent defendant. Instead, the case will be dismissed. Defendant will not
be liable for plaintiff's loss and plaintiff must absorb the full extent of the injuries. This is true regardless of how slight or insignificant plaintiff's negligence
may have been. While contributory negligence used to be the rule in most states,
today only four states follow it—Alabama, Maryland, North Carolina, and
Virginia, and the District of Columbia. The reason for the change is that the "all
or nothing" effect of contributory negligence is considered unduly harsh on the
plaintiff.

Comparative Negligence.   According to the rule of **comparative negligence**, plaintiff's negligence will not defeat the lawsuit. Instead, the jury will allocate the liability between the plaintiff and the defendant depending on their relative degree of culpability based on a total of 100 percent. For example, the jury might find that the restaurant patron who knew her heel was broken was 30 percent responsible and the restaurant that failed to repair the hole in the rug was 70 percent responsible. The plaintiff collects from the defendant a percentage of the damages equal to the percentage of liability attributed to defendant. In the example, plaintiff must absorb 30 percent of the loss but can collect 70 percent from the defendant.

In another example, a hotel guest was raped by an intruder to her room. She had fastened the chain lock on the door, but failed to activate the doorknob lock. The hotel had improperly installed the chain lock so that, once the door was unlocked and cracked open slightly, the chain lock could be easily lifted out of its slot and the door opened. The guest sued the hotel for her damages. The court concluded that each was partially responsible for the incident and allocated damages accordingly. *Ledbetter v. Concord General Corp.*, 665 So.2d 1166 (La., 1996).

In a "pure system" of comparative negligence, the plaintiff will collect the appropriate share of his damages regardless of the percentage of fault attributed to him. Some states that follow the comparative negligence rule provide that, for plaintiff to recover, the percentage of liability allocated to him must be less than that assigned to defendant (maximum 49 percent assigned to plaintiff) (this is known as the "less-than" rule). Other states allow defendant to recover if his percentage of fault is equal to or less than the defendant's (maximum 50 percent assigned to plaintiff). A few states follow a "slight-gross" system in which plaintiff can recover only if his share of the fault is slight and defendant's share is gross.

The Doctrine of Last Clear Chance.   While the contributory negligence doctrine greatly benefits defendants by barring plaintiffs from suing, in certain circumstances, plaintiffs can use the doctrine of last clear chance to support their cases. Ordinarily, a plaintiff who is negligent in a state that follows the contributory negligence rule will be denied recovery against a negligent defendant. But if facts allow the last clear chance doctrine to be applied, it makes no difference if negligent acts of the plaintiff initially put him/herself into peril. The defendant will be liable for failing to prevent the injury.

The doctrine requires exactly what its name implies: that the defendant actually had a last clear chance to avoid the infliction of the injury on the plaintiff.

Four elements must be established before the doctrine will come into play:

1. The plaintiff has been negligent.
2. As the result of this negligence, plaintiff is in a position of peril that cannot be escaped by the exercise of ordinary care.
3. The defendant knew or should have known of the plaintiff's peril.
4. The defendant had a clear chance, by the exercise of ordinary care, to avoid the injury to the plaintiff, but failed to do so.

If any one of these four elements is absent, the doctrine of last clear chance will not apply. Most states that have adopted the comparative negligence rule have abolished the last clear chance doctrine. The reason is as follows: "To give continued life to [last clear chance] would defeat the very purpose of the comparative negligence rule—the apportionment of damages according to the degree of mutual fault." *Spahn v. Town of Port Royal*, 486 S.E.2d 507 (S.C., 1997).

Assumption of Risk

Another legal doctrine whose application has changed considerably in those states that follow the rule of comparative negligence is assumption of risk. Historically, and currently in states that follow the contributory negligence rule, the doctrine benefits the defendant and applies in cases where the plaintiff voluntarily engages in conduct known to present a risk of injury. If plaintiff is injured as a result of that risk, plaintiff, according to the doctrine, cannot successfully sue for the loss. Instead, the plaintiff is said to have assumed the risk, that is, accepted the chance that injury might occur and impliedly agreed not to sue if it does.

To establish assumption of risk, defendant must show that plaintiff had knowledge of the risk, understood the risk, had a choice of either avoiding the risk or engaging in conduct that confronted the risk, and voluntarily chose to take the risk.

Participants in sporting activities are considered to assume the obvious and inherent risks associated with the sport. In *Coleman v. Ramada Hotel Operating Co.*, 933 F.2d 470 (7th Cir., 1991), plaintiff was injured while participating in a timed obstacle course at a company picnic held at a resort owned by defendant Ramada. The first obstacle of the course was mounting a slide backwards. In the process plaintiff fell from the ladder portion of the slide. The court held for Ramada since the dangers associated with the activity were obvious and therefore plaintiff assumed the risk. If, however, the reason plaintiff fell was because a step on the ladder had rotted and weakened, and Ramada had not inspected the ladder for weeks, Ramada would be liable because this was not a normal risk of the activity and therefore, plaintiff did not assume it.

Virtually all states that have adopted the comparative negligence rule had abolished assumption of risk as a total bar to recovery in tort. Instead, assumption of risk is treated as another factor for the trier of fact (jury or judge) to consider when making a comparative negligence evaluation. Thus, in some cases where assumption of risk may apply, the defendant's negligence may be a partial cause of the injury. In such case, an allocation of fault between plaintiff and defendant will be made. "Thus, there is no arbitrary bar to recovery and no sweeping exemption from duty accorded a defendant." *Auckenthaler v. Grundmeyer*, 877 P.2d 1039 (Nev., 1994).

In the following two cases assumption of risk was applied when the doctrine was a total bar to plaintiff"s recovery. As you read the cases consider whether the outcome of the case would be different under the newer rule.

CASE EXAMPLE 5–21

Ball v. Hilton Hotels, Inc.
290 N.E.2d 859 (Ohio, 1972)

It appears from the record that the plaintiff, a resident of Michigan, went to Cincinnati, Ohio, on May 27, 1967, with a reservation to stay at the defendant's hostelry, known as the Terrace Hilton Hotel.

Upon arrival at the hotel, she was informed by the defendant's doorman that there was a downtown area electric power failure and there was no lighting or elevator service in the hotel. The hotel lobby and registration desk were on the eighth floor of the hotel building. The plaintiff checked her baggage with the doorman and then inquired about the use of restroom facilities.

In response to her request, the doorman advised plaintiff the restroom was downstairs; that it would be quite dark on the staircase due to the electric power failure; that plaintiff would not be able to see the doors to the restrooms; and that the doors to the restrooms were located to the right of the bottom of the stairway. The doorman gave the plaintiff a small lighted candle, and she proceeded down the darkened stairway, moving slowly and carefully groping along the handrail.

After arriving at the platform portion of the stairway [apparently the half-way point of the flight of stairs], plaintiff began to grope about for the restroom door and, while so doing, she fell to the bottom of the stair steps and received personal injuries.

In her complaint against the hotel, plaintiff alleges that her personal injuries and resulting damage were directly and proximately caused by the negligence of the defendant in inducing her to enter a hazardous, darkened area of the hotel facility. . . .

Before the defendant would be entitled to a judgment on the theory of assumption of the risk, it must be proven that plaintiff had full knowledge of a condition; that the condition was patently dangerous; and that she voluntarily exposed herself to the hazard created. . . .

[P]laintiff was told that the electric power in the downtown area had failed and there was no light or electric power in the defendant's hotel; that it was dark in the stairway leading to the hotel restrooms; that plaintiff had full knowledge of the darkness when she walked down the stairway with a small lighted candle; and that she moved slowly and carefully as she descended the stairway.

Since it appears there is no genuine issue of any material fact, the trial court correctly determined the plaintiff assumed the risk of her injury and damage when she proceeded into the darkened area of the premises in question. . . .

Ruling of the Court: Judgment affirmed for defendant.

CASE QUESTIONS

1. Identify the elements of assumption of risk and state the particular fact(s) in Ball that satisfy each element.
2. Did the hotel act negligently in directing the plaintiff to the downstairs bathroom? What effect does your answer have on the outcome of the case?

Another example of assumption of risk is provided by the following case in which rowdy crowds spurred the plaintiff to expose himself voluntarily to significant risks.

CASE EXAMPLE 5–22

Eldridge v. Downtowner Hotel
492 So.2d 64 (La., 1986)

[O]n February 7, 1978, Mardi Gras day, plaintiff was the guest of a patron of the Downtowner in the French Quarter. While on the second floor balcony of the hotel, he observed various individuals on other balconies toying with the crowds below by exposing their breasts or "mooning" the crowds by exposing their bare buttocks. Spurred on by the wild atmosphere in the Quarter, plaintiff climbed on the balcony railing and mooned the crowd. While on the railing plaintiff fell to the street below and was seriously injured.

Plaintiff filed suit for 1.75 million dollars arguing that Downtowner was negligent in failing to have a protective screen or a uniformed guard on the balcony to prevent just such accidents as occurred herein. . . .

The record reflects that plaintiff's fall resulted solely from his own conduct. Plaintiff was not pushed off the railing, and he was neither enticed nor encouraged by defendant to sit on the railing. Moreover, the railing was not defective. It is clear, therefore, that plaintiff's fall was in fact caused by his own want of skill, that is, exercising bad judgment by sitting on the railing and in losing his balance. Thus, the question becomes whether Downtowner had a duty to protect plaintiff from his own conduct.

[A] "visitor assumes the obvious, normal or ordinary risks attendant on the use of the premises and owners are not liable for injuries to a visitor when those injuries result form a danger which he should have observed in the exercise of reasonable care."

Here the risk of harm was that of falling while sitting on a railing on a second floor balcony. Such a risk is an obvious and reasonable risk of harm which the defendant had no duty to protect against.

But plaintiff argues that because of the wild atmosphere of Mardi Gras and the fact that traditionally women would expose themselves from the balconies, defendant should have foreseen that an accident was likely and was under an obligation to protect plaintiff from himself. We find no merit in this argument. . . .[A]bsolutely no evidence was offered at trial demonstrating that anyone had ever fallen from the balcony during Mardi Gras or even that people sat on the balcony railings. . . .

For these reasons we hold that the trial court was not required to charge the jury that the defendant had a duty to protect patrons from the type of conduct engaged in by the plaintiff herein. . . .

CASE QUESTION

1. What was the particular risk of injury that plaintiff assumed in this case?

Comparative Negligence and Assumption of Risk

Many states that adopted the comparative negligence rule have abolished the rule of assumption of risk as a total bar to recovery in tort. Instead, assumption of risk is treated as another factor for the trier of fact (judge or jury) to consider when making a comparative negligence evaluation. The following case identifies the inconsistencies between the rules of assumption of risk and comparative negligence.

CASE EXAMPLE 5–23

Auckenthaler v. Grundmeyer, 877 P.2d 1039 (Nev., 1994)

Appellant Lori S. Auckenthaler ("Auckenthaler") and several other individuals were riding horses in an area of Reno, known as Red Rock. . . . Co-respondent Jody White ("White") was a member of the group and was riding a horse owned by Steven Grundmeyer ("Grundmeyer") named Bum. The ride was purely recreational. . . .

During the ride, Bum was acting antsy and nervous and had been threatening to kick other horses that ventured into his proximity. Bum had been recently gelded. Auckenthaler was injured when the horse she was riding strayed too close to Bum. Bum turned and kicked at Auckenthaler's horse, striking Auckenthaler in the leg.

Auckenthaler filed a negligence suit against both White and Grundmeyer. She alleged that White was negligent in continuing to ride a horse that was temperamental and exhibiting dangerous behavior. Auckenthaler also alleged that Grundmeyer was negligent for supplying White with a horse Grundmeyer knew was aggressive and anxious.

White and Grundmeyer moved for summary judgment. They alleged that the appropriate legal standard of care governing participants in recreational activities was not simple negligence, but was instead reckless or intentional conduct [that is, assumption of risk]. . . .

[The district court] established the general proposition that in sporting activities, liability can only be imposed where the participant intentionally injures another player or engages in conduct that is so reckless as to be totally outside the range of the ordinary activity involved in the sport. . . . The purpose for this rule is as follows: by eliminating liability for unintended accidents, the doctrine ensures that the fervor of athletic competition will not be chilled by the constant threat of litigation from every misstep, sharp turn, and sudden stop. On a larger scale, participation in amateur athletics is a socially desirable activity that improves the mental and physical well-being of its participants.

The sole issue on this appeal is whether the district court erred by adopting this standard [and, by granting summary judgment to White and Grundmeyer. . . .

[The assumption of risk rule applied here] occurs where the plaintiff voluntarily accepts known risks involved in a particular situation, and the defendant has no duty of care with respect to the plaintiff. The classic example is the spectator at a baseball game who impliedly understands that the players have no duty to refrain from hitting a ball into the stands. . . .

Horseback riding is a recreational or sporting activity that has inherent dangers. [According to the rule applied by the district court], by choosing to participate, the plaintiff impliedly consents to the inherent risks of the activity and the defendant has no duty or a reduced duty to protect the plaintiff. . . .

The defense of assumption of risk is not favored. It continues to vex and confuse as a masquerade for contributory negligence. . . . In short, we are unable to ascertain any productive reason why assumption of risk should survive the beneficent purposes and effects of Nevada's comparative negligence statute. . . . Thus, there is no arbitrary bar to recovery and no sweeping exemption from duty accorded a defendant. The determination of duty is left to the jury as a factor in the comparative negligence analysis. . . . Within the factual climate of recreational activities or even sporting events, the question posed is whether the defendant participated in a reasonable manner and within the rules of the game. . . . When properly applied, the negligence standard strikes the proper balance between vigorous participation in sports and accommodating litigants injured by unreasonable behavior. The district court erred by adopting the reckless or intentional standard of care. We reverse. . . .

CASE QUESTION

1. What is the primary difference between assumption of risk and comparative negligence?

Summary

Hotels and restaurants face substantial liability for negligence. If a customer is injured by a restaurant or hotel's failure to act reasonably, the business will be obligated to compensate the customer.

For a successful negligence case a plaintiff must prove four elements: (1) the existence of a duty owed by the hotel or restaurant to the plaintiff to act reasonably; (2) a breach of that duty; (3) injury resulting to plaintiff; and (4) proximate cause.

Various legal doctrines are associated with negligence. Those that aid the plaintiff are:

- Res ipsa loquitur, which means "the thing speaks for itself" and relieves the plaintiff of the need to prove specific acts of negligence;

- Higher duty of care owed to children because of their relative lack of judgment and experience;

- The attractive nuisance doctrine, which obligates occupiers of land to exercise reasonable care to protect trespassing children;

- Negligence per se, which, in most states, eliminates the need for a plaintiff to prove negligence where the defendant violated a safety law;

- Strict liability, which renders a defendant liable without fault under limited circumstances;

- Respondeat superior, which obligates an employer to compensate persons injured by the negligent acts of its employees; and

- The doctrine of last clear chance, which applies in states that follow the contributory negligence rule and holds that, even if a plaintiff is negligent, a defendant may be liable if he knew of plaintiff's peril and had an opportunity to prevent the injury but failed to do so.

The legal doctrines related to negligence that aid the defendant include:

- Assumption of risk, which in contributing negligence states, relieves a defendant from liability for injuries incurred by a plaintiff who voluntarily engages in conduct known to present risks of injury;

- Contributory negligence, which relieves a defendant from liability if the plaintiff is at all negligent;

- Comparative negligence, which relieves a defendant from partial liability if the plaintiff is negligent;

- Good Samaritan laws, which restrict exposure to liability for rescuers; and

- Choking laws, which relieve a restaurant from liability for failing to aid a choking patron.

To avoid liability for negligence, hotels and restaurants must be constantly vigilant to ensure, in states that continue to recognize varying standards of duty depending on the status of the injured party, the following: for invitees, that the premises have been inspected, any risks of injury have been removed, and the premises are reasonably safe; for licensees, that known latent defects are disclosed and willful or wanton injury is not caused; and for trespassers, that willful or wanton injury is not caused. In states that no longer recognize the differences between an invitee, licensee, or trespasser, a varying duty of care is owed to all three.

Preventive Law Tips for Managers

- *Always anticipate dangers that may exist at a hotel or restaurant and take the necessary action to eliminate the risks.* Hotels and restaurants are obligated to use reasonable care to protect their patrons from injury. Failure to do so will result in liability. Managers and employees should always be alert to conditions that may present risks. Upon discovery of any such conditions, they should be eliminated. If removal of the condition is not immediately feasible, warning notices should be conspicuously posted.

- *Make frequent inspections of the premises so that dangerous conditions can be detected.* Undetected and uncorrected dangers increase the risk of injuries to patrons. The purpose of regular and thorough inspections is to discover problems before they lead to injury. Once uncovered, they can be corrected and injury avoided.

- *Promptly repair dangerous conditions.* Elimination of dangerous conditions decreases the chances that guests will be injured. Reasonable care should be taken during the repair process to ensure it does not generate injury. For example, while washing a floor, housekeeping should post a sign cautioning passersby that the floor may be slippery.

- *Train employees how to detect dangerous conditions, and include inspection and reporting in their job responsibilities.* The better trained employees are, the more likely they will uncover unsafe conditions. The more employees are responsible to identify unsafe conditions, the less likely accidents are to occur.

- *Carefully examine facilities used by children.* The duty of care owed to youngsters takes into consideration their lack of judgment and thus requires more on the part of the hotel or restaurant than the duty owed to adults. Since children cannot be expected to take precautions for their own safety, hotels and restaurants must be especially careful to ensure facilities likely to be used by them are suitable. Play areas, toys, pinball machines, high chairs, cribs, and similar items must be maintained in a safe condition.

- *Be alert to attractive nuisances, and take precautions to protect youngsters from related dangers.* An attractive nuisance is a condition on property that is appealing to children and likely to attract them even though the property owner or occupier does not invite them. While hotels and restaurants do not ordinarily owe a duty to trespassers, if businesses tolerate a condition that is likely to attract children they must maintain that condition in a way that neutralizes associated dangers. Failure to do so may result in liability.

- *Stay current on laws that relate to your business, and comply with them.* Failure to abide by applicable safety laws may result in liability based on negligence per se. In such cases proof of negligence is not required. Instead, the plaintiff need only prove the existing law and the defendant's failure to comply (plus proximate cause). To avoid overlooking statutes that apply to the hospitality industry, diligently read trade journals, consult regularly with a knowledgeable attorney, and become active in trade associations.

- *Do not rely on compliance with statutes alone to protect your business from lawsuits; in addition, exercise reasonable care to protect patrons from injury.* Compliance with statutes alone may not relieve the hotel from liability. Instead, compliance with laws may be only the beginning of what is required to avoid liability. Analyze risks associated with the establishment and determine what action, in addition to that required by statute, is necessary to eliminate those risks.

- *Choose carefully the suppliers of goods that your hotel or restaurant resells, such as food and gift shop inventory.* The rule of strict products liability enables a buyer of defective goods to sue the seller without regard to negligence. All the plaintiff must prove is that the product was defective when sold and the defect caused injury. To minimize the number of incidents of rancid food in restaurants and defective products in shops, be discriminating in the supplier's from whom inventory is purchased. Check references and reputation, inspect the merchandise when it is delivered, and verify the supplier's financial viability. If you are sued, you may be able to pursue the supplier in strict liability. A supplier who is no longer in business will be of little value in this regard.

- *Select employees carefully and train them well.* An employer may be liable for the acts of its employees. Much potential liability can be avoided by conducting thorough background checks on employees to ensure their suitability and verify their qualifications for the job, and by providing in-depth training to secure their compliance with company rules, policies, and expectations.

- *Aid patrons in need of assistance.* Many states now require a hotel or restaurant to come to the aid of a guest in need. If a hotel guest calls the front desk seeking help for an illness or assault, respond quickly. Lag in reaction time can result in liability. Train front desk personnel on how to handle emergency phone calls. Instruct restaurant and hotel employees on first aid and who to call in the event of emergency.

- *Display prominently the required poster showing first aid procedures including the Heimlich Maneuver.* The Heimlich Maneuver is a procedure that can dislodge food on which a diner is choking. Posters that illustrate the maneuver and contain directions on how to administer it are available, and in some states required. By prominently displaying the poster, necessary information to assist a patron in trouble is always readily available. However, in most states, statutes relieve a restaurant from a duty to apply the Heimlich Maneuver. Promptly summoning medical assistance may be sufficient legally as a response to a choking patron.

Review Questions

1. What does "negligence" mean?
2. Who or what is the "reasonable person"?
3. Identify the four elements of a negligence case.
4. Which two elements of a negligence case must have a cause and effect relationship?
5. What is "res ipsa loquitur"?
6. If the assumption of risk doctrine applies in a case, who wins—the plaintiff or the defendant?
7. What is the difference between comparative negligence and contributory negligence?
8. What duty of care is owed by innkeepers to guests who are children? Does the duty differ at all from the duty owed to adults? If so, how does it differ?
9. What is an attractive nuisance?
10. What differentiates negligence per se from ordinary negligence?
11. What is the difference between an invitee, a licensee, and a trespasser?
12. Identify three circumstances in which liability can result to a hotel for failing to provide adequate security. State how the liability can be avoided.

Discussion Questions

1. In which of the following cases would res ipsa loquitur apply? Why?
   a. Plaintiff was driving his car on hotel property and hit an obstacle in the road.
   b. Plaintiff was sitting at the desk in her hotel room writing postcards when the ceiling light fixture fell on her head and injured her.
   c. Plaintiff tripped in a restaurant.
2. a. Did the plaintiff assume the risk in the following circumstance? Why or why not? Plaintiff was a guest at a hotel with a baseball

field. While playing on the field he tripped on a large hole and was injured.

   b. What is the effect of the risk of loss doctrine in a state that adopted comparative negligence? Why?

3. You are a manager at a restaurant. Your restaurant is sued by a customer who fell on a step at your establishment. What does the element of proximate cause require the plaintiff to establish? How might you dispute proximate cause?

4. Under what circumstances does a hotel or restaurant have strict liability? What can the business do to protect itself against this type of liability?

5. What is the significance of the doctrine of respondeat superior to a hotel or restaurant?

6. How might the duty of care owed by a hotel or restaurant differ depending on whether the plaintiff is an invitee, a licensee, or a trespasser? How might the outcome of a case vary depending on the status of the plaintiff? What is the rationale for such different results?

Application Questions

1. Plaintiff, while about to descend a flight of stairs from a second story restaurant, was engaged in conversation with a companion and failed to survey the steps. An obstacle on the second step caused her to slip and fall, resulting in injuries. The state in which the restaurant was located adopted the rule of comparative negligence. What impact will her negligence have on the lawsuit? Explain fully.

2. Assume in Question 1 that the applicable rule was contributory negligence rather than comparative negligence. What impact would that have on the outcome of the case?

3. A customer at a pizza parlor ate a piece of pizza with a tack in it. Has the customer assumed the risk of the tack? Why or why not? What other negligence doctrine(s) might apply?

4. The Drumlin Hotel has a pond on its property. During the winter the pond freezes and neighborhood children come to play on it. One day in late March the ice was thin and a child fell through and suffered from exposure and frostbite. Will the hotel be liable for the child's injuries? Why or why not? Discuss the issues thoroughly.

5. At a bowling banquet one of the attendees starts to choke on a steak. He is assisted to the bathroom by several of his bowling friends and in the process passes by you as manager. You do not assist him personally, but you do call the police and ambulance. They respond in three minutes. The choking diner is taken to a hospital, where he dies. His wife is

now suing your restaurant for $1 million. What defenses are available to the restaurant?

6. Identify the legal status (invitee, licensee, or trespasser) of each of the following.

   a. A hotel guest.

   b. A person who comes to the hotel to meet a friend who is a guest of the hotel.

   c. A person who enters a restaurant only to use the bathroom.

   d. A person who enters the hotel to attend a meeting being held in a room rented for the day by her employer.

   e. A person who enters the hotel to buy a gift in the lobby gift shop.

   f. A person who enters the hotel to take a shortcut through the building.

   g. A person who enters to rob a guest.

   h. A patron of a restaurant who left his coat and returns the next day to retrieve it.

CHAPTER 6

Negligence and Hospitality Practices—Part 1

CHAPTER OUTLINE

Introduction

Duty Owed Guests in Rooms

Duty Owed Guests and Others in Public Areas

Duty Owed in Restaurants and Dining Rooms

INTRODUCTION

In Chapter 5 we learned what constitutes negligence. We will now examine specific cases dealing with negligence in hotels, restaurants, bars, and related places.

We know that a business owner owes invitees a duty of reasonable care, including the duty to inspect the premises, discover dangerous conditions, and correct them. This, however, does not make a hospitality business an **insurer**, one who is generally obligated to compensate another for all losses. Hotels and restaurants are only liable when they are negligent.

This chapter discusses the precautions the proprietor must take regarding the following areas in hotels and restaurants: guest rooms, furniture, windows, bathroom appliances, lobby, elevators, doors, hallways, stairways, and dining rooms.

Duty Owed Guests in Rooms

Numerous circumstances in guest rooms can lead to liability if a hotel fails to exercise reasonable care. These circumstances include the level of cleanliness; the condition of the furniture, windows, lighting, and heating; bathroom appliances; and the presence of insects or animals.

Cleanliness of Hotel Rooms

Guests expect a clean room when they register. If a guest room is not cleaned well, liability can result. In *Nelson v. Ritz Carlton Restaurant and Hotel Co.*, 157 A. 133 (N.J., 1931), the plaintiff was assigned to a hotel room that had been recently vacated by other guests. The room was very messy. Wastebaskets had not been emptied and the floor was covered with lint and cigarette ashes. The plaintiff left for a few hours to allow housekeeping time to clean. When plaintiff returned, she found that the bed had been changed and clean towels put in the bathroom, but the room had not otherwise been cleaned. She retired for the night. In the morning, the plaintiff got up to answer a knock on the door and stepped on a needle that broke after breaking the skin. She received medical attention but, as a result of the accident, her foot became infected. The plaintiff sued the hotel for negligence and was awarded $2,500 compensation. The court stated that the proprietor of a hotel is required to use due care to have rooms thoroughly cleaned before reassignment. Because the hotelkeeper failed in the performance of this duty, the hotel was liable for resulting injuries.

Beds and Other Furniture

Courts have generally permitted recovery for injuries caused by defective beds and furniture. In a 1909 case, the hotel room was equipped with a bed that would fold up so as to leave the bed in an upright position when not in use. The top of the bed was heavy, weighing about 300 pounds. Plaintiff slept in the bed all night. As he was about to leave the bed in the morning, "the top or upright portion of the bed fell forward upon him, crushing his head down upon his breast and inflicting severe injury." Plaintiff sued the hotel. The testimony presented by plaintiff stopped short of identifying the exact defect in the bed that caused it to fall down and entrap the plaintiff. He used res ipsa loquitur and won the case. *Lyttle v. Denny*, 71 A. 841 (Pa., 1909).

In *Nettles v. Forbes Motel, Inc.*, 182 So.2d 572 (La., 1966) plaintiff, a 5'2" woman, used a dressing table stool to adjust the air conditioner knob located 6'9" above the floor. She was injured when the stool collapsed. The defendants denied liability because the plaintiff knew the stool was not intended for that use. The court rejected this defense, saying the hotel should have foreseen the particular misuse involved here given the height of the air-conditioner control. Further, the testimony revealed that the stools had been improperly assembled by the hotel and the legs on several other stools at the hotel had come loose necessitating repairs. Despite this reoccurring problem the hotel had failed to inspect the remaining stools for soundness.

Furniture used by guests is sometimes abused or just wears out. To what extent should a hotel be liable when furniture collapses and a guest is hurt? The cases hold that the hotel or restaurant must regularly inspect the furniture and discard any that is no longer suitable. Failure to do so will result in liability.

In *Gary Hotel Courts, Inc. v. Perry*, 251 S.E.2d 37 (Ga., 1978), the webbing on a chair seat was missing. The hotel covered the seat with a cushion. When a guest sat on the chair the cushion collapsed, causing him injury. The court held the hotel was liable to the guest because it breached its duty to exercise ordinary care to afford the guest premises that are reasonably safe for use and occupancy. The same result was obtained in *Palagano v. Georgian Terrace Hotel Co.*, 181 S.E.2d 512 (Ga., 1971), where the injury was sustained when a bed in the defendant's hotel collapsed while plaintiff was sitting on it with one foot raised removing his socks. The court said, "There was evidence from which a jury might find that the bed was defective and that such defect could, or should, have been discovered by a reasonable inspection." In another case, the plaintiff was seated in the defendant's restaurant attending a meeting when his chair collapsed, injuring him. The court held res ipsa loqeutur was applicable since the restaurant was in full control of the chair and as such was responsible for its maintenance. *Gresham v. Stouffer Corp.*, 241 S.E.2d 451 (Ga., 1978).

In a case involving a sports bar, the plaintiff was injured when metal bleachers he was sitting on collapsed. The bleachers had been installed four months earlier for use by patrons while watching sporting events on a big screen television. Testimony established that the bleacher manufacturer's assembly instructions called for metal cross-bracing to be installed across the back of the bleachers in an "X." Instead, the metal supports were fastened in a vertical position. The cause of the bleachers' collapse was the improper installation. Although the bar had hired an independent contractor to install the bleachers, the duty to install them safely was a nondelegable duty. Therefore, the bar was held liable for the resulting injuries. *Otero v. Jordan Restaurant Enterprises*, 922 P.2d 569 (N.M., 1996).

In another case, involving a Kentucky Fried Chicken restaurant, a diner, attempting to sit at a table while holding his tray, fell and injured himself when the bench collapsed. Expert testimony suggested that the cause of the collapse was either: a) faulty construction of the bench by the restaurant by using inappropriate, inflexible screws to attach the bench to its frame; or b) failure to occasionally check for loosening bolts which would have been evident by simply jiggling the benches with one's hands. A summary judgment entered in favor of the Kentucky Fried Chicken restaurant was therefore reversed on appeal and a trial ordered. *Bishop v. KFC National Management Co., Inc.*, 473 S.E.2d 218 (Ga., 1996).

Regular inspections for broken or defective furniture will help reduce these types of incidents. Catering and other departments regularly handle portable chairs and tables that are exposed to much wear and tear, making loose screws, nuts, bolts and brackets predictable. Setup crews should watch for needed repairs and carry a screwdriver and wrench. When an item of furniture needing repair is discovered, it should be immediately removed from use until the repairs are completed.

Windows, Window Fixtures, and Screens

The same duty to inspect for defects and remedy them exists in regard to windows and screens. In *Rue v. Warner Hotel Co.*, 186 So. 625 (1939), the plaintiff-guest in the defendant hotel was trying to close a window when it shattered, injuring her arm. Testimony showed that the putty around the window pane was old and decayed, a defect that could have been ascertained by reasonable inspection. The hotel was liable for the oversight. The same results were obtained in another case in which an invitee of a guest was injured by a transom glass that fell when the plaintiff closed the door to the guest's room. Evidence showed that the glass had been broken some time before the accident. Inspection by the hotel would have uncovered this potentially dangerous condition. *Kramer Service v. Wilkins*, 186 So. 625 (Miss., 1939). The doctrine of res ipsa loquitur applied in another case where a transom over the door to the plaintiff's room fell as she was entering and struck her on the back of the head, neck, and shoulders. *Panepinto v. Morrison Hotel, Inc.*, 218 N.E.2d 880 (Ill., 1966). In another res ipsa case, a window shade fell on a guest and injured her, resulting in liability on the hotel. *Hotel Dempsey Company v. Teel*, 128 F.2d 673 (5th Cir., 1942).

Maintaining appropriate fixtures in good condition can protect a hotel from liability. The leading case of *Baker v. Dallas Hotel Company* (see page 121–123), held the hotel potentially liable where a child fell to his death when a window screen that was insecurely fastened fell out. Thus, a directed verdict in favor of the hotel was reversed on appeal and the case was remanded for trial. In contrast, the hotel was not liable in *Schlemmer v. Stokes*, 117 P.2d 396 (1941), where a child pushed through a window screen in a hotel room and fell out. A critical factual difference in this case was that the evidence showed no visible defect in the screen and, despite inspection, neither the plaintiff nor the defendant had found any defects in the screen before the accident. The hotel was therefore not liable to the injured child. Remember, a hotel is not an insurer of its guests' safety; it is only liable when it fails to exercise reasonable care.

Electrical and Heating Hazards

Electrical and heating devices must be maintained in good working order. The early case of *Reid v. Ehr*, 174 N.W. 71 (N.D., 1919), has not been modified through the years. In that case, the plaintiff suffered a shock when she turned on an electric light in her guest room. The court held that the injury was occasioned by the lack of reasonable care on the part of the defendant in maintaining and inspecting the electrical equipment in the room, and so the hotel was liable.

Failure to furnish safe heating can result in an injured guest recovering damages. In *Wilson v. Benoit*, 231 S.W.2d 916 (1950), the court held that the proprietor of tourist cabins was liable when a guest was killed by a gas explosion in his cabin caused by a defective hose connection on the gas heater. The court said the fact that the plaintiff was drunk had no causal connection with the explosion and ruled out a verdict of contributory negligence.

Animals and Insects

The duty of reasonable care owed by hotels and restaurants to their customers applies also to injuries from animals or insects. If a guest is injured by an animal or insect and the hotel or restaurant's negligence led to its presence, liability will result.

The plaintiff in *Williams v. Milner Hotel Co.*, 36 A.2d 20 (Conn., 1944), was bitten by a rat while lying in bed at night. Evidence showed that numerous rat holes existed in the baseboard of the room prior to this event. The defendant claimed that it had taken all necessary precautions by employing a cleaning man and a competent exterminator, and that the room was routinely inspected. The jury held for the plaintiff, apparently relying on the failure of the hotel to remove the rat holes.

The following case involves the equally unpleasant thought of rats in a hotel lobby.

CASE EXAMPLE 6–1

DeLuce v. Fort Wayne Hotel
311 F.2d 853 (Mich., 1962)

. . . The background of the case is as follows: Miss DeLuce [an actress, singer and dancer in films, television, night clubs, and Broadway shows] was a registered guest at the hotel on the date of the accident. On the day after her arrival, arrangements were made by her producer to present a preview of a show for executives of an automotive company at the home of one of the executives. Miss DeLuce had been informed that there was a swimming pool where the performance was taking place, and that she could go swimming if she so desired. She brought her swim equipment, which consisted of a snorkel, a mask, hand fins, and foot fins. Because of the coolness of the weather, she decided not to go swimming. Following the conclusion of the show at 8:30 P.M., a buffet dinner was served, and she, with other performers, afterward left the executive's home at approximately 10:00 P.M. and was taken back to the . . . hotel. When she got out of the car and entered the hotel, she had with her all her music and swimming paraphernalia. She went through the lobby, put

her things on a chair, and went to the desk to ascertain whether she had any messages. She then made a call to see if certain performers in the show had returned to the hotel.

As she went back to the desk, she saw a man in the vestibule, who appeared to be hitting the top of the radiator with one of her swim fins. She ran across the lobby, through the door, and found that the man had thrown her fins down on the floor by the radiator. She reached down to pick them up and felt a sharp bite on her hand. She stood up quickly, and a rat approximately a foot long was hanging from her finger. Calling for help, she opened the door of the hotel with her left hand, rushed out onto the sidewalk, and started to shake the rat, and it fell and ran away. [She later developed postencephalitic Parkinsonism. At the time of the trial, which was two years after the accident, she suffered from that disease, being permanently disabled and incapacitated for the work she had previously carried on.]

Charles B. Nunley, an employee of the hotel, was called as an adverse witness by plaintiff's counsel. Mr. Nunley was a night bellman, whose duties required him to be, at times, in front of the hotel to carry guests' baggage to and from their rooms. There was no doorman at the hotel. Mr. Nunley testified that he often saw rats coming out of the alley around the hotel. The alley was seventy feet from the hotel entrance. He had also seen rats on the sidewalk outside of the hotel, and he had actually chased them off the sidewalk. He testified that the hotel doors had been left open that night, prior to the time Miss DeLuce was bitten by the rat. The vestibule, where she had stepped down to pick up her swim fins, and the lobby floor are level with the sidewalk. When Mr. Nunley was asked whether rats could run right into the hotel when the door was open, he said: "If somebody scares a rat, you know, you can't tell which way he will run." When Miss DeLuce was bitten by the rat, Mr. Nunley was serving food in guests' rooms upstairs, and had just come down on the elevator. The Fort Wayne Hotel produced Mr. Bart Edds as a witness. He testified that he was maintenance man for the hotel and had seen, in the alley next to the hotel, numerous rats flattened out where cars had run over them at night. Ivor Bennett, a former pest-control operator, whose company was employed by the hotel for the extermination of vermin, including rats, testified that the location where the Fort Wayne Hotel was situated was one of the worst rat-ridden areas in the city. He called it the "second worst place" in Detroit for rats.

Other witnesses testified as to seeing rats in the adjacent alley, and also as to seeing the rat clinging to the hand of Miss DeLuce before she ran to the street and shook it off. Rats are ferocious and dangerous carriers of disease and, in Michigan, a bounty is paid for killing them. [The hotel claimed that it should not be liable for the injury unless it knew, or by the exercise of reasonable care should have known, of the presence of rats on its premises.] The issue before us is whether there was an absolute liability on the part of the hotel to keep its premises free from rats, or whether it was subject only to the duty to use due care.

[W]e are of the view the hotel is only liable if the owner knew or should have known of such dangerous condition on his premises. . . .

It is further contended by . . . Miss DeLuce that the evidence of the presence of rats in the alley adjoining the hotel and on the sidewalk in front of the hotel created an affirmative duty on the part of the hotel to protect its paying guests from the foreseeable event that such rats might enter the hotel through its doors, especially in view of the fact that the doors were on a level with the sidewalk, and the hotel took no precautions to keep rats out of its vestibule and lobby. In brief, [the argument is] that under the uncontradicted and uncontested facts of the case, the hotel must have foreseen that a rat might enter the hotel if the doors were left open.

Negligence . . . is ordinarily a question of fact for the jury. It is only where the facts are such that all reasonable men must draw the same conclusion from them that the question of negligence becomes one of law for the court. There is no evidence that any rats had ever been seen in the hotel vestibule or lobby before the night of this accident, or that any guest had ever been bitten by a rat. . . . [W]e are of the view that the question of whether it was reasonably foreseeable that a rat might enter the vestibule or the lobby of the hotel is a question of fact for the jury, and failure of the hotel to use such care as was necessary to avoid a danger, which should and could have been anticipated, would constitute negligence. If, through the hotel's failure to use due care to keep its premises free from rats, the rat in question was on the premises at the time of the accident, the hotel would be [liable].

[T]he case [is] remanded for a new trial.

CASE QUESTIONS

1. What facts presented in the case might establish that the hotel took reasonable care to keep rats out of the hotel?

2. What facts presented in the case will favor plaintiff's argument that the hotel failed to exercise reasonable care to keep the rats out?

In *Cunningham v. Neil House Hotel Co.*, 33 N.E.2d 859 (Ohio, 1940), the plaintiff-guest at the defendant hotel was awakened by a burning and stinging sensation on her right arm caused by an insect bite. The insect that stung or bit the plaintiff was not known or identified, nor was it known where it came from, how long it had been in the room, or the conditions under which it had entered. The plaintiff claimed res ipsa loquitur applied, but the court disagreed, stating that to permit the jury in this situation to draw an *inference* of lack of due care on the part of the hotel would have been mere conjecture. If plaintiff can *prove* lack of due care on the part of the hotel, and proximate cause between that negligence and the inset bite, the hotel will be liable.

In *Brasseaux v. Stand-By Corp. d/b/a Plantation Inn*, 402 So.2d 140 (La., 1981), the plaintiff-guest, while showering, was stung by bees, causing him to fall and injure his left wrist. Beehives were located outside the window to the room. Plaintiff sued the hotel. The manager admitted knowing of the existence of the hives but had not received reports of bees inside any rooms. The court held that if a hotel is on notice of the existence of beehives, it should foresee that bees might get into the hotel and sting a guest. The hotel was negligent for failing to remove the bees and in failing to warn guests of the bees' presence. The hotel was thus liable for defendant's injuries.

Sometimes insect or animal bites occur despite careful action on the part of the hotel. If the hotel was not negligent it will not be liable. In Chapter 5 we studied *Febesh v. Elcejay Inn Corp.*, in which the court held a restaurant was not liable to a guest who suffered a bee sting at an outdoor reception, where no prior incidents of bee stings occurred at the inn and the area was sprayed for bees at least once a day.

Bathroom Appliances and Hot Water

Several cases have originated in hotel bathrooms involving defective appliances and plumbing systems. The same rules of negligence apply. In *Brown Hotel Company v. Marx*, 411 S.W.2d 911 (Ky., 1967), the guest, while turning on the water faucet in his hotel room, cut his hand when the porcelain faucet broke into pieces. The guest sued the hotel and used the doctrine of res ipsa loquitur, eliminating the need to prove the manner in which the defendant was negligent. The evidence established that the hotel failed to make regular inspections of the plumbing fixtures, and the hotel had "mysteriously" lost the shattered faucet fragments. Therefore the hotel was unable to rebut the inference of negligence and so lost the case.

In the following case involving a malfunctioning faucet in a ladies room, the facts did not suggest that the defect would have been discovered by inspection. Therefore the building owner was not liable to plaintiff who was injured by the faucet.

CASE EXAMPLE 6–2

Lonsdale v. Joseph Horne Co.
587 A.2d 810 (Pa., 1991)

[T]he facts reveal that on February 8, 1985, Ms. Lonsdale, in the company of her friend and co-employee/teacher (Ms. Helen DeGaetano), traveled to Monroeville, Pennsylvania, to attend a reading conference. . . .

The conference came to a close at approximately 3:30 P.M., and . . . the two women made their way to the ladies room. While in the restroom facilities, Ms. Lonsdale decided to "run hot water" on her hands. As Ms. Lonsdale described it: . . .

As I turned [the water faucet] on and was holding it there, waiting for the water to come out, it appeared like the round part, the spigot thing, you know that goes around on it, spun around and came back very quickly and with extreme force. . . . [I]t hit my fingers, which were my two fingers here [middle and ring fingers], it came back and hit those fingers. . . . I wasn't really paying that much attention to see how that came back around because, I mean, all I knew, before I knew it, something had hit me very hard, and I really wasn't studying to see how it did that. . . .

When Ms. Lonsdale screamed upon being struck, Ms. DeGaetano went to see what had happened. She did not witness the incident, but upon noticing Ms. Lonsdale's fingers beginning to swell, a ring was removed from the fourth finger of the right hand. The ring was damaged to the extent that a diamond and emerald had been knocked out of their settings and it was no longer circular in shape. . . .

[I]n order to hold the Defendant accountable for the injuries sustained by the Plaintiff, Ms. Lonsdale had to show that the Defendant either knew or, by the exercise of reasonable care, should have known that one of the seven to eight sinks in the ladies' room would malfunction and was likely to cause harm. . . .

At trial, the Plaintiff failed to submit any evidence that the Defendant had knowledge that the faucet handle was defective and involved an unreasonable risk of harm to the user. . . .

Lastly, both the Plaintiff and Ms. DeGaetano testified that on no prior visit to the Horne's ladies' room had they encountered any problem with the faucets.

Taking the testimony of Ms. Lonsdale and Ms. DeGaetano, they being the only witnesses . . . on the question of liability, . . . we have the absence of any showing that any allegedly dangerous condition of the faucet handle could or should have been uncovered by a proper or reasonable inspection. . . .

Since there was an absence of evidence to indicate that the faucet handle was in any way defective we are loathe to say that the condition of the faucet handle would support an inference of negligence on the part of the Defendant.

[Judgment for Defendant.]

CASE QUESTIONS

1. What more would plaintiff have had to prove to establish that defendant was negligent?

2. Why would res ipsa not apply in this case?

In addition to bathroom sinks, showers can malfunction leading to injuries. Excessively hot water has generated a number of negligence cases, one of which is *Wolfe v. Chateau Renaissance*, 357 A.2d 282 (N.J., 1976). Plaintiff, a hotel guest, turned on the shower water and set it at a comfortable temperature before entering. While he was in the shower and rinsing off, and without touching the controls again, very hot water came gushing out unexpectedly. Plaintiff jumped back, hit the back of the tub, and fell, suffering injuries. The court applied res ipsa loquitur and held for plaintiff, noting that the sudden gush of water suggested a malfunction and negligence on the part of the hotel which had exclusive control of the heating plant, pipes and plumbing devices.

Some of these problems can be avoided if housekeeping personnel are instructed to examine the bathroom fixtures routinely, and turn on the water in the shower and sink faucet and let it run a bit. If fixtures appear cracked or broken, or if the water temperature rises substantially, maintenance should be called to inspect. In the following case, such routine inspections saved the hotel from liability.

In *Bearse v. Fowler*, 196 N.E.2d 910 (Mass., 1969), a guest sustained injuries when she slipped and fell in her bathroom at the defendant's motel while trying to shut off the hot water on a shower fixture. The knob failed to respond. The evidence established that the fixture was "brand new;" the motel owner inspected the shower handles daily and had no difficulty in turning them. The owner was not aware of any defect in the fixture and in the exercise of due care would not have discovered any defect. As you should expect given these facts, the court held the motel was not negligent.

A woman fell in the shower stall of her hotel room. She claimed the injury was due to the hotel's failure to both install adequate hand railings or grips in the shower, and to provide adequate slip-resistant devices such as mats or appliques. The court refused to grant the hotel's motion for summary judgment and directed that the case proceed to trial. *Lopez v. Motel 6 G.P., Inc.*, 932 S.W.2d 76 (Tex., 1996).

Another case involved a problem in a ladies room in a J.C. Penney's Department Store that could happen in a restroom at a hospitality facility. Plaintiff entered the only available stall and discovered that the latch to lock the door was missing. She closed the door and placed her pocketbook on the floor of the stall in front of the door so that anyone looking at the outside of the stall would see that it was occupied. "She was in the process of rearranging her clothing when a woman opened the door to the stall forcefully and caused it to hit plaintiff's head." As a result, plaintiff suffered injuries and sued the store. The maintenance manager established that Penny's cleaned and restocked the restroom daily, and performed more comprehensive cleanings weekly which would have revealed the broken latch. There had been no prior broken latches at the store. The court held that, given the store's reasonable maintenance schedule and the lack of similar incidents, the store could not have foreseen the risk and therefore was not liable for plaintiff's injuries. *Parks-Nietzold v. J.C. Penney, Inc.*, 490 S.E.2d 133 (Ga., 1977). Had the store been less vigilant, it likely would have been liable.

Duty Owed Guests and Others in Public Areas

This section deals with a hotel's public areas, such as the lobby, stairs, elevators, bars, doors, and dining rooms. These cases also apply to restaurants, most areas of which are public.

Lobby

Because the lobby is the most frequently used public area of a hotel, special precautions should be taken. Frequent and regular inspections should be made to ensure the walkways are not blocked by suitcases or otherwise, the rugs have no bumps or holes on which people might trip and fall, the furniture is in good condition and able to hold anticipated weight, no intruders are bothering guests, and everything is generally in good order. When hotel employees are repairing or cleaning the lobby floors or furniture, they should place barriers around the work area to protect invitees from related harm.

Elevators

The elevator is an indispensable part of a hotel. Guest rooms are often located on upper floors. Hotels often position restaurants and bars on upper floors to take advantage of the view. As a result, elevators are in great demand and accidents occasionally occur. The type of accidents range from failing to level the elevator with the floor when a guest is exiting, to malfunctioning elevators that plunge down the shaft out of control.

In general, a hotelkeeper who operates an elevator is obligated to use at least ordinary care in its maintenance and operation. In some states, a high degree of care is required.

Self-Service Elevators.   Automatic elevators, also called self-service elevators, are those designed to operate by buttons controlled by passengers without a full-time operator. Guests of all ages and aptitudes who may have little familiarity with elevators will be using them. The manufacturer or contractor installing an automatic elevator, as well as the owner and those under contract to service or inspect it, must act with care because of this fact.

In a self-service elevator case, Briscoe, an employee of a hotel, entered the elevator at the fifth floor, intending to go to the sixth floor. Although he pressed the correct button, the elevator suddenly began a descent, ending with a series of jarring stops at or near the first floor and finally settling on the basement level. Other employees observed Briscoe as he exited the elevator in a somewhat shaken state, suffering apparent back pain. An elevator company had a contract to service and maintain the elevators in the hotel. Briscoe presented evidence showing that the elevator company had deviated from recognized standards of maintenance and argued that res ipsa loquitur should apply. The court agreed based on the evidence presented by plaintiff of deviations from standard maintenance practices. But if defendant could prove that the injury was the result of a manufacturer's design failure rather than negligence in servicing and maintaining the elevator, the inference of negligence created by the res ipsa doctrine would be rebutted. *American Elevator Company v. Briscoe*, 572 P.2d 534 (Nev., 1977).

In another case a woman entered a self-service elevator on the building's third floor intending to go to the ground floor. When the doors shut the elevator plummeted and came to an abrupt stop below the first floor, causing injuries to the passenger. The building owner will be liable if the cause of the injury can be traced to the owner's negligence or to negligence on the part of a repair or maintenance company it may have hired. Liability for the latter would be based on the owner's nondelegable duty to keep the premises safe. *Gaffney v. EQK Realty Investors*, 445 S.E.2d 771 (Ga., 1994).

Freight Elevators.   Remember, hotels and restaurants are not insurers of invitees' safety. If the hotel or restaurant did not cause the injury, it will not be liable. In *Reimer v. Marriott Co.*, 372 S.2d 738 (La., 1979), the plaintiff and others were delivering flowers to be used as table decorations in conjunction with a luncheon they would be attending. A security officer claims he told them that they could not use the freight elevator but the plaintiff persisted, and he told her she would have to wait for a catering manager to take her up. The elevator had an inside steel mesh door that closed from top to bottom and met at the middle. Approximately ten or twelve seconds before the top steel mesh door starts closing, a bell rings and continues ringing until the door is fully closed. About sixty seconds after the steel mesh door has fully descended, the outside door closes automatically unless held open by pushing an "open" button. The plaintiff claims that as she was approaching the elevator with decorations in each hand, the closing inner steel mesh door struck her on the head, causing her to fall and injure herself. The plaintiff sued both the elevator repair company and the hotel.

The court held there was no liability on the part of the elevator repair company because there was no evidence of faulty installation, defective condition, or failure of maintenance. As to the claim against the hotel, there was evidence that the plaintiff knew that the door was closing and that she tried to "beat" the closing door. This was carelessness on the part of the plaintiff. Since she was negligent and the hotel was not, she could not recover.

In another case involving a freight elevator, the hotel was found to be negligent. The plaintiff had used the hotel's freight elevator to make a delivery to the receiving department. Like the elevator in the previous case, the elevator in this case had an upper and lower part to the door and they met in the middle. The door was closed by pulling down on a strap. The length of the strap had been diminished apparently by wear, requiring a higher reach to close the elevator. In the process of closing the door, plaintiff lost his balance. His hand became caught in the door, causing serious injury. The hotel was found to be negligent for its failure to lengthen the strap used to close the door, for its failure to post instructions and a warning, and for the lack of cushioning devices on the edges of the upper and lower portions of the door where they meet. *Chimeno v.*

Fountainbleau Hotel Corp., 251 So.2d 351 (1971). In this case, unlike the previous case, the accident was caused by the hotel's carelessness.

Operator-Assisted Elevators.   *Blackhawk Hotels Company v. Bonfoey*, 227 F.2d 232 (Minn., 1955), concerned a manually operated hotel elevator that fell about forty-five feet, injuring the plaintiff-guest. At the time of the accident the elevator carried nine persons, which was not an overload. The operator could not stop the elevator after leaving the third floor. The elevator was approximately twenty-five years old, was maintained by a service company, and had not been modernized over the years. The hotel contended that the service company should be responsible for the accident because of negligent maintenance of the elevator. The court rejected this position and held that the hotel had a nondelegable duty as to elevators to see that reasonable care was used in furnishing safe elevator transportation.

In another elevator case, the plaintiff alleged that she was injured by the defendant's failure to bring the hotel elevator level with the third floor so that she could alight with reasonable safety. The plaintiff testified that she entered the elevator to go from the lobby to the third floor. When the operator stopped the elevator at plaintiff's floor she glanced down before starting out, but because the elevator and hall were dimly lighted she did not notice whether the elevator floor was level with the hall floor. When she attempted to step out, she struck her foot against the wall of the elevator shaft, which caused her to fall forward, breaking her right arm. The hotel was found liable for breaching its duty to provide passengers a reasonably safe means to exit the elevator. *Jenkins v. Missouri State Life Insurance Co.*, 69 S.W.2d 666 (Mo., 1934).

Supervision of Maintenance.   When an innkeeper leaves the door to an elevator open or unlocked, as where an elevator is undergoing repairs, and a guest falls into the well and is injured, the innkeeper will ordinarily be held liable. *Hayward v. Merrill*, 94 Ill. 349 (1880). This type of accident can be avoided by roping off the area around the elevator and displaying warning signs.

Doors

The duty of restaurateurs and innkeepers to exercise reasonable, ordinary due care to keep the premises reasonably safe applies also to doors.

Crowded Doorways.   In *Schubert v. Hotel Astor, Inc.*, 5 N.Y.S.2d 203 (1938), the court stated that under ordinary circumstances hotels and restaurants need not have a door attendant; but if they are aware that an extraordinary crowd will be gathering, a duty exists to employ an attendant to ensure the safety of patrons entering and leaving. In that case the Hotel Astor was a team headquarters on the day of the Army-Notre Dame football game, an event that attracts a lot of people. In the early evening, not surprisingly, the hotel lobby was congested with people in a "gay, hilarious and carousing mood." The plaintiff, a sixty-three-year-old woman, entered the hotel through the revolving door on her way to a banquet hosted by the hotel and sponsored by the Danish Society. As she had almost completed her entrance, suddenly "there was an awful rush" and several "young fellows" chasing each other inside the hotel lobby ran into the same compartment of the revolving door the plaintiff was in and gave it a hard push. As a result she was struck by a part of the door and suffered a fractured hip and other injuries.

The hotel was held liable because it should have foreseen the large, rowdy crowd generated by the football game and so should have provided a door attendant to help control the crowd's ingress and egress. If an unruly crowd is not foreseeable, an innkeeper or restaurateur cannot be held liable for unexpected conduct of its patrons.

Automatic Doors. In the following case the problem was malfunctioning automatic sliding glass doors.

CASE EXAMPLE 6–3

Landmark Hotel & Casino, Inc. v. Moore
757 P.2d 361 (Nev., 1988)

. . .Ninety-four year old Bertha L. Moore (hereinafter "Moore") was injured when she attempted to enter the Landmark Hotel and Casino in Las Vegas through an entrance with automatic sliding glass doors. Before Moore could pass completely through the entrance, the doors closed on her, knocking her down and injuring her severely. Moore filed a complaint against Landmark Hotel and Casino, Inc.; . . .

We are . . . unable to find merit in Landmark's challenge of the judgment against it. After a jury trial—in which the trial court instructed the jury on the doctrine of res ipsa loquitur as to Landmark, the jury found Landmark liable to Moore, . . .

Landmark . . . argues that the res ipsa loquitur instruction should not have been given because it was not clear that Landmark had exclusive control over the doors that injured Moore. . . . We find Landmark's position unsupported by the record and point out that Landmark admits that there was no evidence of a maintenance agreement, which would have suggested joint control, between

Landmark and the other defendants.

Also unconvincing is Landmark's contention that Moore's accident with the automatic sliding doors was of the type that would ordinarily occur in the absence of negligence. . . .

Automatic sliding glass doors of the type that injured Moore are [very common], affording the public safe ingress and egress to countless facilities on a daily basis. What happened to Moore is unusual; it strongly suggests a malfunction attributable to negligence.

Finally, Moore's expert witnesses testified that the automatic doors that injured Moore should receive thorough mechanical inspections at least every six months, and that they should be inspected weekly to determine if they are working properly. Landmark's assistant chief engineer testified that Landmark did not have any regular maintenance or inspection program for the doors that injured Moore. Such testimony compels the conclusion that the automatic sliding glass doors would not have closed prematurely, and with such disproportionate force, in the absence of negligence on the part of Landmark. . . .

[Judgment for plaintiff.]

CASE QUESTIONS

1. What maintenance procedures should be followed for automatic sliding glass doors?
2. How might the hotel have avoided liability in this case?

Note that the plaintiff in *Landmark Hotel & Casino, Inc.* was ninety-four years old and therefore arguably would take more time than the average person to get through the door and might be more prone than the average person to suffer serious injury in this type of accident. Do these facts lessen the hotel's liability? The answer is no. Hotels and restaurants invite people of all ages and circumstances to their establishments and must anticipate that some guests are more injury-prone than others. They owe a duty to exercise reasonable care to protect the safety and well-being of all their patrons including those who are elderly or injury-prone.

Supervision of Installation and Maintenance.   In *Johnson v. Beavers*, 496 So.2d 1251 (La., 1986), an invitee was hit by a sliding door that was being installed in a hotel. The plaintiff walked through the work area on the way to the bathroom facilities. The employee of the installation company hired by the hotel did not see plaintiff approach. The installer was manually sliding the door to adjust it when plaintiff was hit. Neither the hotel nor the installer placed a warning sign or blockade near or around the work area. Plaintiff sued the hotel and the installer for negligence. They claimed plaintiff was negligent for walking through the work area. Louisiana is a comparative negligence state, and the jury found all parties somewhat negligent, apportioning the liability as follows: the installation company and its employee, 59 percent; the hotel, 21 percent; plaintiff, 20 percent.

In the case of *Bardwell Motor Inn v. Accavallo*, 381 A.2d 1061 (1977), the hotel operator contracted with the defendant to replace a glass panel in the front entrance door. The contractor removed the glass panel and the push bar from the door and left the premises without advising the hotel manager of the condition in which the doorway had been left, without posting any warnings, and without leaving anyone behind to warn people of the danger. A business patron of the hotel fell and sustained personal injuries when trying to open the door. The hotel settled the claim brought against it by the injured man and then sought to recover from the contractor the sum it paid the guest.

The court held that the innkeeper had a nondelegable duty to keep the premises reasonably safe for guests and patrons. The independent contractor owed both the innkeeper and guests the duty of carrying out the job with reasonable care and attention. Because the contractor acted negligently on the job, he was liable not only to guests for any injuries sustained as a result of his failure, but also to the hotel for any loss it sustained. The hotel was thus entitled to reimbursement from the contractor for the money it paid the injured guest.

Hallways

Hallways that are being cleaned can be troublesome, especially when being washed or waxed. In *Bellevue v. Haslup*, 150 F.2d 160 (D.C., 1945), the plaintiff slipped and fell on a hotel hallway floor that was wet from waxing. The defendant maintained that the hotel employee doing the waxing had verbally warned the plaintiff to walk on the dry side of the hallway. Plaintiff denied that any verbal warning was given. Both sides concurred that no warning signs or notices had been placed in the hall. The court found for the plaintiff, holding that the defendant had failed in its duty to keep the hotel in a reasonably safe condition.

When floors are being washed or waxed, barriers and warning signs can prevent an accident, a lawsuit, and the proof problem the hotel experienced in this case.

Care must be taken in the installation and maintenance of hallway carpets. A hole in the rug can trap a shoe heel and result in someone falling. A bulge in a carpet can easily lead to a trip-and-fall accident resulting in injuries and liability. *Carrasquillo v. Holiday Carpet Service, Inc.*, 615 So.2d 862 (Fl., 1993).

Stairways, Steps, and Their Coverings

Guests are entitled to assume that steps and passageways are clear of dangerous impediments and otherwise reasonably safe. Because steps and stairways in a hotel constitute a potential danger to guests, hotelkeepers must do all of the following to avoid liability: see that steps are properly constructed; keep them in good repair; install railings; do not leave items on the steps; provide adequate lighting; and, if carpeted, be sure the carpets are in good condition and safe.

In *Handel v. Rudnich*, 78 So.2d 709 (Fla., 1955), the plaintiff, while descending stairs from the first floor to the lobby, caught her heel on a button protruding from one of the steps and fell to the tile floor below, sustaining serious injuries. Evidence established that a rug had been removed some years ago leaving a button about the size of a silver dollar protruding. The court held for plaintiff, rejecting the contentions of the defendant that the size of the button was not dangerous and that the guest was negligent for using stairs instead of an elevator. A guest who uses stairs is not negligent unless the steps are blocked or barricaded indicating they should not be used.

Another case involved a staple embedded in the carpeting in a hotel conference room. A disc jockey, hired to play for a wedding reception being held in the room, hurt her knee when, while kneeling to plug electrical cords for her equipment into an outlet, the staple pierced her left knee through the cartilage down to the bone. She sued the hotel claiming it was negligent in the maintenance of the carpet. The hotel night janitor testified that during the week leading up to the injury, he had discovered numerous staples while vacuuming because they made a "clinking noise" in the vacuum. He attributed them to construction done for a "Queen of the Universe" pageant held in the room a week earlier. Each night since that event, he picked up fewer and fewer staples. He was eventually satisfied that he had picked up all the staples in the room because he no longer heard the clinking noise. The court determined the hotel used reasonable care to remove the staples and dismissed the case. *Richardson v. Sport Shinko*, 880 P.2d 169 (Ha., 1994).

In *Orlick v. Granit Hotel & Country Club*, 331 N.Y.S.2d 651 (1971), the plaintiff tripped on a short flight of four steps leading to her room. The hotel was negligent on several grounds: no handrail existed; no warning of the stairs' existence was provided; the lighting was poor; and the use of the same carpeting on the foyer, stairway and corridor created an illusion of one level and no stairs. The fact that no previous accident had occurred during the four years since the hotel was built did not constitute a defense.

In the following case, plaintiff's heel became wedged in a gap on a step that the hotel should have discovered.

CASE EXAMPLE 6–4

Fields v. Robert Chappell Association, Inc.
256 S.E.2d 259 (N.C., 1979)

. . . Plaintiff was a registered guest in defendant's motel. She left her room intending to go to the motel office. It was necessary for her to turn to her right and go down a flight of steps. She looked down the steps and saw nothing unusual, except that she saw that the left side was obstructed by the protruding metal handle of a hook that is used to clean swimming pools. She, consequently, did not hold the handrail but moved more to her right towards the wall. There was no handrail on the right side of the step. She fell forward but did not fall all the way down the flight of steps because her foot was caught. She had to pull her shoe loose from the step to get up. There was a deep gash in her leg. She yelled for assistance, and some of the other motel guests gave her first aid before she was taken to a hospital emergency room. After she had been taken to the hospital, another guest went to the stairs where plaintiff had fallen. The stairs were concrete with a metal strip along the front edge of the step. This guest testified that the steps were bloody. She found a piece of plaintiff's shoe heel, the heel cap, wedged between the metal strip and the concrete part of the step. There was a gap between the metal strip and the concrete. Part of the concrete was missing. The witness described it as "a crumbling or an erosion as opposed to a crack." There were similar gaps on several of the steps but on the step where plaintiff's shoe heel had been lodged, the gap was somewhat larger. There was also an eroded area on the top of that step about four inches long that extended back about two inches. It was easier to observe this defect from below than when one looked down the steps from the top. The guest took plaintiff's shoe heel to the motel office and explained what had happened.

Defendant called only one witness, the motel manager. She testified that she was not present on the day the accident occurred. She further testified that the stairs were thirteen years old at the time plaintiff fell and that no repairs had been made after the accident. The motel, including the stairs, was regularly inspected every three months. She had participated in these inspections and had not observed any defects in the "steps prior to the time Mrs. Fields fell, nothing that would be noticeable enough to think you would fall, you know, you might see a crack here or there." She admitted, nonetheless, that the cracks were wide enough to receive the heel of a shoe. . . .

The legal principles that arise on the evidence may . . . be simply stated. The defendant motel operator was not an insurer of the safety of plaintiff, its invited guest. It was, however, required to exercise due care to keep the premises in a reasonably safe condition so as not to expose plaintiff unnecessarily to danger, and to warn her of any hidden perils. It is liable to plaintiff for any injury proximately caused by a breach of that duty. . . .

The evidence all but compels the conclusion that plaintiff fell on defendant's stairs because the heel of her shoe unexpectedly became wedged in a crevice near the front edge of one of the stairsteps. Plaintiff was proceeding in a careful and prudent manner, and the crevice was almost imperceptible to one proceeding down the steps. The wearing away of the concrete and resulting gap between the metal strip and the rest of the step did not occur suddenly. Defendant knew of the condition, should have known that it was dangerous, and yet allowed it to continue to exist without doing anything to warn its guests of the danger. Defendant, thereby, unnecessarily and unreasonably exposed plaintiff and its other guests to a danger that resulted in injury to plaintiff.

CASE QUESTION

1. How could the hotel have avoided the injury and liability in this case?

The following case illustrates another potential stair problem—a step of unusual height. Because users are unaccustomed to the need to lift their feet higher than usual, such steps can cause people to trip and fall.

CASE EXAMPLE 6–5

Robinson v. Western International Hotels Co. 318 S.E.2d 235 (Ga., 1984)

Appellant-plaintiffs Mr. and Mrs. Robinson were registered guests in appellee-defendant's hotel. For an additional fee, they elected to store their vehicle in the hotel's valet parking facility for the duration of their stay. The keys to their vehicle were therefore turned over to appellee's employees who were in charge of the garage facility. When appellants checked out of the hotel, they presented the claim check for their vehicle and were instructed to wait for their car to be brought to them. After a considerable period of time, appellants were told that the keys to their vehicle could not be located. A hotel employee then asked Mr. Robinson to accompany him to the key booth to identify his keys. Mr. Robinson was led through an "employees only" area of the garage. Mr. Robinson and the employee subsequently arrived at the key booth, which was located on a walkway immediately adjacent to the driveway by which vehicles were entering and leaving the garage facility.

When Mr. Robinson reached the key booth, he stepped inside. According to Mr. Robinson, entering the booth from the walkway required that he negotiate a step of unusual height. Once in the booth, Mr. Robinson identified his keys, although he testified that the light was dim. As Mr. Robinson left the booth, he fell. According to his testimony, in attempting to step down from the booth to the walkway he either entirely or partially missed his footing and pitched forward into the driveway.

Mr. Robinson instituted a tort action against [the hotel] to recover for the physical injuries he allegedly sustained when he fell. . . .

The following legal principles are applicable in the instant case: "Where an owner or occupier of land, by express or implied invitation, induces or leads others to come upon his premises for any lawful purpose, he is liable in damages to such persons for injuries caused by his failure to exercise ordinary care in keeping the premises and approaches safe." . . . Further, the innkeeper has a duty to inspect and is liable for such injuries caused by defects as would be disclosed by a reasonable inspection. The basis of the proprietor's liability is his superior knowledge, and if his invitee knows of the condition or hazard there is no duty on the part of the proprietor to warn him and there is no liability for resulting injury because the invitee has as much knowledge as the proprietor does and then by voluntarily acting in view of his knowledge, assumes the risks and dangers incident to the known condition. . . .

Although Mr. Robinson was in an "employees only" area of the hotel at the time of his fall, [the hotel] does not contest that, under the circumstances, Mr. Robinson was its invitee in the parking facility. "The duty to keep the premises safe for invitees extends to all portions of the premises which it is necessary for the invitee to use in the course of the business for which the invitation was extended, and at which his presence should therefore be reasonably anticipated, or to which he is allowed to go." . . .

Appellee relies upon the fact that Mr. Robinson successfully negotiated the walkway and stepped up into the booth as evincing his knowledge of the dangers presented thereby and as militating against his recovery. . . . Mr. Robinson had previously crossed the walkway and stepped into the booth. He fell while attempting to exit the booth. The evidence would authorize a finding that, due to the hazardous factors which existed in the booth area, those who attempted to exit the booth were subjected to "a tendency to surge forward . . . and end up in the drive." Under these circumstances, the mere fact that Mr. Robinson had on a single prior occasion stepped into the booth would not necessarily preclude his recovery for a fall which occurred while attempting to exit it. "[W]e cannot say that under these circum-stances that . . . plaintiff should have had a full ap-preciation of the danger, and that in the exercise of ordinary care [he] should have avoided the in-jury to [himself]. . . . [Judgment for plaintiff.]

CASE QUESTION

1. As this case illustrates, areas intended for employees only are often not as well built or maintained as areas intended for patrons. What precau-tions should hotels and restaurants take to ensure customers are not in-jured in parts of the facility designated for employees?

Escalators

Like stairs, escalators need maintenance attention. Injuries can result if an es-calator is not working properly, if it is overcrowded from too many people, if chil-dren or others are permitted to run or engage in other horseplay while riding, or if scratches, holes, or other damage to the steps develop and go unattended. Likewise, the railings and access areas must be inspected and any dangerous con-ditions removed. A restaurant may be liable where it permits a screw to protrude one inch from the railing of the escalator causing injury to a patron. *Anderson v. Market Street Developers, Ltd.*, 944 S.W.2d 776 (Tex., 1997).

Duty Owed in Restaurants and Dining Rooms

Restaurateurs and hotels with restaurants have a duty to exercise reasonable care to avoid conditions particular to restaurants that can result in injury. Those conditions include slippery floors, foreign substances on floors, overcrowding of tables and chairs, hanging mirrors, and flambe dishes.

Slippery Floors

Accidents caused by slippery floors are not infrequent in dining rooms, ban-quet halls, and bars.

Highly polished and waxed floors are the cause of most slippery floor cases. For example, in *Mitchell v. Baker Hotel of Dallas, Inc.*, 523 S.W.2d 216 (Tex., 1975), the plaintiff slipped while walking on a polished floor at a banquet. The hotel proved that the floor was waxed only twice a year, the latest being three months before the accident, and the floor was inspected on the day of the banquet and the morning after by the banquet director and found not to have been over-waxed, not unduly slick, and in its normal condition. The court held for the hotel; plaintiff failed to prove the hotel was negligent.

Before wax or polish is applied to a floor, be sure the type being used is appropriate for the particular floor, and make sure it is applied consistent with the directions that accompany the product.

In another case the plaintiff, a seventeen-year-old guest of the defendant hotel, was severely injured when she slipped on a wet spot on a wooden walkway at the rear of the lobby. The defendant argued it should not be liable for failing to clean the wet spot because there was insufficient evidence that it had actual or constructive notice of the existence of the moisture. The court said that this point was essentially irrelevant because the evidence established that the floor where the fall occurred was dangerously worn, smooth, and therefore slippery regardless of the wetness, and the entire area was inadequately lighted. This, according to the court, was ample evidence that the hotel had negligently maintained the premises. *194th St. Hotel Corp. v. Hopf*, 383 So.2d 739 (Fla., 1980).

In *Cline v. Texas Hotel*, 392 S.W.2d 594 (Tex., 1965), the plaintiff attended a luncheon along with several hundred other persons. When she left her table, she slipped and fell on the floor, sustaining severe and permanent injuries. She claimed that the type of floor was exceedingly slippery and therefore unsafe. However, she admitted that she had attended many luncheons in the same room and knew that the floor was always "slick" and slippery. For this reason, the court denied her recovery. When as here a plaintiff knows and appreciates the existence of a dangerous condition, plaintiff must take her own precautions to avoid injury.

Foreign Substances on the Floor

Many slippery floor accidents in a dining room, restaurant, or snack bar result from a foreign substance on the floor. As with all negligence cases, the restaurant is not liable unless it failed to exercise reasonable care. Often key in these cases is whether defendant was aware or should have been aware of the existence on the floor of the substance. That was the issue in the following case, which also illustrates once again the principle that a restaurant is not an insurer. Rather, it is liable only if it fails to exercise reasonable care. If the restaurant regularly inspects the floor for spilled or dropped substances and cleans the floor when such substances are found, and someone is nonetheless injured, the restaurant will not be responsible.

CASE EXAMPLE 6–6

Stout v. Restaurant Concepts, Inc.
487 S.E.2d 636 (Ga., 1997)

Gail Stout appeals the trial court's grant of summary judgment to Restaurant Concepts, Inc., doing business as Applebee's Neighborhood Grill

& Bar, in her slip and fall case. Her complaint alleged that when she "left her table which was located in a dimly lit and elevated dining area which could only be exited by traversing a three step tier approximately three feet across" and "moved from the last step to the floor level, in one motion both of her feet went out from under her and she fell to the masonry floor and landed in a wet, greasy puddle that was concealed in the darkness." . . .

Applebee's answered denying liability, and later moved for summary judgment. The motion contended Applebee's had no knowledge of any foreign substance on its floor, Stout did not know what caused her fall, and Stout failed to exercise ordinary care for her own safety. . . .

Mr. Stout's affidavit stated that while he did not see his wife fall, he heard the commotion and helped her up. After she got up, he saw a grease spot on the floor and saw employees of Applebee's cleaning up the spot where his wife fell. . . . Mr. Stout further stated that before his wife's fall, food was continuously carried over the steps to the area where they were seated.

The affidavit of the Applebee's manager on duty that night stated that she had "walked and inspected the entire restaurant" and went into the kitchen for about five minutes when she came out and saw Stout being assisted to her feet. She stated that the steps where Stout fell are wooden with nonskid safety strips and that the floor at the bottom of the steps is tile. She also stated that Applebee's has a policy for inspecting and cleaning the premises by the manager, waiters, and waitresses "constantly monitoring for potentially dangerous conditions, cleaning up, picking up and sweeping the floor as needed." She further stated that this policy was in effect and implemented the night Stout fell as she had visually inspected and monitored the floor throughout the evening.

Additionally, as part of the Applebee's closing procedures, the area had been inspected and cleaned within 20 minutes of Stout's fall, and the manager had again inspected the area about five minutes before Stout fell. The manager further stated that after Stout's fall, she again inspected the area and did not see any foreign substance or debris on the floor; the floor was not wet or greasy.

Another Applebee's employee also provided an affidavit which stated that on the evening in question he had been waiting tables in the area where Stout was sitting, and within five minutes of the time she fell he had walked through the area, visually inspected it, and saw nothing on the floor. He also confirmed the manager's affidavit concerning the implementation of Applebee's inspection and cleaning program that night. . . .

Plaintiff contends the court erred by granting summary judgment to defendant. . . .

[T]o prevail, a plaintiff must show that the owner or proprietor was aware of the substance or would have known of its presence had he exercised reasonable care. . . . Normally a proprietor is permitted a reasonable time to exercise care in inspecting the premises and maintaining them in a safe condition. . . . Applebee's carried its burden with the affidavits from its employees who stated that they had inspected the area shortly before Stout fell and saw no substance on the floor. . . .

Stout failed to carry her burden in responding to Applebee's motion for summary judgment, and the trial court did not err by granting judgment for Applebee's.

CASE QUESTIONS

1. How important to the outcome of the case was the restaurant's floor inspection and cleaning policy?
2. Assuming that plaintiff could prove that she in fact fell on a greasy spot, an allegation disputed by Applebee's, and the grease resulted from spilled food, would the restaurant have been liable for her injuries? Why or why not?

A plaintiff who slipped on a scoop of ice cream dropped by another customer two to four minutes prior to the fall was unsuccessful in her lawsuit against the proprietor for damages because there was insufficient time to discover the unsafe condition. *Schnuphase v. Storehouse Markets*, 918 P.2d 476 (Utah, 1996).

Importance of Enforcing a Policy of Frequent Floor Cleaning

A restaurant may be able to establish that it exercised reasonable care and thus was not negligent where it enforces a policy of frequent inspections of the floor to ensure it is free from spilled foods or beverages. A restaurant was saved from liability for a diner's fall on an unidentified wet spot because of the restaurant's procedure of inspecting the floors of the entire restaurant every 30 minutes. *Daniel v. John Q. Carter Enterprises, Inc.*, 460 S.E.2d 838 (Ga., 1995).

Similarly, judgment was entered against a plaintiff who fell in a restaurant on a lemon peel because of the restaurant's policy and practice that all waiters inspect for foreign substances on the floor and, if they find anything, they pick it up, and that a busboy is always assigned to constantly check for such items during meal periods. *Kauffmann v. Royal Orleans, Inc.*, 216 So.2d 394 (La. 1968). See also *Ochlockonee Banks Restaurant, Inc. v. Colvin*, 700 So.2d 1229 (Fl., 1997) in which a country and western dancer slipped and fell at a restaurant while "spinning and twirling around the dance floor" resulting in a broken ankle. Testimony from the restaurant established that it had a strictly enforced policy that drinks were not allowed on the dance floor; employees monitored the dance floor to ensure patrons did not enter it with drinks; and any spills that did occur were immediately cleaned. This testimony contributed to the appellate court's reversal of a jury verdict in favor of plaintiff.

Where a restaurant has a policy of floor cleaning procedures that ensures safe, nonslippery floors, but the restaurant fails to adhere to that policy, an inference may be drawn that the restaurant was negligent. *BBB Service Co. v. Glass*, 491 S.E.2d 870 (Ga., 1997).

To help avoid liability, hospitality facilities should develop floor maintenance policies designed to achieve floors that are safe for their customers' use. But a policy alone will not suffice to avoid liability. Strict adherence to the policy is necessary for a hotel or restaurant to establish it exercised reasonable care when sued by a guest who trips on the floor.

Placement of Chairs and Tables

If tables in a dining room are so close together that walking between them is difficult, a diner may foreseeably be injured. While exceeding the maximum number of diners that can comfortably be accommodated in a restaurant may be appealing from an income vantage point, it can lead to damages that easily negate any additional profit the extra number of diners might generate. Restaurants and hotels must take precautions to avoid overcrowded dining rooms. The next case addresses the question: How close is too close to place the tables? Note also the discussion about **expert witnesses**, that is, witnesses with superior knowledge about a subject due to education and/or experience.

CASE EXAMPLE 6–7

LaPlante v. Radisson Hotel Co.
292 F.Supp. 705 (Mich., 1968)

. . . Simply stated, the question is whether a jury may find a hotel negligent and an injured plaintiff free from contributory negligence where the hotel, in hiring itself out to stage a banquet for 1,200 paying guests in one of its banquet rooms, allegedly set the banquet tables so close to each other as to leave inadequate aisles and room between seated guests, causing the plaintiff to trip over a chair when attempting to leave the room and thereby injuring herself.

[T]he plaintiff, a semiretired school teacher, sixty-seven years of age, was a guest at the defendant's hotel for the purpose of attending the national convention of a professional education sorority of which she was a member. The convention meetings and related banquets were all held at the defendant hotel.

On August 10, 1967, the convention staged its final banquet, and the plaintiff was in attendance. . . .

Long tables, seating twelve to eighteen persons each, were placed at preset distances apart, which the defendant claims was forty-two inches though the jury could find from evidence the plaintiff introduced that the actual distance between tables was somewhat less. Further, there was evidence that at least at some of the tables, the chairs were back to back to those at the next table. . . .

There was testimony that waitresses were unable to move down the aisles between the long tables, and at the table at which the plaintiff was seated, the plates of food were passed down by the waitresses from person to person from the end of the table. The hotel manager testified this was not a good practice, and he did not permit it, if discovered. . . .

The banquet began at 8:00 P.M., and the plaintiff came to the hall and selected a seat about in the middle of one of the long tables.

Several hours later, at approximately 11:15 P.M., before the banquet program was over and while the lights were dimmed, with a spotlight on the head table . . . the plaintiff decided to leave the banquet hall to meet her son-in-law as prearranged. Moving sideways, she negotiated a path between chairs as the various people moved in toward the table to accommodate her. The jury could find that not realizing the position of the final chair, and believing she had negotiated herself to the main aisle, plaintiff caught her foot on the leg of that last chair and tripped and fell, injuring herself. Based on this evidence and the medical testimony as to the extent of her injuries, the jury awarded plaintiff the sum of $3,500. . . .

The defendant contends that since there was no violation of any statute or ordinance pleaded nor proved, the burden was on the plaintiff to show by expert testimony or otherwise the standard of care to which the defendant's conduct should have conformed. . . .

The issue becomes one of whether a jury should be permitted, without expert testimony, to draw upon their own knowledge, background, and common experience to determine what the standard of care should be and, hence, whether any departure therefrom occurred.

Certainly the nature of the case is not scientifically complicated nor technical. While some training and experience in catering and hotel management may be a necessary prerequisite to the handling of a banquet for 1,200 people, the court is of the view that such training or background is not [indispensable] to the ability to determine what is unreasonable crowding and what is not. The lay juror, knowing no more than the next person about catering procedures, could determine from the evidence in this case whether or not the tables were too close for safety. . . . The rule of evidence applied in determining the appropriateness of opinion "expert testimony" is whether the subject involved is so distinctively related to some science, profession, business, or occupation as to be beyond the ken of the average layman. Here the court is not convinced that expert testimony was required or would necessarily have been helpful to the jury. . . .

The jury could find that the hotel reasonably could foresee that during a banquet commencing at 8:00 P.M. and lasting until after 11:00 P.M., a number of people would leave the hall to go to the restrooms or for other purposes; that with a program in progress, the lights might well be dimmed and vision made more difficult; and that with the crowded or overcrowded conditions, such a fall as occurred might be anticipated. . . .

Ruling of the Court: . . . Judgment for plaintiff.

CASE QUESTIONS

1. Do you agree that the injuries in this case were foreseeable by the hotel? Why or why not?

2. Do you agree that an expert witness was not necessary in this case? Why or why not?

Hanging Mirrors in Dining Rooms

Large plate glass mirrors in a dining room are another factor that can cause injury. A restaurant must be vigilant to ensure such mirrors remain securely attached. In *Deming Hotel Company v. Prox*, 236 N.E.2d 613 (Ind., 1968), a wall mirror measuring 3.5 x 7 feet fell on a guest and severely injured her. She sued the restaurateur claiming res ipsa loquitur. The court upheld the application of that doctrine because the mirror was under the restaurant's exclusive control and management, and the injury would not have occurred if proper care had been exercised.

Ceilings

Improperly built or supported ceilings is another condition that can cause significant injuries and give rise to liability. The following case illustrates this point.

CASE EXAMPLE 6–8

Bank of New York v. Ansonia Associates
656 N.Y.S.2d 813 (Sup. Crt., 1997)

. . . On May 12, 1990, the ceiling collapsed in the croissant shop located in a West Side [of New York City] landmark building. One patron, Miriam Rosa Toigo was killed, and a number of others were injured; thirteen plaintiffs in all have commenced suit. The defendants included owners of the premises, architects, contractors, builders and others. . . .

Evidence established, and both sides' experts agreed that the ceiling which caused the plaintiffs' injuries was a disaster waiting to happen. This is because suspended from the plaster ceiling above the croissant shop were ducts weighing 600 pounds, air conditioners weighing over 200 pounds, a sprinkler system weighing over 1000 pounds, and a hung acoustical tile ceiling, none of which were attached to any structural support other than the plaster ceiling. There was testimony from which it could be found that the owners had numerous opportunities to discover and remedy this dangerous condition over the years. There was also testimony of warning signs such as a falling chunks of plaster, and falling debris.

There was more than ample evidence supporting the jury's finding of negligence. . . .

Serving Flambé Foods

Flaming dishes such as cherries jubilee and baked Alaska add an element of excitement to a menu and a dining room. As the next case tragically illustrates, they also add an element of danger and must be handled with great care if attempted at all. Note in the latter part of the decision the court's discussion on calculating damages.

CASE EXAMPLE 6–9

Young v. Caribbean Associates, Inc.
358 F.Supp. 1220 (V.I., 1973)

This is a tort and breach of warranty action tried by the court without a jury. [Breach of warranty means that a guaranty made by a seller of goods has been broken.] A father and his ten-year-old son seek recovery for mental anguish suffered by the father and bodily injuries suffered by the son brought about in unusual circumstances. The son, Francis Howard Young, was staying with his parents at the defendant, Caribbean Beach Hotel. On New Year's Eve, 1969, the family was having dinner in the hotel dining room. At the end of the meal, the son volunteered to go through the dessert serving line to bring a cherries jubilee for his father. As the son reached the head of the serving line, the waiter in charge of flaming and serving the cherries jubilee found it necessary to kindle the flames by adding more rum to the chafing pan. He took a bottle of hundred-and-fifty-one proof rum, which was stoppered with a narrow "slow pour" spout, and proceeded to pour the rum directly into the pan. As he did so, the spout either dropped out or was popped out by an internal combustion in the rum bottle, and a quantity of volatile rum gushed out. An abnormally high flame resulted that reached out to touch the boy, setting his shirt on fire. The boy suffered severe burns and has undergone considerable treatment for skin and flesh

grafts and plastic surgery. The . . . complaint requests $200,000 compensatory damages for the son and $19,912 medical expenses for the father. The complaint [bases] recovery principally upon negligence of all defendants [the hotel, the serving waiter, and Sears, Roebuck & Company which sold plaintiff the shirt he was wearing], but the breach of warranty . . . allegations were aimed primarily at Sears, Roebuck & Company, the vendor of the allegedly highly flammable boy's shirt.

Initially, and regrettably, I must disallow the father's claim of damages for mental anguish. The anguish of seeing one's ten-year-old son in flames must be horrible and nightmarish, and the continuing anguish of seeing, hearing, and sympathetically feeling the child's ensuing pain and suffering must be, to say the least, debilitating and depressing. However, the general rule is that where the defendant is guilty of no more than negligence, a third party may recover only if he had some fear for his own safety. . . . Perhaps the basis for the rule is a belief that the defendant otherwise owed (and breached) no duty to an unthreatened bystander; or, as a secondary but perhaps preferable explanation, a fear that the causal chain to the bystander will grow so attenuated [weak] that liability will be out of proportion to the wrong. For these reasons, the rule applies even where the bystander is a parent of the victim and so might be expected to suffer particularly deep and genuine anguish . . .

the father has no recovery for what I believe to be an experience of genuine anguish.

The father's right to recover his expenditures for medical expenses and the son's right to recover compensatory damages for his bodily injuries are clear. The hotel is, at the very least, accountable for its serving waiter's negligence in using an improperly stoppered bottle, which permitted the "slow pour" spout either to fall out or pop out, thereby discharging a large quantity of volatile rum. Moreover, as the evidence tended to show, the hotel's serving waiter was negligent in the first place in pouring the rum directly from the bottle and not from an intermediary bowl or pitcher. An experienced maitre d'hotel and chef testified that to pour directly from a bottle was to invite the flame to catch onto the stream of rum and leap from the chafing pan to ignite the vaporous gases inside the bottle, blowing out the cork and turning the bottle into a veritable "flame thrower" or "blowtorch," capable of throwing a flame ten to fifteen feet. Although I need not decide that this in fact did happen, I do find that it was negligent to pour directly from the bottle and not from an intervening bowl or wide mouth pitcher. In a sense, the dessert waiter does not seem morally culpable, for he had not been trained in the proper handling of flambés. Nonetheless, he and his employer should be responsible for the injuries caused to the boy, no matter how inadvertently they came about.

I further find that the negligence of the hotel and its serving waiter was the sole and proximate cause of plaintiff's injuries. The hotel for a time relied in part on the theory that the boy's shirt was itself highly flammable as evidenced by the vigor with which it burned, and that this was an important intervening cause of the holocaust that developed. With this theory in mind, . . . the hotel [sued] Sears, Roebuck & Company. . . . At the trial, however, a written statement of the waiter was produced that indicated that a substantial quantity of the rum had gushed directly onto the boy's shirt. This itself would be more than enough to support the combustion, no matter what the flammability of the shirt fabric might be. [The alleged flammability of the shirt was thus not the proximate cause of the plaintiff's injury.] The . . . complaint against Sears was therefore dismissed. . . . The action then proceeded against the serving waiter and the hotel alone. I also find that the boy was not guilty of contributory negligence. Although there was some testimony indicating that he was warned to stand back, the warning would have been, at the very best, an insufficient caution to a normal boy of plaintiff's age.

With the question of liability settled, I must now address myself to the matter of damages. The father's medical expenses, and reasonably related outlays, have totaled some $12,352.08 to date. In addition, some further surgery will be needed in order to minimize the burn scars on the boy's face and body. Although it is difficult for the medical experts to estimate the costs of these future contemplated operations, the uncontroverted estimate given at trial of $6,000 appears reasonable. The father's total [medical] damages would therefore come to approximately $18,352.08.

The most important and troublesome issue of damages is the award of compensable damages that must be granted to the son for his pain, suffering, permanent disfigurement, and the effect thereof upon his psyche and social adjustment. That his pain was considerable is unquestioned. The boy was on fire for more than several seconds before any one of the astonished bystanders came to his rescue. Before falling to the floor, he tried desperately to tear his shirt off. Finally, after perhaps a full half minute of time, one of the waiters came to his rescue with a tablecloth to snuff out the fire. The father actually saw his son on fire, but was unable to rush to his side because of the crowded dining room. When he reached his son, the waiters were already carrying the boy out of the dining room to the hotel office. An ambulance was called and soon the boy and his father were taken to the hospital emergency room. Supportive and anti-shock treatment was rendered. . . . Much of the treatment consisted of prevention of shock and infection that involved, among other painful manipulations and dressings, debriding of the dead skin tissue, which is a particularly painful process. Doctors are reluctant to give painkillers for fear of causing the patient to become addicted to drugs. The boy was released from the hospital on January 17, 1970, and was flown with a medical attendant to Washington, D.C.

At the Washington Hospital Center, several skin grafts were performed by Dr. Fry. On June 17, the boy was again admitted to the hospital for several injections of steroids into the hypertrophic scarred areas. Hypertrophic scarred areas are scars that are thickened and raised from the healthy, normal skin. There was hospitalization again in October 1970 for further operations to improve the scarred areas.

From my personal observations of the boy's scars, I would say that the scars on his right cheek and beneath his chin are unsightly, as are the scars on his chest and on the backs of both hands. The scar underneath the chin is actually a keloid [a thick scar resulting from excessive growth of fibrous tissue] and is red in color. There are two keloid formations on the chest. There was an attempt to remove one by excision, but the result was a scar worse than the one removed.

The doctor obtained skin for the skin grafts from the boy's left and right thighs. These areas are approximately six inches long and two and-a-half inches wide. These are called "donor sites" that will eventually become less noticeable, but . . . they may always appear as "patches."

The medical testimony was generally that the boy received second and third degree burns over 30 percent of his body's surface. The boy has no injuries to his organs, nor to his eyes. He can make a fist and move his fingers in the normal way. In sum, he has no physical disabilities. The doctors are of the opinion that the scars and keloid on the face and chest areas can be further improved by a combination of excision and injections. One doctor opined that surgery can make noticeable improvements and improve the boy cosmetically. However, there would have to be between three and five hospitalizations to achieve this improvement. The medical consensus is that time alone will show improvement on the scarred areas and that within a few years much of the scars should become less noticeable. . . .

It is no easy undertaking to make a judicial pronouncement that a certain damage award will fully compensate the boy for his pain, suffering and disfigurement. . . . I award the boy $80,000 and the father $18,352.08. . . .

CASE QUESTION

1. How might the result have been different if plaintiff was an adult rather than a ten-year-old boy?

A similar case is *St. Petersburg Sheraton Corporation v. Stuart*, 242 So.2d 185 (Fla., 1971). When the chef added the flambé to the cherries for the fourth time, he did not see any fire in the pan with the cherries. Apparently, however, there was a "little bit of flame that caught the liquid coming out of the bottle." Flames shot out and burned the plaintiff. The court said the chef was negligent and therefore liable for damages.

A restaurant that serves flambé dishes or does any type of tableside cooking with a flame must carefully train its employees on how to prepare the food safely, how to use the related cooking devices, and what to do in the event of a fire.

The court in *Young v. Caribbean Associates, Inc.* ruled that the father could not recover for the mental anguish because the general rule precludes a noninjured party from recovering unless that person had some fear for his own safety. Plaintiff was injured while he was in the serving line. At the time, his father was seated at a table and therefore was not in danger himself. Some states are beginning to allow recovery for mental anguish even in circumstances like the *Young* case where a noninjured relative is not at risk himself.

Serving Hot Liquids

A number of recent cases have involved circumstances where hot tea or coffee served by a restaurant spilled and injured someone. Given that we all expect tea and coffee to be served hot, the question becomes how hot is too hot? In a widely-publicized case, a woman was burned when coffee she purchased from McDonald's drive-through window spilled from its cup which she had placed between her legs while she was driving a car.

In a similar case, two cups of coffee were purchased from a drive-through window at a Burger King. They were served in cups fitted with lids placed in a cardboard container designed to hold four cups, with the two cups placed on opposite diagonal corners. In the front seat of the car was a father driving, a young son in the center, and the mother in the passenger seat. The mother sampled the coffee, found it too hot to drink, and returned the cup to the container which she then set on the floor. As the father made a left turn the coffee spilled causing second degree burns to the son's foot. In the resulting lawsuit, the Burger King restaurant claimed the coffee was served at 175 degrees as required by the Burger King franchisor, noting that customers expect their coffee to be served hot. The court, acknowledging that no duty to warn exists for an obvious danger, determined the issue in this case to be: whether the coffee was so exceedingly hot that serving it without a warning was unreasonable. The court determined this question to be one of fact for a jury to decide. Therefore summary judgment which had been rendered in favor of Burger King by the trial court was reversed and the case was referred to trial. *Nadel v. Burger King Corp.*, 1997 WL 266762 (Oh., 1997).

In another case a woman was scalded while eating in a Chinese restaurant when a teapot containing hot tea fell on her lap from the lazy susan on which the waitress had placed it. The woman claimed the restaurant was aware of at least one prior similar incident and was thus negligent for putting the teapot on the lazy susan rather than the table top. The restaurant claimed the water in the teapot was not unreasonably hot and the injury was not foreseeable. A jury rejected the restaurant's defenses and entered a verdict in favor of the injured plaintiff. That verdict was upheld on appeal. *Babish v. Hunon Szechwann Inn, Inc.*, 1997 WL 410720 (Oh., 1997)

From these cases we learn that it is foreseeable that customers may spill hot drinks purchased at a restaurant and liability can result if the drinks are so hot as to cause burns. The clear message is not to overheat tea, coffee, hot chocolate, and other drinks that must be served hot.

Summary

If a hotel or restaurant is negligent, it faces liability to injured patrons. To avoid liability, hotels and restaurants must be diligent in maintaining their premises in a safe condition. Liability can result from unclean rooms, broken furniture, poorly maintained windows, and unsafe electrical systems. Also exposing hotels and restaurants to lawsuits are uncontrolled rodents, deteriorated bathroom appliances, unsafe elevators, broken doors, improperly installed ceilings, dangerous steps, slippery floors, out-of-control flambé dishes, and excessively hot drinks.

To avoid liability, the establishments must exercise reasonable care to detect dangerous conditions by making regular and frequent inspections of all areas of the hotel or restaurant, correct defects soon after discovery, and properly train employees to perform their job responsibilities without causing injury to others.

Preventive Law Tips for Managers

- *Be sure guest rooms are thoroughly cleaned after each guest leaves and before the next guest is allowed access.* A guest has a legal right to expect the room to be in a clean and safe condition. Failure to clean it before the room is reassigned can result in injuries to the incoming guest, as in the case where the guest stepped on a discarded needle. Inadequate cleaning constitutes negligence and will likely result in liability on the hotel for any resulting injuries to the arriving guest.

- *Regularly inspect the furniture in guest rooms, lobby, and other public rooms to verify they are in good repair and able to withstand expected use.* A hotel may be liable for injuries resulting from collapsing beds and chairs, unsturdy stools, wobbly legs on desks or tables, and other furniture flaws that create risks of injury. These problems should be discovered during frequent inspections, and disabled furniture should be removed from service. Failure to detect and either remove or repair the broken items constitutes negligence.

- *Anticipate likely misuses of furniture and protect against them either by providing written warnings to guests or taking other action appropriate under the circumstances.* We read about a case in which a hotel was liable when a guest fell while standing on an unsteady dressing table stool to adjust the air conditioner knob. While the stool was not meant for standing on, this use was foreseeable given the height of the knob. Be alert to similar foreseeable misuses and take appropriate steps to prevent them.

- *If furniture is purchased unassembled, be sure the assembly is done correctly and no lose screws or other dangerous conditions result.* Furniture assembly requires a certain expertise. Be sure the assembly is done properly and consistent with accompanying instructions so that injury does not result. If an injury occurs, determine what the problem was, inspect all other like furniture still in service, and correct any similar problems.

- *Inspect windows to ensure the glass is not broken and is securely attached, fittings are in good working order, and screens, blinds, and curtains are securely affixed.* A hotel must ensure that the window fixtures in guest rooms and other public rooms are safe. The hotel can foresee that guests will be injured if window glass or fixtures are loose or otherwise unsafe. A regular regime of inspection and repair is necessary to avoid liability.

- *Maintain the heating and electrical systems in a hotel or restaurant in good repair.* The potential injuries from defects in these systems are devastating and require special attention. In-house employees may not have the required skills. Frequent maintenance and check-ups by a company specializing in heating and electricity may be required.

- *Develop a plan to minimize the chance of insects, rodents and other objectionable animals on the premises.* The plan should include: a) regular inspections for rat holes, beehives, and other telltale signs of unwanted critters; b) exterminators if needed; and c) additional precautions required by the particular circumstances of the establishment.

- *Regularly examine the bathroom appliances and check the water temperature to ensure the appliances and plumbing system are in good working order.* Numerous accidents occur in the bathroom. These can result from deteriorating faucets, toilet seats, stall doors, and faulty plumbing systems. Frequent inspections will alert management to unsafe conditions that need repair or replacement. Failure to detect defects and repair them will lead to liability for the hotel or restaurant.

- *Regularly inspect the lobby and other public rooms for unsafe conditions such as walkways blocked by luggage, bumps in rugs, intruders bothering guests, and repairs in progress.* Many people regularly use the lobby. Unsafe conditions will likely cause injury. Precautions must be taken to reduce risks of injury from conditions in the lobby and other public rooms.

- *Develop a maintenance plan for elevators including regular inspections by both in-house employees and a company specializing in elevator maintenance.* Virtually everyone in a sizeable hotel uses the elevators. A faulty elevator is likely to cause injury. As with the electricity and heating systems, the hotel or restaurant may not have the required expertise in-house. The elevator maintenance plan should include regular and frequent inspections by a company with the necessary skill to keep the elevators in good working order. Maintenance is required not just for the elevators used by guests but also for the service elevators.

- *Access to service elevators should be strictly limited.* Often a service elevator lacks amenities of the elevators used by guests and requires training for use. Access to the service elevators should be restricted to those employees who have received the necessary training. Guests and customers should not be allowed to use them. Precautions should be taken to restrict their access.

- *Inspect automatic doors regularly to ensure they are working properly.* Malfunctioning automatic doors will foreseeable cause injury. They should be inspected regularly and any operational problems corrected.

- *If a large, rowdy crowd is expected, increase security at the door and in the lobby.* A boisterous crowd is likely to push, shove, and run, causing injury to others in the vicinity. If such a crowd can be anticipated, the hotel must undertake crowd control efforts. Failure to do so will lead to liability if someone is injured by the unruly crowd.

- *Check stairs for conditions that can cause injury, including deterioration, obstructions, poor lighting, lack of railings, and inappropriate warning of a step's placement.*Countless accidents occur on steps, many of them avoidable. Frequent assessment of the safety of steps in the establishment can greatly decrease the number of incidents.

- *Inspect floors for dangerous conditions, including excessive polish or wax, worn spots, and spilled food or beverages.* Failure to detect and correct these conditions will foreseeable lead to injury and therefore liability. Dining room floors should be inspected before an event or meal. Service personnel should be alerted to inspect the floor for fallen food or debris throughout the meal and while diners are leaving. When selecting new floors, the slipperiness of the tile or covering should be considered.

- *Do not overbook your dining room or other facilities.* Overbooking leads to crowded, unsafe conditions in which guests and patrons may trip and be injured. If your facilities cannot comfortably accommodate an event, do not accept the booking. Clearly inform event planners of limitations on the number of attendees and hold firm to your maximum numbers.

- *Do not serve flambé dishes unless the proper serving utensils are used, emergency equipment is readily available, and your employees have been thoroughly trained on how to control and handle the flames and what to do in an emergency.* Flambé dishes, if not strictly controlled, can lead to serious injury and significant property destruction by fire. Precautions will reduce the chance of injury.

- *Do not serve hot liquids that are so hot as to cause burns.* While customers expect—indeed demand—their tea, coffee, and like drinks hot, remember that customers may spill their drinks on themselves or others nearby. Therefore, the temperature at which such beverages are sold should be such as not to cause burning in the event of a spill.

Review Questions

1. In what rooms of a hotel does the innkeeper's duty to exercise reasonable care apply?
2. What responsibility, if any, does an innkeeper have to maintain the lobby of a hotel in a safe condition?
3. What responsibility, if any, does an innkeeper have to maintain self-service elevators in a safe condition?
4. What risks are associated with flaming foods? What precautions should a restaurant take when serving them?
5. Why do many accidents occur in the shower? What can be done to reduce the number of them?
6. What precautions should a restaurant take when serving hot beverages?

Discussion Questions

1. Identify several circumstances in which liability can result to a hotel for failing to clean a room properly before assigning a new guest to it. State how the liability could be avoided.
2. Identify several circumstances in which liability can result to a hotel for failing to inspect and maintain the furniture in guest rooms properly. State how the liability could be avoided.
3. Identify several circumstances in which liability can result to a restaurant for failing to inspect and maintain the furniture in the dining room and lounge areas properly. State how the liability could be avoided.
4. Identify several circumstances in which liability can result to a hotel for failing to inspect and maintain the windows, window fixtures, and screens properly. State how the liability could be avoided.
5. Identify several circumstances in which liability can result to a restaurant for failing to inspect for and contain rodents, bugs, and animals properly. State how the liability could be avoided.
6. Identify several circumstances in which liability can result to a hotel for failing to inspect and maintain the bathrooms properly. State how the liability could be avoided.
7. Identify several circumstances in which liability can result to a restaurant for failing to inspect and maintain the bathroom properly. State how the liability could be avoided.
8. What precautions should a hotel take to avoid liability for its freight elevator?

Application Questions

1. Sandy is a diner at Reed's Restaurant. While eating, her foot is bitten by a rat. What evidence could Reed's present that might result in a judgment in its favor?

2. Barry is meeting friends at Peter's, a lounge on the thirty-fifth floor of a hotel. While Barry was riding the elevator, it malfunctioned and jerked to a stop. Barry was injured and sued the hotel. What evidence might the hotel introduce that could result in a judgment in its favor?

3. A Rotary Club, which is a service organization of business people, holds its weekly lunch meeting at the Iguana Restaurant. Approximately thirty people attend the luncheons. Must the Iguana provide a door attendant at the restaurant entrance for these luncheons? Why or why not?

4. In one episode of the popular television show "L.A. Law," the door to an elevator on an upper floor at the law firm was left open while the elevator was grounded on the first floor. No warning sign was posted. One of the characters, not realizing the elevator was not waiting at the door, stepped into the shaft and fell to her death. Should the law firm be liable? Why or why not? Does it matter whether or not the law firm owns the building? Why or why not?

5. Jan was a guest at the Hideaway Hotel. As she was walking from her room to the in-house restaurant for breakfast, a maintenance worker was washing the floor. Jan tripped on the wet floor and fell. Is the hotel necessarily liable in this case? Explain.

6. Assume you are the manager of a three story hotel that has stairs leading from all the floors and a raised lobby restaurant requiring guests to climb three steps. Also, the honeymoon suite has a sunken hot tub requiring users to step down four steps. What precautions should you take to avoid accidents on all of these steps.

7. You are the banquet manager at a party house. The guests at a large retirement party will start to arrive in twenty minutes. You are inspecting the premises to ensure everything is in order. What should you be looking for?

8. Ray was walking to the men's room at a restaurant and tripped on a banana peel. What additional facts do you need to know to determine if the resort is liable?

CHAPTER 7

Negligence and Hospitality Practices—Part 2

INTRODUCTION

The previous chapter identified various circumstances in which a hotel or restaurant may be liable for negligent acts. While the breadth of potential liability may have surprised you, it is in reality much greater. This chapter addresses additional situations that can lead to liability, including the condition of outside facilities, swimming areas, fires, security incidents, and medical service.

Duty Owed Guests Outside

A variety of conditions outside a hotel or restaurant can lead to liability if reasonable care is not exercised. These include, among others, valet service, sidewalks, handicap ramps, outdoor sporting facilities, and outdoor lighting.

Outside Door Service

When guests arrive at a hotel by car or taxi, they often stop in front of the establishment, where the door attendant takes their luggage and a valet parks the car. A hotel or restaurant is not, absent foreseeably rowdy circumstances, required to furnish door attendants or valets but if it does, the hotel or restaurant is liable if it is negligent. This rule is illustrated by the following case.

CASE EXAMPLE 7–1

Kurzweg v. Hotel St. Regis Corp.
309 F.2d 746 (N.Y., 1962)

Plaintiff, descending from a cab stopped in the second lane from the sidewalk in front of the Hotel St. Regis, was injured when a car nearer the curb backed up. She sued the owners of both vehicles and the hotel owner, alleging against the latter negligence of the hotel doorman. The hotel owner moved to dismiss the complaint [terminate the lawsuit in favor of defendant without a trial] for failure to state a claim on which relief could be granted. . . .

It is the hotel's contention that it was under no duty by New York law to furnish a doorman, and that therefore failure of the doorman to act cannot bring an action against it. But New York has held liable a person under no duty to act who voluntarily undertakes to act and causes injury through his negligent act. . . . [T]he complaint states a claim upon which relief can be granted. . . .

Grounds

When invitees use the sidewalk of a hotel or restaurant, they must take care where they walk. If they trip and fall due to an obvious defect, the hotel or restaurant will not be responsible. Thus, a wheelchair-bound restaurant patron who tried to maneuver around a trash barrel situated near the restaurant sidewalk, although she recognized passage would be "at best, a tight squeeze", was unable to recover for injuries she suffered when the barrel forced her to fall. *Spagnuolo v. Rudds #2 Inc. d/b/a/ McDonald's*, 221 Mich. App. 358, 561 N.W.2d 500 (Mi., 1997). If, however, the defect is not obvious, as in the following case, the hotel or restaurant may be liable.

CASE EXAMPLE 7–2

Sherman v. Arno
383 P.2d 741 (Ariz., 1963)

. . . The facts . . . are as follows: On March 30, 1958, plaintiff and a friend drove to the Flamingo Hotel for the purpose of lunching at the restaurant operated there. It was a bright sunny Sunday afternoon when they emerged from the restaurant at its south exit to go to plaintiff's car, which she had left in the parking lot across from this exit. There was a driveway between the building wall containing the exit and the parking lot, and because there was quite a bit of traffic on the driveway, she decided not to cross the drive until there was an open space between the moving cars and she had a clear view of her car. A paved walkway (hereinafter referred to as the "walk") ran parallel to and between the building and the driveway in a westerly direction till it met the public sidewalk about sixty-four feet from the exit.

Plaintiff was familiar with the hotel, but she testified that she had never used this walk before, nor had she previously even known it was there. While waiting for traffic on the driveway to clear, she moved along the walk toward the public sidewalk. About fifteen feet from the west end of the walk there was a single step down which plaintiff testified she did not notice or see as she came out of the restaurant. Because her attention was drawn to the automobiles passing by, she continued walking until, as she related at the trial:

"[Plaintiff]. Well, I was walking down the sidewalk and all of a sudden I just, there was not sidewalk there and my—did you want me to demonstrate?

"[Question]. No, just tell us, describe it as best you can.

"[Plaintiff]. I took a step. All I knew, I was just down and I had fallen and hit the edge of my hip against the cement edge of that step."

That plaintiff was severely injured from her fall is not the issue here.

The walk itself is a terra cotta (reddish) color and was "glaring bright" in the afternoon sun on the day in question, according to plaintiff's testimony. Although the sidewalk is relatively level, there is one step at the south exit from the restaurant and two more steps where the west end of the walk intersects with the public sidewalk, in addition to the step where plaintiff's accident occurred. The step where plaintiff fell is approximately four to five inches in height. The riser is painted white and is visible as one approaches from the west, but not from the east as plaintiff approached it. A single white strip, about an inch and a half wide, is painted along the top or nose of the step across the walk. . . . Exhibit 4, a photograph of the step, taken some time after the accident, shows that the white stripe on the step is nearly worn off. The plaintiff testified:

"[Question]. Exhibit 4, Miss Arno, shows a strip of white paint or what has been a strip of white paint along the upper edge of that step. Can you tell us whether or not there was any paint on that step that day as you approached it?

"[Answer]. Well, I can almost positively say there wasn't any paint visible at all."

The basis of plaintiff's action was that defendants were negligent in the construction and design of the step in having it placed in such an unusual and unexpected place on the walk; that they had neglected to keep the white paint on the step properly maintained; and that they were negligent in not having some type of warning to users of the walk that a step was located there.

Defendants maintained, however, that they had exercised the entire duty required of them to use due care in making and maintaining the premises reasonably safe for the customers, and that as the step was openly and obviously visible, no warning was required to be given to any users of the walk. . . .

Here the step upon which plaintiff stumbled was approximately two-thirds of the way down a long walk, and not at the entrance to any building or a mere step down to a parking area or another sidewalk. . . .

There was further evidence that even though designing and building the step in such a place may not have constituted negligence, the step may have been negligently maintained. The photographic exhibits in evidence show that there were at least some times when the paint on the step was so worn that it could but barely be discerned, and plaintiff testified that it was not visible at the time of her fall. . . . This evidence, combined with the fact that there were no other signs or warnings of a step, might properly have been considered in determining negligence on the part of the defendants.

As to the [hotel's] claim that the condition, if dangerous, was open and obvious, we need only examine the location of the step and its relation with the conditions of its surrounding environment. It is evident that the step would be obvious to one traveling the walk toward the step, with the rise in view, in the opposite direction from that in which the plaintiff was walking. However, moving in the same direction as was the plaintiff, the walk could have a "deceptively level appearance." There was evidence that the walk was the same color on both levels; that the white paint on the top of the step was completely worn; that the red terra cotta walk was bright and glary, especially to one just coming out of a building into the bright sunshine

of an afternoon in Tucson, Arizona. The jury might reasonably have inferred a person using this sidewalk might be distracted from the place where he was walking while observing cars passing in the driveway, especially if, as in plaintiff's case, his car was in the parking lot across the drive and he was looking for a place to cross to it, and . . . defendants could have foreseen this. . . .

The jury was adequately instructed on all points concerning the duty of the defendants, as owners of the premises, toward the business invitee. The court explained that a possessor of premises is not an insurer of the safety of business invitees, but is only required to exercise ordinary care to maintain the premises in a reasonably safe condition. The court also stated that the owner is not required to give an invitee notice or warning of an obvious danger existing on the premises, and that if the jury found the condition either obvious or reasonably apparent to an ordinary prudent person in plaintiff's position, then the jury should find for defendants.

Ruling of the Court: [Judgment for plaintiff upheld].

CASE QUESTION

1.   What could the hotel have done to avoid liability?

In *Pincus v. Kiamesha Concord, Inc.*, 263 N.Y.S.2d 895 (1965), the court ruled the plaintiff could not recover when, while taking a shortcut over railroad ties on defendant hotel's premises, he stepped on one that had rotted away, falling and injuring himself. This case is unlike the *Sherman* case because in *Sherman* the plaintiff had the right to assume the sidewalk was safe and conformed to normal engineering principles. In *Pincus* the plaintiff could not assume the railroad ties were safe. Rather, the danger presented by railroad ties is obvious, relieving the hotel of liability.

Other areas of concern on the grounds of a hotel or restaurant include walkways, ramps, and parking lots. The establishment should inspect these areas regularly. If obstructions such as stones, woodchips, or debris are found, they should be removed immediately. Cracks and holes should be repaired. Other unsafe conditions should be eliminated.

A design defect in a handicap ramp at a hotel resulted in a dropoff between the end of the ramp and the road. A guest tripped and fell on the ramp while walking to the parking lot due to the dropoff. The court declined to find that the defect was open and obvious and thus refused to dismiss the case on the hotel's motion for summary judgment. *Anderson v. Turton Development*, 225 Ga. App. 270, 483 S.E.2d 597 (Crt. App. Ga., 1997).

Outdoor Sporting Facilities

Many resorts owe their popularity to outside activities and sports they offer. Are such resorts liable for injuries sustained by a guest while using the sporting facilities? The hotel owes to its guests a duty of reasonable care in the maintenance of all its sports facilities. Even in states that continue to follow the rule of assumption of risk (see discussion on that doctrine in Chapter 5), a guest does not assume the risk that the inn will fail to maintain the sporting facility in a condition that makes it reasonably safe for the guest. Such failure on the part of the hotel will result in liability.

In *Bazydlo v. Placid Marcy Co., Inc.*, 422 F.2d 842 (2nd Cir., 1970), a guest received injuries while using a toboggan slide provided by the hotel. The toboggan jumped from the run and struck a steel pole because the hotel failed to maintain the sidewalls of the run sufficiently to turn the toboggan away from obstructions. The hotel argued that the plaintiff, while utilizing the run, assumed the risk of injury. The court disagreed, saying that despite the assumption of some risk, the plaintiff still had the right to rely on the duty owed by the hotel to maintain the run in a reasonably safe condition. It was the hotel's failure to do so that caused the injury and therefore created liability.

In another case, the plaintiff brought suit against the inn for injuries sustained while ice skating at the resort's rink. Plaintiff alleged that the ice on the rink was defective and dangerous and that the defendant had actual or constructive notice of this. The jury held for defendant, apparently finding that the ice was not in a defective condition or, if it was, the condition should have been obvious to plaintiff, or the inn's operators did now know and reasonably could not have been expected to know about it. *Callahan v. Buck Hill Inn and Golf Club*, 409 N.Y.S.2d 416 (1978).

Resort hotels often offer bicycles for their guests' use. Precautions are necessary and regular periodic inspections should be done to ensure the bikes are in good working order. Bikes should not be issued to a child unless accompanied by a responsible adult. The bikes should be equipped with horns, reflectors, and, if used at night, lights. No more than one person should be permitted to ride the bike at once.

Play areas may also be provided by a hotel or restaurant. Injuries and liability can result from careless selection of equipment, faulty assembly, haphazard placement, and infrequent inspection.

Outdoor Lighting Requirements

The high cost of energy makes it easy to understand why a hotel or restaurant might be tempted to reduce outdoor lighting. Yet even when only a few rooms are rented, the motel itself and any area used by the public must be properly lighted. How much is enough light? The case of *Bowling v. Lewis*, 261 F.2d 311 (4th Cir., 1958), is a good example of a situation where the attempt to save a few dollars on lighting led to a guest's injury and a lawsuit.

The facts are simple. As stated by the court,

> The . . . plaintiff, who was vacationing with his wife and two small children at an ocean front motel, arrived on a Sunday afternoon and used the walk several times until the following Tuesday, when he and his family spent the early evening in an amusement area and returned to the motel when it was very dark and the walk was unlighted. The plaintiff had . . . 18 years' experience driving buses and had very good night vision. He remained in his car with the headlights on to illuminate the walk for his wife and children, and when they had reached the room, he turned off the headlights, waited momentarily to give his eyes an opportunity to adjust to the dark, and proceeded very cautiously along the walk but, nevertheless, tripped over a 10-inch stone in the walk.

Was the guest contributorily negligent by going to his room in the dark? The court ruled that:

> Under the circumstances a guest or lodger is deemed guilty of contributory negligence in using a dark or unlighted stairway or in using a dark or unlighted passageway, as in instances where lighted stairways, or the means of providing light, are available to him. On the other hand, . . . a guest cannot be charged with contributory negligence or assumption of risk merely because he uses a darkened stairway where the elevator is out of commission and the stairway is the only means available for passing between the room and the ground floor, or where, on instructions from an employee, he uses an insufficiently lighted hallway, but exercises care; . . .

Plaintiff was not negligent in this case. He was using the only available means of ingress to his room. There was no one present from whom he could have requested help. He was familiar with the concrete walkway and knew its location; he and his family had used it as a means of ingress and egress several times since their arrival. Plaintiff's wife and the children had safely proceeded along this walkway immediately before the accident. Plaintiff thus had every reason to believe that he could safely negotiate it.

The case of *Rappaport v. Days Inn of America Corp.*, 250 S.E.2d 245 (N.C., 1979), also addresses the duty of a hospitality facility to properly illuminate parking lots. Plaintiff, an eighty-two-year-old woman, fell in the defendant's parking lot as she attempted to go to her room in the darkness. She tripped because she failed to see a six- or seven-inch step up to the walk from the parking lot surface, which was not illuminated in any way. The jury found for plaintiff. An innkeeper is under a duty to keep the premises, including the parking lot, in a reasonably safe condition so as not to expose guests to danger unnecessarily.

Outdoor light fixtures should be inspected daily. If they are not in good working order they should be repaired without delay.

Electronic timers that control exterior lighting must be reset when daylight savings time begins and ends. If clocks are not adjusted immediately, the timing of the lights will be off by an hour and guests may not have adequate light.

Duty Owed Guests in Swimming Areas

Countless millions of Americans swim, and the proliferation of swimming pools at hotels, motels, and clubs has made swimming very accessible to travelers. A swimming pool presents hoteliers with a difficult dilemma. It helps to attract business, but it has high maintenance, energy, and labor costs, and it exposes the hotel to another area of liability. Many states have stringent pool rules that must be followed. Failure to abide by them can lead to liability for pool accidents, as can negligence on the part of the pool operator.

Swimming pool accidents are caused by wet floors, unsafe diving boards, inadequate safety equipment, inadequate supervision, and a variety of other factors.

Exercise Reasonable Care

Consistent with our general principles of negligence, a hotel is not an insurer of guests' safety in and around a hotel pool. The hotel is only liable if it fails to exercise reasonable care. In *McKeever v. Phoenix Jewish Community Center*, 374 P.2d 875 (Ariz., 1962), the ten-year-old daughter of the plaintiff drowned while playing in a pool with her siblings. The shallow area was roped off but the children jumped into the deep end and scurried back to the shallow area several times while playing. The deceased had been left by her father for roughly five minutes when the accident occurred. The trained lifeguard on duty did everything in his power to effect her rescue. All necessary and required safety devices for swimmers were on hand. The court rejected plaintiff's attempt to use the doctrine of res ipsa loquitur and, therefore, plaintiff had to prove all elements of negligence against the defendant. Not surprisingly, the plaintiff lost; negligence had not been established on the defendant's part. The operator of a pool must keep it in a safe condition, have safety equipment available, and, depending on the circumstances and state or local law, have qualified personnel on hand; this the defendant did.

In another pool case, plaintiff was a guest at the Holiday Inn Motel. He was injured when he did a "pike dive" from the side of the pool between the eight-foot and five-foot depth markers. In such a dive the diver enters the water head first, with arms and hands extended above the head in as nearly a vertical position as possible. It is considered a deep water dive. The plaintiff had been a guest for several days and had used the pool during that time. The court decided that the plaintiff was negligent because he knew that the bottom of the pool sloped and that special facilities were available for diving in the pool at the deep end. *Kalm v. Hawley*, 406 S.W.2d 394 (Ky., 1966).

Introduce No New Hazards

A hotel may be liable for leaving maintenance equipment in the vicinity of the pool. In the case of *Tucker v. Dixon*, 355 P.2d 79 (Colo., 1960), the owners permitted pool-cleaning equipment, including large, heavy floats, to remain beside the pool. The evidence showed that the floats were sometimes used as playthings in the pool. The eleven-year-old plaintiff-guest went swimming upon her arrival at the motel. When surfacing from a dive, she hit one of the floats and was injured. The court held for plaintiff because the motel should have known the floats were used in the pool. The motel was negligent for failing to move the cleaning equipment to a place where it would not be easily accessible to swimmers.

Comply With Statutory Requirements

Failure to comply with safety requirements imposed by statutes on pool operators can result in liability under the doctrine of negligence per se.

Modifications Can Create Hazards.   The following is a landmark case that underscores the importance of a pool operator abiding by applicable safety laws both when the pool is first designed and constructed, and during its ongoing use and maintenance. The pool operator must comply with safety laws when repairs and modifications are made. Failure to comply with these laws can lead to terrible consequences for both a patron who is injured as well as the hotel.

CASE EXAMPLE 7–3

Hooks v. Washington Sheraton Corp.
578 F.2d 313 (D.C. Cir., 1977)

This case arose out of the injuries suffered by eighteen-year-old Thomas Hooks when he dove from the three-meter diving board at the Sheraton Park Hotel in Washington, D.C., in June 1971. The pool was equipped with a high performance aluminum "Duraflex" board that propelled Hooks, who was not an experienced diver, into shallow water where he struck his head on the bottom. As a result, Hooks is a quadriplegic. Hooks and his parents sued the operator of the pool, the Washington Sheraton Corporation (hereafter Sheraton) and its parent, ITT, alleging negligence in the construction and operation of the pool. Specifically, plaintiffs alleged that the depth of the water in the diving area of the pool did not comply with applicable District of Columbia regulations and that it was too shallow for a three-meter Duraflex diving board.

[A jury found for plaintiff, who was awarded $4,500,000; his parents were awarded $180,000.]

In its appeal from the finding of liability, Sheraton contends that the . . . court improperly instructed the jury on the standard of care owed by hotelkeepers to their guests, and on the issue of negligence per se. . . .

[W]e affirm the judgment.

The district court began its instructions on the issue of negligence by properly instructing the jury that:

"[T]he owner of a hotel is liable for failure to use reasonable care to keep safe such parts of the premises as he may retain under his control either for his own use or for the common use of the guests or tenants of the hotel.

"It is the duty of the tenants or guests to exercise ordinary care for their own safety. In other words, the owner of a hotel is not an insurer of the safety of his guests, but he does owe to them the duty to exercise reasonable care for their safety."

The court then proceeded to instruct the jury on the general law of negligence, negligence per se, contributory negligence, and assumption of risk. The court's reference to warranty came in the context of the instruction on assumption of risk:

"Before this rule [assumption of risk] is applied to defeat the plaintiff's claim, however, you must be satisfied by a preponderance of the evidence that the danger or hazard that caused the injuries of the plaintiff was open and apparent; that he was aware of it; or that in the exercise of reasonable care, should have been aware of it; and that he voluntarily exposed or subjected himself to whatever hazard or danger might reasonably have been involved.

"You are instructed that the owner or the operator of a hotel warrants to its patrons that the facilities of said hotel are safe for the use by its patrons, free from defects and dangerous designs, and that such facilities can be used in the use and manner for which they were intended without danger or risk of injury and that such facilities are reasonably fit and suitable for their intended use.

"When a patron of such a hotel uses such facilities in the manner and method they were intended to be used, he does not assume the risk of injury and is not chargeable with contributory negligence if he sustains an injury in so doing." [Emphasis added]

It is apparent from the language before and after the sentence relating to warranty that in this sentence the court was explaining to the jury that when using the defendant's pool in the manner for which it was intended, Thomas Hooks did not assume the risk of injury from defects or dangerous design of which he was not aware, and that he was entitled to rely on the hotel's representation that there were no such hidden perils. We think the jury could not have understood the one sentence, delivered in the course of seven pages dealing with negligence, to mean that the hotel owed an "absolute warranty of safety" to its guests. This we think is plain in light of the clear statement at the outset—that the hotel is not an insurer and that it owes its guests a duty of reasonable care. Accordingly, we reject the argument that the instruction improperly imposed upon Sheraton a duty to give its guests an absolute warranty of safety.

Sheraton also contends that the district court erred in instructing the jury on the issue of negligence per se. . . . At trial Hooks offered evidence from which the jury could conclude that the pool failed to meet District of Columbia regulations concerning the depth of water required to be directly under, as well as extending out from, the end of the three-meter diving board.

. . . In an effort to explain any violations, Sheraton called Mr. Brink, the chief of the District of Columbia Bureau of Air and Water Quality, to testify that the plans for the pool had been approved by his bureau.

. . . Sheraton urges us to hold that its evidence of the approval of the plans, the custom of inspection during construction, and the issuance of the operating license for the pool was enough to negative the inference of negligence per se. We disagree.

Mr. Brink testified that he personally approved the plans for the pool in 1960. He also testified that it is the custom for inspectors to check compliance during construction, and that a license to operate the pool would not have been issued unless the pool had been built according to the plans. Mr. Brink did not testify from personal knowledge that the pool was so constructed, nor did anyone else. As it turned out, the pool was not so constructed. The approved plans called for a wooden diving board.

In 1968 Sheraton replaced the original board with a high-performance aluminum "Duraflex" board. Several experts, including the 1976 U.S. Olympic diving coach, testified that this type of board at the three-meter height is unsafe for the inexperienced divers likely to use a hotel pool. A college diving coach said that a "Duraflex" board "has a great deal more of elasticity and projects people higher in the air. . . . [I]f a person's balance is forward at the time [he leaves] that board, it's going to send him a lot farther out."

Moreover, the aluminum board extended five inches farther into the pool than the original wooden board. This seems at first a small modification, but it is of particular importance to the question whether the pool depths violated District of Columbia regulations. The regulations require ten feet of water directly under the board and extending out from it for twelve feet. Thereafter, the bottom may incline toward the surface at a rate of one foot of depth for every three feet of distance from the board. Obviously, as the board extends farther over the water, the distance from the end of the board to the point where the bottom inclines toward the surface is reduced. The area where the bottom slopes up is where the injury occurred. Finally, plaintiffs introduced evidence that on the day of the accident, the pool's water level was several inches low. This, too, would reduce the depth of the water under and out from the diving board. There was no showing that the District of Columbia approved these deviations from the plans approved by Mr. Brink in 1960. We conclude, therefore, that the negligence per se instruction given here was proper under the circumstances. . . .

Ruling of the Court: The judgment [in favor of plaintiff for $4,500,000 and in favor of his parents for $180,000.00] is affirmed.

CASE QUESTION

1.   How could the hotel have avoided liability in this case?

To avoid risks associated with diving boards many hotels have eliminated them. Similarly, pool slides have been removed from many hotels because of injuries caused both to the slider and to people in the pool hit by the slider.

Safety Equipment

Hotels with pools must maintain necessary safety equipment to rescue a swimmer experiencing difficulty in remaining afloat. A hotel was found liable for a guest's drowning where it provided a straight pole but not one with a hook at the end which is used to help raise a submerged swimmer to the surface. In *Harris v. Laquinta-Redbird Joint Venture*, 522 S.W.2d 232 (Tex., 1975), a swimmer at a hotel pool had sunk to the bottom. A rescuer, using the available pole which had no hook, was thus unable to lift him from the water. Instead they were limited to the slower process of pushing him to the shallow area for rescue. The swimmer died by the time the rescue was completed. A city ordinance required that all pools be equipped with a hooked pole. The hotel was found liable based on the doctrine of negligence per se. To avoid liability for this type of negligence, a business must carefully study applicable laws and regulations and do whatever is necessary to comply. If a hotel or restaurant is uncertain as to the meaning of a statute, clarification should be sought from an appropriate source such as the director of the government department responsible for enforcing the particular law or the hotel's attorney.

Act on Superior Knowledge of Dangers

In the following case, the lack of certain safety devices was known to both an injured guest and the hotel, but the hotel had superior knowledge of the danger presented by their absence. In such a case the hotel will be liable for resulting injuries.

Figure 7–1   How might a hotel become liable for negligence in the course of providing the services advertised here? How can liability by avoided?

CASE EXAMPLE 7–4

Coates v. Mulji Motor Inn, Inc.
342 S.E.2d 488 (Ga., 1986)

On April 28, 1981, the West Laurens High School tennis team registered to stay overnight at the Mulji Motor Inn while in Americus, Georgia, for a tennis tournament. Around 9:00 P.M., the entire tennis team, along with the coach and other adult chaperons, decided to go swimming in the motel pool. At approximately 9:15 P.M., seventeen-year-old Javis Coates, a member of the team, drowned.

No one in the group actually saw how the drowning occurred. One student testified that someone had grabbed and pulled him underwater twice; he had gotten out of the pool to complain to the coach about what he at first thought was an antic, and they then noticed Javis Coates in a fetal position on the bottom of the deep end of the pool. After retrieving Coates from the pool, they unsuccessfully attempted resuscitation.

Coates' parents commenced this action against the . . . Mulji Motor Inn, Inc. and the coach, alleging that their negligence resulted in the drowning death of Javis. Following trial of the case, the jury returned a verdict against the [hotel] for $60,000 in favor of the parents; it did not find the coach liable. The trial court, however, subsequently granted the hotel's motion for judgment notwithstanding the verdict. [Coates' parents appealed the judgment.]

Most of the material facts involving the circumstances of the drowning were not in dispute. The motel pool measured 20 feet by 40 feet and had a diving board at the deep end. At the time of the drowning, the pool was not equipped with overhead lights or a safety rope separating the deep and shallow ends. The various depths of the water were marked on the sides of the pool. Although an underwater light located in the deep end of the pool was operational, it was not on during the evening of April 28, 1981, and prior to the drowning the motel guests were unaware of its existence. When the group first went swimming, it was dusk but there still was some natural light; additionally, nearby artificial light provided some illu-

mination of the pool area. A low wall partially surrounding the pool may have cast some shadow over the pool. There was some dispute over the clarity of the water and the visibility of the bottom of the pool at the deep end. Two signs were in place in the immediate pool area, indicating that no lifeguard was provided and that guests swam at their own risk. . . .

[W]e will labor to retain intact the verdict returned by the jury to whom our system has entrusted the dispensing of justice. . . . Questions of negligence are "for the jury except in plain, palpable and indisputable cases, where reasonable minds cannot differ as to the conclusion to be reached."

The motel owner was required to exercise ordinary care in keeping the premises safe. He had a duty to guests to afford premises that are reasonably safe for use, and a duty to inspect which would render him liable for injuries caused by defects which would be disclosed by a reasonable inspection.

In part, [t]he basis of the proprietor's liability is his superior knowledge, and if his invitee knows of the condition or hazard there is no duty on the part of the proprietor to warn him and there is no liability for resulting injury because the invitee has as much knowledge as the proprietor does and then by voluntarily acting in view of his knowledge, assumes the risks and dangers incident to the known condition. It is thus a question of "equal knowledge."

The "knowledge" relates not only to the physical facts, but also to knowledge of the significance of the physical facts. . . . Knowledge includes not only knowledge of the physical condition which can be observed but also an appreciation and comprehension of the danger which the condition presents, . . . [I]n order for a plaintiff to recover, two elements must exist: (1) fault on the part of the owner, and (2) ignorance of the *danger* on the part of the invitee. . . .

Was there any evidence that the motel owner had a superior comprehension of the single or combined effect of the deficiencies in the operation of the pool on the dangers presented? Among those dangers were that there would not be a rope handy to hang on to in case a person could not swim or got into trouble, the swimmer could not be clearly and quickly seen nor perceived from his actions to be in trouble at the bottom of the pool, the swimmer could not clearly see where he was. There was evidence that the motel owner had operated the motel for over a year, had learned how to maintain the pool, knew that the underwater light was there and that it was in part a safety device, knew that there was a steep slope, was experienced in caring for the pool, had observed its use by guests under various conditions, used it himself, and was familiar with its characteristics.

From this background, the jury could find that the innkeeper had superior knowledge of the greater degree of dangerousness, the great risk, which the physical conditions presented.

CASE QUESTIONS

1. What did the court mean when it said, "We will labor to retain intact the verdict returned by the jury to whom our system has entrusted the dispensing of justice."?

2. Give two additional examples of circumstances where both an innkeeper and guest have equal knowledge of the existence of a defect but the innkeeper has superior knowledge of the dangers presented by that defect.

Comply with Pool Safety Procedures

In the following case we see that following safety policies concerning maintenance of swimming pools can protect a hotel from liability. This case, dealing with the unfortunate drowning of a 13 year old, illustrates clearly the difficult task a jury often has in deciding who is liable. As you read the case, determine whether you agree or disagree with the decision of the jury.

CASE EXAMPLE 7–5

Steele v. Inn of Vicksburg, Inc.,
697 So.2d 373 (Miss., 1997)

. . . Thirteen-year-old Tremayne Steele died as a result of a drowning accident in the swimming pool at the Inn. Tremayne was staying as a guest at the Inn with his baseball coach, Jay McKee, and Mr. McKee's son Patrick. Mr. McKee, Tremayne, and Patrick were attending the State Soccer Championship Tournament in Vicksburg, headquartered at the Inn, in which Patrick was participating. . . .

Holiday Inn has a rule requiring that its swimming pool water be kept clear. Mr. Pitzer, manager of the Inn, testified that he had noticed on the Friday before Tremayne's death that the water in the Inn's indoor swimming pool was cloudy due to the large number of children from the soccer tournament swimming in the pool. He had the water treated, but he knew that the water wouldn't clear up in a few hours or overnight. The Inn had a state-of-the-art filtering system and pump which operated continuously. Edmond Gibbs was in charge of maintaining the pool and tested the water regularly to make sure the pH, total alkalinity, calcium hardeners, and EEL reading (copper and ion levels) were all balanced. He also cleaned the pool regularly with a robot and cleaned the filter as needed.

Mr. Gibbs testified that on the day that Tremayne drowned, the pool water was chemically balanced. A pool can be chemically balanced and still be cloudy, but adding chemicals to a balanced water can cause skin and eye burning. The only way to clear up chemically balanced, cloudy water is to let the pool filtration system do its job. . . . While the Inn had the authority to close the pool because of the cloudy water on the weekend of the soccer tournament, Mr. Pitzer decided to leave it open because he did not consider the cloudiness to be a dangerous condition. Linda Marbury testified that she and other guests noticed that the pool water was cloudy on the day that Tremayne drowned, but she had no problem with her children swimming in the cloudy water. Mr. McKee testified that he did not notice the cloudiness while he was at the pool. . . .

Mr. McKee testified that he asked Tremayne if he could swim and that Tremayne said he could. Ms. Steele [Tremayne's mother] testified that Mr. McKee was aware that Tremayne wasn't supposed to swim in deep water and that Tremayne knew not to go in the deep end of the pool. . . .

While the boys were swimming there were signs posted stating that no lifeguard was on duty and to swim at your own risk. McKee and the other parents sat around the pool watching their children, visiting, and drinking beer. Tremayne was the only black child in the pool, so he was easy to spot. However, at some point, Mr. McKee looked up and realized that Tremayne and Patrick were gone. The last time he had seen Tremayne he was playing "Fish Out of Water" . . . a game in which a player cannot be "tagged out" as long as he stays under water. . . .

McKee checked the pool and didn't see either child, so he want back to their hotel room and found Patrick running in the halls. Ms. Steele testified that McKee told her that he was gone for thirty minutes while he put Patrick to bed. He then went to the game room looking for Tremayne. When he didn't find Tremayne in the game room,

Mr. McKee went back to the pool, and a few minutes later, some kids found Tremayne's body at the bottom of the pool. Another guest administered CPR to Tremayne, but was unsuccessful.

Dr. Frank McPherson testified that Tremayne's autopsy report listed the probably cause of death as drowning. He asserted that playing "Fish Out of Water" could cause a child to pass out and breathe reflexively, taking water into the lungs. It could also cause a child to hypoventilate and breathe in water. He stated that it only takes between four and six minutes for a person to die from drowning.

Upon returning to the Inn from the hospital where Tremayne was taken, Mr. Pitzer and Mr. Goodwin, the maintenance chief, tested the water. The tests revealed that all chemical readings were still normal. . . . Mr. McKee also testified that someone threw a penny into the pool, and they couldn't see the penny go to the bottom.

At trial, Ms. Steele's attorney alleged in closing argument that the Inn breached its duty of care toward Tremayne by failing to close the pool or warn of the dangerous condition caused by the cloudy water. He asserted that the cloudy water prevented people around the pool from seeing Tremayne while he was under water, and therefore prevented them from realizing that Tremayne was in trouble and rescuing him. The Inn's attorney argued that because it only takes between four and six minutes for a person to drown, it is speculation to claim that resuscitation efforts would have been more successful had it not been for the cloudy water. The Inn also based its defense on the theory that Mr. McKee was solely at fault for Tremayne's drowning because he failed to properly supervise Tremayne. The jury returned a verdict in favor of the Inn. Ms. Steele appeals. . . .

Tremayne, as a guest of the Inn, was a business invitee, so the Inn owed him the duty to maintain the pool in a reasonably safe condition.

Whether the Inn breached its duty of care was a question for the jury. Ms. Steele is correct in arguing that there was ample evidence to support a jury finding that the Inn breached its duty of care by failing to keep the swimming pool water clear in violation of company policy. They might also have decided that the Inn was negligent in refusing to close the pool or post warnings upon discovering the cloudy condition of the water. However, in the alternative, the jury could have reasonably concluded that the Inn satisfied its duty to maintain safe premises by regularly cleaning the pool, continuously operating a state-of-the-art pool filtration system, and regularly checking and maintaining the chemical balance in the pool water. Based upon the testimony at trial, the jury might also have determined that the cloudy water did not create a dangerous condition. Sufficient evidence was presented at trial to support the jury finding that the Inn did not breach its duty of care.

The jury was also instructed to determine whether any alleged breach of care by the Inn was the proximate cause of Tremayne's death. . . . Again Ms. Steele is correct in asserting that the evidence would have supported a jury determination that the Inn was at least a contributing cause of

Tremayne's drowning. However, substantial evidence was also represented at trial to support a jury finding that Jay McKee's insufficient supervision of Tremayne was the sole proximate cause of Tremayne's death. The jury could also have determined that based upon the short length of time required for a person to die from drowning (four to six minutes) the cloudiness in the pool water was not a contributing factor in Tremayne's death. In other words, the jury could have determined that Tremayne would have drowned even if the water had been clear.

Reasonable minds could differ on the issues of breach of duty and proximate cause in this case. Substantial evidence was presented to support the jury's verdict. This Court should not reverse the jury's verdict based upon Ms. Steele's challenge of the sufficiency of the evidence.

CASE QUESTIONS

1. Had the jury decided the case in favor of Ms. Steele rather than against her, would the court have overruled that verdict? Why or why not?

2. Do you agree or disagree with the jury's verdict? Why?

Warn Guests of Unusual Natural Hazards

A hotel must warn its guests of nonobvious dangers associated with swimming. In a case from Hawaii a hotel warned its guests of such dangers by placing four signs on its 400 feet of ocean frontage which stated that if red flags were posted on the beach that meant dangerous surf conditions existed. The four signs further advised guests to "Please use swimming pools if the red flags are posted." On the day in issue six red flags were placed along the frontage. Plaintiff, claiming to have missed the signs, went swimming in the ocean and was injured when a "huge wave" threw her on the shore. The trial court determined the warning was adequate and dismissed the case without trial. On appeal the court held that the issue of liability was not that clear; if the hotel did not adequately warn plaintiff of the dangers it could be liable. A trial was ordered. *Tarshis v. Lahaina Investment Corp.,* 480 F.2d 1019 (9th Cir., 1973). But in *Adika v. Beekman Towers, Inc.,* 633 So.2d 1170 (Fl., 1994), the court held a hotel owes no duty to guests to warn them of inherent dangers of the ocean. The court thus dismissed a case against a hotel located adjacent to a public beach by the estate of a man who drowned on a day when the water was rough. Said the court, "It may be good practice for a hotel located near the ocean to provide its guests with information on ocean safety, but such a practice is not required under the facts of this case."

At first blush the last two decisions may seem in conflict. A closer look reveals otherwise. In *Adika*, the man drowned due to the ordinary risks associated with swimming in the ocean, which include unexpected rough water and waves. No duty exists on the part of the hotel to disclose or warn of that which should be obvious to guests, and therefore the hotel was not liable. In *Tarshis*, the hotel was aware of an *unusual* risk—ongoing dangerous surf conditions. A hotel must disclose to its guests information about a nonobvious risk. Failure to do so results in liability.

In the following case a hotel may have failed to alert its guests of shallow water beneath a swing near the shore used by children to jump into the water. Since those who used the swing might reasonably expect that the water beneath it would be deep enough to jump into safely, a duty arose to disclose that such was not the case. Since the hotel did not give notice, the judge refused to grant its request to dismiss a case pursued by a person severely injured from using the swing.

CASE EXAMPLE 7-6

Mihill v. Ger-Am Inc.
651 N.Y.S.2d 746 (N.Y., 1997)

Plaintiff Michael Mihill (hereinafter plaintiff) and his parents seek to recover for serious injuries sustained by plaintiff when he jumped or fell into Mirror Lake from a swing located on defendant's property. The swings were on the shore of the lake, approximately three to six feet from the water's edge, and were intended for use by patrons of defendant's hotel. According to defendant's president, the swings were posted with a sign stating, "Do not jump from swings." [The existence of the signs was disputed by several other witnesses.] Despite the claims of defendant's president and night manager that they did not tolerate such activities, there is evidence in the record that neighborhood children used the swings to jump into the lake on a fairly regular basis. Although the water was shallow close to the shore, there was evidently a sharp dropoff 10 to 15 feet out, such that if one swung high enough before jumping, he or

she would arc past the shallow area and land safety in the deeper water.

On the evening of the accident, plaintiff, then age 17, and his friend, Chad Flyte, were . . . on the hotel premises for the purpose of swimming in the lake. Flyte had successfully jumped from a swing into the lake, and plaintiff, who had never swum in that area before and was unaware of the depth of the water or the contour of the lake bed, had begun to swing with the same end in mind. Whether he actually jumped or—as he avers—"chickened out", and was slowing the swing to dismount when his foot caught on the ground, causing him to "flop off" the swing and into the water, is the subject of conflicting deposition testimony. Unfortunately, he apparently entered the water head first, and suffered several injuries rendering him a quadriplegic.

. . . [Given that a dispute existed as to the presence of warning signs near the swings, and the testimony that defendants tolerated children on the swings despite the known danger, defendant's motion for summary judgment is denied.]

CASE QUESTION

1. What should the hotel have done to avoid liability in this case?

Restrict Use or Warn of Hazards in the Water

Another potential danger for ocean swimmers is errant surfboards and other sporting equipment. In *Landrum Mills Hotel Corp. v. Ferhatovic*, 317 F.2d 76 (1st Cir., 1963), a guest completing his ocean swim and about to leave the water was hit in the face with a surfboard owned by the hotel, which permitted the use of surfboards in the swimming area. The hotel was found to have acted negligently by failing to either restrict the area in which surfboards were allowed or warn bathers that surfboards were in use.

Inspect For Glass in Pool Area

In *Bristol v. Ernst*, 27 N.Y.S.2d 119 (1941), the plaintiff's foot was severely cut on a piece of glass at the bottom of a hotel wading pool. In this case the trial judge erroneously charged the jury that the hotel's duty to maintain the pool in a safe condition would not be satisfied by the exercise of ordinary care in the supervision of the pool. Therefore, a judgment in favor of plaintiff was reversed and a new trial ordered. If the glass causing the injury was dropped or placed in the pool just prior to the injury, it could not have been detected nor its presence prevented in the exercise of ordinary care and the hotel would not be liable. To hold to the contrary would make the hotel an insurer of its guests' safety, which is not the intent of the law as we have seen. However, if the plaintiff can prove the glass had been in the pool for awhile, the hotel may have breached its duty to inspect the property for risks at reasonable intervals.

Inspect Lake Bottoms for Hazards

If a hotel invites its guest to swim in a natural body of water, its duty of reasonable care requires it to inspect the bottom for dangerous objects and to remove any found or, depending on the circumstances, warn swimmers, prohibit swimming in the area, or prevent the cause of the dangerous objects—such as boats—from using the swimming area.

In *Montes v. Betcher*, 480 F.2d 1128 (8th Cir., 1973), presented in full in Chapter 5, plaintiff, an experienced diver, dived off a peer at defendant's lake resort. Plaintiff had dived there many times before. On the day in question he hit a jagged piece of concrete and suffered injuries to his scalp and vertebrae. The area was regularly used by both swimmers and boaters. The concrete obstruction was recovered, and it resembled a boat anchor. Defendant never inspected the lake bottom for debris, never raked the bottom, did not erect a warning sign to swimmers, and did nothing to discourage boaters from entering the swimming area.

The jury found these omissions to be negligent and determined the defendant was 90 percent responsible for the accident.

Control Boisterous Conduct of Guests

When boisterous conduct and horseplay are allowed in the pool area, accidents may occur. In *Gordon v. Hotel Seville, Inc.*, 105 So.2d 175 (Fla., 1958), the plaintiff, while swimming face down in defendant hotel's pool, was hit when another swimmer was thrown into the pool by a group of rowdy boys and landed on her. The hotel denied liability. The court ruled that the defendant, as an operator of a swimming pool, owed its invitees the duty to use reasonable care to eliminate unsafe conditions. If the defendant should have been aware of horseplay in the pool and took no steps to stop it, defendant could be liable to plaintiff. If prior to the accident no one in the pool was acting disorderly, the hotel would not be liable. In *Cohen v. Suburban Sidney-Hill, Inc.*, 178 N.E.2d 19 (Mass., 1961), a twelve-year-old youth fell backward off the ladder leading to the diving board at a country club and was injured. At the time, other children were clamoring up the ladder. Three lifeguards were on duty, though none was near the board at the time of the fall and none had observed any horseplay. The court noted that the cause of the fall was as likely that the plaintiff lost his foothold as that supervision was lax. Therefore, plaintiff failed to prove a breach of duty on the part of the owner and the court held for the defendant.

Expect Protection From Guests' Negligence

If a guest is negligent and the pool operator is not, the latter will not be liable when the guest is injured. A hotel without a swimming pool of its own had an arrangement with the owners and operators of a nearby pool to allow its guests to use that pool. Without notifying the pool owners, guests who arrived late one night dived into the deep end of the pool. Unknown to them, the pool was being drained and cleaned, and had only about two feet of water left. The plaintiffs were injured and sued the hotel and pool owners for negligence.

The court determined the plaintiffs failed to exercise ordinary care for their own safety by diving at 5 A.M. without giving the slightest heed to existing conditions. This contributed to the injury and, in a state that followed the contributory negligence rule, defeated plaintiffs' case. *Ryan v. Unity, Inc.*, 55 So.2d 117 (Fla., 1951). (Note: Florida has since adopted the rule of comparative negligence.)

Special Duties

A hotel or restaurant's duty to act reasonably applies in the important circumstances of fire, security, and medical treatment.

Injuries Caused by Fire

Fires present very serious hazards to hotels. Liability can result from inadequate fire safety equipment, delays in notifying the fire department and guests about a fire, and failing to train employees on how to act in a fire.

Innkeepers' concern about fire is heightened as a result of three substantial fires in large hotels in the 1980s that led to many deaths and injuries, much property damage, and many lawsuits. In 1981, fire broke out in the MGM Grand Hotel in Las Vegas, Nevada. Eighty-four people died, almost 700 were injured and approximately 900 lawsuits were brought against the hotel. Many of the cases were settled for considerable sums of money. In 1982, a fire occurred in the Stouffer's Inn in White Plains, New York, killing 26 people. The DuPont Plaza Hotel was the site of a fire in 1986, killing and injuring almost 240. The death toll was due in part to locked exists, obstructed passageways, and inaccessible fire alarms.

Maintain Fire Safety Equipment.   Most states and many localities have passed statutes and building codes listing equipment that all hotels and restaurants are required to have for fire protection. Requirements include fire extinguishers and a duty to test them periodically, sprinkler systems, smoke detectors, fire alarms, smoke and fire dampers, voice communication systems in guest rooms and other public rooms, exit illumination, posting of maps showing exit routes in case of fire, emergency lighting, evacuation plans, employee training, and fire escapes. To accommodate guests who are hearing impaired, alarm systems should include a visual component. Failure to provide required fire safety devices can lead to liability.

In *Pirtle's Administratrix v. Hargis Bank & Trust Company*, 44 S.W.2d 541 (Ky., 1931), the deceased was a guest in the Combs Hotel and died when the hotel was destroyed by fire. Plaintiff charged that the defendant innkeeper negligently failed to provide the hotel with either an iron stairway as a fire escape on the outside of the building or fire fighting equipment, although both were required by statute. The court said that it was a firmly fixed rule that one injured by a violation of a statute may recover from a defendant for any damages sustained, based on negligence per se. In *Moore v. Dresden*, 298 P.465 (Wash., 1931), the defendant hotelkeeper was liable for negligence in failing to maintain adequate fire escapes as required by state law. The court ruled that a hotelkeeper who fails to comply with a safety statute is negligent per se, irrespective of all questions of the exercise of prudence, diligence, care, or skill. If, therefore, the failure to comply with a safety statute is the proximate cause of the injury to a guest, the case is decided in the guest's favor, and all that remains to be done is to assess damages.

Remember, compliance with statutory safety requirements does not guarantee freedom from liability. Rather, these laws set only the minimum standards for fire safety. Innkeepers should view the safety codes as only a starting point and work up from there. For example, since the fire at the MGM Grand in Nevada, the hotel has instituted many fire safety devices not required by law, including a sprinkler system, a computerized alarm system, and monitoring mechanisms, at a cost of more than $5 million. It is safe to assume the hotel regrets not taking these precautions earlier.

Train Staff on How to Respond to a Fire.   When a hotel fire breaks out, the hotel has a continuing duty to exercise reasonable care to protect the safety of its guests. A hotel was found negligent where the night clerk, upon learning of a fire in the hotel, first went to the second floor to look for the fire and only after finding it called the fire department. He then returned to the lobby and attempted to turn on the fire alarm but discovered that it did not work. He next called several of the rooms to alert the occupants. He stopped calling at the direction of the manager, who erroneously believed the fire was under control. The night clerk testified he had not been instructed on how to use the fire alarm. An occupant of one of the rooms died in the fire. His estate sued the hotel and won. The hotel was negligent for failing to notify the fire department immediately, failing to notify guests promptly that a fire existed in the hotel, and failing to train the night clerk on how to use the fire alarm. *Parker v. Kirkwood*, 8 P.2d 340 (Kansas, 1932).

In *Burrows v. Knots*, 482 S.W.2d 358 (Tex., 1972), the hotel was likewise found negligent for failing to timely warn residents of a fire. A guest informed the night clerk "You have a fire," and said she smelled something burning. The clerk, smelling nothing, did nothing. A few minutes later he smelled smoke and investigated, and saw fire coming from the men's restroom. He returned to the office, called the fire department, went outside to move his truck from in front of the hotel, returned to the lobby, and then attempted to go upstairs to warn guests, but the fire blocked his efforts. The estate of a guest who died in the fire sued the hotel. The jury awarded $40,000 for the pain and suffering the guest endured during the ten minutes the death certificate said he survived after the fire began. The court, pointing out that he would have lost consciousness before death and did not suffer pain after becoming unconscious, reduced the verdict to $10,000.

The following case further explains the various responsibilities a hotel has when a fire occurs, and also identifies some of the limits of those responsibilities.

CASE EXAMPLE 7–7

Darby v. Checker Co.
285 N.E.2d 217 (Ill., 1972)

. . . About 8:00 A.M. on Sunday morning, April 15, 1962, the fourth floor of the hotel was swept by fire. The plaintiff, June Hampton, was in room 403 with Alphonso Darby, whom she subsequently married. In her attempt to escape the flames she climbed out the window of the smoke-filled room and clung to bed clothes which Darby had tied to a dresser. She choked from the smoke, became dizzy, fell to the courtyard below and was seriously and permanently injured.

She brought an action for damages against the defendants charging them with negligence and with willful and wanton conduct in operating the hotel without adequate safeguards against fire. A jury returned a verdict in her favor and assessed her damages at $52,500.

In seeking reversal of the judgment the defendants contend that they are entitled to judgment as a matter of law since they were not proved guilty of any negligence proximately causing the plaintiff's injuries and because she was guilty of contributory negligence. . . .

Innkeepers must exercise care to secure the safety of their guests. The defendants agree that the plaintiff was an invitee on their premises and that they owed her the duty of exercising reasonable care for her safety. They assert, however, that her allegations of negligence, . . . were beyond the scope of any duty they owed her. These allegations were: failing to warn the plaintiff of the fire so as to afford her sufficient time to leave the hotel; failing to provide her assistance in leaving; failing to provide a safe, suitable and proper means of leaving the hotel; and failing to extinguish the fire or preventing it from spreading. . . .

The fire started in room 415. This room was on the inside court of the hotel and about 18 feet from the elevator. The fire was discovered by Luke Morris and his wife, residents in room 406, who were aroused by the barking of their dog and the smell of smoke. Mrs. Morris called the switchboard operator and reported that the building was on fire. The operator told her that someone would be up. Mrs. Morris' call was received by Ida Braswell, who worked from midnight to 8:00 A.M. She turned to Geraldine Thomas, the resident manager of the hotel, and to Ardeen Smith, the operator who was to relieve her at 8:00 A.M., and said: "somebody saw smoke upstairs and thinks there is a fire. . . . Let's go to the fourth floor and see if there is a fire up there." She and Thomas, and a resident named McLemore, took the elevator to the fourth floor. Braswell saw smoke coming from room 415. Thomas opened the door. The room was full of smoke and there was a fire in the area of the bed. Thomas closed the door and took the elevator downstairs. . . . Braswell pulled the fire alarm next to the elevator and ran in the opposite direction. She passed all the rooms numbered downward from 415 but knocked on no doors. She "believed" she yelled "fire" as she ran along the corridor. She rushed down the stairway which was adjacent to rooms 401 and 402.

None of the fourth floor tenants who testified at the trial was warned of the fire by hotel employees. Most of them discovered it by opening the doors or windows of their rooms and seeing the smoke and flames. Three tenants said they heard a faint buzz when they opened their doors but all testified that the hotel's fire alarm was inaudible when the doors were closed. The first fireman who entered the building stated that he proceeded through the first floor from the front to the rear and heard no alarm. On the other hand, the fire alarm system was inspected by the Chicago Fire Department less than a month before the fire and found to be in good working order. The hotel em-

ployees testified that after the alarm was sounded it rang loudly for maybe five or ten minutes and then began to fade. After this only a buzzing sound could be heard.

Arlene Smith testified that she was at the hotel's desk checking over the cash on hand when she heard the alarm. Because of prior false alarms she intended to turn it off. A moment or two later as she stepped toward the alarm-box to stop the alarm, she heard Thomas, who had returned to the lobby, cry: "Don't Miss Smith; it's real." The switchboard lighted up and she went to the board. After calling the fire department she attempted to answer the tenants' calls; but the board "went dead." Thomas also tried to talk to the tenants but she too was unsuccessful. The switchboard was alight with calls and she kept saying, "there is a fire; there is a fire" but there was no response. . . .

[P]laintiff discovered the fire when she noticed that the room was uncomfortably warm. She opened the window and saw fire coming out of a nearby window. She awakened Darby and opened the door. Fire and smoke hit her in the face. He pulled her back, closed the door, went to the phone and yelled that there was a fire and they were trapped. He made a makeshift rope out of sheets; tied it to the furniture and helped Miss Hampton out the window. After she lost her grip and fell, Darby went to the stairway and managed to get out of the hotel safely.

Both the hotel manager, Thomas, and the switchboard operator, Smith, had received desk clerk's certification from the Chicago Fire Prevention Bureau. As a prerequisite, instructions were given them concerning the action to be taken in the event of a fire. They were taught that immediately upon learning of a fire they were to call the fire department and then alert the guests to keep them from panicking. Neither Thomas nor Smith complied with this procedure. After they were notified of the fire Thomas took the time to go to the fourth floor to check the accuracy of the report. Smith was indifferent to the report and undisturbed by the alarm. She waited until Thomas returned and confirmed the existence of the fire before she called the fire department or tried to notify the guests. The guests testified they became aware of the fire sometime between 7:30 and 8:00 A.M. The fire department was not informed until 8:10. Firefighters responded to the call at 8:13.

The failure to contact the plaintiff and the conflicting testimony concerning the alarm raised the issue of whether the defendants were negligent in not warning her of the fire. The long delay in notifying the fire department and the casual attitude of the hotel employees supported her allegation that the defendants were negligent in not preventing the fire from spreading. . . .

The [hotel's] defense of contributory negligence . . . is based on the proposition that if Darby was able to get out of the hotel by means of the stairs, the plaintiff could have done so. They state that in leaving the room the way she did she pursued "an obvious course of known danger when an alternative course of known safety was in fact available but steps away." The difficulty the plaintiff experienced in breathing made it necessary for her to leave the room; the fire and smoke in the hallway made exit by normal means seemingly impossible. She found herself in an extremely perilous position caused by an agency beyond her control. In such a situation a plaintiff need not exercise the same degree of coolness, self-possession and judgment necessary under ordinary circumstances. She must be judged by the standard of conduct of a prudent person acting under similar circumstances. . . . That Darby came down the stairs safely is not controlling, for having seen the plaintiff falling from the window ledge and lying in the courtyard below he may have concluded that despite the fire in the hall the stairs afforded the only possibility of escape. He may have also rushed recklessly from the room in a desperate effort to lend assistance to his fiancee. The plaintiff's conduct fell far short of establishing contributory negligence as a matter of law. . . .

The [defendant's request] for a new trial, however, is another matter. The defendants point to several alleged trial errors. . . .

It was error [for the judge] to instruct the jury that the defendants could be found negligent for not putting out the fire. To permit a finding of liability because none of the employees used the fire extinguisher available in the hotel imposed a responsibility not warranted by the evidence. The fire department had instructed the resident man-

ager that extinguishers were to be used only after the department was called and the guests notified. . . . After they verified the fire's existence, further delay in calling the department—by attempting to fight the fire themselves—would have been unjustified. . . . [T]he evidence indicated that the fire was beyond their control when they came upon it.

That portion of the instruction which permitted the finding that the defendants were negligent in failing to provide a safe and suitable means for leaving the hotel was improper. There was no evidence that they did not furnish adequate stairways, elevators, fire escapes or doors and they were under no duty to maintain the plaintiff's upper-floor window as an emergency exit. There was no evidence that they were negligent in the maintenance of these means of egress or that they violated any building ordinance in regard to the number, position or type of these exists. . . .

Instructing the jury that the defendants could be held liable if the jury found that they failed to provide assistance to the plaintiff so she could leave the hotel safely was also error. There was no responsibility on the defendants' part to provide private escorts to able-bodied tenants. If this ambiguous instruction meant that the defendants had the duty to provide directional signs or emergency instructions rather than to see that the occupant of each room was guided to safety by its employees, the evidence, again, was deficient. There was no testimony referring to this subject. . . .

The instruction stated that the plaintiff claimed the defendants were negligent in failing to extinguish the fire and in failing to provide assistance to her in leaving the hotel. Obviously the defendants failed to do these things, but they were not negligent in not doing so. Under the facts of this case they were under no legal duty to put out the fire or escort the plaintiff from the hotel. Nonetheless, the instruction could have led the jurors to believe that because the defendants did not put out the fire and assist her to safety they could find in her favor. . . .

The judgment is reversed and the case remanded for a new trial.

> **CASE QUESTIONS**

1. Identify the actions of the hotel employees in this case that constituted negligence.

2. How could the hotel have avoided liability?

3. What was the court's reasoning for finding that the plaintiff was not negligent? What effect did the emergency circumstance have on that decision?

If a fire is contained and under control, the hotel's duty of due care may not require it to announce the fire to the guests. However, failure to inform guests may increase their peril if the fire gets out of control. The decision of whether and when to tell guests is thus an important one.

In the following case the court held the hotel acted properly in not alerting the guests. Note that the fire department concurred with the hotel that notice was not necessary. The court's decision was based in significant part on the fire department's concurrence.

CASE EXAMPLE 7–8

Taieb v. Hilton Hotels Corp.
506 N.Y.S.2d 810 (N.Y., 1986)

. . . Plaintiffs Bella and Maurice Taieb, French citizens vacationing in the United States, were registered guests of the defendant hotel occupying a room on the 38th floor, when a fire broke out in a lobby utility room housing a shaftway for linen and waste paper chutes, causing a light to medium smoke condition on most of the upper floors. While dressing for dinner, plaintiffs heard sirens and observed [from their window] fire engines on the hotel premises. Without checking with management, Mr. Taieb determined that they should leave the hotel as quickly as possible. On leaving their room, the Taiebs observed smoke at the far end of the corridor, at a distance of approximately 180 feet; the smoke did not obscure their vision in the corridor. Using the stairwell, plaintiffs ran down the 38 flight of stairs—without stopping; for most of the descent, Mrs. Taieb wore no shoes, at her husband's urging, so that she could run faster.

The Taiebs reached the street level and exited without incident.

The fire department, which had been promptly summoned to the scene, confirmed the defendant's decision that evacuation of the hotel was not necessary. The fire itself was localized, contained and extinguished without injury to any [other] guest, and damage to the building itself was quite minimal. Plaintiffs, claiming that Mrs. Taieb developed a phlebitis condition in her left leg as a result of the manner in which she was obliged to flee from the hotel, commenced this action alleging negligence on defendant's part in permitting a fire to break out; in failing to warn plaintiffs as to what was taking place; and in failing to provide a safe and proper means of egress. After a trial, the jury returned a verdict for Bella Taieb in the sum of $150,000 and for Maurice Taieb (for loss of services) in the sum of $20,000.

A hotelkeeper is not liable as an absolute insurer of the safety of his paying guests while they are on his premises, but is obligated to exercise reasonable care under all the circumstances for the safety of his guests. . . . Since we conclude that, as a matter of law, the hotel's overall response to the fire was reasonable and that there was insufficient evidence to support a finding of negligence upon any rational, practical view of the case, we reverse and dismiss the complaint.

To start with, the initial cause of the fire, as indicated by . . . the fire department operations report, is unknown. Plaintiffs' expert opined that an excessive amount of smoke emanated from the lobby level because of deficiencies in cleaning and maintenance procedures, but records produced by the hotel show that the linen chute from the 44th floor down to the lobby closet was cleaned about four months prior to the fire. There is no claim that the stairwell itself was unsafe. No violations were filed against the hotel as a result of the incident.

Since negligence may not be inferred from the fact of the fire (and smoke) alone, it seems to us that plaintiffs' essential theory of recovery at trial was the hotel's failure to advise them of their safety, so as to prevent Mrs. Taieb from injuring herself in attempting to escape from what was perceived as a perilous situation. Certainly, it was reasonable for the hotel to have determined that there was no immediate danger, and that evacuation of some 1700-2000 guests by sounding an alarm might well have caused a general panic. . . . And there is unrefuted testimony in the record to the effect that the hotel's assistant manager, together with staff and fire department personnel, did go through some of the upper floors in an attempt to inform guests that "everything was under control." It is unclear whether plaintiffs' floor was reached in this endeavor, or whether plaintiffs had already embarked upon their descent. In any event, given the rapidly unfolding scenario, and the size of this hotel, we decline to hold that the failure to personally apprise every affected guest that he or she was in a position of safety, and not danger, constitutes an appropriate predicate for tort liability. To impose such a duty upon a hotelkeeper comes very close to making him an insurer of the safety of his guests, and that is not the degree of care required of hotelkeepers. . . . Even assuming that out of due regard for their own safety and upon the information then known to them, plaintiffs were warranted in abandoning the premises, and sustained an injury in the process, that does not equate with a finding that the hotel was culpably negligent.

Security

Appropriately, a primary concern of hoteliers, restaurateurs, and travelers today is that of security. An examination of the various cases and media accounts dealing with attacks, robberies, and rapes of guests in their hotel rooms or on hotel premises accentuates this concern. Personal injury, the loss of life, and loss of property suffered as the result of criminal activity cost the hotel industry millions of dollars in damage payments.

How much security does a hotel, motel, or restaurant owe to guests in the buildings or on the grounds? Is a hotel liable if an intruder attacks a guest in a guest room? In a majority of states, innkeepers have a duty to use ordinary or reasonable care to render the premises safe for their guests. In a significant minority of states, the innkeeper's duty is raised to that of a high degree of care.

While the hotel might argue that the attacker constitutes an independent intervening act negating liability on the hotel, the approach of many courts is summarized in the following quote from the judge in *Banks v. Hyatt Corp.*, 722 F.2d 214 (La., 1984).

[T]ort law has become increasingly concerned with placing liability upon the party that is best able to determine the cost-justified level of accident prevention. . . . [H]olding a negligent innkeeper liable when there is a third-party assault on the premises is sensible . . . because the innkeeper is able to identify and carry out cost-justified ("reasonable") preventive measures on the premises.

Maintain Adequate Staff and Security Procedures.   When a lawsuit grows out of a security incident, the plaintiff must prove that the hotel failed to provide adequate security under the circumstances. Then the question arises as to whether the act of the third party constitutes a new and intervening cause of the injury. If the hotel's laxness on security matters facilitated the criminal's illegal act, causation between the hotel's negligence and the guest's injury will probably exist sufficient to hold the hotel liable. The following case illustrates such a situation.

CASE EXAMPLE 7–9

Nordmann v. National Hotel Company
425 F.2d 1103 (La., 1970)

Mr. and Mrs. Nordmann sued the National Hotel Company for damages that resulted from a robbery and assault committed upon them in a Jung Hotel room in New Orleans between 12:10 A.M. and 1:10 A.M. on October 18, 1965. The Nordmanns, accompanied by a friend and business associate William Mixon, registered into the hotel as paying guests the previous afternoon. That evening, with several other friends, they attended a ball in the hotel ballroom. The hotel contains some twelve hundred guest rooms and there were some twelve to fourteen hundred people at the ball. Shortly after midnight, when the Nordmanns left the ball and started up to their room, they entered a self-serving, automatic-type elevator. They were followed by the man who later robbed and assaulted them. When they left the elevator, they did not notice that this man followed until Mr. Nordmann put the key in the door. At that time, the man thrust a gun in Nordmann's back and pushed them into the room and on the bed. He took such money as Nordmann had in his wallet, fifty dollars, forced him to lie face down on the bed, had Mrs. Nordmann get a razor blade from the bathroom and cut a section of a

venetian blind cord with which he tied Nordmann's hands behind his back. He announced that "It's not just the money I want, that's not all I want." He proceeded to make indecent advances to Mrs. Nordmann, repeatedly slapping and hitting her, and forced her to mix him two drinks. Finally, on her plea to let her mix him another drink or get water for her husband, Mrs. Nordmann was permitted to go back into the bathroom. She described the conclusion of the assault thus: "So, when I got into the bathroom I turned my head, and as I turned my head I could see that he walked over to my husband and pulled his collar loose, and when he did, I don't know what came over me, but the bathroom door was close enough to the knob of the main door, that I said, 'Dear God, don't let that chain be on that door,' because I reached out and I turned that knob and I opened that door and I ran screaming down the hall. That's all that I remember as far as that episode was concerned." The assailant fled down an inside fire escape and has never been captured.

This appeal is from a judgment entered on a jury's verdict for $16,000 in favor of Mrs. Nordmann and for $5,000 in favor of Mr. Nordmann.

. . . The law imposes upon innkeepers at least ordinary or reasonable care to protect their guests against injury by third persons, and some cases call for the exercise of a higher degree of care. In this case the court, by its instructions, held the defendants to a standard of ordinary or reasonable care to protect the hotel's guests from injury by third persons.

The complaint charged the defendants with negligence in the following particulars:

1. Permitting criminals, sex deviates, and vagrants to wander indiscriminately about the hotel;

2. Failure to maintain a competent staff of employees;

3. Failure to maintain adequate security personnel;

4. Failure to summon the police immediately; and

5. Failure to have the hotel security officer investigate the incident as soon as it was reported to a hotel employee.

The evidence was ample to support the jury's verdict. For its twelve hundred rooms, and with a large ball in progress, the hotel had on duty at the time of the robbery and assault only one security officer, one room clerk, and one bellboy. The jury could, with reason, determine that the defendants had failed to perform their general duty to protect their guests. The evidence of the defendant's negligence after the incident was reported is much stronger.

The occupant of the adjoining room was David DuCharme, an insurance adjustor, who happened to be working on some of his papers when his attention was distracted by the happenings. He heard in a male voice the demand for a knife, for a razor blade, and a woman's voice in response, then "the man who had directed the demand for the knife told the woman to cut down the venetian blind cord."

Mr. DuCharme continued to describe in detail just what he had been able to hear of what was happening in the next room. He became convinced that a robbery and assault were taking place. Taking the telephone, he got under the bed covers to prevent his own report from being heard, and got the telephone operator to whom he stated in substance: "I said, 'This is Dave DuCharme in room 1048. There is a holdup or there is a robbery and attempted rape'—I believe were very near the words I used—'going on in the room next to mine.' . . . I said, 'This is an emergency. Call the police immediately. This is an emergency.' And I re-

peated myself, 'There is a robbery and attempted rape going on in the room next to me. It is an emergency. Call the police immediately.'" Instead of taking action herself, the operator responded that, "I will connect you with the room clerk." When the room clerk answered, DuCharme repeated substantially the same report: "I said, 'I have just told the operator, and I am telling you.' I said, 'This is an emergency. I want you to call the police immediately.' And I identified myself again. I said, 'This is Dave DuCharme in room 1048. There is a robbery and attempted rape going on in the room next to mine.' And I repeated myself two or three times again and stated, 'This is an emergency. Call the police immediately.' . . . "The room clerk's response was 'Well, you know, it takes the police fifteen or twenty minutes to get here'," and DuCharme replied, "I didn't ask you any questions about time. I told you this was an emergency and to call the police immediately." DuCharme estimated it took approximately five minutes in which even to report the robbery and assault.

That was only the beginning of the delay. The room clerk admitted that he did not immediately call the police. There were policemen on duty in the ballroom, but they were never summoned. Instead, the room clerk started looking for the security officer or house detective. The jury could have found from the evidence that the police were not actually called until more than forty minutes after Mr. DuCharme notified the telephone operator and the room clerk of the "emergency" and "robbery and attempted rape." When the police finally were called at 1:11 A.M. according to the time precisely stamped by time clock, patrolmen arrived at the hotel within four minutes, but long after the assailant's escape. Indeed, Mr. DuCharme confronted the room clerk with a demand for the reason the police were not notified earlier and met only the desultory response, "We were real busy at the time and we can't be calling the police for everybody that calls down here." There was ample evidence to support the jury's verdict.

In the light of the evidence as to the suffering, mental anguish, shock and injury to the nervous systems of Mr. and Mrs. Nordmann, . . . the damages were modest.

Ruling of the Court: The judgment [for plaintiffs] is affirmed.

1.   Identify all the ways in which the hotel was negligent in this case.

This case is instructive on two points. First, courts will consider whether the staff on duty at the time of a security incident was adequate in number and training to respond to forseeable risks, given the number of guests in the hotel and the events scheduled. Second, when a security incident occurs, hotel staff, once alerted, are expected to respond quickly and appropriately. If the hotel is understaffed, the staff is undertrained, or staff responds poorly, the hotel will likely be liable.

Matching Security to Circumstances.   Ordinary care, which is the duty of care required by an innkeeper for his guests' safety in a majority of states, is not a static, clearly defined concept. One definition will not fit all hotels in all locations at all times. The type of security that would constitute ordinary care in a relatively quiet and tranquil location with a low crime rate might be considered grossly negligent if employed in a high-crime area with a history of muggings and unauthorized entries into guests' rooms. Security thus becomes a relative concept. The precautions necessary must be determined for each individual hotel.

We studied in Chapter 5 that if the hotel or restaurant can anticipate an injury to patrons based on the condition of the premises, the business must use reasonable care to eliminate the condition that created that risk of injury. Likewise, the foreseeability of a criminal attack is an important factor considered by courts when determining whether or not a hotel or restaurant has acted reasonably in the level of security it provides.

The next case identifies various factors that are reviewed to determine if an establishment has provided adequate security. Those factors include community crime rate, crime rate in the immediate area and in similar businesses, presence of suspicious individuals, industry standards, and any particular security problems posed by the establishment's layout. The case also illustrates security concerns faced by hotels with multiple buildings.

CASE EXAMPLE 7–10

Peters v. Holiday Inns, Inc.
278 N.W.2d 208 (Wis., 1979)

. . . In the early morning hours of December 31, 1975, the plaintiff-appellant Francis J. Peters, a motel guest, was assaulted and robbed in his room. Peters commenced this action, alleging the motel was negligent in permitting two intruders access to his room that resulted in his being beaten and robbed. The plaintiff and defendant concede the facts leading up to and culminating in the assault on Peters, although the plaintiff presented additional facts to the court.

Shortly before 3:00 A.M. on December 31, 1975, a car containing four males parked in front of the motel's entrance. The four men sat in the car for a short time before one of the car's occupants entered the motel lobby. The lobby is in the motel's main building, while the plaintiff's room, no. 185, is located in a separate but adjacent structure. The assailant, a former employee of the motel, was known as Elvis to the employees on duty. Upon entering the motel, he asked whether "Uncle George" was working that night and after being told he was not scheduled to work, "Elvis" left the lobby. Rather than exiting the building, the assailant entered the motel's kitchen area, where he stole one of the bellboy shirts.

The activities of the four men were observed by a policeman who was routinely patrolling the defendant's premises in an unmarked squad car. The officer became suspicious after seeing the man who departed earlier from the car return and then observed the auto proceed to the rear of the parking lot near the adjacent motel rooms. The patrolman then entered the motel and questioned the two employees on duty concerning their conversation with "Elvis." The employees informed him that a short time ago, the patrons of room 143 had telephoned the desk to report that a man knocked on their door claiming their room phone was out of order and that he had a message for them from the desk. The patrolman, upon receipt of this information, alertly suspecting something unusual, called headquarters and requested the aid of additional squads that arrived at the scene shortly thereafter.

The imposter "messenger," after being denied entrance to room 143, apparently proceeded to Peters's room, no. 185. The man knocked on the door and repeated the same modus operandi, informing Peters his phone wasn't working and that he had a message for him from the desk. The plaintiff-appellant explains that he looked through the door's one-way viewer and saw a man in the hallway wearing a bellboy's white shirt, the type worn by Holiday Inn personnel. Peters opened the door, believing the message was the 6:30 A.M. "wake-up call" he had requested. Two men pushed their way into the room and held the

plaintiff at gunpoint while one of the assailants searched Peters's pants and room. They found approximately $700 in cash and a set of keys to the plaintiff's bowling alley. The intruders forced Peters to accompany them, apparently intending further criminal activity. The plaintiff was pushed into his own car and, at this time, the police converged upon the vehicle and the four men were apprehended at the scene.

At the time of the assault, the outside entrance to the separate structure housing rooms 143 and 185 was neither locked, monitored by closed circuit television, nor manned by motel staff or security personnel. Further, it is not necessary to pass through the lobby before entering the building. The only security provided by the motel was a dead bolt lock on each room as well as a chain lock and a one-way viewer. It is pointed out that the hallway outside rooms 143 and 185 was well lighted at the time of the assault. It was established by affidavit that the inn did not employ security guards as, in the past five years, there had been few incidents requiring calls to the police for help and the police routinely patrol the motel entrance and parking lot. . . .

In this case, the court is called upon to establish the standard of care to be imposed upon an innkeeper to provide adequate security measures for the safety of his guests. . . .

[T]he proprietor of a place of business who holds it out to the public for entry for his business purposes (including a restaurant) is subject to liability to members of the public while upon the premises for such a purpose for bodily harm caused to them by the accidental, negligent, or intentional harmful acts of third persons, if the proprietor by the exercise of reasonable care could have discovered that such acts were being done or were about to be done, and could have protected the members of the public by controlling the conduct of the third persons, or by giving a warning adequate to enable them to avoid harm.

In our mobile society, travelers carry sums of money because of necessity and the problems caused by the lack of adequate identification for cashing checks in areas away from home. Thus, innkeepers should foresee that necessarily large amounts of monies and credit cards are carried by their guests and, consequently, increased security is required in these days of rapidly increasing assaultive crimes. Certainly hotel patrons can expect that reasonable security will be provided, combined with the friendliness, hospitality, and graciousness so widely advertised by modern hotels. . . .

Thus, the conduct of hotel innkeepers in providing security must conform to the standard of ordinary care. In the context of the hotel-guest relationship, it is foreseeable that an innkeeper's failure to maintain adequate security measures not only permits but may even encourage intruders to rob or assault hotel patrons. Therefore, we hold that a hotel has a duty to exercise ordinary care to provide adequate protection for its guests and their property from assaultive and other types of criminal activity. . . .

Thus, in meeting its standard of ordinary care, a hotel must provide security commensurate with the facts and circumstances that are or should be apparent to the ordinarily prudent person. In other words, an innkeeper's standard of care in providing security will vary according to the particular circumstances and location of the hotel.

Accordingly, as the degree of care that an innkeeper must exercise will vary in relation to the attendant circumstances, relevant factors in deciding whether a hotel has exercised ordinary care in providing adequate security are: industry standards, the community's crime rate, the extent of assaultive or criminal activity in the area or in similar business enterprises, the presence of suspicious persons, and the peculiar security problems posed by the hotel's design. . . . The particular circumstances may require one or more of the following safety measures: a security force, closed-circuit television surveillance, dead bolts and chain locks on the individual rooms, as well as security doors on hotel entranceways removed from the lobby area. . . .

. . . The plaintiff's primary contentions are that the motel was negligent in: (1) allowing suspicious persons to roam about the premises unsupervised during the early morning hours; (2) permitting the suspicious person to gain access to the Holiday Inn uniforms, thus enabling the man to pose as a hotel employee; and (3), as it is not necessary to pass by the motel lobby, the motel failed to provide security personnel, television monitoring equipment, or other security devices, including locks on the outside doors leading to the hallways in the separated motel building where room nos. 143 and 185 were located so as to prevent ingress to all but motel patrons. . . .

We hold, based upon the applicability of the established duty of ordinary care imposed on a hotel to provide security and the facts and circumstances presented by the parties, that reasonable persons could draw competing inferences as to whether the defendant motel provided adequate security. The present case raises a jury question as to whether or not the presence of the assailant in the motel lobby, not for purposes of renting a room, but looking for a certain motel employee at 3:00 A.M., was a suspicious circumstance requiring the motel staff to monitor the intruder's whereabouts.

. . . A hotel's duty to provide reasonable security requires that preventative safety measures must be taken under certain circumstances. . . .

Hotel liability cases requiring a plaintiff to prove the innkeeper's failure to exercise ordinary care commensurate with the circumstances are difficult cases that will present our trial courts with many matters of complex factual proof. . . .

[The case was referred to trial.]

CASE QUESTION

1. If you were on the jury in this case, would you find for the plaintiff or the hotel? Why?

The court in this case mentions various security devices a hotel might use to secure guest rooms. The very basic measures with which all rooms should be equipped are deadbolts, chain locks or other lock or safety device on the doors, and a peephole. The chain on the chain lock should be strong. The peephole, which the court called a one-way viewer, enables the guest to determine who is at the door before opening it. This simple device can protect guests from unknown intruders. The chain locks and dead bolts should be designed so they are easy for the guest to use, and inspected regularly to verify good working order.

Each door or entranceway to the room should be suitably secured. In *Garzelli v. Howard Johnson's Motor Lodges, Inc.*, 419 F.Supp. 1210 (N.Y., 1976) singer Connie Francis was raped at knifepoint in a Long Island Howard Johnson's Motor Lodge. Her assailant gained access to the room through a sliding glass door. Said the court, "The doors gave the appearance of being locked but the testimony showed they were capable of being unsecured from the outside without much difficulty." She recovered $2.5 million in damages for her inability to continue her lucrative career based on the hotel's failure to provide a "safe and secure room".

Match Security to Neighborhood Crime Rates.   When the local crime rate is high, a hotel or restaurant should forsee and anticipate the possibility of criminal activity together with resulting injury or loss to patrons. Appropriate security measures must be adopted. The court in the following case refused to dismiss plaintiff's claim, finding that a jury could determine that the hotel's security precautions were insufficient.

CASE EXAMPLE 7–11

Cyzio v. Rihga International USA, Inc.
660 N.Y.S.2d 271 (N.Y., 1997)

Plaintiff Chester T. Cyzio ("Cyzio") sues defendant Rihga International USA, Inc. ("Rihga") hotel located near Times Square in midtown Manhattan. The complaint alleges that on November 21, 1991, Cyzio registered as a guest at the hotel and that in the middle of the night on November 30th he was viciously and violently assaulted in his room as a result of defendant's negligence in maintaining its hotel security system. Defendant now moves for summary judgment arguing that as plaintiff cannot demonstrate how the assailant gained entry into the building, the plaintiff cannot establish that the alleged failure to provide adequate security was the proximate cause of the attack upon the plaintiff.

In opposing summary judgment, plaintiff relies upon an affidavit from a security expert stating that heightened security is warranted at the Rihga due to its location in a high-crime area and to the ninety-two (92) reported crimes in the eleven months prior to the incident. The expert affidavit also states that the policy described by Rihga's security supervisor at his deposition whereby persons entering the hotel in the middle of the night are not stopped and questioned, even if security personnel did not know whether the person was a guest, is in adequate. The expert also stated that the misplacing of the vincard computer readout showing entries into the plaintiff's room as well as other alleged discrepancies in the security team's handling of the incident are further indications of an inadequate security system. . . .

In a commercial setting such as a hotel, a landlord has a duty to exercise and use reasonable care to protect guests or tenants, while on the premises, against injuries at the hands of third persons who are not employees of the hotel . . . and is required to take reasonable protective measures, including providing adequate security, to protect guests against third party criminal acts . . . particularly where the occurrence of criminal activity on the premises was reasonably foreseeable. (citations omitted.) . . . [A] plaintiff who is assaulted in a commercial building need not demonstrate the manner of the assailant's entry, but need only create questions of fact as to whether the landlord breached its duty to maintain minimal security measures, related to the specific building itself, in the face of foreseeable criminal intrusion upon tenants.

In this case, the deposition testimony of Cyzio himself coupled with the expert's affidavit create issues of fact as to whether the hotel security system was appropriate for this particular hotel, particularly in the middle of the night. The Court also is troubled by the loss of video tapes that defendant claims show the plaintiff entering the hotel and riding in the elevator with an invited guest. Defendant claimed that its security personnel turned the tape over to the police without receiv-ing a police receipt in return. The police, however, have conducted a search and have informed the Court that they do not have such a tape. Plaintiff's expert states that he is familiar with hotel security measures and that it is not standard procedure to turn such tapes over to the police without a receipt. Defendant's security chief, Mr. Higgins, testified that the hotel's security policy is not to question guests or other persons entering the hotel if they are "well dressed or properly dressed and appear to know where they are going; the policy is to question a person entering the hotel only if the person is "behaving suspiciously." Plaintiff's expert states that following such a procedure in the late night or early morning "is tantamount to inviting well-dressed intruders." As questions of fact exist as to the liability of the hotel for plaintiff's loss and injuries, summary judgment [for the hotel] is denied."

CASE QUESTIONS

1. The video tape, if it existed, would be an important piece of evidence for the hotel. How might it have better protected the tape from loss?

2. What policy should the hotel have adopted concerning people who seek to access the guest rooms at night?

Another case in which prior crimes in the vicinity impacted the hotel's duty of care was *Orlando Executive Park, Inc. v. P.D.R.*, 402 So.2d 442 (Fla., 1981). The plaintiff, after registering at a 300-room motel, went to her car to retrieve some papers. She was attacked by a stranger whom she had seen by the registration desk when she registered. The guest was brutalized, sodomized, and left with serious physical and psychological injuries. A year after the attack plaintiff lost her job because of memory lapses, mental confusion, and inability to tolerate and communicate with people, all resulting from the incident. Management was aware of approximately thirty criminal incidents occurring on the premises during the six months prior to the attack, yet the hotel employed only one security guard "from time to time on a sporadic basis." Plaintiff was awarded a verdict in the amount of $750,000. Given the prior criminal incidents at the motel, more security precautions were clearly needed.

Another court found a Club Med resort was not entitled to summary judgment where a former male employee, terminated because of a "bad spirit", entered a female guest's room uninvited at 5:30 A.M. Another guest had reported an intrusion into her room about an hour earlier. Security personnel were aware the former employee had been in the club's disco that night and had not left through the Club's front gate after the disco closed. Two guards tried unsuccessfully to locate him on the premises. Two months prior to the incident two disgruntled employees had damaged the Club's restaurant, entered five guest rooms and stole numerous items. The court declined to rule that the security measures taken by the hotel were sufficient under the circumstances and instead referred the case to trial for a jury to decide. *Grossman v. Club Med Sales, Inc.*, 640 A.2d 1194 (N.J., 1994).

Adequate Security Can Eliminate Liability.   As the next case illustrates, if a hotel takes adequate security precautions but a guest is nonetheless attacked, the hotel will not be liable. As you read this case, assess whether, in your opinion, the security measures were sufficient.

CASE EXAMPLE 7–12

Courtney v. Remler
566 F. Supp. 1225 (S.C., 1983)

The plaintiff was the victim of a brutal assault, robbery and rape while on her honeymoon on Hilton Head Island in Beaufort County, South Carolina. The incident occurred on October 1, 1979, while the plaintiff and her husband were spending the weekend at a motel owned by the defendants. The complaint alleged that the defendants negligently supervised and operated the motel in which the incident occurred, and such negligence was the proximate cause of the injuries, both physical and mental, sustained by the plaintiff.

Findings of Fact

. . . 11. Criminal activity on Hilton Head Island had steadily increased each year since 1975.

12. There had been no assaults or any other crimes against any person occurring on the Islander Inn premises prior to the subject assault. . . .

19. The Islander Inn complex consisted of a main building housing the lobby, reception area, restaurant and lounge. There were four (4) outlying buildings containing guest rooms. Each of the buildings containing guest rooms was rectangular in shape, two (2) stories in height, and had front and rear access doors. In addition, each ground level room had access to the outside via a sliding glass door. . . .

21. Above each guest room door was a fluorescent light which provided the illumination of the hallways and the ability to see through the "observation port" located within the room side of the door. In front of each florescent light was a wooden valance to reflect the light rays directly up and down.

22. The motel room (Room 220) in which the assault occurred, as all rooms, had a fire-rated steel entrance door with a steel door frame. The steel door frame was constructed with a solid metal doorstop which prevented the opening of the door by the insertion of any object between the doorstop and the balance of the frame.

23. The doors were equipped with a door-latch with an automatic locking device. The doors closed and locked automatically.

24. The doorknob on the door was a motel security type which required the use of a key to open the door from the hall. The exterior or hallway-side portion of the doorknob contained "security lips," a mechanism utilized to deter the possible picking of the lock. . . .

26. [The] observation port contained optics providing for magnification and wide vision when looking from the inside to the outside.

27. The door was not equipped with a chain lock or safety chain. . . .

29. The sliding glass door, which provided a second means of access to the outside, contained a locking mechanism which had to be locked manually from the interior. It was the policy of the management to have a sticker or decal affixed to the sliding glass door above the handle and locking mechanism warning all guests to keep doors locked for their protection. It was the further policy of management to have the maids, when cleaning a room, leave all drapes covering the sliding glass door half-way open to allow sunlight to enter the room, and, consequently, this warning decal could easily have been seen. The maids were also instructed by management to replace any decals that either wore off or were torn off. . . .

32. On a twenty-four (24) hour basis, security was provided by "in-house" personnel, including specific staff members and a security conscious awareness program extending to all employees. . . .

39. Between 7:30 and 8:00 P.M. on October 1, 1979, the plaintiff and her husband were in their room, at which time they heard a knock at their motel door. Having been told by friends at their wedding that they would visit them after they arrived on Hilton Head Island, the plaintiff's husband responded to the knock.

40. The plaintiff's husband received no response to his inquiry as to who was there and looked through the "observation port." Seeing no one, he opened the door.

41. Once the door was opened, two (2) black males, armed with pistols and wearing coverings over their heads, forced their way into the room. They bound and gagged the plaintiff and her husband, robbed them of their money, ransacked their luggage and room, and raped and assaulted the plaintiff. . . .

Conclusions of Law

[T]he defendants in the present case argue that they had no duty to protect their motel guests from criminal attacks since the assault and rape of October 1, 1979, could not be reasonably anticipated. The defendants argue that there had never been a crime against a person on the premises until the rape against the plaintiff, although van-dalism incidents had been reported on a few occasions. On the other hand, there can be no question that crime had dramatically increased on Hilton Head Island over the four years preceding the rape attack. Even one of the defendants' witnesses, a county police officer, testified as to the dramatic increase in crime on the island. In addition, during the three month period immediately preceding the attack on the plaintiff, a rape was reported each month on Hilton Head Island. . . . In fact, the Islander Inn added light poles around the perimeter of the premises after discussions about the rape incidents. . . .

The Islander Inn hired a private security guard in May 1979 to guard the premises during the hours of 10:30 P.M. to 7:00 A.M. According to Mr. Kwaiser, all employees were informed of the crime problems on the island and instructed how to react if confronted with a crime. These types of actions by the Islander Inn is an indication of its awareness of the criminal activity on the island. The security guard was presumably hired to protect the guests from late night crimes. As evidenced by its own conduct, Island Inn obviously foresaw the possibility of criminal attacks on its guests and made a determination to combat the attacks. Since the defendants knew or should have known the possibility of criminal acts on their guests, they had a duty to exercise reasonable care to protect against such acts arising.

An innkeeper is not the insurer of safety for his guests. Rather, he owes to his guest the duty of exercising reasonable care to maintain in a reasonably safe condition those parts of his premises which a guest may be expected to use. . . . In the final analysis, the issue is whether, under all the circumstances, the innkeeper in this case provided for its guests reasonable protection against injuries from criminal acts. . . .

[I]t would be incorrect for this court to say the mere fact of a rape is conclusive evidence that security at the Inn was unreasonable. To do such would be to hold the Inn as an insurer of its guests' safety.

. . . There can be no doubt that armed guards in every building, twenty-four hours a day, would have provided the guests with more protection than the security system employed by Islander Inn.

However, it must be remembered that the Inn's function was as a luxury island motel, not a prison. In considering the reasonableness of the security, the court must take into account the purpose and function of the business.

Based on the lack of criminal activity on the premises in the past, one uniformed guard during the nighttime hours is reasonable security for a guest at the motel. The motel is relatively small with 190 total guest rooms. One trained guard could adequately patrol the premises. . . .

The plaintiff also alleges the buildings were negligently designed. This claim is based on the fact that the guest room doors were recessed and this made it difficult for one looking through the "observation port" to see visitors outside the door. Also, the recessed doorways made lighting in the hall inadequate, giving a shadow-effect throughout the hallway. There was testimony from the building architect that the hallways were designed in this fashion to avoid the dreary effect of long, straight hallways. . . . The same type of design is prevalent throughout the industry. The recessed doors do not obstruct the view through the "observation port" if the visitor is standing at the door. The only view that is obstructed is if someone knocks at the door and steps a few feet away from the door. That should caution the guest that something suspicious is happening. Therefore, the design of the building is reasonable.

The lighting in the hallways, although dim, was adequate. . . .

The plaintiff next alleges that the doors to the guest rooms did not provide adequate protection for the guests. The essence of this charge is the failure of the doors to be equipped with "safety chains" or "chain locks." The architect for the motel testified that safety chains were deliberately excluded because they hindered management's entry into a room in case of emergencies. The doors had numerous locking and safety mechanisms which provided adequate protection for the guests. . . .

The Islander Inn, as a whole, was operated and supervised reasonably. The Inn obviously felt a need to protect its guests from criminal attacks by third person, and measures were taken to ensure their safety. The measures were reasonable. The rape incident was a truly unfortunate and horrible experience, but the defendants cannot be held responsible. For this court to hold otherwise would be equivalent to making all motels the insurer of their guests' safety. Therefore, it is

ORDERED, that this action be dismissed.

CASE QUESTION

1. What security measures did the hotel maintain? Why did the court conclude these measures were sufficient? How could security have been improved?

Security Personnel and Firearms.   Should security personnel in a hotel carry weapons? This is a difficult question and there is no easy answer. A gun in the hands of even a well-trained guard can present dangers. If the guard is attacked and subdued, the attacker will have easy access to the firearm and may misuse it. A gun can be a very dangerous instrument in the hands of someone not well trained in its use. An unarmed security guard may be of only limited help in the event of an attack, and the hotel or restaurant that employs the guard risks civil liability for any injuries the guard incurs.

Duty Owed by Hotel to Security Personnel

Just as the hotel is liable to its guests for failing to use reasonable care to protect their safety, it is likewise liable to its security guards. In *Pucalik v. Holiday Inns, Inc.*, 777 F.2d 359 (7th Cir., 1985), a police officer who worked part time at the hotel as a security guard was shot and killed while working at the hotel. At the time of the incident the only entrance to the hotel was through a front, locked door. The court ruled that the officer's death was due to the negligence of the hotelkeeper who failed to repair the front door's self-locking device that had been reported as needing repair. When a guest arrived late at night for a room, the guard opened the door but it did not relock after the guest was admitted. A second person then entered and shot and killed the guard. The court held the hotel owed the guard a duty to use ordinary care in maintaining reasonably safe premises. The jury awarded the guard's family $1,250,000.

Restaurant Security.   Restaurants, like hotels, face security problems. These will be discussed in Chapter 12.

Medical Care

A hotel is not required to offer its guests medical services. To avoid legal complications surrounding the issue of medical care, most hotels today will avoid recommending a particular doctor. Instead, the hotel might provide a list of available physicians and require the guest to select. This eliminates the possibility of a claim against the hotel for negligence where a doctor recommended by a hotel malpractices and the guest is injured as a result.

If a hotel chooses to offer medical services it must exercise reasonable care in the selection of medical personnel and in the provision of the services.

A guest at a Hilton Hotel fell backwards in his hotel room while dressing and hit his head against the wall. He became nauseous and complained to his travel companion of a headache. The latter called hotel management for a doctor and was advised that "some help" would be sent. A woman arrived within a half hour and identified herself as a nurse. After ascertaining the circumstances she recommended the guest remain in bed for twelve hours. By the next day he was in a comatose state. He was taken by ambulance to the hospital where surgery was immediately performed. He suffered permanent brain damage. In fact, the woman who had come to his hotel room was not a licensed nurse. While the hotel had a medical department, a physician was not on call during the evenings. Instead, the woman responded to medical calls "with the full knowledge and consent of the hotel management." Expert testimony established the following: the guest was exhibiting classic symptoms of a blood clot in the brain at the time the woman came to the guest's room; a licensed nurse would have identified the symptoms; a nurse would have sought immediate treatment; and prompt medical care would have averted the brain damage. The court stated that, while the hotel did not owe a duty to its guests to provide medical services, if it undertakes to do so, it must send a doctor "or at the very least a nurse." The appellate court affirmed a judgment against the hotel. *Stahlin v. Hilton Hotels Corp.*, 484 F.2d 580 (Ill., 1973).

Another case involving medical care illustrates proper conduct on the part of a hospitality facility when confronted with a medical emergency. A casino patron/plaintiff had a heart attack while gambling at a blackjack table. The dealer immediately summoned security who responded quickly and, upon assessing the circumstances, called the casino medical station. A nurse arrived at the scene within minutes and immediately instructed security to call an ambulance. She assisted three other patrons in providing CPR. When the ambulance arrived the attendants intubated plaintiff [a procedure in which a tube is inserted into the trachea to help restore the ability to breathe] which caused him to regain a pulse. Plaintiff claimed the casino violated its duty of care to him because the nurse did not intubate him prior to the arrival of the ambulance as a result of which his heart attack was prolonged. The court held that the casino's duty was to summon aid and, until aid arrived, provide reasonable first aid measures. The casino's duty did not require it to provide medical equipment and personnel necessary to perform an intubation. *Lundy v. Adamar of New Jersey, Inc. t/a Trop World*, 34 F.3d 1173 (3rd Cir., 1994).

As with any negligence case, a plaintiff claiming a hotel that offered medical services was negligent must prove proximate cause between the hotel's negligence and the guest's injuries. Sometimes this can be difficult. In *Room v. Caribe Hilton Hotel*, 659 F.2d 5 (P.R., 1981), plaintiff guest, after gambling, retired to his room and began feeling ill. The hotel service directory advertised that a physician was available at all times so the guest called the operator and asked for the doctor. After about four hours the doctor still had not arrived and friends suggested he go directly to the hospital, where he was diagnosed as having a myocardial infarction. He stayed in the hospital for one month. Upon returning to New York, he tried to work but was unable to concentrate because of head pains, poor memory, and other disorders. The plaintiff sued for $1 million for loss of earnings and for pain and suffering inflicted by the hotel's failure to provide him with timely medical care. Plaintiff lost because he failed to establish that, had the hotel doctor arrived soon after plaintiff called for help, he would have avoided the illness. Although the hotel breached its duty to provide promptly the medical treatment it advertised, plaintiff failed to prove that the breach of duty was the proximate cause of his injuries.

Sometimes hotel staff may try to diagnose a guest's problem and suggest home remedies. Personnel should be trained not to do this. A guest whose injury is made worse by such advise will surely sue and is likely to win a resulting lawsuit.

Summary

The potential liability faced by a hotel or restaurant for negligent acts includes virtually every part of the business. As illustrated in this chapter, hospitality establishments will be liable for failing to properly maintain sidewalks and sporting facilities on the premises, and for inadequate lighting inside and outside of the buildings. A hotel offering swimming facilities must use reasonable care to protect the safety of guests who use these amenities. Likewise, precautions must be taken to avoid fire and if fire does break out, to minimize injury to guests. Hospitality facilities must exercise reasonable care to protect the safety of their patrons. Security measures consistent with the risks are required.

If a hotel chooses to offer medical services, it must use reasonable care to ensure that the care giver is qualified, has proper credentials and adequate care is provided.

Only by regular and frequent inspections and prompt repairs of dangerous conditions, can hotels and restaurants avoid liability for negligence.

Preventive Law Tips for Managers

- *Instruct valets how to protect patrons from dangers presented by arriving and departing vehicles.* The unloading area of hotels and restaurants often becomes congested with people and several lanes of traffic. A car pulling out, pulling in, or backing up could foreseeably hit an arriving or departing guest. The valet and other employees who greet arriving patrons at their cars must be alert to the risks and guide both pedestrian and vehicular traffic to avoid accidents.

- *Adequately illuminate all areas in a hotel or restaurant, and be particularly watchful of parking lots and stairs.* Many accidents occur because customers are unable to see where they are walking. Areas particularly prone to accidents due to insufficient lighting are parking lots and steps. Once adequate lighting is installed examine it regularly to ensure the fixtures and bulbs are operable.

- *Be sure sporting facilities are designed safely and maintained properly.* Poorly designed and poorly maintained facilities increase the risk of injury to users. A hotel owes its guests the duty to exercise reasonable care to keep the facilities in a safe condition. While guests assume the ordinary risks associated with a sport, they do not assume the risk that the facilities are hazardous.

- *Hotels with swimming pools must provide rescue equipment, including, without limitation, ropes, rings, poles, and shepherd's hooks.* Failure to provide rescue devices can result in a drowning that was avoidable. The equipment should be kept very close to the pool and readily accessible. It should be examined regularly to assure freedom from defects.

- *Clearly display the depth of the pool.* Clearly posting the depth of pool water can prevent accidents caused by guests diving in water that is too shallow, and by guests proceeding into water that is too deep for ability. The depth should be painted in large numbers and bright colors along the perimeter of the pool. Regularly verify that the depth of the water is consistent with the postings. For pools with unusual depth, such as a pool that has no deep end, signage should also be used to alert unsuspecting swimmers.

- *Provide every possible safety precaution in the pool area.* Always rope off the shallow area to alert swimmers when they are entering the deep end. Demand a life saving certificate from life guards. Be intolerant of horseplay in and around the pool. Clean the water frequently and apply necessary chemicals to prevent the water from becoming cloudy. Use underwater lights in the evening. Verify that the diving board is made from appropriate material and is the proper length. Do not let the water in the pool get low. If the water is low the depth markings will be inaccurate. A diver may be misled into thinking that diving is safe when in fact it is not. Alert guests if a lifeguard is not provided. Use material that is slip-resistant for the floor of the area around the pool. Clean regularly around and in the pool to remove objects that might cause injury to bare feet. Install a telephone close to the pool so that help can be summoned quickly in an emergency.

- *Check the statutes in your state and locality that mandate pool safety features and strictly comply.* Failure to abide by safety laws is negligence per se. The laws in different states and localities vary. Review the applicable laws with a lawyer and make arrangements to obey them.

- *Take every possible safety precaution in beach areas.* Rake the sand along the beach to protect barefoot strollers from foot injuries. Rake the bottom of the area of water into which swimmers walk and dive to remove objects a swimmer might hit. Restrict the areas in which surfboards and like paraphernalia can be used to avoid swimmers being hit by them. Post signs warning of unusual water conditions such as a strong undertow.

- *Check state and local fire safety laws and strictly comply.* Failure to comply with fire safety laws constitutes negligence per se. Fire safety laws often require that equipment such as fire extinguishers be maintained in good condition on the premises and that fire escapes be provided. They also mandate specifications in the construction of new buildings and additions. The laws in different states and localities vary. Review the applicable laws with a lawyer and make arrangements to conform.

- *Train employees thoroughly on what to do in case of fire.* Many lawsuits requiring hotels to compensate guests injured in fires result from employees who fail to timely call the fire department or alert the guests. This problem can be remedied by thorough training and practice drills. Employees should be instructed to call the fire department immediately when a fire is reported. Their next step should be to alert guests in a manner consistent with hotel facilities and policies.

- *If a hotel provides medical services, verify the credentials and capability of the caregiver.* A hotel will be liable if it represents to a guest that a doctor or nurse will be provided when the supposed professional is not certified. A hotel should have referral information on local doctors readily available to give to inquiring guests. Before referring a guest to a particular local doctor, the hotel should confirm the physician's qualifications and standing in the medical community. If the hotel directory advertises 24-hour availability of medical services, they should be offered around the clock.

- *Exercise reasonable care to protect guests from criminal activity.* Make an assessment of the security risks at the establishment and implement a plan to address them. The assessment should include a review of recent security incidents at the hotel or restaurant and in the vicinity, as well as particular risks presented by the premises such as multibuilding layouts and outdoor access to guest rooms. The plan could include such security devices as: security guards; enhanced lighting in the parking lot, in hallways, and in other appropriate places; TV monitors; automatic locks on the doors; chain or safety locks; special door knobs that deter picking of locks; peepholes; door construction designed to prevent unauthorized entry; and computerized keys that change with each guest. The business should also develop an alliance with the local police for advise and back-up help.

- *Instruct employees on how to handle a phone call announcing an emergency.* In the event of an emergency, time is of the essence. If an employee receiving an emergency call does not respond timely and adequately, a patron may be severely injured and the hotel or restaurant may be liable. Adequate training of employees on how to handle emergency calls can mitigate many would-be security incidents.

- *Be alert to suspicious circumstances on the premises.* Employees should be trained to watch for unusual circumstances or suspicious people on the premises, such as an ex-employee who enters the premises late at night or a person in the lobby who approaches guests for no apparent reason. Depending on the circumstances, the person should be watched until the suspicion fades, the person should be asked to leave, or the police should be called.

Review Questions

1. What responsibility, if any, does an innkeeper have to maintain its sporting facilities in a safe condition?

2. Do diners assume the risk that a fire might occur at a restaurant? Why or why not?

3. What kind of safety devices should the operator of a swimming pool keep near the pool?

4. Name four causes of swimming pool accidents.

5. Must a hotel have medical personnel on duty at all times?

6. Is a restaurant an insurer of its patrons safety?

Discussion Questions

1. Identify five circumstances in which liability can result to a hotel for failing to maintain its sporting facilities properly. State how the liability could be avoided.

2. Identify five circumstances in which liability can result to a hotel for failing to provide adequate lighting. State how the liability could be avoided.

3. Identify three circumstances in which liability can result to a restaurant for failing to provide adequate lighting. State how the liability could be avoided.

4. Identify five circumstances in which liability can result to a hotel for failing to maintain its swimming pool properly. State how the liability could be avoided.

5. Identify five circumstances in which liability can result to a hotel for failing to handle a fire properly. State how the liability could be avoided.

6. Identify four circumstances in which liability can result to a restaurant for failing to handle a fire properly. State how the liability can be avoided.

7. Identify three circumstances in which liability can result to a hotel for failing to provide adequate medical services. State how the liability can be avoided.

8. Identify five circumstances in which liability can result to a hotel for failing to provide adequate security. State how the liability can be avoided.

9. Under what circumstances is a hotel with oceanfront property liable to a guest who is injured in the water, and under what circumstances is it not liable?

10. How should the front desk of a hotel respond when a guest calls stating, "This is an emergency."

11. To avoid liability, must all hotels hire security guards? Why or why not?

12. In *Hooks v. Washington Sheraton Corp.*, the 1976 Olympic diving coach testified as an expert witness concerning characteristics of Duraflex diving boards. Why was an expert witness needed in that case but not in *LaPlante v. Raddison Hotel Co.* involving the overcrowded banquet room?

Application Questions

1. Bob is attending a conference of hotel managers. During a break in the program he goes for a walk in a wooded area on the hotel premises. He comes to a large pond. Rather than walk over the bridge that spans the pond, he decides to try to walk across on rocks that are positioned irregularly across the water. While crossing, he falls and is seriously hurt. If he sues the hotel for negligence, should he be successful? Why or why not?

2. Joshua fell in a restaurant parking lot because the lights were dim. At the time he was on his way to attend the wedding reception of a close friend which was being held in the restaurant. The hotel argued he was negligent for exiting his car in the dark. Was Joshua negligent in this case?

3. While swimming at the pool at the Browninger Resort, Ursala, age 31, was hit on the head by Tom, another swimmer, age 11, who had been engaged in horseplay with two friends for a half hour. The lifeguard had requested Tom and his friends to settle down twice during that time but to no avail. If Ursala sues the resort for negligence, what is the likelihood she will win? Why?

4. Juan was sitting in the bar in a restaurant waiting to be seated for dinner. A man he had never seen before mistook him for someone else and, without warning, hit Juan in the face. He was injured and sued the bar for negligence because it failed to prevent the assault. Will the hotel be liable under these circumstances? What additional facts would you like to know before deciding?

5. The Charmin' Motel, located in a medium-crime area, was the site of a rape eight months ago. As a result the hotel installed monitors covering the front and back entrances and the elevators, and requested that the police increase their normal surveillance of the building during the night. Tyrone, a guest at the motel, was assaulted in his room in the middle of the night by two attackers who broke a window to his room to gain entry. Tyrone suffered a broken jaw and the theft of $1000. Is Charmin' Motel liable for his injuries? Explain.

UNIT III

Relationships with Guests and Other Patrons

CHAPTER 8

Guests and Other Patrons

CHAPTER OUTLINE

Introduction

Who Qualifies as a Guest?

Intent of Parties

Guests' Illegal Acts

Termination of a
Guest-Innkeeper Relationship

Landlord-Tenant Relationship

INTRODUCTION

An innkeeper owes certain duties to those who use the hotel's facilities. Those duties vary depending on whether the patron is a guest as that term is defined legally. Not everyone who utilizes or seeks to utilize the facilities of a hotel or inn becomes a guest in the legal sense. Instead, they may be shoppers, restaurant customers, special event-goers, tenants, trespassers, and the list goes on. Whether or not a person qualifies as a guest has legal significance. For example, if property is stolen from a hotel, the extent of the hotel's liability will be directly impacted by whether or not the property owner is a guest. We will study this at length in Chapter 9. A hotel owes certain duties to guests but not to others, for example, to refrain from insulting or humiliating them. We will study this obligation in Chapter 11. As we saw in Chapter 5, a hotel owes to invitees a duty to act reasonably. Guests are invitees. Thus, the outcome of many negligence lawsuits turns on whether or not the plaintiff is a guest.

This chapter explains who qualifies as a guest and discusses the other types of relationships that exist in a hotel.

Who Qualifies as a Guest?

For a person visiting an inn to qualify as a guest, the visit must be for the primary purpose for which an inn operates—rental of rooms suitable for overnight stay. As a general rule, people are not guests unless they require overnight accommodations. People who register at the hotel for rooms are guests. People in the hotel for some other reason do not qualify. For example, a patron of a hotel shop who is not otherwise a guest of the hotel does not become a guest merely by shopping in the hotel. Nor is a passerby who enters the hotel lobby to use the phone a guest. A person who comes to the hotel for the sole purpose of attending a banquet or reception but does not register for a room is likewise not a guest. *Ross v. Kirkeby Hotels*, 160 N.Y.S.2d 978 (1957). Similarly, a person attending a seminar at a hotel but not registering for a room is not a guest. *Augustine v. Marriott Hotel*, 503 N.Y.S.2d 498 (1986).

In the following case a patron in a hotel cocktail lounge who was not a registered guest in the hotel claimed he was shortchanged by the waiter, and then insulted, humiliated, and embarrassed. The liability of the hotel turned on whether the patron qualified as a guest. As we will study in Chapter 11, the hotel in this case will be liable if the patron is a guest; it will not be liable if he is not a guest. You should be able to anticipate how the court ruled.

CASE EXAMPLE 8–1

Wallace v. Shoreham Hotel Corp.
49 A.2d 81 (D.C., 1946)

. . . The substance of the complaint is that plaintiff, in company with his wife and four friends, was a guest at the cocktail lounge of defendant's hotel; that, in payment of the check rendered, plaintiff gave the waiter a $20 bill but received change for only $10; that the waiter insisted he had received from plaintiff a $10 bill and stated publicly for all in the lounge to hear: "We have had people try this before"; that in fact plaintiff had tendered a $20 bill, which fact was later admitted by representatives of the hotel and proper change given plaintiff; that the language of the waiter indicated to those present in the lounge that plaintiff was underhanded and of low charac-

ter and that his demand for change was illegal and comparable to that of a cheat or other person whose reputation for honesty is open to question; that by reason thereof plaintiff was "insulted, humiliated, and otherwise embarrassed." The plaintiff sought judgment for punitive damages of $3,000.

. . . The question thus presented is whether a patron of a cocktail lounge has a cause of action for humiliation and embarrassment resulting from insulting words of a waiter.

It has been held that an innkeeper owes a duty extending to a guest of respectful and decent treatment, and that the innkeeper is liable to a guest for insulting words or conduct. . . . Such duty, however, rests on the peculiar relationship between innkeeper and guest. . . . In the instant case the defendant is an innkeeper. The complaint alleges plaintiff was a "guest" at the cocktail lounge and not a registered guest of the hotel. . . . One who is merely a customer at a bar, a restaurant, a barber shop or newsstand operated by a hotel does not thereby establish the relationship of innkeeper and guest. . . . The situation, as we see it, is the same as if the plaintiff had been the customer of any restaurant or tavern where drinks are served.

[Judgment, therefore, was for the defendant.]

CASE QUESTION

1. What one fact in this case, if changed, would have resulted in plaintiff winning the lawsuit?

Intent of Parties

The innkeeper-guest relationship is a contractual one—the parties exchange the exclusive use of a room for money. An essential element of all contracts is an intention by the parties to enter a contract. Guest status can arise once the intention is formulated, even before the contract is entered. Thus, a transient becomes a guest upon entering a hotel intending to procure overnight accommodations where the innkeeper has a room available. It is not essential that the guest be registered.

How does one determine whether the parties have formulated an intention to enter a contract? The actions of the parties usually evidence whether they have such an intention. A request for a room or an advance registration is sufficient to evidence intent on the part of a transient to become a guest. If the innkeeper registers the traveler and provides a room, this is sufficient evidence of intent on the innkeeper's part to form an innkeeper-guest relationship.

Registration

While registration clearly evidences intent on both the guest's and innkeeper's part to develop an innkeeper-guest relationship, registration is not essential for the relationship to exist. In the following case, two young males registered for a hotel room. A question arose whether the innkeeper intended to contract with two minor females who did not register and who, unknown to the innkeeper, accompanied the two males. One of the females was injured due to the hotel's negligence. If the females qualified as guests the hotel would be liable for the injuries. If, on the other hand, an innkeeper-guest relationship did not exist, the girls would be trespassers and the innkeeper would not be liable.

CASE EXAMPLE 8–2

Langford v. Vandaveer
254 S.W.2d 498 (Ky., 1953)

[Ruth Vandaveer] was severely burned in the explosion of a butane or propane gas heater in a cabin of a motor court operated by the appellant, Clyde B. Langford. . . . Our present inquiry is whether the young lady was a guest.

On Sunday afternoon of January 22, 1950, four young people, C. P. Howe, Bill Nash, Ruth Vandaveer, and Myna Walker, drove to Henderson, Kentucky, from Albion, Illinois, a distance of sixty miles or more. Miss Vandaveer, . . . 17 years old, and Miss Walker, about 15, were students in the high school at Albion and the young men worked in the oil fields near Henderson. The men went into a hotel where Howe's brother was staying, but could not procure accommodations. The party then drove to Langford's Motor Court, a short distance from the city. This was about 8:30 o'clock. The car was stopped in a well lighted place near the entrance of the office and restaurant. Howe met Langford at the door and asked for rooms for four oil men, saying that one of them was then at work but would return early enough to get some rest before checking out time. Langford showed the cabins to the two men, lighted the heaters and explained to them how the valves worked. He and Howe returned to the office and Howe filled out a registration card, giving his address and an automobile license number and signed it "C. P. Howe and party." He filled in the figure "4," showing the number of people in the party and paid $6 for the two rooms. Neither Howe nor Miss Walker testified. Miss Vandaveer and Nash testified he stood by the side of the automobile at all times. It is undisputed that Langford passed twice within ten or fifteen feet of the parked automobile. He says he looked at the car and could have seen anyone in it but saw no one. As the car started over to the cabins he noted that the license number was not the same as that registered and he entered the correct number on the card. (It appears that Howe had given the number of his own car instead of Nash's which he was driving.) Miss Vandaveer testified that when Langford passed the automobile she was sitting on the edge of the back seat looking into the small mirror in front, combing her hair, and Miss Walker was on the front seat doing the same thing. Both were erect and could be easily seen.

According to Miss Vandaveer and Nash, the party entered one of the cabins and then the other where they spent some time together. Then the boys left about ten o'clock to go to work. They planned to return early enough to drive the girls back to Albion in time for school. After they had gone, she and Myna concluded to occupy separate cabins. She took No. 4 and retired about eleven o'clock. Neither had any baggage. On the contrary, Langford and his sister testified that about 11:15 Howe came to the restaurant, ate a sandwich, drank a cup of coffee and then left with three colas. Nash testified he and Howe left the motor court about ten o'clock and worked until seven the next morning. However, there is evidence that immediately following the explosion Howe was there. A man in or about the cabin was heard to say, "I told you not to do that." One of these witnesses, according to Langford, first told him of the presence of the girls on the premises.

The relation of innkeeper and guest is a mutual contractual one, and the existence of intention by both parties is an essential element. It is an exceptional case where that requisite is not clearly established, usually by implication. Ordinarily, where one holds himself out to the public as an innkeeper, and is accustomed to receive all who apply and a transient goes to the [inn] to procure accommodation and receives [same], the relationship is created. But . . . it is not essential that the guest shall have registered . . . though it may be an important circumstance in determining the status.

In the case at bar, the intention of the young lady to become a guest in the legal sense is apparent. The question is whether or not she was intentionally or knowingly *received* as such by the proprietor of the motor court. (Emphasis added.)

[A] person may not impose himself upon the proprietor and become a guest without [the proprietor's] knowledge or intention to receive [the person]. One becomes a guest only if he is received to be treated as a guest and the intention to become such must be communicated to the innkeeper or his agent. [As stated in a prior case,] . . . "a mere guest of the registered occupant of a room at a hotel, who shares such room with its occupant without the knowledge or consent of the hotel management, would not be a guest of the hotel, as there would be no contractual relations in such case between such third person and the hotel proprietor. ". . .

Here we have the acceptance of four men as guests when there were in fact two men and two women. . . . According to the innkeeper's testimony, the young lady slipped into the cabin and occupied the room for the night without the proprietor's knowledge or consent. . . . [In another case,] where a registered guest, without permission from anyone representing the hotel, transferred a room to a woman, she had no right to its possession [and did not qualify as a guest]. . . .

There is no dispute in the evidence that Howe procured the two rooms for four men. But if the proprietor of the motor court saw the young women in the car under the circumstances described and could reasonably have anticipated or understood that they would occupy the cabin, then the jury could find he accepted her as a guest and assumed the legal responsibility owing in such relationship. . . . Ruling of the [appeals] court: [The trial court should not have determined Vandaveer was a guest as a matter of law. Rather, the issue turns on a question of fact and should have been submitted to a jury for determination. Trial ordered.]

CASE QUESTION

1. Assume you are on the jury in this case. Based on the information available, would you hold that plaintiff was a guest? Why or why not?

Delivery of Property

As the court in *Langford* stated, registration at the hotel is not essential for an innkeeper-guest relationship to exist. Some cases hold that a person who intends to register but hasn't yet done so becomes a guest by delivering luggage to a hotel employee. In such cases, the soon-to-be guest evidences an intent to become a guest by giving possession to the hotel employee. The hotel's intent is evidenced by its acceptance of the luggage. The responsibility of the proprietor as innkeeper starts at the moment of the delivery and acceptance of the suitcase.

In one case a jewelry salesman, upon arrival at the MGM Grand Hotel in Las Vegas, checked his luggage and jewelry samples with the bellhop at the door. Thereafter he registered, went to his room, and waited for his luggage. When it arrived he discovered that some of the jewelry samples were missing. The liability of the hotel depended on whether the salesman was a guest when he gave his luggage to the bellhop. The court held the salesman became a guest at the time he made use of the hotel's luggage check service since that service was provided specifically for guests. *Pachinger v. MGM Grand Hotel-Las Vegas, Inc.*, 802 F2d 362 (9th Cir., 1986). Similarly, the innkeeper-guest relationship could begin when the traveler alights from a taxi in front of the hotel and gives the bellhop the luggage, or steps into a hotel van or car at the airport and gives the driver the luggage, assuming a room is available and the traveler intends to register.

In the next case the plaintiff left her luggage at the defendant hotel, although her room reservation did not begin until the next day. Jewelry was stolen from her luggage. The court had to determine whether the parties' intention to enter a contract on the *following* day was sufficient to render the plaintiff a guest on the day the luggage was checked. The court held it was.

CASE EXAMPLE 8–3

Adler v. Savoy Plaza Inc.
108 N.Y.S.2d 80 (1951)

This is an action for the loss of jewelry and personal effects contained in a suitcase which was delivered by plaintiff to defendant for safekeeping. The claimed value of the jewelry was something over $20,000 and the claimed value of the personal effects about $3,300.

The facts are as follows: The plaintiff was accustomed to staying at the defendant's hotel whenever she visited New York and had been a guest of the hotel many times. She and her husband had requested reservations for May 15, 1946. Upon their arrival at 10 o'clock that morning, they were advised that their reservation was for the following day, but that the hotel would try to accommodate them, so they registered, hoping that a room might be assigned during the day. At the same time, they delivered their luggage to the bell captain, and it was deposited in a section of the lobby set aside for the luggage of arriving and departing guests. Plaintiff's husband attended to business during the day while plaintiff was in and out of the hotel. When both returned to the hotel in the afternoon, they found that a room was still not available, so they whiled away some time in the lounge bar and had dinner in the room of a friend who was a guest of the hotel.

All during the day defendant's manager was seeking accommodations for the couple but was unable to locate any in the hotel. He finally secured accommodations for them for the night at the Sherry Netherlands Hotel where they registered at about 8:00 P.M., taking with them two suitcases and a cosmetic case, and leaving the suitcase with the valuables and two matching cases at defendant's hotel.

When plaintiff returned to defendant's hotel the next morning to take up a residence for two or three weeks and requested delivery of her luggage, the large suitcase was missing. During the night the suitcase had been delivered by the night manager of the hotel to an imposter. The circumstances of this delivery are not altogether clear as the night manager was deceased at the time of the trial. Whether there was some complicity on the part of one or more of the hotel employees, as plaintiff suggests, we are not called upon to surmise.

[One of] the questions as to the [hotel's liability for the lost] jewelry, was whether plaintiff was a guest of the hotel.

. . . We are prepared to rule as a matter of law on the admitted facts that plaintiff was a guest.

CASE QUESTIONS

1. Why do you think the court ruled that plaintiff was a guest?

2. What role did her intent to rent a room play in the determination that she was a guest?

3. Suppose plaintiff did not have reservations but the hotel allowed her to leave her bags for the day while she looked for a room elsewhere. Would plaintiff qualify as a guest in this situation?

If, when people deliver baggage to the hotel porter, they do not intend to become guests of the hotel, an innkeeper-guest relationship does not exist. In *Blakemore v. Coleman*, 701 F.2d 967 (D.C. 1983), plaintiffs had come to Washington, D.C. to celebrate President Reagan's inauguration. Before returning home, and after checking out of their hotel, they decided to have lunch at the Jockey Club, an elegant restaurant that was part of the Fairfax Hotel, which was not the hotel in which they had stayed. When they arrived at the restaurant they checked a briefcase and a small carry-on bag with the hotel doorman. After lunch they retrieved their bags from the doorman and discovered a jewelry pouch was missing. The liability of the hotel turned on whether plaintiffs qualified as guests. The court held they were not, stating, "One who is merely a customer at a bar, a restaurant, a barber shop or newsstand operated by a hotel does not thereby establish the relationship of innkeeper and guest."

Even a person who has not yet decided whether to rent a room may, under certain circumstances, be considered a guest. The key issue is whether they came to the hotel for the purpose of benefiting from the services offered by the hotel to guests. This rule of law is illustrated in the following case. Plaintiff, a traveling salesman who frequently stayed at the defendant's hotel, had not yet registered for a room on the date in issue but was considering doing so. He placed his property in a hotel safe deposit box in the meantime. The property was thereafter stolen. Since the innkeeper's liability in such cases turns on whether the property owner is a guest, the court had to determine whether the plaintiff qualified. As you read the case, note that plaintiff's prior business with the hotel was an important factor in the court's decision.

CASE EXAMPLE 8–4

Freudenheim v. Eppley
88 F.2d 280 (Pa., 1937)

. . . [F]reudenheim was the traveling salesman of his diamond firm, and . . . he was accustomed to visiting Buffalo, Detroit, Cleveland, Toledo, Chicago, Indianapolis, Cincinnati, and Pittsburgh. That if trade justified, he stayed at hotels which had vaults for the deposit of valuables and he left his bag containing diamonds in their vaults. . . . Prior to 1930 he came to Pittsburgh eight or nine times a year and stayed at the William Penn [Hotel] two, three, or four days at a time, depending on trade conditions. In 1933 he was twice in Pittsburgh, received his mail at the hotel, but did not stay overnight. On every one of his trips to Pittsburgh he used the vault at the William Penn.

On the morning of December 5, 1933, after visiting other cities, he arrived in Pittsburgh from Cincinnati before 7:00 A.M. After checking his personal bag at the railroad station, he went to the hotel. [He testified]: "I intended to stay here as long as I could do business here." He arrived at the hotel around 7:00 A.M., but the cashier's office, where the hotel had vaults, was not open, and the cashier, Schaller, had not arrived.

His testimony was: "I waited around the lobby until about seven-thirty and around seven-thirty I went back to the cashier's office and saw Mr. Schaller there and he greeted me. I told him I wanted a box, or he said, 'I suppose you want a box. . . .' Whether he knew me by name, I don't know, but he knew me quite well." Continuing the witness said: "Mr. Schaller came out of the cage, which is controlled by a wire door—grill—there, and he brought out a couple of keys and a tag. He tore off part of the tag and gave me the bottom of it, and asked me to sign the upper part, which I did and returned it to him, and he gave me this stub bearing the same number as appears on the part bearing my signature which I gave to him. He then gave me two keys, which were attached to this little ring bearing a metal disc on which is noted the letter 'C.' He then inserted the key which was attached to this ring and opened the box—opened the door—and I put my brief case in which my merchandise had been placed right inside that box. I closed the door and I went downstairs."

In the first place, we have the fact that Freudenheim was known to the hotel as a past guest and that there was the possibility of his lodging at the hotel if trade warranted such stay. There was, therefore, in the mind of both parties that the hotel would have Freudenheim as a guest. He was recognized by the cashier; inquiry was made whether he wanted a box; he was given the box; his merchandise was deposited; . . . This was a service or accommodation which the hotel had extended before and Freudenheim had enjoyed before.

Now it is clear that vault service for valuables is a customary hotel accommodation, and that it was the intention of both parties that Freudenheim should have that accommodation, . . . The responsibility of an innkeeper for the safety of a traveler's property begins at the moment when the relation of guest and host arises, and that relation arises as soon as the traveler enters the inn with the intention of using it as an inn, and is so received by the host. It does not matter that no food or lodging has been supplied or found up to this time of the loss. It is sufficient if the circumstances show an intention on the one hand to provide and on the other hand to accept such accommodation.

Moreover, later on, and before he left, Freudenheim, who was busy with his customers all morning and into the afternoon and took no lunch, did take his dinner in the general dining room of the hotel. It is true he did not take a room and register, but his omission to do so does not put him out of guest protection. . . . It is not necessary that a traveler shall register at an inn as a guest in order to become such, but it is sufficient if he visits the inn for the purpose of receiving [customary services and receives them]. . . .

CASE QUESTION

1. How does this case expand our definition of who qualifies as a guest?

Checking Out

The status of guest is not instantaneously terminated upon check-out but rather continuous for a reasonable period of time while the guest remains on the hotel premises. *Moog v. Hilton Hotels Corp.*, 882 F Supp. 1392 (N.Y., 1995).

Guests' Illegal Acts

A question arises concerning the status of a would-be guest who registers at a hotel giving false information. In a case from Maine, plaintiffs sought damages for personal injuries allegedly sustained when they attempted to escape a fire in the lodging house where they were staying. They had registered as husband and wife but were not in fact married. The defendant lodging house argued that by reason of plaintiffs' misrepresentation, they were trespassers and not guests. Therefore, the argument went, the lodging house owed them no duty to exercise reasonable care.

The court, however, stated that without a demonstration that plaintiffs' illegal act directly contributed to their injuries, neither false registration nor an illegal or immoral purpose in occupying a room would effect their status as guests to whom the defendant owed the duty of reasonable care. Therefore, the plaintiffs qualified as guests and could pursue the case against the lodging house notwithstanding the false registration. *Cramer v. Tarr*, 165 F.Supp 130 (Me., 1958).

In another case from Maine an unlicensed peddler staying at an inn stored his peddler's cart in the hotel stable overnight. Goods were stolen from the cart while the peddler slept. In the peddler's lawsuit against the hotel, the innkeeper denied liability on the ground that the peddler, by peddling without a license, was engaged in illegal activity. In this case too the court held the fact that the peddler was unlicensed was not a bar to the lawsuit because the illegal act of selling without a license did not directly contribute to the theft. *Kimbel's Case* 168 A. 871 (1929).

Termination of a Guest-Innkeeper Relationship

The innkeeper-guest relationship ends when any of the following occurs: (1) the contracted time for the room has elapsed and it is not extended; (2) the bill is not paid when due; (3) due notice is given to vacate the hotel; or (4) the bill has been paid. Guests are allowed a reasonable time after vacating the room to remove their luggage and check out of the hotel, during which they continue to qualify as guests. The length of this period (a half hour, one hour, or longer) depends on the facts of each case.

Landlord-Tenant Relationship

A person who rents a room at a hotel on a long-term basis may have the legal status of a tenant rather than a guest. The innkeepers' responsibilities to a tenant differ from those owed to a guest.

To be a guest the person must be a transient, that is, his stay at the inn is temporary. If the person is staying on a permanent basis, he is a tenant. Whether a hotel patron is a tenant or a guest is determined from a number of factors, including:

- The terms of the contract between the parties (for example, use of the terminology "landlord" and "tenant" rather than "innkeeper" and "guest" suggest the patron is a tenant);

- The extent of control or supervision of the patron's room maintained by the proprietor (the more control and supervision retained by the hotel, the more likely the patron is a guest);

- The rental rate interval, for example, daily, weekly, or monthly, (the shorter the interval the more likely the patron is a guest);

- Length of occupancy (the longer the occupancy the greater the suggestion the patron is a tenant);

- Incidental services offered (for example, frequent housekeeping and room services are often associated with guests but not tenants);

- Whether the room has cooking facilities (cooking facilities are more frequently associated with a landlord-tenant relationship than an innkeeper-guest); and

- The kind of furnishings in the room and who owns them (whereas hotel rooms virtually always are furnished, rooms intended as apartments are less likely to be furnished).

None of these factors alone determines the legal relationship; the more the circumstances resemble a landlord-tenant relationship, the less likely an innkeeper-guest relationship exists.

The following two cases help explain how these factors are applied. In one, a plaintiff had an 11-month, written lease for a room at a hotel. His rent included housekeeping and telephone switchboard services. He was a tenant and not a guest. *Chawla v. Horch d/b/a Master Hotel*, 333 N.Y.S.2d 531 (1972).

In the second case, a patron at a licensed hotel occupied a room that was 12' x 15' and contained a bed and sink. Toilet and bathing facilities were located down the hall and shared with others. Cooking facilities were not provided. Rent was paid weekly. The patron occupied the room for 3$1/2$ months, during which time he had no other residence. When he registered he was required to sign a hotel registration card. He did not make any special arrangements with the hotel concerning the duration of his occupancy. The issue of whether he was a guest or a tenant arose when he was two weeks late with his rent. The legal method of evicting a guest is different from and easier than that for tenants, as is discussed at length in Chapter 10. The hotel used the easier method applicable to guests. The patron argued that he was a tenant and therefore the eviction was invalid. The court determined the relationship was innkeeper and guest, stating,

> [A]ny unilateral intention on the part of the plaintiff to remain at the hotel indefinitely or to make it his home of which [the hotel] had no reasonable notice, would not be determinative in ascertaining what contractual arrangements existed between the parties. . . .
>
> The three month duration of plaintiff's occupancy of the room was not so extended that the trial court was obliged to view it as "permanent". In conjunction with . . . the operation of the premises as a licensed hotel, the rudimentary nature of the accommodations furnished, without cooking, bathing or toilet facilities in the room, is some indication that only a temporary living arrangement was intended. Bourque v. Morris, *460 A.2d 1251 (Conn., 1983).*

Summary

The legal duties owed by an innkeeper to guests are different from those owed to nonguests. A threshold issue in many lawsuits against hotels is whether the plaintiff was a guest in the legal sense. The outcome of the case may depend on the resolution of that issue.

The easiest-to-identify guest is one who has registered for a room on a temporary basis. In doing so, the guest has evidenced an intention to utilize overnight accommodations and the hotel has evidenced its intention to provide the guest a room. The definition of guest has been expanded to include people who mistakenly come to the hotel a day earlier than the first day of their reservations and utilize baggage check services in the interim, people who are in the process of checking in, and regular overnight patrons who, on the day in question, utilize the hotel safe although unsure if they will stay in town overnight but intend to stay at the hotel if they do decide to stay over. While the class of guests has expanded, still necessary is an intention by the guest to use the hotel's accommodations and intention by the hotel to provide the guest a room on a temporary basis.

A hotel guest should be distinguished from a tenant, whose use of a room is longer term than a guest's. The obligation of an innkeeper to a guest differs from that of a landlord to a tenant.

Preventive Law Tips for Managers

- *Recognize that the innkeeper has special obligations to guests.* For this reason, know who qualifies as a guest and who does not.
- *Keep in mind that the following categories of people may qualify as guests:*
  - A person who arrives at the hotel and registers for a room.
  - A person who arrives at a hotel, intends to register, and gives luggage to the bellhop, who accepts it, assuming the hotel has rooms available.
  - A person who arrives at the airport, enters a hotel courtesy van, and gives the driver the luggage which is accepted, assuming the hotel has a room available.
  - A person who arrives at the inn, has reservations for the following day, intends to register as soon as a room is available, and leaves luggage with the bellhop who accepts delivery of it.
  - A regular guest of the hotel who arrives without reservations and, as per prior dealings with the hotel, intends to stay the night if business warrants it.
- *Illegal activity on the part of the guests may not affect their status as guests.* A person injured at a hotel who registers using false information or engages in illegal activity in the room is not thereby any less a guest for

purposes of obligations owed by the innkeeper, unless the illegality was the direct cause of injuries.

- *The innkeeper-guest relationship terminates when certain events occur.* Those events include the contracted time for the room has elapsed; the bill is not paid when due; proper notice is given to vacate the hotel; or a reasonable time has passed following check-out.

- *A tenant is not a guest.* The circumstances of a tenant vary from those of a guest in numerous ways, including: the duration of a tenant's stay usually exceeds that of a guest's; the proprietor's right to enter the room of a guest usually exceeds that for a tenant; the room rates of a guest are usually based on a daily or weekly amount whereas the rates of a tenant are usually weekly or monthly; and a tenant's room will customarily have kitchen facilities included whereas a guest's room is less likely to have them.

Review Questions

1. What role does registration play in the formation of the innkeeper-guest relationship?
2. Under what circumstances can a person who has not registered at a hotel be considered a guest?
3. What is the significance of someone qualifying as a guest?
4. Does a person who is attending a half-day seminar at a hotel without registering for a guest room qualify as a guest?
5. When does an innkeeper-guest relationship terminate?
6. What are some factors that distinguish a guest from a tenant?

Discussion Questions

1. Which of the following qualify as guests?
    a. A patron of a hotel beauty shop who works in an office nearby.
    b. A person who has a reservation at a hotel and enters the hotel's hospitality van at the airport, handing the driver her luggage.
    c. A person who registers for a room for two weeks.
    d. A resident of the area in which a hotel/resort is located who takes tennis lessons twice a week from the professional on the hotel premises.

2. At what point in the hotel check-in process do you think a person should first be deemed a guest? Why? How does your answer compare to the decisions in the cases in this chapter?

3. Under what circumstances might a guest's illegal activity on hotel premises affect the liability of the hotel for injuries to that guest?

4. The Mandarin Hotel provided rooms on a nightly, weekly and monthly basis. Jim rents a room by the week. What additional information would you need to determine whether Jim is a guest or a tenant?

Application Questions

1. Sarah is having her wedding reception at the local Holiday Inn. Her parents contracted with the hotel for the use of a banquet room and catering facilities. Sarah and her then-husband will leave immediately after the reception for their honeymoon in another state. Some out-of-town guests will be staying at the hotel overnight. Who is a guest of the hotel? Why do the others not qualify?

2. Fran flew from her home in Butte, Montana, to New York City. She planned to meet a friend at the airport for dinner. While waiting for the friend she noticed a hospitality van from the hotel at which she had reservations for that evening. She gave her luggage to the driver so she would not have to worry about its whereabouts during dinner. Does Fran qualify as a guest?

3. Mindy had reservations to stay at the Islander Inn for a week. After she was there for three nights she received a call advising that her father was quite ill. She immediately left the Inn and returned home. For what period of time was Mindy a guest? When did she cease being a guest?

4. Jerry made reservations at the Snowway Motel near a ski center. Before the trip he hurt his foot working out on a stairmaster machine and was unable to ski. He told his friend, who decided to go skiing in Jerry's stead. When the friend arrived at the hotel he explained the circumstances to the motel proprietor who agreed to rent the room to the friend. Was Jerry ever a guest of the motel? Why or why not? Does the friend qualify as a guest? Why or why not?

CHAPTER 9

Protecting Patrons' Property

INTRODUCTION

Hotel guests bring a variety of personal property to hotels, including money, jewels, clothing, sports equipment, and cars. Business travelers may bring merchandise samples or inventory for sale. Hotels often provide safes for such property, but guests may choose to leave valuables in guest rooms. Sometimes property may be left in the guest's car parked in a hotel parking lot or property may be left in the lobby, a restaurant, the pool area, or other rooms in the hotel. Unfortunately, guests' property sometimes is stolen. This chapter will discuss the liability of a hotel or restaurant when property disappears.

Risks to Property in the Hotel

Hotel theft is a problem the hospitality industry has not fully solved. This problem puts at risk the safety of guests' property while at the inn.

Hotel Theft

Unfortunately, hotel thefts are not rare. Hotel crime is an industry-wide problem. Most hotel thieves are professionals seeking money, jewels, and credit cards. They travel first class, often registering as guests in the hotel, they plan to burglarize. The many tricks of the thief include "casing" a hotel, and acquiring confidential information from maids, bartenders, or other hotel personnel. These thieves generally do not carry a weapon; if they are surprised in the act, they often convincingly pretend drunkenness.

The "typical" hotel burglar has been described as a well-dressed gentleman in his early 50s who knows good jewelry, good hotels, and the best time to make a hit. He is bold and resourceful, and often quite successful.

Hotels have developed numerous strategies to stem the increase of hotel thefts, including: increasing the number of security personnel; hiring trained professionals; warning guests to lock their rooms and put their valuables in the hotel safe; installing closed-circuit television to monitor hallways; installing electronic lock devices that are changed for each guest using the room; instituting tighter security checks on employees; and, in small hotels, installing electronic lobby doors that can be opened only by the desk clerk when a guest is recognized.

Alliances between the police and hotel security guards can enhance efforts to reduce crime. For example, the New York City Police Department has a hotel unit that concentrates on crimes committed at city hotels. The members of the unit and the security forces at the hotels hold weekly meetings at which they share information and alert each other to potential problems. This policy of hotel security working with local police on a regular basis is very important in keeping hotel security forces well informed about new methods of break-ins, current occurrences, and the latest in detection techniques.

Keys and Locks Offer Limited Security

Handling of keys can contribute to the rate of hotel thefts. Anyone given a key to a hotel room can easily have it duplicated. It is likewise easy for a guest to check out of a hotel and not return the key, permitting it to fall into the wrong hands. Leaving a hotel without returning the key is a widespread practice. A hotel in Kentucky with 227 guest rooms had an average of fifty keys a month carried away, only about one-third of which were eventually returned. In many large cities, an underground market exists for hotel keys. A would-be thief is often willing to pay a good price for guaranteed easy-entrance to hotel rooms.

To help avoid these problems, hotels should not to print the name and address of the hotel or the room number on the key. Many hotels crose code keys so that the number on the keys is not the room number. A good alternative to keys used by a growing number of hotels is electronic punch-cards with the magnetic stripes that allow the hotel to change the "key" every time a new guest occupies the room.

Guests' Insurance Does Not Protect Hotels

Many people are not personally insured against the loss of their valuables. If their property is stolen while they are at the hotel, they are likely to sue the hotel seeking compensation. If a traveler whose property disappears does have insurance coverage and recovers the loss from the insurance company, the hotel is not relieved from liability. Normally the insurance policy provides that the insurance company is subrogated (substituted) to the rights of the guest. This means that the insurance company can sue the hotel to recover the money the insurance company paid to the guest.

Absolute Liability for Guests' Goods

In prior times and according to common law, hotelkeepers were liable for any loss of guests' property occurring on hotel premises. This doctrine was called **infra hospitium**, literally meaning "within the inn." Thus, if property was stolen or otherwise disappeared from the hotel, the innkeeper was liable to reimburse the guest. This strict rule originated several centuries ago when inns were not always safe and the innkeeper was often the culprit. The rule contributed in no small measure to increasing the safety of travel. The hotel industry has changed substantially since those early days. We will see shortly that the rule of absolute liability has likewise been modified.

Exceptions to the Absolute Liability Rule

Almost every rule of law has exceptions, and the common law rule that held the innkeeper absolutely liable for guests' goods was tempered by three: (1) the loss was attributed to an act of God; (2) the loss was caused by an act of the public enemy (in time of war); and (3) the loss was precipitated by the guest. A description of each exception follows.

Acts of God.   An **act of God** is an occurrence over which people have no control, such as an earthquake, lightning, rain, snowstorms, tornadoes, and floods. Even under the common law rule of strict liability, hotels were not liable for damage to guests' property caused by acts of God. Thus, if a flood caused a foot of water in the first story of a hotel, and property of guests assigned to rooms on that floor was ruined, the hotel would not be liable to the guests for the loss. If the guests had insured their property they could pursue the insurance company for compensation, but not the hotel. If the insurance company paid the guest and thereafter attempted to sue the hotel, that lawsuit would not be successful because the hotel is not liable.

If, however, an act of God occurred and loss resulted which could have been avoided by reasonable care on the part of the hotel, the hotel was liable. Suppose a heavy rainfall resulted in water in the hotel's basement ruining skis and other sporting equipment stored there by guests. Assume further the hotel failed to provide sewer traps and shutoff valves in the sewer and drain system. Had these items been installed, the water would not have backed up into the basement. Under these circumstances was the hotel relieved from liability? The answer is no. The act of God was not the proximate cause of the excess water and property damage; the hotel's negligence in failing to install preventive devices was. Therefore, the hotel would have been liable to the guest for the loss.

The Public Enemy.   The second exception to the hotelkeeper's absolute liability for guests' property was loss caused by an act of a public enemy—that is, the adversary of a government, and could include war time and terrorist activities.

Negligent Guest.   The third exception to the innkeeper's absolute liability was the fault of the guest in failing to take precautions to safeguard his own goods. If, for instance, a guest left luggage unguarded in the hotel lobby and the suitcase was stolen, the guest could not recover. Another example involves a guest who, upon going to sleep, left the room door unlocked for a roommate who was returning later. While the guest slept, a fur coat was stolen from the room. The guest, by failing to lock the room door before retiring and knowing that a valuable coat was in the room, facilitated the theft and therefore could not recover its value from the hotel.

Prima Facie Liability Rule—Minority View

Six states have adopted a rule that modifies the common law rule by adding the following provision: Hotelkeepers are liable for property loss only if the loss occurs through their negligence; if the innkeeper can prove that the loss resulted from some other cause, the innkeeper is not liable. This is called the **prima facie liability rule**. The effect of the prima facie rule is this: if the innkeeper can show that the loss of goods resulted from some cause other than neglect by the innkeeper or the hotel employees (for example, if the goods are stolen by robbers without the aid or negligence of the innkeeper), the hotel will not be liable for the loss. If, however, the innkeeper cannot prove that it is free from negligence, the innkeeper will be liable for the loss. The six states that have adopted this rule are Illinois, Indiana, Maryland, Texas, Vermont and Washington. Justification for the rule was stated in an early case from Indiana:

> *Innkeepers, on grounds of public policy, are held to a strict accountability for the goods of their guests. The interests of the public, we think, are sufficiently [served] by holding the innkeeper prima facie liable for the loss or injury of the goods of this guest; thus throwing the burden of proof upon him, to show that the injury or loss happened without any default whatever on his part, and that he exercised reasonable care and diligence.* Laird v. Eichold, *10 Ind. 212 (1858).*

Legislative Limitations to the Absolute Liability Rule

As hotels grew in size and the number of travelers increased, the difficulty of safeguarding property increased. Current law recognizes that absolute liability is unnecessarily burdensome to modern-day hotels and innkeepers. All state legis-latures have adopted statutes to limit hotelkeepers' liability for guests' property losses, provided the hotels follow specific procedures.

Generally, these statutes significantly limit the innkeeper's responsibility for guests' property provided the hotel strictly abides by certain prerequisites. While the details of these statutes vary from state to state, certain common provisions exist, as follows.

1. The hotel must provide safes for the safe-keeping of guests' property.

2. The hotel must post notices announcing the availability of the safes.

3. The hotel must post notices announcing that the hotel's liability is limited.

4. The maximum recovery allowed to a guest for stolen or lost property is prescribed by statute and is usually substantially less than the value of the missing property. For example, a statute may specify that the maxi-mum liability will be one thousand dollars ($1000) regardless of the value of the lost property. If a hotel complies with the statute and a guest's $50,000 ring is stolen, the hotel will be liable to the guest for only $1000.

To qualify for the reduced liability the hotel must strictly comply with the statute's mandates. Because these statutes change the common law, courts inter-pret them in a very exacting way. If the innkeeper deviates from the statute in any manner, the common law rule will apply and the innkeeper will have un-limited liability. Thus, innkeepers must be careful to provide the necessary safe, post the necessary notices in the required places, and otherwise strictly comply with the particular state statute.

In this chapter, laws that restrict innkeepers liability will be called **limiting liability statutes** or **limiting statutes**. Each of the requirements for limited lia-bility will be discussed separately.

Providing a Safe

Almost invariably, the limiting liability statutes require that the innkeeper provide a "proper safe" for guests' valuables. To gain the protection of the limit-ing statutes the hotel safe must be available for guests to deposit their valuables at the time they wish to deposit them. A growing trend is for hotels to provide individual safes in each guest room. The alternative is to provide a safe or safe deposit boxes in a central location, usually in the vicinity of the front desk.

In the following case the hotel provided a central safe but it was not avail-able late in the evening when the plaintiff sought to deposit two diamond rings. What impact do you think that fact had on the hotel's liability? See if your an-swer agrees with the judge's decision.

CASE EXAMPLE 9–1

Zaldin v. Concord Hotel
421 N.Y.S.2d 858 (1979)

Plaintiffs, registered guests, bring suit on a theory of absolute liability for the loss of two valuable diamond rings that disappeared from their hotel room. In its answer, the defendant hotel pleaded [New York's limiting liability statute] by way of defense. Asserting that the hotel's vault was not available to guests at the time they attempted to place the jewelry there for safekeeping, plaintiffs moved for . . . judgment. . . . [W]e hold that a hotel may not claim the limitations on liability afforded it by [the limiting liability statute] at times when it fails to make a safe available to its guests.

[The limiting liability statute] reads: "Whenever the proprietor or manager of any hotel shall provide a safe . . . for the safekeeping of any money, jewels, ornaments, bank notes, bonds, negotiable securities, or precious stones, belonging to the guests . . . and shall notify the guests or travelers thereof by posting a notice stating the fact that such safe is provided . . . in a public and conspicuous place and manner in the office and public rooms . . . and if such guest or traveler shall neglect to deliver such property . . . for deposit in such safe, the proprietor or manager . . . shall not be liable for any loss of such property, sustained by such guest or traveler by theft or otherwise." . . . The statute goes on to limit a hotel's liability for property so deposited with it, whether the loss is sustained "by theft or otherwise," to a sum not exceeding $500.

. . . It is agreed that on Friday afternoon, the plaintiffs William and Shelby Modell, accompanied by their daughter [Anna Zaldin] and son-in-law, checked into the defendant's large resort hotel. No one disputes but that the hotel provided a safe-deposit vault for the use of its guests and that shortly after the plaintiffs' arrival, the daughter requested and was assigned one of its boxes. Plaintiffs allege that she then placed two diamond rings belonging to her mother in the box and that late the following afternoon, she withdrew them from the box for her mother to wear while attending the Saturday evening festivities sponsored by the hotel.

Sometime after midnight, however, upon the conclusion of the hotel's nightclub performance and before retiring, when the Modells and their daughter attempted to redeposit the jewelry, a hotel desk clerk informed them that the vault was closed and that they would have to retain possession of their valuables until it was opened in the morning. The defendant concedes that it would not allow guests access to the vault between the hours of eleven in the evening and eight in the morning. The Modells claim they thereupon secreted the jewelry in their room only to find, upon arising at about 9:00 A.M., that the chain lock with which they had secured the room had been cut from the outside and the rings were missing. They promptly notified the hotel and police of what they took to be a theft.

In now applying the statute to this factual framework, we first remark on the obvious: The statute's wording is plain. . . . [W]hen, as here, a statute is free from ambiguity . . . we must do no more and no less than apply the language as it is written.

Thus read, the statute offers the innkeeper an option: "Provide" a safe for your guests and sharply restrict your liability; or, feel free to do absolutely nothing about a safe and continue the risk of exposure to open-ended common law liability. But, whichever choice you make, since the statute is in derogation of [deviates from] the common law rule, to obtain the benefit of the more circumscribed liability . . . you must conform strictly with its conditions.

The statute fixes no time when a safe may or must be provided. Nor does it mandate availability around the clock. . . . These matters are left entirely up to the hotel. The statute makes no effort to evaluate cost or convenience. Neither does it distinguish between large and small inns, between those that cater to the large convention and those that cater to the individual patron, between those that come alive at night and those that do so in the day, between those that have a wealthy clientele and those that do not. The legislative formula is uncomplicated. It says, straightforwardly, that "whenever" a safe is provided, the liability limitations shall be applicable. Conversely, at those times when an innkeeper chooses not to provide a safe for the use of its guest, he cannot claim the statutory protection. . . .

More specifically, nowhere does [the limiting liability statute] suggest that an innkeeper may provide a safe part of the time and yet gain the benefit of the exemption all the time. . . .

[Judgment for plaintiffs.]

CASE QUESTIONS

1. Did the hotel violate any law by closing the safe during the night?
2. What was the consequence of failing to make the safe available at all hours?

In a Louisiana case, several guests wanting to deposit jewelry in the hotel safe waited for the night clerk for up to 40 minutes in the early morning hours. Without success they went to bed, taking their valuables with them. Following a theft that night from their room they sued the hotel. The court held the hotel liable for the full loss because the front desk was unattended and therefore access to the safe was unavailable. *Durandy v. Fairmont Roosevelt Hotel, Inc.*, 523 F.Supp. 1382 (La., 1981).

Another issue in cases involving limiting liability statutes is the theft-resistant qualities of the safe. If a safe is not adequate to withstand theft or fire, the hotel may not be able to benefit from the limiting statutes. In *Concalves v. Regent International Hotels, Ltd.*, 460 N.Y.S.2d 750 (1983), two plaintiffs each deposited one million dollars worth of jewelry in the hotel safe. The safe consisted primarily of rows of safe-deposit boxes that required two keys to open—one held by the guest, the other by the hotel. These safe-deposit boxes were housed in a room built of plasterboard, with access controlled only by two hollow-core wood doors. The lock on one door was an ordinary residential tumbler lock. The other door had no lock. Plaintiffs claimed that this room was unlocked, unattended, and open to the general public. Also, it was alleged that the card file, showing which box was assigned to which guest and when property had been deposited and removed, was exposed to public scrutiny. Thieves entered the hotel and broke into some of the safe-deposits boxes, including those used by the plaintiffs, and stole the contents. Plaintiffs sued on the grounds that the hotel failed to provide a safe as required by the statute. Each plaintiff sought damages in the amount of $1,000,000. The hotel denied liability based on the limiting liability statute.

The issue in the case was whether the hotel had provided an adequate safe. The court said that in determining whether an appropriate safe was provided, the foreseeable risks—theft and fire—must be considered. The plaintiffs relied on testimony of an expert witness with 29 years experience in design, installation, and sales of safes and vaults. He stated the hotel's facilities could be invaded in less than 30 seconds, and the safe deposit boxes should have been housed in a vault, not a room made with plasterboard and wooden doors.

If the hotel failed to provide a "safe" within the meaning of the law, the hotel is not entitled to the limited liability provided by the statute. Whether the safe provided by the hotel qualified was a question for the jury and so the court ordered a trial to address this issue. Based on the cited testimony, the jury would have good grounds to determine the hotel had not provided the necessary safe.

The requirements identified in that case for the security of central safes would similarly apply to individual in-room safes.

Posting Notice of Availability of Safe

Virtually all limiting statutes require posting of one kind or another. "Posting" means displaying a sign that calls the guests' attention to the availability of a safe and the fact that, by law, the hotel's liability for valuables is limited. Each state's statute identifies the places where the notice must be posted and what the notice must state. The required location and contents vary from state to state.

Strict Interpretation of Posting Requirements.   Failure by a hotel to comply strictly with the posting requirements will result in loss of the limited liability. Instead, the law applied in such a case will be absolute liability as imposed by common law.

In the following case, $35,000 worth of jewelry was stolen from the guest's room. The issue was whether the hotel had properly posted the availability of its safe. If the hotel had complied with the statute it would not owe the guest anything since he failed to utilize the safe. If the hotel failed to comply, it would be liable for the full $35,000.

CASE EXAMPLE 9–2

Insurance Co. of North America, Inc. v. Holiday Inns, Inc.
337 N.Y.S.2d 68 (1972)

. . . This [case] involves the liability of an innkeeper for jewelry that was missing from a guest's room. On August 10, 1968, jewelry valued in excess of $35,000 was found to be missing from a guest's room. . . . After investigation, [the guest's insurance company] paid $35,000 pursuant to an insurance policy and . . . then sued [the hotel] alleging two causes of action, the first based upon an innkeeper's common law liability as insurer of a guest's property and the second grounded on negligence. [The hotel's] answer set up [the New York limiting statute] and the alleged negligence of the guest as defenses to the action.

[The insurance company claimed the hotel] . . . had not fully complied with the posting requirements. The statute provides that an innkeeper may limit his liability by providing a place for the safekeeping of designated valuables and by informing the guests thereof "by posting a notice stating the fact that such safe is provided . . . in a public and conspicuous place and manner in the office and public rooms, and in the public parlors of such hotel, motel, or inn." The statute further provides that the innkeeper shall be relieved of liability in the event a guest neglects to deposit his valuables in such safe. . . . This testimony clearly indicates that appellant had not posted the required notice in all of the public rooms of the motel, although such notices were posted in the guest rooms. . . .

Ruling of the Court: [The hotel is not entitled to the benefit provided by the limiting liability statute; it is liable to the guest for $35,000.]

CASE QUESTIONS

1. In what way did the hotel fail to comply with the limiting statute?

2. Why did the court deny the hotel the benefit of the limiting liability statute when the guest had notice of limited liability by the posting in the guest room?

Insurance Co. v. Holiday Inns teaches that hotels must strictly comply with the posting requirements of the state's limiting statutes. When a hotel fails to post notice exactly as required by the applicable statute, the unlimited liability imposed by common law applies.

Strict compliance is required in most states. A few states are more forgiving. For example, Kentucky has enacted a statute that provides,

[A]ll statutes of this state shall be liberally construed with a view to promote their objective and carry out the intent of the legislature, and the rule that statutes in derogation of the common law are to be strictly construed shall not apply to the statutes of this state.

The effect of this type of statute is illustrated in the case of *Roth v. Investment Properties of Lexington, Inc.*, 560 S.W.2d 831 (1978). Kentucky's limiting statute required hotels to post notice in the office and public rooms of the inn. The hotel in that case had posted only on the doors in each of the guest rooms; it failed to post in the hotel office or public rooms. Further, the law had been changed, although only slightly, in regard to the information to be posted, yet the hotel displayed a copy of the law before the change. The Kentucky court held the innkeeper had sufficiently complied with the statute. This decision was based on the quoted statute, without which such a decision would not have been possible.

Most states require strict compliance with the limiting statute's requirements, as illustrated in *Insurance Co. v. Holiday Inns*.

Conspicuous Posting.   Most limiting liability state statutes require that the posted notice be **conspicuous**, meaning that the notice must be displayed in such a way that a reasonable person is likely to notice it. If, for example, the posted notice in the lobby is obscured by the branches of a decorative tree or a banner announcing a special event, the notice would not be conspicuous. If the print is not easily readable, the notice likewise is not conspicuous. In one case the hotel placed the notice under the glass on a dresser table in the hotel room. The notice was two and one-half inches square and was displayed among promotions describing the hotel and its features. In determining the notice was not conspicuous, the court stated that a guest who glanced at the total display of printed material on the dresser would likely assume its general import was advertising. *North River Insurance Company v. Tisch Management, Inc.*, 166 A.2d 169 (N.J., 1960). However, if the notice is placed alone on the top of a dresser, the posting would likely be considered conspicuous.

In another case a court expressed serious doubts (but did not decide) whether posting notice on the inside of the closet in a motel room was conspicuous. *Fennema v. Howard Johnson Co.*, 559 So.2d 1231 (Fla. App., 1990). Another court refused to consider as conspicuous a notice six inches by three inches and in fine print posted on the inside of the door leading into the guest room. Instead it referred the question to a jury. *Cook v. Columbia Sussex Corp.*, 807 S.W.2d 567 (Tenn. App., 1990).

Some hotels print on registration cards or on the register in which arriving guests sign their names the information required to be posted. This is generally not a permissible substitute for the required posting unless specifically authorized by the limiting statute of the state.

Posting Notice of Hotel's Limited Liability

It is not enough for a hotel to post conspicuously the availability of a safe. Virtually every state's limiting statute requires that the posted notice also inform guests that the hotel's liability is limited. Otherwise, guests are led to conclude erroneously that if valuables are deposited according to the notice, the guest will be protected for the full value of the deposited items. Failure to disclose the hotel's limited liability is thus misleading. If notice of the hotel's limited liability is not provided, the common law rule will apply and the hotel will be fully liable for the loss. The following case illustrates this rule.

CASE EXAMPLE 9–3

Depaemelaere v. Davis
351 N.Y.S.2d 808 (1973)

[O]n April 14, 1971, the plaintiff, a guest at the hotel, requested the use of a safe-deposit box in which he placed an envelope containing $18,000 in cash. Again, on April 30, he deposited another envelope in the safe-deposit box containing $8,000 in cash.

On May 12, 1971, the day before the plaintiff was scheduled to return to Belgium, he requested the safe-deposit box in order to remove the money

therefrom. Upon opening the box, he noticed that a rubber band placed by him around one of the envelopes was askew. He thereupon immediately sat down with his wife on a bench near the hotel desk, opened up the envelopes and counted the money. He found $5,000 in old bills missing from each envelope for a total of $10,000. The loss was immediately reported to the hotel employees and the police department, whose investigation of the loss proved fruitless.

It is alleged by the hotel that the sole key to the box remained in the possession of the plaintiff during the period from April 14 through May 12, except for the brief periods the key was given to the desk clerk for the removal and locking of the box in the safe on April 14, April 30, and May 12.

The process of removing and locking up the safe-deposit box in question was similar to that employed generally by banks. Two keys are required to do so: the customer's key and the hotel master key. Neither key by itself could effect a removal of the box from the safe. However, unlike bank procedures, the box at the time it is removed from the safe and returned to the safe is hidden from the view of the depositor by the safe door that opens in such a manner as to obstruct any view into the room housing the safe. . . .

[The state's limiting liability statute] requires not only that a notice be posted advising the guests of the hotel that a safe is available for the deposit and safekeeping of money, jewels, negotiable securities, and precious stones belonging to the guests, but also that notice be given to the guests of the hotel's limitation of liability imposed by law upon the guests when such facility is used. . . .

The facts with respect to the notices posted by the hotel in the instant case appear to be as follows:

In the guest's room in the hotel, a notice is posted that advises him in legible, clear type: "We have safety-deposit boxes that are available for you without charge. We will appreciate your cooperation."

At the time the guest registered at the hotel, there was printed legibly and clearly on the registration card the following legend: "Money, jewels and other valuables, and packages must be placed in the safe in the office, otherwise, the management will not be responsible for any loss."

It is to be noted that in both of these instances, the guest is not advised of any limitation of liability. . . . The only notices that allegedly notified the guest of this limitation of liability are contained in a notice to guests that is posted at the right-hand side of the registration desk, which notice is not in his direct line of vision and which he will see only if he turns to face that wall; and a notice in one other place vaguely described as being in the lobby of the hotel near the elevators.

These notices, which are on a seven-by-nine-inch card, contained in black large type approximately a quarter of an inch tall a legend that reads as follows: "Notice to guests. A safe is provided in the office for the safe-keeping of money, jewels, ornaments, bank notes, bonds, negotiable securities, and precious stones belonging to guests." There then follows in clear type a space for the posting of daily rates and charges, and then in letters approximately a sixteenth of an inch high or less, the [limitation on liability] provisions of the Law that to my mind are illegible and unreadable except from a distance of ten to twelve inches. . . .

In my opinion, it was the intention of the legislature to see to it that real and effective notice of the hotel's limitation of liability was given to its guests. . . . In the case at bar, I do not regard the posting of the notice setting forth the hotel's limitation of liability as a posting in a "public and conspicuous place and manner," sufficient to effect a limitation of liability. In fact, it is my belief that the notice and warning on the registration card and the notice in the guest's room would lead a guest to the conclusion that he must deposit his valuables in the hotel safe in order to be safeguarded, . . . and that no limitation of liability exists if he complies with this request. . . .

Under the common law, the liability of an innkeeper was that of an insurer of the property of a guest unless it could be shown that such loss was occasioned by the fault or negligence of the guest. As the sections in question are in derogation of the common law rule relative to the liability of innkeepers, they must be strictly construed.

These facts have been established to my satisfaction. The money was deposited as claimed by the plaintiff in this action. Upon his attempted withdrawal of the monies deposited, $10,000 was found to be missing, and no adequate explanation has been proffered by the hotel for the mysterious disappearance of the money. I am of the opinion, therefore, that the hotel's liability for such loss has been established. . . .

Ruling of the Court: Judgment is accordingly awarded to the plaintiff in the sum of $10,000 with interest.

Note: Had the hotel properly complied with the posting requirements, its liability would have been limited by statute to $500.

Other Statutory Mandates

The innkeeper must strictly comply with any other requirements of a state's limiting statute; failure to do so will result in loss of limited liability .In *Florida Sonesta Corp. v. Aniballi*, 463 So. 2d 1203 (Fla., 1985), the guest placed jewelry valued at $85,000 in the hotel safe from which the jewelry was subsequently stolen. The hotel sought to restrict its liability to the statutory limit of $1,000. Unfortunately for the hotel, it failed to abide by a provision of the Florida statute requiring the hotel to give the guest a receipt for the property stating the value. Instead, all of the documentation was retained by the hotel. Said the court, "[T]he hotel's non-compliance with the plain language of the statute, requiring that the receipt be given to the guest depositing valuables, deprived it of the benefit of the limitation of liability. . . ."

Some limiting statutes authorize a hotel to assume financial responsibility for property stored in a safe greater than the limited amount specified in a limiting statute. To do so, the hotel owner or manager must sign a written agreement stating that the hotel is accepting increased liability. Hotels do not normally enter such an agreement absent a very special customer and arrangements with the hotel's insurance company to cover the additional risk.

What Property Belongs in the Safe?

Not all property brought to a hotel by a guest is appropriate for a safe. A critical issue when a guest's property is stolen is whether the stolen items are valuables that the limiting liability statute requires be deposited in a safe. If they are, and the guest fails to use the safe, the hotel will have no liability.

Most state statutes require the following property to be deposited in the safe: money; jewels; ornaments; bank notes; bonds; negotiable securities; and precious stones.

Ambiguities exist. For instance, are cufflinks ornaments? How much money may guests keep in their room? Must they put a watch in the safe?

This problem is illustrated in the case of *Federal Insurance Co. v. Waldorf Astoria Hotel*, 303 N.Y.S.2d 297 (1969), in which the court ruled that cufflinks valued at $175 were not ornaments. The court also held that a watch is neither a jewel nor an ornament; it is instead a timepiece, an article of ordinary wear used daily by most travelers of every social class. A gold money clip was likewise found not to be jewelry in *Chase v. Hilton Hotel Corp.*, 682 F.Supp. 316 (E.D. La., 1988).

However, in a case in the state of Washington involving a very expensive watch, the result was otherwise. In *Walls v. Cosmopolitan Hotels, Inc.*, 534 P.2d 1373 (Wash., 1975), the guest left his $3,685 watch on a nightstand and went down to dinner. When he returned, the watch was gone. The court ruled that the watch was "valuable property" and so should have been deposited in the safe. Since it was not, the hotel was relieved of all liability.

Review of Issues Associated with Hotel Safes

The following case addresses numerous issues associated with jewelry and hotel safes. It includes the need to post the necessary notices in strict compliance with the limiting liability statute. What constitutes conspicuous posting? Does the application of the statute refer to a guest who has removed items from the safe and is checking out of the hotel? In addition, the case raises the interesting issue of whether the notices need be in a foreign language for guests who are not fluent in English. Can this question be anticipated?

CASE EXAMPLE 9–4

Moog v. Hilton Waldorf-Astoria Hotels Corp.
882 F. Supp. 1392 (N.Y., 1995)

Plaintiff Gisela Moog ("Moog") is a German citizen who stayed at the Waldorf-Astoria Hotel in New York City from November 29 to December 1, 1992. Moog arrived at the Waldorf with approximately DM [Deutsche Marks] 615,000 worth of jewelry, which she carried inside a Louis Vuitton bag. Upon arriving at the Waldorf, Moog placed the jewelry in the hotel's safe deposit box. Moog did not, however, fill out an inventory or identify the value of the items that she placed in the safe deposit box.

On the evening of November 30, 1992, Moog accompanied some friends to the opera. Prior to leaving the hotel, Moog retrieved a ruby necklace, five bracelets, two rings, a watch, a brooch, and two pair of earrings from the safe deposit box. Moog did not return the jewelry to the hotel safe deposit box upon her return to the hotel later that evening.

The following morning, Moog went to the hotel lobby to check out. Moog testified that she placed her Louis Vuitton bag with the jewelry on the floor between her legs while she was checking out of the hotel. When she looked down for her bag shortly afterward, the bag was gone. Roger Conway, a plainclothes hotel security officer, was summoned by the front desk clerk and went to assist Moog. . . . Moog has minimal command of the English language. . . .

Moog's first claim for relief is that Hilton-Waldorf was negligent in failing to provide reasonable security at the Waldorf-Astoria Hotel. Hilton-Waldorf argues that liability under this claim is precluded by New York General Business Law

section 200 entitled "Safes; Limited Liability".

In essence, section 200 provides that as long as a hotel proprietor provides a safe deposit box for the storage of valuables and posts conspicuous notice that a safe deposit box is available, a hotel guest who fails to use the safe deposit box cannot hold the hotel responsible if his or her valuables are later lost or stolen. . . . Alternatively, if the hotel guest avails himself or herself of the safe deposit box, the hotel proprietor shall not be liable for any loss sustained by the guest in excess of $1,500 unless otherwise agreed.

The first question here is whether N.Y. General Business Law section 200 was intended to apply to the instant claim, which concerns alleged acts of negligence on the part of Hilton-Waldorf during Moog's check-out from the hotel. N.Y. General Business section 200 was intended to circumscribe an innkeeper's absolute liability at common law for the loss or theft of a guest's valuables while on the innkeeper's premises. . . . While section 200 was designed with an innkeeper's absolute liability at common law in mind, it contains no exception for property lost or stolen as a result of the innkeeper's negligence. Consequently, most courts interpreting this provision have found that its limitation of liability applies even where the substance of the claim is not absolute liability but negligence.

Thus, Moog's first claim fell within the purview of N.Y. General Business Law section 200. This conclusion is not altered by the fact that Hilton-Waldorf's alleged negligence occurred as Moog was preparing to leave the hotel. The statute's limitation of liability applies through the duration of the hotel-guest relationship contemplated by its provisions. . . . Moog's status as a "guest" of the Hilton-Waldorf was not automatically terminated by her checkout, but continued for a reasonable period of time thereafter while she remained on the hotel premises. (Guest is "a transient person who resorts to or is received at an inn for the purpose of obtaining the accommodations which it purports to offer.")

It is undisputed that the Waldorf had safe deposit boxes on the premises and that Moog used a safe deposit box for the stolen jewelry up until the night before her departure. While Moog claims that the value of the stolen jewelry exceeded DM 615,000 or approximately $400,000 at current exchange rates, she failed to inform any employee of the Waldorf at the time she used the safe deposit box, or thereafter, of the value of the contents she deposited, and consequently never entered into the kind of written agreement contemplated by the last sentence of N.Y. General Business Law section 200 which authorizes a hotel to accept greater responsibility than the limiting statute imposes and requires a written agreement. Therefore, according to the provision of the limited liability statute, the most Moog could hope to recover for this claim would be $1,500.

However, because N.Y. General Business Law section 200 was enacted in derogation of the common law rule of absolute liability for innkeepers, it must be strictly construed. The protection against liability that it affords will not be granted unless all of its provisions, including the requirement of con-

spicuous posting of notice, are complied with. While Moog was aware of the Waldorf's safe deposit boxes, she claims that she was never apprised of the hotel's limited liability. She points to evidence that the Waldorf's notices of limited liability are posted in nonconspicuous areas in small, hard-to-read print. Moog also argues that, while a significant number of foreign visitors to the United States are German, the Waldorf's notices of limited liability are provided in English, French, Spanish, and Japanese—but not German.

This Court finds that Moog has raised a material question of fact as to whether notice of the Hilton-Waldorf's limited liability was sufficient to claim the protection of N.Y. General Business Law section 200. An affidavit [submitted by Moog] states that the only notice of limited liability in the Waldorf's lobby was posted by the room key drop-off desk, where guests would see it only after their stay was completed. Moreover, [the affidavit] noted that the posted liability notices on the seventh floor of the hotel, where Moog's room was located, were placed in a recessed doorway across from the elevators where they could not readily be seen by guests. Thus, regardless of what language they were in, the limited liability notices appear not to have been readily visible to patrons using the safe deposit boxes. Such allegations are sufficient to raise questions of fact precluding summary judgment on this claim. . . .

Hotel Guest in Hotel Restaurant

An interesting case involved a hotel guest whose purse was stolen in the hotel restaurant. In the purse were cash and valuables. The guest sued the hotel and lost because, said the court, even in the restaurant she retained her status as guest since it was owned and operated by the hotel. The limiting statute precluded the guest from recovering for lost valuables that were not placed in the safe. *Summer v. Hyatt Corp.*, 266 S.E.2d 333 (Ga., 1980).

Limited Liability for Other Property

What about property not required to be placed in a safe, such as clothes, sporting equipment, inexpensive watches, or merchandise samples? Does a hotel have unlimited liability as to those items? The answer in most states is no, most states have a statute that limits the hotel's liability for these types of property as well.

Clothes and Other Personal Property

The typical limiting statute restricts a hotel's liability for damage or loss of a guest's wearing apparel and other personal property such as a camera, to a specified maximum, for example, $500. This figure may vary from the hotel's maximum liability for lost money and jewels required to be in the safe. If, however, the loss or damage to clothes and other personal property is caused by negligence on the part of the hotel, in most states the hotel is not entitled to the benefit of the statute and will be liable for the full amount of the guest's loss.

The limiting liability statute in Florida treats clothes and personal property a bit differently. Florida's statute relieves the hotel from any liability for loss caused to guests' clothes and personal property unless the hotel was negligent. If it is negligent, the hotel's liability is limited to $500 maximum. This provision is illustrated by a case in which two guests sharing a hotel room in Florida discovered the lock on the room was broken. They called the front desk and requested it be repaired. The hotel sent a repairman but he went to the wrong room. The guests' room was burglarized and property was stolen from each, the total value was $5,722.65. In the lawsuit the guests sought reimbursement for the full value of their loss. The court held the hotel was negligent and so it had some liability to the plaintiff-guests. Based on the Florida limiting statute the liability was limited to $500 for each plaintiff. *Southernmost Affiliates v. Alonzo*, 654 So.2d 1066 (1995).

Door Locks and Window Fastenings

Some states' limiting statutes require a hotel seeking to benefit from limited liability to maintain suitable locks and bolts on doors and fastenings on windows. These devices help deter in-room thefts.

Checkrooms

Some states' limiting statutes differentiate between clothing lost or damaged in the lobby, hallways, and guestrooms, on the one hand, and property lost in a checkroom. While many provisions of limiting statutes may apply only to hotels, those that have a separate section for checkrooms may also cover restaurants because both hotels and restaurants typically have a hat-check area in which patrons or guests can check their coats for safekeeping. In those limiting statutes with separate provisions for a checkroom, the potential liability, while limited, may vary somewhat from the amount applicable to clothes lost elsewhere. Later in this chapter we will look closer at the rules applicable to checkrooms.

Baggage Room

Most states' limiting statutes restrict a hotel's liability for loss or damage caused to guests' property while stored in a baggage or storage room. The hotel's liability will be limited to a specified maximum amount such as $100. If, however, the loss or damage to property stored in the baggage room is caused by negligence on the part of the hotel, it loses the limited liability and will be liable for the full amount of the guest's loss.

Merchandise Samples

The term "merchandise samples" refers to goods for sale brought to a hotel by a salesperson-guest. Even in common law days, the strict liability rule governing an innkeeper's liability for guests' property recognized a distinction between property brought to the hotel for personal use and property brought for commercial purposes. The unlimited liability rule applied only to the former and not the latter.

In an early United States Supreme Court case, a salesman sued a hotel to recover for the theft of his samples. The court held for the hotel, saying:

> *Although Fisher [the salesman] was received by the defendants into their hotel as a guest, with knowledge that his trunks contained articles having no connection with his comfort or convenience as a mere traveler or wayfarer, but which, at his request, were to be placed on exhibition or for sale in a room assigned to him for that purpose, [the innkeeper] would not, under the doctrines at common law, be held to the same degree of care and responsibility, in respect to the safety of such articles, as is required in reference to baggage or other personal property carried by travelers. The defendants, being owners or managers of the hotel, were at liberty to permit the use of one of the rooms by Fisher for such business purposes, but they would not, for that reason and without other circumstances, be held to have undertaken to hold and safely keep them.* Fisher v. Kelsey, 121 US 383 (1887).

Many limiting liability statutes provide that innkeepers have no liability for damage to or loss of merchandise samples unless the innkeeper receives written notice and acknowledges in writing that a guest has such property and its value. If the guest gives the necessary notice, and the hotel makes the required acknowledgement in writing, the statutes customarily limit the hotel's liability. Compliance with the statute is mandatory if the guest seeks to hold the hotel liable, as evidenced in *Associated Mills, Inc., v. Drake Hotel, Inc.*, 334 N.E.2d 746 (Ill., 1975). The plaintiff had manufactured a prototype working model of a new product and used the prototype to demonstrate the benefits offered by the finished product. Plaintiff rented a room at defendant's hotel for display of the model to potential customers. Plaintiff alleged that the hotel, through its agents, had orally agreed to plug and seal the room where the model was being displayed to prevent overnight entry and removal of the model. The hotel had also orally agreed that it would order its employees not to enter or clean the room during the night. The next morning the plaintiff discovered the room had not been plugged, sealed, or locked; it had been cleaned; and the model was missing.

The plaintiff claimed the hotel was liable for $87,000, the value of the prototype, because the hotel had breached its agreement with him. The hotel admitted making the oral agreement with the plaintiff but denied any liability. The hotel claimed the working model was a merchandise sample within the meaning of the limiting statute and plaintiff failed to give written notice of the presence of the model. The hotel further argued that, even if plaintiff had given the required notice and received the necessary acknowledgement from the hotel, the hotel's liability was limited to $250, the maximum amount identified in the Illinois limiting statute for circumstances where the innkeeper is given notice of the presence of merchandise samples. The court agreed with the defendant; plaintiff lost the case.

Limiting statutes further provide that if a guest gives the required notice to a hotel of the presence of merchandise sample and damage or loss is caused by the hotel's negligence, the hotel will have unlimited liability.

Property in Transit

Is the hotel responsible for lost luggage when a guest gives a baggage receipt to a bellhop so that he can pick up the luggage at the airport or similar place? Or when a guest, arriving at the airport, gives luggage to a hotel hospitality van? Without a limiting liability statute, the hotel has unlimited liability in these circumstances. In a New York case which predated that state's limiting statute, a bellhop was sent to pick up a guest's trunk at the railroad station. He made a stop while returning from the station and left the bag unattended. The trunk was stolen along with its contents which consisted of expensive furs and dresses valued at $10,000. The guest sued the hotel for the full value of the lost property and won, based on common law unlimited liability. *Davidson v. Madison Corp.*, 177 N.E. 393 (N.Y., 1931).

Today, most states have limiting statutes that restrict a hotel's liability for guests' property while in transit. In New York liability in this circumstance is limited to $250. These statutes customarily provide that if the loss is due to the hotel's negligence, the hotel's liability is unlimited.

Property Not Covered by Limiting Liability Statutes

The limiting liability statutes do not cover all property that might be stolen or lost in or around a hotel. These statutes apply only to property of hotel guests; they do not cover property of nonguests, such as a coat brought to a restaurant by a patron. The limiting statutes also do not include cars of guests or nonguests.

As we have studied, under common law hotels were liable as insurers for guests' property on the hotel premises. Since parking lots were often not attached to the inn, questions arose whether inns were liable for cars that were stolen or damaged while in hotel parking areas. Today the liability of a hotel or restaurant for cars, property of nonguests and property of restaurant patrons is based primarily on the law of bailments, discussed in detail later in this chapter.

Fire

Just as the innkeeper was liable at common law for virtually all losses to guests' property occurring at the hotel, the innkeeper was likewise liable where the loss was caused by fire. This was true even if the innkeeper was not responsible for starting the fire.

Consistent with the statutory limitations on innkeepers' liability that we have been studying in this chapter, most states have passed laws limiting or eliminating the hotel's liability for damage caused by fire where the fire was not the result of the hotel's negligence. If, however, a fire is caused by the hotel's failure to exercise reasonable care, the hotel will be fully liable for the resulting loss.

Extension of Liability

In a few circumstances the hotel will not be entitled to the full benefit of limited liability provided by statute.

Disclosure of Value

Most states' limiting liability statutes contain an option to enlarge the hotel's liability for goods placed in a safe if the guest has disclosed the value of the goods to the innkeeper and the innkeeper has agreed in writing to assume liability for a greater amount than the statute requires. A hotel will not usually sign such a writing unless the guest pays a fee. But if a hotel does sign a writing and the guests' goods disappear from the safe, the hotel's liability will be greater than it would be without the writing. Even with the writing, many statutes still place a maximum on the innkeeper's liability but the maximum is higher than without the written statement of value.

Estoppel: Loss of Limited Liability

Hoteliers or their agents may make comments to a guest that result in the hotel losing the benefits of a limiting liability statute. This is known as the doctrine of **equitable estoppel**, a legal principle that precludes a person from claiming a right or benefit because that person made a false representation to a person who relied on the statement to his detriment.

Implying Greater Liability   An example of estoppel is the following. A desk clerk at a hotel tells a guest that the hotel maintains safe deposit boxes that she can use free of charge to safeguard her valuables. The clerk further tells the guest that if she deposits the jewelry in one of the boxes, there will be no limit on the hotel's liability if the jewelry is stolen. As a direct result of the clerk's statement, the guest places her jewelry in a safe deposit box. The jewelry disappears from the safe deposit box without explanation. The guest sues the hotel for the full value of the jewelry; the hotel asserts the limiting liability statute as a defense. The guest claims that the desk clerk orally modified the terms of the statute and that the guest incurred the loss only because she relied on the desk clerk's representation. Therefore, the guest argues, the hotel should be estopped (barred) from asserting the statutory liability limitation. Under these circumstances, where the guest relies on the misrepresentation of the hotel's employee, the hotel will likely be estopped from denying liability for the full loss.

Now assume one change of fact in this scenario. When the hotel clerk informs the guest about the safes, the clerk tells the guest that if the jewelry is stolen from the safe the hotel's liability will be limited according to statute. Under these circumstances will the hotel be entitled to the benefit of limited liability? The answer is yes. Although the jewelry might not have been stolen had the clerk not encouraged the guest to put it in the safe, the clerk merely told the guest exactly what the law was. Since no misrepresentation was involved, equitable estoppel does not apply.

Misrepresenting Risk.   The principle of estoppel will also be imposed if the innkeeper or an employee misleads a guest into believing that property can be safely left at a particular place in the inn, causing the guest to disregard posted directions for safekeeping property. The hotel in the following case was estopped for this reason.

CASE EXAMPLE 9-5

Fennema v. Howard Johnson Co.
559 So.2d 1231 (Fla., 1990)

The material facts of this case are undisputed. In August, 1985, plaintiffs Robert J. Fennema and his wife Kimberly A. Fennema came to Dade County, Florida from the state of Washington so that Robert Fennema could become a university professor at Florida International University. They travelled to Dade County in a Chevrolet Camaro and a rented twenty-four foot U-Haul truck which, in turn, towed their 1970 Toyota Land Cruiser; they placed all their possessions in the U-Haul truck. Mr. Fennema drove the U-Haul truck, and Mrs. Fennema drove the Camaro. Upon their arrival in Dade County, they stopped at a Howard Johnson Motor Lodge located at 1430 South Dixie Highway, Coral Gables, Florida, at approximately 6:00 P.M. on August 10, 1985. This lodge was owned and operated by defendants H. William Prahl, Jr. and Robert A. Prahl, under a franchise from the defendants Howard Johnson Company.

Mrs. Fennema went into the motel office and registered for her and her husband. She specifically advised the registration clerk that they had a Toyota Land Cruiser towed by a large U-Haul truck with nearly all their personal belongs in it; she asked where would be a safe place to park this vehicle. The clerk directed her to park the vehicle in a particular area of the motel parking lot behind a building where presumably it would be safe from vandalism or theft. Mrs. Fennema conveyed this information to Mr. Fennema who, in turn, parked the vehicle in the place designated by the clerk. Although there had been numerous incidents of criminal activity including motor vehicle thefts on or about the grounds and parking lot of this motel, the plaintiffs were not provided with this information nor warned of the risks of leaving their vehicle in the lot. The Fennemas thereafter spent the night in the motel without incident, and, the following day, went for a drive in the Camaro. When they returned to the motel at 3:00 P.M. that afternoon, they discovered that the U-Haul truck with all of its contents and the attached Toyota Land Cruiser had been stolen by unknown third parties from the place in the parking lot where the clerk had told them to park it for safekeeping.

Plaintiffs brought a negligence action . . . against defendant innkeepers for the property loss sustained as a result of the above theft in the amount of $177,000. They alleged that the defendants were negligent in failing to warn the plaintiffs that there had been criminal activity in the motel parking lot, and that defendants failed to take other steps to warn their guests and/or to prevent criminal activity from occurring in the parking lot. Plaintiffs also claimed that defendant Howard Johnson, as owner, departed from a standard of care nationally advertised by it, that all defendants knew the parking lot was dangerous, and that, as owners, lessees and operators of the motel, they had an obligation at a minimum to warn their guests. Defendant filed an answer denying any liability for the theft loss and setting up various affirmative defenses, including that plaintiffs' recovery was limited by . . . Florida's limited liability statute. . . .

Plaintiffs [argue that] . . . the statute had no application to their vehicle and its contents under the circumstances of this case. . . .

It is settled in Florida that "[a]n innkeeper owes the duty of reasonable care for the safety of his guest" (person and property) . . . and that an innkeeper's knowledge, as here, of prior criminal activity on or around the grounds of his inn imposes a duty to take adequate security precautions for the safety of his guests and their property. . . . With respect to any damage to or loss of a guest's property, however, an innkeeper's negligence liability is specifically limited by . . . [Florida's limiting liability statute]—provided a copy of that statute is posted "in the office, hall, or lobby or another prominent place of such public lodging . . . establishment." . . .

It does not follow, however, that an innkeeper may, under all circumstances, rely on the . . . statute to limit his liability even if the statute is properly posted at the inn. [W]e conclude that an innkeeper is estopped to rely on the innkeeper's limitation of liability statute if he personally misleads his guest into believing that the latter's property may be safely placed at a particular location in the inn, as this causes a guest to disregard whatever posted statutory procedures there might be for safeguarding a guest's property generally. . . .

[I]n our view, the defendant innkeepers are estopped to invoke whatever protection . . . [the limiting liability statute] may afford. This is so because the defendant's motel clerk affirmatively mis-led the plaintiffs into believing that their motor vehicle and its valuable contents were safe if parked at a particular location in the motel parking lot. Mrs. Fennema specifically informed the motel registration clerk concerning the valuable contents of the plaintiffs' motor vehicle and asked where would be a safe place to park the vehicle; the clerk, in turn, directed the Fennemas to park their vehicle at a particular spot in the motel guest parking lot behind a building where presumably the vehicle would be safe. Plaintiffs had every right to believe and did believe that their vehicle would be safe at that location; they parked their vehicle in the exact spot as directed and later the vehicle was stolen from the spot.

Having affirmatively misled the plaintiffs that it was, in effect, safe to leave their vehicle and its contents at this location in the motel parking lot, the defendant innkeepers are in no position to claim the limited liability protection. . . . Plaintiffs had every right to rely on defendant's affirmative assurance of safety for their property and to believe that these personal assurances of safety overrode whatever statutory procedures might exist for safeguarding guests' property generally. . . . [T]he defendants, by their conduct, are estopped to rely on the protection of the subject statute because they, in effect, misled the plaintiffs into disregarding the procedure stated in the posted statute as being unnecessary, given the motel's personal directive which they followed for safeguarding their property. . . .

CASE QUESTIONS

1. What was the false representation made by the hotel that enabled the guest to invoke the doctrine of estoppel?

2. What was meant by the court's statement, "Plaintiffs also claimed that the defendant Howard Johnson, as owner, departed from a standard of care nationally advertised by it." What was the significance of that statement on the outcome of the case?

Hotel's Negligence

As we have learned, most limiting statutes do not protect an innkeeper in situations where the loss of guests' property is due to the hotel's negligence. The following case illustrates this principle.

CASE EXAMPLE 9–6

Bhattal v. Grand Hyatt-New York
563 F.Supp. 277 (N.Y., 1983)

. . . Plaintiffs, residents and citizens of India, registered as guests in defendant's Grand Hyatt Hotel in Midtown Manhattan on July 19, 1981 and were assigned Room 2946.

Following the customary practice in first class hotels in this City of the sort operated by defendant, plaintiffs turned over to the bell captain various pieces of personal luggage, which are now said to have contained valuables of great significance, and this luggage was duly transferred by defendant's employees to plaintiffs' assigned hotel room.

Plaintiffs did not request that any of their valuables be placed in the safe depository provided by the hotel. . . .

Shortly after arriving at their room with the luggage, plaintiffs left the hotel for luncheon with friends, locking their door with a key provided by defendant. On returning [early] the same evening, plaintiffs discovered that their luggage and the contents thereof were missing.

All things in the modern world which go wrong for reasons other than the application of Murphy's Law, seem to go wrong because of a particular sort of mechanical malevolence known as "computer error." Apparently defendant's front desk relies heavily on computer support, and as a result of computer error, employees of defendant transported plaintiffs' luggage from plaintiffs' room to JFK International Airport, along with the luggage of aircraft crew members of Saudi Arabian nationality, who had previously occupied Room 2946. In other words, the computer omitted to notice that the room had been vacated and relet

to plaintiffs, and hotel employees responding to computer direction, included plaintiffs' luggage along with the other luggage of the departing prior guests. This is not to suggest that the Grand Hyatt-New York is a hotbed house, but apparently it was operating at 100 percent occupancy with no lost time between the departure of the Saudi Arabian aircraft crew members who had previously occupied the room, and the arrival of plaintiffs.

Needless to say, plaintiffs' luggage departed for Saudi Arabia and has not since been seen. A missing pearl is always a pearl of the finest water, and accordingly plaintiffs demand damages in the amount of $150,000. . . .

The [case] presents the question of whether [the limiting liability] statutes limit the liability of an innkeeper in a case where the innkeeper, by his own agents, intentionally and without justification, took custody and control of plaintiffs' luggage and contents, without plaintiffs' authorization, and intentionally, although inadvertently, caused the luggage to be transported to Saudi Arabia. The Court concludes that the statutes do not extend so far as to protect the innkeeper under these facts. . . .

Here, defendant's employees entered plaintiffs' locked room, without plaintiffs' permission or knowledge, and removed their luggage, commingled it with the luggage of the Saudi Arabian aircraft crew members and placed it on a bus headed for Kennedy Airport. The Court infers that if the luggage was not stolen at Kennedy Airport, it arrived in Saudi Arabia and was eventually stolen by a Saudi thief who still had the use of at least one good hand. In this instance, the intentional acts of the defendant clearly constituted conversion [unauthorized exercise of ownership over goods] under New York law.

. . . New York [limiting liability laws] were adopted in the middle of the nineteenth century to relieve an innkeeper from his liability at common law as an insurer of property of a guest lost by theft, caused without negligence or fault of the guest. . . . These statutes and the cases cited thereunder by the defendant extend to the situation where there is a mysterious disappearance of valuable property, either as a result of a theft by an employee of the hotel—or a trespass or theft by an unrelated party, for whose acts the innkeeper is not responsible. The statutes are also intended to protect the innkeeper from the danger of fraud on the part of a guest in a situation where the property said to have disappeared never existed at all, or was taken or stolen by or with the privity of the guest.

The reason for limiting a hotel's liability . . . is to protect against just such a situation. When a hotel room is let to a guest, the innkeeper has lost a large measure of control and supervision over the hotel room and its contents. While housekeeping and security staff can enter the room at reasonable hours and on notice to any persons present therein, essentially, for most of the time at least, property of a guest which is present in a hotel room can be said to be under the exclusive dominion and control of the hotel guest, rather than the innkeeper.

. . . In this case . . . employees of defendant, acting within the scope of their employment and relying on the accuracy of the employer's computer, intentionally converted the luggage of the plaintiffs by removing it from plaintiff's room and delivering it to an aircraft bound for Saudi Arabia. [The limiting statute does not limit the liability of the hotel in this case. Rather, the hotel is liable for the full value of the loss.]

CASE QUESTION

1. What would have been the outcome of the case if the luggage had been stolen by a thief through no fault of the hotel?

Comparative Negligence

Suppose the hotel and the guest are both negligent and the guest's loss is due to the combined negligence. What liability does the hotel have? According to *Vasilios Nicholaides v. University Hotel Associates*, 568 A.2d 219 (Pa., 1990), at least in states that adopted the comparative negligence rule, the hotel's liability will be reduced by the extent of responsibility for the loss attributed to the guest. In that case plaintiff brought a coin collection valued at $34,973 to defendant's hotel. Plaintiff placed the collection in a dresser drawer in his room under some garments. Two days later he discovered the collection missing. The jury determined, without explanation, that both the hotel and the guest were negligent. It allocated to the guest 49 percent of the responsibility for the loss. The guest recovered only 51 percent of his damages.

Nevada's Limiting Statute

The Nevada limiting liability statute is quite different from that found in most other states. Its limitation of liability applies even if the hotel is grossly negligent. Thus, Nevada is very protective of its innkeepers.

An example of the application of this statute is provided by the next case.

CASE EXAMPLE 9–7

Kahn v. Hotel Ramada of Nevada
799 F.2d 199 (Tex., 1986)

. . . Robert D. Kahn, a part-time jewelry broker, traveled to Las Vegas, Nevada, in August, 1983, to participate in a "21" tournament and registered at the Tropicana Hotel. Kahn brought along his personal belongings and some jewelry, which he intended to show to customers in Phoenix, Arizona, after completing the tournament. After the tournament had ended, Kahn surrendered his room and checked out of the Tropicana, but, while awaiting his departure, left his luggage, including a briefcase that contained the jewelry, with a bellman. Kahn contends that he informed the bellman that the contents of the briefcase were "important" and that he saw the bellman place the luggage and briefcase in the hotel baggage room. When he returned to reclaim his luggage less than one hour later, however, Kahn was informed that it could not be located. Later, his briefcase and one valise were found on the second green of the Tropicana golf course, but both were empty. Although certain items of clothing were found in the area where the two pieces of luggage were discovered, neither the jewelry contained in the briefcase nor most of Kahn's other property was recovered. Kahn values the missing property as worth over $50,000.

Kahn alleges that the Tropicana Hotel was guilty of negligence, gross negligence, and other violations of its duties as innkeeper. After completion of discovery, the Tropicana Hotel filed a motion to dismiss . . . contending that the [relevant Nevada limiting] statute limits the common-law liability of innkeepers for the theft, loss, damage, or destruction of any guest's property at $750 unless the hotel expressly waives the limitation. . . .

Under the common law, an innkeeper is responsible for the safety of property entrusted to his care by a guest and may exonerate himself only by showing that the loss or injury suffered by his guest resulted from an act of God, a public enemy, or from the fault of the guest himself . . . Nevada adheres to this view of the common law. Like most, if not all, other states, Nevada has determined that the common law rule is too harsh and has enacted [a statute] to limit its stringency. That statute reads:

1. No owner or keeper of any hotel, inn, motel, motor court, boardinghouse or lodginghouse in this state is civilly liable for the theft, loss, damage or destruction of any property left in the room of any guest of such an establishment because of theft, burglary, fire or otherwise, in the absence of gross [extreme] neglect by the owner or keeper.

2. If any owner or keeper of any hotel, inn, motel, motor court, boardinghouse or lodginghouse in this state provides a fireproof safe or vault in which guests may deposit property for safekeeping, and notice of this service is personally given to a guest or posted in the office and the guest's room, the owner or keeper is not liable for the theft, loss, damage or destruction of any property which is not offered for deposit in the safe or vault by a guest unless the owner or keeper is grossly negligent. An owner or keeper is not obligated to receive or deposit for safekeeping property which exceeds $750 in value or is of a size which cannot easily fit within the safe or vault.

3. The liability of the owner or keeper under this section does not exceed the sum of $750 for any property of an individual guest, unless the owner or keeper receives the property for deposit or safekeeping and consents to assume a liability greater than $750 for its theft, loss, damage, or destruction in a written agreement in which the guest specifies the value of the property. . . .

In interpreting a statute that is both remedial and in derogation of the common law, courts strictly construe the question whether the statute modifies the common law but, if it is clear that the legislature intended to change the common-law rule, liberally construe application of the new rule. Applying these rules to the Nevada statute, we find that the most coherent reading of the statute as a whole makes the $750 maximum applicable when a guest's property is lost as a result of the gross negligence of the innkeeper except when the innkeeper has waived its application. . . .

We recognize that our interpretation of the statute limits to $750 the liability of even a grossly negligent innkeeper who provides his guests no safe. But this interpretation—limiting liability in all instances of negligence except when the innkeeper consents to assume more responsibility—appears to provide the outcome the Nevada legislature in-tended. In the absence of any suggestion that Kahn might have relied on some other reading of the statute, we interpret its awkward language as we think the Nevada legislature intended. . . .

For these reasons, we find that Kahn could not recover more than $750 even if he proved gross negligence. . . .

Liability During Check-In and Check-Out

Should there be a period of time while guests are checking in and out of a hotel that the statute does not apply? When guests first enter a hotel and have not yet completed the registration process, they have not had time to access the safe. When they are packing and preparing to check out, they will likely remove their valuables from the hotel safe. Generally, when goods are stolen or disappear during check-in or check-out, the courts have found the limiting statutes applicable and the hotel not liable for the full loss.

Guest Status

If the person whose property disappears during check-in or check-out is a hotel guest at the time of the loss, the limiting statute applies. In most of the following cases the owner of the missing property was found to be a guest and thus recovery was limited.

A guest of the Hilton Hotel in New Orleans left two rings in her hotel room after washing her hands. She checked out of the hotel that day and did not realize the rings were missing until she was part way home. She immediately called the hotel and an investigation was made. The rings, valued at $10,000, were never found. Like most limiting statutes, Louisiana's applied only to guests. The owner of the rings sued the hotel for their value claiming the innkeeper-guest relationship had terminated before the loss occurred and thus the hotel should be liable for the full value of the jewelry. The court ruled the loss occurred when she left the rings in the room, which happened while she was still a guest. Therefore the hotel was only responsible for $500, the maximum provided by the applicable limiting statute. *O'Rourke v. Hilton Hotels Corp.*, 560 So.2d 76 (La., 1990).

In *Pacific Diamond Co., Inc. v. Hilton Hotels Corp.*, 149 Cal. Rptr. 813 (Ca., 1978), a jewelry salesman had been a guest at the hotel for several days. On the last day of his stay he attended a sales presentation to which he took $150,000 worth of diamonds. After the presentation, he returned to his room to pack and took the diamonds with him. A few minutes before leaving his room, he was beaten and robbed of all the diamonds. He sued the hotel, claiming the limiting statute should not apply since, at the time of the theft, he was about to leave. The court disagreed and ruled the statute was applicable. The salesman should have deposited the diamonds in the safe before he went to his room to pack.

In another case, a jewelry salesman, upon arrival at the MGM Grand Hotel in Las Vegas, checked his luggage and jewelry samples with the bellhop at the door. He told the bellhop that the samples were valuable. After checking in and going to his room, his luggage was delivered but one case of jewelry samples worth $19,000 was missing. He sued the hotel for the value of the jewelry. The hotel defended on the basis that Nevada's limiting liability statute, like that of most states, applies only to guests. Plaintiff argued that he was not a guest at the time he gave the luggage to the bellhop since plaintiff had not yet checked-in. The court held that the innkeeper-guest relationship was established when plaintiff checked his luggage with the bellhop. Therefore the statute applied and the salesman could only recover the statutory amount—$750. *Pachinger v. MGM Grand Hotel-Las Vegas, Inc.*, 802 F.2d 362 (9th Cir., 1986).

Liability After Check-Out

In many cases, guests retain their status after check-out, and limiting liability statutes still apply. In *Nagashima v. Hyatt Wilshire Corp.*, 279 Cal. Rptr. 265 (Cal. App., 1991), plaintiff was in the hotel lobby in the check-out line, having just removed from the hotel safe her jewelry valued at $72,000. While she waited for her turn to check-out, someone grabbed the jewelry from her possession and it was never recovered. The court held the limiting statute applied and so her recovery was limited to $500. In response to plaintiff's argument that application of the statute in her case was unjust, the court suggested she address her argument to the legislature which alone has the power to change the statute.

In the following case the court held that guests who had checked out of a hotel retained their status as guests for purposes of the limiting statute where they left their luggage in the hotel's luggage room while they went shopping for the day.

CASE EXAMPLE 9–8

Salisbury v. St. Regis-Sheraton Hotel
490 F. Supp. 449 (N.Y., 1980)

On the morning of November 22, 1978, Mr. and Mrs. Roger Salisbury concluded a three-day stay at the St. Regis-Sheraton Hotel in New York. While Mr. Salisbury paid the bill and surrendered their room key, Mrs. Salisbury checked their luggage with a bellhop in the lobby. The couple was to spend the day in town and return for the luggage that afternoon. Mrs. Salisbury did not inform the hotel when she checked the luggage that one of their pieces, a cosmetic case, contained jewelry and cosmetics worth over $60,000 and did not ask

that the case be kept in the hotel's safe. . . .

When the Salisburys returned to the hotel to retrieve their luggage at about 4:30 that afternoon, the cosmetic case containing the jewelry was missing. Mrs. Salisbury sued to recover the value of the case and its contents.

It is undisputed that posted conspicuously in the public areas of the hotel was a notice informing guests that the hotel provided a safe for the safekeeping of their valuables, and notifying them of the provisions of the [limiting liability statute] of the New York General Business Law. . . .

The question, then, is whether Mrs. Salisbury ceased to be a "guest" within the meaning of the limiting liability statute when she checked out of the hotel, even though she arranged to have the hotel hold her luggage for the day. . . . The lost luggage was not stored with the hotel for a lengthy period, but simply held for the day as an accommodation to departing guests. . . .

It is not uncommon for a hotel to hold luggage for a few hours after guests check out as an accommodation to them. This would appear to be one of the services that a hotel performs for its guests in the normal course of its business, and there is no reason why it should be deemed to alter the otherwise existing legal relationship between them. Accordingly, we conclude that the limiting liability statutes are fully applicable in the circumstances of this case and preclude any recovery against the hotel for the loss of Mrs. Salisbury's jewelry and limits any recovery for the loss of the case and its other contents to $100.

CASE QUESTION

1. On what basis did the court determine that plaintiffs were still guests at the time of the loss?

Contrary to the foregoing cases, the court in the following case refused to apply the limiting statutes to a check-out situation. The court determined the statute was not intended for such circumstances.

CASE EXAMPLE 9–9

Spiller v. Barclay Hotel
327 N.Y.S.2d 426 (1972)

Plaintiff, a guest of the Barclay Hotel, sued for the value of the property, primarily wearing apparel and jewelry, lost on the steps of the hotel while she was in the process of leaving.

Plaintiff testified that after her two bags were brought to the lobby floor, she asked a bellboy to take them to the cab area and to watch them while she checked out. When she came to the cab area, only one of her bags was there and the bellboy was not present. A search failed to disclose the missing bag or its contents.

No directly contradictory testimony was presented. A representative of the hotel did testify to a telephone conversation in which plaintiff allegedly gave a different version of the event and described the personal property as business samples. However, I accept as substantially accurate plaintiff's trial testimony as to the property that was lost and the manner in which it was lost. . . .

The claim for the items of lost jewelry presents a troublesome problem. [New York's limiting liability statute] excludes recovery by a hotel guest for loss of, among other categories enumerated, jewels, ornaments, and precious stones where the hotel provides a safe for such items, gives appropriate notice of that fact, and the guest does not use that facility. It was conceded that the hotel maintained such a safe and had posted the required notice. . . .

What seems to me decisive here is that [New York's statute] was not designed to apply to a loss occurring under the circumstances of this case. [New York's statute] clearly contemplates a procedure for safeguarding the specified categories of property during a guest's stay at a hotel. Its provisions do not seem to me to be reasonably applied to a loss that takes place when a guest is about to leave, has gathered together her property preparatory to an imminent departure, and is arranging for the transfer of luggage to a vehicle for transportation.

Although that situation presents some conceptual difficulties, I am satisfied that the sensible and fair approach is to consider a loss occurring at that point in time neither in terms of the provisions of [New York's limiting statute], nor in terms of the traditional common law liability of innkeepers, but rather on the basis of the presence or absence of actual negligence. . . .

Having found that the loss here resulted from the negligence of a hotel employee, acting within the scope of his employment, I hold that plaintiff is entitled to recover the value of the lost jewelry. . . .

CASE QUESTIONS

1. On what ground did the court find the hotel liable for the full value of the jewelry?

2. If the missing property had been merchandise samples, what would the outcome of the case have been?

Bailment

A **bailment** is a transfer of possession of personal property from one person to another, with the understanding that the property will be returned. The person giving possession of the property is the **bailor**; the person receiving possession is the **bailee**. For example, if a guest leaves a shirt with room service for ironing, the guest is the bailor, the hotel is the bailee, and the arrangement is a bailment.

The essential elements of a bailment are:

1. *Personal property.* Bailments involve only moveable, tangible objects such as a car, a coat, and the like. The term bailment does not apply to real property (land and buildings).

2. *Delivery of possession.* Possession of the personal property must be transferred to the bailee.

3. *Acceptance of possession by the bailee.* The bailee must knowingly accept possession of the bailed property.

4. *Bailment agreement.* Part of every bailment is an agreement, express or implied, by the bailee to return the bailed goods to the bailor.

Suppose a restaurant patron leaves her coat with a hat check person. Does a bailment exist? The answer is yes. The coat is personal property; possession has been given to the attendant; and the attendant is required to return the coat when the patron (bailor) is ready to leave.

Let us change the facts a bit. Suppose the patron enters the restaurant, removes her coat, and hangs it on an unattended coat rack near the table where she is sitting. Does a bailment exist? The answer is no. Although the coat is personal property, the restaurant has not accepted possession since no one on behalf of the restaurant physically took possession of the coat.

Does a bailment exist when you park your car at a parking lot? The answer is—it depends. A critical factor is whether or not you leave your key with a parking lot attendant. In most circumstances, if you park the car and take the key with you, you have not delivered possession. If, however, you leave the key with the attendant, that person has the ability to move the car and therefore has possession of it. In this latter case a bailment exists.

Affect of Bailment on Liability

The existence or nonexistence of a bailment affects liability. If no bailment exists, neither does liability. For example, if you leave your coat on an unattended coat rack in a restaurant and it is stolen during your meal, the restaurant is not liable. Because the restaurant was not a bailee, it is not responsible for the coat. The following case illustrates this point.

CASE EXAMPLE 9–10

Augustine v. Marriott Hotel
503 N.Y.S.2d 498 (1986)

Plaintiff attended, for a fee, a dental seminar at the Marriott Hotel. The seminar sponsor rented a banquet room, furnished with seats, from defendant.

At the request of the sponsor, defendant furnished a movable coat rack, placing it outside the [seminar] room, in the public lobby.

Plaintiff placed his coat on the rack before entering the seminar. At the noon recess, plaintiff exited the seminar room, but found that the rack had been moved a distance down the lobby and around a corner, near an exit.

Unfortunately, his cashmere coat was missing. He then commenced this action in the Small Claims Part of this court.

Under the common law an innkeeper was an insurer of property, *infra hospitium* [within the hotel facility], of his guests, and liable for the loss thereof or damage thereto unless the loss was caused by negligence of the guest, act of God, or the public enemy.

By statute, such liability has been limited. . . .

The relationship of guest on the part of plaintiff, and that of hotel keeper on the part of defendant, vis-a-vis each other never arose. The occupancy by plaintiff of a private room was never contemplated by the parties.

Plaintiff was a patron of the seminar sponsor, who rented facilities from defendant. The status of plaintiff was like that of a wedding guest of individuals who rent banquet facilities from a hotel. . . .

Therefore, the New York limiting statutes is in no way applicable to the facts presented here.

The relationship of bailor and bailee never came into existence because plaintiff did not entrust his coat to defendant. Not only was there never a delivery to defendant, but defendant never was in actual nor constructive custody of plaintiff's coat.

The sole question remaining is whether defendant owed a duty to plaintiff to provide a guard for the coat rack. Defendant placed the rack in a position near the door to the seminar room, at the request of the seminar sponsor. This created not only an opportunity but an implied invitation on the part of the sponsor, to patrons of the seminar to use the rack.

However, there was no evidence to indicate that users of the rack were led to believe either by the sponsor or by defendant that there would be a guard for the rack. Under the circumstances presented, it was clear that there was merely a rack available for those who wished to use it. Defendant did not lull plaintiff into a sense of security, by which there was created a duty to provide a guard.

There being no duty on the part of defendant, there can be found no breach of duty upon which to underpin a finding of [liability].

Furthermore, a reasonable man would have wondered about the safety of his coat which he hung on a rack in a public lobby of a hotel, without ascertaining if there were a guard.

The claim must be dismissed.

This case illustrates the principle that if no bailment exists, no liability exists. If, on the other hand, a bailment does exist, the bailee is not automatically liable. A bailee is liable only if it fails to exercise the amount of care required by law in tending to the bailed goods. The requisite care varies depending upon the type of bailment. Bailments are classified into three types: 1) for the sole benefit of the bailor; 2) for the sole benefit of the bailee; or 3) mutual benefit. The required level of care differs for each classification.

Bailment for the Sole Benefit of the Bailor

A bailment for the sole benefit of the bailor exists when the bailee receives no benefit from the bailment. For example, assume a computer at your restaurant is not functioning properly. The repair shop is located near where a waiter lives. He agrees at your request to take the computer with him after his shift and deliver it to the shop for repairs. You benefit from this arrangement but, assuming the waiter—the bailee—is not being paid for making the delivery, he does not.

In a bailment such as this for the sole benefit of the bailor, the bailee is obligated to exercise only a slight degree of care over the bailed goods. Stated differently, the bailee is only liable for gross (extreme) negligence.

Bailment for the Sole Benefit of Bailee

A bailment for the sole benefit of the bailee exists where the bailor lends property to the bailee and receives nothing in return. For example, assume that your restaurant is catering four parties this weekend. You are in need of extra serving dishes. A friend of yours owns a restaurant in the business district that is closed on weekends. She agrees to lend you serving dishes for the weekend at no cost. You benefit from this arrangement but your friend, the bailor, does not.

In this type of bailment—for the sole benefit of the bailee—the bailee is required to take great care of the property and exercise a degree of care higher than a reasonable person ordinarily exercises in connection with her own property. Thus, to avoid liability, you would have to ensure the serving dishes are utilized only by trained wait staff to avoid breakage, and are securely placed when not in use to avoid theft.

Mutual-Benefit Bailment

A mutual-benefit bailment, also called a bailment for hire, is one in which both parties receive some benefit from the bailment. Examples of this type of bailment include a traveler renting a car, or a restaurant leasing a pay phone. In the first example, the traveler (bailee) receives the use of the car, and the car rental company (bailor) receives money. In the second example, the restaurant (bailee) receives the use of the phone, and the leasing company that owns the phone (bailor) receives money. In mutual-benefit bailments the bailee's duty is to exercise *ordinary care* over the bailed goods. The difference in the duty owed in a mutual-benefit bailment and a bailment for the sole benefit of the bailor is illustrated in the following case.

CASE EXAMPLE 9–11

First American Bank v. District of Columbia
583 A.2d 993 (D.C., 1990)

. . . First American Bank employed Ronald Armstead as a courier whose duties included making deliveries between the bank's various branch offices and the main office. One afternoon, at approximately 4:20 P.M., Armstead parked the bank's station wagon near the entrance of Branch 13 on 7th Street, N.W., in violation of "No Parking Rush Hour Zone" signs, which were in clear view of Armstead. Four locked bank dispatch bags, marked as such, which Armstead had just picked up from four different branches, were in the rear luggage compartment of the station wagon and in plain view of anyone looking into the vehicle. The dispatch bags contained checks and other valuable documents.

Armstead had received tickets for illegal parking at this particular spot on at least five prior occasions and had been warned against future violations by traffic enforcement personnel. Traffic enforcement personnel had counseled Armstead to park across the street during rush hour to avoid being ticketed or towed. Armstead, who had received numerous parking tickets during his employment with the bank, would simply give the parking tickets to a supervisor for payment. The bank did not reprimand or discipline Armstead, nor did it dock his pay, for the parking tickets.

Within a short time after Armstead entered Branch 13, a parking control aide approached the bank's station wagon and began writing up a ticket for illegal parking. Almost immediately thereafter, a tow truck owned by Transportation Management, Inc. (TMI) arrived at the scene. While the parking control aide was completing the ticket and the tow truck operator was simultaneously preparing to tow the car, one of the employees at Branch 13 alerted Armstead that the bank's vehicle was being towed. Armstead, carrying a dispatch bag, ran out to the vehicle and told the tow truck operator that, as the driver of the vehicle, he was prepared to drive the vehicle away immediately. When the tow truck operator ignored his request to return the vehicle, Armstead asked that he be allowed at least to remove the dispatch bags from the vehicle. The tow truck operator, however, also ignored this latter request, and instead entered the truck and began to drive away with the bank's vehicle in tow. The . . . form filled out by the tow truck operator indicated that the doors, trunk, and window of the bank's station wagon were locked when it was towed from 7th Street. When the tow truck operator arrived at the Brentwood impoundment lot at 4:45 P.M., the dispatch bags were still inside the luggage compartment of the vehicle. The tow truck operator observed the District's lot attendant test all the doors and the rear gate of the vehicle. The lot attendant found them all locked and so certified on the same form.

One and a half hours later, the bank's supervisor of mailroom couriers paid for the vehicle's release and retrieved it from the impoundment lot. The bank supervisor found the driver's door unlocked and one dispatch bag missing. There were no signs of forced entry, nor were there signs of the tape which is customarily affixed to car doors at the impoundment lot. The dispatch bag was never found, nor have the police identified or apprehended anyone who may have removed it from the vehicle. The value of the checks and other papers contained in the dispatch bag was determined to be $107,561. . . . First American brought suit against the District of Columbia and TMI for breach of bailment. . .

The trial court ruled that the District and TMI were gratuitous bailees [bailment for the sole benefit of the bailor] and therefore liable only for gross negligence. The trial court further ruled that First American [was not] grossly negligent. . . . We reverse on the bailment issue.

There is no dispute here that TMI and the District had sufficient possession and control of the bank's vehicle to establish a type of bailment. . . . The question we must resolve is whether the bailment was gratuitous or for hire. A bailee that takes possession of goods solely for the benefit of the owner is a gratuitous bailee and liable only for gross negligence, willful acts or fraud. . . . In contrast, a bailee that receives compensation for its services is held to a standard of ordinary care. . . .

A bailment for hire [mutual benefit bailment] relationship may be created even in the absence of an explicit agreement. . . . All that is required is the existence of a mutual benefit. . . .

The District and TMI actively took possession of the bank's vehicle with the expectation of deriving benefit therefrom. In addition to furthering its interest in insuring the smooth flow of traffic, the District tows and stores illegally parked vehicles for compensation. Likewise, TMI is under contract with the District for the purpose of towing illegally parked vehicles to impoundment lots. Owners of vehicles, on the other hand, receive the direct benefit of having their vehicles safeguarded in the city's impoundment lot until they are ready to retrieve them. As users of the District's roads and highways, they also benefit indirectly from the District's practice of towing illegally parked vehicles that impede the flow of traffic. . . .

We hold, therefore, that the District and TMI are held to the standard of ordinary care when they tow and impound illegally parked vehicles. . . .

In view of the foregoing, we remand this case [for a trial] for a determination of whether the city and TMI exercised ordinary care in safeguarding the bank's vehicle and its contents.

Duty of Bailor in Mutual-Benefit Bailment.   In a mutual-benefit bailment, the bailor has responsibilities as well as the bailee. The bailor is obligated to warn the bailee of any defects in the bailed property that might result in injury to the bailee or interfere with use of the property. This is a form of strict liability; the bailor is liable for failing to disclose defects even if it is unaware of their existence. For example, Jerry rented an automobile for one day. While he was driving the car, the steering gear broke, causing an accident in which he was injured. Jerry had not been warned by the bailor that the steering gear was defective and he sued for injuries. The bailor responded that it did not know of the defect when Jerry rented the car. Notwithstanding the bailor's lack of knowledge of the defect, it is responsible for any loss or injury suffered by the bailee as a result of the defect in the bailed goods. A company in the business of leasing goods, such as a car rental company, should make regular and frequent inspections of its inventory. To avoid liability it must correct any problems discovered or alert the bailee of potential risks.

The case of *Gulf American v. Airco Industrial Gases,* 573 So.2d 481 (La., 1990), involved the rental of a freezer that was represented as having the capacity to quick-freeze a specified number of shrimp per hour. Gulf American, a processor of shrimp, leased the freezer and discovered it could not process the advertised number of shrimp. Instead, it malfunctioned and the frozen shrimp were "extremely dehydrated, white and sometimes came out in clumps of two or three." Gulf American sued the lessor of the freezer for damages. The court held that the lessor, by failing to disclose the freezer's defects, breached its duty as bailor. It was liable to Gulf American for its damages.

Proof in Bailment Cases

A bailor does not usually oversee the bailee. Therefore, when bailed goods are lost or stolen, a bailor typically has difficulty in proving that the bailee failed to exercise the required degree of care. Because of this, bailment law does not require the bailor to prove that the bailee was negligent. Instead, a bailor need only prove delivery of the bailed property to the bailee, acceptance by the bailee, and either a failure on the part of the bailee to return the bailed property, or return of the property in a damaged condition. Such proof establishes a **prima facie** case, that is, a case sufficient to warrant a judgment for the plaintiff if the defendant does not contradict it with other evidence. With such proof a presumption arises that the bailee was negligent (failed to use reasonable care); the bailee will lose the case unless it presents evidence to dispute the presumption of negligence or proves that the loss or damage occurred from a cause other than its own negligence. If the bailee can show that the loss or damage resulted from some other cause or that the bailee exercised reasonable care, the bailee will not be liable for the loss. Application of the presumption is illustrated in the following case.

CASE EXAMPLE 9–12

Value Rent-A-Car, Inc.
v. Collection Chevrolet, Inc.
570 So.2d 1376 (Fla., 1990)

Value Rent-A-Car (Value), . . . left its car in Collection Chevrolet, Inc.'s (Collection) care for repairs. When Value returned to pick up the car, the car and its keys had disappeared. Collection reported the car's disappearance to the police. The police subsequently recovered the car, stripped and heavily damaged.

Value brought suit against Collection for negligence arising from the disappearance of its car. Collection denied having been negligent. . . . Value rested its negligent bailment case upon the stipula-

tion of the parties that: (1) Value delivered the car to Collection; (2) Collection had exclusive possession and control of the car; and (3) Collection failed to return the car to Value. Collection presented testimony about the extensive security measures that existed at the area from where the car was taken. No witness for Collection was able to explain how the car and its keys were removed from Collection's lot. [Value seeks a] verdict based on the general rule that a bailee who has sole, actual, and exclusive possession of the goods is presumed to be negligent if he cannot explain the loss or disappearance of the goods. The trial court [held that] Collection had established due care in its storing of the car, that the evidentiary presumption of negligence had vanished, and that the burden of establishing Collection's negligence had shifted to Value. . . .

Value contends the trial court erred in ruling that the presumption of Collection's negligence, as bailee of the car, vanished, where Collection was unable to explain the loss or disappearance of the car. Collection asserts that proof of its due care overcame the presumption of negligence. Collection further argues that theft of the car was the only logical explanation for its disappearance because the car had been recovered by the police, stripped and vandalized.

As Value correctly argues, and Collection agrees, the well-settled rule in bailment cases is that:

[A] bailee who has the sole, actual, and exclusive possession of goods is presumed to be negligent if he cannot explain the loss or disappearance of the goods, and the law imposes on him the burden of showing that he exercised the degree of care required by the nature of the bailment. . . .

This presumption, however, is a vanishing presumption. Once the bailee introduces evidence of its due care, the presumption of negligence vanishes and the case is decided by the trier of fact [jury] without regard to the presumption. . . .

In this case, the presumption, which was enveloped in a protective bubble, burst, when Collection presented evidence of its due care, that is, its extensive security measures, and the *only* logical inference from the evidence presented was that the car had been stolen. . . .

A ruling that the presumption continues even though the bailee has presented evidence of its due care, would effectively result in the bailee becoming the insurer of the bailed goods. This is not the rule in Florida. Florida agrees with the weight of authority that a bailee is not an insurer of the bailed goods and if the bailee is not negligent or at fault, the risk of loss by theft is on the bailor. . . .

Accordingly, the . . . judgment [for Collection] is affirmed.]

In a Tennessee case, the plaintiff gave the key to his car to a hotel bellboy to park in the hotel parking lot. After going off duty, the bellboy returned to the lot and, without authorization, took the car out for a joyride. Unfortunately, he was in an accident and the car was destroyed. The court held that the hotel was liable for the damage. When the car was originally delivered to the bellboy, a mutual-benefit bailment was created between the plaintiff and the hotel. The hotel was required to return the property to the bailor (plaintiff) when he requested it. Since the hotel was unable to do that, a presumption arose that the hotel was negligent. The presumption arose even though plaintiff did not prove negligence on the part of the hotel. Had the hotel been able to prove that it exercised reasonable care, it would not have been liable. However, it was not able to prove freedom from negligence. Therefore the court ordered the hotel to reimburse the plaintiff for his loss. *Dispeker v. The New Southern Hotel Co.*, 373 S.W.2d 904 (Tenn., 1963).

Items Inside the Bailed Property

Is a bailee liable when valuable property is located inside the bailed property and its presence is unknown to the bailee? For example, suppose you put a valuable ring in the pocket of your leather coat, which you leave with a hatcheck person at a restaurant. You do not inform the attendant of the presence of the ring. The attendant took a break during which the coats were unattended. While the attendant was gone your coat was stolen. The restaurant will be liable for the value of the coat because its employee was negligent by leaving the garments unattended. Will the restaurant also be liable for the value of the lost ring?

The answer becomes obvious if you apply the elements necessary for a bailment. The bailee must knowingly accept possession of the property. In this example the hatcheck attendant knowingly accepted possession of the coat. But did he knowingly accept possession of the ring? The answer, of course, is no; he did not even know of its existence. Therefore the restaurant was not a bailee of the ring and will not be liable for its loss.

Similarly, when you park your car in a parking lot and leave the key with an attendant, if you fail to inform him of a valuable camera in the trunk, no bailment exists as to the camera. If the car is stolen due to the attendant's negligence, the parking lot will be liable to you for the value of the car. The outcome is quite different for the camera. Since no bailment of the camera existed, the parking lot is not liable for its loss.

In the case of *Dumlao v. Atlantic Garage, Inc.,* 259 A.2d 360 (D.C., 1969), the plaintiff checked into a hotel, removed clothing from the back seat of the car, and then delivered the car and key to an employee of the hotel for parking. The guest said there was a set of drums in the trunk, which he had opened when he unloaded his clothing. The bell captain had observed the guest remove a cosmetic case, but could not see if there was anything else in the trunk. He asked if there was any more personal property in the car, but the guest did not respond. The car was then parked by a hotel employee in a nearby garage. A few days later when the plaintiff checked out, the hotel was unable to deliver his car or its contents, nor could it account for its disappearance. The car was located some time later, but the drums were gone. The plaintiff sued the hotel for the loss, claiming the hotel was liable to him as a bailee.

The court determined a bailment existed between the plaintiff and the hotel as to both the car and any contents the hotel employees knew about. An employee would be aware of property in a car if the guest pointed it out or it was in plain view. Here, there was no evidence to show the hotel employee knew that drums were in the trunk. Therefore, there was no bailment of the drums, and the hotel was not liable.

Rules Particular to Bailment of Cars

A hotelkeeper or restaurateur who takes care of a patron's car assumes a great responsibility. The value of an automobile can range from as low as a few hundred dollars to over $100,000. The limiting statutes do not apply to cars. Public parking lots often attempt to limit their liability for stolen or damaged cars by claiming on signs and parking receipts that they are not liable. Because of the quasi-public nature of the accommodations industry, hoteliers are not allowed to limit their liability for loss or damage to bailed property caused by their own negligence. Therefore, such disclaimers of liability on signs or receipts are not effective. The following case clearly illustrates this point.

CASE EXAMPLE 9–13

Ellerman v. Atlanta American Motor Hotel Corp.
191 S.E.2d 295 (Ga., 1972)

Plaintiff, a guest at a motor hotel operated by the defendant, placed his automobile in the defendant's parking facility. He was required by the defendant to leave the ignition key with the defendant's employee, and the latter parked the vehicle in an area unknown to plaintiff. At the time, plaintiff was given a claim check which plaintiff admitted reading. It provided in part as follows: "Liability. Cars parked at owner's risk. Articles left in car at owner's risk. We reserve privilege of moving car to other section of lot. No attendant after regular closing hours." Prior to delivering the ignition key and the car to the attendant, the plaintiff removed a raincoat from the interior, placed it in the trunk of the car, and kept the trunk key. When plaintiff checked out of the hotel, his car was found missing. The car and its contents have never been recovered. Plaintiff's suit sought to recover the value of the items of personality contained in the trunk that he alleged were allowed to be stolen through the defendant's negligence. Plaintiff had been paid by his insurance company for the loss of the automobile. . . .

The defendant contends that the depositing of the automobile with the defendant's attendant under these circumstances does not give rise to a bailment relationship because of the disclaimer of liability printed on the claim check given to plaintiff. He relies upon our decision in [a previous case] as controlling. As we view this issue, [that case] is not in point. [It] dealt with an ordinary parking lot. This case involves a parking facility operated by a motel as a part of its service, and this creates the relationship of innkeeper and guest. . . .

It is recognized that an ordinary bailee by contract may limit or completely exculpate himself from any liability for loss or damage to the bailed property as a result of his own simple negligence.

However, an innkeeper is not an "ordinary" bailee. Many courts and texts have described an innkeeper as a "professional" bailee. . . . Unlike an "ordinary" bailee, the "professional" bailee is often precluded from limiting by contract liability for his own negligence as violative of public policy. The reasoning utilized is that the public, in dealing with innkeepers, lacks a practical equality of bargaining power and may be coerced to accede to the contractual conditions sought by the innkeeper or else be denied the needed services. We think that both the principle precluding the limitation of liability and the reasoning underlying it are sound . . . [A]ny . . . contract purporting to . . . exculpate the innkeeper is contrary to the public interest and policy and cannot be enforced.

A hotel with a parking lot or garage that takes possession of guests' car keys must establish effective security procedures and systems to avoid liability. The high cost of cars dictates the importance of proper management and planning.

An example of negligence on the part of the hotel when acting as bailee is leaving the ignition key in a parked, unattended car, unless the parking lot is carefully monitored at all times. The key facilitates the thief's job. A much better practice is to place all car keys in a specified location accessible only to authorized employees.

We have discussed car bailments as involving transfer of the key. Customarily if a person parks a car in a lot and retains the key, in the eyes of the law he has not delivered possession of the vehicle to the lot owner and therefore no bailment exists. The following case held a bailment existed even though the key was retained by the car's owner. Special circumstances existed that led to the result. Note carefully the court's reasoning for dispensing with the key as the critical factor in creating a bailment of a car.

CASE EXAMPLE 9–14

Allen v. Hyatt Regency-Nashville Hotel
668 S.W.2d 286 (Tenn., 1984)

There is almost no dispute as to the relevant facts. Appellant is the owner and operator of a modern high-rise hotel in Nashville fronting on the south side of Union Street. Immediately to the rear, or south, of the main hotel building there is a multi-story parking garage with a single entrance and a single exit to the west, on Seventh Avenue, North. As one enters the parking garage at the street level, there is a large sign reading "Welcome to Hyatt Regency-Nashville." There is another Hyatt Regency sign inside the garage at street level, together with a sign marked "Parking." The garage is available for parking by members of the general public as well as guests of the hotel, and the public are invited to utilize it.

On the morning of February 12, 1981, appellee's husband, Edwin Allen, accompanied by two passengers, drove appellee's new 1981 automobile into the parking garage. Neither Mr. Allen nor his passengers intended to register at the hotel as a guest. Mr. Allen had parked in this particular garage on several occasions, however, testifying that he felt that the vehicle would be safer in an attended garage than in an unattended outside lot on the street.

The single entrance was controlled by a ticket machine. The single exit was controlled by an attendant in a booth just opposite to the entrance and in full view thereof. Appellee's husband entered the garage at the street level and took a ticket which was automatically dispensed by the machine. The machine activated a barrier gate which rose and permitted Mr. Allen to enter the garage. He drove to the fourth floor level, parked the vehicle, locked it, retained the ignition key, descended by elevator to the street level and left the garage. When he returned several hours later, the car was gone, and it has never been recovered. Mr. Allen

reported the theft to the attendant at the exit booth. . . . The attendant did not testify at the trial.

Mr. Allen then reported the theft to security personnel employed by appellant, and subsequently reported the loss to the police. Appellant regularly employed a number of security guards, who were dressed in a distinctive uniform, two of whom were on duty most of the time. These guards patrolled the hotel grounds and building as well as the garage and were instructed to make rounds through the garage, although not necessarily at specified intervals. One of the security guards told appellee's husband that earlier in the day he had received the following report:

"He said, 'It's a funny thing here. On my report here a lady called me somewhere around nine-thirty or after and said that there was someone messing with a car."

The guard told Mr. Allen that he closed his office and went up into the garage to investigate, but reported that he did not find anything unusual or out of the ordinary.

Customers such as Mr. Allen, upon entering the garage, received a ticket from the dispensing machine. On one side of this ticket are instructions to overnight guests to present the ticket to the front desk of the hotel. The other side contains instructions to the parker to keep the ticket and that the ticket must be presented to the cashier upon leaving the parking area. The ticket states that charges are made for the use of parking space only and that appellant assumes no responsibility for loss through fire, theft, collision or otherwise to the car or its contents. The ticket states that cars are parked at the risk of the owner, and parkers are instructed to lock their vehicles. The record indicates that these tickets are given solely for the purpose of measuring the time during which a vehicle is parked in order that the attendant may collect the proper charge, and that they are not given for the purpose of identifying particular vehicles.

The question of the legal relationship between the operator of a vehicle which is being parked and the operator of parking establishments has been the subject of frequent litigation in this state and elsewhere. The authorities are in conflict, and the result of the cases are varied.

It is legally and theoretically possible, of course, for various legal relationships to be created by the parties. . . . Several courts have found difficulty with the traditional criteria of bailment in analyzing park-and-lock cases. . . .

Tennessee courts generally have analyzed cases such as this in terms of sufficiency of evidence to create a bailment for hire by implication. We believe that this continues to be the majority view and the most satisfactory and realistic approach to the problem, unless the parties clearly by their conduct or by express contract create some other relationship. . . .

In the instant case, appellee's vehicle was not driven into an unattended or open parking area. Rather it was driven into an enclosed, indoor, attended commercial garage which not only had an attendant controlling the exit but regular security personnel to patrol the premises for safety.

Under these facts we are of the opinion that the courts below correctly concluded that a bailment for hire had been created, and that upon proof of nondelivery appellee was entitled to the statutory presumption of negligence. . . .

We recognize that there is always a question as to whether there has been sufficient delivery of possession and control to create a bailment when the owner locks a vehicle and keeps the keys. Nevertheless, the realities of the situation are that the operator of the garage is, in circumstances like those shown in this record, expected to provide attendants and protection. In practicality the operator does assume control and custody of the vehicles parked, limiting access thereto and requiring the presentation of a ticket upon exit. . . .

Appellant made no effort to rebut the presumption [of negligence]. . . . While the plaintiff did not prove positive acts of negligence on the part of appellant, the record does show that some improper activity or tampering with vehicles had been called to the attention of security personnel earlier in the day of the theft in question, and that appellee's new vehicle had been removed from the garage by some person or persons unknown, either driving past an inattentive attendant or one who had absented himself from his post, there being simply no other way in which the vehicle could have been driven out of the garage.

Under the facts and circumstances of this case, we are not inclined to . . . place the risk of loss upon the consuming public as against the operators of commercial parking establishments such as that conducted by appellant. We recognize that park-and-lock situations arise under many and varied factual circumstances. It is difficult to lay down one rule of law which will apply to all cases. The expectations of the parties and their conduct can cause differing legal relationships to arise, with consequent different legal results. We do not find the facts of the present case, however, to be at variance with the legal requirements of the traditional concept of a bailment for hire. In our opinion it amounted to more than a mere license or hiring of a space to park a vehicle, unaccompanied by any expectation of protection or other obligation upon the operator of the establishment. . . .

CASE QUESTION

1. Does this case suggest that parking a car at a typical mall parking lot (large, unattended, not enclosed, owner keeps keys) creates a bailment? Why or why not?

This case is not widely followed by other courts. Most cases involving parking lots require a transfer of the key before a bailment will be found to exist.

Liability for a Patron's Property in a Restaurant, Bar, or Cloakroom

The only portion of many limiting liability statutes that apply to a restaurant or bar covers no-fee checkrooms where the customer is given a receipt for the checked property. In all other circumstances, the only basis for liability for lost property in a restaurant or bar is bailment. As the next case illustrates, if a bailment does not exist, the bar is not liable.

CASE EXAMPLE 9–15

Kuchinsky v. Empire Lounge, Inc.
134 N.W.2d 436 (Wis., 1965)

Kuchinsky entered the Empire Lounge as a customer and hung his coat on a clothes tree near his table. His coat was stolen while he ate.

[In another case] very much in point . . . the plaintiff entered the restaurant kept by the defendant with a party of friends; he removed his overcoat and hung it on a hook affixed to a post near the table at which he seated himself; the attention of neither the defendant nor of any of his employees was called to the coat in any way; and fifteen minutes later, the coat was missing. The court held that the plaintiff had wholly failed to show failure on the part of the defendant to exercise ordinary care.

The rule . . . is that before a restaurant keeper will be held liable for the loss of an overcoat of a customer while such customer takes a meal or refreshments, it must appear . . . that the overcoat was placed in the physical custody of the keeper of the restaurant or his servants, in which cases there is an actual bailment. . . .

In [another case], the plaintiff was a guest at a luncheon held at the defendant's hotel. She hung her mink jacket in an unattended cloakroom on the main floor across from the lobby desk. After the luncheon and ensuing party, the plaintiff went to the cloakroom to retrieve her jacket and discovered it was gone. The court held that no negligence had been established against the defendant and stated: ". . . In any event, we do not feel that it is incumbent upon a hotel or restaurant owner to keep an attendant in charge of a free cloakroom for luncheon or dinner guests or otherwise face liability for loss of articles placed therein. The maintenance of such rooms without attendants is a common practice, and where the proprietor had not accepted control and custody of articles placed therein, no duty rests upon him to exercise any special degree of care with respect thereto. . . ."

Ruling of the Court: [Complaint dismissed]

In another case a restaurant patron whose coat had fallen off his chair was directed by the waitress to hang it in an unattended cloak room. The coat was stolen from the room and the patron sued. The court held the restaurant was not liable because possession of the coat had not been delivered to the restaurant and so a bailment was never created. *Black Beret Lounge and Restaurant v. Meisnere*, 336 A.2d 532 (D.C., 1975).

If a bailment does exist, the hotel or restaurant will be liable if it fails to exercise the necessary care. In the following case the restaurant learned this rule of law the hard way. The case also illustrates a **constructive bailment**, which is a bailment created by law rather than the parties' agreement, due to special circumstances. A constructive bailment, like a mutual benefit bailment, requires the bailee to exercise reasonable care of the bailed good. In this case a constructive bailment was created where a restaurant patron mistakenly left her pocketbook by her table when she departed and it was found by an employee.

CASE EXAMPLE 9–16

Shamrock Hilton Hotel v. Caranas
488 S.W.2d 151 (Tex., 1972)

. . . Plaintiffs, husband and wife, were lodging as paying guests at the Shamrock Hilton Hotel in Houston on the evening of September 4, 1966, when they took their dinner in the hotel restaurant. After completing the meal, Mr. and Mrs. Caranas, plaintiffs, departed the dining area leaving her purse behind. The purse was found by the hotel busboy who, pursuant to the instructions of the hotel, dutifully delivered the forgotten item to the restaurant cashier, a Mrs. Luster. The testimony indicates that some short time thereafter, the cashier gave the purse to a man other than Mr. Caranas who came to claim it. There is no testimony on the question of whether identification was sought by the cashier. The purse allegedly contained $5.00 in cash, some credit cards, and ten pieces of jewelry said to be worth $13,062. The misplacement of the purse was realized the following morning, at which time plaintiffs notified the hotel authorities of the loss.

Plaintiffs filed suit, alleging negligent delivery of the purse to an unknown person and seeking a recovery for the value of the purse and its contents. . . .

[W]e find that there was indeed a constructive bailment of the purse. The delivery and acceptance were evidenced in the acts of Mrs. Caranas' unintentionally leaving her purse behind in the hotel restaurant and the busboy, a hotel employee, picking it up and taking it to the cashier, who accepted the purse as a lost or misplaced item. The delivery need not be knowingly intended on the part of Mrs. Caranas if it is apparent that were she . . . aware of the circumstances (here the purse being misplaced), she would have desired the person finding the article to have kept it safely for its subsequent return to her.

As stated above, the evidence conclusively showed facts from which there was established a bailment with the Caranases as bailors and the hotel as bailee. The evidence also showed that the hotel, as bailee, had received Mrs. Caranas' purse and had not returned it on demand. Such evidence raised a presumption that the hotel had failed to exercise ordinary care in protecting the appellees' property. When the hotel failed to come forward with any evidence to the effect that it had exercised ordinary care, that the property had been stolen, or that the property had been lost, damaged, or destroyed by fire or by an act of God, the appellees' proof ripened into proof by which the hotel's primary liability was established as a matter of law.

Further, this bailment was one for the mutual benefit of both parties. Appellees were paying guests in the hotel and in its dining room. Appellant hotel's practice of keeping patrons' lost personal items until they could be returned to their rightful owners, as reflected in the testimony, is certainly evidence of its being incidental to its business, as we would think it would be for almost any commercial enterprise that caters to the general public. Though no direct charge is made for this service, there is indirect benefit to be had in the continued patronage of the hotel by customers who have lost chattels and who have been able to claim them from the management.

Having found this to have been a bailment for the mutual benefit of the parties, we hold that the appellants owed the appellees the duty of reasonable care in the return of the purse and jewelry, and the hotel is therefore liable for its ordinary negligence.

Appellants urge that if a bailment is found, it existed only as to "the purse and the usual petty cash or credit cards found therein" and not to the jewelry of which the hotel had no actual notice. This exact question so far as we can determine has never been squarely put before the Texas courts. . . . [T]he general rule in other jurisdictions is that a bailee is liable not only for lost property of which he has actual knowledge, but also the property he could reasonably expect to find contained within the bailed property.

We believe appellants' contention raises the question of whether or not it was foreseeable that such jewelry might be found in a woman's purse in a restaurant of a hotel such as the Shamrock Hilton under these circumstances.

. . . It is known that people who are guests in hotels such as the Shamrock Hilton, a well-known Houston hotel, not infrequently bring such expensive jewelry with them, and it does not impress us as unreasonable under the circumstances that one person might have her jewelry in her purse either awaiting a present occasion to wear it or following reclaiming it from the hotel safe in anticipation of leaving the hotel.

We find that the question of whether it is reasonably foreseeable that a woman, under the circumstances of this case, might keep jewelry in a purse, which is determinative of whether there was a bailment of jewelry and whether the negligence in losing the purse was a proximate cause of losing the jewelry, is [a question for the jury. The jury in this case found there was a bailment].

The busboy and cashier assumed possession and control of the purse per instructions of the hotel with respect to articles misplaced or lost by customers. . . . Possession was complete . . . once the bailee assumed possession, he alone had the duty to safeguard the bailed article. . . .

Ruling of the Court: [J]udgment for plaintiff.

CASE QUESTIONS

1. What was the court's reasoning for determining the hotel was liable for the jewelry in the purse?

2. Would a restaurant not connected with the hotel be liable for the jewelry in the purse in a similar factual situation? Why or why not?

In another case plaintiff guest placed in his room a paper bag filled with $9,000 in cash and left the hotel temporarily. The housekeeper found the money while cleaning the room. Seeing no personal effects of the guests in the room, she wrongly assumed he had checked out. Consistent with hotel procedure for lost property, she gave the money to her immediate supervisor, who in turn gave it to the general supervisor. He absconded with the money which was never recovered. The general supervisor had been employed by the hotel for three years and had in that time been given items of value to turn into the office on several occasions. He had always done so until the time in question. The guest sued the hotel; it denied liability for the full $9,000 based on the limiting statute. Plaintiff argued the hotel should be liable, notwithstanding the statute, on a bailment theory since it took possession of the money for safekeeping. The court hedged on whether the law of bailment should supersede the limiting statute but stated that even if bailment law applied, the hotel was not negligent and therefore would not be liable because the housekeeper and her supervisor gave the money to the proper person and that person had always acted responsibly with regard to guests' valuables in the past. The court further held the hotel was not liable for the general supervisor's theft of the money on a respondeat superior theory since, when he stole the money, he was acting outside the scope of his employment. Instead, the hotel's liability was limited by the statute. *Gordon v. Day's Inn*, 395 S.E.2d 876 (Ga., 1990). A significant difference between this case and *Shamrock* is that in *Shamrock* the bailee of the purse was negligent; in this case the court held the bailee was not.

Checkrooms

Many hotels, restaurants, clubs, concert halls, museums, and other public businesses have checkrooms available to safeguard guests' valuables. Checkrooms have an attendant on duty to whom the patron's garment or other property is delivered and who issues an identifying check as proof of receipt of the property. A bailment is thus created. Those coatrooms in which no receipts are given are usually unattended and therefore, typically, no bailment arises. The establishment will thus not be liable for loss or damage. What is the responsibility of a checkroom to guests who leave their possessions?

In *Hackney v. Southwest Hotels, Inc.*, 195 S.W.2d 55 (Ark., 1946), the guest left a camera valued at $300 in the hotel checkroom and was given a receipt for it. On the check was printed a notice that limited the liability of the innkeeper to $25. When the guest sought to retrieve the camera the hotel discovered it was missing. The guest sued for its full value. Notwithstanding the notice on the receipt attempting to limit the hotel's liability, the court held the innkeeper was acting in the role of bailee for hire and ordered the hotel to pay in full. The court stressed the fact that the Arkansas limiting liability statute did not list a checkroom as a place in which the hotel was relieved from the absolute liability of common law and added, "We would be reading into the statute something that is not there if we permitted the hotelkeeper by language on the claim check to limit the extent of his liability concerning property especially entrusted to his care, and concerning which property . . . the legislature did not provide for the limiting of the extent of the liability of the hotelkeeper."

In many states the limiting liability laws do cover attended checkrooms and baggage rooms, thus limiting the restaurant or hotel's liability for losses occurring there. In New York, for example, the maximum liability for a checked item is $200.

If the coatroom is unattended the limited liability statute is not applicable. Since typically no bailment arises when a coatroom is unattended the hotel or restaurant will have no liability for property lost or stolen there. However, the following case establishes that, under certain circumstances, a bailment of a coat may exist even where no checkroom attendant is on duty. Note carefully the court's reasoning for dispensing with the need for an attendant.

CASE EXAMPLE 9–17

Forte v. Westchester Hills Golf Club, Inc.
426 N.Y.S.2d 390 (1980)

Plaintiff Diane Forte was a dinner guest of Mr. LaRue Buchanan and his son at defendant's private country club, Westchester Hills Golf club, Inc., on January 6, 1979.

Miss Forte was concerned about having her full-length raccoon coat hung in the club's cloak room. She personally walked into that room, and saw other fur coats hanging there. The club did not provide an attendant in the cloak room or at the entrance to screen visitors or prevent unwanted guests, although to a limited extent the function of attendant was performed by Doris Cummings, Secretary of the club, who was on duty. No notice disclaiming liability was posted.

Miss Forte was told by Mr. Buchanan that there was no need for concern; the club would be responsible for any loss. Seeing other fur coats in the cloak room and relying upon the assurance of Mr. Buchanan, she gave him her coat to hang up. Miss Forte's coat was missing when Mr. Buchanan later returned to the cloak room after dining; apparently, the coat had been stolen.

Mr. Buchanan had been told a number of times by club employees over the past year, usually in the presence of his wife who also had a fur coat, that there was no need to worry about having coats hung in the cloak room, as the club would bear responsibility for any loss. The club's responsibility was confirmed, or admitted, albeit after Miss Forte's coat was stolen on the evening in question, by an employee of the club, Mr. Abbott (the bartender) who had informed Miss Forte that there was no need for concern; the club would be responsible. Defendant controverts the evidence as to the club's responsibility by offering the by-laws, which are to the contrary. These by-laws however, are not binding upon plaintiff, Miss Forte, who is a [nonmember] guest.

The evidence as to the statement of Mr. Abbott was presented by Mr. Buchanan's testimony. Mr. Abbott was admittedly in charge of the dining room at the time of plaintiff's visit. . . .

The question thus arises as to whether the club is responsible for the theft of Miss Forte's coat. Before liability may be found, a bailment relationship must exist. Ordinarily, there must be (1) an actual delivery of the coat by its owner (as bailor) to the club (as bailee), and (2) circumstances where the bailee retains possession and control of the coat and in which it may be implied that the coat will be returned in proper condition. For the purpose of determining delivery, Mr. Buchanan cannot be considered as a representative or agent of defendant. It is more accurate to consider Mr. Buchanan to be Miss Forte's agent rather than defendant's agent.

The circumstances here are different from those presented in cases involving restaurants and night clubs open to the general public, where bailment is usually found only if there is delivery to an employee-agent of the restaurant or night club. However . . . under the facts presented here, Miss Forte's coat was hung in the cloak room of an exclusive private country club. Miss Forte had seen other fur coats hanging in the cloak room, and Mr. Buchanan had communicated to her the statements as to the club's responsibility. This was her first visit to the club, and she believed her coat would be safe or the club would be responsible. The absence of a notice disclaiming liability is not dispositive, but the country club's case would be stronger if such a notice was posted and seen by its guests. Had Miss Forte seen such a notice, this case would not be in court. . . . There is here an implied invitation for a member or guest to deposit his or her coat in the cloak room. . . .

This Court holds that it was implicit in the relationship between the guest of a member and the defendant country club that the club became bailee of that guest's coat. The bailment was for hire, as opposed to a gratuitous bailment, and required only ordinary reasonable care by the bailee. Monetary consideration was presented in (1) the use of the club's facilities by Mr. Buchanan, a paying member of the club, and his guests, and (2) the dining expenses themselves. The lack of attendants to keep unwanted persons from the club and the lack of any safeguards to protect coats of the members and guests who use the cloak room was ordinary negligence, and defendant is thus liable.

The equities, as well as "substantial justice", are surely on the side of plaintiff. She paid $1,132.92 for her coat, and was quite concerned about the safety of that coat when she asked Mr. Buchanan to hang it up. They both relied upon statements of club employees and the prevailing appearances. The court therefore finds for the plaintiff the amount of $1,000.00 plus costs.

CASE QUESTIONS

1. On what facts did the court rely in determining that the country club had accepted possession of her coat?
2. Although the court did not mention estoppel, did it play a role in the decision?
3. What do you think the outcome of the case would have been if the club had posted a sign in the coatroom disclaiming liability for any loss?
4. Why did the court not award plaintiff the full price she paid for the coat?

The following case addresses many of the issues we have studied—bailments, limiting liability statutes, and conspicuous notice. This case highlights again the courts' restrictive reading of limited liability statutes. As we have seen repeatedly in this chapter, unless all the terms of the statute apply, the limitation of liability is not applicable.

CASE EXAMPLE 9–18

Conboy v. Studio 54, Inc.
449 N.Y.S.2d 391 (1982)

The issue that I must decide is whether the [New York limiting liability statute] provides a monetary haven for a discotheque.

The section states in part:

[A]s to property deposited by guests or patrons in the parcel or check room of any hotel, motel or restaurant, the delivery of which is evidenced by a check or receipt therefor and for *which no fee or charge is exacted*, the proprietor shall not be liable beyond seventy-five dollars, unless such value in excess of seventy-five dollars shall be stated upon delivery and a written receipt, stating such value, shall be issued, but he shall in no event be liable beyond one hundred dollars unless such loss occurs through his fault or negligence. (emphasis supplied)

On January 23, 1982, the claimant, his wife and a group of friends convened for a party at Studio 54 (Studio) in Manhattan. Studio, licensed by the New York City Department of Consumer Affairs as a cabaret, is a discotheque, where patrons dance to recorded music usually played continuously on high fidelity equipment. . . . Often a psychedelic light show accompanies the music and provides background and impetus for the free-spirited patrons who pay $18 per person to dance to the deafening and often overwhelming disco music played continuously on the sophisticated sound system. A cabaret is defined as "Any room, place or space in the City in which any musical entertainment, singing, dancing or other form of amusement is permitted in connection with the restaurant business or the business of directly or indirectly selling to the public food or drink. . . ."

No food is sold or served here—not even a single peanut or pretzel to accompany the alcoholic and soft drinks available for purchase.

The Conboy party checked their coats, 14 in all, with the coatroom attendant. They received 7 check stubs after paying the 75¢ charge per coat. A bailment of the coats was created. Mr. Conboy did not issue a statement concerning the coat's value to the attendant.

After their evening of revelry, they attempted to reclaim their coats. Mr. Conboy's one-month old, $1,350 leather coat was missing. It has not been found and accordingly, he has sued Studio for $1,350.

Under traditional bailment law, once the goods were delivered, the failure of the bailee (Studio) to return them on demand, created a *prima facie* case of negligence. The burden of coming forward with evidence tending to show due care shifted to Studio. Studio did not come forward with any evidence to meet this burden. Mr. Conboy is entitled to a judgment.

Studio, relying on [New York's limiting liability statute], contends that its liability is limited to $75 since no value was declared for the coat. Its argument is incorrect for two reasons.

First, the statute applies to a hotel, motel or restaurant and then only to property deposited by a patron in a checkroom ". . . the delivery of which is evidenced by a check or receipt therefor and for which no fee or charge is exacted. . . ." The statute offers innkeepers and restaurant proprietors who comply with it a reduction of the innkeeper's common law insurer-liability as to guest's property deposited with them. Compliance with the terms of the statute relieves the innkeeper or restaurant owner of this common law responsibility, where applicable. The statute is in derogation of the common law and is therefore strictly construed.

That being said, it need only be noted that the statute offers its protection to restaurants, hotels and motels, not discotheques which appear to be modern-day versions of dance halls.

Simply put, a discotheque may qualify as a restaurant but there is no logic in giving it that classification unless one of its principal activities is the furnishing of meals. Certainly, Studio should not be classified as a restaurant, because it serves no food. A licensed cabaret, such as Studio, is permitted to engage in the restaurant business but is not required to.

The term "restaurant" was first used in America to refer to dining rooms found in the best hotels and to certain high-class a la carte restaurants. Today, a restaurant would be thought of as an establishment that sells food and drink or where meals may be purchased and eaten. The limitations on liability set forth in the statute are therefore not applicable here. . . . It may be illogical to condition limitation of liability on the sale of meals, but that is what the statute says and it is for the legislature to change, not this Court.

Even if I might have concluded that Studio could be treated as a restaurant, it still would not have benefitted from the liability limitation provided by the statute because of the fact that a charge was exacted for each coat checked.

Studio claims however that their liability may nevertheless be limited by the posting of a sign in the courtroom. The sign states: "Liability for lost property in this coat/check room is limited to $100 per loss of misplaced article.". . .

[T]he posting of the sign [is not] a useless act, for it may still function as a common law disclaimer. To bind Conboy to this limitation, I must find however that he had notice of the terms of the disclaimer and agree to it. Studio did not establish that the sign was posted in a conspicuous manner. I hold that Conboy is not bound by the posted disclaimer of liability.

As to damages, Conboy is entitled to the "real value" of the coat. Real value, especially with respect to used clothing or household furnishings that are lost or damaged is not necessarily its market value which presumably would reflect a deduction for depreciation. In fact, the real value may be measured by the price paid when new for the lost or damaged goods.

One commentator has offered a reason that the strict market value approach is not favored:

No judge buys his clothing second hand and none would expect any owner to replace his clothing in a second hand store. Hence no judge expects to limit the cost of replacing clothing to a market no one should be expected to use.

I therefore hold that Conboy may be compen-sated on a basis that will permit him to replace the very same coat purchased new—$1,350.

Judgment for claimant in the sum of $1,350.

CASE QUESTIONS

1. Why did the limiting liability statute not apply in this case?
2. Why did the disclaimer sign hung by Studio 54 not relieve the discotheque from liability?
3. If Conboy's coat was three years old rather than one month, do you think the court would have awarded him its full value of $1,350?

Concessionaires

Often a hotel or perhaps a restaurant will contract with a concessionaire (an independent contractor) to operate the checking facilities (luggage and coats). Usually the concessionaire pays the hotel a fee for the business opportunity. Such an arrangement saves the hotel from having to manage and staff the checking operations. Several plaintiffs whose checked property was not returned from concessionaire have argued that the concessionaire is not entitled to the benefits of the limiting statutes because those statutes were designed to protect only innkeepers and restaurateurs. Courts have upheld this argument in *Aldrich v. Waldorf Astoria Hotel, Inc.*, 343 N.Y.S.2d 833 (1973); and *Jacobson v. Belplaza Corp.*, 80 F.Supp. 917 (N.Y., 1949).

Summary

The liability of hotels and restaurants for their guests' and patrons' property has changed over time. The common law imposed unlimited liability on inns and food establishments. Most states have since passed limiting statutes which significantly reduce this liability.

For money, jewels, and securities, the requirements of limiting statutes typically require that hotels provide safes, post notices in prescribed places announcing the availability of the safes, and post notices in prescribed places announcing the hotel's limited liability. The specifics of these statutes vary from state to state. Only if the hotel strictly complies with the statutory requirements will it benefit from limited liability.

For other property a guest brings to a hotel, such as clothes or sporting equipment, limiting statutes provide limited liability for hotels unless the loss is caused by the hotel's negligence. If it is, the hotel will typically be liable for the full value of the missing property. An exception is the state of Nevada, which limits the liability of innkeepers even when they are negligent.

For property not covered by the limiting statutes, the liability of a hotel or restaurant is based on laws regarding bailment. If no bailment exists, the business is not liable for loss or theft of property. If a bailment does exist, the hotel or restaurant will be liable for the loss only if it failed to exercise the requisite degree of care for the bailed goods. The amount of care required varies depending on whether the bailment is for the sole benefit of the bailor, the sole benefit of the bailee, or is a mutual benefit bailment. If the hotel or restaurant applied the care required, the establishment will be free from liability even though property was lost.

Preventive Law Tips for Managers

- *Identify the Specific Requirements of Your State's Limiting Liability Statute and Follow Them.* The limiting statutes relieve a hotel from common law strict liability. The statutes are generally not applicable unless the hotel follows their mandates exactly. Most states' statutes require that the hotel provide a safe and post notice conspicuously in specified places of the availability of the safe and the hotel's limited liability. To qualify under the statutes, a hotel safe must be secure and capable of withstanding burglary attempts. It should be available to guests 24 hours a day. Anything less jeopardizes the relief from full liability offered by the statutes.

  The posted notices must not only inform the guest of the safe's availability but must also state that, if goods are lost or stolen from the safe, the hotel's liability will be limited. The notices must be posted each and every place the statute requires. For example, if the statute mandates posting by the registration desk, in the lobby, and in guest rooms, posting in less than all three locations is inadequate in most states and will not protect the hotel from unlimited liability. The notice must also be conspicuous, meaning easy to read and easy to find. A notice hidden behind lobby furniture or in a nonobvious place in the guest room will not satisfy the statute. In these circumstances the hotel will be liable for the full value of the lost property.

  Individual states may have additional requirements. For example, some states require "suitable" locks or bolts on the doors and "suitable" fastenings on windows and transoms in guest rooms. Check your state statute carefully and make sure your establishment is in compliance. Loss through inadvertence or carelessness of the very significant benefit offered by these statutes is inexcusable.

- *Train Appropriate Employees How to Use the Safe.* If a guest is unable to place valuables in the safe because the staff does not know how to operate it, the safe is not "available" to the guest as required by statute and the hotel will have unlimited liability. Supervisory employees who work at the front desk should be well trained on use of the safe and the importance of its availability around the clock. If an employee does not correctly operate the safe or fails to follow hotel procedures for its use, thefts may be facilitated. In addition, the guest who owned the property will be very dissatisfied.

- *Instruct Employees about the Hotel's Limited Liability and the Importance of Their Not Overstating That Liability.* The consequence of an employee exaggerating a hotel's liability for property stored in a safe may be that the hotel has unlimited liability. The only way to avoid the principle of estoppel from curtailing the limiting statutes' applicability is by ensuring your employees do not misstate the hotel's liability. Training and frequent reminders about the benefits of the statutes and what constitutes appropriate comments to guests about liability should minimize this potential problem.

- *Limit the Authority of Employees to Sign Documents Accepting Greater Liability than Provided by Statute.* The limiting statutes allow a hotel or restaurant to accept liability beyond the statutory maximum. To incur such liability the hotel must sign a document acknowledging receipt of specific property and agreeing to expanded liability. To avoid loss of limited liability, the hotel should restrict significantly the employees authorized to sign such documents. Unauthorized employees should be informed about such agreements, their own lack of authority, and the identifies of those who are authorized to sign. This will prevent inadvertent loss of the statute's benefit.

- *Adopt Procedures to Limit Thefts of Property from the Safe.* While the limiting liability statutes remove much of the liability a hotel would otherwise have when property is missing from the safe, such losses are costly to the hotel in terms of good customer relations. Efforts should be made to minimize this loss. Security measures concerning the safe should be reviewed and updated regularly. The number of employees with access to the safe should be limited (but not too limited because guests must have access whenever requested for limited liability to apply). Tight control should be maintained of keys to the safe and records that identify contents of the safe. Other security measures appropriate to your establishment should be instituted.

- *Regularly Review Procedures Followed in Checkrooms to Minimize Chances of Theft.* Many thefts in hotels and restaurants occur in the baggage checkroom or the coat check area. Access to these rooms should be limited. Attendants should be instructed not to leave unless another attendant is available. They should be trained always to require a receipt or other proof of ownership before returning goods. The checkrooms should be equipped with security devices to enable the attendants to notify security unobtrusively if a theft is in progress.

- *Develop and Strictly Enforce Procedures for Parking Guests' Car.* Employees assigned to parking customers' cars should be screened for driving abilities and criminal records for theft or crimes relating to driving, such as driving while intoxicated and reckless driving. Their training should stress the importance of driving patrons' cars carefully. The establishment should have procedures for handling car keys designed to avoid loss or theft. The hotel should maintain adequate insurance to cover its potential liability for violation of a bailee's responsibilities.

- *If the Coat Room Is Unattended, Hang a Sign Stating the Hotel is Not Liable.* In *Forte v. Westchester Hills Golf Club, Inc.,* the court held, based on the particular circumstances of that case, that a bailment existed even though the coat room at the club was unattended. The judge suggested that, had the club hung a sign disclaiming liability, it might not have been liable. By displaying such a sign, an establishment in otherwise similar circumstances may be able to avoid liability. The sign alerts the customer that the establishment will not cover the loss; instead, the patron leaves the goods at his/her own risk.

- *Adopt Procedures Enabling the Hotel or Restaurant, When Acting as Bailee, To Prove Reasonable Care.* The law of bailment creates a presumption of negligence on the part of the bailee if the bailor can prove delivery, acceptance, and either damage to the goods or inability by the bailee to return them. The bailee can rebut the presumption of negligence by showing it used reasonable care while in possession of the goods. Procedures for ensuring safety should be developed and enforced so that the hotel can prove it exercised reasonable care.

- *If a Concessionaire Operates the Checkrooms, the Contract Should Require Safety Procedures be Utilized and Insurance be Obtained.* A concessionaire can damage the hotel's reputation. A guest is hardly ever aware that a service is being offered by someone other than the hotel or restaurant. When guests' property is stolen, the guest views the wrongdoer as the hotel, not the concessionaire. The hotel thus has a public relations interest in ensuring the concessionaire does not engage in conduct likely to alienate patrons. The hotel should be vigilant to ensure the concessionaire's practices maximize security and minimize theft. The contract should require specified security procedures be followed and also that the concessionaire purchase insurance to cover its unlimited liability.

Review Questions

1. According to common law, what is the innkeeper's liability for a guest's lost or stolen property?
2. What is an "act of God," and what is its relevance to a hotel's liability for guests' property?

3. What is a limiting liability statute?

4. What two key facts must be included in a notice posted pursuant to most limiting liability statutes?

5. Which of the following types of property are covered by the limiting liability statutes that require hotels to maintain a safe?

   a. Jewelry

   b. Cash

   c. A laptop (portable) computer

   d. Diamond cufflinks

   e. Expensive sporting equipment

   f. Clothes

6. What is the consequence for a guest failing to put valuables in a safe?

7. Can guests and innkeepers contract for a greater coverage for guests' valuables than allowed by statute?

8. What is estoppel? What is its relevance to a hotel's liability for lost property?

9. At what point in the check-in process does a limiting liability statute become effective?

10. What is a bailment? What is the difference between a bailment for the sole benefit of the bailor and a bailment for the sole benefit of the bailee?

11. If you leave a watch with the jeweler to be repaired, who is the bailor and who is the bailee?

12. Does a bailment exist between a hotel and a guest when the guest goes out for the evening and leaves property in her room?

Discussion Questions

1. Describe two possible circumstances in which a hotel that provides a safe to its guests does not satisfy the statutory requirement for a safe.

2. The Mandan Hotel posts the notice required by the limiting statute in the bathroom of guest rooms on the inside door of the medicine cabinet. Has the hotel posted the notice conspicuously? Why or why not? Suppose the notice is placed inside the top dresser drawer near the stationery. Is this conspicuous posting? Why or why not?

3. Jan ate dinner at the Demrich Restaurant. After dinner she paid the cashier and went home without realizing she had left her purse at the restaurant. What liability does the restaurant have if the cashier does not notice the purse and it is stolen? What liability does the restaurant

have if the cashier takes possession of the purse intending to notify Jan that it is at the restaurant?

4. Compare the liability of a hotel and a concessionaire for coats checked in a cloakroom.

Application Questions

1. A limiting statute requires that a hotel post the necessary notice in the registration area, in the hotel lobby, and in the guest rooms. If a hotel posts the notice in the registration area and in guest rooms but fails to post in the lobby, will the hotel be entitled to limited liability? Why or why not? Does the state in which the hotel is located affect your answer?

2. A guest arrives at a hotel and informs the desk clerk that she has with her a large amount of cash. She expresses concern for its safety, and the clerk recommends she place it in a hotel safe deposit box. When she hesitates, he assures her that the money will be protected and further, even if it does become lost the hotel will be fully liable. Relying on this assurance, she deposits the money in a safe deposit box. When she sought to retrieve the money it had disappeared and has not been recovered. Is the hotel entitled to limited liability under these circumstances? Why or why not?

3. Terry is a law book salesperson. She is attending a conference of lawyers and has brought with her approximately $5000 worth of book samples. What must she do vis-a-vis the hotel to obtain maximum protection for the books?

4. Sandra is talking to the front desk clerk in the process of checking out. While she is reviewing the bill, someone steals her briefcase, which was on the ground near her feet. The briefcase had in it various documents she needed for work, a spare pair of glasses, and a pair of cufflinks with emeralds in them. Will the hotel be liable for the loss of any of these items? Why or why not?

CHAPTER 10

Rights of Innkeepers

CHAPTER OUTLINE

INTRODUCTION

This chapter focuses on the innkeeper's rights concerning selection, entry into, and moving of a guest's room; the right to evict guests; and the right to pursue a nonpaying guest.

While patrons are the lifeblood of hotels and restaurants, an unruly or belligerent customer can interfere with the enjoyment of other patrons and damage the operation of the business. Hotels and restaurants may not want to serve such people.

In this chapter we will investigate the circumstances under which a hotelkeeper or restaurateur can refuse a guest accommodations or a meal and evict a guest. The chapter discusses how to evict and how not to evict. This is a sensitive area of the law; a wrong move can lead to a lawsuit accusing the proprietor of assault, false arrest, slander, or false imprisonment.

Sometimes patrons do not pay their bills or pay by fraudulent means. The law arms hospitality proprietors with various methods to obtain payment, including the innkeeper's lien and criminal charges of theft of services, possession of stolen property, forgery, and issuing a bad check. This chapter discusses these legal rights and remedies.

As you read the cases in this chapter, you will likely note that many are relatively old. This is because many of the issues in this chapter have not been the subject of recent lawsuits. The older cases remain viable precedents.

Right to Exclude Non-guests

Generally innkeepers and restaurateurs extend an implied invitation or license to all, including nonguests, to enter their facility. Therefore, the public's presence on the premises, even though not as the result of an express invitation, does not constitute trespass. This implied license can be revoked by the innkeeper for people other than guests at any time. Therefore, persons entering a hotel who are not guests and do not intend to become one are required to leave the premises if asked. Similarly, a restaurateur can ask a person in a restaurant to leave who is not interested in eating or drinking but rather is just lingering, loitering, or otherwise "hanging out". A person who has been requested to leave and fails to do so after being given a reasonable opportunity, thereby becomes a trespasser.

The operator may use reasonable force to evict a trespasser but only after the trespasser has been asked to leave and refuses to do so. The amount of force that can be used is limited by law. Only that amount of force as is reasonably necessary to remove the trespasser from the premises is permitted. Excessive force will subject the hotelier or restaurateur to liability; the trespasser will be able to sue the business for injuries that result.

In the following case the innkeeper avoided the need to use force by calling the police.

CASE EXAMPLE 10–1

People v. Thorpe
101 N.Y.S.2d 986 (1950)

Defendants are charged with the offense of disorderly conduct in violation of . . . the Penal Law. They are members of a religious group known as Jehovah's Witnesses. Each of these defendants asserts that he is a minister of the gospel and preaches from door to door under the direction of the Watchtower Bible and Tract Society, Inc., a corporation established by law for religious purposes.

Defendants entered the Endicott Hotel located at 81st Street and Columbus Avenue, New York City, at 10:30 A.M. on Saturday morning, February 4, 1950. Defendant Thorpe proceeded to the second floor and defendant VanDyk to the top floor of the hotel. Each went from door to door down the hotel corridors, knocking to gain the attention of the hotel guests, and, upon the door being opened, sought to impart to each person thus approached the religious doctrines advocated by the Jehovah's Witnesses. Literature was tendered by the defendants consisting of a book, booklet, and magazine. Contributions, if not actively solicited, were certainly encouraged and, in any event, were admittedly accepted.

Defendants continued their mission until halted by the hotel manager. They conducted their activities as quietly as possible and seemingly without undue annoyance of the hotel residents. When the hotel manager learned of their presence, he asked defendants summarily to desist. The defendant Thorpe explained that he considered it his constitutional right to preach from door to door, which was, he claimed, established as an appropriate method of preaching in accordance with the tenets of his faith. Defendants refused to leave the hotel, whereupon a police officer was summoned who, upon arrival, informed defendant Thorpe that the hotel management had a right to insist that the defendants' activities stop and that they forthwith leave the hotel. Defendant replied that he had a right to stay there and, admittedly, told the officer then in uniform, "If I was to leave, he would have to put me under arrest."

In the meantime, the hotel manager located defendant VanDyk pursuing his activities on one of the upper floors. He was requested to leave the hotel. Defendant VanDyk thereupon went down to the hotel lobby with the manager, the police officer, and defendant Thorpe, who had been escorted by the policeman to the street. The hotel manager admonished defendants that they could not return to the hotel. . . . Defendants insisted that it was their right to preach in the hotel and, admittedly, "returned shortly to the hotel with the intention of resuming their preaching activity.". . .

It is urged that a conviction will result in abridgement of the liberties of press and worship guaranteed by the United States Constitution.

It was long ago held that "from the very nature of the business, it is inevitable" that a hotel owner "must, at all reasonable times and for all proper purposes" have "control over every part" of the hotel, "even though separate parts thereof may be occupied by guests for hire." . . . The hotel management rightfully may exercise control designed to serve the convenience, comfort, or safety of guests and their property. A person who is not a guest "has in general no legal right to enter or remain" in the hotel against the will of the management.

The hotel management may guard against the possible dangers and annoyances of trespassers or unsolicited visits, and to that end it may, and it is common knowledge that it usually does, exclude all uninvited visitors from the private hotel corridors and from gaining access to the private accommodations of the hotel guests, regardless of whether the one excluded is actually engaged in an otherwise lawful mission, be it commercial, political, or religious.

It was entirely proper for the hotel management to enforce that policy here. That some or even many of the hotel guests may not have found the preaching activities of the defendants objectionable did not deprive the hotel manager of the right to compel observances of such policy. . . .

Greater vigilance is normally demanded and expected of a hotel in the adoption of measures designed to serve the comfort, convenience, and especially the privacy of its guests, as well as their safety and the safety of their property.

The hotel manager, hence, rightfully halted the defendants' preaching activities and justifiably summoned police aid in ejecting them from the hotel. After they were ejected, and notwithstanding that they were admonished not to return to the hotel by the police officer, the defendants, nonetheless, did return for the express purpose of proceeding with their activities, announcing that they proposed to do so unless arrested. . . . Defendants' conduct, "at the very least, was such that it tended to disturb the public peace and quiet and to occasion a breach of the peace. That, under our cases, is sufficient.". . .

Ruling of the Court: The defendants are found guilty.

Since the decision in the *Thorpe* case in 1950, Congress has enacted the Civil Rights Act of 1964, which was expanded by the Civil Rights Act of 1991. The 1964 Act, which we studied in Chapter 3, legislatively proclaims that hotels and restaurants have the status of places of "public accommodation" and as such cannot discriminate against persons because of race, color, religion, or national origin. Could Thorpe successfully argue today that he was denied equal access to the hotel because of religion in violation of the Civil Rights Act? The answer would be no, provided the hotel barred all door-to-door solicitors and not just religious proselytizers. The reason access was denied was not Thorpe's religion but rather his action of engaging in door-to-door solicitations. Discrimination on that basis is not illegal.

Refusing a Guest Lodging

The general rule is that a hotel cannot refuse accommodations to anyone seeking them. This is true regardless of the hour of the guest's arrival. Some states impose by statute a fine for refusing accommodations. The reason for this rule is steeped in history. In olden days, the means of travel was horse and buggy, the number of hotels was very limited, and thieves were prevalent in the night. If a traveler was refused accommodations at one hotel, he might not arrive at the next hotel until very late at night and would thus be exposed to considerable risk.

Several exceptions to the general rule exist. In those circumstances a hotelkeeper can legitimately refuse to provide lodging. If a hotel has no vacancies it may refuse a would-be guest. "No vacancies" can exist even though some rooms are not occupied provided those rooms are legitimately out of service, as where they are being painted, refurbished or repaired, or the unoccupied rooms are being held for reservations. A hotel that refuses accommodations to someone seeking a room and later accepts a different guest will have to explain its actions if challenged by the person who was turned away. Without a good explanation the hotel may be liable for violation of its duty to the would-be guest or for discrimination.

The hotelkeeper can also refuse persons who are criminals, intoxicated, disorderly, unclean (not bathed), or suffering from a contagious disease. The explanation for the innkeeper's right to exclude these categories of people is the hotelier's duty to protect the well-being of its other guests. The courts have also allowed innkeepers to refuse known persons of bad reputation because of the effect such guests may have on the stature of the hotel. Likewise, the innkeeper can deny a room to a prospective guest who is not able or willing to pay in advance a reasonable price for a room for the duration of the intended stay. If the person seeks an available room for five days but can only prove ability to pay for one, the innkeeper must provide him with a room for one night.

A hotel can also refuse to accommodate guests with firearms, explosives, or pets. In recent years all states have adopted statutes that forbid refusing services to a person with a seeing eye dog. Many of these statutes have been expanded to include service animals which aid sighted but otherwise disabled people. The Americans With Disabilities Act, a federal law discussed in Chapter 3, likewise requires a hotel to accommodate seeing eye dogs and other service animals.

The Consequences of Wrongful Refusal

What are the consequences of wrongfully refusing a guest? The excluded guest can sue the hotel for damages, which may include any additional expenses of staying elsewhere. If the refusal is based on race, color, religion, sex, or disability, most state statutes have penalty clauses requiring the hotel to pay a fine for the wrongful exclusion in addition to any damages suffered by the would-be guest. The remedy under the federal civil rights law is an injunction barring further illegal discrimination.

Age

Age is not a protected class in places of public accommodation under federal civil rights law or most state laws. Therefore, a restaurant could refuse to serve a young person if it was so inclined. While most restaurants would have little motivation to refuse service to a child accompanied by an adult, they may be less willing to serve a table full of young people, perhaps because of concern for rowdiness or for inability to pay. A few jurisdictions have statutes prohibiting discrimination against young people in places of public accommodation. An example is Washington, D.C. (D.C. Code Section 1-2519).

The innkeeper is in a situation different from the restaurateur. The innkeeper has a common law duty to provide accommodations to anyone seeking them, except people within the exceptions just discussed in the section of this chapter entitled "Refusing a Guest Lodging." Thus, a young person is entitled to hotel accommodations unless an exception applies.

In Chapter 4 we studied that a minor can cancel a contract and, in many states, avoid partial or even full payment. Is an innkeeper at risk for not being paid when a room is rented to a minor? The answer is no, for two reasons. First, as we studied, although minors may cancel their contracts, they remain liable for the reasonable value of necessities received. Food and shelter are normally considered necessities. Further, parents are liable for necessities furnished to their minor children. Thus, if the minor refuses to pay, the hotel can pursue the minor's parents.

Selecting Accommodations for a Guest

All hotel rooms are, in fact, different even though they may be furnished identically and of the same size. In many instances the room location is important to a guest—its view, proximity to the lobby, the floor it is on, or other factors affect its appeal. The determination of what room will be assigned a guest has always been the innkeeper's prerogative. The following case illustrates this rule.

CASE EXAMPLE 10–2

Nixon v. Royal Coach Inn of Houston
464 S.W.2d 900 (Tex., 1971)

. . . On December 4, 1968, Virginia Key Nixon was twenty-eight years of age, married, and in the employ of General Electric Company of Dallas as a systems analyst. On this particular day her work required her to come to Houston. She drove her automobile from Dallas to Houston and, arriving after it was dark, checked in the Royal Coach Inn alone at approximately 8:30 P.M. A motel employee directed her to the room to which she was assigned, which was some distance away from the main desk. After depositing her luggage in her room, she left the hotel to eat outside the motel area. Approximately one hour later, she returned to the motel, parked her car in the parking lot in the rear of the motel, and entered the building. She ascended the stairs and, while in the process of unlocking the door to her room, was attacked by an unknown assailant. She testified that though she did not lose consciousness, everything went black, and then she started screaming. It was at this time that she saw an unidentified man running down the hall in the direction of the main desk. Her screams brought no assistance, but she was able to reach the office switchboard through the phone in her room. Individuals came to her assistance in response to her phone call.

In her original petition, appellant [Nixon] alleged that appellee [the motel] was negligent [for] . . ."(1) billeting a single woman in a remote room in a desolate area of the motel."

An innkeeper is not an insurer of the safety of its guests. An innkeeper's responsibility to his guests is limited to the exercise of ordinary or reasonable care. We are cited to no authority that requires an innkeeper to assign any guest to a particular room or to any particular part of a hotel or motel. Nor has our attention been directed to any part of the record that would indicate that the appellant was in fact billeted in a remote or desolate area of the motel. . . .

Ruling of the Court: The judgment of the trial court is affirmed for the defendant.

Changing a Guest's Accommodations

Once a room is assigned to a guest, can an innkeeper require the guest to change rooms? Only two cases have been reported on this issue and both allow the innkeeper to change the room. In an early Canadian case, *Doyle v. Walker*, 26 U.C.Q.B. 502 (1867), the plaintiff-guest sued the defendant hotel for trespassing and taking his goods from the room he was originally assigned to another one. The court said the hotelkeeper has the sole right to select the room for the guest and, if expedient, to change it. This ruling was followed in *Hervey v. Hart*, 42 So. 1013 (Ala., 1906), in which the court said an innkeeper would not be liable for moving a guest "if he offered plaintiff proper accommodations in lieu of the room previously assigned to him." Further, the hotelkeeper does not become a trespasser while transferring the guest's belongings.

It is not good policy to change a room or move a guest's possessions without permission. The practice should be avoided unless the reasons are compelling. If a room change does become necessary, a better approach would be to ask the guest to move. If the guest refuses, alert the guest before the transfer occurs that the change will be affected by hotel personnel.

Entering a Guest's Room

Most courts hold that when guests are assigned a room, they are to be the sole occupants during the time that it is set apart for their use. The innkeeper retains the right of access only for such reasonable purposes as may be necessary in the conduct of the hotel as, for example, normal maintenance and repair, imminent danger, nonpayment, and when requested by the guest.

When imminent danger exists, an innkeeper or the police may enter a guest's room to address the emergency circumstance. *People v. Love*, 84 N.Y.2d 917, 620 N.Y.S.2d 809 (N.Y., 1940). Further, the emergency condition may impose a duty on the innkeeper to enter a guest's room to eliminate the danger. Failure to do so can result in liability. For example, in *Gore v. Whitmore Hotel Co.*, 83 S.W.2d 114 (Mo., 1935), the plaintiff, a pedestrian on the sidewalk adjacent to a hotel, was severely injured when he was pushed off the sidewalk and into a moving taxi by other people on the sidewalk. They were attempting to avoid being hit by a large paper bag containing water that had been thrown from a window of the hotel. For the several days leading up to the incident, which coincided with a large convention at the hotel, there was a "regular deluge" of falling water-filled bags whenever a passerby appeared on the street. Sometimes water was poured out of pitchers from the windows to the streets below. There was no evidence identifying the room from which the bags had been thrown. The court said that, under the circumstances, the hotel was obligated to exercise reasonable care to identify the offenders and the room used by them, and halt the dangerous activity. Because the hotel had the right to send its employees into the rooms each day to service them, the jury found that the hotel had the means to ascertain from which rooms the pillows and laundry bags were missing and thereby identify the wrongdoers and attempt to stop them.

Evicting a Guest

Under certain circumstances an innkeeper has the right to withdraw hotel privileges and evict a guest, provided no more force is used than is necessary. **Evict** means to remove someone from property. The following are grounds for eviction.

Failure to Pay the Hotel Bill

Failure to pay one's hotel bill is grounds for eviction. The eviction is ordinarily carried out by asking the guest for the amount due and requesting the guest to leave by a certain hour if the bill is not paid. If the guest fails to pay after such a demand, the hotel may evict. The reason for this rule is as follows. Innkeepers are understandably interested in maximizing the occupancy of the rooms in order to increase income. The innkeeper can thus be expected to properly clean a room of a guest who is delinquent on paying so the room can be rented to another guest. *People v. Lerhinan*, 455 N.Y.S.2d 822 (N.Y., 1982).

In the following case the guest refused to pay for food he received at the hotel restaurant. In response the hotel refused to serve him food, which action was upheld by the court.

CASE EXAMPLE 10–3

Morningstar v. Lafayette Hotel Co.
211 N.Y. 465 (1914)

The plaintiff was a guest at the Lafayette Hotel in the city of Buffalo. . . . He . . . purchased some spareribs, which he presented to the hotel chef with a request that they be cooked for him and brought to his room. This was done, but with the welcome . . . [food] there came the unwelcome addition of a bill or check for $1, which he was asked to sign. He refused to do so, claiming that the charge was excessive. [Remember, the year was 1914. A dollar was worth much more then.] That evening he dined at the [hotel] cafe, and was again asked to sign for the extra service, and again declined. The following morning, Sunday, when he presented himself at the breakfast table, he was told that he would not be served. . . . He remained at the hotel till Tuesday, taking his meals elsewhere, and he then left. [He then sued the hotel claiming the hotel wrongfully refused to serve him.] An innkeeper is not required to entertain a guest who has refused to pay a lawful charge. Whether the charge in controversy was excessive, was a question for the jury. . . .

Overstaying

Occupying a room beyond the agreed time is grounds for eviction. The contract for a room is for a definite time, be it one day, a week, or longer. When the period is over, the hotel has met its obligation under the contract and, if requested by the hotel, the guest must leave. If the guest fails to depart, the contract is breached and the guest becomes a trespasser. The hotel can then do one of two things: either assume that a new contract exists on a day-to-day basis obligating the guest to pay the cost of the room; or, if the hotel has made other commitments for the room, evict the guest. A good practice that most innkeepers have adopted is to print or stamp the date of departure on the registration card and on a copy given to the guest with an oral reaffirmation of the departure date. This helps to ensure that both the hotel and guest have the same understanding of the duration of their relationship.

Three states—Hawaii, Louisiana, North Carolina—as well as Puerto Rico have passed statutes that codify the common law position and make a holdover guest a trespasser. For example, Hawaii's statute specifies: "Any guest who intentionally continues to occupy an assigned bedroom beyond the scheduled departure without the prior written approval of the keeper shall be deemed a trespasser." This modifies the common law slightly in that the statute does not require the innkeeper to request overstaying guests to leave prior to evicting them.

North Carolina's statute requires the innkeeper to issue a written statement specifying the time period during which the guest may occupy an assigned room and to have the guest initial it. At the end of the period specified, the innkeeper automatically has the right to lock the former guest out of the room. The statute denies the former guest the right to enter to reclaim any personal property and permits the innkeeper to remove it. The statute also authorizes the innkeeper to use reasonable force in preventing the lodger from reentering the room.

Puerto Rico requires the innkeeper to call the police to physically remove a holdover.

In the 47 states that do not have statutes specifically covering the rights of innkeepers with regard to overstays, innkeepers should proceed with caution when evicting the guest so as to reduce the possibility of lawsuits.

Persons of Ill Repute

In the following case, decided in 1923, the court upheld a hotel's right to evict a guest because she was a prostitute. Watch for the description of the method used by the hotel for the eviction and the court's decision on the acceptability of that method.

CASE EXAMPLE 10–4

Raider v. Dixie Inn
248 S.W. 229 (Ky., 1923)

Appellant, Thelma Raider, applied to the Dixie Inn, at Richmond, for entertainment, and paid her board and lodging for a week in advance, saying that her home was in Estill county and she had come to Richmond, at the expense of her mother, to take treatments from a physician. At the end of the week she paid in advance for another week, and so on until the end of a month, when she went downtown, and on returning was informed by the proprietor and his wife, who are appellees in this case, that she no longer had a room at that hotel, and remarked to her that no explanation was due her as to why they had requested or forced her removal. Alleging that she was mortified and humiliated by the words and conduct of the proprietors of the hotel, appellant, Raider, brought this action to recover damages in the sum of $5,000. Appellees answered, and denied . . . harsh or improper conduct on the part of the proprietors of the hotel, but admitted that they had required appellant to vacate her room and to leave the hotel, and gave as their reason for so doing that she was a woman of bad character, recently an inmate of a house of prostitution in the city of Richmond, and had been such for many years next

before she came to the Inn, and was in said city a notoriously immoral character, but that appellees did not know her when she applied for entertainment at their hotel, but immediately upon learning who she was and her manner of life had moved her belongings out of the room into the lobby of the hotel, and kindly, quietly, and respectfully asked her to leave; that they had in their hotel several ladies of good reputation who were embarrassed by the presence of appellant in the hotel and who declined to associate with her and were about to withdraw from the hotel if she continued to lodge there; that appellant had not been of good behavior since she had become a patron of the hotel.

"Plaintiff says that she is advised that these defendants (the Dixie Inn) had a legal right to remove her, and that she does not question that right, but that she was removed as a guest for hire from said Dixie Inn at a time that was improper and in a manner that was unduly disrespectful and insulting, and that she was greatly mortified and humiliated thereby, and suffered indignity because of the wrongful manner in which she was removed from said Dixie Inn as herein set out and complained of."

. . . As a general rule a guest who has been admitted to an inn may afterwards be excluded therefrom by the innkeeper if the guest refuses to pay his bill, or if he becomes obnoxious to the guests by his own fault, is a person of general bad reputation. . . .

It appears, therefore, fully settled that an innkeeper may lawfully refuse to entertain objectionable characters, if to do so is calculated to injure his business or to place himself, business, or guests in a hazardous, uncomfortable, or dangerous situation. The innkeeper need not accept any one as a guest who is calculated to and will injure his business. . . . A prize fighter who has been guilty of law breaking may be excluded. . . . Neither is an innkeeper required to entertain a card shark; . . . persons of bad reputation . . . drunken and disorderly persons; . . . one who commits a trespass by breaking in the door; . . . one who is filthy or who subjects the guests to annoyance. . . .

It therefore appears that the managers of the Dixie Inn had the right to exclude appellant from their hotel upon several grounds without becoming liable therefor, unless the means employed to remove her were unlawful. . . .

[T]he only remaining question is: Did they do so in a proper manner, or did they employ unlawful means to exclude her? The averments of the petition show she was not present at the time they took charge of her room and placed her belongings in the lobby of the hotel, where they were easily accessible to her; that when she came in they quietly told her that they had taken charge of her room, but gave no reason for doing so. We must believe from the averments of the petition that very little was said, and that the whole proceeding was very quiet and orderly. As they had a right to exclude her from the hotel, they were guilty of no wrong in telling her so, even though there [may have been] other persons present in the lobby at the time they gave her such information, which is denied.

The averments of the petition as amended "that appellees removed appellant from the hotel in an improper manner and were unduly disrespectful and insulting" are mere conclusions of the pleader, and are not supported by the statement of facts found elsewhere in the petition.

The petition . . . did not state a cause of action in favor of appellant against appellees.

Judgment [in favor of the hotel] affirmed.

What constitutes an objectionable character is a debatable question, and the hotelier relying on this ground for eviction should proceed carefully. The decision in *Raider v. Dixie* probably would not be followed today unless the prostitute was practicing the illegal trade in the hotel.

Intoxication and Disorderly Conduct

Intoxication alone is not an adequate reason in most states for eviction. However, a hotel has the right to evict a person who is intoxicated and disturbing other guests. There must be a disturbance of the peace, disorderly conduct, threat to other guests, damage to the room, or the like. In circumstances where the intoxicated person threatens the well-being of other guests, a hotel may be negligent for failing to remove the disorderly person.

Disorderly Conduct

A sober person engaged in disorderly conduct can likewise be evicted. An interesting example involving unusual disorderly conduct concerns a television station that sent a camera crew to a restaurant that had been cited for health code violations. The instructions given the camera crew were to enter unannounced "with cameras rolling," apparently in an effort to catch on camera unsanitary practices. The television crew entered as directed with bright lights glaring. Some diners hid under the table, others left without paying their bills, and those waiting to be seated left without being served. The restaurant ordered the crew to leave and sued for damages on the grounds of trespass. A verdict in the restaurant's favor for $1200 was upheld on appeal. *Le Mistral, Inc. v. Columbia Broadcasting System*, 402 N.Y.S.2d 815 (N.Y., 1978).

Contagiously Ill Guests

According to common law, hotel operators had the right to evict a guest who contracts a contagious disease that is easily spread. The innkeeper was obligated to use extreme care to avoid aggravating the guest's condition, which generally meant the innkeeper should summon the assistance of a public health official, a doctor, or an ambulance if the condition necessitated. According to the American With Disabilities Act, which became effective in 1992 and was discussed at length in Chapter 3, a debilitating contagious disease may constitute a disability which is defined as, "A physical or mental impairment that substantially limits one or more of the major life activities of such individual." The Act bars innkeepers and restaurateurs from withholding their services on the grounds of disability if a reasonable modification can be made to accommodate the disability. Arguably, if the disability is a contagious disease, the innkeeper can continue to exclude would-be guests because to provide them a room would expose many others to the illness, violating the innkeeper's duty of reasonable care for guests' well-being. This exposure would therefore be an unreasonable accommodation.

Breaking House Rules

Hotels are entitled to adopt reasonable rules to ensure order and safety on the premises, and to prevent immorality, drunkenness, and other forms of misconduct that can offend guests or bring the hotel into disrepute. These rules, often called house rules, might, for example, include prohibitions against walking in the lobby in a wet bathing suit, wearing shorts in the lobby after 6:00 P.M., or having pets in guest rooms (other than seeing eye dogs or service animals which must be allowed by statute). An innkeeper can evict a guest for failing to comply with a house rule. Such rules should be posted in conspicuous places, including guest rooms. All rules concerning the use of a pool should be displayed poolside.

Persons Not Registered

When a person is not or has never been a guest of the hotel, the innkeeper can evict that person for violating house rules or even without cause. In the next case a hotel had a rule prohibiting unregistered guests above the lobby. A nonguest ordered to leave the hotel because she was suspected of engaging in prostitution challenged the hotel's right to evict her. The court upheld the hotel's right to prohibit on the premises those people who fail to abide by its rules.

CASE EXAMPLE 10–5

Kelly v. United States
348 A.2d 884 (D.C., 1975)

. . . Between the months of January and March 1974, appellant was seen by the chief of security at the Statler Hilton Hotel on approximately five occasions. He first noticed her in the hotel bar speaking with a guest with whom she later went upstairs. On one occasion when she was in the lobby all night, a police officer assigned to the vice squad told the hotel's security officer that appellant was a prostitute and showed him a copy of her criminal record and her mug shot.

On March 18, hotel security officers again noticed appellant in the hotel. At that time she was once more observed going upstairs with a guest. After about an hour in the guest's room, she came out of the room alone. She was stopped by the hotel security officers and informed of the hotel policy of not allowing any unregistered guests above the lobby. She was also told of the conversation with the police vice squad officer and was read a "barring notice." [That is, a notice that orders someone to remain off the premises. Disregard of the barring notice constitutes the crime of unlawful entry which is the equivalent of trespass. The notice said: You are hereby notified that you are not permitted entry in the Statler Hilton Hotel, 1001 Sixteenth Street, Northwest. In the future, if you return to the Statler Hilton Hotel and gain entry, you may be subject to criminal prosecution for unauthorized entry.] Furthermore, she was told that if she returned to the hotel, she would be arrested and charged with unlawful entry.

On August 19, security officers were called to the fifth floor of the hotel. They waited outside one of the rooms until appellant emerged with two male companions. She was then placed under arrest.

Appellant . . . argued that the [unlawful entry] statute [quoted below] was not applicable to a hotel and accordingly a hotel could not issue a valid barring notice. . . .

It is a general rule that: . . .

[Where a person does] not enter the hotel as a guest nor with the intention of becoming one, [it is] his duty to leave peaceably when ordered by the [innkeeper] to do so, and in case of his refusal to leave on request, [the innkeeper] was entitled to use such force as was reasonably necessary to remove him. . . .

It necessarily follows that if a hotel has the right to exclude someone, and he or she receives appropriate notice of his exclusion, that person's subsequent presence in the hotel is without lawful authority. Thus he or she is subject to arrest for the crime of unlawful entry. The unlawful entry statute of Washington, D.C. provides:

"Any person who . . . being [in or on any public or private buildings] without lawful authority to remain therein or thereon shall refuse to quit the same on the demand of . . . the person lawfully in charge thereof, shall be deemed guilty of a misdemeanor."

In the instant case, appellant concedes that she was warned not to return to the hotel. She also admits that she was in the hotel on the evening of August 19, 1974. Consequently, under the authorities cited above, with which we agree, her entrance into the hotel was unlawful. . .

Appellant's other grounds for reversal, namely that the hotel policy was unreasonably and discriminatorily applied and that the government's evidence was insufficient, are without substance.

Ruling of the Court: . . . judgment . . . for the defendant.

As illustrated in the next case, the rights of a guest are not assignable, that is, transferable; therefore, a registered guest cannot give another person the status of guest.

CASE EXAMPLE 10–6

Hennig v. Goldberg
68 N.Y.S.2d 698 (1947)

. . . Defendants were innkeepers, and plaintiff occupied a room in their hotel. . . . [D]efendants, in [plaintiff's] absence, changed the lock of the room which she occupied, so that upon her arrival at the hotel in the early morning of February 20, 1946 and again in the early afternoon of February 25, 1946 she was unable to gain admittance. [She sued the hotel for forcible entry.]

. . . Furthermore, I find that plaintiff occupied the room—which had been assigned to one Bihovsky, who had dwelt in it for some time and had paid the February 1946 rent in advance in full—without permission from defendant or any one representing the hotel, that she had not registered as a guest, and that the permission to use the room which she had obtained from the guest Bihovsky gave her no lawful right to the room and did not even put her in possession inasmuch as Bihovsky's rights as a guest were not assignable or transferable.

. . . Obviously [the relevant statute] was never intended to make it necessary for an innkeeper to resort to court proceedings . . . to remove from his inn, or from a room in his inn, one who came in without his permission, express or implied. This is simply a case in which defendants found plaintiff in a room in which she did not belong and changed the lock so that she could not again gain access to that room. In so doing defendants were within their strict legal right, although I think it probable that they acted as they did because they wished to rent the room to someone who would pay a daily rather than a monthly rate. . . . [Defendants] acted lawfully and are not answerable in damages to plaintiff.

Judgment may be entered in favor of defendants dismissing the complaint. . . .

Persons Without Baggage

In times past, a hotel could refuse to provide a room to a would-be guest who did not have any luggage. The concern was that the would-be guest was not a traveler in need of a room but rather a person intending to use the room for prostitution or some other immoral or illegal purpose. Today such a rule would likely not be sustained by a court. The mere absence of luggage does not in itself indicate an immoral or illegal intent. Reference is nonetheless still made in some statutes to the idea that a person arriving at an inn without luggage might be refused. For example, in Alabama's statute defining criminal fraud against hotels and restaurants, included as illegal is the obtaining of accommodations by the "false or fictitious show or pretense of any baggage" (Code of Alabama, Section 34-15-19).

Business Competitors

If a business competitor comes to a hotel seeking accommodations they cannot be refused. But a business competitor who comes to a hotel to solicit customers can be enjoined, meaning a court order can bar them from continuing such solicitations. In *Champie v. Castle Hot Water Springs Co.*, 233 P. 1107 (Ariz., 1925), the hotel maintained a livery business supplying its guests with horses. The defendant, a competitor in the livery business, likewise supplied horses to the hotel's guests using the hotel's property to carry on its business arrangements with the guests. The hotel sued and the court granted the injunction, prohibiting defendant from taking any horses on defendant's property. Said the court,

> *Has an innkeeper the right to refuse a competitor access to his premises, for the purpose of competition, when the presence of the latter is requested by one of the former's guests?. . . . [I]t has never been held that they must furnish their private facilities for the use of a competitor in business. Cases involving the same general principles as the one at bar have frequently arisen, and it has been held almost invariably that the owner of the premises is within his rights in excluding a competitor therefrom.*

Suppose a hotel offers food and room services, and a guest orders food to be delivered at the hotel by a competitor. Can the hotel refuse admittance to the competitor, making the delivery impossible? The answer seems to be yes, because such services will lower the hotelkeeper's total volume of business and therefore constitute outright competition.

If the hotel chooses to grant permission to the competitor to carry on business at the inn, the hotel can charge a fee for the privilege of using the hotel's premises and for access to the guests.

Suppose the hotel does not offer food. Can the inn select one or a few exclusive food preparers and exclude others from doing business on the premises? The answer is yes. The hotel has a legitimate interest in protecting the level of service provided. As we have studied, the hotel has duty to exercise reasonable care for the well-being of its guests. By selecting certain companies that will be allowed to offer food to the guests, the hotel is furthering this obligation. It also has a rightful interest in maintaining its reputation which could be adversely affected by allowing unknown or substandard food providers on the premises.

Without the hotel's legitimate interest in its guests' well-being and its own reputation, the hotel would not be able to restrict guests' choice of purveyors. This point is illustrated in *Eagle Springs Water Co. v. Webb & Knapp, Inc.*, 236 N.Y.S.2d 266 (1962). A landlord of a commercial building restricted to one the providers of bottled water allowed on the premises. That one provider gave the landlord a share of fees paid by the tenants. The landlord's main purpose in excluding other bottled water companies was its own financial interest. The court held this was an insufficient reason to allow the landlord to restrict tenants' choice and exclude competitors.

Illegal Eviction or Detention

Evicting someone from a hotel or restaurant for cause is proper. It should be carried out considerately; no harsh words or force should be used unless absolutely necessary. A wrongful eviction can result in liability not only for physical injuries but also for mental and emotional distress. *Lopez v. City of New York*, 357 N.Y.S.2d 659 (1974).

Excessive Force.   Unnecessary agitation or force in the course of an eviction can lead to liability for the torts of assault or battery.

Assault, in tort law, means intentionally putting someone in fear of harmful physical contact such as making a fist in a way suggestive of an imminent punch. The tort of **battery** means causing harmful physical contact to a person. Intentionally punching someone in the face is an example of the tort of battery. Battery occurs where a hotel or restaurant owner or employee grabs a patron and pushes him/her out of the premises without good cause. *Jones v. City of Boston*, 738 F.Supp. 604 (Mass., 1990).

In the following case the hotel owner was liable to a patron for battery in the course of a wrongful eviction.

CASE EXAMPLE 10–7

Hopp v. Thompson
38 N.W.2d 133 (S.D., 1949)

This is an action to recover damages for assault and battery. Defendant [Appellant] owns and manages the Thompson Hotel in Sisseton. On the evening of June 21, 1946, plaintiff [Respondent] entered the hotel and a fracas occurred in which both parties were injured. Plaintiff brought the action to recover his damages and defendant filed an answer denying liability. Defendant also pleaded a counterclaim for the damages which he claims were sustained by him. The jury returned a verdict for plaintiff in the sum of $10,249 upon which judgment was entered and defendant appealed.

The first question presented is the sufficiency of the evidence to justify the verdict of the jury. Respondent testified that he entered the hotel in response to the invitation of a guest; that appellant, without just cause, ordered him to leave the hotel; that he started to leave, as ordered, when appellant assaulted and beat him with a piece of iron pipe thereby causing unconsciousness, severe cuts and bruises on his scalp and body, and injuries to his brain. His claim to damages consists of hospital and physicians' expense, loss of time, pain and suffering, both present and future, besides exemplary and punitive damages.

Appellant denied all of these contentions of respondent. He testified that respondent was a stranger to him and was not a guest at the hotel. That when respondent entered the hotel it was about 11 o'clock in the evening which was closing time; that respondent started to go upstairs and as he did so appellant repeatedly asked him who he was and what he wanted to which respondent made no reply; that appellant then told respondent to come down and go home; that respondent still refused to go and thereupon appellant tapped him lightly on the shoulder and told him to get out; that respondent did not leave as ordered and that appellant told him that appellant would call an officer; that when appellant picked up the telephone receiver respondent assaulted him and took the receiver from him. At this time appellant says he picked up a short piece of pipe, tapped respondent on the shoulder with it and again ordered him to leave and that respondent still refused to go; that a scuffle ensued in which appellant hit respondent on the shoulder and respondent grabbed appellant by the neck with both hands; that during this time appellant struck respondent on the back of the head with the pipe; that the parties were on the floor part of the time; that appellant called for help, which came, and then the struggle ended. Appellant contends that he struck respondent only to subdue him and that he used no more force than he thought was necessary for that purpose.

It is the general rule that an innkeeper gives a general license to all persons to enter his house. Consequently, it is not a trespass to enter an inn without a previous actual invitation, but, where persons enter a hotel or inn, not as guests, but intent on pleasure or profit to be derived from intercourse with its inmates, they are there, not of right, but under an implied license that the landlord may revoke at any time. . . . The respondent did not enter the hotel as a guest nor with the intention of becoming one and it was his duty to leave peaceably when ordered by the landlord to do so, and in case of his refusal to leave on request

appellant was entitled to use such force as was reasonably necessary to remove him. . . .

Here respondent denies that he refused to leave when ordered to do so. He also denies that he knowingly assaulted or beat appellant. He testified that he walked toward the desk, then turned to go out, and that the next thing he remembered he was standing outside on the street covered with blood. This record presents a substantial conflict in the evidence. The jurors are the exclusive judges of the weight of the evidence and the credibility of the witnesses and therefore this court could not substitute its judgment for the verdict. . . .

The judgment [in favor of Respondent/Plaintiff] is affirmed.

CASE QUESTIONS

1. The jury believed the guest's version of the facts. Based on that version, what did the hotel manager do wrong? How should he have handled the situation?

2. Why did the Appellate Court refuse to substitute its own opinion for that of the jurors?

The following case provides another example of the tort of battery. In this case it was committed by an overzealous bouncer at a club whose job required that he restrict the number of people allowed to enter.

CASE EXAMPLE 10–8

Durand v. Moore
879 S.W.2d 196 (Tex., 1994)

. . . Lewis was a doorman at Durand's nightclub when he assaulted a customer waiting to enter the club. Durand complains that Lewis was not acting in the course and scope of his employment when the assault occurred. . . .

On April 19, 1991, Craig Lewis, an employee of Durand, was assigned to the front door of the club. His job included checking IDs, enforcing the dress code, and coordinating the admission of customers into the club.

That night or early morning April 20, Michael Moore and Lawrence Ward went to the club. The club was filled to capacity, and both men waited in line for customers to leave. However, doorman Lewis did not admit customers into the club in waiting-line order. Instead, he selected several persons from the line behind Moore and Ward. Ward, and then Moore, left the line and complained to Lewis. Ward turned away and walked toward his car, but Moore remained and continued the discussion with Lewis. There was conflicting testimony whether Moore and Ward were loud and abusive and whether Durand personally quieted them down just before the assault.

Without provocation, Lewis grabbed a tall cocktail glass filled with a drink and struck Moore on the side of the head shattering the glass. While Moore struggled to restrain Lewis and ward off further attack, Lewis struck Moore several more times with a flashlight. Ward returned and attempted to break up the struggle, but Lewis struck him in the face with the flashlight, breaking Ward's nose. Ward retreated as Durand and others pulled Lewis and Moore apart. Ward called the police. An ambulance arrived, and Moore and Ward received first aid. Ward was later treated at a hospital. Moore declined treatment. Moore sued Durand and Lewis . Lewis defaulted. After a bench trial, the court found Durand liable under respondeat superior. Durand appeals.

In general, to impose liability upon an employer for the tort of his employee under the doctrine of respondeat superior, the act of the employee must fall within the scope of the general authority of the employee in furtherance of the employer's business and for the accomplishment of the objective for which the employee is hired. . . .

When an employee commits an assault, it is for the trier of fact to determine whether the employee ceased to act as an employee and acted instead upon his own responsibility. . . .

It is not ordinarily within the scope of a servant's authority to commit an assault on a third person. . . .

The nature of the employment may be such as necessarily to involve at times the use of force as where the employee's duty is to guard the employer's property and to protect it from trespassers so that the act of using force may be in furtherance of the employer's business, making him liable even when greater force is used than is necessary.

The master who puts the servant in a place of trust or responsibility, or commits to him the management of his business or the care of his property, is justly held responsible when the servant through lack of judgment or discretion, or from infirmity of temper, or under the influence of passion aroused by the circumstances and the occasion, goes beyond the strict line of his duty or authority and inflicts an unjustifiable injury on a third person. . . .

[T]here was evidence that Lewis had the responsibility to control the admittance of customers into the club. There was evidence that Lewis admitted, ahead of Moore and Ward, two spendthrift customers who had "paid the light bill last month." Lewis' assault of Moore immediately followed their discussion of why Lewis was giving preferential treatment to certain customers. We find that this evidence was probative that Lewis' assault of Moore was overzealous enforcement of the criteria and procedures used to select waiting customers for admittance into the club. . . .

[The evidence was sufficient to support the verdict against Durand. Judgment affirmed.]

In another case involving assault by a bouncer at a club, the plaintiff patron had too much to drink. The bouncer escorted the plaintiff to the front door, took from him the drink he had just purchased, and threw it away. The plaintiff attempted to push the bouncer away but was seized by two other employees who pushed plaintiff out the front door. While plaintiff's arms were pinned by the two men, a third employee, the head doorman, repeatedly hit plaintiff in the face with his fists. A jury found the employees were acting within the course of their employment and decided the case in plaintiff's favor. On appeal the decision was affirmed. *Country Road, Inc. v. Witt*, 737 S.W.2d 362 (Tex., 1987).

In a case of battery also involving discrimination, the court interpreted the tort of battery broadly to ensure the restaurant was held responsible even though the patron was not injured. The manager of a restaurant snatched a black patron's dinner plate just as the latter was being served because the manager refused to serve African-Americans. The patron chose to sue the restaurant for battery rather than discrimination. The jury found that the manager "forcibly dispossessed plaintiff of his diner plate" and "shouted in a loud and offensive manner" that plaintiff could not be served there. The court, finding that a battery had occurred, stated, "Under the facts of this case, we have no difficulty in holding that the intentional grabbing of plaintiff's plate constituted a battery. The intentional snatching of an object from one's hand is as clearly an offensive invasion of his person as would be an actual contact with the body." *Fisher v. Carrousel Motor Hotel, Inc.*, 424 S.W.2d 627 (Tex., 1968).

In this case Fisher could have also sued for discrimination on the basis of race in violation of the Civil Rights Act of 1964 and, depending on the law of Texas, for discrimination in violation of a state civil rights law. Why did he sue for the tort of battery rather than violation of civil rights laws? One reason may be that the remedy for a violation of the federal civil rights law is not monetary; it is instead an injunction that prevents the wrongdoer from continuing the discrimination. The remedy for a battery case is compensation for the resulting injuries.

Verbal Abuse.   Evictions can be carried out verbally without the use of force. Such was the case in *Milner Hotels, Inc., v. Brent*, 43 So.2d 654 (Miss., 1949), in which an eviction for cause was handled very badly. The plaintiff-guest paid the room rent for her husband, daughter, and herself weekly. The rent was paid up for one more day when the plaintiff tried to pay for an additional week. Her money was refused and she was told to vacate her room by the manager, who said in an angry voice, loud enough for others in the lobby to hear, "We do not want you here." The plaintiff was also locked out of her room. She was embarrassed and distressed over the alleged damage to her reputation.

The plaintiff had recently been a witness in a case against the corporation that owned the hotel. The manager of the hotel later admitted to plaintiff that he had been ordered to evict her because of her involvement in that case.

The plaintiff sought punitive damages which, as the court said, are only awarded if the defendant committed a wrongful act, intentionally, willfully, and with gross disregard of plaintiff's rights. The court determined that the manager spoke the words used here with intentional malice and in gross disregard of the plaintiff's rights, and awarded plaintiff punitive damages.

These cases involving both excessive force and verbal abuse underscore the importance of affecting an eviction properly.

How to Evict

To review, a hotel or restaurant can evict a guest for nonpayment of a bill, overstaying, intoxication coupled with disorderly conduct, serious or contagious illness, or breaking house rules. Also, business competitors seeking to solicit customers can be excluded. In addition, a hotel can evict nonguests and a restaurant can evict those who are on the premises who have not and do not intend to order food or drink.

Ideally, physical force and harsh words can be avoided when an eviction is made. Good practice requires the innkeeper or restaurateur in the first instance

Applicable Property

To what property does the lien apply? Courts have held that most property a guest brings to the hotel is covered by the lien. Innkeeper's liens have been held valid on such diverse items as a piano, valuables in a safe-deposit box, stolen property, and automobiles. *Chesham Auto Supply v. Beresford Hotel*, 29 Times L.R. 584 (1913). Covered property is not limited to articles necessary for travel; merchandise samples of traveling salespeople may be subject to the lien. It does not, however, extend to a person's necessary wearing apparel and certain personal jewelry such as wedding rings. Those items are exempt and the guest is entitled to them.

The innkeeper's lien extends to personal property brought to the hotel by the guest even if the guest does not own it provided the innkeeper does not know it is owned by someone else. Innkeepers cannot place a lien on property that they know belongs to a third party or is stolen. The goods of one spouse are not subject to the innkeeper's lien when the indebtedness is that of the other spouse. *Geobel v. United Railways. Co. of St. Louis*, 181 S.W. 1051 (Mo., 1915).

Applicable Charges

When innkeepers have a lien on the personal property of their guest, the innkeeper's right to possession is greater than the guest's. If the guest attempts to take the property away, he can be charged with theft.

Items on a guest's bill to which the lien applies include the guestroom charge, service charges for delivery of a guest's baggage to and from the hotel, valet service, C.O.D. charges, room service and the like. However, the innkeeper cannot enforce the lien when the services were rendered by an independent contractor such as a doctor or the owner of one of the shops in the building. Nor can the independent contractor enforce the lien; it is particular to the innkeeper.

Termination of the Lien by Payment or Sale

An innkeeper's lien terminates when the bill is paid. The hotelkeeper must then return any property seized pursuant to the lien. If payment is not made, the innkeeper can sell the property and use the proceeds to satisfy the bill, as well as expenses associated with the sale including advertising and storage of the goods pending sale. Many states mandate the procedure to be followed when goods subject to the lien are sold. The objective of these statutes is to ensure, for the benefit of the guest, that the sale generates the greatest possible proceeds. A typical statute requires the innkeeper to publish notice of the sale in a local newspaper at least two weeks prior to the sale date, including a description of the goods to be sold. The innkeeper is further required to send notice of the sale to the nonpaying guest. This allows the guest one last opportunity to pay the bill before the sale occurs and retrieve the possessions.

Many statutes direct how the proceeds must be applied. A typical statute provides that the innkeeper can retain the amount of the unpaid bill and expenses incurred in arranging and advertising the sale. Any surplus must be paid to the guest. If the innkeeper cannot locate the guest, the surplus money can be paid to a designated public official such as the chief fiscal officer of the city in which the sale oc-curred. That officer is required to hold the money until the guest retrieves it. The hotel is thus saved from having to keep track of the surplus money indefinitely.

The Innkeeper's Lien and Due Process

Over time, all of the states enacted legislation adopting the lien. Beginning in 1970 a series of cases called into question the validity of the innkeeper lien. These cases questioned whether the lien satisfies the due process clause of the federal Constitution, a clause that precludes the taking of property without the opportunity for a court hearing. The concern was that the lien allows innkeepers to take guests' property summarily, that is, without a hearing in court at which the guest could contest the bill or the allegation of nonpayment. The United States Supreme Court seemed to clarify the issue by holding that the due process clause of the Constitution applies only when *government* seeks to take property and is not applicable when a lien exists and neither party to it is a governmental entity. Thereafter some states, through their state constitutions, expanded the right of due process to cover not just government transactions but private trans-actions as well. In those states, an innkeeper cannot enforce the lien (sell the goods) without giving the allegedly nonpaying guest an opportunity for a hear-ing in court. In all other states the innkeeper's lien is enforceable without the ne-cessity of going to court.

A brief review of the cases that raised the due process issue follows. The issue arose in the state of California in the case of *Klim v. Jones*, 315 F.Supp 109 (Cal., 1970). The plaintiff worked irregularly as a painter and had limited financial means. He was a boarder at the Junior Tar Hotel and paid $10 per week for his room. One day he was awakened by the manager and told his rent was due. Plaintiff denied owing any rent. When plaintiff left the room, the manager pad-locked it and refused to release plaintiff's property which included clothing, un-derwear, painting tools, an electric frying pan, a coffee pot, a lamp, and personal papers including plaintiff's driver's license, birth certificate, Navy transcript and bank book. Plaintiff needed his belongings for work and identification. He sued the hotel seeking an injunction ordering the hotel to release his belongings. The court ruled that the California innkeeper's lien statute was "constitutionally infirm for its failure to provide for any sort of hearing prior to the imposition of the innkeeper's lien, thus depriving the boarder of property without due process of law." That court did not hold that due process applied only to government tak-ings. Instead, the court held that due process applies between an innkeeper and a guest, and mandates a court proceeding before the innkeeper can enforce a lien on the guest's property. Similar holdings followed in other cases in various states.

The next significant case in the development of lien law and due process was *Flagg Brothers v. Brooks*, 436 U.S. 149 (1978), decided by the United States Supreme Court. Brooks and her family had been evicted from their apartment and their belongings had been stored at the Flagg Brothers Storage Co. ware-house. Brooks failed to pay her storage bill and Flagg threatened to sell her stored belongings. She brought an action against Flagg, seeking a declaration that such a sale would violate her due process and equal protection rights. The Supreme Court held that the due process provision of the U.S. Constitution protected only against infringement by governments; a private matter as in this case between a creditor and a debtor in no way involved the state and so did not create a constitutional issue. The court thus denied Brooks' claim that the sale by the storage company violated a constitutional right.

Distinctions Between Due Process Requirements of the Federal Constitution and State Constitutions

A third case involving liens and due process was *Sharrock v. Dell Buick-Cadillac*, 408 N.Y.S.2d 39 (1978). The plaintiff and defendant disagreed over a bill concerning work done on a car, and plaintiff refused to pay. The defendant imposed on the car a garage lien, which is similar to an innkeeper's lien, and turned the car over to an auctioneer for sale. The plaintiff challenged the sale in court.

Based on stare decisis, the New York court was obligated to accept the ruling of the Supreme Court and so held there was no basis for finding the New York lien statute violative of the U.S. Constitution. However, the court, uncomfortable with the lack of a court hearing before a person's property is seized and sold, went on to say that the due process clause of the *state* constitution does not require government action. The court thus held that the sale of the car by the repair shop without a court proceeding violated the due process mandates of the state constitution. *Sharrock* drew a distinction between the right to *possess* property subject to a lien and the right to sell that property. The repair shop could maintain possession of the car without going to court. However, the car could not be sold until the due process requirements of the state constitution are satisfied.

The New York State legislature has since repealed the hotel lien law.

To review the present status of innkeepers liens, the United States Supreme Court has clearly stated that possessory liens such as the innkeeper's lien do not violate the due process protections of the U.S. Constitution unless the government is a party to the lien. The states are free to extend due process protection beyond government infringement, as New York did. Therefore, innkeeper liens are as valid today as they were under common law, except where due process rights have been enlarged by state constitution or state statute. In those states a court order is required before a guest's property can be sold.

Defrauding the Hotelkeeper or Restaurateur

All states and the District of Columbia have passed criminal statutes that seek to protect the innkeeper and restaurateur from guests who attempt to leave without paying. The name given to the crime varies from state to state and includes theft of services, larceny, and fraud. These statutes criminalize nonpayment where the perpetrator sought services with the intention of avoiding payment. Many of the statutes provide different penalties depending upon the amount and value of the goods or services received by the absconder. For example, in Massachusetts, for a defendant who receives food, entertainment or accommodations in excess of $100, the maximum jail sentence is two years. In New York, theft of services from a hotel or restaurant is punishable by a fine up to $1,000 and imprisonment up to one year without regard to the value of the services stolen. As evidenced by the penalties, states regard this type of crime quite seriously.

Intent to Defraud

To establish a defendant's guilt, the prosecutor must prove two elements at trial: (1) defendant obtained food or lodging without paying for it; and (2) defendant intended to avoid payment. Proving a defendant's intentions is often difficult. To aid the prosecutor, many state crime statutes create a presumption of an intent not to pay. In these states, once the prosecutor proves that the defendant received food or accommodations without paying, a presumption arises that defendant intended to avoid payment. The defendant can present evidence to rebut the presumption. If the defendant does not, the evidence of nonpayment, together with the presumption, is sufficient for conviction. In the following case the presumption did not apply.

CASE EXAMPLE 10–9

State of Utah v. Leonard
707 P.2d 650 (Utah, 1985)

The defendant, Steven Charles Leonard, appeals from his jury conviction of theft of services. . . . He argues that the evidence was insufficient to support the verdict; . . .

On February 10, 1981, the defendant checked into the Tri-Arc Travel Lodge in Salt Lake City. . . . He paid for the first night's lodging in cash. On February 11, 1981, he again paid his full hotel bill in cash. After the payment on the 11th, no more payments were made. By February 14th, the accumulated bill for the defendant's room was over $100. When the defendant did not respond to the hotel's requests for him to contact the desk to pay the accumulated bill, his hotel room was locked. On February 15th, the defendant and another male, James Borland, reported to the front desk supervisor that they were locked out of their room. Defendant promised to pay the outstanding

$352.40 owed on the hotel and restaurant bills that were in his name the following day when he could go to his credit union for the necessary money. The defendant was let back into his room.

The following day the resident hotel manager called the defendant's room. The person who answered the phone responded to the defendant's name and promised to pay the bill. Instead the defendant and Borland vacated the room. The defendant was arrested shortly thereafter and charged with theft of services. . . .

The defendant was convicted of obtaining services by deception. . . . [The relevant statute] provides: A person commits theft if he obtains services which he knows are available only for compensation by deception, threat, force, or by any means designed to avoid the due payment therefore."

Fraudulent intent is the gravamen of the offense of theft of services. Without [the requirement of] proof of a criminal state of mind, the law would imprison people for mere failure to pay a debt, a practice not sanctioned in this or any other state of this nation. . . . The rule is that a person who in good faith accepts the benefit of services for which he plans to pay later cannot be convicted of theft even though he subsequently does not recompense the provider of services. The remedy in such case is a civil suit for breach of contract. Obviously, however, a defendant's denial of a fraudulent intent at the time of receiving the services is not binding. As is often the case, circumstantial evidence may speak louder than words.

The defendant made an implied promise to pay for the lodging and services provided the nights of February 12th, 13th, and 14th. However, the implied promise to pay and the subsequent failure to pay the bill, standing alone, are legally insufficient to show the elements of deception . . . the prosecution must prove fraudulent intent by

more than just a mere failure to pay. Some additional evidence is required to sustain a finding of fraudulent intent. In short, a conviction cannot be sustained merely on proof that a person acquired lodging and failed to pay for it.

Numerous types of circumstantial evidence may show fraudulent intent. For example, circumstantial evidence that a defendant had no money and no prospect of acquiring sufficient money when it was time to pay might be sufficient, as would express false promises, or deception as to the identity of the renter. However, evidence that establishes no more than a breach of an express or implied contract is not sufficient to prove the crime of theft of services, and a jury should be so instructed.

[Reversed and remanded.]

CASE QUESTIONS

1. Why is failure to pay an outstanding bill not sufficient, standing alone, to establish fraudulent or criminal intent?

2. What additional evidence is necessary to establish a fraudulent or criminal intent?

Failure to pay resulting from some cause other than intentionally avoiding payment is not criminal. For example, if a restaurant patron placed her purse on the floor while dining and it was stolen while she ate, she may have no other money with her and be unable to pay her bill. She will not be guilty of a crime because her inability to pay was not by design.

In *Manley v. State*, 633 S.W.2d 881 (Tex., 1982), proof of intent not to pay was missing. The appellant and his three children were diners in the Grubsteak Restaurant. The children's spaghetti was cold and sticking together. The appellant and the other child complained about their food as well. The waitress had the dinners recooked but they still were not satisfactory. When the bill was brought to the table appellant requested an adjustment. The waitress left to talk to the cook and did not immediately return. Appellant, apparently exasperated, left his card at the cash register with the following note on the back. "Call me when you decide. Res: 937-5300." The restaurateur immediately had the patron arrested for theft of services. At trial the cook admitted that whoever prepared the spaghetti did not wash and separate it to keep it from sticking. The customer was convicted but the conviction was reversed on appeal. The appellate court stated,

> *While the customer might be colored irritable and impatient and inconsiderate for not waiting to settle the dispute, we cannot conclude he "absconded" [an element of the crime; meaning he intentionally left without paying]. He left his name, business address and telephone number of his business and residence. . . . [W]e cannot conclude that the evidence is sufficient to establish the requisite intent to commit the offense.*

In *State v. Croy*, 145 N.W.2d 118 (Wis., 1966), the court reached a different result for good cause. The defendant had secretly left the hotel without informing the management of his departure. He left his luggage in the room in an apparent attempt to mislead the hotel about his status. When he left he owed the bills that had accumulated for room, board, long-distance telephone calls, and related items. The statute in Wisconsin provides that a crime is committed if a person who "had obtained food, lodgings or accommodations at any hotel, motel, . . . intentionally absconds without paying for it." The defendant was found guilty at trial. The appellate court found sufficient evidence to support defendant's conviction. The defendant's attempts to mislead the innkeeper plus the extent of the bills strongly suggested the defendant intended to avoid payment.

Fraudulent Payment

Additional statutes also protect the innkeeper and restaurateur from conniving patrons. Most states criminalize the act of knowingly issuing a bad check. A bad check is a check for which the maker has insufficient funds in the bank, or a check written on an account that has been closed. If a customer pays for dinner or a room with a bad check and knows the check is bad, the restaurant or hotel can pursue the patron on criminal charges. Although the statutes vary from state to state, the crime is typically a misdemeanor subjecting the customer to fines of up to $1,000 and jail up to one year.

In addition, patrons who pay their bills with a credit card they know is stolen and who sign the card owner's name on the receipt may be committing the crimes of possession of stolen property and forgery. The crime of criminal possession of stolen property is committed when a person knowingly possesses stolen property with intent to benefit herself or someone else other than the owner. Forgery is the unauthorized alteration, completion, or making of a written instrument such as a credit card receipt or a check with intent to defraud or deceive. Most states designate forgery and criminal possession of stolen property as either high-level misdemeanors or felonies.

Hotels and restaurants are also often the victims of thefts of such items as ashtrays, silverware, glasses, towels, and the like. To avoid this type of theft some hotels nail or otherwise affix the radios, televisions, and remote control devices to the desks and dressers in guest rooms. If a guest does steal property, she is liable for the crime of larceny which is either a misdemeanor or felony depending on the state involved and the value of the goods stolen.

False Arrest

When a hotel or restaurant believes it is the victim of one of these crimes it should proceed cautiously. Overreaction can result in liability to the guest for **false arrest**, that is, the tort of intentional and unprivileged confining of another person. If time permits, the restaurant or hotel manager, rather than handling the matter in-house, should call the police. When officers arrive, the manager will explain the basis for believing a crime has occurred. The police will then take over the investigation. If, however, the suspect is likely to escape if no action is taken until the police arrive, the hotel or restaurant may want to act on its own. Again, caution is advised. In many states hotels and restaurants will be liable for detaining a person unless in fact that person has committed a crime. Therefore, hotel or restaurant management should not restrain a person unless the manager is quite sure the person in fact engaged in criminal activity.

Summary

The law gives the innkeeper the exclusive right to determine what room will be assigned to what guest, and, if necessary, to switch the room during the guest's stay at the hotel.

To protect the reputation of a hotel or restaurant, and to protect other patrons from unnecessary disturbances and injuries, a restaurant can refuse to serve anyone for any reason except race, color, natural origin, religion, sex, marital status, and disability. A hotel can evict guests who fail to pay their bill, are unruly, ill with contagious diseases, break house rules, or stay beyond their scheduled departure date. When evicting a guest, the hotel should attempt to avoid the use of force, but if force does become necessary, no more force should be used than necessary to effect the eviction.

If a hotel guest fails to pay the bill, the hotel may be able to enforce an innkeeper's lien against the guest's property. If a restaurant patron or hotel guest attempts to leave without paying, the business can press criminal charges for theft of services or larceny. If the guest pays with a stolen credit card or bad check, the guest can be prosecuted for possession of stolen property, forgery, or issuing a bad check.

Preventive Law Tips for Managers

- *Do not refuse accommodations to a guest unless one of the permissible reasons for refusing accommodations exists.* The common law rule provides that a hotel may not refuse accommodations to a guest. With few exceptions, anyone seeking a room is entitled to one. A hotel can legally refuse to provide a room only if the prospective guest is unable to pay, intoxicated, disorderly, suffering from a contagious disease, unclean, a known criminal or otherwise notorious, accompanied by a pet (other than a service animal), or in possession of a firearm or explosives. The hotel can also deny accommodations if it is full. Absent one of these circumstances, the hotel must provide rooms for all who seek them.

- *Do not change a guest's room unless absolutely necessary, and then only after informing the guest and requesting cooperation.* The law allows an innkeeper to change a guest's room. Guests are foreseeably troubled and inconvenienced by such moves and so room changes should be avoided whenever possible. If a room change does become necessary, the best practice is to inform the guest and request cooperation. In addition to winning goodwill, such an approach can cushion anger generated by a surprise relocation that could result in a lawsuit for trespass or infliction of emotional stress, albeit unfounded.

- *Do not enter a room assigned to a guest except for maintenance, imminent danger, nonpayment, or upon request.* When guests are assigned a room they are the sole occupants for the duration of their stay; the innkeeper is not free to come and go in the room. The permissible reasons for hotel staff to enter are limited to cleaning, repairs, emergencies, or when requested by the guest, as when room service is called.

- *Do not evict a guest unless the ground is one recognized by law: inability to pay, overstaying, bad reputation, intoxicated and disorderly, contagious disease, or breaking house rules.* Generally, once a guest is granted a room, she is entitled to occupy it during the scheduled stay, and the hotel cannot expel her. A few exceptions exist, enumerated above. In those circumstances a hotel can evict a guest. Eviction for any other reason can lead to liability.

- *When evicting a patron, do not use any more force than is necessary.* When evicting a patron the innkeeper or restaurateur should attempt to avoid the use of force. If appropriate, the patron should be invited to leave peaceably. If the patron refuses and repeated urging does not change her mind, and if circumstances permit, the innkeeper or restaurateur should summon the police. If circumstances do not permit, the patron can be physically removed from the premises but the hotel can use only that amount of force as is reasonably necessary. Use of a greater amount of force can result in liability on the hotel for battery.

- *When making an eviction, do not make derogatory remarks to the guest.* Insulting commentary during an eviction is inappropriate and serves only to worsen an already difficult situation. If the comments are false and overheard by passersby, the hotel may be liable for slander. If a guest wants to know why she is being evicted, she should be told the reasons without additional comment. Whenever possible, the encounter at which the innkeeper or restaurateur informs the guest of the eviction should occur in an office or private room away from the hearing of others. The innkeeper will be well-advised to have an additional employee present who can testify later if necessary concerning the propriety of the eviction process.

- *Hotels cannot evict long-term boarders who qualify as tenants without a court order.* To evict a tenant the hotel/landlord must pursue a lawsuit for eviction. The law provides a summary proceeding for this purpose. Eviction without a court order violates a tenant's rights and may lead to liability.

- *Restaurants should not refuse to serve a diner on the basis of race, national origin, color, religion, marital status, sex, or disability.* A restaurant, unlike a hotel, is not legally obligated to serve all who seek service. With the exceptions enumerated, the restaurant can refuse to serve anyone it chooses. Liability under civil rights laws will result if the restaurant discriminates on the prohibited grounds.

- *A hotel should not sell property subject to an innkeeper's lien without first determining whether state law requires a hearing for due process purposes.* While the federal constitutional right of due process does not require a hearing before an innkeeper sells property subject to an innkeeper's lien, some states have interpreted due process clauses in their constitutions as requiring such a hearing. Determine the applicable state law before selling guests' property and comply with it.

- *Train employees to detect stolen credit cards, forgeries, bad checks.* Unfortunately, some hotel and restaurant patrons attempt to avoid payment by use of stolen credit cards, forgeries, bad checks, or simply by failing to pay the bill. To help reduce the number of such incidents, employees should be trained to recognize these occurrences. Police are usually willing to address an employee training session on these issues.

- *Before pressing criminal charges, be sure the evidence supports a finding of a wrongful act and a criminal mental state.* To prove someone guilty of crimes involving fraud against a hotelier or restaurateur, the prosecutor must prove beyond a reasonable doubt that the defendant committed a wrongful act and had the required criminal mental state (intentionally or knowingly, depending on the crime). If the evidence suggests an innocent explanation for nonpayment, such as the patron's wallet was stolen while at the restaurant, criminal charges should be avoided. Wrongfully accusing someone of a crime can result in liability.

Review Questions

1. Under what circumstances can a hotel refuse to provide accommodations to someone seeking a room?
2. What precautions should a hotel take before moving a guest to another room?
3. Under what circumstances can an innkeeper enter a room assigned to a guest?

4. Can a hotel refuse to allow competing businesses to solicit its guests on its premises? Why or why not?

5. Name five legal grounds for eviction of a guest from a hotel.

6. How much force can a hotel use when evicting a guest?

7. What are the consequences to a hotel of using excessive force when evicting a guest?

8. Under what circumstances can a restaurant refuse to provide dinner to a would-be guest?

9. What is the difference between the torts of assault and battery?

10. What benefit does an innkeeper's lien provide to an innkeeper?

11. Under what circumstances does the federal Constitution require a court proceeding before a lien can be enforced?

12. If a district attorney is prosecuting a defendant for theft of hotel services, what are the elements of a crime that the prosecutor must prove?

13. What acts constitute the crime of issuing a bad check?

Discussion Questions

1. Jan and Dave have dinner reservations at the Del Rio Restaurant for 7:30 P.M. They arrive at the restaurant at 7:45 P.M. Must the Del Rio honor their reservation?

2. Terry and Cindy, both waitresses at Hillary's Restaurant, were having a dispute. Terry made a gesture suggesting she was about to throw a plate at Cindy. Cindy was frightened and ran from the room. Has Terry committed any tort? If so, which one? What are the elements of that tort?

3. What is required of an innkeeper who is enforcing an innkeeper's lien?

4. What is the due process issue associated with an innkeeper's lien?

5. What are the differences between a hotel's right to refuse to provide a room to a would-be guest and a restaurant's right to exclude?

6. What would the necessary components be of a house rule prohibiting pets on the premises? Where should the rule be posted?

Application Questions

1. George was drinking at a hotel bar. He became intoxicated and left the bar around 10:00 P.M. While walking through the hotel lobby he stopped a woman seated on a couch and tried to engage her in conversation. She requested that he leave but he failed to go. This encounter was observed by a security guard. What action should the guard take? Discuss various possibilities.

2. Steve operates a restaurant. His girlfriend recently broke up with him for another man. The "other man" sought dinner at the restaurant. Steve refused to seat him. Is Steve legally entitled to refuse service to the man? Why or why not?

3. Tyrone and Jeff walked into a corner grocery store at 1:55 A.M. to buy beer. At 2:02 they took their selections to the cash register. The clerk refused to sell the beer because the law in the town prohibited alcoholic sales after 2:00 A.M. Tyrone, refusing to take no as an answer, left money on the counter and told the clerk, "Here's ten dollars for the beer and an extra $2 for your trouble. If there's any problem we're staying at the Polex Motel down the street, room 312." Based on their prior purchases of beer, Tyrone and Jeff believed ten dollars was generous to cover the cost. Unknown to Tyrone and Jeff, the actual cost of the beer was $15.00. Have they committed the crime of larceny? Why or why not?

4. Several diners at the Olympia Restaurant have complained of stolen coats in the last few days. A regular customer known to the manager entered the store with a new coat. The manager deduced that the customer was the thief and detained him pending an investigation. Was the manager's action in detaining the customer legal? Why or why not?

5. Barry is a guest at the Midway Inn. He paid his bill with a stolen credit card and signed his name on the receipt. Identify all the crimes that Barry has committed in this transaction.

CHAPTER 11

Guests' Rights

CHAPTER OUTLINE

Introduction

Basic Rights of Guests

Protection Against Illegal Searches

Proper Handling of Mail

Rights Concerning Rates and Fees

INTRODUCTION

The law endows guests with a variety of rights. Disregarding any of these rights by the innkeeper can lead to liability to the hotelier.

Among the rights guests have are the following: the right to occupy hotel rooms without disruption; the right to be treated respectfully and not be insulted or humiliated by hotel staff; the right to be free from false arrest or detention without cause; certain rights of privacy; the right to be informed of fees and charges before they are imposed; and the right to have hotel employees handle guests' mail appropriately. The extent of these rights will be discussed in this chapter.

Basic Rights of Guests

Guests have certain basic rights recognized by law which include the following: the right to occupy their room undisturbed, the right to privacy in their room, the right not to be insulted, and the right not be falsely arrested based on inaccurate information provided by the innkeeper.

Right to Occupy Assigned Room

A guest assigned a room in a hotel has the right to occupy the room without disruption from the innkeeper. An exception to this rule is where the innkeeper has legal grounds to remove the guest, as discussed in the previous chapter. An example would be nonpayment of the bill. An innkeeper who wrongfully excludes a guest from the room will be liable to the guest for damages.

The hotel in the following case violated a guest's right in this regard.

CASE EXAMPLE 11–1

Perrine v. Paulos
224 P.2d 41 (Cal., 1950)

Two young women were evicted by defendants from a hotel in Los Angeles. Returning from work one evening, they found padlocks on their rooms. They could not get to any of their personal belongings or clothing. They could not find other accommodations and had to sleep in their automobiles for three nights. Then, on demand of their counsel, they were permitted to again occupy their rooms.

The case was tried by the court, with judgment for plaintiffs for $500 each for general damages; and $500 more each, exemplary [punitive] damages. . . .

The evidence establishes without contradiction that defendants owned the hotel and that plaintiffs were guests.

At common law, innkeepers were under a duty to furnish accommodations to all persons in the absence of some reasonable grounds. . . .

An innkeeper who refuses accommodations without just cause is not only liable in damages, but is guilty of a misdemeanor. In such cases, exemplary damages may be assessed.

In this case, no showing whatever was made by defendants in excuse or in justification of their treatment of plaintiffs. They just locked them out.

Ruling of the Court: The judgment is affirmed. . . .

Right to Privacy in Guest Room

A guest has the right to occupy the room without invasion by the innkeeper or any other unauthorized person. There are four exceptions to this rule when the innkeeper is authorized to enter the guest room. They are: (1) normal maintenance (including housekeeping) and repair; (2) imminent danger; (3) nonpayment; and (4) when requested to enter by the guest, such as to respond to a guest's room service order. Thus, hotel employees can enter only at such times as is necessary in the general conduct of the hotel or in attending to the needs of the guest.

The guest's right to privacy obligates the innkeeper to take steps to prevent not only unauthorized employees from entering the guest's room, but also unauthorized nonemployees. In the following case the hotel's caution was rewarded.

CASE EXAMPLE 11–2

Campbell v. Womack
345 So.2d 96 (La., 1977)

Plaintiff, Elvin Campbell, is engaged in the sand and gravel business. Since the nature of his business often requires his absence from his home in St. Farncisville, Mr. Campbell generally obtains temporary accommodations in the area in which he is working. For this purpose, Mr. Campbell rented a double room on a month-to-month basis at the Rodeway Inn in Morgan City, Louisiana. The room was registered in Mr. Campbell's name only.

From time to time, Mr. Campbell would share his room with certain of his employees; in fact, he obtained additional keys for the convenience of these employees. It also appears that Mr. Campbell was joined by his wife on some weekends and holidays, and that they jointly occupied his room on those occasions. However, Mrs. Campbell was not given a key to the motel room. On one such weekend, Mrs. Campbell, arriving while her husband was not at the motel, attempted to obtain the key to her husband's room from the desk clerk, Barbara Womack. This request was denied, since the desk clerk found that Mrs. Campbell was neither a registered guest for that room, nor had the registered guest, her husband, communicated to the motel management his authorization to release his room

key to Mrs. Campbell. Plaintiffs allege that this refusal was in a loud, rude, and abusive manner. After a second request and refusal, Mrs. Campbell became distressed, left the Rodeway Inn, and obtained a room at another motel. Mr. Campbell later joined his wife at the other motel and allegedly spent the weekend consoling her. Shortly thereafter, suit was filed against the Rodeway Inn and desk clerk, Barbara Womack. . . .

The motel clerk was under no duty to give Mrs. Campbell, a third party, the key to one of its guest's rooms. In fact, the motel had an affirmative duty, stemming from a guest's rights of privacy and peaceful possession, not to allow unregistered and unauthorized third parties to gain access to the rooms of its guest. . . .

The additional fact that Mrs. Campbell offered proof of her identity and her marital relation with the room's registered occupant does not alter her third-party status; nor does it lessen the duty owed by the motel to its guest. The mere fact of marriage does not imply that the wife has full authorization from her husband at all times and as to all matters. . . . Besides, how could Mrs. Campbell prove to the motel's satisfaction that the then present marital situation was amicable? This information is not susceptible of ready proof. . . .

CASE QUESTION

1.   How did the court in this case interpret the guest's right of privacy?

In another case the hotel was less diligent. A battered wife sought shelter in a Holiday Inn against her husband's abuse. Upon arrival, she informed the front desk that her husband had beaten her, requested that no calls be put through to her room, and that no one be informed of her presence at the inn. Her husband, however, convinced the hotel manager to not only unlock her door for him but also to cut the safety chain when she refused to unhook it. While in the presence of the manager, her husband stated he was going to kill his wife. Later that day, he beat her so severely she died in her sleep from her injuries. Her sister sued the hotel, among others. The hotel claimed it was not liable and sought summary judgment. The court denied the motion, and held that a jury would be empaneled to determine whether the hotel should be held responsible for the woman's death. *Thetford v. City of Clanton*, 605 So.2d 835 (1992). While the outcome of the jury trial is unknown, the hotel generally has a duty to protect the privacy of its guests and to refuse admittance to a guest's room without the guests permission. As this case illustrates, disregard of this duty can have grave consequences.

A guest's right of privacy in his room is not recognized in all states. For example, an Indiana court held that the state does not recognize a right of privacy as to a guest's room number and, therefore, a hotel is not liable when it gives the number to an unauthorized third person. In *Ellis v. Luxbury Hotels, Inc.* 666 N.E. 2d 1262 (Ind., 1996) a hotel informed a guest's estranged husband of the guest's room number where the husband represented himself to be the guest's brother seeking to help the guest with supposed car trouble. The hotel was not liable to the guest's date who was attacked by the husband when the latter sought to enter the room.

Another privacy issue that recently surfaced involves employees creating peepholes through which they are able to observe guests in their hotel rooms. Such conduct intrudes on guests' right to privacy. The following case, which received much media coverage, details how this phenomenon can occur.

CASE EXAMPLE 11–3

Carter v. Innisfree Hotel, Inc.
661 So.2d 1174 (Ala., 1995)

Paul Carter and Wendy Carter sued Innisfree Hotel, Inc. ("Innisfree") [a management corporation that managed the Travelodge Hotel] [and others] alleging various claims arising out of an alleged "peeping Tom" incident during their stay at the Birmingham Civic Center Travelodge Hotel. The trial court entered a summary judgment in favor of all defendants. The Carters appeal from the summary judgment as it relates to Innisfree. . . .

On February 25, 1993 . . . the Carters [traveled to attend a concert and] decided to rent a room for the night at the Birmingham Civic Center Travelodge. They checked into Room 221 that afternoon, and, after purchasing fast food, went back to their room to eat and relax. While in the room, they heard knocking and scratching sounds, which ap-

peared to emanate from behind a wall near the bathroom; the wall was covered by a mirror. However, they assumed that the sounds were from a neighboring room. They conducted their private marital activities that afternoon, including sexual intercourse, without regard to the strange noises. Wendy was undressed in front of the mirror for nearly two hours that afternoon, while applying her makeup and fixing her hair in preparation for the concert. Before the concert, while Paul was brushing his teeth in front of the mirror, he noticed two scratches in the mirror at eye level. He did nothing about the scratches at that time. The Carters went to the concert as they had planned.

After the concert, Paul again looked into the mirror and saw the scratches. He then removed the mirror and found two round, dime-sized scratches on the back of the mirror. Upon closer inspection, Paul found a large hole in the wall behind where the scratches were placed on the mirror. There was a hollow space approximately 1.5 feet wide between the Carters' wall and the wall of the adjoining room, which allows for maintenance workers to repair wiring and plumbing pipes. After looking at the hole closely, the Carters noticed a hole in the wall of the adjoining room that was covered by the mirror in that room. There was black electrical tape stuck onto the mirror of the other room; when Wendy pulled the tape off, the Carters discovered scratches on that mirror as well. . . .

Paul then telephoned the police and asked them to investigate; they were not able to identify the alleged "peeping Tom." After the police left, the Carters checked out of the hotel and drove back to Huntsville. Paul testified that he has suffered chronic nervousness and sleeplessness since the incident. Wendy testified that she and Paul have had strains in their marriage resulting from nervousness and paranoia she has suffered due to the incident. . . .

Nora Wood, a manager employed by Innisfree, stated that she inspects the Travelodge's rooms on a daily basis but said she did not know of the holes and scratches until the Carters complained about them.

The Travelodge customer who rented the adjoining room during the Carters' stay testified that he did not spy on the Carters. However, the record does not indicate whether he was absent from his room during the time the noises occurred. The record indicates that security guards, maintenance workers, housekeepers, and management personnel employed by Innisfree all have access to master keys that open the hotel rooms.

Invasion of Privacy

. . . Because the scratched mirror and the hole in the wall of Room 221 gave a secret viewing access into Room 221 from the adjoining room, a jury could find a wrongful intrusion into the Carters' right to privacy, and a jury could reasonably infer that the intrusion arose through the actions of Innisfree's agents, who have control over the hotel. The Carters need not prove the actual identity of the "peeping Tom," nor need they demonstrate actual use of the spying device, although, as we have already stated, a jury could reasonably infer from the evidence that the mirror and hole had been used to spy on them. There is no need for the Carters to establish that they saw another's eyes peering back at them through their mirror. . . . There can be no doubt that the possible intrusion of foreign eyes into the private seclusion of a customer's hotel room is an invasion of that customer's privacy. . . . Even if it is proven that a third party, someone other than an agent of Innisfree, caused the holes and scratches, Innisfree may be held liable for the invasion of the Carters' privacy. It had an affirmative duty, stemming from a guest's right of privacy and peaceful possession, not to allow unregistered and unauthorized third parties to gain access to the room of its guests. . . .

Negligence/Breach of Contract

. . . A jury could reasonably conclude from the evidence that Innisfree, through reasonable inspections, could have prevented the scratched mirrors and the holes behind those mirrors. . . . The jury could conclude that Innisfree had a contractual obligation to the Carters, its customers, to provide them with security, which, at the least, would mean a room free from fear that they were being viewed through their mirror. The jury could also find that Innisfree negligently failed to fulfill this duty, by allowing viewing access to the Carters' room through its failure to inspect the wall and to replace the scratched mirror. The trial court erred in entering the summary judgment for Innisfree on these claims. . . .

Protection Against Illegal Searches

A guest's right to privacy in the guest room occasionally conflicts with the police's interest in searching a hotel room as part of a criminal investigation. The rights of the guest and the responsibilities of the innkeeper in this situation are greatly impacted by the guest's privacy rights.

Report of Illegal Activity by Innkeeper

When a guest is assigned a room in a hotel, he has exclusive right to the room subject to the exceptions discussed in this chapter. If a hotel employee, in the course of legally entering a guest's room, finds evidence of illegal activity, what should the hotel do? Permitting that activity to proceed unabated may endanger other guests, in violation of the innkeeper's duty to exercise reasonable care to protect their safety, and may also jeopardize the hotel's license to carry on business, as we will see in Chapter 15. The hotel should report the illegal activity to the police. Is the hotel violating any rights of the guest by informing the police? The answer is no, provided the hotel employee was legally in the guest room when the illegal activity was discovered.

In *Engle v. State*, 391 So.2d 245 (Fla., 1980) a member of the hotel housekeeping crew discovered automatic rifles under the bed and some marijuana in an ashtray. She reported her findings to her manager, who reported them to the police. The hotel did not violate any obligation owed to the guest by making the report to the police.

Search Warrant

Once the police are called, they cannot legally search the room on the strength of permission given by the hotel manager or owner alone. Instead, the police must obtain a **search warrant**, which is an order from a judge commanding a police officer to search a designated place for evidence of criminal activity. If a search is made of a hotel room without a search warrant, the search invades the guest's privacy. Before issuing a search warrant, a judge must be satisfied that the police have probable cause to believe the search will uncover evidence of a crime. **Probable cause** consists of facts sufficient for a reasonably intelligent and prudent person to believe that evidence of a crime is located in the place the police want to search.

The warrant requirement provides a buffer between individuals and the police that helps ensure that people's privacy rights are not violated. The **exclusionary rule** holds that evidence obtained in a warrantless search will not be admissible in court. The prosecutor will not be able to use such evidence to help prove the defendant's guilt.

In the *Engle* case, discussed above, the police searched the hotel room for the weapons and the marijuana without first obtaining a search warrant. The defendant asked the court to suppress the evidence which the court did. Similarly, where a motel owner permitted police to search a hotel room occupied by a guest without his permission and without a search warrant, vines of marijuana found in the room were suppressed and the criminal action against the guest. *People v. Greig*, 619 N.Y.S.2d 444 (1994). When evidence is suppressed, the charges will be dismissed unless the police have other evidence against the defendant.

Would the innkeeper be liable in a case like *Engle* or *Greig* where the police, relying on information provided by a hotel employee, made an illegal search without a warrant? The answer is no. The hotel is not liable for the acts of the police; they are not employees or agents of the hotel. Thus, while the search without a warrant constitutes an invasion of the guest's privacy, the hotel cannot be held liable for that wrong.

Effect of Termination of Occupancy on Privacy Rights

As we have seen in this chapter, the guest's right to exclusive use of the room ends if the guest fails to pay as agreed or if the occupancy period expires. The right to occupy the room reverts from the guest to the innkeeper, who is entitled to enter the room, remove any remaining property of the guest, and prepare it for the next guest.

Just as the guest's right to occupy the room ends, so too does the guest's expectation of privacy. Thus, if any evidence is found in the room while the hotel is preparing it for the next guest and the police are called, they can search without a warrant and the evidence will not be suppressed. In *People v. Lerhinan*, 455 N.Y.S.2d 822 (1982), the guest was two weeks overdue in payments so the innkeeper entered the room and removed the belongings. The hotel manager discovered liquor and tools that had been stolen from the hotel. He called the police, who investigated without a warrant. The guest was arrested the next day. His request to suppress the evidence was denied because, at the time the incriminating items were discovered, he no longer had the exclusive right to occupy the room and thus had no expectation of privacy.

In another case a guest rented a room for a week. Near the end of the period he was in a car accident and was hospitalized. Drugs were suspected and the police wanted to search the defendant's hotel room. The police guarded the room but did not enter it prior to the end of the rental period. A few hours after the rental period had expired, the motel owner permitted the police and a drug-sniffing dog to search the room. Marijuana was discovered in an open shaving kit and was seized by the police. Defendant's efforts to suppress the marijuana were unsuccessful. Said the court, "A motel guest's reasonable expectation of privacy within a motel room runs concurrently with the lease of that room. The expiration of defendant's lease, therefore, ended his reasonable expectation of privacy in the motel room and gave the motel owner the right to enter the room. The owner could give consent to the police to search the room at that time." *State of Texas v. Porter*, 940 S.W.2d 391 (Tex., 1997).

Consent to Search

Consent is an exception to the requirement that the police obtain a search warrant. If a guest voluntarily agrees to permit the police to enter the room and search it, the police are free to do so. Evidence discovered in this situation will not be suppressed.

For the consent to be valid, the person agreeing to the search must have authority to give consent. Clearly, a guest has the authority to consent to a police search of his own room.

Suppose the guest is not in when the police arrive seeking permission to search. If they ask the innkeeper for approval and he consents, is the search valid? The answer is no. During the time a room is assigned to a guest, neither the innkeeper nor any employee of the hotel has the authority to consent to a search unless the guest expressly authorizes one of them to do so, which is unlikely to occur. If the police make a search of a guest's room relying only on consent granted by the innkeeper or a hotel employee, any evidence found will be suppressed. Will the hotel be liable to the guest? It is possible that a court would find the hotel invaded the guest's privacy in this situation.

Disturbing the Peace

Suppose a condition in a guest's room is disturbing to other guests. A hotel employee enters the room to quell the disruption and discovers evidence of a crime. Is this an illegal search requiring suppression of the evidence? Since the innkeeper has a duty to protect guests from interference by others, the innkeeper is entitled to enter the room where the disturbance is occurring. Any evidence in plain view found by the innkeeper while legally in the guest's room will not be suppressed. That issue is explored in the following case.

CASE EXAMPLE 11–4

People v. Henning
96 Cal. Rptr. 294 (Cal., 1971)

Sometime after ten o'clock P.M. (the curfew hour), on the evening of December 25, 1969, the desk clerk of Hillside Inn called the police department asking assistance concerning a disturbance in one of its rooms. An officer responded. He was told that a guest had complained about a disturbance at room 109, where a group of juveniles and adults were pounding on the door demanding admittance. The officer and a hotel employee went to the room. No one was then present in the outside hall, but inside "a very loud radio" was turned on. The officer knocked on the door repeatedly and called the name of the defendant Henning, to whom the room was registered. There was no response whatever, and there was no diminution of the radio's sound output. At the officer's request, the hotel employee unlocked the door. The officer again knocked on the door, with a similar lack of response within. The door was then pushed slightly ajar. The officer testified, "At that time I could see in, and I could see the lower half of a male's body extended in a prone position over the end of the bed fully clothed." The man was lying face down. Fearful that the man was

in trouble, the officer entered to "check on his welfare." Upon the entry, in plain sight on the floor, on a table, and protruding from the prone man's pocket, the officer saw, and recognized the nature of, a portion of the narcotics and dangerous drugs that were later the subject of Henning's motion to suppress. The man partially on the bed was Henning, who appeared to be in a deep sleep.

From this evidence, it could reasonably be concluded that the officer entered Henning's room with consent of the hotel employee; that the initial purpose of the entry was to silence a loud radio that was annoying the hotel's guests; and that upon seeing Henning prone and in an unusual position on the bed, an additional purpose developed—concern for the man's safety. It may clearly be inferred that the officer at no time prior to the entry had a purpose to arrest anyone or to search the room. And he may reasonably be considered as an agent of the hotelman, who understandably did not wish, unattended, to risk a hostile confrontation in silencing a source of annoyance to the hotel's guests.

We have no hesitancy in concluding that a hotelkeeper himself may enter a rented, but presently unoccupied, room when reasonably necessary to quiet a "very loud radio" that is presenting a substantial annoyance to other guests. Indeed, it has been held that an innkeeper is under an obligation not to harbor persons dangerous to the peace and comfort of those for whose comfort he is bound to provide, . . . to protect his patrons from annoyance, . . . and to exercise proper care for the safety and tranquility of the guest.

It seems most reasonable for the hotel people to have called upon a police officer for assistance, rather than risk violence in pursuit of their duty of care for the nighttime comfort, tranquility and quiet of their guests. If so, then it was equally reasonable for the police officer, on request and with their consent and under the facts before us, to assist in such an undertaking.

The additional purpose of the officer, upon observing the condition of Henning within the room, was clearly without Fourth Amendment or other fault. Reason tells us, and valid authority holds, that an entry is proper when a police officer reasonably and in good faith believes such entry to be necessary in order to render aid to a person in distress. . . .

[A] reasonable inference could be, and was, properly drawn by the court that the officer acted only in aid of the hotel management late at night to quell a disturbance—a loud radio—in the room. . . .

[W]e must conclude that there was substantial evidence in support of the superior court's order denying Henning's motion to suppress evidence.

CASE QUESTION

1. If the radio had not been playing loudly, would the evidence have been suppressed?

Previously we determined that a hotel employee is not authorized to consent to a search of the room of a current guest. In this case, the court, in upholding the validity of the search, relied in part on the fact that the hotel employee had consented to the search of the guest's room. The reason why the hotel employee could consent here is that a disturbance was occurring in the room. When a guest's activities in a room annoy others outside the room, the guest should anticipate that the innkeeper will need to quiet the disruption and thus the guest's expectation of privacy is diminished. Entry by the innkeeper in such circumstance is permissible. The innkeeper can seek the help of law enforcement and entry by both will be authorized.

Emergency Situation

Another circumstance under which an innkeeper is permitted to admit police into a guest's room is where reasonable grounds exist to believe that the guest is in distress and in need of assistance. In *State v. Wright*, 607 P.2d 19 (Ariz., 1980), the police were called to a hotel in response to a report of a disturbance. Guests in one room had been awakened by pounding on the door of the adjacent room. When the police arrived, two people were outside the room where the disturbance occurred. They explained they were trying to arouse their friend who had been drinking heavily earlier in the evening. No response was made to the officer's knocking. He obtained a key from the innkeeper and entered. The occupant was unconscious on the bed. His pulse was weak. An ambulance was called. Drugs were found on the table in the room. In the resulting criminal case for possession of drugs, the occupant claimed the police entry into the room was unauthorized and therefore the drugs should be suppressed. The court rejected this argument, holding that the police can enter in an emergency where the occupant is or is reasonably believed to be in need of imminent aid.

Search of Items Mislaid by Guests

A related privacy problem involves mislaid or forgotten luggage of a guest. Can an innkeeper who finds a guest's mislaid briefcase open it to help determine the true owner? The answer is yes. In such a case the owner's right to privacy must yield to a reasonable search of the briefcase by the manager to determine the owner. If the innkeeper instead fails to verify ownership of the briefcase and gives it to someone other than the owner, the innkeeper will be liable to the true owner for breach of its duty as bailee, as discussed in Chapter 9. It follows that hotel management personnel who open a lost or mislaid briefcase would not be invading the owner's privacy or making an unauthorized search. The following case illustrates the various issues that can arise in this situation.

CASE EXAMPLE 11–5

Berger v. State
257 S.E.2d 8 (Ga., 1979)

The assistant manager of the Hyatt Regency Hotel was given a briefcase that had been found in the main lobby. It was closed but not locked. It was not an unusual occurrence to find several misplaced briefcases each day in the hotel. He opened the briefcase to find if it contained any identification of its owner. It contained a wallet, a large amount of "business papers," and "bundles of money." Two men who inquired about the briefcase were directed to his office. One man, the defendant, stated that it was his briefcase. The manager asked him if he had any personal identification. The defendant told him his identification was in the wallet in the briefcase. The manager stated that it was hotel policy that identification must be made from the person and not from the lost object, and "if the person can't identify themselves, obviously we can't give it out." The manager was particularly concerned about this item because of the large amount of cash it contained. Both men were getting "agitated" and "a bit loud."

Police officers Derrick and Cochran were employed by the hotel as security personnel while they were off duty. Officer Derrick received a call over his "beeper" and was directed to report to the assistant manager's office. Officer Derrick testified that when he arrived, the assistant manager briefed him on the situation, and he identified himself to the defendant and asked him if the briefcase was his. The defendant stated that it was. Officer Derrick asked defendant if he had "any identification, driver's license or anything like that." The defendant said it was in the briefcase. . . . According to Officer Derrick, the briefcase was unlocked and the top was mostly down. He opened up the case, pulled out the billfold and left the briefcase open. Officer Derrick asked the defendant to write out his signature for comparison purposes. "As I was looking at the signatures on the driver's license and . . . the signature on the piece of paper, the case was right in front of me, and I noticed there was a bag of what I thought was marijuana inside the case in the back of it . . . and [the defendant] saw me see the marijuana . . . that's when he said . . . "I don't want you to search the briefcase.". . .

The defendant testified that when he was asked for identification by the assistant manager, he took his wallet out of the briefcase and told the manager what was in it, and at that time the officers came in. He stated the briefcase was closed and the wallet was in his hand. When asked for identification, he showed Officer Derrick his driver's license, and he signed his name to let the officer make a comparison. He testified that Officer Derrick said: ". . . yeah, that's you all right . . . but that doesn't prove this is your briefcase. . . . I am going to have to look in it. . . . It was closed. . . . I said I would prefer that you do not look in it." Although [the defendant] repeated his request not to look in the briefcase, the officer opened it and searched through the briefcase until he found the marijuana, cocaine, and $7,000 in cash. [Defendant tried to suppress the money and drugs on the ground that the search was illegal.] The court denied the motion to suppress. Defendant brings this appeal.

Defendant argues that . . . [he] had a reasonable expectation of privacy in his briefcase that was protected by the Fourth Amendment. . . .

Here the defendant was not arrested, nor did he have the briefcase "in his possession." The briefcase had been misplaced. Innkeepers of this state have a statutory liability to guests for property coming into their possession. . . . It is not an unauthorized search for hotel management personnel, including security personnel, to open unlocked items found on their premises in an attempt to determine ownership so that the lost or misplaced property can be returned to its proper owner.

In the instant case, the incriminating evidence came into possession of the law enforcement authorities inadvertently and unmotivated by any desire to locate incriminating evidence. Assuming without deciding that Officer Derrick was acting as a police officer, we find nothing unlawful about a police officer opening an unlocked, lost, or misplaced item to determine ownership. The marijuana was then in plain view, and the officer was authorized to confiscate the contraband. . . .

Ruling of the Court: Judgment affirmed. [The drugs found in the briefcase were admissible against the defendant in his trial for illegal possession of controlled substances.]

CASE QUESTION

1. Why was the search of the briefcase not a violation of defendant's constitutional right against unreasonable searches?

Unclaimed Lost Property

What is the responsibility of an innkeeper or restaurateur when lost property is found and no one claims it? Many states have statutes that prescribe a procedure for disposing of such items. Typically, the hotel is required to inform the police of the finding or deposit the property at the police station. Failure to do so may constitute a crime. See for example New York Personal Property Law §252.

Protection Against Insults

Though the use of insulting and abusive language is objectional and can evoke anger, the courts have been slow to regard it as a basis of civil liability as between individuals. Most states do not recognize abusive language, without more, as amounting to a tort. However, if the language is beyond abusive and qualifies as outrageous, it may constitute the tort of intentional infliction of emotional stress. For this tort, the words must be "so extreme in degree, as to go beyond all possible bounds of decency and to be regarded as atrocious and utterly intolerable in a civilized community." *Vinson v. Linn-Mar Community School District*, 360 N.W.2d 108 (Iowa, 1984). In addition, for a successful lawsuit, the plaintiff must have suffered severe or extreme emotional distress.

However, some courts have allowed recovery for a lower threshold of abusive language in cases where an innkeeper and guest are involved. The reason is that the innkeeper, carrying on a business of a public nature, is expected to extend to guests respectful and decent treatment, and to refrain from conduct that would interfere with their comfort or humiliate and distress them. *DeWolf v. Ford*, 86 N.E. 527 (N.Y., 1908), was one of the earliest cases in point. Here the court said,

> *One of the things that a guest for hire at a public inn has the right to insist upon is respectful and decent treatment at the hands of the innkeeper and his servant, so that is an essential part of the contract, whether express or implied. This right of the guest necessarily implies an obligation on the part of the innkeeper that neither he nor his servants will abuse or insult the guest or indulge in any conduct or speech that may unnecessarily bring upon him physical discomfort or distress of mind.*

No similar duty is owed to a nonguest. In *Jenkins v. Kentucky Hotel Co.*, 87 S.W.2d 951 (Ky., 1935), the plaintiff, who was a nonguest, was waiting in the lobby for her brother, who was attending a banquet. The hotel detective approached the plaintiff and, in a rude and menacing manner, told her erroneously that no such meeting was going on in the hotel and ordered her to leave. Fearing bodily harm, she left. A few minutes later she returned and went directly to the room where the meeting was being held. The court held that although the detective's manners were rude and highly objectionable, "bad manners are not actionable." The court stated, "[A]ppellant was at most a mere licensee, and that if she had been requested in a proper manner to leave the lobby and had failed to do so, reasonable force could lawfully have been used to eject her."

In another nonguest case the plaintiff, a patron of a lunch counter, was accused by the waitress of leaving without paying for his food when in fact he had paid. The court denied recovery, saying the waitress' statements were not so "outrageous or atrocious as to exceed all possible bounds of decency as is required". *Henderson v. Ripperger*, 594 P.2d 251 (Kan., 1979). In accord is *Wallace v. Shoreham Hotel Corp.*, printed in full in Chapter 8, page 234–235.

In *Jones v. City of Boston*, 738 F. Supp. 604 (Mass. 1990), plaintiff, a black man, was a patron at the Sports Saloon in the Copley Square Hotel. After he spoke with a group of white women the bartender allegedly said to them, "What did I tell you about talking to niggers?" Jones sued the hotel for his resulting emotional distress. In Massachusetts, to collect damages for emotional distress, the plaintiff's emotional injury must be severe. The court in this case held, "Although there is not question that referring to a person as a 'nigger' is outrageous," plaintiff was unable to show that his distress was severe.

In another case polite treatment of a guest helped to save the hotel from liability. We also learn more about what does not qualify as sufficient humiliation to support a lawsuit. A clerical error resulted in hotel checking plaintiff out of his room one day before his reservation was to expire. Another guest was given posses-sion of the room. When plaintiff returned to the hotel in the early morning hours, he was unable to occupy his room. Plaintiff sued for "indignity, abuse and humilia-tion." According to his testimony, the desk clerk was not discourteous or abusive. Said the court, "[I]t is difficult to find any degree of humiliation in an incident which unfolded in a deserted hotel lobby at 3:00 A.M. witnessed by a solitary and apologetic desk clerk. . . . It is the publicity of the thing that causes the humilia-tion." Plaintiff's case was thus dismissed. *Pollock v. Holsa Corp.*, 454 N.Y.S.2d 582 (NY, 1982).

Protection Against False Arrest

Neither a hotelkeeper nor a restaurateur is under any duty to prevent the ar-rest of a guest by police officers who are seemingly acting within their authority. However, if the arrest is due to a false statement by the hotel, restaurant or their agents, the establishment could be liable. In *Nensen v. Barnett*, 134 N.W.2d 53 (Neb., 1965), a hotel employee falsely told a police officer that a guest had breached the peace, which led to her arrest. She successfully sued the hotel for **false arrest** which is unauthorized restraint of a person.

A hotel or restaurant commits the tort of false arrest or imprisonment when it detains a person illegally. Only if the person in fact has committed a crime, can the establishment legally detain that person.

The plaintiff in *Jacques v. Childs Dining Hall Co.*, 138 N.E. 843 (Mass., 1923), accompanied by her aunt, entered the defendant's restaurant and proceeded through the crowded facility up one flight of stairs to the ladies' lounge. As the aunt did not desire anything to eat, the plaintiff went alone downstairs to the dining area and was served. Upon receiving her bill she returned to her aunt and together they walked towards the door to leave. As they passed the cashier's desk, plaintiff paid for the food she ate. As they started to leave the restaurant, the cashier called them back by ringing a bell and beckoning plaintiff. The cashier questioned the plaintiff as to why the bill covered only one meal. She replied that her aunt had not eaten in the restaurant and again started to leave. The cashier commanded her to wait. The head waiter and then the manager were summoned. The plaintiff and her aunt were detained and questioned for some twenty-five minutes. Finally the cashier approached plaintiff, who was then with the manager, and said he (the cashier) had mistakenly mixed up plain-tiff's check with someone else's. Plaintiff was then allowed to leave.

Like many states, Massachusetts, the state in which the case occurred, autho-rizes a restaurant to detain a person if it has reasonable cause to believe she did not pay money owed, provided the detention lasts for only a reasonable amount of time and is carried out in a reasonable manner. If, however, the person is de-tained without reasonable cause or for an unreasonable amount of time or in an unreasonable manner, she is entitled to recover for her damages. In the *Jacques* case, the court determined the detention was based on inattention and carelessness of the cashier, which falls short of reasonable cause. Therefore the case was decided in favor of plaintiff.

This case underscores the principle that a hotel or restaurant cannot with impunity interfere with its patrons' freedom of movement or accuse them of illegal acts. It can do so only if it has reasonable grounds to believe the patron has acted illegally.

Rights Concerning Rates and Fees

Legal mandates and good practice require that room rates and other fees be disclosed to guests before they are incurred. A hotel cannot impose charges for services not provided.

Right to Advance Notice

Guests have a right to know, prior to contracting for a room, the fees and charges a hotel will impose. They should be made clear to avoid unhappy or angry guests at check-out time. Many states require that rates be posted in each room and signs containing prices not be misleading.

Right to No Extraneous Fees

Guests also have the right not to be charged for services they did not receive. For example, a statute in New York provides that "no charge or sum shall be collected or received by any hotelkeeper for any service not actually rendered." Contrary to this statute, the Waldorf Astoria charged all guests a 2 percent fee for "sundries" (miscellaneous items), which covered messenger services that some guests used and others did not. The hotel's right to impose the fee was successfully challenged by the State Attorney General, the chief legal officer of the state. The court's decision follows.

CASE EXAMPLE 11–6

State of New York v. Waldorf-Astoria
323 N.Y.S.2d 917 (1971)

Petitioner brings this special proceeding . . . to permanently enjoin and restrain the respondents from conducting and transacting their business in a persistently fraudulent and illegal manner, and to direct restitution to all consumers of the amount charged for services not rendered . . . pursuant to [statute]. . . .

The General Business Law does require every hotel to post "a statement of the . . . charges by the day and for meals furnished and for lodging." It further provides that "No charge or sum shall be collected or received by any such hotelkeeper or innkeeper for any service not actually rendered."

Between December 2, 1969 and May 21, 1970 the respondents did add to each bill of each customer a 2 percent charge for sundries. . . .

Respondents argue that there was no violation of the General Business Law because it only prohibits charges "for any service not actually rendered" and that message services in fact were rendered. However, even respondents admit that all of their customers did not receive special, costly messenger service. They contend that 77 percent did receive such service but admit that 23 percent did not. None of their customers received any explanation or itemization of the charge for sundries. All of them were charged this 2 percent during the period in question. . . .

The business of an innkeeper is of a *quasi* public character, invested with many privileges and burdened with correspondingly great responsibilities. . . . The charge for message services delineated as sundries was fraudulent and unconscionable. Accordingly, petitioner's application is granted to the extent that respondents are permanently enjoined from engaging in the fraudulent and illegal acts and practices complained of herein.

The amount of money to be refunded is admitted. The petitioner, by its Bureau of Consumer Frauds and Protection, investigated the records of the respondents and claims that the 2 percent charge for sundries during the period in question involved 64,338 customers and amounts to $113,202.83. Frank A. Banks, vice-president and manager of respondent, in an affidavit of June 10, 1971, states that during the period in question transient room sales amounted to $6,329,484. The 2 percent charge would therefore be over $126,000. However, the exact amount is not important, as the respondents are ordered to refund to each and every customer during the period in question all charges for unexplained sundries. These refunds are to be made within 60 days of the date of service of the judgment herein with notice of entry. Within 30 days thereafter canceled vouchers or copies thereof will be exhibited to the petitioner. . . .

CASE QUESTION

1. What alternate arrangements for payment of the fee might the hotel have made to avoid liability for returning the money?

Hotels should ensure that they do not impose fees for services not actually rendered. If the hotel intends to charge for certain services, it should charge only those guests who utilize the services. If the demand is insufficient to cover the costs of providing the service, the hotel should reassess whether it wishes to continue offering that service.

Telephone Charges

At one time, telephones in guest rooms were considered a courtesy offered by a hotel for the convenience of guests. There was no duty on the part of hoteliers to supply telephone services. Today, failure to have a telephone in the room may violate the innkeeper's duty to keep the room safe for guests and to provide them adequate security.

A telephone may be the only source of communication in an emergency situation. It might be used to give instructions to guests trapped in their rooms during a fire, or to summon help by a guest who suddenly takes ill and is unable to leave the room. In numerous situations telephones are necessities in a hotel room, not a luxury or merely a convenience.

In the past, the charges that hoteliers could impose on guests for phone service were severely restricted by both state and federal regulation. Local and intrastate calls were regulated by state public utility commissions that allowed only a very small surcharge. Interstate and international calls were regulated by the Federal Communication Commission, which allowed no surcharge at all. As a result, hoteliers avoided installing elaborate telephone systems because they lost money on telephone services. More recently, however, most states have eliminated regulations limiting the surcharge that hotels may impose on local and intrastate calls, thus providing hotels with a source of revenue.

The charges now imposed for phone calls made from hotel rooms are an irritant to many guests. Also annoying is the lack of predictability of the amount of the charge; they vary significantly from hotel to hotel. Some states, including New York, now have a "truth-in-dialing act" that requires the hotel to display a sign on or near the principal room phone stating the amount of any surcharge imposed. The sign must be conspicuous. Violations can result in fines of various amounts.

In states where surcharge regulations still exist, hoteliers are bound to conform to them and may not impose a surcharge greater than that allowed by the state regulatory authority.

Proper Handling of Mail and Packages

Hotel guests often receive mail and packages at the hotel. Sometimes mail arrives after guests depart. In either case guests have a right to have the mail handled properly by the innkeeper. This right can be construed from the nature of the hotel business. The innkeeper can anticipate that mail will be sent to guests and should develop procedures accordingly. An example of procedures that fulfill the hotel's responsibility to guests include the following: 1) when a package is received for a guest, a notice is placed in the guest's mailbox informing him of receipt by the hotel of the package; 2) the "call" light in the guest room is illuminated, alerting the guest to call the front desk; and 3) the package is not released unless the person claiming it exhibits identification. In a recent case the above procedures were followed, except the claimant exhibited a room key instead of identification and the hotel delivered the package to that person. The hotel later discovered that person was not the addressee. The hotel may be liable to the intended recipient for negligent handling of the package. See *Bottoms & Tops International, Inc. v. United Parcel Service and Marco Polo, Inc.*, 610 N.Y.S.2d 439 (1994). A related issue involves facsimile machines, which are common today and permit instantaneous transmission of letters and documents. If the hotel provides a facsimile machine for guests to use, procedures should be established to ensure guests can send and receive faxed documents reliably.

The following case illustrates the problems a hotel can encounter if proper procedures are not followed. The innkeeper agreed to refuse delivery of a package expected by a departing guest. Unfortunately, a hotel employee accepted delivery and stored the package. The hotel was found to be a bailee with a duty to exercise reasonable care.

CASE EXAMPLE 11–7

Berlow v. Sheraton Dallas Corp.
629 S.W.2d 818 (Tex., 1982)

Berlow, a designer and manufacturer of jewelry, frequently authorized her parents (the Soifers) to represent her in showing and selling jewelry to fashionable department stores. In January, 1978, Berlow authorized the Soifers to show ten pieces of jewelry in Dallas. Berlow arranged to have a package containing the jewelry delivered by United Parcel Service (UPS) to her parents at the hotel. The package was marked "insured" on the outside and showed Berlow's return address. The package did not arrive at the hotel during the four-day stay of the Soifers. During their stay, each of the Soifers asked frequently about it at the front desk and, before checking out, the Soifers informed front desk personnel that this was a very important package, although they deliberately refrained from telling them the contents or value of the package. They asked that the hotel refuse delivery of it, and personnel at the front desk agreed to refuse its delivery. Agreeing to and subsequently refusing delivery of packages upon the oral instructions of guests to front desk attendants was standard procedure for the hotel. Contrary to its agreement, however, when the package arrived the hotel took delivery of it, stored it at the front desk for a month, and then turned it over to the United States Post Office (USPO) without postage, marked "Return to Sender." This, too, was standard procedure for the hotel in dealing with packages stored at the front desk. No attempt was made to determine if the Soifers had been recent guests at the hotel, nor to contact Berlow. The package was lost. At trial, Berlow testified that the fair market value of the jewelry was $10,231.

[T]he jury found that the hotel was negligent in its acceptance, care, and handling of the package, and that this negligence both increased the risk of loss of the package and was the proximate cause of the loss. The jury refused, however, to find the hotel grossly negligent. . . . Additionally, the jury found that the hotel did not substantially perform its agreement to refuse delivery of the package by delivering it to USPO and that Berlow's loss was suffered because she relied on the hotel's promise to refuse the package. Finally, the jury found that the hotel, acting as a reasonable and prudent person, should have foreseen that the package contained property of substantial dollar value. The jury awarded Berlow $10,231, the fair market value of the jewelry. . . .

The hotel argues that the bailment of the package was merely gratuitous and, as a gratuitous bailee, it can be held liable only for gross negligence. Because we find for reasons explained below that the bailment of the package was a bailment for mutual benefit and not a gratuitous bailment, the hotel was liable for its ordinary negligence.

. . . We find that a bailment was established as a matter of law, that the bailment was one of mutual benefit as a matter of law, and that there was some evidence to support the jury's findings on negligence, proximate cause, and damages. . . .

In order to constitute a bailment there must be a contract, express or implied, delivery of the property to the bailee, and acceptance of the property by the bailee. Uncontroverted evidence showed that the hotel, rather than refusing delivery, took possession of Berlow's package and stored it on the premises, under lock and key, for one month. Assuming custody of the package in this manner established an implied contract to bail the package. Delivery of the package and acceptance of it by the hotel were stipulated; thus bailment of the package was established as a matter of law.

That the bailment was one for mutual benefit and not merely gratuitous was also established as a matter of law. A bailment is for the mutual benefit of the parties, although nothing is paid directly by the bailor, where property of the bailor is delivered to and accepted by the bailee as an incident to a business in which the bailee makes a profit. The Soifers were paying guests at the hotel. It is not unusual for patrons to have packages delivered to them at a hotel, and, in this case, the evidence showed that the practice occurred frequently enough that the hotel developed standard procedures for dealing with packages. Although no direct charge was made, the price paid for the room also included the incidental services provided by the hotel. This provided consideration for the implied agreement to bail Berlow's package and established a bailment for mutual benefit as a matter of law.

Having entered into a bailment for mutual benefit, the hotel became liable for its ordinary negligence. The jury found that the hotel was negligent in its acceptance, care, and handling of the package, and there was some evidence to support this finding. The evidence showed that the hotel violated its own standard procedure, as well as its express agreement with the Soifers, to refuse delivery of packages when requested to do so. The evidence also showed that the package was stored for one month, during which the hotel made no attempt to contact the Soifers or Berlow, then delivered to USPO without postage. This raises some evidence upon which the jury could find the hotel negligent.

[T]he hotel argues that, as a matter of law, it was not negligent. According to the hotel, because the package was delivered to USPO for return to Berlow, the liability for any loss rested with USPO as a subsequent bailee and not with the hotel. We do not agree. While the evidence showed that Berlow's package was lost while in the custody of USPO, it also showed that the hotel gave the package, which was insured when delivered to the hotel by UPS, to USPO without insurance or postage. This was evidence of negligence by the hotel, sufficiently strong to require submission of the issue to the jury. The hotel, therefore, did not establish its non-negligence as a matter of law.

There was also some evidence to support the jury's finding that the hotel's negligence was a proximate cause of Berlow's loss. . . .[B]ecause the package was given to USPO without postage, the jury could find that the hotel should have reasonably foreseen that the package would never reach Berlow.

Likewise, there was some evidence to support the jury's finding that it was foreseeable that the package contained property of substantial dollar value. . . . [T]he jury could find it reasonable for the hotel to foresee that guests would bring or deliver items of value to the hotel. . . .

Because there was some evidence on each element of recovery on Berlow's theory that she and the hotel entered into a bailment for mutual benefit, the trial court erred in granting the hotel's motion for judgment notwithstanding the verdict; thus judgment should be rendered for Berlow. . . .

[J]udgment rendered in favor of Berlow for $10,231.

CASE QUESTION

1. Assume that the hotel employee with whom the Soifers made arrangements for return of the package was not on duty when it arrived or had been terminated before it arrived. What procedures might the hotel have instituted to ensure the Soifers' wishes were nonetheless honored?

Summary

Guests have a variety of rights which innkeepers must honor or risk liability. Those rights include the right to occupy the guest room without disturbance; right against unauthorized police searches; right against insulting treatment by hotel employees; right to be free from unlawful arrest or restraint by the hotel staff; right to disclosure of information concerning fees and charges for the room, phone, and other services; and right to proper handling of mail, facsimile transmissions, and incoming packages.

Preventive Law Tips for Managers

- *Do not disrupt a guest's occupancy of the room except for good and exceptional cause.* A guest has the right to occupy the hotel room without interference from the innkeeper. Once a room is assigned to a guest, the innkeeper can enter only for normal maintenance, imminent danger, nonpayment, disruption of other guests, and when requested by the guest. Entering the room at other times or forcing a guest out of a room without cause violates this right and entitles the guest to damages from the hotel.

- *If police ask you for permission to search the room of a current guest who is not in arrears in payment, remind the officer that you do not have legal authority to consent to a search.* A police officer in pursuit of a defendant may not know or recall in the heat of an investigation that an innkeeper lacks authority to consent to a search of a guest's room. If police request authority to search an occupied room, ask to see the warrant. If they do not have one, remind them that by law an innkeeper does not have that authority (unless one of the exceptions apply) and any evidence obtained will be suppressed. In response, most officers will apply for a warrant.

- *Do not give lost or mislaid property to someone claiming to be the owner without verifying that person's identity and ownership.* An innkeeper has a duty to exercise reasonable care in tending to lost or mislaid property. The duty of reasonable care encompasses the return of the goods to its owner. If a hotel gives the merchandise to someone other than its rightful owner, the hotel may be liable to the owner. To avoid that happening, the innkeeper should require proof of ownership before giving the goods to anyone.

- *Train employees to be polite and respectful of guests; stress the importance of avoiding insulting or abusive language.* Offensive or humiliating comments made by a hotel employee to a guest can result in liability for the hotel. Employees should be trained to address guests respectfully and avoid insulting comments.

- *Train employees on how to handle a suspected theft properly.* Guests have the right not to be falsely accused of improper conduct by hotel staff. Employees should be taught proper procedures for handling suspicious activity. Those procedures might include any of the following, depending on the circumstances: contacting the manager or other supervisory employee; investigating further; and contacting the police.

- *When investigating suspected criminal activity, do it confidentially, informing only those who need to know, and reasonably, with minimal disruption to the guest.* Conducting an investigation improperly can lead to liability. The investigation should be done within a reasonable amount of time from when suspicion arose. The treatment of the suspect during the investigation should be respectful and reasonable. The investigation should be no broader than necessary to determine the truth or falsity of the suspected activity.

- *Do not impose any charge on a guest's bill for services not utilized by the guest.* A guest can legally be charged only for those services which he utilized while a guest at the hotel. Additional charges are not authorized. The hotel's billing procedures should be reviewed to ensure guests are not charged for unused services.

- *Disclose information concerning the fees for in-room telephone use.* Most hotels charge a fee for the use of phones located in hotel rooms. The fees vary and guests are often uncertain as to the amount of the charges in a given hotel. Some states require that information identifying the charges be disclosed in writing near the phone. Compliance with these statutes is necessary to avoid fines. In states that do not statutorily require disclosure of this information, good practice calls for its disclosure. Unpleasant disagreements at check-out are thereby avoided.

- *Develop procedures to ensure that mail addressed to guests and prior guests is properly handled, and follow those procedures carefully.* A hotel may be liable when mail or packages sent to guests or prior guests are not delivered to the addressee. The hotel should adopt procedures for handling the mail to ensure it reaches the intended recipient. Those procedures should include: (a) maintaining a record of the guest's home address; (b) determining the proper method of forwarding mail to a prior guest (U.S. mail, UPS, etc.); (c) providing funds for postage and insurance; and (d) developing rules for proper handling during the period between receipt of the mail by the hotel and forwarding of it to the guest.

Review Questions

1. What obligation, if any, does a hotel have to refrain from using abusive or insulting language to a guest?

2. Will a hotel be liable to a guest if an employee falsely informs the police that the guest has committed criminal activity?

3. Under what circumstances can an innkeeper enter a guest's room without consent?

4. What constitutional rights are at risk when the police search a hotel room for evidence?

5. If a police search violates a constitutional right, what happens to any evidence that is seized in the search?

6. Who issues a warrant?

7. What must a police officer prove in order to obtain a warrant?

8. Who has the authority to consent to a search of a hotel room that has been assigned to a guest? Who does not have that authority?

9.   What restrictions does a hotel have concerning the fees it charges?

10.   What obligation, if any, does a hotel have concerning mail, packages, and facsimile messages received by the hotel and addressed to guests?

Discussion Questions

1.   According to the exclusionary rule, incriminating evidence found during an illegal search cannot be used against the defendant. Often, without that evidence, the defendant will be acquitted. How do you feel about the exclusionary rule?

2.   In what way does a guest's expectation of privacy vary depending on whether he is still a guest or has checked out? Why does the expectation of privacy vary in these circumstances?

3.   Why can a hotel employee look into a mislaid briefcase before returning it to a guest who claims ownership of it? Why does this not violate the owner's right of privacy?

4.   You are the assistant manager of a hotel. You have been assigned the task of devising procedures for handling mail delivered to the hotel for guests, both current and past. What are the legal issues you will need to address and what procedures will you recommend?

Application Questions

1.   Jan and Dean are friends and are both guests at the Morbury Hotel. While they were in the lobby after returning from a stroll through downtown, Jan called Dean insulting names. Dean was embarrassed and annoyed about the incident. Has the hotel violated any obligation owed to Dean? Why or why not?

2.   Connor and his wife are guests at a hotel. During their stay and while Connor was supposed to be attending a business meeting, he was arrested for sale of illegal drugs. The police went immediately to the hotel and received from the innkeeper permission to search the room. During the search the police found illegal drugs and drug paraphernalia. Can they be used against Connor at trial? Why or why not? Does the hotel have any liability to Connor in this circumstance? Why or why not?

3.   Elisha was a guest at the Billet Hotel. As she was checking out she discovered she was charged for various items she had thought were free. The hotel had not informed her previously that a fee would be imposed. She was angry and demanded to see the manager. Is the hotel legally entitled to collect these fees? What should the hotel have done to avoid this problem?

UNIT IV

Special Topics

CHAPTER 12

Liability and the Sale of Food and Alcohol

INTRODUCTION

Studies suggest that one out of every three meals is eaten away from home. If restaurants serve unhealthy food, a serious health risk results. To encourage safe practices, the law imposes liability on restaurants that serve inedible food and requires that claims made about the food be truthful.

Alcohol likewise creates hazards. Driving while intoxicated leads to death on U.S. highways every year. In addition, intoxicated persons are frequently belligerent and cause disturbances. To limit alcohol abuse, the law regulates its sale. Violations by liquor vendors can result in loss of their license to sell alcohol, liability for resulting injuries, and criminal penalties.

A bar or restaurant has a duty to provide reasonably safe premises for its patrons. If a disturbance or attack is foreseeable, as where a belligerent patron remains on the premises or prior security incidents have occurred, the owner must take action to protect the customers from harm. Disregarding this duty can result in liability for damages.

This chapter will examine the laws applicable to the sale of food and alcohol and the duty of a restaurant or bar to protect the safety of its patrons.

Warranty of Merchantability

The **Uniform Commercial Code** (UCC) is a set of rules designed to simplify and modernize the law governing the sale of goods. Virtually all states and the District of Columbia have adopted it. The UCC imposes an implied warranty that the goods are "merchantable" in all contracts for the sale of goods, including food, where the seller is a merchant. UCC 2-314. (This is a typical UCC cite. The numeral "2" identifies which of the UCC's nine articles is referenced. The number following the dash refers to a section within the referenced article.) **Merchantable** means the goods are at least average quality and fit for their ordinary purpose. If you buy a book bag and it tears when you put two books in it, it is not fit for its intended purpose and thus is not merchantable. This warranty of merchantability is implied in all contracts for the sale of goods made by a merchant; it exists even if the parties never mention it in their negotiations. The warranty renders manufacturers and sellers of food virtually insurers that the food is wholesome and free from dangerous substances. The basis for imposing this liability is a public policy for protection of consumers.

Merchantable Food

Food, to be merchantable, must be fit for human consumption, that is, it should not make you ill when you eat it. To pass muster, food does not have to be nutritional or taste great; it merely must be eatable.

Objects in Food

A pizza served with a tack in it is not merchantable. The restaurant that served the pizza will be liable to a customer injured by the tack based on breach of the warranty of merchantability.

Foreign/Natural Test.   In some states, whether an object found in food constitutes a breach of warranty is determined by the **foreign/natural substance test**. If the object is natural to the food product, the warranty is not violated. If, however, the object is foreign, the warranty is breached.

A case illustrating the application of this test is *Mix v. Ingersoll Candy Co.*, 59 P.2d 144 (Cal., 1936). The plaintiff was injured by a chicken bone while eating chicken pot pie. The court held the defendant was not liable since chicken bones were natural to chicken. Similarly, chicken bone slivers in chicken soup and nutshell pieces in nut breads are natural substances and, under the foreign/natural test, do not violate the warranty of merchantability.

Where the item in the food that causes injury is a foreign object, that is, unrelated to the make-up or ingredients of the product, its presence breaches the warranty and the restaurant will be liable for resulting injuries. A plaintiff who swallowed pieces of glass lodged in ice cream while eating a banana split successfully sued the restaurant that sold the ice cream. *Deris v. Finest Foods, Inc.*, 198 So.2d 412 (La., 1967).

Some states have found this test too limiting and have redefined what qualifies as foreign and as natural. In these states, something that may be natural in the product's original state may not be considered so in its manufactured state. Thus, a woman who broke her tooth on a bone in a "boneless chicken sandwich" was entitled to damages for her resulting injury notwithstanding the state in which the incident occurred followed the foreign/natural test. *Meladay v. Wendy's of New Orleans, Inc.*, 637 So.2d 1094 (La., 1996). Said the court, "When a product undergoes the manufacturing process and is marketed as a particular type of product, i.e., a can of tuna, a foreign substance is any substance not associated with that finished product. Thus, a 'fish eye lens,' although natural to a tuna fish, is not considered a 'natural' object in a can of tuna meat. Likewise, we hold a piece of bone is a 'foreign' object in a manufactured boneless chicken breast."

Reasonable Expectation Test.   An alternate test applied by some states is the **reasonable expectation test**, which examines whether an object found in food ought to have been anticipated by the consumer. If the object should be anticipated, its presence in the food does not constitute a breach of the warranty. If, on the other hand, its presence is not reasonably expected, it does constitute a breach. Under this test, more circumstances are likely to constitute breach of the warranty than under the foreign/natural test because some objects may be natural but nonetheless unexpected. The outcome of the application of the reasonable expectation test is not always clear because reasonable people might disagree about what should be reasonably anticipated. See if you agree with the judge's decision in the following case.

CASE EXAMPLE 12–1

Webster v. Blue Ship Tea Room, Inc.
198 N.E.2d 309 (Mass., 1964)

. . . On Saturday, April 25, 1959, about 1 P.M., the plaintiff, accompanied by her sister and her aunt, entered the Blue Ship Tea Room operated by the defendant. The group was seated at a table and supplied with menus.

This restaurant, which the plaintiff characterized as "quaint," was located in Boston on the third floor of an old building on T Wharf, which overlooks the ocean.

The plaintiff, who had been born and brought up in New England (a fact of some consequence), ordered clam chowder and crabmeat salad. Within a few minutes she received tidings to the effect that "there was no more clam chowder," whereupon she ordered a cup of fish chowder. Presently, there was set before her "a small bowl of fish chowder." She had previously enjoyed a breakfast about 9 A.M. that had given her no difficulty. The fish chowder contained haddock, potatoes, milk, water, and seasoning. The chowder was milky in color and not clear. The haddock and potatoes were in chunks (also a fact of consequence). She agitated it a little with the spoon and observed that it was a fairly full bowl. . . . It was hot when she got it, but she did not tip it with her spoon because it was hot . . . but stirred it in an up and under motion. She denied that she did this because she was looking for something, but it was rather because she wanted an even distribution of fish and potatoes. She started to eat it, alternating between the chowder and crackers which were on the table with . . . [some] rolls. She ate about 3 or 4 spoonfuls then stopped. She looked at the spoonfuls as she was eating. She saw equal parts of liquid, potato, and fish as she spooned it into her mouth. She did not see anything unusual about it. After 3 or 4 spoonfuls she was aware that something had lodged in her throat because she couldn't swallow and couldn't clear her throat by gulping and she could feel it. This misadventure led to two esophagoscopies at the Massachusetts General Hospital, in the second of which, on April 27, 1959, a fish bone was found and removed. The sequence of events produced injury to the plaintiff that was not insubstantial.

We must decide whether a fish bone lurking in a fish chowder, about the ingredients of which there is no other complaint, constitutes a breach of implied warranty under applicable provisions of the Uniform Commercial Code. . . . As the judge put it in his charge, "Was the fish chowder fit to be eaten and wholesome? . . . [N]obody is claiming that the fish itself wasn't wholesome. . . . But the bone of contention here—I don't mean that for a pun—but was this fish bone a foreign substance that made the fish chowder unwholesome or not fit to be eaten?"

The plaintiff has vigorously reminded us of the high standards imposed by this court where the sale of food is involved . . . and has made reference to cases involving stones in beans, . . . trichinae in pork . . . and to certain other cases, here and elsewhere, serving to bolster her contention of breach of warranty.

The defendant asserts that here was a native New Englander eating fish chowder in a "quaint" Boston dining place where she had been before; that [f]ish chowder, as it is served and enjoyed by New Englanders, is a hearty dish, originally designed to satisfy the appetites of our seamen and fishermen; that this court knows well that we are not talking of some insipid broth as is customarily served to convalescents. We are asked to rule in such fashion that no chef is forced "to reduce the pieces of fish in the chowder to minuscule size in an effort to ascertain if they contained any pieces of bone." "In so ruling," we are told (in the defendant's brief), "the court will not only uphold its reputation for legal knowledge and acumen, but will, as loyal sons of Massachusetts, save our world-renowned fish chowder from degenerating into an insipid broth containing the mere essence of its former stature as a culinary masterpiece." Notwithstanding these passionate entreaties we are bound to examine with detachment the nature of fish chowder and what might happen to it under varying interpretations of the Uniform Commercial Code.

Chowder is an ancient dish preexisting even the appetites of our seamen and fishermen. . . . The word "chowder" comes from the French *chaudiere* meaning a "cauldron" or "pot." In the fishing villages of Brittany . . . *faire la chaudiere* means to supply a cauldron in which is cooked a mess of fish and biscuit with some savoury condiments, a hodge-podge contributed by the fishermen themselves, each of whom in return receives his share of the prepared dish. The Breton fishermen probably carried the custom to Newfoundland, long famous for its chowder, whence it has spread to Nova Scotia, New Brunswick, and New England. . . . Our literature over the years abounds in references not only to the delights of chowder but also to its manufacture. A namesake of the plaintiff, Daniel Webster, had a recipe for fish chowder that has survived into a number of modern cookbooks and in which the removal of fish bones is not mentioned at all. One old time recipe recited in the New English Dictionary study defines chowder as "A dish made of fresh fish (esp. cod) or clams, stewed with slices of pork or bacon, onions, and biscuit. Cider and champagne are sometimes added. Hawthorne speaks of

". . . [a] codfish of sixty pounds, caught in the bay, [which] had been dissolved into the rich liquid of a chowder." A chowder variant, cod "Muddle," was made in Plymouth in the 1890s by taking "a three or four pound codfish, head added. Season with salt and pepper and boil in just enough water to keep from burning. When cooked, add milk and piece of butter." The recitation of these ancient formulae suffices to indicate that in the construction of chowders in these parts in other years, worries about fish bones played no role whatsoever. This broad outlook on chowders has persisted in more modern cookbooks. "The chowder of today is much the same as the old chowder. . . ." The all-embracing Fannie Farmer states in a portion of her recipe, fish chowder is made with a "fish skinned, but head and tail left on. Cut off head and tail and remove fish from backbone. Cut fish in 2-inch pieces and set aside. Put head, tail, and backbone broken in pieces, in stewpan; add 2 cups cold water and bring slowly to boiling point. . . ." The liquor thus produced from the bones is added to the balance of the chowder. . . .

Thus, we consider a dish that for many long years, if well made, has been made generally as outlined above. It is not too much to say that a person sitting down in New England to consume a good New England fish chowder embarks on a gustatory adventure which may entail the removal of some fish bones from his bowl as he proceeds. We are not inclined to tamper with age-old recipes by any amendment reflecting the plaintiff's view of the effect of the Uniform Commercial Code upon them. We are aware of the heavy body of case law involving foreign substances in food, but we sense a strong distinction between them and those relative to unwholesomeness of the food itself, e.g., tainted mackerel[on the one hand] . . . and a fish bone in a fish chowder [on the other]. Certain Massachusetts cooks might cavil at the ingredients contained in the chowder in this case in that it lacked the heartening lift of salt port. In any event, we consider that the joys of life in New England include the ready availability of fresh fish chowder. We should be prepared to cope with the hazards of fish bones, the occasional presence of which in chowders is, it seems to us, to be anticipated, and which, in the light of a hallowed tradition, do not impair their fitness or merchantability . . . We are most impressed by *Allen v. Grafton*, 170 Ohio St. 249, 164 N.E.2d 167, where in Ohio, the Midwest, in a case where the plaintiff was injured by a piece of oyster shell in an order of fried oysters. Mr. Justice Taft (now Chief Justice) in a majority opinion held that "the possible presence of a piece of oyster shell in or attached to an oyster is so well known to anyone who eats oysters that we can say as a matter of law that one who eats oysters can reasonably anticipate and guard against eating such a piece of shell. . ."

Thus, while we sympathize with the plaintiff who has suffered a peculiarly New England injury. . . .

Judgment for the defendant.

CASE QUESTION

1. The court's decision was based in part on its belief that people who eat fish chowder anticipate and expect that it will contain occasional bones. Do you agree? Do you think the decision would have been different if the plaintiff came from Nebraska?

In a similar case, the court, relying on *Webster*, ruled that an occasional piece of clam shell in a bowl of clam chowder should be reasonably expected. The court therefore decided in favor of a grocery store that sold a can of clam chowder to plaintiff, who injured a molar when she bit down on a piece of clam shell while eating the soup. *Koperwas v. Publix Supermarkets, Inc., 534 So.2d 872 (Fla., 1988).*

Trend Toward the Reasonable Expectation Test

In judging the merchantability of food, courts recently have been favoring the reasonable expectation rule over a strict application of the foreign/natural test, at least in part because even the presence of natural substances can sometimes render food unfit. The Florida court explained it well in *Zabner v. Howard Johnson's, Inc.*, 201 So.2d 824 (Fla., 1967):

> *The reasoning applied in [the foreign/natural] test is fallacious because it assumes that all substances which are natural to the food in one stage or another of preparation are, in fact, anticipated by the average consumer in the final product served. It does not logically follow that every product which contains some chicken must as a matter of law be expected to contain occasionally or frequently chicken bones or chicken-bone slivers [just] because chicken bones are natural to chicken meat and both have a common origin. Categorizing a substance as foreign or natural is not determinative of what is unfit or harmful in fact for human consumption. A nutshell natural to nut meat can cause as much harm as a foreign substance, such as a pebble, piece of wire or glass. All are indigestible and likely to cause the injury.*

The plaintiff in *Zabner*, while eating maple walnut ice cream, suffered punctured gums and fractured teeth from the presence in the ice cream of a walnut shell. The court held the shell, although a natural substance, could not be reasonably anticipated and thus its presence violated the warranty of merchantability.

In a case from the State of Washington, plaintiff ordered a crab melt open sandwich which consisted of a toasted English muffin topped with shredded crab meat, melted cheese, and chopped parsley. Plaintiff bit into the sandwich and swallowed a one-inch piece of crab shell. Surgery was necessary to remove the shell from plaintiff's esophagus. If Washington followed the foreign/natural test, the shell would have been deemed natural and the restaurant would not have been liable. But the state adopted the reasonable expectation rule. The court held the presence of the shell would not be reasonably anticipated and so constituted a breach of the warranty of merchantability. *Jefferies v. Clark's Restaurant Enterprises, Inc.*, 580 P.2d 1103 (Wash., 1978).

In *Johnson v. C.F.M., Inc.*, 726 F.Supp. 1228 (Kansas, 1989), plaintiff purchased from a convenience store a cup of coffee that contained a considerable amount of coffee grounds. She became ill when she drank it and sued the store. Had the court applied the foreign/natural test, it would have dismissed the case. Instead, the court applied the reasonable expectation test and referred the case to trial, leaving it up to a jury to decide whether the coffee grounds should have been reasonably anticipated.

In *Jackson v. Nestle-Beach, Inc.*, 569 N.E.2d 1119 (Ill., 1991) plaintiff bit into a Katydid, a chocolate-covered pecan-caramel candy, and broke a tooth on a hard pecan shell embedded in it. Had the court applied the foreign/natural test, the case would have been dismissed. Instead the court applied the reasonable expectation test and referred the case to trial.

Consider a case in which the state applies the reasonable expectation test and the object found in the food is foreign. In most such cases the object will be unexpected, so the food vendor will be liable for breach of warranty. For example, human blood would not be expected in biscuits and gravy purchased from a restaurant. A plaintiff found same when she opened the styrofoam container in which her take-out breakfast was delivered. The preparer had not sufficiently bandaged a cut on her arm. *Flagstar Enterprises, Inc. v. Davis*, 997 WL 564475 (Ala., 1997). Likewise, two AA batteries would not be expected at the bottom of a Diet Coke can. Their presence constitutes a breach of the implied warranty of merchantability. A verdict in plaintiff's favor in the amount of $554,000 was upheld on appeal. *Vamos v. Coca-Cola Bottling Company of New York, Inc.*, 627 N.Y.S.2d 265 (N.Y., 1995).

The following case also illustrates this point.

CASE EXAMPLE 12–2

Coulter v. American Bakeries Co.
530 So.2d 1009 (Fla., 1988)

. . . The uncontroverted evidence presented at trial revealed that appellant had purchased doughnuts manufactured by appellee and sealed in their original package. She opened the package in her automobile and in the course of driving to her destination consumed several pieces of one doughnut by breaking them off with her fingers and popping them into her mouth. Because of an abscessed tooth and sore jaw, instead of chewing the doughnut with her teeth, appellant would sip milk through a straw allowing the doughnut to dissolve in her mouth. In fact, it was the dissolving nature of the doughnut which had prompted appellant to purchase that particular product. Shortly after she began consuming the doughnut, she felt something

stick in her throat and immediately ceased ingestion. It was later discovered through x-rays the same day that appellant had consumed a piece containing a metal wire and caused her subsequent injury.

A complaint was filed alleging breach of implied warranty in that the doughnuts were unfit for human consumption. . . .

In a breach of an implied warranty action based on the presence of a harmful substance in food, the test of whether the presence of the harmful substance constitutes a breach of implied warranty is whether the consumer can reasonably expect to find the substance in the food as served. . . .

Applying the foregoing to the instant case, there was simply no evidence that appellant could have expected to find a wire in the doughnut. . . . [J]udgment in favor of appellant.

In an occasional case a foreign object may be determined to be reasonably expected by the diner. In *Clime v. Dewey Beach Enterprises, Inc.*, 831 F. supp. 341 (Del., 1993), plaintiff suffered a serious illness from eating raw shellfish that contained bacteria. Expert testimony established that most people who eat that bacteria suffer only minor digestive tract discomfort. However, if the diner has a compromised immune system or liver disease, he will suffer a more severe reaction. Plaintiff had a liver condition and sued the restaurant for breach of warranty of merchantability. Expert testimony established that the bacteria was common in the waters off North America and taken in by filter feeding organisms such as clams. The court thus found that one who eats raw clams should expect the presence of substances that are indigenous to clams in their natural state, including the bacteria at issue in this case.

Other Grounds for Breach of Warranty of Merchantability

Foreign or unexpected objects in food are not the only basis for liability based on the sale of food. Other grounds include improper food handling and preparation that result in unwholesome food, that is, food not fit for human consumption or harmful if eaten. If the food is unfit, the warranty of merchantability is breached.

Class Action

A restaurant's failure to properly handle or prepare food could result in not just one customer becoming ill but in some cases many will be sick. If numerous people are made sick from the same unsanitary and unhealthy food handling practices, they may be able to ease the expense of the lawsuit by bringing a **class action**. This is a proceeding pursued on behalf of many people who were injured by the same cause, and whose cases raise legal issues in common. Due to the decreased expense and relative ease of participating in a class action, potential plaintiffs who might not otherwise sue will assert a claim in a class action, thus expanding the liability exposure for the defendant. In *McFadden v. Staley*, 687 So.2d 357 (Fl., 1997), the complaint alleged that several hundred people contracted salmonella poisoning or other gastrointestinal ailments as a result of unsanitary and unsafe practices at defendant's restaurant. The court authorized those who became ill to pursue the case against the restaurant as a class action.

Hot Beverages

Food establishments need to exercise caution when serving hot beverages. An elderly woman won a multimillion dollar verdict against McDonald's after she was scalded by spilling hot coffee on her lap. A judge later reduced the amount of the verdict, but the fast-food restaurant nonetheless was forced to pay the plaintiff for her injuries. Numerous similar lawsuits followed involving not only coffee but also hot tea and other hot beverages.

To avoid liability in this type of case, a restaurant should take several precautions. The temperature at which the drink is served should not be such as will cause burns if spilled. Cooler than near-boiling will suffice. Automatic tea and coffee makers can be preset to dispense the drink at a safe-to-dispense temperature. Hot beverages served at a buffet should be capped when handing them to customers. The caps should have a lift-off tab so customers can add sugar and cream without having to remove the cap. Wait personnel should avoid placing hot beverages near a child. Finally, if the drink is extremely hot, warn the customer either orally when the beverage is served, or in writing by placing a notice on the cup. McDonald's now places a warning on its cups that reads, "Caution: Contents Hot." Cups at Starbucks, the coffee chain, states, "Careful, the beverage you are about to enjoy is extremely hot." Both notices alert the customer to be cautious.

Pork and Trichinosis

It is well known that uncooked pork often contains a parasite that can cause trichinosis, a life-threatening disease. When the pork is properly cooked the parasite dies and the threat of trichinosis is eliminated. In *Horn v. South Shore Service, Inc.*, 529 N.Y.S.2d 129 (1988), plaintiff Theresa Horn purchased a beef product from defendant butcher, South Shore Service, Inc. which was intended to be eaten without cooking. Unknown to Horn, South Shore had combined some raw pork with the beef. The pork contained trichina spirulis. As intended, Horn ate the beef product without cooking it. As a result she developed trichinosis. She sued South Shore and its supplier, Scaminaci, for breach of the warranty of merchantability.

The facts strongly supported Horn's claim that South Shore breached the warranty of merchantability by selling raw pork mixed in a product intended to be eaten without first cooking it. The facts as to Scaminaci support a different outcome. Scaminaci denied that it breached the warranty and the court agreed. The pork itself was not unfit for human consumption; cooking it would have eliminated the trichinosis problem. Therefore Scaminaci did not sell a defective product. While South Shore misused the raw pork by mixing it with beef intended to be eaten raw, Scaminaci could not have foreseen the butcher's improper use and so was not liable for South Shore's breach.

Proof Problems

A plaintiff in a breach of warranty action must prove that the food purchased at defendant's establishment was the cause of an injury. When a person eats in a restaurant or buys take-out food and later becomes ill, is that sufficient proof that the food from the restaurant caused the illness? The answer, of course, is no. The food that made plaintiff sick may have originated in plaintiff's refrigerator. Or the illness may have been caused by something other than bad food. To win the case, plaintiff must prove that the food was purchased from defendant's establishment, the food was unwholesome, and it caused the illness. In the following case plaintiff failed to prove that the food was unfit for human consumption.

CASE EXAMPLE 12-3

Renna v. Bishop's Cafeteria Co. of Omaha
218 N.W.2d 246 (Neb., 1974)

Plaintiff seeks to recover damages as a result of being served food which was allegedly unwhole- some, adulterated, and not fit for human consumption. . . .

Plaintiff had breakfast at Bishop's Cafeteria in Omaha at approximately 9:20 A.M., October 25, 1968. Plaintiff, who was 63 years of age, had eaten a light lunch and a light evening meal the previous day and had nothing else to eat until this breakfast which consisted of several grapefruit sections, two fried eggs, hash browns, a roll, and a cup of coffee. He had eaten lightly the day before pursuant to his physician's instructions, preparatory for a cholesterol test which was made approximately an hour before his breakfast at Bishop's. Plaintiff testified the eggs were on the cool side and didn't taste just right. He began to experience stomach pains about 12:30 P.M. that day. These pains were mild at first but shortly became more severe and he began to feel nauseated, vomited, and experience diarrhea. He was admitted to the hospital at approximately 6 P.M. that day.

Doctor Maurice F. Stoner, who had been plaintiff's personal physician for a number of years, diagnosed plaintiff's affliction as acute pancreatitis, and stated his opinion that the precipitating cause was the food purchased at Bishop's Cafeteria. He found no evidence of either food poisoning or food infection in treating plaintiff, but the hospital did not look for such evidence. Doctor Stoner stated in regard to acute pancreatitis there is an underlying cause which no one understands and a precipitating cause. The precipitating cause could be alcohol, gallstones, emotional upset, or a hearty meal. The doctor felt the meal which plaintiff consumed at Bishop's Cafeteria was a hearty meal. It was his testimony that a wholesome meal could be the precipitating cause and could bring on the symptoms of pancreatitis. He also testified that fasting followed by a hearty meal could bring on symptoms of pancreatitis, whether the food was wholesome or otherwise. Plaintiff's doctor was unable to state with reasonable medical certainty that plaintiff consumed infected or poisoned food on October 25, 1968. He had no opinion as to whether plaintiff was suffering from food poisoning or food infection when he examined plaintiff at the hospital. He further testified that it would be speculation to say plaintiff had food poisoning or food infection.

A restaurateur engaged in serving food to paying guests for immediate consumption on the premises impliedly warrants that the food so served is wholesome and fit for human consumption and is liable for injuries to such person proximately caused by a breach thereof without proof of negligence. . . . Before this rule becomes applicable, however, there must be proof that the food sold is unwholesome and not fit for human consumption. Plaintiff wholly failed to produce proof to sustain this issue.

True, plaintiff experienced difficulties approximately 3 hours after consuming his breakfast. His personal physician diagnosed his ailment as acute pancreatitis and testified the precipitating cause was the food consumed at Bishop's Cafeteria. However, he could not say that this meant the food was unwholesome, or tainted in any way. He testified a wholesome meal could have had the same effect. Doctor Stoner had no opinion as to whether plaintiff was suffering food poisoning or food infection when he examined him at the hospital. He further testified it would be speculation to say that food poisoning or food infection was present. The most plaintiff proved is he became ill following the ingestion of his breakfast at Bishop's. This, however, does not prove that the food eaten was unwholesome. His medical evidence indicates his condition could have been brought on because he ate a hearty breakfast after fasting.

The judgment [in favor of the cafeteria] is affirmed.

CASE QUESTIONS

1. How did the testimony of the plaintiff's doctor support the defendant's position?
2. Give two examples of facts that would have established that the food was unwholesome.

In a case in which plaintiff alleged flu-like symptoms from the presence of a worm in a can of string beans purchased at a grocery store, the court dismissed the complaint due to plaintiff's failure to prove the cause of her illness was the worm. Said the court, "The mere fact that the plaintiff became nauseous about one-half hour after consuming some of the contents of the can is insufficient [to avoid dismissal of the complaint.] There are many different causes of nausea, vomiting and stomach distress. Moreover, the report of the plaintiff's own examining physician, in describing her visit to his office the day after the alleged incident, makes no reference to the incident." . . . *Valenti v. Great Atlantic & Pacific Tea Company*, 615 N.Y.S.2d 84 (1994).

Similarly, a diner at a Kentucky Fried Chicken noticed that his chicken "smelled kind of funny" and "didn't taste right." A day and several meals later, he developed severe abdominal pains. A doctor stated that his condition was consistent with improperly cooked poultry or meat but "chicken was at the top of the list" of culprits. Plaintiff had eaten bacon since his KFC meal. The trial court dismissed the case, ruling that the proof of proximate cause was insufficient. The appellate court reversed and ordered that the case proceed to trial so that a jury could decide whether the evidence of proximate cause was sufficient. *McCarley v. West Quality Food Service*, 948 S.W.2d 477 (Tenn., 1997).

Restaurant as Insurer of Wholesomeness

As we have stated, the law renders a restaurant a virtual insurer of the fitness of the food it serves. The court in the previous case referenced this when it stated that a restaurant that serves unwholesome food is liable "without proof of negligence". This means that if the food is not fit for human consumption, the restaurant is liable regardless of cause. For example, assume a restaurant serves cereal in unopened, portion-size boxes delivered from the manufacturer. Unknown to the restaurant, the cereal in one of the boxes is unwholesome. A customer who becomes ill from the cereal should be successful in a lawsuit against the restaurant even though the restaurant was not negligent. If the restaurant can prove the cereal was unwholesome when it was delivered to the restaurant by the supplier, the restaurant should win in a breach of warranty lawsuit against the supplier.

Privity of Contract

Under common law, a direct contractual relationship was required between the plaintiff and the defendant in a breach of warranty action. The relationship between parties to a contract is called **privity of contract**. If you go into a store and purchase a can of corn and the corn is unwholesome and makes you ill, you will be able to sue the store because you had a contractual relationship with it. If, however, you ate the corn as a guest at a wedding reception held at a restaurant, you are not in privity of contract with the restaurant and so your right to sue the restaurant may be questioned.

Some states have relaxed the requirement of privity to some extent. In *Conklin v. Hotel Waldorf Astoria*, 161 N.Y.S.2d 205 (1957), a hotel guest invited a friend to lunch at the hotel. The friend was injured by a piece of glass in a roll. The bill for the meal was paid by the hotel guest. When the friend sued the hotel, it denied liability on the ground she was not in privity of contract with the hotel. The court rejected this argument, holding that the hotel, by accepting the plaintiff's order, impliedly contracted with her even though she did not pay the bill. Another state with a more rigid approach to privity might have held against the plaintiff.

When the UCC was adopted, the states were in disagreement about how much to relax the privity rule. To accommodate all positions, the UCC contains three different rules concerning privity; each state selects the one it prefers. The effect is uneven application of the law. The most restrictive option limits the benefits of the warranty to the buyer, the buyer's family, and the buyer's household guests. The broadest alternative covers any person who may reasonably be expected to consume the food. UCC 2-318.

Strict Products Liability

To alleviate the privity requirement, most states have adopted a cause of action called strict products liability based in tort law rather than contracts so that privity is not required. To sue in strict products liability, a plaintiff must prove only three elements: (1) defendant sold a product in a defective condition, such as food that was unwholesome; (2) plaintiff was injured; and (3) the injury was caused by the defect. Strict products liability eliminates the requirement of privity and enhances a plaintiff's chances of success in a lawsuit based on defective food.

A restaurant unknowingly bought eggs contaminated with salmonella. The presence of the salmonella deemed the eggs defective. An employee of the restaurant ate some of the eggs and became ill. The employee could sue the restaurant for strict products liability although the employee was not in privity with the supplier. *Bacci Restaurant v. Sunrise Produce Co.*, 1995 WL 774387 (Conn., 1995).

Another strict products liability action involved a hamburger purchased by a diner which contained a hard piece of plastic. The customer choked on the plastic as she tried to eat the hamburger, resulting in serious injuries. *Williams v. McDonald's of Torrington*, 1997 WL 276308 (Conn., 1997). The presence of the plastic made the hamburger defective.

If the cause of illness is inherent in the food, poses no threat to most people, and the restaurant took precautionary measures to protect diners from the illness the food will not be considered defective. Therefore, the restaurant will not be liable for strict products liability when a customer becomes ill. A patron of a Louisiana restaurant died from eating oysters that contained a rare bacteria that poses no threat to a healthy person but can be lethal to someone with a weakened immune system. His family sued the restaurant and the restaurant's suppliers. The court dismissed the action against both defendants. The bacteria was in the oysters when they were harvested from the sea and affected very few people. The restaurant took many precautions to prevent contamination of the oysters. Restaurant employees carefully stocked and refrigerated the oysters, and restaurant personnel used approved sanitary procedures for shucking them. Similarly, the supplier followed state regulations, purchasing oysters only from licensed fishermen who harvested from state-approved oyster beds. *Simeon v. The Sweet Pepper Grill*, 618 So.2d 848 (La., 1993).

Negligence

An additional basis for suing a restaurant that serves unhealthy food is negligence. For example, a restaurant that served a glass of water to a diner was liable for negligence where the water was contaminated with chlorine cleaning solution and the guest became ill as a result. But for an employee's carelessness, the water would not have contained detergent. *Waddell v. Shoney's, Inc.*, 664 So.2d 1134 (Fl., 1995).

Choice of Action

A diner who is served defective food may have three bases on which to sue: breach of warranty, strict products liability, and negligence. How does the plaintiff determine in a given case which cause of action to pursue? Some states by statute limit the plaintiff to a choice of one ground to sue for unhealthy food. Absent such a statute, the plaintiff will usually include in the complaint all three causes of action, hoping to prove at least one of them. For example, a restaurant diner who found a roach on his pizza sued the restaurant and referenced all three causes of action is his complaint. *Cooke v. Pizza Hut, Inc.*, 1994 WL 680051 (Del., 1994). The plaintiff will collect her damages only once even if she can prove more than one ground for recovery.

Customers with Allergies

Restaurants must abide by guests requests for elimination of certain ingredients from their food. These requests are often prompted by allergies. If the restaurant fails to honor the request and the customer suffers an allergic reaction from having eaten the offending food, the restaurant may be liable. In one case, a child's mother sent back a first serving of ice cream because it contained nuts to which the child was allergic. The restaurant merely scraped off the nuts and squirted some fresh whipped cream on top and returned the ice cream to the customer. The child ate the ice cream and went into anaphylactic shock from the residue of the nuts.

When food is rejected by a patron for any reason, wise policy mandates that substitute food be served and that it be presented on a clean dish. From a food allergy standpoint, if only the offending ingredient is removed and the balance of the food is returned to the customer on the same plate, the residue may cause an allergic reaction.

False Food Claims

Restaurants often make various claims about the food they sell. These representations may refer to health or nutritional benefits, methods of preparation, or other attributes. The law requires that such representations be truthful. False claims can lead to prosecution.

Truth-in-Menu Laws

Most states have laws seeking to eliminate misleading food advertisements and labels. Some states have laws that specifically outlaw untruthful statements on menus. Other states have general statutes that bar "unfair trade practices" that have been interpreted to apply to fraudulent food claims. For example, orange juice made from concentrate cannot be promoted as "fresh." Long Island duck must originate on Long Island. Similarly, syrup billed as "made in Vermont" must have been made in Vermont. Kentucky Fried Chicken was forced to rename its "Lite and Crispy" chicken to "Skinfree Crispy" and pay a fine of $25,000 because the number of calories in the product was virtually identical to the original recipe. Fish or other products that have been frozen cannot be sold as "fresh." Maine lobster is considered sweeter tasting and is more expensive than many lobsters caught elsewhere. If a lobster was not caught in Maine, it cannot be advertised as Maine lobster.

Food Labeling

As the public has become more concerned about health issues, including cholesterol and fat gram intake, health claims can sell a food product. Food producers have tried to capitalize on that interest. Too frequently, manufacturers have stretched the truth or made claims they cannot substantiate.

An example of questionable claims that have been the subject of lawsuits include an advertisement for margarine, a product with a significant fat content, saying it was a "headstart to a healthier heart" and it "does your heart good". Similarly advertisers have overused and misused words such as "light," low-calorie," "low fat," and "low sodium."

A federal labeling law was passed in 1990 called the Nutrition Labeling and Education Act of 1990, 21 United States Code, Section 343. The Food and Drug Administration (FDA), a federal agency charged with overseeing the food and pharmaceutical industries, has promulgated regulations to enforce the act which have an effective date of May 1994. The regulations include the following:

1. Mandatory nutritional labels for all packaged foods.

2. Standardization of serving sizes. This is significant because information such as fat grams and calories are based on serving sizes. Before the effective date of the act, food purveyors used varying serving sizes, making comparison shopping difficult. Companies often used an artificially small serving size, making the nutritional information such as calories and grams look unjustifiably appealing.

3. Regulation and standardization of words such as "light," "cholesterol-free," and "low calorie."

4. Mandatory labeling of fat content by weight, specifying both total fat and saturated fat.

5. Mandatory labeling of fiber content by weight.

6. Mandatory labeling of the content of the following as percents of the U.S. Recommended Daily Allowance (RDA): total fat, saturated fat, cholesterol, sodium, carbohydrates, and fiber.

7. Limitations on health claims. The statute specifies the permissible food/disease-avoidance relationships. Furthermore, it permits only claims that the food "may" or "might" reduce the risk of disease.

Special regulations were promulgated for restaurants. Whenever a restaurant makes a claim about the nutrient content (for example, "low sodium" or "light") or the healthfulness of a food product (for example, "fiber helps to prevent cancer"), the restaurant is required to provide to patrons upon their request the information required to be on a label of packaged food. As initially adopted, these regulations did not apply to health and nutrient content claims made on menus but rather only those made on signs, placards, or posters in the restaurant. The menu exclusion was challenged in court by a public interest consumer group. It noted that almost half the American food dollar is spent on food consumed away from home, and argued that restaurant menus often contain misleading or false representations about the nutritional and health value of the food. The court held the exclusion of menus from the regulations was unauthorized. As a result, all restaurants that make health or nutrient content claims on their menus must now provide the mandated nutritional information. *Public Citizen, Inc. v. Shalala*, 932 F. Supp. 13 (D.C., 1996).

However, the information is still not required to be included on the menu. Instead, the information need only be available "upon request."

Claims by restaurants that food has certain nutrient content can be based upon information from nutrient data bases, cookbooks, analyses, "or by other reasonable bases that provide assurance that the food or meal meets the nutrient requirements for the claim." 21 C.F.R. §101.10.

Further, if a restaurant uses as descriptors of its menu items any terms defined by the Act or regulations, the restaurant must comply with those definitions. Thus, if a restaurant promotes a menu item as "light," that item must meet the standard for that term as developed by the FDA.

Kosher Foods

Some Jewish people eat only kosher food; that is, food prepared consistent with religious requirements. For example, those requirements mandate for meat the method of slaughter and the time within which processing must occur following slaughter. They also prohibit certain foods regardless of method of slaughter or preparation, such as pork and seafood without scales or fins (lobster, crab, scallops).

When food is labeled as kosher, the label suggests the food has been prepared in accordance with those requirements. People who keep kosher have a right to expect that a restaurant advertising kosher food will serve food prepared as required by religious rules.

The preparation of kosher food is supervised by a rabbi (Jewish clergy) or a representative selected by the rabbi. Without the rabbi's verification that the food has been properly prepared to merit the designation of kosher, it cannot be advertised as such.

Laws in most states prohibit advertising food as kosher unless it is. Promoting non-kosher food as kosher violates these laws. In New York and Florida, two states with large Jewish populations, this type of fraud constitutes a crime.

Relationships Between Fast-food Operations and Hotels

An expanded relationship is developing between fast-food restaurants and hotels. For example, some Marriott Hotels now offer Pizza Hut pizzas on their room service menu. Although most Marriotts already have restaurants and room service, brand name pizza has proven to be a popular item, benefiting both Marriott and Pizza Hut. The relationship between the two companies is a contractual one. According to the terms of the contract, the pizza is prepared by Marriott employees. For consistency purposes, Pizza Hut has an interest in ensuring that Marriott employees prepare the pizza in the same way that other Pizza Hut pizzas are made. Therefore, Pizza Hut trains the Marriott employees and provides the ingredients. In return for the training and the right to use the Pizza Hut name, Marriott pays Pizza Hut a licensing fee.

Suppose a Pizza Hut pizza prepared by Marriott employees is unwholesome in some way, perhaps because it contained a tack, and a guest was injured while eating it. Who would be liable? The hotel? Pizza Hut? Both? The answer is that the hotel will most likely be the only one liable, assuming the defect originated there. This is so because the hotel is not an agent of Pizza Hut nor are the employees of Marriott employees of Pizza Hut. The basis of Marriott's liability would be breach of warranty of merchantability, strict products liability, and negligence in the preparation of the food.

In two circumstances, however, Pizza Hut might also be liable. If the defect originated with Pizza Hut, as where Pizza Hut supplies Marriott with the cheese for the pizza and the tack was in the cheese, Pizza Hut and Marriott will both be liable for breach of warranty of merchantability, strict products liability, and possibly negligence. The other circumstance in which Pizza Hut might be liable is where it failed to train Marriott employees properly and the poor training led to the defect. The basis for the liability in this situation would be negligence. Absent these two situations, only Marriott will be liable.

The Marriott-Pizza Hut connection is not the only marriage between fast food and hotel chains. The economy hotels are the fastest growing segment of the lodging industry but few have restaurants. They often encourage family restaurant chains to open an outlet near their buildings. In these situations the hotel and restaurant are two separate, unconnected businesses and, as long as they remain so, neither will be liable for the negligence or breach of warranty of the other. Likewise, the hotel would not be liable in strict products liability for food sold by the restaurant. Days Inn in downtown Atlanta included food from nearby Wendy's on its room service menu. While normally two separate businesses are not liable for each other's wrongful conduct, a guest who became ill from unwholesome food served by a local restaurant endorsed by the hotel may claim the hotel was negligent for endorsing an allegedly substandard restaurant. To avoid this kind of liability, a hotel that includes food on its room service menu from a restaurant not operated by the hotel should make periodic inspections of the restaurant to ensure proper operations. This will help to avoid and defend against accusations of negligence. In the alternative the hotel can include a notice on its menu informing guests that the hotel has no relationship with the restaurant and is not liable for acts of the restaurant.

Smoking Restrictions

Many states and localities are adopting laws that restrict or prohibit smoking in many public buildings, including restaurants. These laws are based on findings that breathing secondhand smoke (smoke caused by others' tobacco) is a carcinogen and significant health hazard for nonsmokers as well as smokers. Typically, the laws that restrict but don't prohibit smoking require that a restaurant designate a nonsmoking area and allocate a certain percentage of seating capacity to it, such as 70 percent. Often restaurants want to maximize the permissible smoking section to accommodate their smoking patrons. An issue in a recent case was whether a restaurant could include in the calculation of total square footage of the dining area a room designated for private parties and only intermittently available for public dining. If the room was included in the calculation, the permissible smoking area would be enlarged. The court held that such a room can be included. *Bleiburg Restaurant, Inc. v. NYC Dept. of Health*, 658 N.Y.S.2d 574 (1997).

An avid cigar-smoker challenged New York City's anti-smoking law, one of the toughest in the nation, as it relates to cigars. He claimed no reliable scientific study established that secondary cigar smoke was harmful. A court rejected his claim, finding sufficient basis for the belief that secondary cigar smoke subjected nonsmokers to health risks. *Beatie v. City of NY*, N.Y.L.J., 8/7/96.

Generally, the enforcement officer for smoking regulations is the county board of health, and the penalty is a fine of several hundred dollars.

Alcoholic Beverages and the Hospitality Industry

The government has long been concerned about the sale of alcohol. Those who abuse alcohol risk injury to themselves and to others because an intoxicated person has diminished physical coordination and loses inhibitions. The injuries might result from a car accident, a fight, or other mishap. To curb such incidents, each state highly regulates the sale of liquor. Regulations include limitations on who can sell it, who can buy it, and even on the days and times it can be sold.

To obtain a license to sell alcohol, a restaurant or hotel must apply to the state. In most states, to qualify for a license the applicant must prove he has not abused liquor in the past, whether as a consumer, a seller, a driver, or otherwise;

has not been convicted of a felony; and is otherwise of good character and fitness.

A liquor license, once granted, may be revoked or suspended by the state if the licensee violates the liquor laws. In most states, sales are prohibited to people under age 21, visibly intoxicated persons, and habitual drunkards.

Sales to anyone on this prohibited list may result in suspension or revocation of a liquor license. It can also lead to civil liability for resulting injuries and, particularly in the case of serving a young person, criminal liability for which penalties include jail and a fine. Great care should be taken to avoid illegal sales.

Sales to Underage Patrons

People under age 21 often try to finagle their way into a bar to be served. A licensee (a bar or restaurant with a liquor license) must develop and strictly enforce rules and procedures to ensure that proper proof of age is obtained before alcohol is served. Frequent reinforcement by management of the importance of verifying age is necessary in the effort to reduce incidents of underage service. State statutes often provide a defense to a charge of serving someone under 21 where the young person displayed to the licensee an identification card with a photograph "apparently" issued by a governmental entity and the licensee had implemented a written policy requiring such identification. Interestingly, in many states it is illegal for people under 21 to misrepresent their age or present false identification. In such states, young people presenting false IDs or otherwise claiming to be older than they are face criminal prosecution.

Sometimes a person of legal age purchases alcohol and gives it to someone underage. You may think that the licensee is not liable in these situations. If the licensee had no reason to know that the underage person would gain access to the alcohol, the seller will not be liable. For example, in *Jones v. B.P. Oil, Inc.*, 632 So.2d 435 (Ala., 1994), a person bought beer from a convenience store. After exiting the store and proceeding beyond the sight of the sales clerk, he gave some of the beer to his underage friend who was driving. A car accident resulted, and the injured party sued the convenience store. The store was held not liable due to the absence of evidence that the store owner knew or should have known that the purchaser would share it with an underage person.

If, however, the circumstances are such that the licensee should have known that the adult purchased the beverages for the minor's use, the sale may be illegal. In one case a minor asked his adult neighbor to purchase beer for him. The neighbor agreed and together the two went to a beer distributor. An employee of the distributor approached the car and the neighbor placed the order. After the beer was put in the car the employee sought payment. The neighbor looked at the minor, who took money from a mug he was holding and handed it to the neighbor who in turn gave it to the employee. Apparently the amount was insufficient because the employee returned to the car seeking additional money and again the neighbor looked to the minor, who withdrew additional money from the mug. After leaving the store and consuming the beer, the minor climbed an electrical transmission tower, came into contact with a high voltage line, was burned, and fell 100 feet to the ground resulting in serious injury. Pennsylvania, where the case occurred, holds a licensee liable to a minor if the minor is served alcohol and is injured as a result. The minor's parents sued the beer distributor for damages. The trial court dismissed the case, holding that the sale by the beer distributor was made to the neighbor and not the minor. On appeal the case was referred to trial on the ground that a jury might determine that the beer distributor should have known the actual purchaser was the minor. *Thomas v. Duquesne Light Co.*, 545 A.2d 289 (Penn., 1988).

This case instructs us that licensees must be alert to circumstances where an apparent purchase by an adult is in reality an illegal purchase by a minor. Failure to detect such illegal purchases can result in liability and loss of license.

Often the laws that prohibit underage drinking include an exception for an academic course in which tasting alcohol is required for instructional purposes. Part of your curriculum may include such a course on bartending.

Sales to People Who Are Visibly Intoxicated

Sales of alcohol to people who are visibly intoxicated is illegal. To quality as illegal the person's appearance or actions must indicate he is intoxicated. A factual determination of intoxication cannot be made solely on the basis of how much alcohol a person has consumed because the effects of alcohol may differ greatly from person to person. Thus, where the evidence in a case suggested the patrons were served four or five bottles of beer and an equal number of whiskey shots within two hours preceding the incident that resulted in injury, this was not sufficient to establish that defendant was visibly intoxicated. *Shar v. Schmidli*, 653 N.Y.S.2d 468 (1997).

Although intoxication is sometimes difficult to detect, that may not be a defense to a charge of illegal sale. While the sale is only illegal if the customer is "visibly" intoxicated, bartenders and wait personnel are expected to be familiar with indicia of intoxication. Servers must be trained to identify them. They include slurred speech, bloodshot and watery eyes, flushed face, and poor coordination which is often evidenced by difficulty in performing such acts as making change or handling money, lighting a cigarette, or walking without staggering or stumbling. Evidence of intoxication can also include being overly friendly, boisterous, loud, argumentative, aggressive, crude, and annoying to other customers, to mention only a few. Good training videotapes, developed by the National Restaurant Association and the American Hotel and Motel Association, are available to instruct bartenders and wait personnel on how to recognize intoxication. Training materials also cover such topics as how to manage the dispensing of alcoholic beverages, how to manage customers' consumption of alcoholic beverages, how to prevent service to underage or intoxicated customers, how to prevent an intoxicated customer from driving, and what to do if those efforts fail. In addition to initial employee training, frequent refresher courses are an important component of alcohol service training. Employee meetings provide a good opportunity to reinforce the message that alcohol must be served responsibly. Some states, for example Maryland, have laws that require all establishments that serve alcohol to be certified in an alcohol awareness training program.

Errors in who a licensee serves not only put at risk the license to sell alcohol, it also can lead to liability for injuries caused by the wrongly served patron.

Sales to Habitual Drunkards

Sale of alcohol to known habitual drunkards is prohibited. A habitual drunkard is someone who regularly imbibes alcohol and frequently becomes intoxicated. A licensee who serves a known habitual drunkard risks losing his license and may be liable for injuries caused by such person.

Proof of Intoxication

In a lawsuit, intoxication is usually proved in one of two ways. The first, used primarily when a criminal charge of driving while intoxicated is involved, is by showing the percent by weight of alcohol in the person's blood, called the BAC level. The BAC is determined by analyzing the person's blood, breath, urine, or saliva. The most frequent method used is a breathalyzer or intoxilyzer, a device that utilizes a breath sample of the person believed to be intoxicated to make the determination. The test must be done within a few hours of an arrest. In most states, if the percent by weight of alcohol is .10 or higher, the person is legally intoxicated. In an increasing number of states, the number is .08. As the number of alcohol-related accidents increase, more states are considering lowering the percentage rates.

The second way intoxication can be proved is by the indicia of intoxication discussed previously in this chapter. The witnesses can include anyone who observed the patron in an intoxicated state, such as the bartender, wait staff, other customers, and the police.

Alcohol Vendor's Liability under Common Law

Under common law, in most states the licensee was not liable for damages caused when it served alcohol to someone who was under 21, visibly intoxicated, or a habitual drunkard and that person was injured or caused injury to another. Thus, if a wrongfully served customer left a bar, drove a car, and on the way home caused an accident in which the patron or someone else was injured, the bar was not liable. According to this common law rule, the proximate cause of the injuries was the *consumption* and not the *sale* of the liquor. The injured person in the example could sue only the drunk driver; the bar or restaurant that sold the alcohol to the driver was not liable.

As the number of alcohol-related accidents have grown, most states have found the common law rule unsatisfactory. Said one court, "With today's car of steel and speed it becomes a lethal weapon in the hands of a drunken imbiber. The frequency of accidents involving drunk drivers are commonplace. Its affliction of bodily injury to an unsuspecting public is also of common knowledge." *Ohio Casualty Insurance Co. v. Todd*, 813 P.2d 508 (Okla., 1991). A person able to prevent alcohol abuse is the licensee, that is, the bar or restaurant. The common law rule did nothing to encourage the server to prevent patrons from abusing alcohol. Another concern with the common law rule was that many intoxicated persons who cause injury have little money with which to compensate those they injure. The owner of a restaurant or bar is more likely to have insurance and assets.

Alcohol Vendor's Liability under Dram Shop Act

Over time, public policy came to demand more responsibility on the dispenser of alcohol resulting in legislation in many states called **Dram Shop Acts** ("dram shop" is an outdated term for a bar). These acts impose liability on a restaurant or bar for certain injuries resulting from illegal sales. The objectives of dram shop laws are to discourage proprietors from selling alcohol illegally and to afford compensation to victims whose injuries emanate from the unlawful sale of alcohol.

The potential liability is very significant. Some illegal sales have resulted in verdicts that have financially ruined the bar or restaurant that wrongfully served alcohol.

The following quote from *Rappuport v. Nichols*, 156 A.2d 1 (N.J., 1959), explains well the rationale for holding the bar or restaurant liable.

> *When alcoholic beverages are sold by a tavern keeper to a minor or to an intoxicated person, the unreasonable risk of harm not only to the minor or the intoxicated person but also to members of the traveling public may readily be recognized and foreseen; this is particularly evident in current times when traveling by car to and from the tavern is so common-place and accidents resulting from drinking are so frequent. . . .*
>
> *Today, the hazards of travel by automobiles on modern highways have become a national problem. The drunken driver is a threat to the safety of many. It is understandable that early cases did not recognize any duty of an innkeeper to the traveling public because a serious hazard did not exist. [Presumably because at one time cars were not yet invented, and once they were, initially they were not accessible to many people.] It is a well established, sound principle of legal philosophy that the common law is not static. Under the skillful interpretation of our courts, it has been adapted to changing times and conditions of our civilization. . . .*
>
> *The increasing frequency of serious accidents caused by drivers who are intoxicated is a fact which must be well known to those who sell and dispense liquor. This lends support to those cases which have found the automobile accident to be "the reasonably foreseeable" result of furnishing liquor to the intoxicated driver.*

Liability of the bar or restaurant is not restricted to car accidents. Any injury will suffice, including, for example, those resulting from fights.

Alcohol Vendor's Liability to the Patron

When a licensee makes an illegal sale and the person wrongfully served is injured, is the licensee liable to the patron? The answer varies, depending on the state. In most states, dram shop acts do not impose liability for injuries to wrongfully served customers. In these states the act imposes liability only for injuries to a third person. An explanation is provided in *Tobias v. Sports Club, Inc.*, 474 S.E.2d

450 (S.C., 1996). "In our view, a rule which allows an intoxicated individual to hold a tavern owner liable without regard to his own actions in continuing to consume alcohol promotes irresponsibility and rewards drunk driving." In that case, a bar patron drank to excess and was injured in a car accident he caused while driving home. The court affirmed a jury verdict in favor of the bar. In *Jackson v. PKM Corp.*, 422 N.W.2d 657 (Mich., 1988), the plaintiff was injured in a single vehicle accident while driving home from defendant's bar. She claimed that, prior to the accident, she was served alcohol notwithstanding she was visibly intoxicated. The court dismissed the case on the grounds that neither common law nor the state dram shop act imposes liability on a licensee for injuries to a wrongfully served patron.

In *Fisher v. O'Connor's, Inc.*, 452 A.2d 1313 (Md., 1982), plaintiff was allegedly served at defendant's bar after reaching a "visibly intoxicated" condition. While intoxicated, he fell from his stool and permanently injured his leg, requiring the use of a brace and crutches. His action against the bar was dismissed because neither Maryland's dram shop act nor common law permits the patron to sue the licensee.

In *Cuevas v. Royal D'Ibervilee Hotel*, 498 So.2d 346 (Miss., 1986), the plaintiff was attending a medical technician's convention at the defendant hotel where she allegedly was served alcohol after becoming visibly intoxicated. She fell over a railing 30 feet to the lobby floor. Her action for damages against the hotel was likewise dismissed.

A minority of states allow the wrongfully served patron to sue the licensee for resulting injuries. These actions are based not on dram shop acts but on negligence of the licensee. In *Lyons v. Nasby*, 770 P.2d 1250 (Colo., 1989), plaintiff, the decedent's personal representative, claimed the decedent was served at defendant's restaurant when he was visibly intoxicated. While intoxicated he drove his car off a mountain road and was killed. In holding that the plaintiff could sue the restaurant in this circumstance, the court stated,

> We have stated before that a reasonable person would foresee that an inebriate will act without prudence, control or self-restraint. . . We agree that voluntary intoxicated is a self-indulgent act. We also note that a person who voluntarily consumes alcohol to the point of intoxication is at the very least partially responsible for his injuries. However, the fact that the patron has acted in an unacceptable manner should in no way lessen the equally unacceptable conduct of a tavern owner. One who stands behind a bar and serves drink after drink to a visibly intoxicated customer engages in behavior which is as opprobrious as that of the customer. . . . Insulating tavern owners from liability does not send the message that they, as well as their patrons, must be accountable for their actions.

In accord is *Klingerman v. Sol Corp. of Maine*, 505 A.2d 474 (Maine, 1986). Decedent was served an excessive amount of alcohol at defendant's Ramada Inn and died of alcohol poisoning. The court, after determining that the decedent's personal representative could not sue under the state dram shop act, held that plaintiff could sue for negligence.

Whether or not the bar is liable to the patron, a licensee that makes an illegal sale of alcohol faces fines and license suspension. If the illegality is selling to a minor, the bar might also be guilty of a crime.

Alcohol Vendor's Liability to Third Parties

Although licensees in most states will not be liable to a wrongfully served patron injured from the alcohol, licensees can be held liable to others who are injured from the patron's intoxication. For example, if a licensee serves a visibly intoxicated patron who, while driving home, hits another car causing injury to its driver, the licensee will be liable to that driver. Similarly, if an underaged patron is served and, as a result of the alcohol, injures another in a fight, the licensee will be liable to the injured person. For example, in *Grayson Fraternal Order of Eagles v. Claywell*, 736 S.W.2d 328 (Ky., 1987), a visibly intoxicated patron drove from the premises of the licensee and collided with another car, killing one person and seriously injuring another. The court held that the licensee would be liable to the deceased's estate and the person injured.

The potential liability under dram shop acts is very significant. To protect against this liability, tavern keepers should do everything possible to avoid illegal alcohol sales. Employee training is critical. If an error is made, the barkeeper should discourage the wrongly-served patron from driving home. Many restaurants and bars today contract with companies that provide rides home to intoxicated patrons and in some circumstances drive the customer's car home as well.

The practice of managers overseeing service decisions made by bartenders and wait personnel can help to limit liability. In one case involving a proceeding to revoke a restaurant's liquor license, alcohol had allegedly been served to a visibly intoxicated customer. The manager observed the customer's condition and immediately removed the bottle of beer. Based on the facts, the court found for the restaurant. Similar action in a dram shop case might save the licensee from liability.

Alcohol Vendor's Liability to Passengers in Patron's Car

Often when injury results from a car accident, the injured party is a companion of the wrongfully served patron and a passenger in the patron's car. If the passenger did not contribute to the driver's intoxication, the bar or restaurant will be liable. In most states, dram shop acts are interpreted as not imposing liability for the companion's injuries if she caused the driver's intoxication, that is, if the passenger purchased the alcohol and gave it to the driver or encouraged the latter to drink more than he could tolerate. In the following case the court discusses the circumstances under which a passenger's action against the licensee will and will not stand.

CASE EXAMPLE 12-4

Goss v. Richmond
381 N.W.2d 776 (Mich., 1985)

Plaintiff alleged in his dram shop action that defendant Le-Rob, a licensed seller of alcoholic beverages, illegally sold intoxicating liquor to a visibly intoxicated person, defendant Robert Richmond. Richmond allegedly drove his automobile off the road and struck a tree. Plaintiff was a passenger in the Richmond automobile and suffered serious injuries.

Plaintiff testified that he and Richmond purchased pitchers of beer in "rounds," each taking turns buying pitchers. The trial court held that buying such "rounds" amount to buying drinks for defendant Richmond. The court held that, by doing so, plaintiff was noninnocent party under the dram shop act and was thus precluded from proceeding under the act. . . .

Plaintiff argues that his participation in bringing about the injury-producing intoxication should not bar recovery. . . .

The objective of the Legislature in enacting the dram shop act was to discourage bars from selling intoxicating liquors to visibly intoxicated persons and minors and to provide for recovery under certain circumstances by those injured as a result of the sale of intoxicating liquor. . . . To permit one who has been an intentional accessory to the illegality to shift the loss resulting from it to the tavern owner would lead to a result we believe the Legislature did not intend. A person who buys drinks for an obviously intoxicated person, or one whom he knows to be a minor, is at least as much the cause of the resulting or continued intoxication as the bartender who served the consumer illegally. In short, barring recovery by a wrongdoer by holding that the wrongdoer is not among those to whom the Legislature intended to provide a remedy advances both purposes of the act, to suppress illegal sales and to provide a remedy for those injured as a result of the illegality.

Plaintiff next argues that the "innocent party" doctrine as applied in this case denies him equal protection of the laws. Plaintiff claims that, because he could recover if he and defendant Richmond, instead of buying "rounds," would each have purchased their own pitchers and drank side by side, the "innocent party" doctrine as applied in this case creates an arbitrary distinction between persons of the same class. . . .

The material question when a defendant claims a plaintiff is not an "innocent party" under the dram shop act is whether the plaintiff actively participated in the intoxicated person's inebriation. . . .

We do not find the distinction between persons who purchase "rounds" and those who merely accompany the allegedly intoxicated person to be arbitrary. A person who purchases a pitcher of beer knowing that the allegedly intoxicated person will drink therefrom is a more direct participant in the other's intoxication and more directly encourages the other's intoxication than a mere drinking companion. Buying in "rounds" conceivably sets the pace at which the allegedly intoxicated person will consume alcohol and conceivably encourages the allegedly intoxicated person to consume his "fair share."

[Judgment for the licensee] Affirmed.

In *Pollard v. Village of Ovid*, 446 N.W.2d 574 (Mich., 1989), the intoxicated driver's passenger was killed when the car missed the entrance of a bridge and crashed into a wall. The passenger's estate was denied recovery against the bar in which the two had been drinking because the passenger had, on several occasions during the evening, obtained glasses of beer for the driver, and further, had purchased alcohol he and the driver drank while in the car.

In *Prunty v. Keltie's Bum Steer*, 559 N.Y.S.2d 354 (N.Y., 1990), plaintiff passenger had bought "at least one drink" for the driver. The one drink was found to be sufficient to preclude plaintiff's dram shop action against the bar. In *Estate of Darby v. Monroe Oil Co., Inc.*, 488 S.E.2d 828 (N.C., 1997), the passenger, together with several others, were expelled from a bar in which they had been drinking and decided to have a party at one of their houses. The decedent drove his car with the others as passengers to a convenience store to purchase alcohol. Many in the group, but not decedent, contributed money to purchase the beer. When the group left the store en route to the party, decedent turned his keys over to a companion and became a passenger. The driver ran off the road, hit a tree, and all were killed. The court determined that the deceased passenger contributed to the driver's intoxication and thus was denied recovery against the seller of the alcohol. In another case plaintiff passenger had been barhopping with the driver for approximately six hours before the accident but had not purchased any of the driver's drinks. The plaintiff in that case was not prevented from suing the bar. Said the court, "A denial of recovery . . . must be supported by a much more affirmative role than that of drinking companion." *Russell v. Olkowski*, 535 N.Y.S.2d 187 (1988). Similarly, in *Griffin Motel Co. v. Strickland*, 479 S.E.2d 401 (Ga., 1997), the court refused to preclude a lawsuit by the estate of a drinking companion of an intoxicated driver where the companion was a passenger in the car and was killed in a one-car collision caused by the alcohol. No evidence was presented that the passenger had furnished alcohol to the driver.

Two Licensees Serving One Patron

More than one bar or restaurant may be liable in a given case. For example, if a visibly intoxicated person is served first at one bar and then a second one, both will be liable to a third person injured by the patron. The injured person cannot, however, recover twice for the same injuries. Instead, the liability will be allocated between the two bars. If, however, the drinker was not visibly intoxicated while at the first bar, it will not be liable.

Apportionment of Liability Where Plaintiff is Negligent

Where the person injured by the illegally-served drinker is negligent in such a way as to contribute to the cause of the accident, the injured person's recovery will be reduced accordingly. Thus, as in a comparative negligence case (see Chapter 5), the jury will allocate a percentage of the liability to the plaintiff. His recovery against the bar will be reduced by that percentage. *Adamy v. Ziriakus*, 659 N.Y.S.2d 623 (1997).

States without Dram Shop Acts

A few states do not have dram shop acts. Some of them have created a common law basis for holding the licensee liable when an illegally-served patron causes injury to a third party. Other states preclude all actions against the tavern owner for injuries caused by illegal sales. In these states even third parties injured by a wrongfully served patron will not be able to collect from the licensee for their injuries.

Liquor Liability Insurance

A licensee can purchase insurance to cover dram shop liability. This insurance is often called liquor liability insurance or dram shop insurance. The cost is based on numerous factors, including the volume of alcohol sold by the licensee, prior incidents of liability for illegal sales, the nature of the establishment, hours it is open, and the geographical area.

Some states require that liquor license applicants have either liquor liability insurance or a liability bond to cover liability.

New Demands from Convention Sponsors

Companies that sponsor events at hotels or restaurants may be liable to someone injured by an illegally served attendee at the event. For example, in a Florida case, an employer that sponsored a meeting at a hotel was held liable for the employee's alcohol-related accident. The employee had numerous drinks throughout the evening at the hotel bar, including three purchased by the president of his company. The employee lived in the area and so drove home following the evening's activities. The accident occurred on his way home and resulted in the death of two people in the other car. The case occurred in Florida, which exempts licensees from liability in dram shop situations in which the injury was caused by a visibly intoxicated patron. The family of the one of the deceased sued the employer, alleging negligence. A jury trial resulted in a sizeable verdict against the employer. This case underscores yet again the importance of prudent alcohol service for all involved. Companies planning events at a licensee's establishment are being encouraged to demand evidence of the licensee's liquor liability insurance coverage. Further, the host companies should ask for provisions in their contracts obligating the licensee to supervise the liquor service, follow responsible alcohol service procedures, serve alcohol only to those legally entitled to drink, and hold the company harmless (compensate them) for any liability incurred as a result of alcohol at the function.

Strategies to Avoid Liability

As we have seen, liability for illegal alcohol sales can lead to money verdicts against a bar or restaurant and revocation of the liquor license. This liability must be taken very seriously by all licensees. We have already discussed important steps to help reduce liability. These include employee training and refresher courses, oversight of sales by a supervisor, and insisting on driving home intoxicated customers. Other practices that can contribute to reduced risk of liability include the following:

- Adopt internal policies and rules concerning alcohol sales and publish them in an employee newsletter if the licensee has one, and near the employee lounge or near the punch-in clock.

- Promote alternatives to liquor such as bottled waters and distinctive coffees and teas. Train service personnel to offer guests both a wine menu and a water/coffee/tea menu, or combine the two. Treat bottled waters as bottled wines in all aspects of sales and service. Consider the possibility of a special "house" water carrying the licensee's name and logo.

- Offer "minidrinks," that is, less alcohol at a lower price. Frozen drinks with just a touch of alcohol can be fun and appealing.

- Offer non-alcohol wine and beer which, as the name suggests, contain no alcohol.

- For specialty drinks that contain more than the normally expected one to one-and-a-half ounces of liquor, state the quantity of alcohol on the beverage menu.

Alcohol Sales in Hotel Guest Rooms

Many hotel licensees now sell alcohol through vending machines or other mechanical devices in guest rooms. Access to the machine or device is restricted by means of a key or magnetic card. The prohibition against illegal sales applies to these devices. The innkeeper must not provide the key or magnetic card to anyone who is under 21, visibly intoxicated, or a habitual drunkard.

Miscellaneous Regulations on Licensees

Various statutory mandates apply to licensees, depending on the state involved. States have gone to great lengths to control the sale of alcoholic beverages. The purpose of these laws is to foster and promote temperance in the consumption of alcohol, and respect for and compliance with the law. They are enforced by a state agency authorized to issue, suspend, and revoke liquor licenses. The name given to that agency varies from state to state, and will be referred to here as the liquor authority. The penalties for failing to abide by these laws include suspension or revocation of the liquor license and fines. Remember, these regulations vary from state to state.

Age of Alcohol Servers.   Most states specify a minimum age (usually 18 or 19) for workers in establishments that serve alcoholic beverages. No one under that age can be on the wait staff, or sell, dispense, or handle alcohol beverages. Lower minimum age requirements apply to dishwashers or busboys in establishments that serve alcohol. The objective of these regulations is to limit the exposure to alcohol of persons younger than the legal drinking age.

Restrictions on Alcohol Sales on Sunday.   In many locations, alcohol is prohibited from being sold on Sunday before noon. Also, sales for off-premises consumption, such as purchases from a liquor store, may be prohibited all day. The objective of this law is to further the recognition of a sabbath day.

Warnings to Pregnant Women.   Licensees must display a sign close to where alcohol is dispensed stating the following: "Government Warning: According to the Surgeon General, women should not drink alcoholic beverages during pregnancy because of the risk of birth defects." The objective of this law is to caution pregnant women about the risks to the fetus from drinking alcohol.

Prohibition of Illegal Gambling.   A licensee cannot permit the bar or restaurant to be used for illegal gambling. The objective of this law is to prevent illegal conduct from occurring where alcohol is sold.

Prohibition of Disorderly Conduct.   A licensee cannot permit disorderly conduct, such as fighting, solicitation for purposes of prostitution, or lewd or indecent sexual acts or performances in the bar or restaurant. The objective of this law is to minimize the disorderly and illegal conduct that may occur where alcohol is served.

Maintenance of Prescribed Records.   A licensee is required to maintain records of its suppliers, documenting the extent of its daily alcohol purchases and information about the vendor. The objective of this law is to permit the liquor authority to track liquor purchases and sales and determine the volume of sales of particular licensees.

Restrictions on the Type of Alcohol Sold.   States usually offer various types of liquor licenses, including licenses for on-premises consumption, which a restaurant would likely have; licenses for off-premises consumption, which a liquor store would have; licenses authorizing the sale of beer and wine only; licenses authorizing sales of alcohol for one day only; and other types. A licensee with a limited right to sell must abide by the limitations. For example, a licensee with a wine and beer license cannot sell mixed drinks.

Limitations on Sales Promotions.   The licensee may be restricted from utilizing specials such as "two for ones", and novelties such as gifts or prizes, in the sale of alcohol. The purpose of these laws is to encourage moderation in the intake of alcohol. For that reason, these practices should be discouraged even where legal. Under discrimination laws, bars are restricted from having a "ladies night" during which drinks are offered at a reduced price to women but not men. Many bars disregard this prohibition.

Prohibition on Signs That Imply Alcohol Improves Athletic Prowess. The licensee may be prohibited from displaying signs that suggest athletes or others recommend drinking alcohol. The purpose of this law is to discourage over-indulgence.

Proximity to School or Church.   A licensee cannot be located within certain distances, such as 200 feet, from the entrance of a school or place of public worship. The objective is to protect the well-being of students and the tranquility of churches.

Liability for Injuries to Patrons

Restaurateurs and tavern keepers (referred to here collectively as restaurateurs) has a duty to protect a patron from injury caused by another patron when the injury is foreseeable. Restaurateurs have been held liable in several circumstances for failure to control activity on their premises.

Failure to Eject Quarrelsome Patron

One circumstance in which a restaurateur is often found liable is when a patron is injured in a fray with a person who is allowed to remain on the premises despite a known propensity for fighting. The question in cases where the injured patron sues the restaurant is whether the restaurateur had knowledge of the patron's combative tendencies or could have reasonably foreseen the coming attack. If not, the restaurateur will most likely not be liable. In *Stevens v. Spec Inc.*, 637 N.Y.S.2d 979 (1996), plaintiff, a nightclub patron, was struck in the face with a beer bottle by a member of the band during a dispute that started when plaintiff failed to move from the stage area when requested. Plaintiff sued the nightclub claiming it provided insufficient security for the safety of its customers. The court dismissed the case, finding that the altercation was spontaneous and unexpected. Although there had been "three or four" fights in the nightclub within a ten-month period prior to the evening in question, none was similar to the incident in which plaintiff was hurt, and none involved the band member who struck plaintiff.

In two cases involving attacks in restaurant drive-through lines the incidents were found to have occurred "instantly and without warning," thereby relieving the restaurant of liability. In *Callen v. Cale Yarborough Enterprises*, 442 S.E.2d 216 (S.C., 1994), plaintiff was hit with a piece of lumber by a man who was a passenger in the car in front of him. Plaintiff testified the incident occurred quickly and without notice as a result of an argument. The court, noting that the restaurant did not serve alcohol and "does not fit the description of an operation which attracts or provides a climate of crime," held for the restaurant. Similarly, in *Griffin v. V&J Foods, Inc.*, 546 N.W.2d 579 (Wis., 1996), the court dismissed a lawsuit against a restaurant where the plaintiff was shot by a robber while waiting in a drive-through lane. The employee at the window testified that she knew the attacker and had never had trouble with him in the past. Further, the attack occurred "so suddenly that it could not have been prevented by additional security measures. . . ".

If a patron is known to the proprietor as a troublemaker, or circumstances suggest that a disturbance is likely, the owner must take steps to protect other patrons. Failure to do so can lead to liability. In *McFadden v. Bancroft Hotel Corp.*, 46 N.E.2d 573 (Mass., 1943), a military organization held its annual convention in the hotel operated by the defendant. The plaintiff, a conventioneer, was assaulted without provocation while in the grill room. The assailant had attracted attention prior to the attack on plaintiff by hollering, loudly cursing, "swaying around," arguing with other patrons, and threatening to hit one of them. This conduct was observed by several hotel detectives. In the plaintiff's lawsuit against the hotel, the court held for the plaintiff, noting that the hotel had a duty to exercise reasonable care for the safety of its patrons. Because the hotel's agents had witnessed the assailant's erratic behavior prior to the attack, they should have foreseen an incident and removed him from the grill room before the assault.

If restaurant employees are unable to remove the troublemaker, the police should be summoned. In *Dubak v. "Q" Lounge, Inc.*, 559 A.2d 424 (N.J., 1989), a bar was held liable for failing to call the police when the bouncers' repeated efforts to halt a fight were unsuccessful.

In *Shank v. Riker Restaurant Associates, Inc.*, 216 N.Y.S.2d 118, *aff'd.* 222 N.Y.S.2d 683 (1961), an unidentified "hoodlum" using abusive language had been creating a disturbance in the restaurant for over twenty minutes before the plaintiff's entry. At one point he asked for a glass of water and then "drop kicked" it against the kitchen door-spreading water and pieces of glass over a wide area. Despite this conduct he was not ejected by the manager. When plaintiff arrived, the hoodlum first insulted her by calling her vile names, then knocked her to the floor and shoved a heavy metal counter stool into her head, causing a severe fracture of her skull. Plaintiff won her case against the restaurant because it was negligent for not taking action to evict the ruffian when the disturbance began.

The restaurant's duty to intercede or call the police is a strict one. Failure to take remedial action can result in an award of punitive damages. The restaurant in the following case was ordered to pay punitive damages for its failure to intervene in a foreseeable disturbance even though the plaintiff was found partially responsible for her injuries.

CASE EXAMPLE 12–5

Gould v. Taco Bell
722 P.2d 511 (Kan., 1986)

. . . Rosie Gould and her friend, Theresa Holmberg, . . . drove to a Taco Bell restaurant. . . . They arrived at the restaurant at approximately 11:30 P.M. There were six people who all sat together in the booth. After ordering their food, Gould and Holmberg sat down in a booth across from the group. Karen Brown was one of the individuals in that group.

Brown and her companions began engaging in loud, crude and vulgar conversation, designed to be overheard and to shock Gould and Holmberg. Neither Gould nor Holmberg made any comment to Brown or her companions during this conversation. At one point, a Taco Bell employee told the group to quiet down, but the conversation grew louder.

Eventually, the group got up to leave but prior to reaching the exit, Brown stopped and said, "Those two white bitches over there think they're hot shit." Gould was shocked and asked, "Are you talking to us?" When Brown responded, "Yes," Gould requested her to "please come over here and repeat yourself."

Brown responded by suddenly dashing to Gould's booth and striking her in the face with a clenched fist, knocking her sideways and bruising her face and nose. Gould, shocked, called Brown a "nigger." Brown then began hitting Gould with her fists with renewed effort. This beating continued for about thirty seconds until Holmberg inter-

vened by moving between Gould and Brown. She told Brown, "We don't want any trouble." Gould and Holmberg began moving toward the door but Brown kept saying "Come on, hit me, bitch. Come on, I want to fight." Gould and Holmberg continued to insist they did not want to fight, but when they reached the door of the restaurant Brown began beating on Gould again.

During this second exchange, Mark Wills, the assistant manager at the restaurant, watched the altercation as he came out from behind the counter. Wills did not try to stop Brown because he did not want to get involved and for fear Brown would strike him for interfering. Nor did he call the police, since he didn't feel the situation warranted such action. However, Wills did tell Brown, "Why don't you just leave? You did this two weeks before in here."

[A fight in the parking lot ensued.] . . . Holmberg screamed for someone to call the police. The Taco Bell employees did not respond. Holmberg was finally able to break away and ran inside to the food counter and asked Wills (who had followed her back inside) if she could use the phone to call the police. Wills advised her the phone was not for public use. Holmberg threatened to jump over the counter and use the phone. Wills finally reluctantly called the police. . . .

This scared Brown and her companions and they got in their car and left.

Gould filed the present action against Taco Bell, alleging Taco Bell failed to provide security measures sufficient to protect Gould. . . .

The jury found Gould 49% at fault and Taco Bell 51% at fault. They awarded Gould $500 in actual damages and $10,000 in punitive damages. Taco Bell appeals the jury's findings. . . .

A proprietor of an inn, tavern, restaurant, or like business is liable for an assault upon a guest or patron by another guest or third party where the proprietor has reason to anticipate such an assault and fails to exercise reasonable care to forestall or prevent the same.

The duty of a proprietor of a tavern or inn to protect his patrons from injury does not arise until the impending danger becomes apparent to him, or the circumstances are such that a careful and prudent person would be put on notice of the potential danger. . . .

It is not required that notice to the proprietor of such an establishment be long and continued in order that he be subject to liability; it is enough that there be a sequence of conduct sufficient to enable him to act on behalf of his patron's safety. . . .

The evidence in this case was sufficient to establish such a "sequence of conduct." Thus, we hold the jury's verdict against Taco Bell for Gould's injuries is supported by the evidence. . . .

Punitive damages are permitted whenever the elements of fraud, malice, gross negligence, or oppression mingle in the controversy. . . .

Punitive damages are allowed not because of any special merit in the injured party's case, but are imposed to punish the wrongdoer for malicious, vindictive, or willful and wanton invasion of the injured party's rights, the purpose being to restrain and deter others from the commission of like wrongs. . . .

Taco Bell argues its conduct could not be wanton because it had no reason to know that harm was imminent. This argument is not supported by the facts. The evidence at trial indicated that the shift manager, Mark Wills, saw Karen Brown strike the plaintiff while the plaintiff was still sitting in the booth, but he did nothing. As the parties moved toward the door, Wills came out from behind the food counter to an area within a few feet of the assailant and the plaintiff. He again failed to call the police or attempt to intervene, but instead observed a second attack upon Gould. It was not until Gould's friend, Theresa Holmberg, broke away from Karen Brown and ran inside and threatened to jump over the counter in order to phone the police that Wills finally called the police.

Evidence was also presented that Mark Wills believed Karen Brown had been the cause of a disturbance in the restaurant a couple of weeks before the present incident occurred, yet he failed to intervene or call the police when she began attacking Gould.

In addition, Mark Walters, the store manager, testified that since he became manager of the restaurant in August 1981, the late night patrons had been "destructive" and "uncontrollable." He stated that the late night business in Taco Bell originated in the neighboring bars and that the customers were rowdy and used loud, vulgar, and obscene language, and engaged in verbal fights and occasional physical fights. He also testified there was not sufficient help to handle such crowds and that Taco Bell's written policy was to call the police in case of disruptive customer behavior.

These facts indicate that Taco Bell was aware of the "imminence of danger" yet failed to intervene or warn plaintiff of such danger. There was substantial evidence to support the jury's award of punitive damages.

The judgment of the trial court is affirmed.

CASE QUESTIONS

1. In what three ways did Taco Bell fail to control the activity in its restaurant in this case?
2. Why was Taco Bell liable for punitive damages?

In a related situation, a diner in a restaurant was paralyzed from the waist down in a drive-by shooting. The perpetrator was the estranged husband of a waitress on duty at the time of the shooting. Five months earlier, the estranged husband had threatened to shoot a male employee who had been harassing the waitress. Restaurant management was aware of the prior incident. The paralyzed patron argued that the restaurant was therefore on notice of the estranged husband's violent tendencies and had breached its duty to her by not providing better security. The court noted that the estranged husband did not display a gun during the prior incident and the harassing employee had been fired, thereby eliminating the threat of such incident recurring. The court held the restaurant was not on notice that the estranged husband might attempt to kill his wife or act violently toward customers. The court therefore determined that the restaurant had not violated its duty to act reasonably to protect its patrons and dismissed the complaint. *Hillcrest Foods, Inc. v. Kiritsy*, 489 S.E.2d 547 (Ga., 1997).

To review, if the restaurateur or bar owner cannot reasonably foresee injury to a patron, the owner's responsibility to take steps to prevent attacks is limited. If, however, circumstances suggest that patrons are at risk of being accosted, the restaurant or bar must take reasonable action to protect the customers and prevent the attack.

Failure to Provide Adequate Security

A related instance in which a restaurant or bar may be liable to a patron for injuries caused by another customer is where the tavern keeper fails to provide a staff adequate to police the premises. Liability will turn on whether the restaurant took sufficient precautionary measures based on the foreseeability of the incident. If the restaurant is known to be the site of assaults, robberies, or similar incidents in the past, the owner is on notice that patrons may be in danger and has a duty to protect them.

In *Early v. N.L.V. Casino Corp.*, 678 P.2d 683 (Nev., 1984), plaintiff was attacked in the restroom of a casino restaurant and suffered physical and psychological injuries. The court found the attack was foreseeable, noting that the crime log books for the casino showed ninety-two crimes known to have been committed on the premises in the two years preceding the attack on plaintiff.

The court further found the casino took inadequate precautions to protect guests against foreseeable attacks. The security guards were given no formal training sessions, written materials, or security manuals. Few if any security staff meetings were held. On some occasions no guards patrolled the casino entrance at night. The chief of security was unable to attend monthly hotel security chiefs' meetings because of low staffing. This was woefully inadequate for the risks involved.

Shootings and fights frequently occurred at the defendant bar in the following case. The owner failed to take steps necessary to protect the customers.

CASE EXAMPLE 12–6

Stevens v. Jefferson
436 So.2d 33 (Fla., 1983)

Earl Sidney Jefferson was shot and killed in a bar by a fellow patron. Stevens owned and operated the bar. Jefferson's widow alleged and proved that previously there had been numerous shootings and fights in the bar, that the owner had failed to train or equip employees to maintain order, and that no security personnel had been employed when the owner knew or should have known that his patrons were being exposed to risk of harm from fights or shootings by other patrons. In effect Mrs. Jefferson showed that Stevens either created a dangerous condition or allowed one to exist by the manner in which he ran his establishment. She did not allege, however, that Stevens knew of any dangerous propensities of Jefferson's assailant, and Stevens contends that Jefferson cannot prevail because of that lack of knowledge. We disagree.

The proprietor of a place of public entertainment owes his invitee a duty to use due care to maintain his premises in a reasonably safe condition commensurate with the activities conducted thereon. . . . We have stated that the proprietor of a liquor saloon, although not an insurer of his patrons' safety, is bound to use every reasonable effort to maintain order among his patrons, employees, or those who come upon the premises and are likely to produce disorder to the injury or inconvenience of patrons lawfully in his place of business. . . . A determination as to whether this duty has been vi-

olated will, of necessity, depend upon a review of the facts of each individual case. Additionally, the risk of harm must be foreseeable. This foreseeability requirement has often been met by proving that the proprietor knew or should have known of the dangerous propensities of a particular patron. . . . But specific knowledge of a dangerous individual is not the exclusive method of proving foreseeability. It can be shown by proving that a proprietor knew or should have known of a dangerous condition on his premises that was likely to cause harm to a patron. . . .

To affix liability against a tavern owner for injuries to patrons intentionally inflicted by third parties, a risk of harm to his patrons must be reasonably foreseeable. . . .

A tavern owner's actual or constructive knowledge, based upon past experience, that there is a likelihood of disorderly conduct by third persons in general which may endanger the safety of his patrons is also sufficient to establish foreseeability. . . .

It is incumbent upon the plaintiff to prove legal causation. . . . Mrs. Jefferson met her burden by showing that the bar was a "rough" place with a history of fights and gunplay and that the owner had terminated all security service and had left the premises in the charge of a female employee who could not maintain order. Under these facts a jury could determine that a foreseeable risk of harm to patrons existed, that the risk was either created or tolerated by Stevens, that he could have remedied the danger but failed to do so, and that because of that failure to perform his duties Jefferson was killed.

CASE QUESTIONS

1. What circumstances made violence at this establishment forseeable?
2. What action should a restaurant or bar owner take to protect patrons when the restaurant has been the site of many fights?

In *Taco Bell, Inc. v. Lannon*, 744 P.2d 43 (Colo., 1987) the plaintiff was injured in the course of an armed robbery at a restaurant and suffered a gunshot wound. The restaurant argued that it could not have foreseen the particular inci-

dent because robberies occur randomly and without notice of the time or man
ner. The court rejected this argument, noting that the restaurant had experienced ten armed robberies during the prior three years. The court held that harm
to customers was foreseeable and so the restaurant was required to institute security measures. Said the court,

> To establish that an incident is foreseeable, it is not necessary that an owner or occupier
> of land held open for business purposes be able to ascertain precisely when or how an in-
> cident will occur. Rather, foreseeability includes whenever it is likely enough in the set-
> ting of modern life that a reasonably thoughtful person would take account of it in
> guiding practical conduct.

The restaurant argued that security measures would be costly and create an
economic burden. The court rejected this defense, saying,

> To be sure, such measures would result in some economic burden on Taco Bell and a
> predictable corresponding increase to customers in the cost of Taco Bell's food products.
> For the most part however, we believe that these potential measures—which, according
> to the evidence might include making sure the restaurant is well illuminated, installing
> highly visible video cameras, keeping [only] small amounts of cash in the registers, post-
> ing signs notifying potential robbers of the small amount of cash kept on the premises,
> training employees in methods for dealing with in-progress robberies, and locking non-
> public entrances during nighttime hours—are relatively inexpensive.

Attention to security issues is a must to avoid liability. A restaurant's security
plan should include thorough training of employees on how to handle a disturbance, and frequent assessments of the foreseeable risks and the precautionary
practices needed.

No Duty to Comply with Demands of Robber

In an unusual case, a patron at a fast-food restaurant who was held hostage
by an armed robber was injured when a restaurant worker failed to comply with
the robber's demands for money. The customer sued the restaurant to recover for
her injuries. The court held that a restaurateur has no duty to comply with a robber's unlawful demands even though compliance might lessen the danger to
other persons on the premises. *Kentucky Fried Chicken of California, Inc. v. Brown*,
927 P.2d 1260 (Ca., 1997).

Safety Concerns Particular to Food Preparation

Some aspects of food service present particular safety risks to employees. The
restaurateur has a duty to exercise reasonable care to minimize these risks.
Kitchen areas are inherently dangerous. Each piece of equipment can cause serious injuries if misused, such as meat cutters, grills, deep-fat fryers, knives, and
stoves. We discussed in Chapter 6 the hazards associated with flaming foods,
which can cause injury to employees or customers. Another danger is dropped
food, which can result in slip-and-fall cases.

A direct relationship exists between the quality of an accident-prevention program and the frequency and severity of accidents. Employee training is imperative.

Summary

Various laws protect patrons of restaurants and bars against such dangers as adulterated and mislabelled food.

Those that dispense alcohol must avoid sales to patrons who are visibly intoxicated, underage, or habitual drunkards. Illegal sales can result in revocation of a liquor license, criminal sanctions, and dram shop liability, requiring the licensee to compensate a third person injured by the patron. In some states the licensee might also be liable to compensate the patron. Employee training programs concerning service of alcohol are necessary and should be reinforced with frequent refresher courses.

A restaurant or bar owes it patrons the duty of exercising reasonable care to avoid security incidents. If the proprietor is aware of belligerent tendencies of a patron, the customer should be expelled. If fights or other security incidents have occurred in the past, precautions such as security personnel, bright illumination, and video cameras may be necessary. Attention to security matters and frequent security audits are necessary to avoid liability. Local police are usually glad to assist and advise.

Food preparation and service present particular safety issues that should be addressed. These include potentially dangerous equipment, flambe dishes, and dropped food.

Preventive Law Tips for Managers

- *Inspect food carefully before it is served to ensure it is fit for human consumption.* A restaurant that serves inedible food will be liable for breach of the warranty of merchantability. Liability will result even if the restaurant is not aware that the food is unwholesome. To minimize the chances of serving unhealthy food, all food should be carefully inspected before it is used as an ingredient in a recipe and before it is served. Any unfit food, including adulterated food, foreign objections, and natural objects that a customer may not expect and that can cause injury, should be removed.

- *Cook pork thoroughly to destroy the parasite that causes trichinosis.* Uncooked pork often contains a parasite that can cause the life-threatening disease of trichinosis. The parasite is killed upon proper cooking of the pork. To ensure restaurant patrons are not exposed to the risk of the disease, all pork should be thoroughly cooked before serving.

- *Be sure all claims made about food offered at a restaurant are accurate.* The law requires only truthful claims be made about food offered to restaurant patrons. Descriptions on menus such as "fresh," "made in Vermont," or "zero cholesterol" must be truthful. If a restaurant uses words that are standardized by regulations of the Food and Drug Administration (FDA) pursuant to the Nutrition Labeling and Education Act of 1990, such as "light" or "low-calorie," the food item must meet the FDA standards. If food is promoted as kosher, it must meet the requirements mandated for that designation.

- *If a hotel promotes food from a restaurant not operated by the hotel, it should inspect the restaurant periodically to verify that sanitation, food preparation, and management standards are being met.* A guest injured by food from a restaurant promoted by a hotel may have a cause of action against the hotel if the latter has not assessed the operational practices of the restaurant on a regular basis. To protect itself from liability, a hotel that encourages its guests to dine in a particular restaurant should satisfy itself periodically that the restaurant is worthy of the endorsement.

- *Comply with smoking restrictions imposed on restaurants.* Many states and localities have adopted smoking restrictions that require restaurants to set aside a certain percentage of seating capacity for use by nonsmoking diners. A few localities have outlawed all smoking in restaurants. Know the law in your area and do whatever is necessary to comply.

- *To avoid loss of a liquor license, comply strictly with state restrictions on serving alcoholic beverages.* A restaurant or bar cannot serve alcohol without a license from the state. In most states to the following people are illegal: a visibly intoxicated person; someone under age 21; and a habitual drunkard. If a licensee does not strictly comply with these laws, the state can suspend or revoke the license. Most states are unyielding in their enforcement of the alcoholic beverage control laws. Stringent compliance is the only way to preserve a liquor license.

- *Another reason for avoiding illegal sales is dram shop liability.* Dram shop acts, adopted by most states, render a bar or restaurant liable when a person is injured by someone to whom the licensee sold alcohol illegally. To avoid this potentially financially devastating liability, the licensee should do all of the following: do not sell to persons in the prohibited categories; train employees on how to manage alcohol sales, how to detect if someone is intoxicated, and how to handle requests from customers who cannot legally be served; reinforce the training regularly; offer alternatives to alcohol such as "minidrinks" containing less alcohol, bottled waters, and fancy coffees and teas; and provide a "ride-home" service for patrons who appear incapable of driving safely.

- *Determine what additional regulations your state imposes on licensees and comply with them.* States have adopted various restrictions and regulations for its liquor licensees. Examples of such regulations include a minimum age for wait personnel in licensed restaurants and bars; required warnings to pregnant women about the effect of alcohol on the fetus;

and prohibition of illegal gambling and disorderly conduct at the licensed premises.

- *Eject patrons with known propensities for fighting.* A bar or restaurant may be liable if one patron causes injury to another patron in circumstances in which the injury was foreseeable and adequate security measures were not undertaken. To reduce the possibility of injury, customers who are known to pick fights should be denied entrance to the establishment.

- *Immediately stop a fight that breaks out in a bar or restaurant and eject the participants.* If customers start fighting, the altercation should be stopped immediately and the participants ejected. Failure to end the brawl can result in liability. If the licensee is unable to stop the fighting, the police should be called.

- *Provide staff sufficient to address foreseeable problems.* A bar or restaurant must provide a staff sufficient to handle foreseeable difficulties. For example, if a large crowd is expected on a given day, or if the establishment has been the site of fighting in the past, the bar should have on duty a staff sufficient in size and training to handle associated problems. Failure to provide adequate staff can result in liability if one customer injures another.

- *Come to the aid of a customer who has been injured.* If a customer is injured while on the premises, the bar or restaurant should aid the patron in obtaining help. The assistance required might include any of the following, depending on the circumstances: call the police; call an ambulance; call someone the customer requests you to call; allow the customer to use the phone; eject the troublemaker.

- *Adopt procedures for use and maintenance of kitchen appliances to minimize injuries to employees.* Kitchens by necessity contain many potentially dangerous appliances and utensils including stoves, grills, meat cutters, knives, and deep-fat fryers. Procedures should be adopted for their use and maintenance to ensure maximum safety. Other components of a good risk-reduction plan are employee training and frequent overseeing of the area by managers.

Review Questions

1. What states have adopted the Uniform Commercial Code?
2. What does the warranty of merchantability guarantee?
3. What is the difference between the foreign/natural test and the reasonable expectation test?
4. What disease can be contracted by eating uncooked pork?
5. What does "privity of contract" mean? How does it impact a lawsuit involving the warranty of merchantability?

6. What is strict products liability?

7. What is meant by "truth-in-menu"?

8. What impact does the 1990 Nutrition Education and Labeling Act have on restaurants?

9. What is kosher food?

10. What changes have been made from the common law rule concerning liability of a bar or restaurant for injuries caused by an intoxicated patron?

11. Why do some states limit smoking in restaurants?

12. The law prohibits the sale of alcohol to certain categories of people. Identify those categories. What penalties do states impose for illegal sales?

13. What is meant by dram shop liability?

14. When a patron who is visibly intoxicated continues to drink at two different licensees and then is in a two-car accident injuring the driver of the second car, which licensee is liable to the driver of the second car?

15. Identify three strategies for limiting dram shop liability.

16. What behaviors might alert alcohol service personnel that a patron is visibly intoxicated?

17. Identify five regulations some states impose on liquor licensees.

18. What factors determine the price of liquor liability insurance?

19. Under what circumstances is a restaurant liable when one patron injures another?

20. What safety precautions are necessary to avoid injuries occurring to employees in a restaurant kitchen?

Discussion Questions

1. If you are the manager of a restaurant, would you prefer that the foreign/natural test or reasonable expectation test apply? Why?

2. Do you agree with the decision in *Webster v. Blue Ship Tea Room, Inc.* involving the bone in the fish chowder? Why or why not?

3. Dan ate breakfast at a restaurant known as Pam's Breakfast Shop. He later became ill. Are these facts sufficient to establish that Pam's Breakfast Shop sold unwholesome food? Why or why not?

4. Must a plaintiff suing for breach of the warranty of merchantability show that the defendant was negligent? Why or why not?

5. What differentiates strict products liability from the warranty of merchantability?

6. What steps should a restaurant manager take to be sure that the menu contains no inaccurate statements?

7. In most states a patron who is illegally served alcohol and thereafter injured as a result cannot sue the licensee who made the illegal sale. A third person injured by the patron can sue the licensee. What is the rationale for distinguishing between the two?

8. Under what circumstances should a restaurateur foresee injuries to a patron?

Application Questions

1. Mandy, manager of a cafeteria at a large corporation, purchased a new freezer for the kitchen. It operated at a temperature a few degrees above the setting. Is the freezer merchantable? Why or why not?

2. A hotel chain and a well-known hamburger fast-food chain are negotiating a contract which would authorize the hotel to use the fast-food chain's name on the hotel's room service menu to promote the sale of hamburgers. What terms will the hamburger company want to include in the contract? Why? What terms will the hotel want included? Why?

3. Jerry had been drinking all evening at the Bonger Bar and became visibly intoxicated. The bartender continued to serve him. Thereafter Jerry left the Bonger Bar and, still visibly intoxicated, went to Gordon's Restaurant, where he had another drink. While driving home from Gordon's, Jerry drove his car in the wrong lane and crashed head-on with another car. Both Jerry and the driver of the other car suffered serious injuries. Both sued Gordon's and Bonger Bar. Who is liable to whom?

4. A bartender at the Rascal Cafe, which is located in a state with a drinking age of 21 and a dram shop act, served a female who was 19 years old. She had only one drink. Due to the effects of the alcohol, she failed to stop at a red light and hit a pedestrian who was crossing the street. Is the cafe liable to the pedestrian for the injuries? Why or why not?

5. Assume in the previous question that no one from the Cafe asked the patron for proof of age. What penalty might the Cafe face?

6. Jim owns a bar in an upscale part of town. It is patronized primarily by business people who stop in for a few drinks after work. No fights or disruptions have ever occurred and no patron has ever been unruly. One night a man started threatening other customers. Jim immediately approached the man and told him to leave. While Jim was escorting him to the door, the man punched another customer who suffered a broken nose. The patron sued Jim's bar for his injuries. Is the bar liable under these circumstances?

CHAPTER 13

The Travel Agent and the Airlines—Rights and Liabilities

INTRODUCTION

At one time the American travel industry catered primarily to three categories of travelers: the wealthy, business people, and government officials. This is no longer the case. United States citizens have developed one of the highest per capita incomes in the world. As a result, travel is now within the reach of many. As the travel industry serves more people, it becomes more complex and the problems inherent in arranging travel also grow.

There was an Alka-Seltzer® television commercial in which a vacationing couple is seen sitting beside a swimming pool in a state of extreme agony. As the camera retreats, it becomes obvious that their vacation paradise is undergoing extensive construction and earth removal. The man shouts over the roar: "I asked the travel agent, 'Where can we go for a little peace and quiet? He says, 'Mr. Fields, I've got just the place! A peaceful little cottage in the heart of the Mellow Mountains.'" The sounds of construction increase. "My head . . . my stomach . . . I need some Alka-Seltzer." The travel industry felt so maligned by the ad that they pressured Alka Seltzer's advertising agency to change the commercial. But the picture it presented was not entirely fiction. Sometimes paradise gets paved.

Travel agents do not just sell tickets; the travel agent also dispenses travel information and advice on all aspects of a trip, including the best way to get there, where to stay, where to eat, and what to anticipate en route and upon arrival. Most travelers put their trust in the travel agent and expect to be notified of important information or risks affecting their trip. Unfortunately, that trust is sometimes misplaced.

The consumer rights movement has had a large impact on the travel industry. Travelers are very aware that they may be entitled to compensation when their travel plans go awry. Many disappointed travelers try to find that recompense in court via litigation against the negligence of the travel agent, or against one of the many third-party suppliers that make up the travel industry.

This chapter discusses the rights of the traveler and the liabilities of the travel agent and the airlines when travel plans fail.

The Make-up of the Travel Industry

The travel industry is composed generally of the following four groups.

1. Suppliers of travel services, such as hotels, resorts, airlines and other types of transportation.
2. Travel wholesalers that combine the services offered by suppliers into "package tours."
3. Travel agents who sell both specific services and package tours.
4. Travelers themselves, who usually deal with the travel agent but who sometimes buy services directly from either the supplier of travel services, or, far less often, from the travel wholesaler.

To fully comprehend this chapter you need to know a bit about two topics: agency law and tariffs. An introduction to each follows.

Agency Law

In some cases in this chapter the issue arises whether the travel agent is an agent of the supplier of travel services (such as the hotel, airline, bus company, etc.), or, in the alternative, an agent of the traveler. The answer, as we will see, can determine the outcome of the case and depends on the facts.

Agency means a relationship in which one person acts for or represents another based on authority voluntarily given by that other person. Such relationships involve two parties: a principal and an agent. The **principal** is the person who authorizes someone else (an agent) to act on his behalf and controls the method used by the agent to do the authorized tasks. The **agent** is the person so authorized, the one who represents or acts for the other consistent with the principal's directions. A classic example of a principal/agent relationship is an employer (principal) and employee (agent). By using agents, a principal can conduct multiple business transactions simultaneously in different locations.

When an agent acts on behalf of a principal and within the scope of the authority given by the principal, the principal is legally bound by the agent's acts, and the agent is not. Thus, where a travel agent acts as an agent for an airline and arranges plane reservations for a traveler, the airline and not the agent is required to provide the transportation.

When an agent acts outside the bounds of delegated authority the principal is not bound and the agent may be liable for fraud for misrepresenting the authority he had. Thus, where a travel agent has not been authorized by an airline to sell its tickets but the travel agent sells tickets on the airline's flights notwithstanding, the airline is not required to honor the tickets. The travel agent will be liable to the traveler for losses incurred.

Agency law requires that the agent disclose the identity of the principal so that the agent's client can investigate the reputation or credit of the principal if the client is so inclined. Thus, where a travel agent is acting as an agent of a tour operator when selling a trip to the client, the travel agent must inform the client of the tour operator's identity. If the agent fails to disclose either the identity of the principal or the fact that the agent is acting for another party, the client can legally assume the agent is acting on his own behalf. In this circumstance the agent will be liable as a principal. A case in point is *Siegel v. Council of Long Island Educators, Inc.*, 348 N.Y.S.2d 816 (1973). Ten plaintiffs sued a travel agent in Small Claims Court for three days of lost touring time and other inconveniences suffered during a trip to Israel, caused by the agent's poor planning and failure to make reservations. When planning the trip, the travel agent disclosed that he was acting as an agent for a travel wholesaler but did not disclose the latter's identity. The travel agent argued that, since he was acting as an agent of the wholesaler, the wholesaler should be liable. The court held the travel agent was liable and the wholesaler was not because the travel agent did not disclose the identity of the wholesaler to the plaintiffs.

Similarly, in *Van Rossem v. Penney Travel Service, Inc.*, 488 N.Y.S.2d 595 (NY, 1985), newlyweds were advised on their honeymoon departure day that the wholesaler of their trip had gone bankrupt. Fortunately, the wholesaler had paid for their airline tickets. Unfortunately, the wholesaler had not paid for the hotel. The couple opted to take the trip and pay anew for their accommodations. Upon their return, they sued the travel agency which claimed the wholesaler alone should be liable. The travel agency had not informed the couple that it was acting as an agent for a wholesaler nor the identity of the wholesaler (the principal). As a result, the travel agency was liable.

An agency relationship must be distinguished from that of an independent contractor. **Independent contractors** are people who contract to do work for someone else but are engaged in an independent business for themselves. The only part of the work controlled by the party who hires an independent contractor is the outcome. Independent contractors furnish their own supplies and equipment, pay their own expenses, set their own hours of work, and are paid fees or commission, not salary. Independent contractors may or may not be agents, depending on the facts. The acts of independent contractors who are not agents will not bind the person who hires the independent contractor.

Tariffs

The tariff system is referenced in many cases in this chapter. A **tariff** is a rule or condition of air travel that binds the airline and passengers. Passengers are bound by tariffs even though they do not know about them and do not expressly agree to them. Tariffs are developed by the airlines and must be approved by a government agency. That agency was originally the Civil Aeronautics Board, which is no longer in existence. The relevant agency today is the Department of Transportation.

Tariffs on file with the Department of Transportation, if valid, control the services provided by the airline. Tariffs cover such items as limitations on the airline's liability for damaged baggage, procedures for filing a claim, rules for reservations and check-in times, limits on the airline's liability for schedule changes and flight delays, and personal injury liability limitations. Some of these tariffs contain very one-sided language favoring the airline. Copies of tariffs are available upon request at airports, although few passengers are aware of this and few ask to see them. Tariffs are binding on passengers whether or not they are aware of the rules.

The following case provides insights into the role of tariffs in travel law.

CASE EXAMPLE 13–1

Fontan-de-Maldonado v. Lineas Aereas Costarricenses
936 F.2d 630 (1st Cir., 1991)

The appellant, Ms. Enriqueta Fontan de Maldonadov ("Fontan"), is an American citizen who lives in Puerto Rico. She planned a vacation in Costa Rica and booked a ticket, through a travel agent, to fly on a Costa Rican airline, Lineas Aereas Costarricenses, S.A. ("the Airline"). An employee of the Airline, she alleges, told her travel agent that she need take only her birth certificate, not her passport. But, because she did not take her passport, her return journey became a nightmare, with officials in Panama (where she had intended a stop-over) refusing to accept her, the Airline shunting her from one country to another, and her eventually spending the night on the floor of a Venezuelan airport. She sued the Airline, claiming that its bad advice about the travel documents amounted to negligence. The Airline replied that the ticket says such documents are the traveler's, not the Airline's, responsibility and that its tariff holds it free of liability for bad advice about which documents are needed. . . .

The relevant provision in the Airline's tariff says that passengers "shall comply with all . . . travel requirements of countries to be flown from, into, or over," and that the Airline "shall not be liable for any . . . information given by any . . . employee . . . to any passenger in connection with obtaining necessary documents . . . or for the consequences to any passenger resulting from his/her failure to obtain such documents. . . ." As required by law . . . the Airline has filed its tariff with the Department of Transportation, which regulates the rates and services of international airlines serving the United States. Fontan concedes that if this tariff provision is valid, she cannot prevail. Tariff provisions are binding on a passenger, even if the passenger did not actually know of them. . . . Fontan argues that the tariff is a nullity because it offends . . . public policy.

It is well-established law that a federal court may not hold a tariff provision unlawful as offending against public policy unless the agency empowered to reject the tariff has first had a chance to consider the question. . . . If the agency has not yet considered the issue, courts, under the doctrine of primary jurisdiction, will normally stay [suspend] the lawsuit so that the party asserting the invalidity of the tariff provision may challenge it before the agency. . . . Of course, if the agency has already announced its views, there is no need to apply the doctrine. . . . But, as far as we are aware, neither the Department nor its predecessor, the Civil Aeronautics Board, has considered the lawfulness of a tariff provision of the kind here at issue. . . .

Since we do not consider the tariff provision so obviously reasonable that the Department of Transportation could not lawfully set it aside, nor so obviously unreasonable that the Department would have to do so, the Department must consider the question in the first instance.

The Airline says that we can affirm the district court's decision on an alternative ground, namely, that conditions printed on Fontan's ticket made her responsible for proper documentation. It is the tariff, however, not the ticket, that constitutes the contract. . . . If the Department of Transportation were to find the tariff provision unreasonable, and for that reason void, the ticket would not help the Airline.

Accordingly, we . . . remand with instructions to stay the proceedings for a reasonable time to permit Fontan to challenge the validity of the tariff before the department.

So ordered.

Remedies for Small Damages

The amount of damages suffered by a traveler whose plans have gone awry is not always large. The cost of a lawsuit may discourage such travelers from suing the party responsible for the disruption, whether that party was the travel agent, airline, or travel service supplier. Two developments reduce the cost of suing and therefore both encourage would-be plaintiffs to sue and increase liability exposure of those in the travel industry. These developments are Small Claims Court and class action lawsuits.

Small Claims Court

Many travel cases are brought in Small Claims Court, a forum that encourages people to act as their own advocates without a lawyer. To aid that process, Small Claims Court dispenses with formal rules of evidence and procedure that govern trials in other courts. The maximum amount of money a plaintiff can seek in Small Claims Court is relatively small and varies from state to state but is typically around $3,000. Judges in Small Claims Court are often more sympathetic to consumers than to those in control of the situations that give rise to the controversy. As you read the small claims cases in this chapter see if you detect such an attitude.

Because rules of procedure and evidence are relaxed in Small Claims Court, and because lawyers are not necessary, many plaintiffs who might be discouraged from suing by the complexities of a lawsuit decide instead to pursue their case. As a result businesses, including those in the the hospitality industry, have a much greater exposure for their shortcomings than if Small Claims Court did not exist.

Class Action Suits

A **class action suit** is a legal device in which all people who have suffered losses from the same cause jointly sue the defendant. It is a financially attractive option for plaintiffs because the cost of the lawsuit is spread among many plaintiffs instead of just one. A class action was pursued on behalf of persons who purchased a vacation package from Club Med. The complaint alleged that the seller had promoted the accommodations as luxurious, but instead they lacked electricity, air conditioning, hot and cold running water, and operable toilets. *King v. Club Med, Inc.*, 430 N.Y.S.2d 65 (1980). In *Guadago v. Diamond Tours and Travel, Inc.*, 392 N.Y.S.2d 783 (1976), the judge granted permission to five plaintiffs to represent a class action. The plaintiffs claimed that the defendants—Club Islandia, two Long Island travel agencies, a Long Island tour organizer, and a New York tour wholesaler—misrepresented the nature and quality of accommodations at a Jamaican resort and sued for fraudulent misrepresentation and breach of contract. The class was comprised of 400 people who took three separate charter tours during a three week period. Said the court, "[C]lass action relief may well be necessary to vindicate the rights of members of the class, whose individual claims are otherwise too small (under $500) to warrant independent litigation against the impressive legal strength of the defendants." Two factors make this decision and other similar class action cases significant. First, these cases allow a class to sue jointly rather than requiring each traveler to shoulder independently the costs of a lawsuit. Second, by defining the class as including travelers on three separate charter tours rather than limiting the class to just one, the potential liability for the travel industry defendant is enlarged.

The Rights of the Traveler

When travel plans do not turn out as represented and purchased, the law is quite supportive of the traveler and provides a remedy in many circumstances.

Baggage Claims—Domestic and International

When travelers hand their baggage to an airline to have it transported to their destination, they are entering into a contract with the airline. This contract binds the airline to deliver the baggage to the destination and to restore it to the traveler upon arrival. If the airline fails to deliver the luggage at the destination, it has breached its contract with the traveler. Under normal contractual circumstances, the traveler would be entitled to recover from the airline the value of the lost baggage and its contents. However, because of the frequency of loss or delayed delivery by the airlines, the airlines would suffer a significant financial burden if travelers were able to recover the full value of lost property in every case. So rules have been adopted to protect the airline from unlimited liability.

According to the Air Transport Association, U.S. airlines recently handled over 659 million bags a year. The best estimate is that 350,000 to 400,000 a year are misrouted and not picked up from the carousel. The airlines report that 75 percent of those lost bags are reunited with their owners within twelve hours, and an additional 20 percent are delivered within five days. The remaining 5 percent still amounts to a significant number. The concept of limiting the airline's liability for this lost luggage is similar to the limiting liability statutes applicable to innkeepers when guests' property is lost or stolen, as we saw in Chapter 9. One set of laws for limiting liability applies to international flights and another set of laws applies to domestic flights. Both will be reviewed in this chapter. In both, the passenger is entitled to compensation only for lost property; compensation for emotional stress is not permitted, nor is punitive damages.

International Flights.   International flights are governed by the Warsaw Convention, an international treaty that sets the limits of liability for lost, stolen, damaged or misdelivered baggage. Under the Convention, the limitation on liability for checked luggage is $9.07 per pound up to forty-four pounds, or just about $400; the limit for carry-on baggage is $400. The passenger is informed of the limitation on the airline ticket. (See Figure 13-1). In exchange for limited lia-

ADVISE TO INTERNATIONAL PASSENGERS ON LIMITATION OF LIABILITY

Passengers on a journey involving an ultimate destination or a stop in a country other than the country of origin are advised that the provisions of a treaty known as the Warsaw Convention my be applicable to the entire journey, including any portion entirely within the country of origin or destination. For such passengers on a journey to, from, or with an agreed stopping place in the United States of America, the Convention and special contracts of carriage embodied in applicable tariffs provide that the liability of certain carriers, parties to such special contracts, for death of or personal injury to passengers is limited in most cases to proven damages not to exceed U.S. $75,000 per passenger, and that this liability up to such limit shall not depend on negligence on the part of the carrier. The limit of liability of U.S. $75,000 above is inclusive of legal fees and costs except that in case of a claim brought in a state where provision is made for separate award of legal fees and costs, the limit shall be the sum of U.S. $58,000 exclusive of legal fees and costs. For such passengers traveling by a carrier not a party to such special contracts or on a journey not to, from, or having an agreed stopping place in the United States of America, liability of the carrier for death or personal injury to passengers is limited in most cases to approximately U.S. $10,000 or U.S. $20,000.

The names of carriers, parties to such special contracts, are available at all ticket offices of such carriers and may be examined on request. Additional protection can usually be obtained by purchasing insurance from a private company. Such insurance is not affected by any limitation of the carrier's company. Such insurance is not affected by any limitation of the carrier's liability under the Warsaw Convention or such special contracts of carriage. For further information please consult your airline or insurance company representative.

NOTICE OF BAGGAGE LIABILITY LIMITATIONS

Liability for loss, delay, or damage to baggage is limited unless a higher value is declared in advance and additional charges are paid. For most international travel (including domestic portions of international journeys) the liability limit is approximately $9.07 per pound for checked baggage and $400 per passenger for unchecked baggage. For travel wholly between U.S. points federal rules require any limit on an airline's baggage liability to be at least $1250 per passenger. Excess valuation may be declared on certain types of articles. Some carriers assume no liability for fragile, valuable or perishable articles. Further information may be obtained from the carrier.

CARRIER RESERVES THE RIGHT TO REFUSE CARRIAGE TO ANY PERSON WHO HAS ACQUIRED A TICKET IN BIOLATION OF APPLICABLE LAW OR CARRIER'S TARIFFS, RULES OR REGULATIONS
SUBJECT TO TARIFF REGULATIONS

Figure 13–1   Limitation of liability stated on the back of an airline ticket. (*Courtesy of United Airlines*)

bility, the airline is presumed to be responsible when luggage is missing or lost. The airline can rebut this presumption if it can show it took all possible precautions to avoid the loss. Further, passengers have the option of purchasing insurance to cover loss in excess of the convention's maximum.

The following case provides some background about the Warsaw Convention. In it, the traveler's lost property considerably exceeded the $400 maximum allowable. As you read the case, note particularly the requirements the airline must follow to avail itself of the limited liability.

CASE EXAMPLE 13–2

Lourenco v. Trans World Airlines, Inc.
244 N.J.Super. 48 (N.J., 1990)

. . . On January 24, 1988 plaintiffs and their two minor daughters were passengers on T.W.A. flight 33 from Nassau, Bahamas to J.F.K. Airport in New York City. The Flight was cancelled due to technical difficulties. The Lourencos and their children were later flown to Miami, Florida on Bahamas Air. The group then boarded a Pan American flight to J.F.K.

Their luggage, last seen in Nassau, was shipped separately and lost. It was delivered to plaintiff's home three days later. Plaintiffs allege the luggage was broken into and that $9,232.59 worth of jewelry and other valuables is missing.

Plaintiff, Mario Lourenco, is an employee of T.W.A. Neither he nor his wife made a special declaration of the value concerning the contents of their luggage. Plaintiffs did not request special handling of the baggage or purchase special insurance covering the full value of their possessions. . . .

Defendant did not state the weight and number of pieces of luggage on plaintiffs' ticket or baggage check. The total weight of the items missing is stipulated as less than (50) fifty pounds.

T.W.A. argues that its liability is limited by the Warsaw Convention. . . . The Convention is an international treaty that limits the liability of airlines for death, injury, property damage or loss and delay. It applies to all international transportation of persons, baggage or goods performed by aircraft for hire. The carrier is liable for loss or damage to any checked baggage occurring during transportation by air, including the period baggage is in the charge of the carrier whether in an airport or on an aircraft. Liability is limited to $9.07 per pound of lost baggage, except in cases of willful misconduct. The parties agree the baggage was in international flight and is governed by the Warsaw Convention.

In return for limited liability, the air carrier is presumed liable to a passenger unless the carrier can show that it had taken all necessary measures to avoid damages, or that it was impossible for it to take such measures.

The Convention permits an airline to limit its liability if the provisions of Article 4 are complied with. Article 4 of the Convention states:

1) For the transportation of baggage, other than small personal objects of which the passenger takes charge himself, the carrier must deliver a baggage check.

2) The baggage check shall be made out in duplicate, one part for the passenger and the other part for the carrier.

3) The baggage check shall contain the following particulars:
   (a) The place and date of issue;
   (b) The place of departure and of destination;
   (c) The name and address of the carrier or carriers;
   (d) The number of the passenger ticket;
   (e) A statement that delivery of the baggage will be made to the bearer of the baggage check;
   (f) The number and weight of the packages;
   (g) The amount of the value; . . .

(h) A statement that the transportation is subject to the rules relating to liability established by this convention.

4) The absence, irregularity, or loss of the baggage check shall not affect the existence or the validity of the contract of transportation which shall nonetheless be subject to the rules of this convention. Nevertheless, if the carrier accepts baggage without a baggage check having been delivered, or if the baggage check does not contain the particulars set out at (d), (f), and (h) above, the carrier shall not be entitled to avail himself of those provisions of the convention which exclude or limit his liability.

The Warsaw Convention is binding on a passenger, if the passenger has notice of its provisions. Notice, ordinarily printed on the airline ticket, gives the passenger an opportunity to declare that the value of his baggage is in excess of standard limits. The passenger can then pay a supplementary fee to cover the excess and increase his potential recovery to the declared value. The passenger is also free to make a special contract with the airlines or purchase insurance.

Plaintiffs received written notice of the Convention's applicability. The defendant did not, however, write down on the baggage check the number of pieces or weight of plaintiffs' luggage as required by subsection (3)(f) of Art. 4. The parties agree that defendant complied with all other provisions of Art. 4.

What are the consequences to an airline if it does not strictly comply with subsection (3)(f) of Art. 4? The cases demonstrate a considerable split in authority.

The courts in the State of New York generally hold that when the claim check or ticket does not indicate the number and weight of the packages, the carrier cannot avail itself of the limitation [of liability].

The weight of federal authority, however, holds that the carrier's failure to record the number and weight of a passenger's luggage is a technical and insubstantial omission. . . .

The economic interest of passengers to be adequately compensated for lost baggage competes with the airline's interest in controlling costs and curtailing litigation. The Convention's limits on liability have been criticized as unconscionably low. Nations in the Third World have complained that the limits of liability are too high. Compromises have been reached in setting the present limits; . . .The economic policy choice, however, is not for this Court to make.

As an international treaty the Warsaw Convention remains "the supreme law of the land." It is not for Courts to "indulge in judicial treaty-making," or to decide if the U.S. Airline Industry, no longer in its infancy, still needs special protection. The Court's function is to construe the Convention, determine its meaning and apply it fairly. Whether the treaty is construed strictly or liberally the polestar should be to effectuate its evident purpose. There is populist appeal in subjecting the airlines to unlimited liability for lost baggage. This is not, however, the evident purpose of the Treaty. . . .

This Court holds that the failure to record the weight and number of plaintiffs' luggage on the baggage check is a technical and insubstantial omission and should not deny defendant the benefit of the limitation of liability provisions of the Warsaw Convention. . . .

The difficulty presented by the instant case is that the plaintiffs' luggage was lost, found and returned; with jewelry and other valuable items missing.

The Treaty bases damages on weight, not the actual value of the lost baggage. A pound of jewelry, or for that matter clothing, is obviously worth more than the $9.07 allowed. The plaintiffs were well aware of the worth of their jewelry, and the modest recovery permitted under the Convention for lost baggage, before they checked their luggage with the airline. They chose to run the risk of its loss without benefit of insurance or special declaration. Since the Court has decided that the Warsaw Convention's limitations of liability apply and the plaintiffs have stipulated that the missing items weighed fifty (50) pounds or less, it follows that defendant's liability is limited to a total of $453.50.

CASE QUESTION

1. On what principle did the court base its decision that the Warsaw Convention's limitation of liability applied?

The limitation of liability also applied in a case involving the lost luggage of a marketing director for a sporting goods company. The contents included 1500 t-shirts and 120 pairs of soccer shoes. The company sought damages in the amount of $15,728; the court held the company was bound by the limitation of liability in the Warsaw Convention. *Abbaa v. Pan Am*, 673 F. Supp. 991 (Minn., 1987). The convention's limitation of liability was held inapplicable in *Schedlmayer v. Trans International Airlines, Inc.*, 416 N.Y.S.2d 461 (1979), a Small Claims Court case. The plaintiff, upon request, gave her hand luggage to a flight attendant for storage in the front of the plane during a charter flight from Austria to New York. After the plane was in flight, the plaintiff remembered that she had left a camera and $1,300 in currency in the bag. During a stopover she asked the stewardess to return her bag but was told that she could not get it until the aircraft landed at its final destination in New York. Upon arrival in New York, the plaintiff retrieved her luggage and immediately discovered that, although the camera was still there, the currency was gone. The airline refused to reimburse her for the loss and the plaintiff sued. A threshold issue in the case was whether the Warsaw Convention applies to charter flights. The court held that it did.

The determination of the extent of the airline's liability centered on Article 4 of the Convention which provides: "If the carrier accepts baggage without a baggage check having been delivered . . . the carrier shall not be entitled to avail himself of those provisions of the convention that limit his liability." The court held that when the flight attendant took the bag from the passenger, the airline took control of it so it then assumed the status of checked baggage. Since the stewardess failed to issue a claim check, as required by the Convention, the defendant airline could not take advantage of the limitations of the Convention and so was liable to the plaintiff for the full amount of her loss.

Another factor that will bar an airline from the advantages of the Convention's limited liability is "willful misconduct." The following case helps to define willful misconduct in reference to misplaced or damaged luggage on international flights. In *Compania De Aviacion Faucett v. Mulford*, 386 So.2d 300 (Fla., 1980) the Mulfords, who had boarded a flight on the defendant airline in Cuzco, Peru with a destination of Lima, Peru, had been informed by the airline's employees that their luggage was on board their flight when in fact the luggage had been removed. It was not returned to the Mulfords until after they returned home. The court held that the airline had "deliberately or recklessly" given the Mulfords misinformation. The court thus held that the airline engaged in willful misconduct rendering the limiting liability provisions of the Warsaw Convention inapplicable. The airline was thus ordered to pay damages beyond the limits of the Convention.

Willful misconduct was also found in a case where plaintiffs exited a plane during a stopover in Rio de Janeiro, Brazil. The plane was continuing to New York. Plaintiffs' luggage was not unloaded. Plaintiffs, New York residents, were at the beginning of an 18-day trip and had with them only the clothes they were wearing. Despite plaintiffs' urgent requests during the layover that airline personnel search the baggage compartment for plaintiffs' suitcases, the airline refused. It claimed the search would have taken an hour and it did not want to delay the departure of the flight. The airline's lost-and-found agent assured plaintiffs their luggage would be returned to Rio de Janeiro within two days. However, plaintiffs' itinerary required they leave Rio de Janeiro the next day. Plaintiffs' luggage was never recovered. They sued for the full value of their belongings; the airline claimed the Warsaw Convention's limitation of liability applied. The court found the airline's refusal to attempt to locate plaintiffs' luggage was willful misconduct and therefore the Convention's limitation of liability did not apply. Said the court, "[The lost and found agent's] callous disregard for plaintiffs' plight and willful renunciation of its contractual obligation to its passengers [to safely transport and deliver luggage] was motivated by selfish economic interest and justifies a finding of willful misconduct under the provisions of the Warsaw Convention." The court, however, rejected plaintiffs' claim for damages based on physical inconvenience, discomfort, and mental anguish. *Cohen v. Varig Airlines*, 405 N.Y.S.2d 44 (1978).

Occasionally, a traveler's luggage will be damaged during transport. To obtain recovery for damaged baggage requires that the traveler follow strictly the prerequisites identified in the tariffs. One such requirement is that notice be given to the airline within a specified number of days after receipt of damaged luggage. Failure to give timely notice is fatal to the lawsuit. In *Onyeanusi v. Pan Am*, 952 F.2d 788 (3rd Cir., 1992), Pan Am transported plaintiff's mother's body from Pennsylvania to Nigeria. The casket arrived late; the body and casket were damaged. Plaintiff complained to the airlines two months later, considerably in excess of the two-week notice period permitted by tariff. The plaintiff's lawsuit was thus dismissed.

Domestic Flights.   The Warsaw Convention does not apply to domestic flights. Limits of liability for lost luggage on domestic flights are covered by tariffs which, as we have seen, are developed by the airlines and approved by the Department of Transportation. By law, since 1987, the lowest maximum liability an airline can include in its tariff is $1,250. As with international flights, airlines must offer passengers the option of purchasing insurance coverage above the tariff's maximum.

Before boarding a flight, passengers are required to pass through a security check in the airport consisting of metal detectors and x-rays of carry-on luggage. During the check the passenger is separated from his bags. An interesting case involved a passenger who grabbed the wrong hand baggage after proceeding through the security system. Upon discovering the mix-up, he reported it to the airlines, but his baggage was never returned. He sued the airlines in Small Claims Court seeking the value of his lost goods. The airline claimed that, since it was required by law to perform the security checks, it should not be held liable for property lost during a check. The court determined the value of the passenger's lost property was $950 and ordered the airlines to pay, stating that although the airlines are required to conduct security screenings they have a duty to safeguard the passenger's hand baggage during those checks. *Tremaroli v. Delta Airlines*, 458 N.Y.S.2d 159 (1983). Said the court,

> *The traveling public is warned not to pack valuables in checked luggage which is stored within the aircraft's freight and luggage compartments during the flight's duration. Accordingly, valuables are encouraged to be packed in hand baggage intended to be carried aboard the plane to be kept within the passenger's view and control. Yet, the passenger and his hand baggage are separated as both go through the required security measures. The passenger, indeed, is placed in a catch-22 situation in need of a safe place to carry his travelers cheques, credit cards, travel and business documents, identification, airline tickets, eyeglasses and jewelry. . . .*
>
> *Thus, the security system of an airline should operate in such a manner that it is accountable to the public for the return of hand baggage. . . .*

Interestingly, the airline hired an independent security company to perform the security checks. The airline's contract with the security company contained a provision that required the latter to "indemnify and hold harmless" (compensate) the airline for any liability the latter incurred from the security checks. As a result, the security company was required to reimburse the airline for the $950. awarded to the plaintiff.

In another factually similar case, the alarm sounded when the plaintiff went through the metal detector. She was "briefly inspected" and permitted to continue to the airplane. By then, her handbag was no longer on the conveyor. A search was unsuccessful. She sued the airlines for the value of jewelry contained therein—$431,000. In this case, the court held the airline's liability was limited by its tariff amount of $1,250 on the basis that plaintiff was a ticketed passenger at the time of the loss. *Wackenhut Corp. v. Lippert*, 609 So.2d 1304 (Fl., 1933). Another plaintiff was likewise restricted to the maximum recovery stated in the tariff. The airline transported cremated remains from Georgia to Puerto Rico, and held them in its warehouse pending retrieval by the family. Prior to that time, the box containing the remains disappeared. *Cubero Valderama v. Delta Air Lines, Inc.*, 931 F. Supp. 119 (P.R., 1996).

Traveling with Animals

For purposes of determining an airline's liability for mishandling property, pets are treated in the same way suitcases are. In *Young v. Delta Airlines, Inc.*, 432 N.Y.S.2d 390 (1980), the plaintiff's pet dog died while in the custody of the airline. The plaintiff sued not only for the value of the dog (it was an expensive breed), but also for compensation for the emotional disturbance she suffered as a result of the dog's death, and punitive damages.

The court dismissed the claims for mental suffering and punitive damages, noting that these types of damages are not recoverable where an airline mishandles a traveler's property. Concerning compensation for the value of the dog, the court held recovery was limited to $500 by applicable tariffs. The dog was classified as the plaintiff's personal property and stood in the same position as an inanimate piece of luggage.

We have seen that a passenger can purchase insurance from the airlines to cover the value of property in excess of the maximum provided in the Warsaw Convention or the airline's tariffs. Could the dog owner have purchased insurance with the airline to cover the value of the dog so as to increase the amount of her recovery in the event of the animal's death? Must the airline sell such insurance? It seems so. Based on the *Young* case, holding that the dog has the same status as luggage, it would follow that the airline would have to sell the insurance to cover the dog as it would for any other baggage.

In *Gluckman v. American Airlines*, 844 F. Supp. 151 (NY, 1994), plaintiff's golden retriever died as a result of heat stroke caused during a flight delay that resulted from mechanical difficulties. The delay was in Arizona on a June day when the temperature was 115 degrees fahrenheit. The dog had been maintained in the airplane's baggage compartment which was unventilated. The court denied recovery to plaintiff for emotional distress and loss of companionship of the pet. Plaintiff also sought recovery for pain and suffering *of the dog*. The facts established that, upon removal from the baggage compartment, "the dog's face and paws were bloody; there was blood all over the crate; and the condition of the cage evidenced a panic effort to escape." Notwithstanding the apparent distress of the dog, the court rejected this cause of action as well.

Refunds on Tickets

Sometimes circumstances entitle a traveler to a refund on airline tickets, but getting that refund can be difficult.

In *Levine v. British Overseas Airways Corp.*, 322 N.Y.S. 2d 119 (1971), the plaintiffs purchased round trip tickets from the Comet Travel Agency for the itinerary of New York-London-Amsterdam-Copenhagen-Stockholm-London-New York. Plaintiffs paid Comet for the tickets which in turn paid the airlines, British Overseas Airway Corporation (BOAC). The Stockholm leg of the trip was cancelled. Plaintiffs returned their ticket directly to BOAC and sought a refund of $86, which the airline did not deny was due. However, consistent with a practice adopted by many airlines, BOAC sought to make refund payments directly to the travel agent (Comet) and deduct therefrom the travel agent's commission for the cancelled portion of the trip. Plaintiffs objected seeking payment of the refund directly from BOAC.

The court sided with the plaintiffs and stated that once the travel agent paid the fare to the carrier, the traveler has a valid claim for restitution against the carrier. While the travel agent was an agent for the plaintiffs when purchasing the tickets, once the travel agent had completed the ticket purchase, all authority to act for the customer ended. Therefore Comet was not authorized to accept refund money on plaintiffs' behalf, and so the court ordered the airline to refund the money directly to the plaintiff.

In *Antar v. Trans World Airlines, Inc.*, 320 N.Y.S.2d 355 (1970), the plaintiff was the victim of fraud perpetrated by the travel agent, Peters. He sold to the plaintiff a trip for six to Israel which supposedly included air fare and hotel. Plaintiff paid the travel agent more than $8,000 in return for which Peters delivered to plaintiff six TWA airline tickets issued on blank ticket forms. Thereafter the travel agent disappeared without paying TWA for the tickets. TWA refused to honor them because, although the travel agent had been an authorized agent of TWA until two weeks prior to plaintiff's ticket purchase, TWA had revoked the agency. Plaintiff sued TWA. The court, noting that TWA was not a party to the fraud, held for the airline; plaintiff was not entitled to a refund from TWA.

Remember, when an alleged agent is not authorized to act for the supposed principal, that principal is not bound and the alleged agent is liable for fraud. Here plaintiff could sue Peters for fraud. Unfortunately, plaintiff will likely have difficulty finding Peters.

Rights of Handicapped Travelers

Vinogradov, the great Russian philosopher, said that social change can only be made by legislating the change. In the United States, this maxim is constantly being proved. The school desegregation and other civil rights cases of the 1950s and 1960s stand as examples of this rather dismal truth. See Chapter 3 for a discussion of the civil rights laws as applied to hotels and restaurants. When we examine the transportation industry, we see that the airlines and other carriers have been slow to accommodate the disabled.

Until a short time ago, few laws impacted the decision of commercial airlines and other forms of transportation on whether to provide transportation to handicapped people. When the carrier decided to deny transportation, the reason usually given was simply that planes, trains and buses were not equipped to transport the handicapped.

The Americans With Disability Act (ADA) became effective on January 26, 1992, and The Air Carrier Access Act (ACAA) in 1986. The ADA is discussed at length in Chapter 3. The ACAA was adopted to prevent what Congress called the "humiliating and degrading" practices of airlines. It states that, "[N]o air carrier may discriminate against any otherwise qualified handicapped individual, by reason of such handicap, in the provision of air transportation." What effect do these statutes have on the 43 million Americans who are disabled travelers?

The law is quite clear that disabled people can use the airlines if they meet minimum requirements concerning mobility designed to ensure personal and public safety. Discrimination against handicapped people meeting these minimum requirements will result in liability, as evidenced in the following case.

CASE EXAMPLE 13–3

Tallarico v. Trans World Airlines, Inc.
881 F.2d 566 (8th Cir., 1989)

Polly Tallarico, who is fourteen years old, has cerebral palsy which impedes her ability to walk and talk. She generally uses a wheelchair, but is able to move about on her own by crawling. Although Polly is able to speak only short words, she is able to hear and understand the spoken word. She communicates by use of a variety of communication devices such as a communication board, a memo writer and a "Minispeak."

On November 25, 1986, the day before the Thanksgiving holiday, Polly arrived at Houston's Hobby Airport intending to fly to St. Louis, Missouri, unaccompanied. When the TWA ticket agent, Richard Wattleton, learned that Polly intended to fly alone he contacted Lynn Prothero, acting TWA station manager, and asked for directions as to how he should handle the situation. Wattleton had learned from the limousine driver assisting Polly that she could not speak or walk. Wattleton . . . [informed Prothero] that Polly could communicate by use of a communications board. From this information, Prothero determined that Polly would not be allowed to fly unaccompanied and informed Wattleton of her decision. This decision was apparently made on the basis of Prothero's conclusion that Polly could not take care of herself in an emergency and could not exit the plane expeditiously. As a result of this decision, Polly's father had to fly to Houston to accompany Polly to St. Louis.

The Tallaricos brought suit alleging that TWA violated the ACAA by denying Polly the right to board the plane because of her physical handicaps. The jury found for the Tallaricos awarding damages in the amount of $80,000. The district court entered judgment notwithstanding the verdict on the issue of damages reducing the award to $1,350 which is equivalent to the Tallaricos' actual out-of-pocket expenses.

. . . The ACAA states that "[n]o air carrier may discriminate against any otherwise qualified handicapped individual, by reason of such handicap, in the provision of air transportation.". . .

[A] "qualified handicapped person" is a handicapped individual (1) who tenders payment for air transportation, (2) whose carriage will not violate Federal Aviation Administration regulations, and (3) who is willing and able to comply with reasonable safety requests of the airline personnel, or if unable to comply, who is accompanied by a responsible adult passenger who can ensure compliance with such a request. . . .

The evidence at trial showed that Polly had tendered payment for air transportation, that her carriage would not violate any FAA regulations (in fact she had flown alone before), and that she was capable of complying with the reasonable safety requests of airline personnel. The evidence demonstrated that Polly is able to crawl on her knees or her hands and knees, that she has normal intelligence, and that she is capable of communicating her needs. Polly has a variety of ways of communicating including the use of communication boards which contain the letters of the alphabet and some short phrases; a memo writer, an electronic typewriter-like device; and a "Minispeak," a portable computer with an electronic voice attached. Polly is able to fasten her own seat belt as well as put on an oxygen mask. In addition, Polly's mother testified that she was confident that Polly could crawl to the bathroom (and, presumably, an exit) on the plane if necessary. . . .

The jury awarded the Tallaricos $80,000. The district court then granted judgment n.o.v. in favor of TWA as to $78,650 of the damages award. The court concluded that there was insufficient evidence to support the total award and that as a matter of law, the award was not sustainable. The court determined that $1,350 of the award was compensation for out-of-pocket damages as a result of TWA's refusal to allow Polly to board and the remainder was damages for emotional distress. . . .

In this case the proof of the emotional distress which Polly suffered after TWA denied her boarding came from the testimony of her mother, her father, the assistant director for Polly's school and the driver who was with Polly when the incident occurred. Theodore Sherwood, the driver who took Polly to the airport, testified that Polly was with him when he was told she would not be allowed to board the aircraft. He stated he noticed that Polly was getting disturbed as she listened to his conversations with TWA employees. Sherwood also testified that he felt it necessary to call Polly's school to see if someone there could talk to Polly and calm her down because after the incident she was crying and upset about what had happened. Polly's father testified that Polly was very angry and upset about the incident. In addition, he stated that since the incident Polly has seemed more withdrawn, quiet and reserved. Polly's mother also testified that Polly was upset about what happened and that Polly was anxious about the situation and concerned about having to fly back to Houston after the Thanksgiving holiday. Susan Oldham, the assistant director of Polly's school, testified that prior to the incident Polly was very outgoing and socialized well with the other students. After the incident, Ms. Oldham testified, Polly seemed more withdrawn and would spend large amounts of time by herself in her room after school was over. Ms. Oldham stated that when she asked Polly if something about her trip home had upset her, Polly replied that what had happened had made her feel badly and had hurt her feelings.

We find that sufficient evidence was presented to support the jury's award of $80,000. Consequently, we reverse the district court's judgment n.o.v. . . .

We agree with the district court that the Tallaricos failed to present sufficient evidence to support an award of punitive damages and similarly do not reach the question of whether punitive damages would be allowed under the ACAA.

CASE QUESTION

1. How could TWA have avoided the liability in this case? Include in your answer not just changes in their handling of plaintiff's situation but also steps to avoid liability in future cases involving disabled passengers.

Other provisions of the Air Carrier Access Act include the following requirements: air carriers must design new and renovated terminals to accommodate people with disabilities; airlines must provide fully accessible services in all existing airport facilities; airlines cannot require passengers with assistive devices to undergo special security procedures if the person using an aid clears the system without activating it, but airlines are entitled to examine assistive devices they believe may conceal a weapon; airlines must allow passengers with disabilities to store canes and other assistive devices close to their seat, and cannot count that equipment toward a person's limit of carry-on luggage; if space in the baggage compartment is insufficient to accommodate all travelers, priority must be given to wheelchairs and other assistive devices; and personal mobility equipment stored during flight in the baggage compartment must be among the first items removed from the compartment upon arrival at the destination.

Handicapped travelers must make known their needs to the airlines. Travel providers need not guess what the needs of the handicapped person are. In *Adiutori v. Sky Harbor International Airport*, 880 F. Supp. 696 (Ariz., 1995), the plaintiff had severe arthritis which made walking very difficult and required the use of two canes. When his connecting flight was cancelled, he was rerouted, requiring him to change terminals, a distance of one and a half miles. He requested a wheelchair and that was provided. A skycap pushed him in the chair from his plane to the bus stop where he caught the bus to the new terminal. Upon arrival at the bus stop, plaintiff was told, "This is where you get off. This is where the bus stop is." Plaintiff exited the chair without help and without request for further assistance. At the waiting area all seats for bus passengers were occupied. Plaintiff stood in pain for twenty minutes while waiting for the bus. He refused the offer of an elderly woman to relinquish her seat to him. The bus that arrived was not handicapped accessible. He entered it with difficulty but without requesting assistance.

Soon thereafter, plaintiff suffered a heart attack. He sued the airline, claiming the attack was caused by the lack of assistance in making the terminal change. The court held for the airline, noting that applicable laws and regulations "do not force air carriers to provide unrequested assistance to handicapped individuals. . . . Furthermore, it is a violation of [applicable laws] to force handicapped individuals to accept services they do not request. . . ." Addressing the requirements of the Americans With Disabilities Act, the court noted that the airport had two wheelchair accessible shuttle vans available 24 hours a day, seven days a week. They could be summoned by passengers from special phones located at ground transportation areas or by airport personnel upon request by a handicapped passenger. Because plaintiff failed to request help, his claim against the airline was dismissed.

Special Rights of Airlines

Because of the nature of air travel, with the ever-present dangers associated with adverse weather conditions and passenger safety, certain rules apply to airlines only.

Right of Airlines to Cancel Scheduled Flights

Many airline flights are cancelled each day, usually with a bona fide reason. Still, with each cancellation many travelers' schedules are disrupted. A great deal might depend on the traveler being in the right place at the right time.

In normal contract situations, cancellation would constitute a breach of the airline's contractual duty to transport the passenger to the designated destination and liability would result. However, there are conditions under which the airline is not bound to fly. In such cases cancellation of a flight will not result in liability for breach of contract. One of those conditions is mechanical problems with the aircraft. An airline will not be liable for breach of contract where it cancels a flight due to mechanical problems. *Cenci v. Mall Airways, Inc.*, 531 N.Y.S.2d 743 (1988). Another circumstance in which cancellation of a flight will not result in liability for breach of contract is poor weather. This is illustrated in the following case.

CASE EXAMPLE 13–4

Johnson v. Northwest Orient Airlines
642 P.2d 1067 (Mont., 1982)

On December 12, 1979, plaintiff bought a round trip Missoula-Billings ticket from Northwest. On December 22, 1979, plaintiff's scheduled return date, Northwest issued the plaintiff a boarding pass for the Billings-Great Falls-Missoula- Spokane flight. But weather conditions at take-off time, 9:50 A.M., prevented Northwest from landing in Missoula. Therefore, all Missoula passengers were placed on a Billings-Helena flight and were then taken by bus from Helena to Missoula. Plaintiff was offered a check for $29.70, the savings on his alternative transportation. The check was returned several months later, after this suit was initiated.

Plaintiff alleges he arrived home eight hours late because of the flight cancellation. He earned $153,000 in 1979, working 3,000 hours at $50 an hour. As an insurance agent, he claims his weekends are particularly lucrative, earning him more than $100 an hour for ten hours a day. He is seeking $1,000 damages for the loss of a ten-hour day and $122 refund for his plane fare. . . .

The [lower] Court determined there were no material issues of fact and that Northwest was entitled to judgment as a matter of law.

Did weather conditions in Missoula prevent the plane from landing? Northwest needs three miles of visibility to land in Missoula. Common sense dictates that only the weather conditions existing prior to take-off, 9:50 A.M., are pertinent. In this case, plaintiff's own exhibit from the National Weather Service shows there was only one and one-half miles of visibility at 9:52 A.M. Therefore, weather clearly prevented Northwest from landing in Missoula.

Did Northwest have a legal right to cancel the Billings-Missoula flight in light of the poor weather? Civil Aeronautics Board regulations govern rights and liabilities between airlines and passengers and cover this issue. Those regulations authorize airlines to cancel flights when necessary. Therefore, Northwest acted within its legal authority in canceling the Billings-Missoula flight.

Did Northwest have a right to refuse plaintiff a seat after a boarding pass had been issued? As noted above, the flight was properly cancelled due to adverse weather. [A] Civil Aeronautics Board Tariff does not require advance notice to be given of flight cancellations. Therefore, Northwest properly excluded plaintiff, even after a boarding pass had been issued.

[W]e believe there are no material issues of fact and that Northwest is entitled to judgment as a matter of law.

CASE QUESTION

1. Why do you think the law relieves an airline from liability for breach of contract when a flight is cancelled due to weather conditions?

The fact that weather conditions or some other acceptable reason caused the cancellation is not the end of the inquiry. To avoid liability the airline must assist passengers in locating alternate flights to reach their destination. Liability will result if the airline fails to aid passengers adequately in making other arrangements.

Sometimes an airline's efforts to aid a passenger whose flight has been cancelled or delayed are frustrated by the negligence of another airline. Liability in such a case may fall on the second airline and not the one that cancelled the flight. Airlines are required to aid travelers whose flights with other airlines are cancelled. In *Levy v. Eastern Airlines and Pan American Airlines*, 449 N.Y.S.2d 906 (1982), plaintiff's family's flight on Eastern Airlines was delayed due to bad weather. Before he left home plaintiff was notified by phone of the delay and offered seats on a Pan American flight leaving 20 minutes earlier. He agreed and the Eastern representative confirmed the Pan American reservations. When plaintiff and his family arrived at the airport the Pan American representative denied knowledge of the reservations. Plaintiff contacted an airport Eastern representative who contacted Pan American by phone and again confirmed the reservations. Plaintiff's family went to the Pan American gate and again attempted to board. The Pan American ticket agent at the gate failed to check whether confirmed reservations existed for plaintiff and summarily denied them boarding. The plane left without plaintiff and his family. Plaintiff sued both Eastern and Pan American. Concerning Pan American, the court held it had failed to satisfy its duty under an applicable tariff rule to assist passengers from other airlines' cancelled flights. Pan American was thus liable.

Plaintiff also claimed that Eastern was liable. The court held Eastern complied with its obligation to assist in finding alternate travel arrangements. Plaintiff further argued that Pan American was acting as Eastern's agent and therefore Eastern should be liable to plaintiff for Pan American's inappropriate actions. The court held no agency relationship existed between the two airlines but rather Eastern was acting as an agent of plaintiff. Therefore Eastern was not liable.

Rights of Airline Captains

Passengers in flight are confined by the aircraft for the duration of the trip. If anyone on the plane seeks to jeopardize the safety of the passengers—by hijacking, assault, or otherwise—the option of calling the police is not available. The result is that the occupants of the plane can readily be placed at risk. To address this issue, the law gives the pilot significant latitude in deciding to remove a ticketed passenger from the plane prior to take-off.

The following case addresses the extent of the pilot's authority to remove travelers who are suspected of being hijackers.

CASE EXAMPLE 13–5

Zervigon v Piedmont Aviation, Inc.
558 F.Supp.1305 (N.Y., 1983), aff'd w/out
opinion, 742 F2d 1433 (1983)

Eight plaintiffs, who were removed from an airplane owned and operated by defendant, Piedmont Aviation, Inc., ("Piedmont"), which was about to depart from Tampa, Florida, to New York City, were each awarded $7,500 damages by a jury. Piedmont now moves for judgment notwithstanding the verdict ("nov").

The Plaintiffs allege that their involuntary removal was discriminatory and in violation of [the law]. Piedmont justified its action upon the ground that in the opinion of the captain of the airplane plaintiffs' continued presence thereon (1) "would or might be inimical to the safety of [the] flight," and (2) presented the possibility that they "would cause disruption or serious impairment to the physical comfort or safety of other passengers or [the] carrier's employees," as provided under Piedmont's tariff filed with the Civil Aeronautics Board. . . .

A trial court may correct a jury verdict only if after so viewing the evidence it is convinced that the evidence is so strong and overwhelming in favor of the prevailing party that reasonable and fair-minded persons, in the exercise of impartial judgment, could not render a verdict against it.

The issues must be considered against the totality of the facts as they existed at the time the captain took his action. His decision cannot be viewed in isolation separate from events that preceded it but in proper perspective as of the time of their occurrence and in relationship to one another. Whether a captain properly exercised the power to remove a passenger . . . "rests upon the facts and circumstances of the case as known to the [captain] at the time [he] formed [his] opinion and made [his] decision and whether or not the opinion and decision were rational and reasonable and not capricious or arbitrary in the light of all those facts and circumstances." The fact that the safety and well being of many lives are dependent upon his judgment necessarily means that the captain is vested with wide discretion. "This is understandable when one considers that an airline usually must make such decisions on the spur of the moment, shortly before takeoff, without the benefit of complete and accurate information." Thus, "the reasonableness of the carrier's opinion . . . is to be tested on the information available to the airline at the moment a decision is required. There is correspondingly no duty to conduct an in-depth investigation into a ticket-holder's potentially dangerous proclivities."

We thus consider the evidence against the applicable law. The eight plaintiffs and their band boy left LaGuardia Airport, New York City, on the morning of March 28, 1981, on a Piedmont airplane for Tampa, where they were to perform at a dance concert that evening. They were ticketed to return to New York the next morning at 7:05 on Piedmont Flight 372. After completing their performance, and following a brief stopoff in the early hours of the morning at a hotel, they arrived at the Tampa airport where they waited in an embarkation room preparatory to boarding the 7:05 A.M. plane. While there and waiting to enplane, the group, by their loud and boisterous manner, attracted the attention of Mr. Luis Ramos, another passenger. Mr. Ramos and his wife heard one of the group say to another in Spanish "when we arrive in the capital they will ask us for our experience on this flight," which Mr. Ramos regarded as unusual.

After the passengers were seated on the plane, it left the gate and readied for the takeoff. The members of the musical group were seated generally in the same area in the rear of the plane. However, before reaching the runway, the band boy assaulted a stewardess by grabbing her hand, twisting it and she screamed. She was visibly shaken and reported the incident and her concern about the group to the captain, George Sturgil, who immediately called airport security and returned to the gate, where he ordered the band boy removed from the plane. Following the band boy's removal, the plane again taxied for the takeoff. It returned a second time to the gate, however, to remove a bass instrument that erroneously was thought to belong to the band boy.

While the plane was at the gate for the second time, Mr. Ramos, who had observed the band boy being taken off the plane by a police or security officer, said to a passenger seated next to him, Mr. Herbert Hill, that the band boy "belong[ed] to a group of musicians, like eight or ten, who were talking in the waiting room. And one of them said to another, 'when we arrive in the capital, they will ask us about our experience on this flight.'" Hill understood Ramos to say "[W]on't the people be surprised when we get to the capital with this aircraft." The use of the word "capital" suggested to Hill that the plane would not land as scheduled, and "rang a bell" in his head that it was Havana, Cuba, where the plane would be forced to land. Thereafter, Hill signalled a stewardess and at his request Ramos repeated the statement to her. She then apprised the captain of it, who immediately left the cockpit and went to where Hill and the Ramoses were sitting. Ramos then repeated his story to the captain. Captain Sturgil returned to the cockpit and ordered the removal of the plaintiffs. Mr. and Mrs. Ramos and Mr. Hill all testified that the overheard statement made them apprehensive that a highjacking to Cuba was in the making.

There can be no doubt that as a matter of law the captain's decision was reasonable and appropriate. The facts known to him provided a sufficient basis for concluding that plaintiffs' continued presence on the aircraft would or might be inimical to the safety of the flight. From the totality of circumstances, the captain was completely justified in believing that there existed a potential highjack threat. As commander of the aircraft, he was charged with the responsibility for the one hundred persons aboard: both passengers and crew alike. If he had decided otherwise, and continued the flight with the plaintiffs on board, his inaction might well have subjected the flight and passengers to grave danger. Indeed, with the information conveyed to him and the prior incident of an assault upon a crew member, if the captain had not taken the action he did he may well have faced a charge of dereliction of duty. Overall, his decision to remove the plaintiffs, therefore, was both reasonable and prudent. There is not the slightest basis to the charge that the action was not taken in good faith. The contention that he should have questioned each member of the group before ordering their removal is unrealistic. He had sufficient indicia of conduct centering about the members of the group that "would or might be inimical to the safety of [the] flight" to warrant forthwith action. He did not have to tempt fate so that the prospect of highjacking became reality.

Moreover, the captain's action was justified under the terms of the tariff filed with the Civil Aeronautics Board. The information conveyed to him by the flight attendant as to the conduct of the group was sufficient to alert him to the "possibility . . . that [the plaintiffs] would cause disruption or serious impairment to the physical comfort and safety of other passengers." Therefore, the Court grants defendant's motion and sets aside the jury's verdict. The complaint is dismissed and a verdict directed in favor of the defendant. So ordered.

CASE QUESTION

1. Why does a pilot need the authority to remove passengers from a flight?

The following case confirms the wide latitude given to the pilot to exclude troublesome passengers from a flight.

CASE EXAMPLE 13–6

Sarah Rombom v. United Airlines
867 F. Supp. 214 (1994)

On August 3, 1992, plaintiff, Sarah Shepard Rombom ("Rombom"), boarded a United flight in Chicago destined for New York. Rombom and her traveling companion, Lani Adelman ("Adelman"), however, were removed from the plane before it departed and arrested by the Chicago Police Department.

Both sides agree on the following facts. Plaintiff claims that after she and Adelman boarded the flight, they engaged in conversation with three men seated in the row behind them. The group became friendly, photographs were taken, and one of the men massaged Adelman's hand between the seats. . . . As the aircraft left the gate, a flight attendant had to stop reading the flight safety instructions to ask Rombom, Adelman, and the three men to be quiet. . . .

The parties disagree about what then ensued. United claims that the group refused to comply with the flight attendant's requests to be quiet, and continued to act in a rambunctious manner during and after the safety instructions. The flight attendant sought assistance from the head flight attendant, defendant Joyce Cunningham, who notified the pilot, defendant K. S. Burbech, of the situation. Burbech instructed Cunningham to tell the offending passengers that they would be removed from the aircraft if they failed to behave properly. Cunningham relayed this message to Rombom and her associates, who allegedly reacted to this ultimatum by becoming even more ill-mannered.

Cunningham reported this response to Burbech, who decided to return to the gate. At the gate, members of the crew requested that the five offending passengers disembark. The group refused, and asserted that they would deplane only if escorted off by the police. The police were then summoned to escort the passengers off the plane. At this point, the three men deplaned quietly and were not arrested. Rombom and Adelman, however, had a sharp exchange with the police officers, who arrested the women for disorderly conduct.

Plaintiff describes quite a different scenario. She rejects United's characterization of her conduct as disruptive and a safety problem. To the contrary, Rombom alleges that it was Cunningham who acted inappropriately and unprofessional, in a rude and aggressive manner toward her and Adelman. . . .

Rombom and Adelman were taken to a holding cell at the airport. They were later transported to another jail in downtown Chicago, where they were placed with "hard core criminals." Rombom was scared that she would be raped because the words "Lesbian love" were written all over the walls of her cell. Rombom and Adelman were released on bail later that evening. The charge against Rombom and Adelman was subsequently withdrawn.

Rombom sued United, the pilot, and the head flight attendant in the Supreme Court of the State of New York, New York County, claiming that as a result of the defendants' actions she suffered "great mental and physical distress, of a temporary and permanent nature, was humiliated, made sick and injured her character and reputation and otherwise suffered grievous harm." Rombom demanded five million dollars in compensatory damages, and punitive and exemplary damages in the amount of three million dollars. . . .

Under federal law, the pilot has discretion to refuse to transport a passenger who poses a threat to the safety of the flight. Whether the pilot properly exercised his discretion to deny Rombom passage by returning to the gate rests on the facts and circumstances of the case as known to the airline at the time it formed its opinion and made its decision [to deny transport to a passenger] and whether or not the opinion and decision were rational and reasonable and not capricious or arbitrary in light of the facts and circumstances. They are not to be tested by other facts later disclosed by hindsight. . . .

Nothing in the record even remotely suggests that Captain Burbech's decision fell outside the spectrum of reasonable conduct. At best, Rombom alleges that the Captain overreacted to the threat Rombom and her companions posed. . . .

As noted, Rombom alleges that well after she ceased to pose a safety threat, the flight crew decided to have her arrested. Rombom argues that this decision was motivated by spite. . . .

An air carrier is authorized to refuse transportation to a passenger "when, in the opinion of the carrier, such transportation would or might be inimical to safety of the flight." Federal regulations place this authority in the pilot's discretion. . . .

For the reasons stated above, United's motion for summary judgment is partially granted with respect to any claims based on (1) the arguments plaintiff had with the flight attendants concerning her behavior, and (2) the pilot's decision to return to the gate.

Overbooking

Because so many people make airline reservations and then do not appear for the flight, airlines will frequently deliberately overbook a flight. This practice ensures that the plane will fly as close to capacity as possible. Airlines are not the only travel service suppliers that overbook; hotels also do it, as we discussed in Chapter 4.

A problem arises, of course, when there are fewer no-shows than expected. The result is insufficient seats on the plane (or rooms in a hotel) to accommodate everyone with a confirmed reservation. In such instances, the airline will "bump" some passengers, denying them transportation.

According to the Department of Transportation, for a three month period, the airlines paid 127,500 passengers to give up their seats. The 10 major airlines bumped an additional 10,917 people involuntarily while boarding 90,918,016—a rate of 1.2 bumpings for every 10,000 passengers.

What are the rights of the person who is bumped? An involuntarily bumped traveler may be entitled to damages for breach of contract and, in those cases where the carrier fails to assist the traveler in making alternate plans, to punitive damages.

In *Lopez v. Eastern Airlines, Inc.*, 677 F. Supp.181 (N.Y.,1988), Lopez, a lawyer, was bumped from an 8:00 P.M. flight on which he had confirmed reservations and rescheduled on a midnight flight, disrupting his plans by four hours. He sued the airline for $2,500; he was awarded $450 for breach of contract. The court determined the airline had breached its contract with him and so he was entitled to damages. He used his original ticket for the later flight so he suffered no out-of-pocket loss. The court based the award of $450 on plaintiff's inconvenience, loss of time, anxiety and frustration. In addition to the breach of contract claim, Lopez had also sued for the tort of fraudulent representation concerning his confirmed reservation. The court denied this claim on the ground that, "[T]he practice of overbooking in the air transportation industry was public information, openly discussed by the carriers, the Civil Aeronautics Board and publications of national circulation. Therefore the limitations of a 'confirmed' reservation should have been known by plaintiff."

When overbooking occurs, the law specifies how a determination will be made as to who will be denied seating. The airlines must first ask for volunteers who agree to wait for a later flight, usually in exchange for free airline tickets for a subsequent trip. Thereafter the airline must apply its priority rules which all airlines must develop and file with the Department of Transportation. This process is explained in the next case.

CASE EXAMPLE 13–7

Goranson v. Trans World Airlines
467 N.Y.S.2d 774 (1983)

This small claim is based on TWA's bumping of the plaintiff, Arlene Goranson, from her scheduled flight to London as part of a vacation tour for which she had contracted. The Court holds TWA liable for bumping as a common law breach of contract and awards compensatory damages in the amount of $1,500. . . .

Plaintiff, Arlene Goranson, contracted with TWA for a flight to London as part of a tour to

Great Britain and other places in Europe that was leaving on April 18, 1982. She is an intelligent woman having a genuine interest in gardening and is a member of various horticulture associations. She therefore had a special personal interest in visiting the Savill Gardens which was scheduled as part of the tour. She saved for this trip and waited many years before taking it. She selected TWA because of its representations as to reliability and responsibility. One of many such representations in TWA's brochures promoting the tour read:

Remove Uncertainties the TWA Way

Have you ever been stranded at an airport because you couldn't get on a plane? Have you ever had to travel miles out of your way to catch a "bargain" flight? If not, think about it. It's not the best way to begin a carefree vacation. Consider: *with TWA there are no charter risks, no standby blues or airport gambles. Every flight is scheduled, carrying with it the TWA reputation of reliability. You know in advance exactly where you'll fly from and when.* Maybe you'll pay a few dollars more for peace of mind, but don't you think it's worth it? (Emphasis by TWA)

When she arrived at JFK Airport on the evening of the scheduled departure date, TWA was unable to provide her with the previously confirmed space due to overbooking. Reliability and peace of mind, promised to her, vanished except for the printing in the advertisements.

She could not obtain transportation to London for two days and she arrived in London on the following Monday, missing the first two days of her tour which included the Savill Gardens. She asked permission from TWA during the tour to return to London at the end of the tour to see the places that she missed. However, TWA refused this proposal. She was required to return to the United States with the remaining passengers as scheduled. TWA offered to pay her $400 being the maximum set forth in the [Civil Aeronautics Board] regulations, but she refused and brought this small claim action for $1,500.

The two issues presented are: (1) whether TWA was liable because of overbooking and subsequent bumping as a simple common law breach of contract; and (2) whether the amount of damages is exclusively governed by, and cannot exceed that allowed by, CAB regulations.

In 1976, Justice Powell, in *Ralph Nader v. Allegheny Airlines, Inc.*, 426 U.S. 290, 294, 96 S.Ct. 1978, 1982, 48 L.Ed.2d 643 (1976), discussed the necessity of overbooking and the airlines contention that it was a desirable practice:

Such overbooking is a common industry practice, designed to ensure that each flight leaves with as few empty seats as possible despite the large number of "no-shows"—reservation-holding passengers who do not appear at flight time. By the use of statistical studies of no-show patterns on specific flights, the airlines attempt to predict the appropriate number of reservations necessary to fill each flight. In this way, they attempt to ensure the most efficient use of aircraft while preserving a flexible booking system. . . . At times the practice of overbooking results in oversales, which occur when more reservation-holding passengers than can be accommodated actually appear to board the flight. When this occurs, some passengers must be denied boarding ("bumped"). The chance that any particular passenger will be bumped is so negligible that few prospective passengers aware of the possibility would give it a second thought. . . .

The CAB's current policy embodied in its Oversales Regulations, however, is (1) to allow oversales, (2) to leave it to the carrier to ensure that bumping is minimized, (3) to provide a regulated amount or minimum compensation to the aggrieved passenger, and (4) to recognize the passengers optional right to recover damages in a court of law.

The inconsistency of the CAB's approval of the bumping practice, along with the implied recognition that it is a breach of contract, has proven to be troublesome.

Under CAB regulations, in the case of "deliberate overbooking," the airline must now follow a defined procedure. . . . It must first request volunteers who are willing to relinquish their reserved space in return for compensation and second, it must arrange for comparable transportation for a passenger denied boarding.

The airline may then deny boarding to a passenger in accordance with its own boarding priority rules. The airline, however, must then provide compensation for those involuntarily denied boarding. The amount of this compensation as set forth in the tariff varies for each case, but the maximum is $400.

This Court now concludes that when TWA refused to provide plaintiff passage on the plane that she had tickets—when she was "bumped," and when TWA did not provide plaintiff with the first two tour days she contracted for, in each instance, there was a common law breach of contract for which there is a traditional state court remedy.

Accordingly, TWA is liable for overbooking and bumping as simple common law breach of contract and plaintiff Arlene Goranson is awarded actual compensatory damages without regard to TWA's tariff or to any CAB regulation.

With respect to the damage issue, courts have held that damages may consist of a wide variety of elements, including expenses for substitute or alternate transportation, meals, compensation for humiliation, outrage and inconvenience. . . .

Plaintiff's actual damages are related to her loss of two days of traveling and vacation in England where she had intended specifically to see the Savill Gardens and related attractions. She is therefore entitled to recoup these two days in England, with TWA paying her expenses as damages.

The Court therefore calculates her damages as the cost of round trip air transportation to London ($800), ground transportation to and from airports for the round trip ($100), hotel and meals for 3 days in England ($400) and tour expenses ($100). This totals $1400. Plaintiff is also entitled to recover for her extreme inconvenience, aggravated by TWA's refusal to allow her to return to England at the end of the tour to see the attraction she missed on her first 2 days. Since the Court's small claim jurisdiction is only $1500, only $100 additional can be allowed for inconvenience.

Judgment is therefore entered for Plaintiff for $1500 plus costs.

In *Smith v. Piedmont Aviation, Inc.*, 567 F.2d 290 (5th Cir., 1978), the airline was liable for failing to follow its priority rules. Plaintiff was denied seating on his confirmed fight because it was overbooked. Piedmont used a first-come first-served basis to determine who would be bumped. However, Piedmont's rules required priority be given based on the time and date the passenger booked the reservation. The boarding agent testified that had he abided by the airline's priority rule, the record check to ensure compliance would have delayed the flight several hours. Plaintiff nonetheless won the case. The basis for the airline's liability was its disregard of its own priority rules.

The plaintiff in this case also sought punitive damages based on the following additional facts. Plaintiff originally rejected alternate flights offered by Piedmont because they would have caused him to miss a rehearsal for a wedding in which he was the best man. He thrice demanded a charter flight to his destination. The Piedmont agent finally responded, "I don't know when you're going to get it through your thick head we're not going to charter you a flight."

The court refused to award punitive damages finding no malice on the part of Piedmont. Instead the court termed the agent's statement "a reaction obviously provoked by [plaintiff's] repeated unreasonable requests for a charter flight." The court further noted, "Although he missed the rehearsal, plaintiff performed flawlessly as groomsman." An important point working in Piedmont's favor on the issue of punitive damages was that it assisted plaintiff in securing alternate travel arrangements.

In other cases courts have ruled that a traveler who is bumped from a domestic flight is not entitled to punitive damages. *West v. Northwest Airlines, Inc.*, 995 F.2d 148 (9th Cir., 1993). Similarly, a passenger who is refused seating on an oversubscribed international flight is not entitled to punitive damages, based on the limitations of liability provided in the Warsaw Convention. The Convention was discussed previously in this chapter and governs international flights. *Harpalani v. Air-India*, 634 F. Supp 797 (Ill., 1986).

Punitive damages were awarded in *Bottenstein v. Connecticut American Bus Lines*, 509 N.Y.S.2d 248 (1986), involving bus transportation. The case was brought in Small Claims Court. Defendant bus company failed to honor plaintiffs' confirmed bus tickets home from an overnight trip to Atlantic City because the bus was overbooked. Defendant also failed to help plaintiffs find alternate means of transportation. Plaintiffs found a ride on Greyhound and sued defendant for compensation for their expenses home, reimbursement for their ticket on defendant's bus, and punitive damages. The court held for the plaintiff on all counts, stating that the defendant's failure to assist plaintiffs in "secur[ing] some safe alternative means of transportation is not to be countenanced, and shows a reckless and willful disregard towards the plaintiffs in derogation of their contract for safe passage."

Liability for Consequences of Traveler's Lack of Visa

When people travel to countries other than their place of residence, certain documents are often required for entry. These may include a passport and a visa. The airline tariffs provide that the traveler and not the airline is responsible to determine what documents are required and to secure them. In two cases a traveler did not have the necessary documentation and was denied either travel on the plane or entry into the foreign country. In both cases the airline was sued. In both cases the airline's tariffs clearly stated that the responsibility for obtaining the necessary travel documents rests with the passenger. As a result, both cases were decided in favor of the airline.

In *Chukwu v. British Airways*, 915 F. Supp. 454 (Mass., 1996), the plaintiff, although ticketed, was not allowed to board his flight because he did not have the required visa. The airline refunded the cost of the ticket. Plaintiff sought damages for "unreasonable psychological traumatic experiences." The court dismissed the case finding that the airline's tariff permitted it to deny boarding to a passenger whose travel documents were legally insufficient.

A plaintiff in another case was permitted to board a plane to Turkey and was transported there. Upon arrival she was taken into custody by Turkish officials because she did not have the necessary visa to enter the country. Following her ordeal she sued the airline, claiming it should have informed her of the visa requirement. The airline's tariff places the requirement of securing the necessary travel documents on the passenger, and relieves the airline from advising the passenger concerning necessary documentation. The tariff further relieved the airline from liability for the consequences to a passenger of failing to acquire a visa. Therefore, the case was decided in defendant's favor. *Aquasviva v. Iberia Lineas Aereas de Espana*, 902 F. Supp. 314 (Puerto Rico, 1995).

Liability for Negligence

Airlines, like other hospitality businesses, are liable for negligence that causes injury to a guest. Examples of the type of negligent acts that can result in liability to an airline include: 1) failing to properly latch the door of a serving cart that swung open on take-off and struck a passenger's knee; and 2) improper monitoring by flight attendants of compliance with regulations concerning use of overhead luggage racks, resulting in a suitcase falling on a passenger's head. *Gee v. Southwest Airlines*, 110 F.3d 1400 (9th Cir., 1997).

Liabilities of Travel Agents and Charter Tour Companies

There are over 40,000 travel agents in the United States and they play a key role in the travel industry. While in the past they functioned as mere ticket dispensers, today they are information specialists on whose expertise the traveling public heavily relies.

In this section we will examine the parameters of the retail travel agent's liability in day-to-day business conduct. These liabilities include both the travel agent's own actions, those of the agent's employees, and under certain circumstances, those of third-party suppliers that a travel agent recommends to clients.

Liability for Own Actions

Like any other business person, the travel agent will be held liable to clients for wrongful acts, including torts such as negligence and fraud. The reason for this liability is that travel agents represent themselves as experts in making travel arrangements and customers rely on that expertise. Travel agents must exercise reasonable care in making a client's travel arrangements and must not intentionally mislead a client.

Provide Accurate Information.   If the travel agent gives false or incomplete information, the traveler may experience great inconvenience. In such a case the travel agent may be liable. In the next case both the travel agent and the airline misled the plaintiff traveler. Both were required to compensate the plaintiff.

CASE EXAMPLE 13–8

Burnap v. Tribeca Travel
530 N.Y.S.2d 926 (N.Y., 1988)

In this small claims case, the court has been asked to decide when a ticket is a ticket. It all began when Mr. Boston and Ms. Burnap pur-

chased two round-trip tickets from Tribeca Travel agency for Paris, back in August of 1987. The travel agency booked them on Continental Airlines departing on September 16, 1987 and returning from Paris on September 26, 1987.

Perhaps it did not bode well for their trip that the tickets did not arrive until September 15, 1987, but nevertheless they took off at the scheduled time on September 16, 1987.

Once in Paris they called to confirm their return flight three days before (Sept. 23) and they arrived at the airport on September 26, 1987 for their return flight in what they thought was a timely fashion, i.e., since the tickets indicated the departure time was 11:00 A.M. they arrived about 10 minutes before 10:00 and were informed that the flight had been rescheduled for 10:00 A.M. and that given customs and security they could not make the flight. Since both Mr. Boston and Ms. Burnap had obligations in New York and Continental had no other flights that day, they purchased two one way tickets to New York on American Airlines.

Once back in New York, they wrote to Tribeca Travel requesting that they be reimbursed for the return tickets they had bought from American Airlines and Tribeca refused. Mr. Boston and Ms. Burnap sued Tribeca, and Tribeca in turn sued Sofa Travel (its agent) and Continental Airlines. . . .

[T]hrough its president, Larry Handel, Tribeca Travel denied responsibility. Mr. Handel testified that the time of the return flight from Paris had been changed by Continental Airlines on September 5, 1987. Mr. Handel indicated that he wrote the ticket himself on September 4, 1987. He acknowledged however that the ticket was not delivered until September 15, 1987. When asked why the ticket was not altered to reflect the change in time between September 4 (when it was written) and September 15 (when it was hand delivered) Mr. Handel had a number of explanations which are presented here, not necessarily in the order argued. The first of those was that the change occurred over a holiday week-end (Labor Day). The second was that he did not have a computer on which to receive notice of the change. Third, he stated that the cost of the tickets ($440) was substantially less than the market price (over $1,200). Finally Mr. Handel argued that anyone who travels nowadays must count on delays and problems and that they must learn to take it in stride. Hence this decision since it seems clear to the Court that no monetary award alone will suffi-

ciently indicate to the travel agent that while travel delays and hassles these days are more the rule than the exception, that he has some obligation to prevent them where he is responsible.

Following Mr. Handel's testimony Mr. Stuart Pollack, the General Manager of Continental Airlines, testified that Continental had rescheduled the time of the return flight from Paris to New York on September 4, 1987. As was their standard procedure for such changes (or "Ques" as they call them), the change was relayed by computer to Tribeca travel agents on September 5, 1987. He offered into evidence a computer printout with an accompanying explanation of the various codes contained in it which indicated that the information concerning the change in flights had been sent to the Continental Reservations Agents in Paris. When questioned about why Mr. Boston and Ms. Burnap had not been told of the time change when they called to reconfirm their flight in Paris, he responded that the code on the printout indicated that the travel agent had already been notified and therefore there was no need to tell them.

Neither the airline nor the travel agent acknowledge any responsibility for the failure to notify Boston and Burnap. Mr. Handel [president of Tribeca] implied that the purchase of a ticket at a bargain rate creates less of a contract than if it is purchased at full face.

Mr. Handel seems to view the purchase of an airline ticket as no different from buying a subway token: Caveat emptor [let the buyer beware] and *if* the train comes, get on it quick! These arguments notwithstanding, the Courts have recognized that the purchase of an airline ticket creates a contract between the parties. Here the travel agent held himself out as being in the business of selling tickets. Both claimants responded and purchased tickets. Clearly part of the contract created by the purchase is being able to rely on the date and times of flight departures as they are given on the ticket.

The travel agent claims that he had no computer in his uptown office and therefore did not receive the transmission from Continental Airlines indicating that they had changed the time of departure. This is no defense since he had a computer in his other office and more importantly, he had an obligation to inform the passengers who purchased tickets and relied on him to provide them valid and proper tickets in exchange for the requested fare. Moreover, Sofa who worked for them and had provided the tickets in question acknowledged that they had a computer.

Nor can Continental Airlines be viewed as blameless. They sent the information to Paris and failed to notify Boston and Burnap when they called to confirm. Sofa on the other hand had no direct dealings with claimants. Tribeca, which sued Sofa, failed to establish any responsibility on [Sofa's] part for any of these occurrences.

However, Tribeca and Continental are both liable to claimants. Continental must pay claimants

for the balance of the tickets paid for that were unused because claimants were not informed of the scheduled change. Judgment is awarded against Continental, in the amount of $440.

Tribeca Travel bears greater responsibility since it drew up the ticket but never corrected it to reflect the actual departure time. Since the claimants return tickets cost $1,384 and Continental is liable for the unused half of the tickets, judgment is awarded against Tribeca Travel in the amount of $944. [The difference between the cost of the return tickets and the amount Continental was required to pay].

CASE QUESTIONS

1. What should Tribeca Travel agency have done in this case to avoid liability?
2. What could Continental Airlines have done in this case to avoid liability?
3. Why do you think Tribeca Travel Agency was ordered to pay more than Continental Airlines?

In *Das v. Royal Jordanian Airlines*, 766 F.Supp. 169 (N.Y., 1961), the travel agent issued airline tickets to a client for travel from New York City to Calcutta, India. The agent handwrote on the tickets "confirmed." In fact the travel agent knew the client was "wait listed" (on a waiting list without a confirmed reservation). When the client arrived for the flight he was denied a seat and sued the agent for breach of duty of due care. The court held for the plaintiff and awarded him both the cost of the tickets and money for emotional distress.

Investigate Third-Party Suppliers.   Travel agents have a duty to do the following vis-a-vis service providers (hotels, charter companies, tour operators, etc.) they recommend: investigate their operations; discover material information about them that is reasonably available; and disclose that information to their customers. Travelers are legally entitled to expect that travel services recommended by a travel agent will be reliable and suitable. Failure of a travel agent to adequately investigate can lead to liability, as the agent in the following case learned.

CASE EXAMPLE 13–9

Josephs v. Fuller (Club Dominicus)
451 A.2d 203 (N.J., 1982)

This is an action by John and Regina Josephs against a resort known as Club Dominicus and a travel agency known as Richard's Travel Service, brought because defendant's resort accommodations were substandard.

It is uncontested that defendant Richard's Travel Service (Richard's) recommended and arranged for plaintiffs to spend their vacations at Club Dominicus in the Dominican Republic, and that the accommodations provided by Club Dominicus were far below standard.

It appears, further, that Richard's is independent from Club Dominicus except for the commissions received for booking vacations.

Richard's moved for dismissal at the end of plaintiff's case on the ground that plaintiff had not proved any facts upon which liability of a travel agent could be based. (It should be noted that defendant Club Dominicus is not involved at this point of the litigation because it is in default for failing to answer the complaint.)

Richard's argues that it was simply an agent for a disclosed principal and, as such, owed no duty to plaintiffs. The only party owing any duty to plaintiffs [according to Richard's] was the disclosed principal, Club Dominicus, and that party is the only one liable for a breach.

For the reasons enunciated herein, Richard's motion [to dismiss] is denied.

Defendant is mistaken in its contention that because it was paid by Club Dominicus it was the agent of Club Dominicus only, and since its principal was disclosed to the plaintiffs, it owed no duty to the plaintiffs. . . .

Defendant's position is that, even if it was negligent in booking a vacation at a resort about which it knew nothing, it is not liable because it owed no duty to the plaintiffs. This is clearly wrong.

Since defendant's commissions were paid by Club Dominicus, those commissions would not be earned without plaintiff's patronage. The pecuniary benefit bestowed on defendant by plaintiff forms the basis of a legal duty.

As a travel agent, [defendant] owed a certain duty to [its customers]. A travel agent is a special agent, akin to a broker, which engages in a single business transaction with the principal.

[I]t would seem absurd to hold that defendant Richard's had no duty to acquire any knowledge of the facilities it was booking. Plaintiffs could well have made their own arrangements, choosing a resort at random. But rather than risk a substandard vacation, they took advantage of the service offered by defendant. As it turned out, defendant had little or no more knowledge than the plaintiffs.

This court, therefore, holds that when a traveler relies on the recommendations of a travel agent and suffers damage because of accommodations so totally unacceptable that any reasonable travel agent would have known not to make such recommendations, the travel agent is liable.

A travel agent was liable when a hotel he recommended to a customer was "closed, chained and guarded" upon the traveler's arrival. Said the court, "A travel agency has a duty to his customer to not only use reasonable care in making travel reservations, but also in confirming them prior to the date of the trip." *Barton v. Wonderful World of Travel, Inc.*, 502 N.E.2d 715 (Ohio, 1986).

A travel agent was liable to his customer where the agent failed to confirm that a tour advertised as including two meals a day in fact included the meals. After the client paid $1,032 for two people and the agent sent the money to the tour operator minus the agent's commission, the agent learned the trip did not include the meals. Thereafter, upon the agent's representation to the customer that the trip could be cancelled with a full refund, the customer chose to cancel rather than pay an additional $300 for the meals. In fact, the money was not refundable. The customer thus lost $1,032. The travel agent was liable to the customer for this amount based on breach of contract and negligent performance of his duties. Said the court, "Defendant's contractual obligation included verifying and confirming that such tour with the enumerated components and at the stated price was actually available before he sold it." *Pellegrini v. Landmark Travel Group*, 628 N.Y.S.2d 1003 (1995).

In another case the travel agent was found liable for failing to have sufficiently investigated the status of the charter company with which the agent made reservations for plaintiff and her four children to fly. Plaintiff's trip to Puerto Rico occurred without incident. When she and her family arrived at the airport ready to board the flight home, she learned the air carrier had gone out of business. She sued the travel agent, seeking the cost of the tickets she purchased from another air carrier for the flight home. "There was no testimony of efforts made [by the travel agent] to assure the performance [by the charger company] and no evidence that the travel agent provided the [traveler] with information about any risks associated [with a charter]." The court held the travel agent was liable for cost of the return flight tickets because it failed to ascertain the reliability of the charter company it recommended. *Rodriguez v. Cardona Travel Agency*, 523 A.2d 281 (N.J., 1986).

Similarly, a travel agent was found liable for having insufficiently researched a tour operator it recommended. The tour company went bankrupt resulting in the loss of a client's vacation money. The court ordered the travel agent to compensate the traveler for the loss. *Douglas v. Steel*, 816 P.2d (Ok., 1991).

Travel agents are well advised to suggest travel insurance to their customers. Such insurance compensates the would-be traveler for the cost paid for the vacation if the trip is cancelled for certain reasons, including bankruptcy of the travel provider. Having recommended the purchase of travel insurance can assist a travel agent's defense when sued by a customer whose plans were frustrated by a supplier's bankruptcy. In *Creteau v. Liberty Travel, Inc.*, 600 N.Y.S.2d 576 (1993), plaintiffs traveled to St. Croix. Part way through their two-week vacation, both the airline and a subsidiary that made plaintiff's hotel arrangements went bankrupt. The hotel had not been paid and plaintiffs had to pay anew for the hotel and their flight home. They sued the travel agent for the money they double paid. The court held the travel agent was not liable to the plaintiff for the airline's bankruptcy. This case is distinguishable from the two prior cases because the agent was aware that the financial condition of the airlines was questionable and had so informed the plaintiffs. They chose to retain their travel plans nonetheless. An additional factor noted by the court as a basis for finding no liability was the travel agent's repeated recommendation that the plaintiffs purchase travel insurance. The recommendation was included with a written confirmation plaintiff received of his itinerary with the invoice for the trip, and again with the tickets.

In the following case travelers accused a tour operator of failing to properly investigate the hotel accommodations provided on the tour. The tour operator, however, had researched the hotel, and so was not liable to the clients.

CASE EXAMPLE 13–10

Wilson v. American Trans Air, Inc.
874 F.2d 386 (7th Cir., 1989)

. . . American Trans Air (American) is a charter tour operator headquartered in Indianapolis, Indiana. It regularly plans and operates tours to the Cayman Islands. Participants in these tours are offered accommodations at the Holiday Inn Grand Cayman International Beach Resort (Holiday Inn Grand Cayman), operated by Humphreys (Cayman) Ltd, under a franchise agreement with Holiday Inns, Inc. American sometimes sponsors two or three trips to the Cayman Islands per month and has included, as an option, accommodations at the Humphreys hotel in its tours since at least 1976. One employee of American always accompanies the tours to the Caymans and stays with the tour group at the Humphreys hotel.

Mr. and Mrs. Wilson participated in an American tour to the Cayman Islands in October 1984. They chose to stay at the Humphreys hotel. On October 30, Mrs. Wilson was assaulted by an intruder entering her second floor hotel room through a balcony door while she was asleep. The intruder attempted to rob and rape Mrs. Wilson, and she suffered bodily injuries during the attack.

The majority of participants in these tours apparently do not choose to purchase an optional "ground package" that includes accommodations at a local hotel (in this case, Humphreys). However, promotional materials for this trip did include references to accommodations at the Holiday Inn Grand Cayman. In addition, brochures, rate cards, and other promotional material are provided to American by Humphreys at American's request. The Wilsons also assert that, since 1978, American has published advertisements for 131 tours specifically offering accommodations at the Humphreys hotel.

American did conduct basic research regarding its tours. It attempted to gain information about the political stability and climate of the destination country. It apparently did not inquire into guest safety and security at the hotel. The Wilsons allege that there was substantial criminal activity involving guests at the Humphreys hotel in the months preceding the attack on Mrs. Wilson, but American disclaims any knowledge of such activity.

The Wilsons maintain that American is liable to them because it breached its duty as a charter tour operator to investigate proposed accommodations for safety and to warn prospective patrons of any dangerous conditions discovered during the investigation. The Wilsons submit that this duty arises out of contractual language contained in American's travel brochure, the federal regulations governing charter tour operators, and tort law.

The Wilsons ground their contract argument in the following language found in the advertising newsletter that American distributed to potential customers:

Responsibility of American Trans Air: This tour program is planned and operated by American Trans Air, Inc. . . . as *principal* and tour operator . . . American Trans Air is responsible for making all arrangements for transportation, provided that *in the absence of negligence on the part of American Trans Air*, the responsibility does not extend to any assumption of liability for any personal injury or property damage arising out of or caused by any negligent act on the part of any hotel, other air carrier or anyone rendering any of the services or accommodations being offered in connection with this Public Charter. . . .

The Wilsons . . . note that the contract states that American is the principal and is responsible for any negligent act of its own with respect to the accommodations offered in connection with the tour. The Wilsons assert that this duty required American to make some reasonable investigation into the safety of any accommodations that it promoted and recommended and to warn prospective patrons of any danger at the hotel that might affect them.

We cannot accept the Wilsons' contention. . . .

[W]e note that a charter tour operator, as the principal responsible to tour participants for all the services and accommodations offered in connection with the charter tour, cannot disclaim liability for injuries arising out of its *own* negligence. A charter tour operator, as principal, employs independent contractors such as airlines and hotels to provide transportation and accommodation services to its patrons. Although a principal generally cannot be held liable for the torts of an independent contractor, [the] law does allow a principal to be held liable for the torts of a hired independent contractor when the consequences of the principal's own negligent failure to select a competent contractor caused the harm upon which the suit is based. This negligent selection theory would allow liability to be imposed upon American for its own negligence as principal, liability that it did not disclaim under its contract and cannot disclaim under the applicable federal regulation.

Although the Wilsons' allegation that American breached a duty to investigate the safety and security of the hotel accommodations that it included in its tour package can be construed as a claim based on negligent selection theory, their claim cannot

survive. American chose Humphreys to provide the hotel accommodations in its tour package. Humphreys operated a Holiday Inn. The hotel was located on Seven Mile Beach on Grand Cayman Island, British West Indies—a British Crown Colony. There is nothing in the record that indicates that the Holiday Inn Grand Cayman was located in a high-crime area, that the hotel experienced more safety and security problems than other resort hotels on the island, or that the level of criminal activity involving guests at the Holiday Inn Grand Cayman was unusually high for a large beach resort. In addition, American stated that, in considering guest safety and security at hotels included in its tour packages, it "rel[ied] on the general reputation" of the hotels involved. American also knew that Humphreys had security guards on the premises, and it had received no notice of any guest complaints regarding safety and security at the Holiday Inn Grand Cayman. An officer of American had visited the island and engaged in face-to-face negotiations over rates and payment policies with representatives of the hotel. Under such circumstances, American had no duty to make specific inquiries into guest safety or security at the Holiday Inn. . . .

The judgment of the district court [in favor of American] is affirmed.

CASE QUESTIONS

1. On what principal did the court base its judgment?
2. Based on the court's holding, how does the liability of a tour operator for a guest's safety compare with that of an innkeeper?

In another case, vacationers in Jamaica were robbed and one was raped at gunpoint. Among the parties sued was the travel agent who made the arrangements for air travel and lodging. The court, noting that a travel agent is not an insurer or guarantor of its customers' safety, stated that the agent is not obligated to investigate safety factors of lodging accommodations unless requested by the customer to do so. However, the court also stated that "where the agent has knowledge of safety factors or where such information is readily available, a travel agent has the duty to inform the customer of those factors." *Creteau v.*

Liberty Travel, Inc., 600 N.Y.S.2d 576 (N.Y., 1993). Based on the court's somewhat conflicting statements, travel agents would be well-advised to make inquiry of recommended destinations to ensure their relative safety.

Death of a college student on a Mexican party train led to a lawsuit by her parents against the tour operator that arranged the itinerary, transportation, and lodging. The deceased was killed on an unsafe platform when walking from one train car to another. Three prior deaths of college students had occurred on the party train, a fact known to the tour operator but not disclosed to the tour participants. The court refused to dismiss the lawsuit against the tour operator. While it noted that a travel agent or tour operator cannot be "reasonably expected to divine and forewarn of an innumerable litany of tragedies and dangers inherent in foreign travel," the court nonetheless found the tour operator in this case may have violated its duty to disclose information. *Maurer v. Cerkvenik-Anderson Travel, Inc.*, 890 P.2d 69 (Ariz., 1994).

Liability for Breach of Contract by Third-Party Service Suppliers

When a customer purchases a trip from a travel agent and the trip as portrayed does not materialize, the agent may be liable for breach of contract.

In the following case, the travel agent was found liable to a client for a breach of contract where the client's vacation was spoiled by the wholesaler's failure to reserve hotel rooms.

CASE EXAMPLE 13–11

Odysseys Unlimited, Inc. v. Astrol Travel Service
354 N.Y.S.2d 88 (1974)

Following an earlier practice, in the summer of 1972 the Paterson and Majewski families began to plan a joint vacation over the Christmas holiday. In doing so they relied upon Astral Travel Service ("Astral") an agency with which they had previously dealt. They looked forward to spending a few days with their five children in the Canary Islands, of course not anticipating the discomfort, inconvenience and disappointment they would suffer. . . .

Astral (a retail travel agent) suggested to Dr. Paterson and Mr. Majewski a package tour prepared by Odysseys (a wholesale agency). The tour, entitled "Xmas Jet Set Sun Fun/Canary Isle," was scheduled to depart December 26, 1972 by jet for Tenerife, Canary Isles, . . . staying at the "delux Semiramis Hotel" and returning on January 1,

1973 by jet. Majewski and Paterson accepted this trip costing $1,375.90 and $1,076.80 respectively and made their down payments to Astral. Astral withheld its commission and forwarded the balance along with the reservations to Odysseys who in turn confirmed the reservations to Astral. . . . An information sheet . . . furnished details of the trip and referred to the accommodations at the "Five-Star Hotel Semiramis."

On December 26, 1972 the group flew off to the Canary Islands. They arrived at the airport in Tenerife at about dawn and waited about two hours . . . before they were taken to the Hotel Semiramis. At this point the passengers had been en route some thirty hours. While at the airport they saw Mr. Newton, President of Odysseys, who accompanied the group tour. (The inference may reasonably be drawn that he went along because he anticipated the difficulties which were shortly to be encountered.) Two hundred fifty weary but expectant guests arrived at the Semiramis and were presented with a letter from the hotel . . . advising them that there were no accommodations available to their group. Dr. Paterson confronted Mr. Newton with this letter and the latter acknowledged that there was no space available and that he was looking for others. For about four hours, two hundred fifty people (including baggage) were in the lobby of the Semiramis until they were divided into groups and directed to other [hotels]. The Paterson and Majewski families were brought to the Porto Playa Hotel which was not fully ready for occupancy because it was under construction and without the recreational facilities and conveniences available at the Hotel Semiramis. Portions of the Porto Playa Hotel were enclosed in scaffolding. Paterson and Majewski testified that work was done in their rooms, water supply uncertain, electric connections incomplete, etc., etc. throughout their stay.

The court is convinced that prior to the group's departure Mr. Newton was aware that there were no reservations at the Semiramis Hotel for his charges. He testified that on either December 18th or 19th, 1972 he knew of the overbooking at the hotel. . . . In his letter of January 12, 1973 addressed to tour members, Mr. Newton confirms the fact that he had been aware of some "problem with overbooking by that hotel" (Semiramis Hotel) and states that his agent "had the foresight to have arranged for alternate accommodations". . . . [T]he reservations for the tour were not confirmed and, therefore, the hotel was not obligated to accommodate the members of the group. . . .

Majewski and Paterson sue in contract and negligence seeking recovery of their payments for their trip and for their ordeal. Their claims spring from a breach of contract by Astral for its failure to furnish the hotel accommodations agreed upon. Majewski and Paterson are entitled to recover from Astral for the breach of contract. Damages in the usual breach of contract action should indemnify a party for the gains prevented and losses sustained

by the breach; to leave him in no worse, but put him in no better, position than he would have been had the breach not occurred. . . . However, when a passenger sues a carrier for a breach of their agreement concerning accommodations the [i]nconviences and discomforts which a passenger suffers . . . are to be considered in the assessment of the damages. . . .

The agent should be held responsible to: (a) verify or confirm the reservations and (b) use reasonable diligence in ascertaining the responsibility of any intervening `wholesaler' or tour organizer. Because the contract was violated and the accommodations contracted for not furnished, a more realistic view for awarding damages to Majewski and Paterson would include not only the difference in the cost of the accommodations but also compensation for their inconvenience, discomfort, humiliation and annoyance.

Odysseys attempted to mitigate the damages to Majewski and Paterson by offering proof as to the difference in value between what they received (at a four-star hotel) and what was agreed upon (a five-star [hotel]). However, this evidence is without force because the hotel at which they stayed was under construction, its recreational facilities were non-existent and its location was not nearly as desirable as that of the Semiramis. The proverbial expression about a picture being worth a thousand words has particular application to Exhibits [presented by plaintiffs] to reveal what Majewski and Paterson expected and what they found. Paterson and Majewski are entitled to the return of the total sum each paid for the trip as damages to them and their family for the inconvenience and discomfort they endured. . . .

On Astral's cross-claim against Odysseys for breach of contract, concerning the Majewski and Paterson claims . . . Astral is entitled to a judgment against Odysseys in the amount of $2,452.70 less $308.30 which Astral retained as its commission, because Odysseys failed to perform its contract and it was Odysseys which was responsible for the fate which befell Majewski and Paterson.

At first it may seem unfair that the travel agent is liable to the client for the dereliction of the wholesaler. But remember, the party who dealt face-to-face with the client and who contracted to arrange the travel itinerary was the travel agent; the client may not have had any direct dealings with the wholesaler and may not know how to contact the wholesaler. Also, the travel agent is not without a remedy. Note in the last paragraph of the previous case, the judge said that the travel agent was able to collect from the wholesaler the money the agent was required by the court to pay to the client. Thus the liability ultimately rests with the party at fault, the wholesaler. However, if the wholesaler goes bankrupt or has discontinued business and cannot be located, the travel agent will suffer the loss.

Not every traveler makes arrangements through a travel agent or airline office. Some travelers use charter companies that offer reduced rates for those who do not mind traveling without a lot of frills. The charter company is liable if it breaches its contract to provide transportation.

CASE EXAMPLE 13–12

Musso v. Tourlite International, Inc.
500 N.Y.S.2d 969 (1986)

When Thomas Wolfe wrote *You Can't Go Home Again* it is clear he had no reference to Mr. Musso, the plaintiff in this case. On the other hand, given what happened to Mr. Musso, he undoubtedly felt the sentiments of Wolfe's title during the events.

Mr. Musso's travels began with his decision to purchase charter airline tickets from Tourlite Inc. to pay a visit to Italy, from whence he came. He bought round trip tickets for himself and his wife and they flew to Rome with no incident.

Mr. Musso was aware of the rules of the charter which required a confirmation of the return flight at least 72 hours prior to departure (which he complied with and there is no dispute as to the fact that this was done). He was also required to arrive at the airport three hours in advance of the flight.

Mr. Musso testified that he and his wife arrived at the airport for their return flight on August 3, 1985 at 10 A.M. The flight was scheduled to depart at 1 P.M., but when he inquired at the information counter, Mr. Musso was informed that the flight was delayed until 3 P.M. The person at the booth instructed him to get on line at about 1:30 P.M. Mr. Musso remained at the airport and joined the line at 1:30 as he had been instructed.

There was only one line for charter flights. When he finally arrived at the front he was told by the person behind the counter that while they had his reconfirmed reservation the plane was full and that it was ready to leave, and that he would therefore not be able to board it. Later, he was told by a representative of the charter company (Tourlite) that he might be able to catch the following week's charter. Upon hearing that Mr. Musso, who from his description remained calm in the face of being told that he had no flight home, decided that he would make other arrangements. He rented a car, drove into Rome where he checked into a hotel overnight, and bought two Alitalia tickets to New York for the following day.

Once he returned to New York, Mr. Musso sued Tourlite, the charter company, in Small Claims Court for the cost of the airline tickets. . . .

The rights of an airline passenger are provided for in Civil Aeronautics Board regulations, which establishes the obligations of airlines. While the flight here was not on a scheduled airline, and was booked through the charter company, it is clear that the purchase of airline tickets creates a contract between the purchaser and the provider of service. Tourlite agreed to bring Mr. Musso and his wife to Italy and back providing they complied with certain conditions. As the facts indicate Mr. Musso fulfilled his end of the bargain—he reconfirmed, he appeared promptly for departure, but was told there was no room for him on the plane.

Tourlite, in its defense, offered the testimony of the Director of Customer Service, Hans Elsevier. Mr. Elsevier, who was not present in Rome at the time these events occurred, testified that on the day in question, the flight manifest [a list of a plane's passengers] indicated twenty-seven vacant seats. He stated that while Tourlite had a representative present, the seating for the plane is done by a "handling agent." The manifest also indicated that the Mussos were confirmed on the flight in question. He said that a representative of Tourlite was stationed in front of the counter to assist passengers with difficulties. However, Mr. Musso testified that he had not encountered any such person although he had looked for someone. Mr. Elsevier admitted that he had no idea why Mr. Musso had not been permitted to board the plane.

None of the arguments advanced by defendant Tourlite relieves it of its contractual responsibility to the plaintiff here. The testimony indicated Mr. Musso complied with his part of the contract by reconfirming. He appeared at the airport, and waited on line. Since Mr. Elsevier was not present at the time of these events it is difficult to accept his hearsay testimony that a representative of Tourlite was there and was assisting those on line.

Mr. Musso is therefore entitled to recover from Tourlite the cost of his Alitalia airline tickets ($1100) and the additional cost for the rental car ($55) that he needed to go back into Rome to spend the night, together with interest from August 1985.

No Liability for Third-party Suppliers' Negligence

Travel agents are not liable for the negligence of a hotel, resort, or other service provider booked for a client by the agent. Thus, the agent who made reservations for a customer at a Club Med resort was not liable to the vacationer who suffered injuries due to the resort's negligence. *Stein v. Club Med Sales, Inc.*, 658 N.Y.S.2d 639 (1997). Likewise, a bed-and-breakfast reservation service was not liable to a customer who fell at the inn because it failed to have railings on steps. *Manes v. Coats*, 941 P.2d 120 (Alaska, 1997).

Similarly, where a traveler on a European bus tour sustained injuries due to the negligence of the bus company, the travel agency that arranged the tour was not liable for the injuries. *Dorkin v. American Express Co.*, 351 N.Y.S.2d 190 (1974).

Tour operators also are not liable for the negligence of independent contractors which provide services to those on a tour. Thus, a tour operator responsible to coordinate transportation, hotel accommodations, and certain special events was not liable when a tour participant took a "booze cruise" and was served too much alcohol which caused him to leap overboard to his death by the ship's propellers. *Smith v. West Rochelle Travel Agency, Inc.*, 656 N.Y.S.2d 340 (1997).

Nor are tour operators generally liable when a tour participant is injured during sightseeing at a place not under the control of the tour operator. In *Loeb v. Tauk Tours*, 793 F.Supp 431 (N.Y., 1992), the plaintiff, while a member of a tour offered by defendant, fell near their lodge while visiting the Grand Teton National Park in Moran, Wyoming. The tour operator claimed it was not responsible for any dangerous condition on which plaintiff tripped, nor did it have control over the area surrounding the lodge and therefore it should not be liable. Plaintiff argued that since the tour operator selected the tour sites and provided supervision, it had a duty to warn of foreseeable risks such as rocky slopes and steep trails. The court rejected plaintiff's position and held that a tour operator has no duty to warn or protect tour participants from a possible hazardous condition that may exist on the property of others.

Disclaimers by the Travel Agent

Travel agents frequently insert disclaimers in their written materials. A **disclaimer** is a term in a contract that attempts to avoid all liability on the part of one party to the contract. The effectiveness of disclaimers in limiting the liability of travel agents is questionable. The courts have not looked favorably on attempts by travel agents to relieve themselves from liability for negligence or other wrongful conduct and have usually limited the enforceability of disclaimers. As a result, such clauses are generally invalidated under various legal theories, including insufficient notice to the customer, lack of specificity in the language, inequality of bargaining power, and, perhaps most important, offensiveness to public policy.

A travel agent, rather than inserting a disclaimer in contracts with clients, should use instead an explanatory clause that defines the relationship between all the parties involved and properly sets out what liabilities attach to each. In such a clause, travel agents can make clear to clients that suppliers of travel services are not agents of the travel agent and so the travel agent should not be liable if the supplier is negligent or breaches a contract or otherwise disrupts the client's travel plans. Such a clause enhances the client's understanding of the relationships involved and may aid the travel agent in avoiding a lawsuit.

However, an explanatory clause, like most disclaimers, will not relieve travel agents from their own or their employees' negligence or wrongful conduct.

Insurance

Mistakes and poor judgment can happen in any business, although with good management their occurrence should be limited. A travel agent or travel wholesaler can purchase insurance to cover its loss when errors are made. The objective of insurance is to minimize the effects of errors made by travel agents and their staffs.

While many types of insurance coverage are available, "errors and omissions" covers any adverse judgment and the cost of defending a lawsuit resulting from the travel agent's failure to fulfill its obligation to a client as well as from the conduct of third-party travel service suppliers. Insurance, however, should not be used as an excuse for poor management techniques or shoddy business practices. Clients are entitled to better, and with each lawsuit the cost of the insurance is likely to escalate.

Rental Cars

The car rental business is an important component of the travel industry as it provides travelers with mobility and relieves them from reliance on public transportation. Car rentals presents potential problems for travelers and the rental companies, including overbooking and liability for accidents.

Overbooking

A traveler who flies into a strange city expecting a car to be waiting for him and discovers the rental company cannot fill the reservation will have a major headache. A few states have enacted consumer protection laws that deal with un-filled car rental reservations. These laws state that, if a company fails to provide a car to a customer with a confirmed reservation, the company may be subject to a fine. Each rental company has a contingency plan for unfilled reservations. Most have adopted a compensation policy for travelers whose car reservations cannot be filled and who rent a car from another company at a higher price. The amount the rental companies will pay is the difference between their contract price and the higher price the customer pays to the other company.

Accidents in Rental Cars

When a rental car is involved in an accident, questions arise as to whether the rental company is liable to someone injured as a result. Generally the rental company is not liable except where it negligently entrusts the vehicle to a lessee. **Negligent entrustment** means providing a product (in this circumstance, a car) for use by another person knowing that person is likely to use the product in a dangerous manner. A car rental company is liable for negligent entrustment only when it has reason to know the lessee is incompetent to drive the car. If it has such knowledge and the lessee is in an accident, the car rental company may be liable for the damages. As the following case illustrates, the law gives consider-able leeway to the rental company.

CASE EXAMPLE 13–13

Drummond v. Walker,
643 F.Supp. 190 (D.C., 1986), aff'd
861 F2d 303 (1988)

This action arises out of a car accident which occurred early in the morning on August 6, 1984. Plaintiff alleges that defendant Kenneth Scott, while driving a car rented from defendant Americar, fell asleep at the wheel and struck a guardrail on Route 70 near Hagerstown, Maryland. Plaintiff, a passen-ger in the car, suffered facial injuries in the accident.

Scott did not actually execute the rental agree-ment for the car. Defendant Charlene Walker rented the car for Scott on August 2, 1984, because Scott lacked the appropriate identification and credit necessary to rent the car. When Walker rented the car, the American manager gave the keys to Scott, who drove the car away from the American lot. Walker never took possession of the car.

In . . . her complaint, plaintiff alleges that American is liable for her injuries by virtue of American's negligent entrustment of the car to Scott. She contends that the entrustment was negligent because Scott lacked proper identification and did not possess a credit card. Plaintiff further suggests in her opposition to the instant motion that American was negligent in entrusting the car to Scott whom they knew to be slightly under 21 years of age. American has a policy of not renting to drivers under 21 years.

. . . [P]laintiff alleges that defendants American and CFM are liable for her injuries through the negligent acts of their agents. Plaintiff argues that Scott and Walters were American's agents by virtue of the rental agreement. Plaintiff also contends that CFM, who supplies rental cars to American, is liable for American's negligence by virtue of the contract between them. . . .

Even if American's employees knew that Scott would be driving the car, that he lacked proper identification and credit, and that he was under 21 years of age, such knowledge would still be insufficient to establish a prima facie case of negligent entrustment. One liable for negligent entrustment is

> [o]ne who supplies, directly or through a third person, a chattel for the use of another, whom the supplier knows or has reason to know to be likely because of his youth, inexperience, or otherwise, to use it in a manner involving unreasonable risk of physical harm to himself and others . . . is subject to liability for physical harm resulting. . . .

Generally, negligent entrustment of a vehicle to an incompetent driver is imposed only where the owner entrusts the vehicle to one whose appearance or conduct is such as to indicate his incompetency or inability to operate the vehicle with care. In order to impose liability in other cases, where the incompetency of the driver is not apparent to the owner of the vehicle at the time of entrustment, it must be affirmatively shown that the owner had at that time knowledge of facts and circumstances which established the incompetency of the driver.

The negligent entrustment rule is considered a harsh rule because it imposes liability on an owner for the negligence of a driver over whose conduct he is unable to exercise the slightest degree of supervision or control. Its application has, therefore, been held limited to situations where the owner had knowledge that the driver did not know how to drive, was physically or mentally incapable of operating a motor vehicle, was intoxicated or who had the habit of becoming intoxicated, or was a minor with a record of reckless driving.

In order for defendant American to be liable for negligent entrustment it would have to be established that defendant Scott belonged "to a class which is notoriously incompetent to use chattel safely" and that his incompetency was the proximate cause of plaintiff's injury. None of the facts presented by plaintiff, even if known by American, would indicate that Scott belonged to a notoriously incompetent class. The fact that Scott was under the age of 21, or lacked adequate identification or credit does not reflect directly on his ability to operate a car competently. American would not be on notice by virtue of these facts that Scott was not a safe driver. Therefore, [the cause of action based on negligent entrustment] must be dismissed.

Similarly, [the other claims in the complaint] must also be dismissed. The rental of a car creates a bailment relationship between the parties. Neither the relationship between American and Walker and Scott, nor the relationship between CFM and American, entailed sufficient control over the agent by the principal to create an agency relationship.

Consequently, this action is dismissed.

CASE QUESTION

1.   Why was the car rental company able to avoid liability in this case?

A similar issue arose in *Nielson v. Ono and Dollar Rent-A-Car*, 750 F. Supp. 439 (HI., 1990). Here too the court held the rental company had not negligently entrusted the vehicle. Yoshiko Ono, a Japanese national with a valid Japanese driver's license, rented a car from defendant Dollar-Rent-A-Car. While driving the car she lost control of it causing it to cross from a northbound lane into a southbound lane, striking plaintiff's vehicle. Plaintiff sued Dollar claiming it negligently entrusted the vehicle to Ono, noting that Ono, as a foreign citizen, was presumably unfamiliar with local driving and traffic laws. The court rejected plaintiff's claims and held for Dollar stating,

> *Plaintiff does not allege Ono was intoxicated or otherwise physically or mentally impaired when Dollar turned the car over to her. Additionally, there is no proof that she appeared unusually young or inexperienced. Finally, plaintiff has made no showing that Ono rented cars from Dollar on other occasions, thereby putting Dollar on notice of her alleged incompetence as a driver . . . [F]oreign citizenship alone cannot constitute notice of a driver's incompetence.*

Negligent Rental of a Defective Car

Another circumstance that can give rise to liability on the part of the car rental company is knowingly renting a vehicle that has mechanical problems. In *Betancourt v. Manhattan Ford Lincoln Mercury, Inc.*, Feb. 18, 1994, N.Y.L.J. 1 (col. 3), the plaintiff was forced to make an emergency stop on the side of a busy unlit highway because the car he rented malfunctioned. While so situated he was hit and killed by a passing truck. The rental company was aware at the time it rented the car to plaintiff that it had a history of overheating and leaking engine coolant. The lower court dismissed the case. The appeals court reversed the dismissal and reinstated plaintiff's complaint, finding sufficient evidence to refer the matter to a jury for trial.

Unauthorized Drivers

A problem that car rental companies often confront is unauthorized drivers. Authorized drivers include the lessee and anyone else the rental company approves in writing. Everyone else is an unauthorized driver. Virtually all car rental contracts include a provision forbidding operation of the rental car by an unauthorized driver, as well as a provision stating that insurance coverage applies only to authorized drivers. If you rent a car and allow a friend to drive who has not been approved by the rental company, your friend is an unauthorized driver. If the friend is in an accident with the car, the rental company's insurance will not cover resulting injuries. You will be liable to the rental company for damage to the car. You, in turn, may be able to recover from your friend. Travelers who rent cars can avoid these problems by ensuring the rental cars are driven only by authorized drivers.

In the following case a question arose whether the driver was authorized. Take note of the court's unwillingness to interpret the contract to include an implied (unwritten) term that would allow as permissible drivers people who are not expressly authorized by the rental company but granted permission to drive by an authorized driver. Thus, a valet was not an authorized driver even though he parked a rental car with the permission of the authorized driver.

CASE EXAMPLE 13–14

Travelers v. Budget Rent-a-Car Systems, Inc.
901 F.2d 765 (9th Cir., 1990)

The facts are not in dispute. In October 1985, while vacationing on the island of Maui in Hawaii, Albert Mellon rented a car from Budget Rent-A-Car. The rental agreement stated that Budget would provide liability insurance for Mellon and any other authorized driver. Budget was self insured.

Several days after renting the car, Mellon and his wife drove to Mama's Fish House, a local restaurant of some renown. On arrival, Mellon turned the rental car over to Brent Jones, a valet parker in Mama's employ. The Mellons partook of piscine fare; Mr. Mellon had the mahi-mahi, Mrs. Mellon the shrimp.

After a satisfying dinner, Mellon dispatched Jones to retrieve the car. Jones drove the car to the restaurant entrance, where while still seated behind the wheel—he opened the passenger side door for Mrs. Mellon. As Mrs. Mellon stood beside the open door, Jones got out of the car. The car lurched backward. The open door struck Mrs. Mellon, dragged her along the ground and caused numerous injuries.

The Mellons filed suit against Mama's and Jones. That suit was settled when Travelers Insurance, Mama's insurer, tendered its full policy limit of $300,000. Budget, as owner and insurer of the car that struck Mrs. Mellon, also paid her $15,000 pursuant to Hawaii's no-fault insurance statute. Travelers then instituted the present suit seeking a declaration that Budget must also indemnify Travelers for half of the expenses of defendant Mama's and Jones and up to $100,000 of the settlement. Travelers' claim is derived from its insured, Jones, who, it argues, was also insured by Budget because he used the car with Mellon's permission.

. . . The district court held that, because Jones did not have Budget's permission to drive the car, he was not insured by Budget. Consequently, the court granted . . . judgment in Budget's favor.

Travelers appeals. . . .

To allow Travelers to recover from Budget on the basis of the rental agreement would require an act of interpretive legerdemain [trickery or magic]; the language of the contract could not be clearer. The rental agreement provides liability coverage "only for Renter and any Authorized Driver . . . for bodily injury . . . arising from use or operation of Vehicle as permitted by this Agreement." As to what is permitted by the agreement, it states explicitly that the

Vehicle shall not, under any circumstances, be used or operated by any person: (a) Other than Renter or any Authorized Driver which shall by definition include only the Additional Driver shown on the reverse side hereof, and any driver who is a member of Renter's immediate family, his employer, his employee, or his partner provided such driver has Renter's prior permission and is a qualified, licensed driver of at least 21 years of age, . . .

Brent Jones is neither the Renter nor an Authorized Driver as provided by the rental agreement. Under the plain terms of the contract Budget provides no coverage for the accident at Mama's Fish House. . . .

Travelers . . . asks us to read into the rental agreement an implied term providing liability coverage to anyone who drove the car with Mellon's permission. The company points to cases from other jurisdictions that have found such an implied term. . . .

For one thing, an implied term providing liability coverage to anyone other than the renter or an authorized driver would be directly contrary to the express language of the contract. It is elementary contract law that a court will only supply a term where the contract does not address the dispute between the parties. . . . Where the language of a contract is clear and addresses the issue before the court, the court may not interpret the contract by supplying an implied term. . . . The Budget-

Mellon rental agreement is definite and unambiguous on this point; the contract excludes insurance coverage for the events at Mama's parking lot. There is no occasion to supply an implied term, and that should be the end of the matter as far as Hawaii contract law is concerned.

Travelers nonetheless points to cases from other jurisdictions that have found an implied permittee term under circumstances similar to those here. According to these courts, car rental companies must expect that some renters will allow other people to drive the rental car in violation of the agreement. Therefore, the rental companies are deemed to have consented to the breach. . . .

To recite such reasoning is to criticize it. The idea that a party may not rely on a contract term because the other side can be expected to violate it cuts at the very heart of contract law. Contracts enable parties to define their mutual rights and responsibilities; they are useful only insofar as each side can count on being able to hold the other to the terms of the agreement. If a contract provides anything at all, then, it is the reasonable expectation that the parties will fulfill their obligations, either voluntarily or under judicial compulsion. For a court to deny enforcement of a contract term because breach is foreseeable defeats the purpose of having a contract, effectively withdrawing that particular issue from regulation by mutual assent. . . .

The rule Travelers advocates is also dangerous because it adds a heaping measure of uncertainty where certainty is essential. Insurance companies, like other commercial actors, need predictability; they write their contracts in precise language for that reason, and they calculate their premiums accordingly. When insurance contracts no longer mean what they say, it becomes exceedingly difficult to calculate risks. Insurance companies can predict with a fair degree of accuracy the risks involved when a car "may only be used or operated by an Authorized Driver." What are they to make of "it is foreseeable and inevitable that rental vehicles . . . will be operated in violation of a restrictive lease agreement"? Just how many other risks will some court find foreseeable and inevitable? Increasing uncertainty through judicial meddling raises insurers' costs of doing business; inevitably those costs are passed on to customers. . . . [Judgment for Budget] Affirmed.

Age Discrimination When Renting Cars

Many car rental companies have refused to rent a car to a person who is under age 25. The reasons given for the refusal are high insurance premiums for this age group and high accident rates. The law in many states prevents car rental companies from refusing to rent a car to someone who is at least 18 years of age, provided insurance coverage is available. Most such statutes provide that any additional insurance costs imposed because of the age of the driver can be passed on to the driver. While some car rental companies continue to resist rentals to those under 25 a recent case in New York upheld the law requiring rentals to those who are at least 18. *People v. Alamo Rent A Car,* 3/28/97 N.Y.L.J. 1 (col. 3) (1997).

Summary

Airline travelers have certain rights when they travel, including: the right to limited compensation when an airline loses their luggage; the right to rerouting assistance from an airline when flights are cancelled; and the right of handicapped travelers to access this means of transportation.

Travel agents must exercise reasonable care in making a client's travel arrangements and must not intentionally mislead a client. A travel agent may be liable for giving false or incomplete information and for failing to investigate third-party suppliers. A tour operator may be liable for failing to provide promised accommodations.

Car rentals are an important service available to travelers. Car rental companies will be liable to people injured by a driver of a rented vehicle if the rental company knew at the time of the rental that the driver was incompetent. A traveler will be liable to the rental company if he permits an unauthorized driver to drive the car who then has an accident.

Preventive Law Tips for Managers

- *If employed by the airline industry, regularly review your company's system of baggage control to minimize the number of suitcases that are misrouted.* Failure to deliver luggage to a passenger's destination breaches the airline's contract with the traveler to transport the luggage as well as the passenger to the destination. Although the law provides limited liability, thereby sparing the airlines from the need to compensate passengers for the full value of the loss, reimbursement at the limited liability rates can be costly. Further, loss of passengers' luggage generates bad will and will likely cause lost business in the future. Taking precautions to minimize the incidents of lost luggage will save the company from unnecessary lawsuits and liability.

- *If employed by the airline industry, regularly review your company's baggage check procedures to ensure compliance with the Warsaw Convention for international flights.* Lack of compliance can result in loss of limited liability. The convention requires that the airlines do the following for international flights: 1) prepare a baggage check receipt in duplicate, giving the passenger one copy and retaining the other; and 2) include on the receipt the following information: place and date of issue, place of departure and destination, name and address of the carrier(s), the number of the passenger ticket, a statement that delivery of the baggage will be made to the bearer of the baggage check, the number and weight of packages, the amount of the value, and a statement that the transport of the luggage is subject to the rules relating to liability established by the Warsaw Convention.

- *If employed in the airline industry, do not mislead passengers concerning the whereabouts of lost luggage.* Intentionally giving passengers false information about the whereabouts of their luggage can lead to loss of limited liability. Be truthful and accommodating when passengers inquire about misplaced baggage.

- *If employed in the airline industry, ensure your company's rules and facilities for transporting animals protect the well-being of the animal.* An airline may be liable for injury to pets in flight. While pets are considered for airline liability purposes the equivalent of baggage entitling the airlines to limited liability, animals have needs that suitcases do not. Those needs should be met to the extent possible.

* *If engaged as a travel agent, double check the times of your clients' flights and give them accurate information.* If the travel agent gives incorrect information about the times of a flight or fails to update a client about a change in departure time, the travel agent may be liable for the clients' inconvenience and cost for alternate travel. Diligence in verifying information can avoid this problem.

* *If engaged as a travel agent, do not misrepresent a client's status on a flight.* If a travel agent informs a client that he has a confirmed seat when in fact the client is on the waiting list, the travel agent may be liable for inconvenience and added expense caused to the client by the misrepresentation. The travel agent should always give the client truthful information only.

* *If engaged as a travel agent, investigate thoroughly any travel wholesaler you recommend to a client.* A travel agent may be liable to clients for the failure of a travel wholesaler to provide the intended trip. The basis for this liability may be negligence or breach of contract. An agent will be liable in negligence for the wholesaler's failure to perform if the agent did not adequately investigate the wholesaler. The agent may also be liable on a breach of contract theory when the wholesaler fails to perform in whole or part. Although in such cases the travel agent may be able to obtain compensation from the wholesaler, bad will is generated by the unhappy clients. Further, if the wholesaler has gone out of business, compensation may not be obtainable. A thorough check into the wholesaler's business operations, experience, and past tours can help ensure reliability by the wholesaler and freedom from liability for the travel agent.

* *If engaged as a travel agent, investigate thoroughly any travel services you recommend to a client.* A travel agent may be liable to clients for the nonperformance or substandard performance of any travel service or accommodation recommended by the agent. Before recommending a hotel, bus, train, limousine services, sightseeing tour, or other service, the agent should familiarize himself with the company's services and reliability to ensure they are suitable for the client. An inappropriate recommendation can lead to liability for the travel agent.

* *If a flight is cancelled, the airline should offer assistance to passengers in making alternate arrangements.* The law recognizes that bad weather and other circumstances can present safety issues for air travel, and the airline will not be liable for breach of contract where circumstances dictate cancellation of a flight. However, the law also recognizes that passengers' travel plans will be disrupted by the cancellation and so imposes on the airlines a duty to aid passengers in locating alternate flights. Failure to assist the displaced passengers in this regard can lead to liability.

- *If employed in the airline or travel agent industry, accord handicapped patrons the rights provided under the Americans With Disabilities Act and the Air Carrier Access Act.* These Acts require generally that handicapped persons be given access to places of public accommodation including travel agents' offices and air transportation. The law also requires that airlines make necessary accommodations for disabled passengers provided they are able to travel without presenting a risk to themselves or others.

- *In the event of overbooking, the airline should offer assistance to passengers in making alternate arrangements to reach their destinations.* The law recognizes that overbooking will occur on occasion as a result of the airlines' attempts to run their business as efficiently as possible. To avoid liability to bumped passengers, the airlines should assist them in finding alternate transportation. Also, when determining who to bump, the airline should follow its priority rules.

- *If employed in the car rental business, regularly review your procedures to ensure the number of unfilled reservations is kept to a minimum.* When a car rental company overbooks its fleet and is unable to accommodate customers with reservations, it is in breach of contract and liability and penalties will follow. To minimize this occurrence, frequent review of procedures should be undertaken.

- *If employed in the car rental business, do not rent a car to someone who is obviously incompetent to drive.* A car rental company will be liable for negligent entrustment where it rents a car to someone who obviously is incapable of driving lawfully. The car rental company should require a valid driver's license. If the would-be renter appears intoxicated or high on drugs, the rental company should investigate further. If it rents to someone it should have known was not qualified and that person is in an accident with the car, the rental company may be liable for resulting injuries.

- *If employed in the car rental business, inspect your fleet of cars regularly for mechanical problems.* If a car develops such a problem, remove it from service until the problem is fully repaired. A car rental company that rents a vehicle known to contain mechanical problems may be liable if an accident results. To avoid this liability, inspect the cars regularly and repair any problems found to exist.

Review Questions

1. Name the four groups that compose the travel industry.
2. What differentiates Small Claims Courts from other courts?
3. If an agent acts with authority for a principal, who is legally bound by the acts of the agent?

4. What is the difference between an agent and an independent contractor?
5. What is a tariff?
6. What is an airline's responsibility when it takes custody of a passenger's luggage?
7. What should be included on the baggage check an airline gives to a client on an international flight?
8. What treaty binds the United States and other countries on matters involving international plane flights?
9. Why should a travel agent be familiar with the places he recommends?
10. What is a disclaimer and how do the courts treat them?
11. What obligation, if any, does an airline have to passengers when it cancels a flight due to bad weather?
12. Under what circumstances can a pilot remove a person from a plane and refuse to provide him transportation?
13. What is the consequence of a person representing himself as an agent of a disclosed principal when the "agent" has not been authorized by the principal to act as an agent?
14. What is errors and omissions insurance coverage?
15. What Acts protect rights to disabled passengers?
16. What is negligent entrustment?

Discussion Questions

1. How does Small Claims Court increase the potential liability of the travel industry?
2. How does one distinguish between an agent and an independent contractor?
3. Why does the Warsaw Convention require that a passenger have notice of its provisions?
4. A travel agent has made arrangements through a travel wholesaler for a client's tour. The wholesaler fails to make hotel reservations and as a result the client must stay in an inferior hotel. Why should the travel agent be liable to the client when the party who failed to provide services was the wholesaler?
5. How might airport security checks be modified to ensure that passengers and their carry-on luggage do not become separated?

Application Questions

1. Theresa is a pilot for ABC Airlines. Does either Theresa or the airlines qualify as a principal or an agent? If so, which qualifies as which? Why?

2. Melanie contracted with a travel agent for the purchase of a charter trip to England. The travel agent made the necessary arrangements with the charter company and recommended a one-day side trip which the client agreed to purchase. While the client was on the side trip, she was injured because a step on the company's bus was rotted. Further, the airline overbooked the client's return flight which resulted in a two-day delay in the client's arrival home. What potential liability, if any, does the travel agent have in these circumstances?

3. Jeremy had confirmed reservations on a flight from New York City to Boston. The airline overbooked the flight. How should the airline determine whether or not Jeremy will get bumped?

4. Tyrone was struck by a car while roller skating on the sidewalk. The car was a rental car. Under what theory might Tyrone attempt to hold the car rental company liable for his injuries? What would he need to prove to establish his case? How could he prove that?

CHAPTER 14

Employment

CHAPTER OUTLINE

INTRODUCTION

The employer-employee relationship is fertile ground for lawsuits against the employer. These cases seek to enforce employment laws and take one of two forms, either a lawsuit by the employee or an action brought by the government against an employer.

Employment law is far-reaching and affects employees' wages; prohibits discrimination on the grounds of race, religion, color, national origin, sex, pregnancy, age, and disability; and requires the employer to verify worker eligibility for employment in the United States. We will study each of these topics in this chapter.

Fair Labor Standards Act

The Fair Labor Standards Act (FLSA) is a federal law passed in 1938. It mandates minimum wages, one and one-half pay for overtime work, equal pay for equal work, and restrictions on child labor.

Nothing in the law requires employers to pay employees for vacations, holidays or sick days, although such paid time off has become the norm.

Minimum Wage

The FLSA requires that, with few exceptions, employers involved in interstate commerce pay employees at least the minimum wage set by Congress. The minimum wage is increased from time to time as Congress sees fit. As of September 1, 1997, the minimum wage is $5.15 an hour. States may specify a minimum wage higher than Congress. If so, employers in those states must pay the higher amount set by the state.

Low Sales Exception to Minimum Wage Requirement.   Excepted from the minimum wage requirement are employers with less than $500,000 in annual sales. In the following case the court had to decide whether a hotel and adjacent restaurant were two separate businesses, each of which fell below the threshold amount for FLSA coverage (then $362,500), or one business subject to the act.

CASE EXAMPLE 14–1

Brock v. Best Western Sundown Motel, Inc.
883 F.2d 51 (8th Cir., 1989)

Ronald and Beverly Halling appeal the District Court's determination that their motel and restaurant business violated the minimum wage provisions of the Fair Labor Standards Act (FLSA). The Hallings do not dispute that their business has paid some of its employees less than the federal minimum wage, and has failed to pay the required overtime premium of one and one-half times the federal minimum wage for work in excess of 40 hours a week. The only issue in dispute is whether the Hallings' business is exempt from the provisions of the FLSA.

Ronald Halling owns the Best Western Sundown Motel, which generates an approximate annual sales volume of $265,000. Beverly Halling owns an adjoining restaurant, Grandmother's House, which generates an approximate annual

sales volume of $190,000. If the motel and the restaurant are taken to be separate enterprises, both would be exempt from the operation of the FLSA, in that both have an annual sales volume of less than $362,500, the minimum required for application of the FLSA. The Secretary of Labor contends that the motel and restaurant form a single enterprise (with a total income over the $362,500 threshold) . . . in that they are related activities performed through unified operation and common control for a common business purpose.

The District Court held for the Secretary. The Court found that the motel and restaurant are physically connected, that each business operates without regular payment of rent on property owned jointly by the Hallings, and that the establishments share a telephone, laundry facilities, and advertising. The Court further found that Ronald often did work in the restaurant and once signed the restaurant's income-tax return, while Beverly frequently did work at the motel. The Court also found the Hallings jointly hired a couple to manage the motel and restaurant together. . . .

The Hallings' arguments generally dispute the District Court's interpretation and construction of testimony, but they provide [no basis to conclude] that the District Court committed error. On the facts found by the District Court, we have little

trouble affirming its legal conclusion that the Hallings' motel and restaurant constitute a single enterprise under the FLSA. . . . [T]he Hallings' establishments are clearly under the common control of the same owners, with substantially overlapping operations. . . .

Affirmed.

Tips Exception to Minimum Wage Requirement.   Another exception to the minimum wage requirement applies to employees who routinely receive at least $30 per month in tips on the job. For those employees an employer can credit a percentage of the tips against the hourly minimum wage requirement. As of September 1, 1997, up to 59 percent of the minimum wage can be replaced by tips. For example, a restaurant owner could pay a waiter $2.13 (41 percent of the minimum wage) rather than $5.15 an hour. However the credit cannot exceed the tips actually received by the employee. For the restaurant to take advantage of the tip credit and pay the waiter only $2.13 per hour, the waiter must receive a minimum of $3.02 per hour in tips. Some states have minimum wage laws that impact these figures. Tip pooling among tipped employees, including wait personnel, counter help, bus help, and bartenders is permitted under the FLSA for purposes of the employer utilizing the tip credit to reduce an employee's pay below minimum wage. Several states have laws that prohibit tip pooling for this purpose.

Training Wage Exception to Minimum Wage Requirement.   An employer can pay a training wage below minimum wage to a limited class of employees. The training wage is 85 percent of minimum wage, which as of September 1, 1997, is $4.38 per hour. The only employees to whom this wage applies are workers between the ages of 16 and 19 who are entering the workforce for the first time. The employer can pay the training wage in lieu of minimum wage for a maximum of 90 days. Thereafter the employer must pay minimum wage.

Overtime Pay

FLSA requires that certain employees who are paid on an hourly basis and who work more than 40 hours in one week be paid at least one and one-half times their regular pay for the hours in excess of 40. For example, if a receptionist at a restaurant is paid $6 per hour and works 45 hours in one week, the employer must pay $9 per hour for the last five of those hours.

Exempt Employees.   The statute contains an exemption to the overtime and minimum wage requirements for executive, administrative, and professional employees. Employers often seek to avoid overtime pay for employees believed to be within the exempt categories. Employees denied overtime pay may contest their classification as an executive.

To qualify for the exemption, the employee must meet a duties test and a salary test. To qualify as an executive, the employee must be managing the business or part of it, must regularly direct the work of two or more employees, and either: a) be paid a salary (as opposed to an hourly wage) of at least $250 per week; or b) have the authority to hire, fire, or promote and be paid a salary of at least $155 per week.

Concerning the duties portion of the test, the issue is not strictly a question of how much time is allocated to managerial duties as opposed to other tasks. Rather, the court will also evaluate such factors as the importance of the managerial duties as opposed to other responsibilities, the frequency with which the employee exercises discretion, and his relative freedom from supervision.

In *Dole v. Papa Gino's of America, Inc.*, 712 F. Supp. 1038 (Mass., 1989), a chain restaurant claimed its lowest level manager, whose job title was Associate Manager, was an executive position and therefore exempt from overtime pay. The job, an entry-level position, included work that regular crew members do (preparing pizzas, salads, and other food, running the cash register, waiting on customers, cleaning), tasks described by the company as "learning by doing," and studying company manuals to prepare for management tests. Associate Managers perform little or no supervision of other employees, are not in charge of a restaurant, and do not supervise shifts. Not surprisingly, the court determined the position of Associate Manager was not an executive position.

Concerning the salary test, for an employee to qualify for the exemption from minimum and overtime pay, his compensation must be a predetermined amount and cannot be based on the number of hours worked. The amount of pay must not be reduced for variations in the quantity or quality of work performed. Thus, a salaried employee is not exempt from overtime pay if his pay is reduced when he works fewer hours than expected or his work product does not meet expectations. *Martin v. Malcolm Pirnie, Inc.*, 949 F.2d 611 (2nd Cir., 1991).

In addition to executive employees, also exempt from the overtime and minimum wage requirements of the FLSA, are administrative and professional employees. To qualify as administrative employees, workers must generally exhibit discretion and independent judgment, spend at least 50 percent of time at work on office or nonmanual work relating to management policies or general business operations, and earn a salary of at least $250 per week. The test for professionals is similar except the 50 percent criteria applies to performing work requiring specialized study. The duties and salary tests also apply to these employees.

Another category of employees is exempt from the overtime provisions but not the minimum wage requirement. Often called the "miscellaneous exemption," this grouping includes seasonal workers, camp employees, domestic workers, movie theater workers, agricultural employees, taxi drivers, and amusement workers.

Time Worked

The FLSA identifies what constitutes time worked for purposes of determining the number of hours for which an employee is entitled to hourly pay and for determining whether an employee has worked overtime. The following are counted as time worked: coffee and snack breaks; meetings to discuss daily operations problems; rest periods of 20 minutes or less; travel from job site to job site or to customers; required training; and clearing a cash register or totaling receipts after regular work hours.

Equal Pay for Equal Work

A provision of FLSA, called the Equal Pay Act, requires that men and women who do the same job, or jobs that require equal skill and responsibility, be paid the same or according to the same pay schedule. An issue that often arises is whether jobs are the same. The test is whether they have a "common core" of tasks, or, stated otherwise, whether "a significant portion" of the two jobs is identical. In one case the court found two jobs to be substantially equal even though one required some travel and minor additional responsibilities. *Fallon v. Illinois*, 882 F.2d 1206 (7th Cir., 1989). While the Act protects both men and women, most cases have involved situations where a woman was paid less than a man.

Comparable Worth

The Equal Pay Act applies only when two people are doing the same job, or jobs that require the same skills and responsibility. Sometimes men and women work at jobs that are quite different and one is paid more than the other, yet the value of their work to the employer is more or less equal. **Comparable worth** refers to jobs requiring different skills and responsibilities that have equal value to the employer. Courts have rejected the argument that comparable worth requires equal pay. If adopted, courts would be required to evaluate the worth of different jobs and rank them according to their relative values, something courts seem ill-equipped and unwilling to do. Advocates of equal pay for jobs of comparable worth argue that it would address the undervaluation of jobs traditionally associated with women, something that is not addressed by the Equal Pay Act.

In 1989, comparable worth was again rejected in *International Union v. Michigan*, 886 F.2d 766 (6th Cir., 1989). In that case the employer, the state of Michigan, had done its own market studies and was aware of wage disparities in its own pay system between jobs predominantly filled by females and different jobs of comparable worth filled by men. The plaintiffs, state employees, claimed that by perpetuating the system the employer discriminated against female workers. In denying plaintiffs' claims, the court stated,

> *[Laws prohibiting unequal pay are] not a substitute for the free market, which historically determines labor rates. . . . Mere failure to rectify traditional wage disparities that exist in the marketplace between predominantly male and predominantly female jobs is not actionable.*

Retaliatory Discharge

If an employee believes she is being paid unfairly, and complains or commences a lawsuit under the FLSA, the employer is often irritated and sometimes antagonistic toward her. The EPA addresses this phenomenon by prohibiting an employer from discharging or otherwise discriminating against such an employee. 29 U.S.C. §215(a)(3). Thus, where a restaurant discharged a manager for complaining about the restaurant's break policy and nonpayment of overtime compensation, the discharge violated the FLSA. The court awarded the terminated manager in excess of $52,000 for unpaid overtime, back pay, and other compensatory damages. *Brown v. Pizza Hut of America, Inc.*, 113 F.3d 1245 (10th Cir., 1997).

Restrictions on Child Labor

Many employees in most hotels and restaurants are young, often high school or even junior high students. The FLSA provides a minimum age for employees, restricts the number of hours younger employees can work, and limits the tasks they can perform. The minimum age is 14; an employer cannot legally hire a person younger than that. During school weeks, an employee who is 14 or 15 cannot work more than 18 hours a week and not more than three hours on a school day. During the school year, these employees cannot begin work earlier than 7:00 A.M. or end later than 7:00 P.M. During vacation, that same employee cannot work more than eight hours a day or more than 40 hours a week. The workday cannot begin earlier than 7:00 A.M. or end later than 9:00 P.M.

Some states have additional, stricter rules that further limit the hours young people can work. For example, in New York, 16 and 17 year olds are limited to four hours of work per day except for Fridays, Saturdays and Sundays when they can work eight hours. The maximum number of hours a week they can work while school is in session is 28, and if the employer wants them to work beyond 10:00 P.M., parental permission is necessary as is verification from the school that the employee's academic standing is satisfactory. Violators can be fined $1000 for the first violation, $2000 for the second, and $3000 for the third.

The federal law as well as some state laws limit the types of work young employees can do. For example, under the FLSA a worker between the ages of 16 and 18 cannot operate baking machines, meat grinders, or power driven knives used for meat processing. As an example of a state law, an employee in New York under age 16 cannot operate a slicing machine or paint the exterior of a building.

Violations of the FLSA

An employee whose rights under the FLSA have been violated can pursue the case with the Wage and Hour Division of the U.S. Department of Labor, an agency charged with overseeing enforcement of laws that protect employees, or file a lawsuit against the employer seeking damages. If the employer's actions are willful, the employer can be criminally prosecuted by the U.S. Justice Department, a branch of government charged with prosecuting federal crimes. Penalties include fines and jail.

At-Will Employment

Employment arrangements between employers and employees are considered "at-will". This means the employment contract between an employer and an employee is indefinite in duration and can be terminated at the will of either party. Stated more starkly, either the employer or the employee can terminate the employment without liability to the other at any time, for any reason, or for no reason. If, however, an employment contract contains an express provision stating that an employment arrangement will exist for a specified period of time, a party will be liable for early termination. In *Parker v. John Q. Hammons Hotels, Inc.*, 914 F. Supp. 467 (N.M., 1994) a management trainee was terminated for making a profane statement to a fellow employee and for other misconduct. He sued the hotel claiming breach of his employment contract. That contract did not contain a provision stating his employment would last for a specific time period. The court held that the employment relationship was at-will, enabling the hotel to terminate it any time without obligation to the trainee. His lawsuit was thus dismissed.

Illegal Job Discrimination

Notwithstanding an employer's right to terminate an employment contract based on the at-will doctrine, an employer cannot discriminate against workers on the basis of race, skin color, religion, sex, national origin, disability, age if the employee is at least 40 years old, or pregnancy. These categories are called **protected classes.** In some locales, discrimination on the basis of sexual orientation is likewise illegal.

Discrimination in employment is the basis for many lawsuits. The Civil Rights Act of 1991 and the Americans With Disabilities Act, have enhanced employees' rights. Continued enforcement of the employment provisions of the Civil Rights Act of 1964 also underscores the need to treat all employees and applicants fairly.

Title VII of The Civil Rights Act of 1964

The statute that outlaws most grounds for discrimination is Title VII of the federal Civil Rights Act of 1964. It reads as follows,

> *It shall be an unlawful employment practice for an employer (1) to fail or refuse to hire or to discharge any individual or otherwise discriminate against any individual with respect to his compensation, terms, conditions, or privileges of employment, because of such individual's race, color, religion, sex, or national origin. 42 United States Code Section 2000e-2(a).*

For example, a restaurant violates Title VII by hiring only males as wait personnel and refusing to hire females, as would a hotel that refuses to hire anyone who is Norwegian. Often acts of discrimination are not as obvious as these examples. Instead, the discrimination can be very subtle and therefore difficult to detect as well as prove. Title VII outlaws both **disparate treatment** discrimination, which is intentional discrimination based on considerations of race, color, religion, sex or national origin, as well as **disparate impact** discrimination, which involves neutral practices that unintentionally result in unequal treatment. For example, an employer's no-beard policy was found to discriminate against black males because they suffer in substantially greater numbers than white males from a skin disorder that makes shaving difficult. In enforcing the no-beard policy, the employer had not intended to restrict employment opportunities for black males, but the effect of the rule was to do exactly that. *Bradley v Domino's Pizza*, 939 F.2d 610 (8th Cir., 1991).

Other statutes we will study also prohibit discrimination. For example, discrimination against people with disabilities is prohibited by the Americans With Disabilities Act, and discrimination against U.S. citizens employed abroad by U.S. companies is prohibited by the Civil Rights Act of 1991. Likewise, discrimination on the basis of age is prohibited by the Age Discrimination in Employment Act. The referenced Acts are federal laws. State statutes prohibit discrimination on grounds in addition to those covered by the federal laws including martial status, arrest record, and in some locales, sexual orientation.

Title VII covers employers with 20 or more employees. It created the Equal Employment Opportunity Commission (EEOC), a government agency that is charged with enforcing Title VII's mandates.

Filing a Complaint

Before a Title VII action can be brought in federal court, a discrimination charge must be timely filed with the EEOC which has state and regional offices throughout the country. It has specific rules and procedures for filing and strict time limits. Generally, an employee must file a claim with the agency within 180 days after the alleged discriminatory act. Thereafter an EEOC staff attorney or investigator will meet with the employee and make an initial assessment whether the case is justified and should proceed. If the EEOC determines there is no reasonable basis to believe the charges are true, the agency will decline to pursue the claim. Despite this determination, the employee can proceed with a lawsuit in court against the employer. If the EEOC chooses to pursue the claim, it will prepare a complaint, forward it to the employer, and then meet with the employer in an effort to reach a resolution.

Due to a large caseload, the EEOC has a sizeable backlog of cases and cannot fully pursue every claim. If the agency fails to act on a claim within 180 days of filing, the employee can request a right-to-sue letter authorizing the worker to file a lawsuit in federal court against the employer. Once the employee receives a right-to-sue letter he has only 90 days to file the lawsuit.

Remedies

The remedies available to a successful plaintiff in a Title VII case are substantial and were recently expanded. Until 1991, the remedies were limited to the following:

- An injunction precluding the employer from continuing the offending conduct;
- An order requiring the employer to adopt a policy forbidding discrimination and mandating implementation of the policy;

- Attorney's fees, thereby relieving the plaintiff of this substantial expense; and

- Back pay where plaintiff was terminated and unable to find a comparable job. **Back pay** refers to the difference between: a) what plaintiff would have earned in the absence of discrimination, and b) what plaintiff earned in alternative employment or, if plaintiff did not seek another job, what plaintiff could reasonably have earned had he looked for employment.

Compensatory and punitive damages were generally unavailable in discrimination cases prior to 1991. The only exception was for plaintiffs in cases involving *intentional* job discrimination based on race or skin color.

The categories of plaintiffs to whom a judge can award compensatory or punitive damages in a Title VII case was greatly expanded by the Civil Rights Act of 1991. All employers should take notice. That act authorizes compensatory and punitive damages as a remedy for plaintiffs seeking redress not only from intentional discrimination based on race or skin color, but also those victimized by intentional discrimination based on sex, religion, and national origin. Note that age discrimination is not included; a plaintiff in such a case is still not entitled to compensatory or punitive damages.

Compensatory damages include back pay, future monetary losses, emotional pain, suffering, mental anguish and other nonmonetary losses.

Whereas plaintiffs in race and skin color cases can collect unlimited damages, the Civil Rights Act of 1991 places a cap on the amount an employer will be obligated to pay in any one suit. For employers with 15 to 100 employees, the maximum is $50,000; for those with 101 to 200 employees, $100,000; 201 to 500, $200,000; and for those with more than 500, the maximum is $300,000. These caps do not apply to back pay awards; those are limited only by the amount of pay lost.

Punitive damages can be awarded only in those circumstances in which the employee can show that the employer engaged in illegal discrimination "with malice or with reckless indifference to the federally protected rights" of the employee.

Another remedy authorized by the Civil Rights Act of 1991 is compensation for expert witness fees. This is an important remedy since most discrimination cases require one or more expert witnesses, such as a specialist on sexual stereotyping in a sex discrimination case. Each expert witness must spend time reviewing the case, researching particular issues, preparing with the plaintiff's attorney, and testifying. As a result their fees are typically quite high.

Defense of Bona Fide Occupational Qualification

A **bona fide occupational qualification** (BFOQ) relieves an employer from liability for disparate treatment (intentional) discrimination where selection of an employee based on sex, religion, or national origin is reasonably necessary for the normal operation of the employer's business. This defense is construed narrowly by the courts. To qualify, two elements are necessary: 1) the job in issue must require a worker of a particular sex, religion or national origin; and 2) such requirement must be necessary to the essence of the business operation. An example of a BFOQ is hiring only women to model women's make-up.

Another example of a BFOQ is a rule promulgated by the Federal Aviation Administration that requires pilots who reach age 60 to retire. In an age discrimination lawsuit brought by a 60-year-old pilot who wished to continue flying for Federal Express, the court determined that, "At some age everyone reaches a level of infirmity or unreliability that is unacceptable in a pilot in air transportation. That age will vary from person to person but cannot yet be predicted in a specific individual." The court thus determined that mandatory retirement at age 60 did not constitute discrimination. *Coupe v. Federal Express Corporation*, 121 F.3d 1022 (6th Cir., 1997). Unlike a pilot's position, where safety is not an issue for the requirements of a job, a mandatory retirement age of 60 does not constitute a BFOQ and will likely constitute illegal discrimination. See, for example, *EEOC v. Johnson & Higgins*, 887 F. Supp. 682 (N.Y., 1995), in which a 62 mandatory retirement age for directors of an employee benefits consulting firm was found to constitute age discrimination and not to qualify as a BFOQ.

Note that BFOQ is not a defense to a claim of racial discrimination.

Defense of Business Necessity

Business necessity may relieve an employer of liability for disparate impact (unintentional) discrimination. If a neutral selection criterion has a disparate impact on a protected class but constitutes a business necessity, the criterion will not violate the Civil Rights Act of 1964. **Business necessity** means that the criterion has an obvious relationship to job performance. An example of a business necessity is speaking fluent English for a person with a job requiring communication with English-speaking people. Some job applicants from other countries may not meet this job requirement and can be excluded from consideration as a result. Like BFOQs, business necessity is defined narrowly.

Race

As we have seen, race is one of the grounds on which Title VII outlaws discrimination. The statute's main objective concerning race was to eliminate discrimination against blacks. Sadly, racism pervaded our society and mandated this remedial legislation. Its application however is not restricted to any one racial or minority group. In the words of the United States Supreme Court, the prohibition against discrimination in employment on the basis of race bars "discriminatory preference for any racial group, minority or majority." Additional examples of racial groups include Caucasian, Hispanics, Asian, American Indians, and Eskimos.

The outlawed discrimination includes not only refusals to hire, resistance to promote, and unjustified firings, but also other types of discrimination such as refusal to allow an employee to wear an Afro-American hairstyle and terminating a white employee for associating with a black colleague.

An interesting application of Title VII is found in *Vaughn v. Texaco*, 918 F.2d 517 (5th Cir., 1990). The plaintiff was a black attorney. Her supervisor, while unhappy with her work, was advised by the department manager not to relay his dissatisfaction to her but rather to "let it ride" to avoid charges of race discrimination. Plaintiff thus missed the opportunity to improve her performance through constructive criticism and counseling from her supervisor. Plaintiff was terminated when the department manager, in a cost-cutting effort, was forced to terminate the two lowest rated employees. The court held that the employer's failure to constructively criticize and develop the plaintiff was motivated by race and violated Title VII.

An employer can defend against a claim of discriminatory firing by establishing a legitimate, nondiscriminatory reason for the termination. A charge of discrimination made by a white dining room supervisor was dismissed in the following case because the employer could establish misconduct on the employee's part.

CASE EXAMPLE 14–2

Singh v. Shoney's, Inc., 64 F.3d 217 (5th Cir., 1995)

Delores Singh (Singh) filed a complaint against her former employer Shoney's, Inc. (Shoney's), alleging that she was fired because of her race. . . . The district court granted summary judgment in favor of Shoney's. We affirm.

Singh, a white female, was hired by Shoney's in September 1981. At the time of her termination in January 1993, Singh held the position of Dining Room Supervisor in a Shoney's restaurant in New Orleans, Louisiana. Her duties included hiring, firing, supervising, disciplining, and training the hostesses, waitresses, and salad bar attendants who worked in the restaurant.

In January, 1993, defendant's corporate office received a "petition" signed by 36 workers employed at the same restaurant as Singh. The petition alleged that Singh had been engaging in offensive, racially-discriminatory conduct toward subordinate employees. Shoney's responded to the petition by sending its Vice-President of Personnel, John Southerland, and its Equal Employment Opportunity Manager, Juanita Presley (both of whom are black), to New Orleans to investigate the allegations. Southerland and Presley interviewed 44 employees at the restaurant, including Singh. Based on these interviews, Shoney's concluded that Singh had en-

gaged in offensive, inappropriate conduct in the workplace, and terminated her employment.

During the course of the investigation, it came to Shoney's attention that the manager of the restaurant, Terry Dumars, a black male, had also engaged in inappropriate conduct in the workplace, and he was terminated. Dumars was replaced with a white male, and Singh was replaced with another white female.

. . . In order to make out a prima facie case of discrimination, a plaintiff alleging discriminatory discharge must show (1) that she is a member of a protected group; (2) that she was qualified for the job that she formerly held; (3) that she was discharged; and (4) that after her discharge, the position she held was filled by someone not within her protected class. Once the plaintiff establishes a prima facie case of discrimination, the defendant must articulate a legitimate, nondiscriminatory reason for the discharge. If the defendant states a legitimate reason, the plaintiff must show, by a preponderance of the evidence, that the reason provided by the defendant was a pretext for discrimination. . . .

Singh failed to make out a prima facie case of racial discrimination on this record, because she was replaced by a white female. Moreover, Shoney's has stated a legitimate nondiscriminatory reason for discharging Singh. . . . Shoney's reasonably believed the allegation contained in the petition, and acted on it in good faith.

CASE QUESTION

1. Why is is necessary for a terminated employee seeking to establish discrimination to show she was replaced by someone not within her protected class?

Also constituting discrimination based on race is the creation or tolerance by an employer of a work environment that significantly and adversely affects the psychological well-being of an employee because of the employee's race. A black police officer successfully sued his employer alleging he had endured racial slurs and other offensive racially-oriented incidents in the locker room, in lineups, during training, and throughout the workplace during his 16-year police career. He reported the incidents to the chief of police, who mandated that all police officers view a video on people's perceptions of themselves and others. The video was not directly related to discrimination. The chief did not investigate the reported occurrences and took no disciplinary action. The court, while holding that "a few isolated incidents of racially oriented harassment or hostility is insufficient to establish a violation," determined that the police department violated Title VII by permitting a racially hostile environment. *Ways v. City of Lincoln*, 871 F.2d 750 (8th Cir., 1989).

The police department defended the suit in part on the basis that it had a written policy against racial harassment. The court held the existence of a policy alone, without committed efforts to enforce it, will not relieve an employer of liability for discrimination.

In *Schwapp v Town of Avon*, 118 F.3d 106 (2nd Cir., 1997), a police officer alleged a hostile work environment based on twelve racially hostile comments and jokes made during his twenty-month tenure. The incidents included a comment by his supervisor that the plaintiff officer had to accept the fact that he was working with racists and should not be so sensitive. The court determined these incidents would amount to a hostile environment and denied summary judgment to the police department.

The lessons from the last two cases are equally applicable to hospitality employers. They have an obligation to ensure the workplace is tolerant and accepting of all races. To escape liability for permitting a hostile work environment, it is not enough for an employer to have on record a policy prohibiting such conduct. The employer must take steps to train employees about the policy and enforce it.

National Origin

National origin, another protected class, refers to the country where people were born or from which their ancestors came. For example, a refusal to hire workers of Spanish ancestry violates Title VII. The law also protects "hyphenated-Americans", such as Italian-Americans, Polish-Americans, and Mexican-Americans. National origin discrimination was established in a case involving the Westin Tucson Hotel. Plaintiff was a Nigerian-born African-American who was employed in the hotel's laundry. He tried six times unsuccessfully to transfer to other jobs for which he was qualified, primarily in the accounting department. When he asked about his status, he was told by the head of housekeeping, "Go back to Africa where you came from. We don't have any job for you here"; and by the Director of Human Services, he "should go to a black business to find a job." Plaintiff was awarded employment in the accounting department of the hotel, back pay, and attorney's fees. *Odima v. Westin Tucson Hotel*, 53 F.3d 1484 (9th Cir., 1994).

Employer tolerance of ethnic slurs or jokes by employees or supervisors also constitutes discrimination based on national origin.

Employers often prefer to hire an employee who is fluent in English. People from other countries may not speak English well. Refusal to hire someone whose English is faltering may constitute illegal discrimination on the basis of national origin. However, if the ability to speak English is a business necessity for the job, an employer who refuses to hire an applicant not well versed in English is not discriminating illegally. An example of English fluency being a business necessity is a job that requires communication with English-speaking patrons, such as wait personnel in restaurants or a hotel concierge.

In *Stephen v. PGA Sheraton Resort, Ltd.*, 873 F.2d 276 (11th Cir., 1989), plaintiff, a black male of Haitian origin, was a purchasing clerk for a Sheraton Resort. His duties included delivering supplies to many of the departments at the resort. His inability to understand English resulted in the misdelivery of supplies and at least one employee having to obtain her own supplies. Plaintiff was terminated from the clerk position and offered a lesser-paying job in housekeeping which involved setting up for banquets. The court held for the Sheraton, determining that plaintiff's termination "rested on proper concerns of business necessity. . . . [T]he employer took the contested employment action for a legitimate non-discriminatory reason."

If fluency is not required for the job, as is the case for housekeeping personnel at a hotel or dishwashers at a restaurant, refusal to hire on this ground would be illegal.

In the following case the hotel refused to promote a Hispanic employee because of her limited capacity to speak English. The court denied her claim of illegal discrimination, finding the hotel's requirement of fluent English was a business necessity.

CASE EXAMPLE 14–3

Mejia v. New York Sheraton Hotel
459 F.Supp. 375 (N.Y., 1978)

This is an employment discrimination case pursuant to Title VII of the Civil Rights Act of 1964. . . .

Plaintiff alleges in her complaint that she was discharged on June 24, 1975 from her position as a chambermaid with the Sheraton Hotel on account of her Spanish surname and the fact that her primary language was Spanish and that two years earlier she was denied a promotion to a front office cashier position for the same reasons.

The defendants deny any discriminatory purpose or effect of their conduct and assert that . . .

the reason why plaintiff was not promoted to the front office cashier position which she sought was that she was not qualified by reason of the paucity of her English language ability and her lack of familiarity with office procedures.

The facts established herein are the following.

Plaintiff is a female Dominican national who came to the United States in about 1970 as the holder of a visa entitling her to become employed in this country. Her education and schooling occurred abroad in a Spanish school and she never had any education in the English language until she arrived in this country. The plaintiff was employed as a chambermaid in the housekeeping department of the Sheraton Hotel from on or about October 29, 1970 to on or about June 24, 1975. During her employment, whatever ability she possessed to understand, speak and write English she acquired through courses that she had taken in English at New York University during a period of three months after her arrival here.

The defendant [is] New York Sheraton Hotel. . . .

Commencing in April 1973 the plaintiff enrolled in an Industry Training Program, a program jointly sponsored by plaintiff's Union and the city's hotel industry to train hotel employees for positions within the hotel industry. . . . A week after her training she applied for a position as a front office cashier. Such a job was never tendered to her. . . .

In 1974 there was an opening in the cashier's department and plaintiff spoke to the manager but she was told that she would have to learn to speak better English because the position required a greater aptitude than the plaintiff possessed. . . . The management found that the plaintiff's language barrier was a stumbling block to a front office post for the plaintiff, a post that would necessarily bring her in contact and communication with the guests of the hotel. . . .

Following her discharge, plaintiff resorted to the EEOC charging that she was discriminated against because . . . of her national origin and was not promoted because she was Spanish. . . .

The evidence in the case established beyond peradventure of doubt a serious past and current inability on the plaintiff's part to articulate clearly or coherently and to make herself adequately understood in the English language. She continued taking English courses after her discharge in the summers of 1975, 1976 and 1977 with minimal improvement. Her instructor's latest report card for the 1977 session recites that she was a poor student and definitely should not go on to [the next] level as she could not do the written work and that pronunciation was also a problem. . . . Plaintiff's exhibition on the witness stand emphasized the current existence of an English language deficiency that made it quite difficult for the Court, the reporter and counsel to understand what she was saying in her testimonial responses.

The requirement of the hotel for greater English proficiency than the plaintiff can exhibit was significantly related to successful job performance and did not operate to exclude minority applicants at a higher rate than applicants who are not of that minority group. There is no doubt that the plaintiff was not sufficiently qualified to be placed in a position in the front office cashier's department. The defendants found her not acceptable for such employment in a legitimate, nondiscriminatory manner. . . . Plaintiff's Hispanic origin . . . formed no part of defendant's refusal to place her in the front office cashier's department. Business necessities precluded a person of plaintiff's qualifications from being placed in the front office cashier type occupation in a large public hotel. The Sheraton Hotel employs about 650 persons, more than a third of whom are of Hispanic origin. . . . Although plaintiff cannot be faulted for her eagerness to advance from the position of a chambermaid to the front office of the hotel, the evidence conclusively shows that she was never sufficiently qualified and therefore was not eligible for the position she sought in the defendant's front office. . . .

Accordingly, the complaint herein is dismissed. . . . Judgment for defendant.

CASE QUESTION

1. Why was fluency in English important in the job plaintiff sought? Why was it less important for her job as a chambermaid?

National Origin and Accent Discrimination

A person from another country may be knowledgeable about English but speak with an accent. Said one court, "Accent and national origin are inextricably intertwined." An employer can refuse to hire a would-be worker based on accent only if it materially interferes with job performance. The connection between accents and illegal discrimination based on national origin is new legal ground. The law in this area is very important to managers in the accommodations industry, where so many employees are foreign-born.

A plaintiff who proves he has been discriminated against solely because of his accent has proven illegal discrimination based on national origin. *Ang v. Proctor & Gamble Co.*, 932 F.2d 540 (6th Cir., 1991). A professor was denied tenure (a permanent teaching position) because students complained her accent was difficult to understand. She sued the school district claiming discrimination on the basis of national origin. The court found for the school district stating, "Unlawful discrimination does not occur when a plaintiff's accent affects his ability to perform the job effectively." *Forsythe v. Board of Education, Hays, Kansas*, 956 F. Supp. 927 (Kans., 1997). But if the accent does not interfere with the ability to perform the job, the employer cannot refuse to hire or promote on that basis. A bank employee was denied a promotion to Loan Officer because of his accent. The court determined that his accent would not have interfered materially with his performance. The award, which was upheld on appeal, included back pay, lost future pay, expert witness fees, attorney's fees, compensation for emotional distress, and expenses for medical and psychiatric treatment necessitated by the discrimination. *Xieng v. People's National Bank of Washington*, 844 P.2d 389 (Wash., 1993).

Religion

An employer cannot discharge or refuse to hire a person because of religion, including all aspects of religious observance and practice. This rule can sometimes present difficulties for employers. For example, some workers celebrate sabbath in such a way that work is precluded. Some celebrate it on Saturday and others on Sunday. Accommodating religion-based requests for days off can complicate an employer's work schedule. Must an employer oblige employees' requests for days off to celebrate religious holidays? An employer has an affirmative duty to attempt to accommodate the religious observances and practices of its employees, unless the employer can demonstrate that such an accommodation would cause undue hardship to the business. An employer who is unable to reasonably satisfy the religious needs of an employee can escape liability if it can show it made a good-faith attempt to accommodate those needs or that to do so would cause undue hardship.

Reasonable accommodation requires an employer to give unpaid time off for religious holidays if the employee's services are not needed at work. Further, if paid leave is allowed for other purposes, unpaid leave may not qualify as a reasonable accommodation. An employer is also required to accept schedule changes arranged by the employees unless there is a good reason not to permit the substitution, as where the substitute lacks necessary skills to do the job. Another reasonable accommodation an employer might provide is a means of communication among employees to facilitate their finding substitutes, such as a bulletin board.

A manicurist and a skin specialist sought a day off without pay to observe Yom Kippur, a Jewish holy day, which fell on a Saturday, the busiest day in the salon business. The employer, noting that the employees already had customers booked for appointments on the day in question, denied the request. Neither employee came to work on Yom Kippur, and both were terminated from their jobs. They sued, claiming discrimination based on religion. The employer was unable to show that it tried to accommodate the employees' religious practices or that it would suffer an undue hardship by granting the day off. The employer was thus liable for religious discrimination. *EEOC v. Ilona of Hungary, Inc.*, 108 F.3d 1569 (1997).

In the hospitality industry, Saturdays and Sundays, the days on which many religious observances fall, are busy and therefore important business days. Accommodating employees who need these days off on a regular basis may cause a hardship to employers. Factors that can support a claim of undue hardship include lack of availability of alternate employees, lost efficiency to the operation caused by the absence of the observant employee's skills, and costs necessarily incurred by employers such as paying a premium to encourage other employees to work on the weekend, and lost patronage.

Sex

Title VII outlaws discrimination in employment on the basis of gender. An employer cannot refuse to grant women or men a benefit of employment based on their sex. For example, paying men more than women for the same job responsibilities is discrimination based on sex. This occurred in a case involving a restaurant franchisor that hired several personnel recruiters, one of whom was a female. The restaurant paid her less money than her male counterparts because she "was not the breadwinner" and "didn't need to make as much as a man." This constituted discrimination. Further, since the wrongful conduct was willful, by statute the restaurant was required to pay double the amount of back pay awarded to plaintiff. *Scribner v. Waffle House, Inc.*, 976 F. Supp. 439 (Tex., 1997)

Hiring only one gender for a particular job generally constitutes discrimination. For example, a restaurant cannot hire only males as wait personnel. The EEOC brought a discrimination action against Joe's Stone Crab Restaurant, a well-known Florida eatery that did exactly that. Women were prevalent in other positions at the restaurant. Stated the court, "While women have predominated among Joe's owner/managers, as well as among the laundering, cashiering and take away staff, women have systematically been excluded from the most lucrative entry level position, that of server." The court thus held the restaurant's hiring practices violated Title VII. *EEOC v. Joe's Stone Crab, Inc.*, 969 F. Supp. 727 (Fl., 1997). Now both men and women fill the ranks of servers at the restaurant.

A related case involved Hooters, a 204-restaurant chain in 40 states with a theme of scantily clad women performing most jobs involving customer interaction including wait personnel, bartenders, and receptionists. Males were hired only as managers or kitchen help. The company was charged with gender discrimination in a class action lawsuit brought by males who had applied for wait jobs and had either been refused on the basis of their sex or hired to work in the lesser-paid kitchen jobs. The case was settled for $3.75 million and a commitment by Hooters to hire males as bartender assistants, greeters at the door, and in a new "staff position" which involves clearing tables and bringing condiments to the table. The staff position will earn more than what bussers customarily make and will share in tips. The principal server remains a female-only position. The settlement thus expands the opportunities for males to obtain employment at Hooters and earn more than minimal pay. It also preserves the primary wait position for women only. Had the case proceeded to court, Hooters might have been directed to modify its theme to permit male waiters.

In another case, a hotel that refused to hire women as bartenders "patently offended" Title VII. *Krause v. Sacramento Inn*, 479 F.2d 988 (9th Cir., 1973). Likewise, an airline that utilized inferior pay scales for stewardesses as compared to stewards acted illegally. *Leffey v. Northwest Airlines, Inc.*, 567 F.2d 429 (1976).

An airline that required women flight attendants to be single but hired married men for the same position acted illegally. *Sprogis v. United Air Lines, Inc.*, 444 F.2d 1194 (7th Cir., 1971). Similarly, an employer cannot refuse to hire women with preschool-age children if it hires men with preschool-age children.

An employer cannot use the argument that a particular job is dangerous as a basis to hire only men. An objective of Title VII is to permit each woman to make that decision for herself. The United States Supreme Court held that an employer discriminated illegally when it excluded women of child-bearing age but not men of similar age from jobs requiring exposure to lead, which had the potential to damage both male and female reproductive systems. *International Union, United Automobile Workers v. Johnson Controls, Inc.*, 117 S. Ct. 1196 (1991).

The protection against sexual discrimination is not limited to females but rather also protects males. A male guest service agent at a Pennsylvania Sheraton Hotel had a basis to sue when he was able to show that his reassignment to a phone operator position was motivated by considerations of gender. *Davis v. Sheraton Society Hill Hotel*, 907 F. Supp. 896 (Pa., 1995).

Establishing that an employer's discriminatory acts are based on sex can sometimes be difficult. Statements made by management that women in general are simply not competent to perform a particular job are classic examples of evidence that helps to establish a gender discrimination case. The following comments, made by an employer who was hiring for the position of collections manager, help to prove a case of gender discrimination: "Women cannot get tough enough with customers and collect the money," and "This job requires a man to do it." *Haynes v. W.C. Caye & Co.*, 52 F.3d 929 (11th Cir., 1995).

In another case a discharged female sales representative attempted unsuccessfully to establish that her termination was due to sex discrimination. One of the circumstances she cited as establishing discrimination was her supervisor's scheduling a lunch meeting at Hooters restaurant. The court, while referring to the meeting site as "grossly unprofessional" found the meeting locale insufficient to support a discrimination verdict. *Ray v. Tandem Computers, Inc.*, 63 F.3d 429 (5th Cir., 1995).

To establish a case of discrimination for failing to hire or promote based on gender, plaintiffs must establish that they are qualified for the position they seek. An employer can refuse to hire or promote a person who lacks the skills necessary to perform a job adequately. In *EEOC v. Marion Motel Associates*, 763 F. Supp. 1334 (N.C., 1991), plaintiff, an employee of defendant motel, sought promotion to general manager. When the position was assigned to a man, she sued for gender discrimination. The court decided the case in favor of the hotel, finding that plaintiff was not qualified for the position. In making that determination, the court referenced testimony that established that plaintiff was occasionally tardy for work, failed to alert off-site management of excessive absences of the general manager, and "was reluctant to perform tasks over and above her regular job duties."

Gender-Differentiated Grooming Standards

A number of cases involve male employees who were fired for failing to comply with grooming standards imposed on men but not women. The plaintiffs in these lawsuits claim the personal appearance regulations discriminate on the basis of sex. The law is now quite clear that minor differences in an employer's appearance rules for men and women that reflect customary modes of grooming for one sex but not the other do not violate Title VII. The objective of Title VII is to equalize employment opportunities. Discrimination based on sex characteristics that are unchangeable is prohibited, but discrimination based on factors of personal preference that an employee can modify does not restrict employment. Thus, requiring that male employees have short hair but imposing no similar restriction on female employees is not sex discrimination. A male employee who was terminated for violating such a hair policy has no basis on which to sue his former employer. *Tavora v. New York Mercantile Exchange*, 101 F.3d 907 (2nd Cir., 1996). Likewise, a prohibition against men wearing earnings while women are permitted to do so, does not violate the discrimination laws. *Capaldo v. Pan American Federal Credit Union*, 43 EPD Section 37,016 (1987). Said the court, "[A]n employer is permitted to exercise legitimate concern for the business image created by the appearance of its employees."

An employer cannot require one sex to wear a uniform and not the other where both are doing the same job. A bank that required female tellers and office and managerial employees to wear uniforms while permitting men to work in customary business attire was liable for sex discrimination. While the employer gave each woman one uniform, the workers were required to purchase replacement uniforms, pay income tax on the one provided by the employer, and pay for cleaning and maintenance. The court explained the defendant had several options: permit women to wear "appropriate business attire;" require the male employees to wear uniforms; or make uniforms optional for both men and women. Said the court, "Title VII does not require that uniforms be abolished but that defendant's similarly situated employees be treated in an equal manner." *Carroll v. Talman Federal Savings & Loan Association*, 604 F.2d 1028 (7th Cir., 1979).

Sexual Harassment

Sexual harassment is a form of sexual discrimination and constitutes a violation of Title VII. Sexual harassment includes two types of illegal action: 1) unwelcome sexual advances or requests for sexual favors in return for job benefits; and 2) verbal or physical conduct of a sexual nature that creates an intimidating, hostile, or offensive work environment. The former is called **quid pro quo** sexual harassment; the latter, **hostile environment** sexual harassment.

Examples of quid pro quo sexual harassment include firing a female worker who rejects her supervisor's advances, *Sparks v. Pilot Freight Carriers, Inc.*, 830 F.2d 1554 (11th Cir., 1987); denying a woman a promotion and/or training opportunities because she rejects her boss' advances, *Henson v. City of Dundee*, 682 F.2d 897 (11th Cir., 1982); demoting a female employee for the same reason, *Carrero v. New York City Housing Authority*, 890 F.2d 569 (2d Cir., 1989), and conditioning the grant of a two-week leave of absence for a female employee on her performing oral sex on her supervisor. *Nichols v. Frank*, 42 F.3d 503 (9th Cir., 1994).

An example of a hostile work environment is one in which female employees are exposed to persistent lewd remarks and ubiquitous pinups. *Robinson v. Jacksonville Shipyards, Inc.*, 760 F. Supp. 1486 (Fl., 1991). Said the court, "Pornography on an employer's wall or desk communicates a message about the way he views women, a view strikingly at odds with the way women wish to be viewed in the workplace." In *Splunge v. Shoney's, Inc.*, 97 F.3d 488 (11th Cir., 1996), the following clearly constituted a hostile environment: male employees grabbed at the female plaintiffs, commented extensively on their physical attributes, showed them pornographic photos and videotapes, offered them money for sex, favored other employees who had affairs with them, and speculated aloud as to their sexual prowess. Also constituting hostile environment sexual harassment are the following circumstances: a waitress' supervisor, on at least a dozen occasions, bumped into her from behind and rubbed against her or ran his hands over her buttocks at the pie cooler or in other behind-the-counter spaces; he inquired about her sex life; and he led other employees to believe he was having an affair with her. *Knabe v. Big Boy East*, 114 F.3d 407 (3rd Cir., 1997).

Casual or isolated incidents of discriminatory conduct such as a few sexual comments or slurs will not constitute a hostile environment. However, conduct less severe than that in *Splunge v. Shoney's, Inc.* will cross the threshold and result in liability.

While the offending employee in each of these cases was male and the victim female, sexual harassment can be perpetrated by females against males, males against males, and females against females. The types of activity that can constitute sexual harassment are many and include insults, pressure for sexual activity, repeatedly asking someone out on a date when the invitee has indicated a lack of interest, suggestive sounds, obscene gestures, lewd pictures, touching, pinching, brushing against someone, coerced sexual intercourse, and giving personal gifts. Cases have established common patterns of victims' reactions to sexual harassment, including distraction, inability to work, anger, anxiety, depression, sleeping problems and other physical ailments.

Unwelcomed Conduct. A critical factor for sexual harassment is that the activity be unwelcome by the employee and the harasser knows it is unwelcome. If the conduct is desired, it is not harassment.

Consent alone does not establish that the conduct is welcome. An employee may begrudgingly consent to unwelcome acts because of fear of losing a job or promotion. In *Meritor Savings Bank v. Vinson*, 477 U.S. 57, 106 S. Ct. 2399 (1986), a bank employee agreed to have sexual relations with a bank vice-president because she feared losing her job if she refused. The encounters continued for a period of years. She later sued the bank for sexual harassment. The bank defended in part by claiming the relationship was voluntary. The court responded, "The correct inquiry is whether respondent by her conduct indicated that the alleged sexual advances were unwelcome, not whether her actual participation in sexual intercourse was voluntary." The court referred the case back to the court with original jurisdiction to determine whether the acts were unwelcome. Note that the court did not rule that the long-term aspect of the relationship merited a presumption or inference that it was welcome.

In some circumstances the unwelcome nature of the conduct can be implied from the nature of the activity, such as coerced sexual intercourse. In other circumstances the conduct's offensiveness will be less clear and the employee must relay that it is not appreciated. If a supervisor asks an employee out on a date for the first time, the request is normally not sexual harassment, even if the employee refuses. If, following the refusal, the supervisor continues to pester that employee for a date, the requests may constitute sexual harassment. Similarly, if the supervisor had previously been rebuked by the employee for other types of sexual conduct, the invitation for a date may be sexual harassment.

At least one case has held that the employee need not verbalize the unwelcome nature of sexually suggestive conduct; consistent demonstration through actions is sufficient notification. In *Chamberlin v. 101 Realty, Inc.*, 915 F.2d 777 (1st Cir., 1990), the court held an employee adequately relayed the unwelcomed nature of her boss' advances where, on several different occasions, she failed to respond to his sexual innuendos, changed the subject when he suggested intimacy between them, and pulled her hands away when he reached for them across a restaurant table at lunch.

Employer Liability. Employers such as hotels and restaurants have often attempted to avoid liability by claiming that a supervisor's harassing conduct should not be attributable to them. The liability of an employer depends in part on the type of sexual harassment involved. For quid pro quo sexual harassment (where a supervisor conditions a job, job benefits, or the absence of a job detriment on an employee's submission to sexual conduct), the harasser's employer is liable. The theory of the employer's liability is respondeat superior, that is, the employer is liable for the wrongful acts of an employee (supervisor) done in furtherance of the employee's job responsibilities (granting job benefits or detriments).

The employer is not automatically liable in a hostile environment case. To establish liability on the employer the plaintiff must prove that the employer knew or should have known of the harassing conduct either because of its pervasiveness or because plaintiff complained to management. Plaintiff also must show that the employer, if advised of the harassment, failed to take prompt remedial action in response to the complaints. The following case illustrates appropriate response by an employer to a sexual harassment complaint. As a result, the employer escaped liability.

CASE EXAMPLE 14–4

Gregg v. Hay-Adams Hotel
942 F. Supp. 1 (D.C., 1996)

. . . Plaintiff Debra Denise Gregg is currently employed as an Assistant Pastry Chef at the Hay-Adams Hotel in Washington, D.C. She was hired as such in June of 1993 and has remained in this position since that time. She alleges that within a few months of her hiring, the Executive Chef of the Hotel, Patrick Clark, began to make suggestive remarks toward her, culminating in unwelcome physical contact. . . .

On April 14, 1994, some eight months after the harassment allegedly began, Gregg complained about Clark to Payroll/Personnel Assistant Toya Roberts. Independently, another coworker, Victoria Dade, also complained about Clark to Roberts that very day. There had never been a sexual harassment complaint by any hotel employee prior to this date.

Still on April 14, 1994, Roberts reported the complaints to Human Resources Director Jeffrey Lea, who instructed Roberts to prepare a memorandum regarding the charges—which she delivered to him the next day. In the memo, Roberts reported, among other things, that she told Gregg she would assist her and urged Gregg to take down notes concerning the events.

On Friday morning, April 15, 1994, Lea met with Urs Aeby, the General Manager of the hotel who then ordered an immediate investigation of the complaints. Aeby then met with each of the two women to inform them that all appropriate steps would be taken to provide them a harassment-free workplace, and he further assured them that they would not be subject to retribution. Statements were taken from Gregg, Dade, and several other employees who might have knowledge of the events. Clark was told generally about the allegations but not about who had made them.

On April 26, 1994, less than two weeks after the complaints, Aeby issued Clark a "formal and final written warning." The letter stated that the investigation revealed behavior "verging on harassment" and that even with respect to unsubstantiated allegations, Clark had "shown a serious lack of judgment." The letter further warned him that any retributive acts could be punishable by termination of employment.

There have been no subsequent sexual harassment accusations since the April 14, 1994 charges. . . .

Gregg attempts to place liability on the employer by arguing that the hotel "violated its expressed company policy regarding sexual harassment to refrain from sexually discriminating against plaintiff by allowing its agents and employees to make sexual advances towards plaintiff and by creating an intimidating hostile and offensive work environment." Gregg neither alleges, nor has evidence to suggest, that the employer actually knew or had reason to know of the harassment [prior to Gregg's complaint], nor that the Hotel approved of it. . . . When a company, once informed of allegations of sexual harassment, takes prompt remedial action to protect the claimant, the company may avoid Title VII liability.

Turning to the issue of whether the hotel actually did respond in an appropriate and timely fashion to Gregg's complaint, the court finds that defendant did so, and to a degree which would remove it from any Title VII liability.

It is undisputed that the Hotel took the following actions:

1. When Gregg reported her complaints to the Payroll/Personnel Assistant, Sonya Roberts, she

immediately carried the news to the Human Resources director.

2. Gregg (and another woman who complained) was assured that she would be helped.

3. Within a week of the allegations, four interviews, plus statements by complainants were taken to confirm or disaffirm the charges.

4. The General Manager of the Hotel notified Clark of the allegations, and personally assured Gregg that sexual harassment would not be tolerated.

5. Clark was issued a "formal and final warning," placed in his personnel file, on April 26, 1994, less than two weeks after the complaint was made.

6. The warning to Clark stated that further behavior would result in the immediate termination of his employment.

7. Clark was also threatened with termination should he retaliate against those who complained about him.

8. Clark apologized to Gregg.

9. The Hotel re-issued its sexual harassment policy, ran seminars on sexual harassment (with mandatory attendance for all employees), and Gregg was told to report any further harassment or retaliation directly to the Human Resources Director or the General Manager.

10. A new Human Resources Director, Graciela Lewis, made several visits to the kitchen to ensure the working environment was comfortable there.

11. Gregg admits there was no further harassment after April 14, the date of her first and only complaint to the hotel.

These steps are substantial enough both in action and effect to negate Title VII liability. . . .

An employer may be liable for sexual harassment not only when supervisors initiate the harassment but also when co-workers or customers harass an employee. For an employer to be liable for sexual harassment administered by non-supervisory co-workers, the employer must be aware of the harassment, as where it is occurring openly and blatantly, or where the harassed employee reports it to the superior.

In a case involving sexual harassment by patrons, a Las vegas casino cocktail waitress reported harassing comments by customers to her boss who did nothing in response. The casino defended its inaction by claiming that inappropriate comments, sexual or otherwise, by patrons is inevitable in a job that requires constant contact with the public, particularly in a city that is a "fun" destination where people sometimes drink to excess and often lose more money than they should. The court clearly rejected these circumstances as a defense to the waitress' discrimination action. Said the court, "[E]mployers are liable for failing to remedy or prevent a hostile or offensive work environment of which management-level employees knew or in the exercise of reasonable care should have known." *Powell v. Las Vegas Hilton Hotel & Casino*, 841 F. Supp. 1024 (1992).

An employer that takes prompt and substantial action to protect employees from customer harassment will thereby avoid liability. In one such case a professional mime performed for Circus Circus Casino in the character of a life-size children's wind-up toy. She was sufficiently convincing in this role that casino patrons occasionally tried to touch her to determine if she was human. When the mime discussed her concerns about this circumstance with her supervisor, he assigned a large man dressed in a clown costume to accompany her when she performed. Further, a sign was prepared for her to wear that read, "Stop: Do not touch". Further, other casino employees were alerted to call security if they saw that she was being harassed and to direct customers not to touch her. Thereafter, a customer touched the mime despite another employee warning the customer three times not to do so. The mime sued the casino, claiming it did not take sufficient precautions to protect her against sexual harassment by the customers. The court disagreed, finding the casino took reasonable and sufficient steps to protect the mime from customer harassment. *Folkerson v. Circus Circus Hotel & Casino*, 107 F.3d 754 (1997).

In another case involving harassment by customers, an employer was held liable where it forced an employee to wear a sexually provocative uniform that the employer could reasonably forsee would subject the employee to sexual harassment by customers and did subject her to such conduct. *E.E.O.C. v. Sage Realty Corp.*, 507 F. Supp. 599 (N.Y., 1981). Employers such as bars and casinos, who require waitresses to wear short skirts and low-cut tops may incur liability when the scant clothing foreseeably provokes harassing behavior by the clientele.

To limit the occurrences of sexual harassment, employers should develop a company policy clearly establishing that sexual harassment will not be tolerated. The policy should be posted and published to all employees. It should include a complaint procedure that authorizes employees to file complaints with a high-level employee not in their line of supervision. Complaints should be treated seriously and investigated thoroughly. When warranted, appropriate and prompt remedial action should be taken, including the following: in a quid pro quo case, changing the work site of the harasser, terminating the harasser, and denying him/her a promotion; in a hostile environment case, mandating that the objectionable conduct stop (such as requiring that pinups be removed and lewd comments cease), and penalizing those who caused the hostile environment through adverse job action and/or required training about sexual harassment.

Pregnancy

The increasing number of women of childbearing age who enter the labor force prompt the question of an employer's obligation to a pregnant employee. Part of Title VII, called the Pregnancy Discrimination Act, makes it unlawful for an employer to treat medical conditions relating to pregnancy and childbirth less favorably than other disabilities, unless justified by business necessity. (42 U.S.C. Section 2000e.) The basic principle of the Act is that women who are pregnant or affected by related conditions must be treated the same as other applicants and employees on the basis of their ability or inability to work. A woman is therefore protected against such practices as being fired or forced to take a leave of absence just because she is pregnant. Women who are pregnant and able to work must be permitted to work on the same condition as other employees.

If the pregnancy becomes disabling and the woman is not able to work for medical reasons, she must be accorded the same rights, privileges, and other benefits as other workers who are disabled. An employer could not terminate a pregnant woman whose doctor requires her not to work if the employer allows workers with other disabilities to take a leave of absence. This is an important right for the worker since, with a leave of absence, the employee preserves her right to the job, seniority, and benefits. If the employee is terminated and later rehired, she loses the seniority and benefits she accumulated prior to the termination.

If an employer is imposing adverse job action on all employees, the employer can include the pregnant woman among those affected. For example, if the pregnancy coincides with a slowdown in the employer's business during which the employer is cutting hours of all employees, as, for example, a summer resort in the fall, the employer can legally cut the pregnant employee's hours as well.

In a case involving business necessity, an airline's policy of removing flight attendants as soon as their pregnancy became known was challenged by a pregnant stewardess. The court upheld the airline's policy. Fatigue and nausea often accompany pregnancy and could render a flight attendant unable to perform job responsibilities in an emergency, thus risking the safety of passengers. Although different women have different physical reactions to their pregnancies, the airline would not be able to predict which pregnant stewardesses would suffer from ailments and which would not. Therefore the policy of not allowing pregnant stewardesses to work met the business necessity exception. *Levin v. Delta Air Lines, Inc.*, 730 F.2d 994 (5th Cir., 1984).

Reinstatement policies for employees returning to work after giving birth must be the same as for employees returning to work after absences due to other temporary disabilities. The EEOC has declared that an employer cannot prohibit an employee from returning to work for a specified length of time after childbirth. Instead, individualized determinations of the time needed for recovery should be made in the same manner used for other disabilities.

An issue of abortion rights was raised in a case involving a busser at a Holiday Inn who became pregnant and so informed her manager and fellow staff members. She also discussed with her manager and some co-workers that she had not ruled out the possibility of an abortion. According to the Food and Beverage Director, "We have a very Christian staff in that restaurant who were very offended by [the busser's discussion of a possible abortion]." The busser was disciplined for creating an "uproar" among the staff and advised if she spoke of an abortion again at work she would be terminated. She ultimately was fired. The court held that discharging an employee on the basis of a statement that she is considering an abortion, has had one, or intends to have one, constitutes illegal pregnancy discrimination. The court also determined that the busser had adequately presented a claim of religious discrimination since her belief that abortion was morally permissible as opposed to the Christian employees who objected to abortion was identified as the cause of staff uproar and contributed to her termination. *Turic v. Holiday Inn*, 842 F. Supp. 971 (Mich., 1994).

Age

As medical developments have expanded life expectancy, the American work force has aged and issues of age discrimination take on greater importance. An employer may prefer a 25-year-old for a wait job over a 60-year-old. Can the employer fire or refuse to hire the older person? The answer is no; if an employer fires the older worker because of age, the employer will be liable for age discrimination. A federal law called the Age Discrimination in Employment Act (ADEA), 29 U.S.C. Sections 621-634, bars an employer from discriminating against an employee on the basis of being 40 years of age or older. The purpose of the ADEA is "to promote employment of older persons based on their ability rather than age; to prohibit arbitrary age discrimination in employment; and to help employers and workers find ways of meeting problems arising from the impact of age on employment." The ADEA makes it unlawful for an employer to refuse to hire, discharge, or discriminate with respect to compensation or conditions of employment because of a person's age.

The ADEA attempts to balance the needs of seasoned workers with those of the business community. As with all the discrimination laws, the ADEA does not prevent an employer from making employment decisions based on legitimate reasons other than age. Also, an employer can refuse to hire older workers if it can show that youth is a legitimate business necessity.

Age discrimination was proved where plaintiff, a 61-year-old male, interviewed for a salesperson job with defendant, a company that sells spices. He had held the job previously and been very successful at it, winning the top sales award. He had continuously ranked among the top sales representatives. He had been terminated when the company discontinued its sales force and used a food broker instead. He then worked for the broker selling the same spices he had sold for defendant. He applied for his old job when the company reversed the decision to use a broker. In response to a 59-year-old applicant's inquiry as to pay, defendant's interviewer stated, "Normally I hire younger people and start them out at $17,000 per year." Plaintiff was not rehired. Other older applicants were also rejected. The person hired did not have experience in the sale of spices. The nondiscriminatory reasons given by defendant for not hiring plaintiff were "various and always changing". Based on these circumstances, the court upheld the jury's finding that plaintiff was the victim of age discrimination. *Newhouse v. McCormick & Co., Inc.*, 110 F.3d 635 (8th Cir., 1997).

In the following case, two hotel employees claimed that they were fired because they were each over 40 years old. A want ad placed by the restaurant and comments made by the owner established illegal age discrimination.

CASE EXAMPLE 14–5

EEOC v. Marion Motel Associates
763 F.Supp. 1338 (N.C., 1991)
. . . The Plaintiff, on behalf of claimants Aileen Peterson and Effie C. Petersen, alleged that the Defendant . . . terminated their employment on the basis of their ages. . . .

The evidence established that both claimants were over 40 years of age during their employment by the Defendant. Gary F. Hewitt, owner and manager of the Defendant Park Inn, testified that he was satisfied with the work of claimant Effie C. Petersen. While there was some testimony as to claimant Aileen Peterson's tardiness in reporting to work, it appears that she also generally met the legitimate expectations of Defendant. Moreover, the evidence was that Hewitt expressed his desire to replace claimants Aileen Peterson and Effie C. Petersen with younger employees. According to the testimony, although Hewitt was an experienced businessman, he caused an unlawful advertisement to be published in *The McDowell News* which announced vacancies in all supervisory and desk clerk positions and urged "young, energetic persons" to apply for employment at the Park Inn. Hewitt testified that when claimant Effie Petersen offered to learn additional tasks for the second shift, he replied, "You can't teach an old dog new tricks." The evidence further established that the job application used by the Defendant contained a notice regarding prohibitions under the Age Discrimination in Employment Act (hereinafter "the Act"). . . .

The Court sent the issues covering the age discrimination claim of Aileen Peterson and Effie Petersen to the jury. The jury responded in the affirmative to the issue, "[D]id the Defendant . . . terminate the employment of claimant Aileen Peterson and claimant Effie C. Petersen because of their age?"

The evidence was that Hewitt was an experienced businessman with knowledge of the Act. Hewitt used job application forms at the Park Inn that contained a notice regarding the Act's prohibitions. As stated above, Hewitt placed an advertisement in *The McDowell News*, that was in violation of federal law. Moreover, the Court heard the testimony about Hewitt's age-biased comment to Effie Petersen and the circumstances regarding her departure. The Court finds that the totality of the evidence establishes a course of conduct [establishing violation of the Act]. . . .

[Judgment for plaintiff affirmed.]

Retaliatory Discharge

It is illegal for the employer to retaliate against an employee who files a complaint with the EEOC or otherwise objects to or protests an employer's violation of civil rights laws. Such an illegal discharge is called a **retaliatory discharge**. For example, an employer cannot dismiss, demote, or refuse to promote a worker on the ground that he filed a discrimination claim with the EEOC. An example of a retaliatory discharge is provided in *Brady v. Sam's Town Hotel & Gambling Center*, 110 F.3d 67 (9th Cir., 1997). Plaintiff had been employed by defendant as a poker dealer until June 1991. Thereafter, he testified against defendant in a discrimination lawsuit brought by another employee. Subsequently, plaintiff reapplied for a poker dealer's position at defendant's casino. He was told by the poker room manager that "I don't even know if they're gonna want to hire you back because of the involvement with the [discrimination case]." Further, defendant normally followed a policy of rehiring dealers who had previously worked at its casino before hiring new dealers. When defendant thereafter experienced two poker dealer openings, it hired new dealers rather than defendant. The court held these facts would support a finding of retaliatory discharge.

Another form of prohibited retaliatory personnel action is writing a negative job reference for someone who files a discrimination complaint. In *Hashimoto v. Secretary of the Navy*, 118 F.3d 671 (9th Cir., 1997), a budget analyst for the Navy filed a complaint against her immediate supervisor alleging race and gender discrimination. She thereafter sought a position with the Army and asked her supervisor for a reference. He provided one but it was not flattering. The court concluded that the negative reference was motivated by "retaliatory animus" and thus violated Title VII.

Mixed Types of Discrimination

Sometimes an employer will discriminate against a worker on more than one illegal ground. As you read the following case, see how many illegal bases for discrimination you can find. While the case is quite long it provides an excellent review of most of the discrimination topics we have discussed.

CASE EXAMPLE 14-6

EEOC v. Hacienda Hotel
881 F.2d 1504 (9th Cir., 1989)

On May 30, 1986, the Equal Employment Opportunity Commission ("EEOC" or "the Commission") initiated this employment discrimination action against appellant defendant Hacienda Hotel ("Hacienda" or "the Hotel"), in El Segundo, California. The Commission alleged that the Hacienda, its General Manager (Frank Godoy), its Executive Housekeeper (Alicia Castro) and its Chief of Engineering (William Nusbaum), had engaged in unlawful employment practices against female employees in the Hacienda housekeeping department by sexually harassing them, terminating them when they became pregnant, failing to accommodate their religious beliefs, and retaliating against them for opposing Hacienda's discriminatory practices. Relief was sought and obtained on behalf of five current and former Hacienda maids, all but one of whom were undocumented aliens, who were alleged to have been victims of appellant's discriminatory employment practices during 1982 and 1983. We affirm.

[Facts of the case involving Teodora Castro:]

The Hotel hired Teodora Castro in June 1980. Teodora became pregnant in late 1981 and continued to work for defendant. During the course of her pregnancy, both Alicia Castro and Nusbaum made numerous crude and disparaging remarks regarding her pregnancy. Nusbaum, for example, told Teodora that "that's what you get for sleeping without your underwear;" he also asked why she was pregnant by another man and made comments about her "ass." Nusbaum often subjected her to sexually offensive remarks in the presence of Alicia Castro, who merely laughed. Alicia Castro herself told Teodora that she did not like "stupid

women who have kids," and on many occasions called her a "dog" or a "whore" or a "slut."

In late 1981 and early 1982, Teodora Castro complained to Frank Godoy and Jose Ortiz, the union representative, about Nusbaum's and Alicia Castro's comments, but the situation did not improve. On June 30, 1982, Teodora Castro was terminated, as Alicia Castro admitted in her deposition and at trial, because of her pregnancy. She was rehired in November 1982, following the birth of her child.

Teodora Castro is also a Seventh Day Adventist who observes the Sabbath on Saturdays. Prior to her termination, she had been given Saturdays off. After she was rehired in November 1982, however, Alicia Castro informed her that she would have to work Saturdays. Teodora reminded the Executive Housekeeper that she needed Saturdays off in order to observe her Sabbath, but Alicia Castro denied her request. On December 17, 1982, Alicia Castro terminated Teodora for refusing to work on her Sabbath. During this time period, another maid in the Housekeeping Department, who was less senior than Teodora, was permitted to have both Saturdays and Sundays off after she had been attacked on the way home from work while waiting for public transportation, which was inadequate on weekends.

Following her termination, Teodora immediately sought employment. After another pregnancy, she finally secured new employment at another hotel in May 1984. Between May 1984 and the date of the trial, Teodora Castro earned less than she would have earned had she remained employed by the Hacienda.

[Facts of the case Involving Maria Elana Gonzales:]

Maria Elana Gonzalez was a maid in the Hacienda Housekeeping Department from October

27, 1980, to September 21, 1982. Gonzalez is a Jehovah's Witness and observes her Sabbath on Sundays. In early September 1982, Gonzalez requested that she be given Sundays off in order to observe the Sabbath. Alicia Castro initially granted Gonzalez's request; two days later she changed her mind and told Gonzalez that she had to work Sundays or quit.

Gonzalez filed a union grievance complaining of Castro's refusal to accommodate her religious beliefs. Gonzalez also informed the General Manager of the Hacienda Hotel, Frank Godoy, of Alicia Castro's refusal to adjust her schedule. Godoy told Gonzalez that he would speak with Castro regarding her request. Alicia Castro subsequently told Gonzalez that because she had complained to Godoy, she would never have Sundays off and that she should be grateful that she had a job. Castro also told Gonzalez that she was going to "make life so difficult for her that she would not know her head from her feet."

During the month of September 1982, Castro issued four disciplinary warnings to Gonzalez and terminated her on September 21, 1982. Following her termination, Gonzalez sought other comparable employment.

[Facts of the case Involving Flora Villalobos:]

The Hotel hired Flora Villalobos in April of 1980. After she became pregnant in early 1982, she was regularly subjected to sexually offensive remarks from Alicia Castro and Nusbaum. Castro often called her a "dog" or a "whore," and Nusbaum told her that women "get pregnant because they like to suck men's dicks." On many occasions, Nusbaum threatened to have her fired if she did not submit to his sexual advances. Castro witnessed some of Nusbaum's behavior and laughed at his sexual remarks. On October 31, 1982, when Villalobos was approximately seven months pregnant and still able and willing to work, Castro terminated her employment because of her pregnancy. Villalobos had obtained a statement from her doctor indicating that she was able to continue working until two or three weeks before her estimated delivery date of December 28, 1982.

On February 9, 1983, Villalobos provided Castro a written statement from her doctor indi-

cating that she was able to return to work immediately. Villalobos was not rehired until April 8, 1983. The Hotel hired two maids, one rehire and one new employee, while Villalobos was awaiting rehire.

[Facts of the case Involving Leticia Cardona:]

Leticia Cardona was employed by the Hotel from May 15, 1981, to September 28, 1982. After she became pregnant in early 1982, she was subjected to sexually offensive comments by Alicia Castro and Nusbaum. In September 1982, when Cardona was six months pregnant, Castro told her that she was too fat to clean rooms and fired her on September 28, 1982. Although at trial Castro testified that Cardona was terminated for poor work performance, Castro had previously admitted in a deposition that she terminated Cardona pursuant to her practice of terminating pregnant employees. Cardona's notice of termination form, which was completed by Castro, states that she was terminated because of her pregnancy.

In December 1982, after the birth of her baby, Cardona returned to the Hotel and requested her job back, but Castro refused. Castro testified that Cardona was not rehired because she was a poor worker.

[Facts of the case Involving Mercedes Flores:]

Throughout her term of employment from October 8, 1978, to March 10, 1983, William Nusbaum made sexual advances and offensive sexual comments to Mercedes Flores. Nusbaum regularly offered, for example, to give her money from his paycheck and an apartment to live in if she would "give him [her] body." He also assured her that she would never be fired if she would have sex with him. Flores claimed to have heard Nusbaum make offensive sexual comments to other maids, including complainants Cardona, Castro, and Villalobos. On one occasion, for example, she heard him say to Villalobos: "You have such a fine ass. It's a nice ass to stick a nice dick into. How many dicks have you eaten?" . . .

[Pregnancy Discrimination]

Alicia Castro admitted that it was her practice to terminate pregnant employees rather than permit them to take temporary leaves of absence, although she did not terminate other employees who were similarly temporarily disabled because of illness or injury. Alicia Castro specifically admitted that she terminated claimants Castro, Villalobos, and Cardona because of pregnancy.

Appellant argues that it should not be held liable for pregnancy discrimination because no one suffered any "damage" as a result of an application of the discriminatory policy. In particular, appellant contends that Teodora Castro and Villalobos were rehired following their pregnancies without loss of seniority or other benefits, while Cardona would not have been reinstated in any event because of her poor work performance. . . .

Even if no employee suffered a "tangible loss" of an "economic nature," i.e., a loss of seniority or wages or other monetarily quantifiable employment benefits, appellant's implementation of a policy or practice under which pregnant employees were treated differently from other temporarily-disabled employees with similar capacity for work would still be a violation of both the letter and spirit of Title VII's prohibition against pregnancy discrimination. Appellant overlooks, moreover, the district court's ultimate determination that at least one of the pregnancy discrimination claimants, Flora Villalobos, actually did lose wages because of appellant's discriminatory policy. . . .

[Religious Discrimination]

The district court found that Teodora Castro and Marie Elena Gonzalez informed Alicia Castro of their religious beliefs and requested that their schedules be adjusted such that they would have a day off on their Sabbath, that their supervisor, Alicia Castro, denied their requests, threatening them with discharge if they did not work on their Sabbath, and that Teodora Castro was actually dismissed for refusing to work on her Sabbath. These findings are clearly sufficient to establish appellees' prima facie case of religious discrimination. . . .

[The] Hacienda made no effort whatsoever to accommodate the religious beliefs of both these women. Alicia Castro admitted that she never asked any maid if they would volunteer to work nor did she make any effort to rearrange the schedule of the maids according to the religious needs of the employees within the housekeeping department. The record also reflects that there was at least one voluntary substitute, Teodora's sister, who was willing to work for her. . . .

[T]he Hacienda failed reasonably to accommodate the religious practices of Teodora Castro and Maria Elena Gonzalez, and that it terminated Teodora Castro because of her religion, in violation of Title VII. . . .

[Retaliatory Discharge]

The district court found that Maria Elena Gonzalez established a prima facie case of retaliation. When Alicia Castro found out that Gonzalez had spoken with Frank Godoy, she told Gonzalez that now she would never have Sundays off and threatened to make her life very difficult. Within less than an month of her complaint to Godoy, Castro issued three written warnings to Gonzalez and fired her.

Appellant contends, however, that Gonzalez was fired for poor work performance and not for any retaliatory reasons. . . . [D]uring trial, Alicia Castro testified that she fired Gonzalez for poor work performance. The court below, however, explicitly found that Alicia Castro was not a credible witness. . . .

[Sexual Harassment Claim]

Hacienda argues that the sexually harassing conduct in which Castro and Nusbaum were proven to have engaged was not sufficiently severe or pervasive to be actionable. Appellant also contends that it could not be held liable for the acts of Nusbaum and Castro of which it had no notice. Finally, Hacienda argues that its policy against discrimination and its internal grievance procedures should shield it from liability for sexual harassment. We consider each of Hacienda's contentions in turn.

There is no dispute in this case that the acts of sexual harassment complained of occurred, and that they were unwelcome. The contested issue is whether the harassment was sufficiently "severe or pervasive" to alter the terms and conditions of the claimants' employment and to create a sexually hostile work environment. As the record reveals, Nusbaum repeatedly engaged in vulgarities, made sexual remarks, and requested sexual favors from the complainants. The complainants' direct supervisor, Alicia Castro, also frequently witnessed, laughed at, and herself made these types of comments. Castro had direct authority to hire, discharge, and discipline housekeeping employees, and Nusbaum threatened at least one of the claimants that he would have Castro fire her if she did not submit to his sexual advances. . . . [W]e agree with the district court's conclusion that the complainants were subjected to severe and pervasive sexual harassment that "seriously tainted" the working environment and altered the terms and conditions of their employment. . . .

[E]mployers are liable for failing to remedy or prevent a hostile or offensive work environment of which management-level employees knew, or in the exercise of reasonable care should have known.

Under this standard, Hacienda can be held liable for Castro's and Nusbaum's actions. The general manager of the Hacienda, Frank Godoy, had actual knowledge of allegations of harassment, as did Alicia Castro, a supervisor with authority to hire, discharge, and discipline employees in the housekeeping department. The court also found, by implication, that appellant should have known . . . of the harassment because it was severe and pervasive and "seriously tainted" the complainants' working environment. Finally, appellant failed to take prompt remedial action when it was notified of its employees' allegations. . . . [A]ppellant could be held liable for Castro's and Nusbaum's conduct.

Appellant's remaining argument, that the complainants failed to pursue internal remedies under appellant's general nondiscrimination policy, can be disposed of quickly. . . . Where, as here, the employer's discrimination policy does not specifically proscribe sexual harassment, and its internal procedures require initial resort to a supervisor who is accused of engaging in or condoning the harassment of which the employee complains, it would be plainly unreasonable to require discrimination claimants to exhaust such procedures as a predicate to suit. In any event, this court has held that a Title VII plaintiff need not exhaust her employer's internal remedies.

[Undocumented Aliens]

Appellant argues that the district court erred in awarding back pay to Teodora Castro, Flora Villalobos, and Maria Elena Gonzales, all of whom were undocumented alien workers when they were subjected to appellant's discriminatory employment practices. The Hacienda also challenges the district court's calculation of the back pay awards. . . .

The district court in this case assumed that Title VII, including its remedial provisions, applied to the undocumented aliens who were subjected by appellant to various forms of employment discrimination. It is basically undisputed that all of the employees who were awarded back pay for the Title VII violations in this case were in the United States, were not subjected to deportation proceedings, and were available for employment throughout the back pay period that could readily be calculated with certainty. Under our existing case law, then, the district court did not err in concluding that Castro, Villalobos, and Gonzalez were entitled to back pay in this case despite their status as undocumented aliens.

[Back pay]

We turn now to appellant's arguments that the district court abused its discretion in calculating the back pay awards in this case. . . . In awarding back pay, the district court is required to attempt to make victims of discrimination whole by restoring them to the position in which they would have been absent the discrimination. Title VII also requires mitigation of damages, however, by providing that "amounts earnable with reasonable diligence [by the employee]" be deducted from a back pay award. The back pay award in this case was well within the court's discretion. . . .

[Injunctive Relief]

Appellant's final arguments challenge the district court's decision permanently to enjoin appellant from "engaging in any employment practice which discriminates on the basis of sex, religion [or otherwise violates employment laws]." . . . Appellant contends that injunctive relief . . . was an inappropriate and unneeded sanction because there is no reasonable expectation that the alleged violations will recur. . . .

Even if the individual complainants have been made whole by the relief awarded by the district court, this court has recognized that the EEOC has a right of action [for an injunction] that is independent of the employees' private rights of action. This is because the EEOC is not merely a proxy for the victims of discrimination, but acts also "to vindicate the public interest in preventing employment discrimination." By seeking injunctive relief, the EEOC not only deters future unlawful discrimination but also seeks to protect aggrieved employees and others similarly situated from the fear of retaliation for filing Title VII charges. . . .

An employer that takes curative actions only after it has been sued fails to provide sufficient as-surances that it will not repeat the violation to justify denying an injunction. Appellant's recent efforts to train managerial employees regarding discrimination problems and the absence of further EEOC charges in recent times are encouraging and laudable; however, the district court did not abuse its discretion by awarding permanent injunctive relief on the facts of this case.

For all of the foregoing reasons, the judgment of the district court is AFFIRMED.

The Civil Rights Act of 1991

We have already seen that the Civil Rights Act of 1991 (CRA91) enacted some significant changes to discrimination law. It increased the categories of discrimination for which a plaintiff can be awarded compensatory and punitive damages. It permits a successful plaintiff to collect expert witness fees from the defendant. Many businesses opposed CRA91 because these factors motivate victims of discrimination to pursue lawsuits.

CRA91 provides plaintiffs with other benefits as well. These additional advantages affect United States citizens employed abroad, mixed motive cases, burden of proof in discrimination cases, training about discrimination, and "glass ceilings."

U.S. Citizens Employed Abroad. Prior to the CRA91, protection against discrimination did not apply to citizens of this country employed abroad by an American company. In *EEOC v. Arabian American Oil Co.*, 111 S. Ct. 1227 (1991), decided before the adoption of CRA91, a U.S. citizen working in Saudi Arabia for an American Company was denied protection of Title VII. CRA91 clearly states that the Civil Rights Act of 1964, including Title VII, was intended to apply to such citizens. An exception is provided for the circumstance where compliance would violate the law of the foreign country. For example, if a United States employer is doing business in a country that prohibits women from working more than a certain number of hours per week, the employer could not be faulted for discriminating against women when hiring for a job requiring more than that number of hours.

Mixed Motive Cases. Not infrequently, acts of discrimination are motivated by more than one factor, only one of which is illegal. Prior to the CRA91, an employer could avoid liability for discrimination by proving that it would have made the same adverse decision concerning the employee's work status even if the illegal consideration, such as gender, had not played a role. The CRA91 significantly modifies this rule. Now, if a termination or other adverse employment action is motivated even in part by illegal discrimination, the action is illegal. The opportunity for the employer to escape liability by showing the same decision would have been made regardless of the illegal consideration has been eliminated. CRA91 provides, "An unlawful employment practice is established when the complaining party demonstrates that race, color, religion, sex, or national origin was a motivating factor for any employment practice, *even though other factors also motivated the practice.*" (Emphasis added.)

A successful plaintiff in a mixed motive case is not entitled to compensatory or punitive damages, or back pay. The remedies are limited to injunction, declaratory judgment, attorney's fees, and court costs.

Training. CRA91 creates a Technical Assistance Training Institute designed to provide assistance and training regarding the Civil Rights Act of 1964, the CRA91, and the Americans With Disabilities Act (which is the subject of the next section in this chapter). Failure by an employer to take advantage of the technical training, and misunderstandings by an employer of the Acts' requirements, are *not* defenses to violations.

Glass Ceiling. **Glass Ceiling** refers to artificial barriers that have held women and minorities back from promotion to management and decision-making positions in business. To address the underrepresentation of women and minorities, CRA91 established a Glass Ceiling Commission to study the manner in which businesses fill management positions.

The report, issued in 1995, concluded that substantial barriers still exist for women and minorities at the highest levels of business. The Commission found that white males hold 96 percent of all senior management positions at the level of vice president or higher. Major contributors to this circumstance include persistent bias, negative stereotypes, prejudice concerning women and racial minorities, and inadequate laws. Among the Commission's recommendations for removing these barriers are the following:

1. Chief executive officers must demonstrate commitment to diversity.

2. Affirmative action should be used as a tool to ensure equal opportunity to compete for upper management positions. **Affirmative action** refers to employment programs designed to remedy discriminatory practices in hiring.

3. Senior managers and directors should be sought from nontraditional sources and backgrounds.

4. Businesses should prepare minorities and women for senior positions (provide training, mentoring, etc.).

5. Businesses should provide training to sensitize employees about gender, racial, ethnic, and cultural differences.

6. Recognizing that women are still primarily responsible for home and family, companies should adopt policies that accommodate the balance between work and family.

Companies should review their policies and practices, and modify them where needed to facilitate the achievement of diversity and the advancement of all segments of the workforce.

Americans With Disabilities Act

The Americans with Disabilities Act (ADA), which became effective in 1992, is an uncompromising proclamation of this country's commitment to equal opportunity for the disabled. The expected impact of this law can be gleaned from estimates that put the number of Americans with disabilities at 43 million. Many employers in the past have declined to hire people with disabilities because of fear that they will be unable to perform the job or be absent frequently or require a lot of assistance. Such fears are based on stereotypes and should not be the basis for employment decisions. The ADA seeks to eliminate the barrier of those stereotypes for disabled persons who are able to perform on the job.

We saw in Chapter 3 the ADA's provisions requiring accessibility to places of public accommodation. In this chapter we study its employment provisions. They apply to all phases of employment, including hiring, advancement, discharge, compensation, training, and other terms of employment. To the hospitality industry, the ADA can mean fundamental changes in personnel policies.

In short, the ADA provides that an employer cannot refuse to hire or otherwise discriminate against a disabled person who can, with reasonable accommodation, perform the essential functions of a job. A **disability** is defined as a physical or mental impairment that substantially limits a person's ability to walk, see, hear, perform manual tasks, learn, work, or care for themselves. **Essential functions** are the core responsibilities of a job as distinguished from marginal or incidental assignments. The ADA applies to employers with a minimum of 15 employees; it does not apply to employers with less than 15 workers.

Essential Functions

In determining what functions are essential to a job, a court will consider the following: the employer's judgment as to which functions are essential; written job descriptions drafted before the job was advertised or interviewing began; and the amount of time on the job needed to perform the function.

The following are reasons that may render a job function essential: the reason the position exists is to perform that function; only a limited number of employees are available who can perform the task; the function may be highly specialized and the reason for hiring a particular person is her expertise or ability to perform that function.

In *Polesnak v. R. H. Management Systems, Inc.*, 1997 WL 109245 (1997), a general manager of a Burger King was terminated due to obesity (he weighed 600 pounds) which qualified as a disability. He had always received excellent reviews evidencing his ability to do the essential functions of the job. The employer thus violated the ADA and was liable to pay plaintiff back and future wages that plaintiff lost due to the illegal discharge.

Reasonable Accommodations

What constitutes a reasonable accommodation depends on the facts of each individual case. The ADA may require an employer to do any of the following: modify facilities to make them accessible, such as enlarging doors to make them negotiable in a wheel chair; modify schedules to coordinate with public transportation; acquire equipment, such as magnifiers for the visually impaired; provide sign language interpreters for the hearing impaired; or modify exams and training programs for the visually impaired or learning disabled. While employers have expressed concerns about the cost of accommodations, studies have concluded that over 70 percent of accommodations cost less than $500 and 50 percent cost less than $50. Some tax incentives are available for providing accommodations. Employers are not required to provide personal use items such as hearing aids or eye glasses.

Undue Hardship

Where the accommodations required to enable the employee to perform the essential job functions are not reasonable, but rather impose an undue hardship on the business, the employer can legally refuse to extend employment to the disabled person. An **undue hardship** is an act that requires significant difficulty or expense on the part of the employer, taking into account such factors as the nature of the business, cost, and the business' resources. For example, a night club that features live music need not discontinue the music to accommodate a would-be waiter who is hearing impaired and unable to hear customers' beverage and food orders over the sound of the band. To eliminate music would change the format of the business and constitute an undue hardship.

The employer's duty to provide reasonable accommodation applies not only to applicants for employment but also to employees already on staff who are or become disabled and cannot perform their original jobs. Reasonable accommodation in these circumstances can include, in addition to the accommodations listed above, reassigning employees to a vacant position for which they are qualified. If accommodations are unavailing and no alternate position is available, the employer is not required to continue the employment.

Preference Not Required

An employer is not required to give preference to a disabled person but can instead hire the most qualified applicant. For example, two people apply for a typing job for which speed is needed to perform successfully. One applicant has a disability and types 50 words a minute. The other has no disability and types 70 words a minutes. The employer can hire the faster typist because she has the best qualifications.

An employer cannot make employment decisions based on inability to perform *nonessential* functions of the job, which are marginal tasks that do not qualify as essential functions. Change the facts of the typing example a bit: both applicants type 70 words per minute; a nonessential function of the job is answering the phone; the disabled person is unable to hear and so cannot answer the phone. Can the employer hire the other applicant because of the disabled person's inability to answer the phone? The answer is no because answering the phone was not an essential job responsibility.

ADA Impacts on Application Process

The ADA permeates all aspects of the hiring decision. At the preemployment interview an employer cannot ask job applicants about the nature of a disability. Prohibited questions include: Do you have a disability? How severe is your disability? What medications are you taking? Have you been hospitalized recently? The employer can inquire whether the applicant can perform the essential functions of the job and can ask the applicant to demonstrate ability to perform those functions. Depending on the job, permissible questions might include: Can you lift and carry a 20-pound tray? Will you please demonstrate your ability to do this?

An employer cannot require that an applicant submit to a medical exam prior to extending a job offer. However, the offer can be conditioned on the results of a medical exam, but only if all incoming employees in the same position are required to be examined regardless of disability. The information obtained from the test must be kept confidential and in a file *separate* from the employee's employment file. The only people entitled to see the medical report are first aid personnel, supervisors who need the information to determine necessary restrictions and accommodations, and government officials investigating compliance with the ADA.

Drugs and Illnesses

Drug tests are treated differently from medical exams. An employer can require a test to detect illegal use of drugs as part of the application process. An applicant for employment who uses illegal drugs is not protected by the ADA. An employer can discriminate against such a person when making employment decisions. However, if a would-be employee abused drugs in the past but has since been rehabilitated or is enrolled in a supervised rehabilitation program and does not currently use them, she is a person with a disability and cannot be denied a benefit of employment on that ground.

Persons afflicted with AIDS and people who are HIV positive are considered disabled for purposes of protection under the ADA. The ADA does not require a restaurateur to hire as a food handler a person with an infectious or communicable disease that is transmitted to others through food handling. For a disease to qualify, it must be on a list developed by the Secretary of Health and Human Services (hereinafter, the Secretary) that is required to be updated annually. AIDS is not transmitted through food handling and is not on the list. A restaurant that refuses to hire a food handler with AIDS because of the disease violates the ADA.

Diseases that are on the list include hepatitis A virus, salmonella typhi, staphylococcus aureus, and staphylococcus pyogenes. An employer can refuse to hire a would-be food handler who has these illnesses. With the list the Secretary published symptoms that may indicate the presence of one of the listed diseases. The symptoms include diarrhea, vomiting, open skin sores, boils, fever, dark urine and jaundice.

The Secretary also commented, "The failure of food employees to wash hands (in situations such as after using the toilet, handling raw chicken, cleaning spills, or carrying garbage, for example), wear clean gloves, or use clean utensils is responsible for the foodborne transmission of [bacteria or viruses]."

Past Disabilities and Caregivers

The Americans With Disabilities Act protects not only people with disabilities, but also those with a past disability. For example, an employer cannot refuse to hire a recovered cancer patient. Also protected are those people who have a relationship or association with a disabled person, such as a spouse or parent. Although the employer may fear that an applicant with a disabled child might be absent frequently, that relationship cannot be used as a reason for rejecting the applicant. If the applicant is hired and does take excessive leave, she can be terminated for that reason.

Pursuing an ADA Case

The ADA encourages would-be plaintiffs to mediate and settle their complaints rather than litigate. A person wishing to pursue a claim under the ADA can file a complaint with the Equal Employment Opportunity Commission or pursue the case individually. The potential liability a defendant faces in a lawsuit is significant and includes the following: a) compensatory damages including emotional pain, suffering, mental anguish, and loss of enjoyment of life; b) punitive damages; c) attorney's fees; d) expert witness fees; e) reinstatement where an employee was wrongly terminated; and f) back pay. The ADA encourages employers to attempt reasonable accommodation by relieving them from liability for compensatory damages where they made a good faith effort in consultation with the disabled person to identify and make a reasonable accommodation. For a plaintiff to win punitive damages, she must prove that the employer acted with malice or reckless indifference to the rights guaranteed under the ADA.

Case Law Applying the ADA

The responsibilities of employers to disabled employees and job applicants are triggered only when the disabled person is able to perform the essential functions of the job with or without reasonable accommodations. Thus, the termination of a food server did not violate the ADA where the server suffered from panic attacks when the restaurant became crowded causing a "complete inability to function". In those circumstances, she was unable to perform the essential functions of her job: serving food. The attacks occurred notwithstanding an accommodation made by the employer assigning the server to the least busy workstation. *Johnston v. Morrison, Inc.,* 849 F. Supp. 777 (Ala., 1994).

Similarly, a slot attendant at a casino suffered a neck injury deeming him unable to perform the essential functions of his job which included carrying heavy bags of coins. Termination of his employment was therefore not discrimination under the ADA. *Van de Pol v. Caesars Hotel Casino,* 979 F. Supp. 308 (N.J., 1997).

Mandatory Verification of Employment Status

Entrance to this country is restricted by law. While tourists are permitted to come in large numbers, only a limited number of people can enter each year for other purposes. To immigrate to the United States to attend school, work, or otherwise live here requires permission from the Immigration and Naturalization Service (INS), the government agency responsible for overseeing the immigration laws. An **immigrant** in the United States is someone from another country who enters this country with authorization from the INS. One who enters this country without the necessary approval is an **illegal alien.**

Immigration Reform and Control Act

The Immigration Reform and Control Act (IRCA), 8 U.S.C. Sections 1324a and 1324b, is a federal law passed in 1986 that applies to employers with more than three employees. It enlists employers in the effort to prevent illegal aliens from working in this country. IRCA requires employers to verify the employment status of employees they hire. An employer must complete and retain a form called the Employment Eligibility Verification Form, commonly referred to as Form I-9. The primary purpose of this form is to verify that the individual is authorized to work in the United States. The employee must present identification and proof that she has permission from INS to work here. The employer is required to examine the document(s) to determine if, in the words of the statute, it "reasonably appears on its face to be genuine." No later than three days following the date of hire the employer must sign form I-9 verifying under penalty of perjury that the employer has verified that the individual is not an unauthorized alien. The employee must also sign attesting to legal status. The employer must retain the form for three years following the date of hire or until one year after the employee leaves, whichever is longer. Form I–9 is shown on page 475.

If the employee is unable to locate the necessary documents, the employer may allow 21 days for the employee to secure them. If the employee has not produced them by the end of the 21 days, the employer must terminate her. Failure to sever the employee will subject the employer to a penalty up to $1000 even if the employee's legal status is later confirmed. If an employer illustrates a pattern or disregard for the required verifications, the penalty increases to $3000 for each offense.

When reviewing documents to satisfy IRCA, it is the employer's responsibility to check the expiration dates. An expired document is not adequate proof of a person's status.

U.S. Department of Justice
Immigration and Naturalization Service

OMB No. 1115-0136
Employment Eligibility Verification

Please read instructions carefully before completing this form. The instructions must be available during completion of this form. ANTI-DISCRIMINATION NOTICE. It is illegal to discriminate against work eligible individuals. Employers future expiration date may also constitute illegal discrimination.

Section 1. Employee Information and Verification. To be completed and signed by employee at the time employment begins

Print Name: Last	First	Middle Initial	Maiden Name

Address (*Street Name and Number*)	Apt.#	Date of Birth (*month/day/year*)

City	State	Zip Code	Social Security #

I am aware that federal law provides for imprisonment and/or fines for false statements or use of false documents in connection with the completion of this form.	I attest, under penalty of perjury, that I am (check one of the following): ☐ A citizen or national of the United States ☐ A lawful permanent resident (Alien # A _____) ☐ An alien authorized to work until _____ / _____ / _____ (Alien # or Admission # _____)

Employee's Signature	Date (*month/day/year*)

Preparer and/or Translator Certification. *(To be completed and signed if Section 1 is prepared by a person other than the employee.) I attest, under penalty of perjury, that I have assisted in the completion of this form and that to the best of my knowledge the information is true and correct.*

Preparer's/Translator's Signature	Print Name

Address (*Street Name and Number, City, State, Zip Code*)	Date (*month/day/year*)

Section 2. Employer Review and Verification. To be completed and signed by employer. Examine one document from List A OR examine one document from List B <u>and</u> from List C as listed on the reverse of this form and record the title, number and expiration date, if any, of the document(s)

	List A	OR	List B	AND	List C
Document title:	_____		_____		_____
Issuing authority:	_____		_____		_____
Document #:	_____		_____		_____
Expiration Date (*if any*):	___ / ___ / ___		___ / ___ / ___		___ / ___ / ___
Document #:	_____				
Expiration Date (*if any*):	___ / ___ / ___				

Certification - I attest, under penalty of perjury, that I have examined the document(s) presented by the above-named employee, that the above-listed document(s) appear to be genuine and to relate to the employee named, that the employee began employment on (*month/day/year*) ___ / ___ / ___ and that to the best of my knowledge the employee is eligible to work in the United States. (State employment agencies may omit the date the employee began employment).

Signature of Employer or Authorized Representative	Print Name	Title

Business or Organization Name	Address (*Street Name and Number, City, State, Zip Code*)	Date (*month/day/year*)

Section 3. Updating and Reverification. To be completed and signed by employer

A. New Name (*if applicable*)	B. Date of rehire (*month/day/year*) (if applicable)

C. If employee's previous grant of work authorization has expired, provide the information below for the document that establishes current employment eligibility.

Document Title: _____ Document # _____ Expiration Date (if any): ___ / ___ / ___

I attest, under penalty of perjury, that to the best of my knowledge, this employee is eligible to work in the United States, and if the employee presented document(s), the document(s) I have examined appear to be genuine and to relate to the individual.

Signature of Employer or Authorized Representative	Date (*month/day/year*)

Form 1-9 (Rev. 11-21-91) N

Figure 14–1   Employment Eligibility Verification Form, commonly referred to as Form 1-9

LISTS OF ACCEPTABLE DOCUMENTS

LIST A		LIST B		LIST C
Documents that Establish Both Identity and Employment Eligibility	**OR**	Documents that Establish Identity	**AND**	Documents that Establish Employment Eligibility

LIST A	LIST B	LIST C
1. U.S. Passport (unexpired or expired)	1. Driver's license or ID card issued by a state or outlying possession of the United States provided it contains a photograph or information such as name, date of birth, sex, height, eye color, and address	1. U.S. social security card issued by the Social Security Administration (*other than a card stating it is not valid for employment*)
2. Certificate of U.S. Citizenship (*INS Form N-560 or N-561*)		2. Certification of Birth Abroad issued by the Department of State (*Form FS-545 or Form DS-1350*)
3. Certificate of Naturalization (*INS Form N-550 or N-570*)	2. ID card issued by federal, state, or local government agencies or entities provided it contains a photograph or information such as name, date of birth, sex, height, eye color, and address	3. Original or certified copy of a birth certificate issued by a state, county, municipal authority or outlying possession of the United States bearing an official seal
4. Unexpired foreign passport, with I-551 stamp *or* attached *INS Form I-94* indicating unexpired employment authorization		
5. Alien Registration Receipt Card with photograph (*INS Form I-151 or I-551*)	3. School ID card with a photograph	4. Native American tribal document
6. Unexpired Temporary Resident Card (*INS Form I-688*)	4. Voter's registration card	5. U.S. Citizen ID Card (*INS Form I-197*)
7. Unexpired Employment Authorization Card (*INS Form I-688A*)	5. U.S. Military card or draft record	6. ID Card for use of Resident Citizen in the United States (*INS Form I-179*)
8. Unexpired Reentry Permit (*INS Form I-327*)	6. Military dependent's ID card	7. Unexpired employment authorization document issued by the INS (*other than those listed under List A*)
9. Unexpired Refugee Travel Document (*INS Form I-571*)	7. U.S. Coast Guard Merchant Mariner Card	
10. Unexpired Employment Authorization Document issued by the INS which contains a photograph (*INS Form I-688B*)	8. Native American tribal document	
	9. Driver's license issued by a Canadian government authority	
	For persons under age 18 who are unable to present a document listed above:	
	10. School record or report card	
	11. Clinic, doctor, or hospital record	
	12. Day-care or nursery school record	

Illustrations of many of these documents appear in Part 8 of the Handbook for Employers (M-274)

Form 1-9 (Rev. 11-21-91) N

FPI-RBK

Figure 14–1 (continued)

The penalty for hiring an illegal alien is a cease and desist order, which requires the employer to halt the illegal hiring, and a fine that ranges from $250 to $2,000 for each unauthorized alien for a first offense. Fines can range up to $5,000 per illegal worker for a second offense, and up to $10,000 per illegal worker for a third offense. The law makes repeated offenses prohibitively expensive.

When the IRCA was under consideration by Congress, various minority groups feared that employers would attempt to avoid liability by refusing to hire all aliens. While the Civil Rights Act outlaws discrimination based on national origin, it does not include noncitizens or a protected class. To prevent discrimination against immigrants who are authorized to work, IRCA prohibits discrimination in employment based on citizenship status, which means an employer cannot refuse to hire, based on lack of citizenship, a qualified alien authorized to work. Interesting, IRCA provides a preference in hiring and recruiting for a United States citizen over an alien "if the two individuals are equally qualified."

Family and Medical Leave Act

The Family and Medical Leave Act (FMLA) addresses a problem that employees often face—obtaining time off from work to care for sick children or other family members. The FMLA, effective in 1993, entitles eligible employees to up to 12 weeks of leave per year for childbirth, adoption, foster placement, or to care for a child, spouse, or parent who has a serious health condition, or for the employee's own serious health situation. To be eligible, an employee must have been employed for at least 12 months before the leave commences and have worked at least 1,250 hours during that 12 month period. Employers covered by the FMLA are those who carry on their payroll 50 or more employees for each working day for each of 20 or more weeks in the year. Upon returning from the leave, an employee must be reinstated to the position held before the leave or to an equivalent position with equivalent pay, benefits, and other terms of employment.

Summary

Employment laws cover virtually every aspect of the employer-employee relationship.

The Fair Labor Standards Act mandates minimum wages, one and one-half pay for overtime work, equal pay for equal work, and restrictions on child labor.

The Civil Rights Act of 1964, Title VII, prohibits discrimination on the basis of race, color, religion, sex, and national origin. Other laws prohibit discrimination on the basis of pregnancy, age (over 40), disability, marital status, arrest record and lack of citizenship.

The Immigration Reform and Control Act requires employers to verify the employment status of employees, primarily to prevent illegal aliens from working in this country.

Preventive Law Tips for Managers

- *Unless your business is exempt, pay your employees the applicable minimum wage.* The Fair Labor Standards Act (FLSA) imposes an obligation on employers to pay a minimum wage. As of September 1, 1997, the minimum wage is $5.15. Some exceptions apply, including employers whose annual sales are less than $500,000, and employees who receive part of their pay in tips.

- *Pay employees one and one-half times their hourly wage for hours they work in excess of 40 per week.* The FLSA requires this time-and-a-half pay for time worked in excess of 40 hours in any given week. This rule does not apply to qualifying managerial, administrative, or professional employees.

- *Utilize the same pay scales and ranges for male and female employees who perform the same job.* The Equal Pay Act, a provision of the FLSA, requires equal treatment in pay of men and women who do the same jobs.

- *Do not hire anyone under age 14.* The FLSA prohibits the employment of young people under age 14.

- *If you hire young workers, verify the applicable restrictions on their hours and duties and abide by them.* The FLSA and laws in many states restrict both the hours certain teenage employees can work and the types of tasks they can perform. Do not assign these workers to illegal hours or prohibited responsibilities. The hours can be confusing because they differ by age groups and change for school days, weekends, and holidays. Careful attention to the various restrictions are required to avoid fines and unwanted negative publicity.

- *Do not discriminate on the basis of race.* Race is a protected class. Employees should not be treated differently for any reason because of their race. Racial groups include African-Americans, Caucasians, Orientals, Native Americans, Eskimos, and Native Hawaiians.

- *Do not discriminate on the basis of national origin.* National origin is a protected class. Employees should not be treated differently for any reason because of their country of origin.

- *Do not discriminate on the basis of accent or inability to speak English unless mastery of the language is a job necessity.* Generally, discrimination against a person who cannot speak English well or who speaks with an accent constitutes discrimination on the basis of national origin. If, however, performance of the job requires knowledge of English and ability to speak it well, someone who cannot understand it or who cannot be understood is not qualified, and so failure to hire that person would not be illegal discrimination.

- *Do not discriminate on the basis of religion.* Religion is a protected class. Employees should not be treated differently because of their religion. If an employee needs a modified work schedule to comply with religious observances, the employer is required to make a reasonable effort to accommodate the employee. If accommodation would cause the employer undue hardship, the employer can refuse to oblige the employee's religious needs and will not be liable for religious discrimination.

- *Do not discriminate on the basis of sex.* Sex is a protected class. Employees should not be treated differently because of their sex.

- *Do not tolerate sexual harassment.* Sexual harassment is a form of sex discrimination. Managers should be vigilant to minimize the incidence of quid pro quo and hostile environment sexual harassment.

- *Do not treat pregnancy or childbirth differently from any other disability.* The Pregnancy Discrimination Act, which is part of Title VII, requires that pregnant employees be treated the same as other employees. An employer cannot treat pregnant employees differently from employees with other temporary disabilities in regard to opportunities to continue to work, leave arrangements, or reinstatement rights.

- *Take steps to ensure your work site is free from illegal discrimination.* Develop and strictly enforce an antidiscrimination policy. Sponsor training sessions for all employees on what constitutes illegal discrimination and the company's intolerance of it. Identify one or more persons to whom complaints can be made and include someone outside the line of employees' supervision such as a representative of the personnel department. When a complaint is made, react to it promptly by investigating thoroughly and taking appropriate corrective action. Consult the employee who complained before initiating remedial action.

- *If you employ United States citizens abroad, do not discriminate on the basis of race, skin color, religion, sex, or pregnancy.* The Civil Rights Act of 1991 outlawed discrimination against United States citizens working abroad for American companies.

- *Do not discriminate against employees because they are 40 years old or older.* The Age Discrimination in Employment Act (ADEA) renders people age 40 or older a protected class. They should not be treated differently in employment because of their age. A preference for youth is an illegal basis on which to make job decisions unless youth is a business necessity.

- *Abide by the Americans With Disabilities Act (ADA).* Do not discriminate on the basis of disability. The ADA requires employers to make reasonable accommodations for applicants or employees who are able, with or without accommodations, to perform the essential functions of the job. Examples of reasonable accommodations include enlarging doors to accommodate wheel chairs and modifying schedules to coincide with public transportation. People protected by the ADA include not only those with disabilities, but also those with a past disability and those responsible for the care of a disabled person.

- *Do not make employment decisions based on nonessential functions of a job.* The ADA provides that a disabled person is qualified for a job if she can perform the essential functions of that job with or without reasonable accommodations. An employer who refuses to hire a qualified disabled person because that person is unable to perform nonessential functions has violated the ADA.

- *Accurately write job descriptions so they include all essential functions of the job.* Job descriptions are one source of information for identifying what the essential functions of a job are. To ensure applicants are not excluded because of inflated descriptions of job responsibilities, and to ensure applicants are qualified with or without accommodations to perform the essential functions, the job description should accurately describe the duties of the job.

- *Do not ask questions about a person's medical condition or disability at an interview.* The employer can inquire whether an applicant can perform the functions of the job and can ask that she demonstrate the ability to do so. Questions about the person's medical condition, disability, medication, or hospital stays violate the ADA.

- *If an employee on staff becomes disabled, attempt to find another job with an opening that she is qualified to perform.* The ADA requires that employers attempt to reassign an employee who becomes disabled while employed.

- *Do not require an applicant to submit to a medical exam prior to offering that person a job.* The ADA precludes an employer from mandating a pre-offer medical exam. An offer, once made, can be conditional on the results of a medical exam provided all incoming employees are required to submit to the exam.

- *Keep as confidential information obtained from a medical exam.* This information cannot be kept in an employee's employment file but instead must be kept in a separate file. The only people entitled to review it are first aid personnel, supervisors who need the information to determine necessary restrictions and accommodations, and government officials investigating compliance with the ADA.

- *If your business is accused by an employee of illegal discrimination or if it is investigated for illegal discrimination by the EEOC or a state agency, prompt remedial action may mitigate the outcome.* Whenever a complaint or investigation is made, your attorney should be consulted on how best to handle it. Prompt corrective action may rectify the illegal discrimination and minimize the negative impact on the business.

- *Do not discharge employees or take other adverse job action against them because they complained about illegal discrimination or filed a complaint with the EEOC.* Such a discharge or adverse action is retaliatory and is itself illegal discrimination.

- *Verify the employment status of each employee you hire within three days of the date of employment.* The Immigration Reform and Control Act (IRCA) seeks to minimize the number of illegal aliens employed in this country. Employers are required to examine their worker's employment documents to verify authorization to work in the United States. Any employee who cannot produce the necessary proof within 21 days of employment must be terminated.

• *Do not discriminate against immigrants who are authorized to work in this country.* The IRCA prohibits an employer from refusing to hire a qualified alien on the ground she is not a citizen.

Review Questions

1. What statute imposes a minimum wage requirement on employers?
2. Name two exceptions to the minimum wage requirement.
3. How much in wages is an employee entitled to be paid for working in excess of 40 hours a week?
4. Name five protected classes.
5. What is Title VII?
6. To what do the initials EEOC refer?
7. Name four remedies available for a Title VII violation.
8. What must a plaintiff prove to establish a retaliatory discharge?
9. Name two racial groups other than African-Americans and Caucasians.
10. Under what circumstance can an employer refuse to hire an applicant who speaks only minimal English?
11. In the category of age, who is included within the protected class under federal law?
12. What are the two types of sexual harassment? Provide an example of each.
13. Name five types of activity that can constitute sexual harassment.
14. In what ways can an employee relay the unwelcome nature of sexually harassing conduct?
15. What type of discrimination against a pregnant worker is prohibited by the Pregnancy Discrimination Act?
16. What is the "glass ceiling"? What has Congress done about it?
17. To what aspects of employment does the Americans With Disabilities Act apply?
18. What is the difference between essential functions of a job and non-essential functions?
19. Who can an employer require to submit to a medical exam before making a job offer?
20. What does the Immigration Reform and Control Act require of an employer? What is the penalty if the employer fails to comply?

Discussion Questions

1. What is the difference between the legal concepts of equal pay and comparable worth?

2. What do you think prompted the laws that impose a minimum age for employment and restrict the hours an employee under specified ages can work?

3. What impact will the expansion of remedies for discrimination under the Civil Rights Act of 1991 likely have on employers' hiring and firing practices? Why?

4. Why do you think Congress placed a cap in the Civil Rights Act of 1991 on the amount of compensatory damages a court can award to a plaintiff in most civil rights cases?

5. Why is discrimination based on an accent the equivalent of discrimination based on national origin?

6. Why are minor differences in grooming rules for male and female employees acceptable?

7. The dining room manager of a restaurant is hiring wait personnel. A person who walks with a limp applies. The manager is concerned about the applicant's ability to handle the physical demands of the job. What can the manager ask the applicant during the interview, and what can the manager not ask?

Application Questions

1. An employer has an aversion to red hair. She refuses to hire anyone with that color hair. Is this illegal discrimination? Why or why not?

2. Lee is opening a Thai restaurant. He refuses to hire anyone who was not born in Thailand as chef, dishwashers, and wait personnel. Is this illegal discrimination against applicants of other nationalities?

3. Marti is an observant Jew and celebrates eight religious holidays that do not coincide with legal holidays. Does Title VII require that her employer give her time off for these holidays? Why or why not?

4. Allison's boss continually makes sexually suggestive comments to her and often brushes against her when she is in his office. She has asked him to stop but he continues. She reported his conduct to the vice-president for personnel. He felt she was exaggerating the facts and did not investigate or take any action.

    a. What should the vice-president have done?

    b. Is the company Allison works for liable for sexual harassment under these circumstances?

5. The female manager of the Crayster Hotel terminated the male night supervisor because his work was marginal and she preferred working with females. Is the termination illegal discrimination? Why or why not?

6. Kyle, who is deaf, has applied for a job as a bookkeeper at the Brookside Hotel. The bookkeeper is required to maintain financial records of the business and prepare financial reports for management. The information is obtained primarily from guest invoices, bills, and receipts. Most of the required reports are submitted in written form. The bookkeeper is also required to attend two staff meetings a week at which the general manager orally informs the staff of developments at the hotel. The general manager frequently consults informally with the bookkeeper concerning financial matters.

   a. What accommodations could the hotel make to enable Kyle to handle the job responsibilities?

   b. Will the hotel be obligated to make those accommodations or can it refuse to hire Kyle because of his disability? Why?

7. The Bystone Restaurant, a 25-table family restaurant with a strong business of take-out ice cream, has advertised for a manager. Among the applicants are a woman in a wheelchair with a bachelor's degree in restaurant management and two year's experience as an assistant manager at a similar restaurant, and a man with a masters degree in restaurant management and five year's experience, three as an assistant manager and two as a manager. Must the employer give preference to the disabled female? Why or why not?

8. The Nimark Hotel is hiring a business manager. Of all the applicants, the two most qualified are a citizen of the United States and a citizen of France legally authorized to work in this country. According to the Immigration Reform and Control Act, if the two are equally qualified, which one should be offered the job?

CHAPTER 15

Regulation and Licensing

CHAPTER OUTLINE

INTRODUCTION

The law regulates various aspects of the hotel and restaurant business. We have seen throughout this book numerous circumstances in which the law significantly impacts the manner in which a hotel or restaurant is operated. In this chapter we will see even more examples, including the law of trademarks, copyrights, anticompetitive activities, franchising, registration of guests, rates charged for rooms, recycling, licensing requirements, and zoning.

Regulation of the Marketplace

Numerous regulatory laws impact the marketplace in which hospitality establishments do business. These laws apply to trademarks, copyrights, antitrust concerns, and franchising.

Trademarks and Service Marks

Many successful businesses are emulated by other companies desiring to trade on the familiar name, style, and image portrayed to the public. If you decided to open a fast-food restaurant specializing in hamburgers, you would probably make considerably more money if you called it McDonald's rather than, say, Sue's Hamburgers. However, the name McDonald's, when used in the fast-food industry, is a trademark, which means the owner has the exclusive right to its use. If you use the name without the owner's permission, you will be illegally infringing on McDonald's trademark.

A **trademark** is, generally, any word, name, symbol (such as McDonald's yellow arches), or device adopted and used by a manufacturer or merchant to identify its goods and distinguish them from goods sold or manufactured by others. A **service mark** is similar to a trademark except that it identifies services rather than goods. A company can obtain a trademark or service mark in its name or logo simply by using it in connection with its business. The company can also register it with the federal Patent and Trademark Office located in Washington, D.C., which notifies other potential users that the name has been appropriated. The ownership of the mark, however, is acquired by use and is unaffected by failure to register. When two companies are using the same name, the test to determine who has the rights to the name is who used it first.

Someone who uses another's trademark or service mark in connection with a similar product or service without permission will be liable for trademark infringement. For example, Burger King has a trademark on the name "Chicken Tenders" for battered and fried chicken breast pieces. Defendant who sold a chicken breast meat product under the same name was thereby liable for trademark infringement. *Burger King Corporation v. Pilgrim's Pride Corporation*, 934 F. Supp. 425 (Fl., 1996).

An infringement occurs not only when a second company uses the identical name, but when another company uses a similar name which is likely to confuse consumers and divert business from the trademark owner. In 1963, a federal court in Raleigh, North Carolina, found that a restaurant was imitating Howard Johnson's trade name by using the name "Henry Johnson's." The court enjoined (prohibited) Henry Johnson's from using that name. *Howard Johnson Co. v. Henry Johnson's Restaurant*, Civil Case 1258 U.S.D.C. (N.C., 1964).

The law on trademarks and service marks is found in the Lanham Act, Section 43(a), 15 U.S.C. 1125 [a], which prohibits the passing off of services by one person under the guise that they are the services of another. The statute states that,

> *any person who shall affix, apply, or annex, or use in connection with any . . . services . . . a false designation of origin, or any false description or representation, includ-*

ing words or other symbols tending falsely to describe or represent the same . . . shall be liable to a civil action by any person . . . who believes that he is or is likely to be damaged by the use of any such false description or representation.

To prove a trademark infringement case, the plaintiff must show two things: 1) ownership of a distinctive mark or name; and 2) defendant's use of a similar mark or name that is likely to cause confusion as to the source of products or services. The test for infringement is whether the second user's adoption of the name is confusingly similar to the original user, that is, will consumers be diverted from the first user and do business with the second because they were misled by the trade name? The more alike are the names and products being offered by the two companies, the more likely a trademark infringement will exist. Similarity in names and services was the basis for a finding of infringement in re Dixie Restaurants, Inc., 105 F.3d 1405 (1997). The trademark owner used the name "Delta" in its hotel, motel, and restaurant business. A new restaurant sought to use the name "The Delta Cafe". The court noted that the services offered by each party were identical (restaurant operation) and the dominant element in the cafe's name (Delta) was identical to the trademark owner's name.

Even the script used to promote a name can add to the likelihood of confusion. In the case of *Tisch Hotels, Inc., v. Americana Inn, Inc.*, 350 F.2d 609 (7th Cir., 1965), the court ruled illegal the use of the word "Americana" by a Chicago hotel company that adopted that name without permission from a luxury hotel that had a trademark on the name. Said the court, "Not only did the defendant pirate the name, but it also adopted plaintiff's fanciful presentation of the name in all details, namely, 'americana' all in lowercase letters with a white line extending through the first "a" and a five-point star as the dot over the i."

Another way to prove likelihood of confusion is to show actual confusion by customers who were misled. While actual confusion is not essential, it provides the court or jury with positive proof of the existence of substantial likelihood of confusion.

Penalties for infringing a trademark include an injunction prohibiting further infringement; giving back of profits diverted from the trademark owner; and fines. The effects of an injunction are illustrated in *Gas Town, Inc. of Delaware v. Gas Town*, 331 F. Supp. 626 (Conn., 1971). The Marathon Oil Company of Ohio had registered the name Gas Town as a trademark. Eighteen months later a corporation with 200 service stations in New England, New York and Louisiana used Gas Town as the name for its stations. The Marathon Oil Company sued for trademark infringement. A federal court issued an injunction barring the second corporation from using the name, and ordered it to remove the Gas Town signs from its 200 stations. The corporation thus had to pay for new signs and new advertising to introduce the public to its new name, no small expense.

Prior to adopting a trade name, a business can and should conduct a trademark search. Such a search, done quickly and easily by computer with the assistance of an attorney, will disclose whether the desired name is already in use.

The following case illustrates the application of many of these rules.

CASE EXAMPLE 15–1

Gilbert/Robinson, Inc. v.
Carrie Beverage-Missouri, Inc.
758 F.Supp. 512 (Mo. 1991)

Plaintiff Gilbert/Robinson, owner of HOULI-HAN'S restaurants, initiated this action alleging service mark infringement . . . based on defendants . . . use of the service mark MIKE HOULIHAN'S on their bars.

. . . In April 1972, plaintiff began to use the service mark HOULIHAN'S OLD PLACE to identify its bar and restaurant located in Kansas City, Missouri. . . .

Since April 1972, plaintiff has opened establishments under the name HOULIHAN'S or HOULIHAN'S OLD PLACE in 22 different states. Currently, these establishments number 55, including three in metropolitan St. Louis. There are also 10 franchise HOULIHAN'S locations in the United States. In approximately 1983, plaintiff discontinued the use of OLD PLACE in its signs and advertising for the company-owned HOULIHAN'S because the majority of its customers refer to the establishments simply as HOULIHAN'S. . . .

Since 1972, plaintiff has spent nearly $27 million in advertising and promoting its HOULIHAN'S establishments nationwide and those establishments have yielded nationwide sales in excess of $1 billion during that time. Advertisements for HOULIHAN'S bars and restaurants have appeared on television, radio and in newspapers and magazines throughout the United States.

In 1982, defendant Carrie Beverage Incorporated opened a bar which it operates in the Grand Avenue shopping mall in downtown Milwaukee, Wisconsin under the service mark MIKE HOULIHAN'S. The names in the service mark MIKE HOULIHAN'S refer to Michael Heyer and John Houlihan, who are the sole shareholders of defendant Carrie Beverage, Inc. . . .

During the fall of 1984, plaintiff announced that it would open another HOULIHAN'S in St. Louis Union Station in December 1985. In August 1985, plaintiff learned of defendant's plans to open a MIKE HOULIHAN'S in the St. Louis Centre

shopping mall in downtown St. Louis, Missouri. Plaintiff . . . informed defendants of plaintiff's rights in the HOULIHAN'S marks and insisted that defendants change their mark. . . .

Five months after [defendant] had opened its MIKE HOULIHAN'S bar in St. Louis, plaintiff opened its restaurant utilizing the service mark HOULIHAN'S and HOULIHAN'S OLD PLACE in the Union Station complex in St. Louis, Missouri.

Plaintiff presented strong evidence of a nationwide reputation. Plaintiff's expert, Marshall Scott, testified that HOULIHAN'S is a well-known name inside and outside the restaurant industry and across the county. . . . To customers seeking food and beverage services in Missouri and across the nation, HOULIHAN'S means plaintiff's HOULIHAN'S

Substantial actual confusion resulted from defendants' use of the name MIKE HOULIHAN'S in St. Louis Centre. Both plaintiff's and defendants' establishments experienced instances of actual confusion by customers and vendors, including misdirected telephone calls, misdirected vendor deliveries, and misdirected service calls . . . Although the frequency of actual confusion has diminished over time, it continued up through the time of trial.

HOULIHAN'S is the distinctive word in the HOULIHAN'S marks as well as in the name MIKE HOULIHAN'S. The HOULIHAN'S marks are displayed in standard block lettering. MIKE HOULIHAN'S is also displayed in block lettering, which is slightly scripted. The HOULIHAN'S and MIKE HOULIHAN'S marks are similar in appearance.

HOULIHAN'S and MIKE HOULIHAN'S are in direct competition for bar revenues. The bar is a very important part of plaintiff's business. . . .

A survey was conducted at plaintiff's request to determine the likelihood of confusion of customers with respect to whether HOULIHAN'S and MIKE HOULIHAN'S are part of the same operation. The survey was conducted by a firm which specializes in consumer surveys. The survey was conducted in an unbiased and scientific manner, utilizing generally accepted survey techniques. Impartial interviewers drew responses from a relevant pool of potential consumers. The questions posed were not leading, misleading or biased, and the recordation was handled in an unbiased manner. . . .

Of the 200 respondents interviewed, more than two-thirds, 67.5%, believed that both establishments were owned or affiliated with the same company. Moreover, more than four out of five respondents who said they think that both establishments are owned by or affiliated with the same company cited the name as the reason they came to that conclusion. . . .

Specifically, the ultimate issue is whether defendant's design so resembles plaintiff's mark that it is likely to cause confusion among consumers as to whether plaintiff has sponsored, endorsed or is otherwise affiliated with the defendant. . . .

In order to claim ownership of a distinctive mark or name, a party must demonstrate that his use of the mark has been of such a quality and for such a duration that it has come to identify goods bearing it as originating from that party. . . .

The exclusive right to use the mark belongs to the first person who appropriates it and uses it in connection with a particular business. Any doubts as to confusion are to be decided against the newcomer. . . .

In order to constitute an infringement, it is not necessary that the trademark be literally copied. Neither is it necessary that every word be appropriated. There may be infringement where the substantial and distinctive part of the trademark is copied or imitated. . . . The similarity of marks is to be determined by looking at the total effect of designation rather than by comparing individual features. . . .

Although names are not identical, similarity will deceive almost as much as precise identity. Nice and careful discrimination between the names cannot be expected from a busy public.

The right to operate under one's own name is not unlimited: The first user of the name is entitled to protection. A family name cannot be used to appropriate the business of another. . . . It is true that there are some minor differences between the two marks. Defendants' mark is in a slight script. Further, defendants use the word MIKE in front of the word HOULIHAN'S. However, the use of a modifying word is not sufficient to dispel the likelihood of confusion, when the most prominent word in the name appears in both.

[T]he similarity and competitive proximity of the products is an important factor in determining likelihood of confusion. The greater the similarity, the greater the likelihood of confusion. . . .

In this case, both plaintiff and defendant operate facilities with bars . . . and the two facilities are located within one mile from each other. . . .

Surveys are often used to demonstrate actual consumer confusion. Courts frequently give substantial weight to properly conducted surveys, unless they are seriously flawed. . . .

In this action, the Court finds that the survey is valid and was properly conducted. The survey demonstrated that more than two-thirds of those persons polled believe that HOULIHAN'S and MIKE HOULIHAN'S were affiliated in some manner. . . this factor weighs strongly in favor of finding trademark infringement on the part of defendant. . . .

Plaintiff has proven uncontroverted evidence that in 1972 it appropriated the name HOULIHAN'S for its restaurant and has since used the name continuously. Plaintiff's appropriation and use of the name was prior to that of defendants, who first began use of the name in 1982. Therefore, plaintiff has acquired trademark rights in that name. It is further the conclusion of this Court that plaintiff has established that defendants' use of the mark MIKE HOULIHAN'S is likely to cause confusion as to the source of the products sold by defendants. . . . Therefore plaintiff is entitled to relief.

JUDGMENT AND ORDER

. . . [D]efendant is permanently enjoined [barred] from using his trademark MIKE HOULIHAN'S . . . effective ninety days from the date of this judgment.

You may wonder why the court did not order defendant to stop use of the name Mike Houlihan's immediately rather than in ninety days. The reason for the delay is to allow defendant time to adopt a new name and make necessary arrangements to change its signs, menus, advertising materials, and any other items on which it promotes its name.

Likelihood of Confusion.   Remember, the test for infringement is likelihood of confusion. Absent a likelihood of confusion, no infringement exists. If the trademark owner and second user do not compete in the same markets so that the public is unlikely to confuse one for the other, the use of the mark by the newcomer may not be illegal. In *Steak & Brew, Inc., v. Beef & Brew Restaurant, Inc.,* 370 F.Supp. 1030 (Ill., 1974), the plaintiff, which operated a chain of restaurants under the name Steak & Brew, attempted to prevent the defendant, which operated a restaurant named Beef & Brew, from using the word "Brew" in its name. Defendant operated only one restaurant, which was in Rock Island, Illinois; the closest restaurant in plaintiff's chain was 100 miles away. The facts in the case established that defendant had innocently adopted the name without knowledge of plaintiff's use, and Steak & Brew was unknown in the Rock Island, Illinois area. The court stated that ordinarily the use and registration of a trademark will bar a subsequent business from using the same name. However, when two parties employ the same mark on goods of the same class, but they operate in remote and separate markets, the second user may legally continue to use the name. An exception to this rule is where it appears that the second adopter has selected the mark to benefit from the reputation of the first user or to forestall the expansion of the first user's business.

Another reason the court found no infringement in the *Steak & Brew* case is that the word "brew" is descriptive and in common use. Therefore, it is not subject to exclusive appropriation. Ordinarily a company cannot gain trademark rights in a word that is part of the English language and commonly used. Such a word could achieve trademark protection only upon proof that it attained a secondary meaning, that is, the public identifies the term or phrase with the company using it. Thus, for example, Kentucky Fried Chicken cannot prevent another restaurant from using the word "chicken" or "fried chicken" in its name. However, the public has come to recognize the phrase Kentucky Fried Chicken as the name of a chain of fast-food restaurants. Therefore no other company could name itself Kentucky Fried Chicken. On this basis also, the court ruled there was no basis for a finding that the defendant's use of the name "Beef & Brew" violated trademark law. Defendant was allowed to continue using the name but only for the one restaurant in Rock Island.

Another case in which no likelihood of confusion was found was *Dunfey Hotels Corp. v. Meridien Hotels Investments Groups, Inc.,* 504 F. Supp. 371 (N.Y., 1980). The Dunfey Corporation operated a hotel under the name Parker House. It objected when the Hotel Parker Meridien New York started to use the name Parker Meridien in connection with its hotel. The court held that the degree of similarity between the two marks was not great, and the Parker House failed to prove likelihood of actual confusion.

Similarly, where two companies independently and concurrently developed several restaurants under the name John Q's, the plaintiff, with one in Cleveland, could not prevent the defendant from opening one in Cincinnati, 240 miles away. Plaintiff failed to present evidence that the restaurant in Cincinnati would be patronized by customers of the Cleveland restaurant or any other evidence that confusion would result. Further, there was no evidence that the defendant attempted to deceive the public or capitalize on plaintiff's name. *Stouffer Corp. v. Winegardner & Hammons, Inc.*, 502 F.Supp. 232 (Ohio, 1980).

Public Domain.   According to the trademark law, a valuable trademark may be lost if the word becomes a part of the language, that is, in common usage. When this happens, the word goes into the **public domain**, meaning it has become so commonly used that it loses its trademark protection. Over the years, this has happened to such notable trademarks as Aspirin, Mimeograph, Linoleum, Dry Ice, Escalator, and Kerosene. In each instance, what began as a trademark ended as a frequently used word in normal parlance. Doubtless, the English language has been enriched, but the manufacturer is the poorer—penalized, ironically, because its product became too popular.

How does the law determine that a trademark has gone into the public domain? While the point in time is rarely clear, the main prerequisite is that the public has come to consider the word as the generic name for the thing itself, rather than as an indication of a specific manufacturer or that manufacturer's specific product. For example, a court held that "Toll House" was no longer a trademark, largely because so many consumers used that term to describe a kind of cookie rather than one specific maker of the cookie. *Nestle Co., Inc. v. Chester's Market, Inc.*, 571 F.Supp. 763 (Conn., 1983). For the same reason, "Shredded Wheat" lost its status as a trademark, *Kellogg Co. v. National Busciut Co.*, 305 U.S. 111, 59 S. Ct., 109 (1988).

Trademark Registration.   We have seen that a trademark can be registered with the federal Patent and Trademark Office. Although registration is not necessary for trademark protection since rights accrue from mere use of a name, registration helps to discourage unauthorized use and makes a trademark infringement case easier to prove. It protects the mark nationwide.

The process of registration includes: submission of various documents to the Patent and Trademark Office; publication of the proposed mark by that office to alert others with similar names; opportunity for objection to registration by others who might already be using the name; and, if there is no objection or if there is and the applicant wins, issuance of a registration certificate which completes the registration process.

Once a trademark is registered, the owner should include with the name, usually after the last letter, the following insignia ® (the capital letter "R" in a circle). This alerts the public that the word is a registered trademark and cannot be used by others. Most states have registration procedures that protect a business' name on a state-wide basis. The process is easier and less expensive than federal registration. Which registration is appropriate depends on the geographical area in which the business anticipates using the name. If the business owners foresee opening other similar businesses with the same name in more than one state, or if they anticipate franchising the operation, federal registration should be pursued.

One case that encompasses many trademark principles is *Holiday Inns, Inc., v. Holiday Inn*. The defendant undertook a course of action calculated to associate itself in the public eye with plaintiff trademark owner and intentionally mislead the traveling public. The case presents historical background on a giant of the hotel industry, states the test of what constitutes trademark infringement, and discusses the rights of the traveling public not to be deceived.

CASE EXAMPLE 15–2

Holiday Inns, Inc.,
v. Holiday Inn
364 F.Supp. 775 (S.C., 1973)

This action is brought by the plaintiff, Holiday Inns, Inc., . . . the largest company in the restaurant and lodging business in the United States, hereinafter referred to as "the Chain." The suit is for . . . service mark infringement against the defendant Holiday Inn, a South Carolina corporation that operates a motel and restaurant at Myrtle Beach, South Carolina, under the name of Holiday Inn. This defendant has counterclaimed, alleging [trademark] infringement and unfair competition, and seeks cancellation of certain of plaintiff's [trademark] registrations. . . .

This matter was heard before the court without a jury . . . [T]he court makes the following finding of facts:

1. The plaintiff Holiday Inns, Inc., . . . is a corporation . . . founded in 1952 and since that time has grown to the point that it is now the largest factor in the restaurant and lodging business in the United States. . . . The Plaintiff's principal business is providing restaurant and lodging services operating under the name Holiday Inn. These services are provided either through company owned facilities or facilities franchised by the Chain. At present the Chain has a facility in almost every major city in the United States, including 33 in the State of South Carolina. The Chain presently owns or franchises approximately 1,300 facilities in the United States.

2. The Chain's original concept was to establish a network of motels and restaurants spanning the entire country upon which the traveling public could rely in obtaining satisfactory services. The facilities affiliated with the Chain are readily recognizable, with quality controls exercised by the Chain and many similar services available at all facilities, such as free use of baby cribs, no charge for children under 12 when sleeping in the room with the parent, kennels for pets, etc.

3. The Chain had developed and prominently displays on each facility a large sign, generally referred to as the "great sign." This sign is one of the major features by which travelers generally identify a motel as belonging to or affiliated with the Chain. This sign is quite large, but in some cities smaller versions are used in order to comply with local zoning restrictions. The sign has a green background with the name HOLIDAY INN in large distinctive script lettering, a large star at the top and smaller stars by the name HOLIDAY INN, a large orange arrow starting at the bottom of the sign and running in a sort of semicircle with the point indicating the location of the facility. There is always an attraction panel near the bottom of the sign. . . .

5. In the promotion of its services, the plaintiff also uses certain slogans, one of which is YOUR HOST FROM COAST TO COAST. . . .

7. The above registered service marks of plaintiff are well known to the American traveling public. They have been extensively used and advertised in promoting plaintiff's services and the services of its franchisees. Numerous advertisements have appeared in magazines, newspapers, on radio and television and billboards, as well as a house magazine and a directory of member facili-

ties of which more than ten million are printed and distributed each year. . . .

8. The *defendant* Holiday Inn was incorporated in 1960 (Emphasis Added). . . .

10. The defendant's facility grew over the years to its present 87 units. . . .

12. The plaintiff first learned of defendant's facility in 1956 when a franchisee of plaintiff, who was constructing a motel facility in Myrtle Beach, received a letter from defendant's lawyer objecting to the proposed usage of HOLIDAY INN within the Myrtle Beach area. Plaintiff's franchisee obtained permission from plaintiff to operate the facility within the plaintiff's system under the name HOLIDAY LODGE. This facility has been operated continuously since 1956. . . . A great sign was erected in front of the facility presenting the words HOLIDAY LODGE in large script lettering above the words HOLIDAY INNS OF AMERICA SYSTEM. . . .

15. In 1968 the defendant's general manager ordered a sign constructed and placed in its parking lot immediately across the street from its facility. He requested the sign maker to design a sign which would resemble, but not exactly duplicate, the plaintiff's "great sign" and delivered to the sign maker one of plaintiff's brochures to use as a guide. . . . [T]he signs are so similar that the traveling public would be easily confused and upon seeing defendant's sign would conclude that it was a franchisee of plaintiff or affiliated with it. The colors of the two signs are almost identical. The use of stars, the big arrow, the attraction panel, and the script of Holiday Inn are so similar that the court can only conclude that defendant erected his sign with the intent and purpose of infringing the rights of the plaintiff and unfairly competing with it. . . .

23. Confusion has developed as a result of the similarity of names and there have been mix-ups in bills, letters, reservations, deliveries, etc. . . .

26. . . . [C]onfusion has been deliberately and systematically nurtured by the defendant in an effort to profit from the national recognition and goodwill of the plaintiff. . . .

Conclusions of Law

. . .2. Upon review of the evidence the court is compelled to conclude that the defendant's course of conduct proves it guilty of . . . service mark infringement. . . .

3. The test for trademark infringement . . . is whether . . . imitation of the registered mark is "likely to cause confusion, or to cause mistake, or to deceive." The test is to be applied with regard to the effect of the marks on an ordinary purchaser having an indefinite recollection of the mark to which he has been exposed on a previous occasion.

[T]he sign erected by the defendant in 1968 is substantially identical to the plaintiff's "great sign" and although differences are obvious when pictures of the two signs are compared side by side, the effect of the defendant's sign was obvious and was likely to cause confusion, mistake or to deceive the public. . . .

4. The script form in which defendant presents its name Holiday Inn is substantially identical to the distinctive script used by plaintiff. . . . Although there may be slight differences in the location of the stars, the overall effect is such as is likely to cause confusion, mistake and to deceive the public.

5. Defendant's slogan, YOUR HOST ON THE COAST and YOUR HOST WHILE AT MYRTLE BEACH, differs from the plaintiff's slogan, YOUR HOST FROM COAST TO COAST, and if these slogans alone were the basis of the plaintiff's complaint, this court would not find them to be an infringement. However, when considered with the other acts of the defendant, . . . the court must conclude that the use of these slogans by the defendant was an effort to trade upon the goodwill of the plaintiff and represent an infringement of its protected mark, YOUR HOST FROM COAST TO COAST.

6. Although intent is not a necessary element of trademark infringement, there can be no question of defendant's intent to infringe upon the plaintiff's marks. . . .

7. The plaintiff's [trade]marks are famous throughout the United States and are becoming well known in many other countries. Great effort and expenditure of funds by the plaintiff have not only built up its successful business but have created in the mind of the public strong recognition of its name and service marks. . . . These property rights of the plaintiff are entitled to broad protection. . . .

10. The defendant has asserted and this court finds that it is the prior user of the name Holiday

Inn in Myrtle Beach, South Carolina. . . . The defendant is entitled to continue the use of the name Holiday Inn within the city limits of Myrtle Beach, South Carolina, but this court will not prevent the plaintiff from operating its facilities now known as Holiday Lodge . . . in Myrtle Beach. . . .

Now, Therefore, It Is Ordered, Adjudged and Decreed:

1. The defendant [is] hereby perpetually enjoined and restrained from:

a. Using either directly or indirectly a script identical to or any colorable imitation of plaintiff's script Holiday Inn on the outside of its building, on any billboards or on any advertising material.

b. Using directly or indirectly its version of plaintiff's "great sign" or any colorable imitation thereof.

c. Using directly or indirectly the slogan YOUR HOST WHILE AT MYRTLE BEACH or YOUR HOST ON THE COAST or any colorable imitation thereof.

d. Using directly or indirectly any sign, script, slogan or star design, color combination or other indicia of plaintiff that suggests or tends to suggest a connection with the plaintiff.

2. The defendant shall have ninety (90) days from the date of this order to comply and defendant's attorney within such time shall submit to the court evidence of compliance.

3. The defendant has the right to continue using the name Holiday Inn within the town of Myrtle Beach, South Carolina. . . .

And it is so ordered.

Copyright

A **copyright** is the exclusive right of an author or other copyright owner to reproduce and license (authorize) the reproduction of literature, art, music, drama, sculpture, choreography, motion pictures, computer software, and other audiovisual works including broadcasts of sporting events. Generally, the copyright is initially owned by the creator of the work. The rights associated with a copyright are separate from the work itself. Indeed, the artist can sell the work but retain the copyright. Thus, a restaurant owner who purchases a copyrighted painting cannot reproduce it onto placemats without permission of the copyright owner. Normally, the copyright owner will charge a fee for the permission, thus enabling the owner to benefit repeatedly from the creating talent utilized in the work. If, however, the artist sells the *copyright*, the purchaser becomes the copyright owner and can reproduce the work without further authorization.

A copyright owner can transfer some but not all of the rights included within a copyright. In *Wilcox v. Raintree Inns of America, Inc.*, 76 F.3d 394 (10th Cir., 1996), a professional freelance photographer took photographs for use by a company in business to promote the 1989 American Ski Classic and the 1989 World Alpine Ski Championships in Vail, Colorado. According to the terms of the contract between the photographer and the promotion company, the latter was entitled to use the pictures for "promotional purposes" only. Any additional use would require further consent of the photographer. The promotion company thereafter gave six of the photographs to Raintree, a hotel in Vail. Raintree used these photographs, without any further discussion with or payment to the photographer, as part of a display in its hotel lobby during the Alpine Ski Championship competition. The photographer filed suit, claiming the hotel's use of the pictures violated his copyright. The court determined that the display in the Raintree lobby was intended to promote the World Alpine Ski Championships and therefore was within the grant of rights given by the photographer. The use of the photos did not, therefore, violate the photographer's copyright.

A copyright comes into existence automatically when the work is created. Prior to March 1, 1989, the law required the copyright owner to place a copyright notice on the work when it was first made available to the public in order to retain the copyright. Failure to include the notice resulted in loss of copyright. The required notice consisted of three parts: a) the letter "c" in a circle—©; 2) the name of the copyright owner; and 3) the year of first publication. Due to a change in the law, the copyright notice is no longer necessary, although it is strongly recommended to discourage unauthorized copying.

Illegal Satellite Reception

An area of copyright law that has been the subject of litigation in the hospitality field is the use of satellite dishes to receive and exhibit audiovisual programming without the permission of the program's copyright owner. Such use infringes the copyright on the programs. In one case a Holiday Inn was sued for copyright infringement by various cable stations including Home Box Office, Inc. (HBO), ESPN, Showtime, and The Movie Channel, Inc. The hotel had installed a satellite system enabling it to receive copyrighted programming without paying for it. The Holiday Inn in turn offered to its guests the opportunity to view the programming in their rooms for a fee. No part of the proceeds was paid to the cable stations. The stations claimed the interception and exhibition of the copyrighted programs without their permission constituted copyright infringement. The court agreed and issued an injunction against the hotel requiring it to stop. *Home Box Office, Inc. v. Corinth Motel, Inc.*, 647 F. Supp. 1186 (Miss., 1986).

Another case involved the satellite interception by several bars of a blacked-out football game. The National Football League (NFL) contracts with the television networks for the broadcast of its games. The contract states that, if a game is not sold out 72 hours before the start, it cannot be broadcast within 75 miles of the home team's field. The defendant bar owners used satellite dishes to receive transmissions of the blacked-out games without the approval of the NFL, which owned the copyright. The bar owners were thus able to exhibit the blacked-out games to their patrons. The NFL sued the bars. The court held the unapproved exhibition of the copyrighted games constituted an unauthorized reproduction of the work and issued an injunction against the bars. *National Football League v. McBee and Bruno's, Inc.*, 792 F.2d 726 (8th Cir., 1986).

Another basis on which to pursue a business that exhibits television programming without authority is the Communications Act, a federal law that prohibits the interception of cable or satellite transmissions without authority from the sender of the transmission.

Pay-for-view programming requires viewers to pay a fee to obtain access to the show. As illustrated in the following case, a bar or restaurant that obtains access without payment of the fee views the show illegally in violation of the Communications Act.

CASE EXAMPLE 15–3

Cablevision Systems Corp. v. 45 Midland Enterprises, Inc.
858 F. Supp. 42 (N.Y., 1994).

Plaintiff has a franchise to provide cable television in Port Chester. Defendant operates a tavern/restaurant, which intercepted the Home Box Office ("HBO") signals for the February 6, 1993, boxing match between Riddick Bowe and Michael Dokes without having paid the required fee. . . .

Defendant subscribed to and was authorized to receive basic service, which did not include HBO signals. To authorize receipt of the HBO signal, plaintiff provides a decoder box to the customer. The box unscrambles the signal. Plaintiff related that a market exists for unscrambling devices, which are not authorized by plaintiff and which will however permit reception of HBO signals, and explained that a subscriber to basic channels, who was displaying a premium channel such as HBO, was employing an unauthorized converter-decoder device to gain access to the premium channel.

Robert Weber, plaintiff's audit investigator, visited [defendant] on the evening of February 6, 1993. Fifty-six (56) individuals were present along with two (2) television sets. The televisions were displaying the introductions of the boxers to the Bowe-Dokes match, which was scheduled for live broadcast that evening. Weber noted that the sets were tuned to channel 6, which is the HBO channel in Port Chester. He also observed what he described as a cable television converter-decoder device near the television in the area of the bar. This device was not of the type and color which plaintiff provided to authorized subscribers. . . .

The evidence was sufficiently convincing to persuade me that defendant violated the statue by unauthorized interception of a cable television signal on February 3, 1993. . . .

In a related factual situation, a bar that had not paid the pay-for-view fee exhibited a videotape of a restricted boxing match that had been made and brought to the bar by a patron who apparently had paid to view the match at home. The eatery was sued for violation of the Act and found liable. Kingvision Pay Per View, Ltd., v. 900 Club, 1996 WL 496600 (Ill., 1996).

We learn from these cases that companies in the business of selling pay-for-view rights customarily send investigators to bars and restaurants at the time restricted programming is broadcast to determine if the business is illegally exhibiting the limited-access show. A sports bar or like establishment seeking to attract customers by showing restricted events must first obtain the necessary license and pay appropriate fees. Failure to do so will result in liability leading to payment of damages, fines, attorney's fees for the opposing party (in addition to one's own), and an injunction.

Music Performances

Many restaurants and hotels offer musical entertainment. The music may be live, on a juke box, or presented by a disc jockey. Live presentations may involve a single performer on weekends only, a band that plays every night of the week, or any combination thereof. Most music is copyrighted. The performer(s) may, during any performance, play the music of many different copyright owners. How does the restaurant or hotel know from whom permission must be obtained and how can it manage the many different authorizations that may be required? While at first blush it may appear that the process of obtaining permission can be very complex and time-consuming, a system has been developed that streamlines it.

Most owners of copyrights on musical compositions belong to one of three associations which collect copyright fees for its members. Hotels and restaurants need only deal with these organizations and not with each composer individually. The two main organizations are the American Society of Composers, Authors and Publishers (ASCAP), and Broadcast Music, Inc. (BMI). Both license (grant for a fee) on a nonexclusive basis the public performance rights of its members' copyrighted works. A hotel or restaurant must have a license from these organizations to use the works in their collection. Since an establishment cannot easily restrict its musical offerings to the works controlled by one organization or the other, in most circumstances hotels or restaurants will need a license from both.

ASCAP and BMI distribute most of the receipts from license fees, minus overhead, to their members as royalties for the use of their compositions. The allocation among members is based on detailed weighted formulas.

ASCAP.   The license fees charged to hotels and restaurants, bars, and clubs by ASCAP are not based on the particular songs actually performed. Rather, they are based on a combination of factors that include the number of nights a week the establishment offers music, seating capacity, and whether admission is charged.

ASCAP controls such a large part of the performance rights of the music industry that it could exercise monopoly power if limitations were not imposed. The law has thus imposed restrictions on its ability to dictate fees. The process for determining the license fee a user must pay is as follows. The hotel or restaurant submits a written application to ASCAP. It responds in writing advising the business of the proposed fee. A sixty-day negotiation period follows in which the restaurant or hotel can object to the fee and the parties then attempt to reach a mutually agreeable compromise. If they are unsuccessful, the hotel or restaurant can apply to the federal district court in New York for a determination of a reasonable license fee. The mandated negotiation period and the right of the music user to seek a court determination of a reasonable fee lessens substantially the bargaining power ASCAP would otherwise have.

BMI.   License fees charged by BMI are determined through negotiations between BMI officials and established trade associations such as the National Restaurant Association. For hotels and restaurants, the fees are determined based on annual expenditures for musicians and entertainers. For concert halls, fees are determined by seating capacity. For other establishments such as ballrooms, fees are based on a percentage of gross annual income.

Consequence of Performing Music Without a License.   If a restaurant or hotel fails to obtain the necessary licenses for musical performances, it will be liable for copyright infringement. A dance-club restaurant paid a fine of $5,000 for each song played in its establishment for which it did not have authorization. *T-Boy Music Publishing, Inc. v. Jayoffer, Inc.*, 87 F.3d 1322 (9th Cir., 1996).

Before bringing a lawsuit, ASCAP or BMI will inform the proprietor that a license is necessary and encourage its purchase. If the owner refuses to pay the applicable fee and continues to provide musical entertainment, a lawsuit by ASCAP or BMI against the hotel or restaurant is likely. Both organizations are zealous in pursuing their members' rights.

BMI discovered that a restaurant was playing its members' music on a jukebox without cost to customers to enhance their dining experience. The restaurant did not have a license to do so. BMI attempted to remedy the circumstance without a lawsuit by making "repeated written and telephonic requests, as well as one personal visit, to urge Blueberry Hill Restaurant to enter into a licensing agreement and to warn of the consequences of failing to do so." After defendants failed to respond to these numerous entreaties, plaintiffs filed the instant action. The restaurant was ordered to discontinue playing protected music without a license and to pay damages to BMI. *BMI v. Blueberry Hill Family Restaurants, Inc.*, 889 F. Supp. 474 (Nev., 1995).

Not infrequently, a restaurant will play the radio as background music for its diners' enjoyment. The music played on the radio is copyrighted. Radio stations customarily have a license with BMI and ASCAP to play protected songs. The following case addresses the circumstances in which a restaurant may violate the copyright laws for using radio music in this way.

CASE EXAMPLE 15–4

Cass County Music Company v. Port Town Family Restaurant
55 F.3d 263 (7th Cir., 1995)

The plaintiffs . . . own copyrights to six songs that are the subject of this suit. The defendant was the owner of the Port Town Family Restaurant located in Racine, Wisconsin. The restaurant is a free-standing building accommodating up to 128 patrons with a public dining area of approximately 1500 square feet. The restaurant is equipped with a "radio-over-speaker" sound system that provides a consistent level of background music throughout the dining area.

On the night of March 13, 1992, two investigators employed by ASCAP had dinner in the Port Town Family Restaurant . While dining, the investigators heard some of the plaintiffs' songs played over the restaurant's sound system. The source of the music was a radio broadcast of WMYX-FM, a Milwaukee station. The radio station is an ASCAP licensee. The license between ASCAP and WMYX-FM prohibits retransmissions of the station's broadcasts. . . .

The ASCAP licensing fee for establishments that play music four to seven nights a week and seat between 76 and 150 patrons is $327 per year. From May, 1985, until December 1991, ASCAP repeatedly and unsuccessfully approached the Port Town Family Restaurant about the need for the restaurant to obtain an ASCAP license in order to continue legally to play background music.

The plaintiffs subsequently brought this action against the restaurant owner. They allege copyright infringement on the basis of the public performance of the six copyrighted musical compositions. The plaintiffs requested an injunction prohibiting further performances, $1000 damages for each infringement, and costs including reasonable attorneys' fees. . . .

The Copyright Act contains an exemption that allows the use of ordinary ["home-type"] radios and television sets for the incidental entertainment of patrons in small businesses or other professional establishments, such as taverns, lunch counters, hairdressers, dry cleaners, doctors' offices, etc. . . .

There are two ways in which an establishment could fall outside the exemption. First, if any non-home-type components are used, then the entire system must be considered a non-home-type system. Second, if the establishment has configured the home-type equipment in a way not commonly used in a home, the exemption is lost. The critical factors are the type and sophistication of the equipment used, the size of the area in which the broadcast is audible, and whether the equipment has been altered, augmented, or integrated in some fashion. . . .

The Port Town Family Restaurant's music system utilizes, in addition to a Radio Shack receiver, a separate control panel containing five selector switches, nine speakers recessed into the dropped acoustic tile ceiling, and concealed wiring. Each speaker consists of as" aluminum grille, an 8" loudspeaker, and a 70-volt (70-V) loudspeaker line matching transformer. Without the addition of the transformers, the receiver is designed to drive only four speakers over moderate lengths of speaker cable. However, with the 70-V transformer attached to each speaker, . . . the receiver effectively can power up to forty speakers wired in parallel, thirty-six speakers more than the receiver was designed to handle without overloading. . . . The restaurant's nine speakers are evenly spaced within the 1500 square-foot dining area. . . . The set up . . . provides background music that is consistent and evenly audible throughout the public seating area.

The system at issue here cannot be characterized fairly as "homestyle", that is, commonly found in homes. The receiver clearly is used beyond the normal limits of its capabilities. Accordingly, the Port Town Family Restaurant is not exempt from compliance with the Copyright Act.

Antitrust Problems

The economic system of the United States is based on free and open competition. It seeks to ensure new businesses can enter the market and all businesses can compete on a more or less equal basis. The reason for promoting competition is the belief that it motivates producers to make better products and to sell them at lower prices, thereby benefiting consumers. Certain laws, called **antitrust laws**, attempt to ensure that open competition is preserved.

An important federal antitrust law is the Sherman Antitrust Act, passed in 1890 and supplemented by a second Act in 1914 called the Clayton Act. These remain the two key federal antitrust laws today. The United States Supreme Court described the objective of the Sherman Act as follows:

> *The Sherman Act was designed to be a comprehensive charter of economic liberty aimed at preserving free and unfettered competition as the rule of trade. It rests on the premise that the unrestrained interaction of competitive forces will yield the best allocation of our economic resources, the lowest prices, the highest quality and the greatest material progress, while at the same time providing an environment conducive to the preservation of our democratic, political, and social institutions. But even were that premise open to question, the policy unequivocally laid down by the act is competition.*
> **Northern Pacific Railroad v. United States**, *356 U.S. 1, 78 S. Ct. 514 (1968).*

The Act states the following:

> *Every contract, combination . . . or conspiracy, in restraint of trade or commerce among the several states . . . is hereby declared illegal. . . . Every person who shall monopolize any part of the trade or commerce among the several states . . . shall be deemed guilty of a felony, and, on conviction thereof, shall be punished by a fine [and/or imprisonment] . . . 15 U.S.C. §§ 1,2.*

The specific activities that restrain competition and are addressed by the antitrust laws are listed below. Some are **per se violations**, which means they are always illegal. Others are subject to the **rule of reason**: they are not always illegal, but rather their benefits (such as economic efficiency) are balanced against their anticompetitive effects in a particular case. If the benefits outweigh the negatives, the activity will be permitted. If the anticompetitive impact is too great, it will be outlawed.

Penalties.   Penalties for violation of antitrust laws are significant and include **dissolution**, which means requiring a business to terminate its operations; **divestiture** which means requiring a business to terminate of its operations; criminal penalties including jail and substantial fines; and **treble damages**, that is, payment of three times the loss suffered by an injured plaintiff.

Some hotels and restaurants have violated antitrust laws. In 1977, four hotel firms and the Hawaii Hotel Association (a trade association of hotel owners) were charged with criminal violation of price-fixing laws. All pled no contest, an alternative plea to guilty or not guilty allowed in some states. Defendants Sheraton Hawaii Corp. and Hilton Hotels were fined $50,000 each, and Cinerama Hawaii Hotels and Flagship International were each ordered to pay $25,000, while the trade group was fined $10,000.

Application of The Per Se Rule.   The following is a list of activities that restrain competition and are per se violations of antitrust laws.

- *Price-fixing agreements*, in which competitors agree among themselves to sell goods at a certain price and not lower.
- *Territorial division agreements*, in which competitors assign each other a territory and agree not to compete in the others' territories, thereby each obtaining a territorial monopoly.
- *Group boycott*, in which two or more sellers refuse to do business with a particular person or company, intending thereby to eliminate competition or block entry to a market.
- *Resale price maintenance agreements*, in which a manufacturer determines the price at which the retailer must sell.
- *Price discrimination*, where a seller of goods charges different prices to different buyers for the same product (not applicable to services).
- *Exclusive dealing contracts*, in which a seller (usually a wholesaler) forbids a buyer (usually a retailer) from purchasing the products of the seller's competitors.

The following case is an example of the application of the Sherman Act and the per se rule to a group boycott situation. It also raises the disturbing question about the liability of a hotel for the acts of its high-level employees. Hotels have attempted to avoid antitrust liability by giving detailed instructions to their employees about what they can and cannot do. This case establishes that instructions are not enough; the hotel must also conduct follow-up checks to ensure employees are carrying out the instructions.

CASE EXAMPLE 15–5

United States v. Hilton Hotels Corporation
467 F.2d 1000 (Ore., 1972)

This is an appeal from a conviction under an indictment charging a violation of section 1 of the Sherman Act.

Operators of hotels, restaurants, hotel and restaurant supply companies, and other businesses in Portland, Oregon, organized an association to attract conventions to their city. To finance the association, members were asked to make contributions in predetermined amounts. Companies selling supplies to hotels were asked to contribute an amount equal to one per cent of their sales to hotel members. To aid collections, hotel members, including [Hilton Hotels Corp.] agreed to give preferential treatment to suppliers who paid their assessments, and to curtail purchases from those who did not.

The jury was instructed that such an agreement by the hotel members, if proven, would be a per se violation of the Sherman Act. [Hilton Hotels Corp.] argues that this was error. . . .

[T]he conduct involved here was of the kind long held to be forbidden. . . ."Throughout the history of the Sherman Act, the courts have had little difficulty in finding unreasonable restraints of trade in agreements among competitors, at any level of distribution, designed to coerce those subject to a boycott to accede to the action or inaction desired by the group or to exclude them from competition."

[T]he necessary and direct consequence of defendants' scheme was to deprive uncooperative suppliers of the opportunity to sell to defendant hotels in free and open competition with other suppliers, and to deprive defendant hotels of the opportunity to buy supplies from such suppliers in accordance with the individual judgment of each hotel, at prices and on terms and conditions of sale determined by free competition. . . .

The primary purpose and direct effect of defendants' agreement was to bring the combined economic power of the hotels to bear upon those suppliers who failed to pay. The exclusion of uncooperative suppliers from the portion of the market represented by the supply requirements of the defendant hotels was the object of the agreement, not merely its incidental consequence.

[Hilton Hotel Corp.'s] president testified that it would be contrary to the policy of the corporation for the manager of one of its hotels to condition purchases upon payment of a contribution to a local association by the supplier. The manager of [Hilton's] Portland hotel and his assistant testified that it was the hotel's policy to purchase supplies solely on the basis of price, quality, and service. They also testified that on two occasions they told the hotel's purchasing agent that he was to take no part in the boycott. The purchasing agent confirmed the receipt of these instructions, but admitted that, despite them, he had threatened a supplier with loss of the hotel's business unless the supplier paid the association assessment. He testified that he violated his instructions because of anger and personal pique toward the individual representing the supplier. . . .

The court instructed the jury that a corporation is liable for the acts and statements of its agents "within the scope of their employment," defined to mean "in the corporation's behalf in performance of the agent's general line of work," including "not only that which has been authorized by the corporation, but also that which outsiders could reasonably assume the agent would have authority to do." The court added:

"A corporation is responsible for acts and statements of its agents, done or made within the scope of their employment, even though their conduct may be contrary to their actual instructions or contrary to the corporation's stated policies."

[Hilton] objects only to the court's concluding statement.

Congress may constitutionally impose criminal liability upon a business entity for acts or omissions of its agents within the scope of their employment. Such liability may attach . . . even though [the conduct] may have been contrary to express instructions. . . .

In enacting the Sherman Act, Congress was passing drastic legislation to remedy a threatening danger to the public welfare. . . . The statute was designed to be a comprehensive charter of economic liberty aimed at preserving free and unfettered competition as the rule of trade. It rests on the premise that the unrestrained interaction of competitive forces will yield the best allocation of our economic resources, the lowest prices, the highest quality and the greatest material progress, while at the same time providing an environment conducive to the preservation of our democratic, political and social institutions.

With such important public interests at stake, it is reasonable to assume that Congress intended to impose liability upon business entities for the acts of those to whom they choose to delegate the conduct of their affairs, thus stimulating a maximum effort by owners and managers to assure adherence by such agents to the requirements of the Act. . . .

Violations of the Sherman Act are a likely consequence of the pressure to maximize profits that is commonly imposed by corporate owners upon managing agents and, in turn, upon lesser employees. In the face of that pressure, generalized directions to obey the Sherman Act, with the probable effect of foregoing profits, are the least likely to be taken seriously. And if a violation of the Sherman Act occurs, the corporation, and not the individual agents, will have realized the profits from the illegal activity. . . .

For these reasons we conclude that as a general rule a corporation is liable under the Sherman Act for the acts of its agents in the scope of their employment, even though contrary to general corporate policy and express instructions to the agent. . . .

The purchasing agent was authorized to buy all of appellant's supplies. Purchases were made on the basis of specifications, but the purchasing agent exercised complete authority as to source. He was in a unique position to add the corporation's buying power to the force of the boycott. [Hilton] could not gain exculpation [freedom from liability] by issuing general instructions without undertaking to enforce those instructions by means commensurate with the obvious risks. . . .

Ruling of the Court: [Conviction of Hilton for violating the Sherman Act] Affirmed.

CASE QUESTIONS

1. In what way does a group boycott such as the one in this case restrict competition?

2. Why was the hotel liable for the conduct of an employee who was acting contrary to his supervisor's directives?

Application of the Rule of Reason.   The following is a list of activities that may restrain competition and are judged according to the rule of reason.

- *Territorial restrictions*, in which a manufacturer restricts the territory in which a dealer can sell, thereby restricting other dealers from competing.

- *Monopoly*, in which one firm controls the market for a particular product with the intent of excluding competitors.

- *Tying arrangements*, in which a seller conditions the sale of a product on buyer's agreement to purchase some other product produced or distributed by the seller.

- *Mergers*, in which two businesses are combined into one, resulting in a substantial limitation of competition.

An interesting case in which the rule of reason was applied in a tying arrangement was *Martino v. McDonald's System, Inc.*, 625 F.Supp. 356 (Ill., 1985). McDonald's, the fast-food hamburger operation, required its franchisees (owners of individual restaurants; see discussion later in this chapter) to sell Coca-Cola and no other cola drink as a condition for allowing the franchisees to use the McDonald's name. The reason for the requirement was McDonald's interest in a standard menu at all its restaurants, and in a linkage with a product known and popular among consumers.

Some franchisees wanted to sell Pepsi-Cola because they could buy it for less. They sued McDonald's, seeking to have the Coca-Cola requirement declared illegal as a tying arrangement. The court held the restriction was *legal* based on the rule of reason. The court noted that McDonald's is by no means a monopoly in the fast-food industry; McDonald's does not dominate the cola market; competition was not substantially lessened by McDonald's Coca-Cola requirement; McDonald's does not have a financial interest in the profits of the Coca-Cola Company; and its reasons for imposing the restriction were reasonable.

The following case explores restrictions against monopolies. We discussed in Chapter 10 that a hotel can prohibit from its premises competitors in the services the hotel offers. We learn from the following case that the resulting exclusive right to sell to hotel guests is not considered an illegal monopoly. Similarly, a sports stadium can prohibit spectators from bringing in food from outside sources. Such a prohibition does not violate the antitrust laws although it gives the stadium the exclusive right to sell food during the event to those in attendance.

CASE EXAMPLE 15–6

Elliott v. The United Center
126 F.3d 1003 (1997)

Millions of spectators have attended games and other events at the United Center, home of the world-famous Chicago Bulls, as well as the Chicago Blackhawks, circuses, ice shows, concerts, and in 1996 the Democratic National Convention. But ever since the United Center opened, it has had a policy that prohibits all patrons of the center

from bringing food into the arena. This, according to Thornton Elliott and his co-plaintiffs, has given a "monopoly" on food sales to the Center. Elliott [the plaintiff] and his colleagues are licensed peanut vendors who, up until the time the United Center imposed this policy, turned a respectable profit selling peanuts outside the stadium. They brought this suit under section 2 of the Sherman Act, claiming that the United Center's food policy constitutes an illegal attempt to monopolize food sales inside the arena and in the surrounding geographic area. The district court was unpersuaded and dismissed the case. We agree. . . .

According to the complaint, ever since the United Center implemented its food policy in September 1994, patrons are inspected for food when they enter the stadium, and if any is found, it is confiscated by stadium security. If a fan buys a bag of peanuts from Elliott, therefore, she must consume it before she enters the United Center, unless she wants to risk contributing it to the "illegal food" stash collected by the security personnel. Worse yet, if she has a hankering for peanuts during the Bull's game, her desires will go unfulfilled because the United Center does not offer peanuts for sale in the stadium (except little bags of peanuts for the circus elephants). This policy has cost Elliott dearly . . . the average sales of peanuts have dropped to approximately one-fifth of sales in previous years. Predictably, some vendors have gone out of business, and the remaining ones are struggling to survive. . . .

[Plaintiffs] conceded that the United Center might have had a legitimate business reason to prohibit certain kinds of food, such as cans, bottles, or alcoholic beverages in general, in the interest of maintaining order in the facility, but plaintiffs claim that no such reason could be advanced for the blanket food ban. The complaint points out the United Center's monopoly over the presentation of live National Basketball Association games and live National Hockey League games in the Chicago market, and implicitly argues that the Center is, through the food policy, attempting to extend its monopoly to the alleged food concession market. . . . Plaintiffs claim the fewer the food concessions, the higher the price the United

Center can charge for food its patrons consume, and the more consumers will suffer. . . .

The United Center can recoup the cost of putting on an event in any of a number of ways. It can charge very high ticket prices, and allow unlimited numbers of food concessions in and around the stadium, or it can charge somewhat lower ticket prices and restrict the number of concessions (thereby earning some of its profits from food sales.) . . . The United Center is obviously not monopolizing the market for peanuts: it is staying strictly out of the peanut business. Prices and output of peanuts in the area are totally unaffected by the United Center's policies.

The logic of Elliott's argument would mean that exclusive restaurants could no longer require customers to purchase their wines only at the establishment, because the restaurant would be "monopolizing" the sale of wine within its interior. Movie theaters, which traditionally (and notoriously) earn a substantial profit of their revenue from the sales of candies, popcorn, and soda, would be required by the antitrust laws to allow patrons to bring their own food. . . . Elliott's principal point is that the customer knows that once he is ready to walk through the entry gate, he may not have with him any "outside" food. The same could be said of any of the establishments we have just mentioned: once inside a restaurant, or a movie theater, the customer is at the mercy of the place he has chosen. The price of the refreshments or the wine is just one part of the price of the evening out.

[The facts here do not present a] violation of the antitrust laws. . . . We therefore conclude that the district court correctly dismissed Elliott's complaint . . . Affirmed.

Franchising

Towns and cities look more and more alike as each have hotels, restaurants, and stores with the same names. This phenomenon is based in part on large businesses expanding the number of its company-owned outlets, and in part on franchises. A **franchise** is an arrangement in which the owner of a trademark, service mark, or copyright licenses others, under specified conditions, to use the mark or copyright in the sale of goods or services. As we have seen, use of another's service mark, trademark, or copyright without permission constitutes infringement. The **franchisor** is the owner of the mark or copyright; the **franchisee** is the party to whom the right to use it is given. Examples of franchises include Wendy's, Dunkin Donuts, Tony Roma's, Day's Inn, and Super 8 Motels.

Nature of the Franchise Relationship

The relationship between the franchisor and the franchisee is a contractual one. By contract, the franchisor authorizes the franchisee to utilize the trademark, service mark, or copyright. In return the franchisee customarily agrees to pay the franchisor an initial sum of money and a percentage of profits on an ongoing basis. The better known the business name is, the higher will be the fees paid by the franchisee. The contract customarily requires the franchisee to maintain certain standards and the franchisor to provide various kinds of technical assistance.

Because the relationship is a contractual one and not an employment relationship or a principal/agent relationship, the franchisor customarily is not liable for the acts of a franchisee. Thus, if a fast-foot franchisee negligently prepares a meal in such a way that a customer is injured, the franchisor will not be liable; only the franchisee is responsible. The reason is that the franchisee and not the franchisor is the owner and operator of the business. This principle is illustrated in *Choice Hotels International, Inc. v. Palm-Aire Oceanside, Inc.*, 95 F.3d 41 (4th Cir., 1996). A hotel franchisee was negligent in the maintenance of a balcony railing. A two-year old guest fell seventy feet to the ground when deterioration caused the railing to give way. The guest sued both the franchisee and the franchisor. The court held the franchisor was not liable.

The franchisor would be liable only if the franchisor's agents participated in the day-to-day operations and management of the business or, where a patron is injured by a product, if the franchisor made or sold the item that caused the injury.

Benefits to the Franchisee

The franchisee stands to benefit from a franchise relationship in several ways. The use of the franchised name is usually valuable. In addition, the franchisor is typically required to provide technical help to the franchisee, including market research to decide where to locate the business, advise on layout and design of the building, employee training, recipes, accounting methods, information on suppliers, and other assistance that may be needed. Another important benefit is group advertising. Often each franchisee will contribute a sum of money for promotions, and the franchisor prepares print and broadcast advertisements. The individual franchisee thus receives the benefit of an expensive advertising campaign for a fraction of the cost. Further, the franchisee may receive an exclusive territory within which the franchisor will not license another franchisee to operate.

An exclusive territory is very valuable to a franchisee because it protects the business from competition from a nearby franchisee. If a franchisee receives an exclusive territory, it will be stated in the contract. If the contract does not include a provision identifying an exclusive territory, the franchisor can authorize another franchise operation to open in close proximity. In *Payne v. McDonald's Corp.*, 957 F. Supp. 749 (Md., 1997), a McDonald's franchisee was frustrated when the franchisor authorized two additional restaurants within two miles of his eatery. He sued the franchisor for breach of contract. The court stated, "The problem faced by plaintiffs in claiming a breach of contract by McDonald's is their inability to point to any provision in the express and unambiguous agreements between the parties which has been breached by McDonald's." A provision in the contract stated, "[N]o exclusive, protected or other territorial rights in the contiguous market area of the restaurant is hereby granted or inferred."

A franchisee is well-advised to attempt to negotiate a provision in the franchise agreement granting an exclusive territory. Without it, the franchisee's patronage may be invaded by a like business resulting in a considerable lost income.

Benefits to the Franchisor

The franchisor benefits financially from the fees paid by the franchisee. The franchisor also benefits from the additional exposure of the name resulting from the franchisee's use. The more the name is known and accepted by the public, the greater the franchise fee the franchisor can command from subsequent franchisees. The value of the name is preserved in part by contract provisions requiring the franchisee to maintain certain standards including size of building, interior and exterior design, cleanliness, use of logo, and restrictions on products sold. These standards requirements provide consistency and public acceptance for a franchise operation. For example, although each McDonald's restaurant is individually owned, we have a certain expectation of what we will find if we go to one, and whichever outlet we choose we will likely find what we expect.

Fraud and Breach of Contract by the Franchisor

If a franchisee pays the franchise fees and the franchisor fails to promote the name, provide technical assistance, or otherwise comply with its contractual obligations, the franchisee may be the victim of fraud or breach of contract. To reduce the chances of this happening, a would-be franchisee should thoroughly investigate a franchisor before investing in a franchise.

Disclosure Requirements for Franchisors

When the concept of franchising first began, unscrupulous franchisors often took the money of unsuspecting franchisees' and failed to provide the promised services. To protect franchisees against this occurrence, both federal and state laws have been passed requiring franchisors to disclose detailed information about their business at least ten days before accepting any money from the franchisee.

The information typically required to be disclosed includes:

- The name and address of the franchisor;
- The business experience of persons affiliated with the franchisor;

- Whether any such person has been convicted of a felony;
- The length of time the franchisor has conducted a business of the type to be operated by the franchisee;
- The franchisor's most recent financial statement, and information about any material changes in the finances since it was prepared;
- A copy of the franchise contract typically used by the franchisor;
- A statement of all fees that the franchisee will be required to pay;
- The proposed application of the fees by the franchisor;
- Whether any franchisees have sued the franchisor;
- Circumstances under which the franchise agreement can be terminated;
- The number of franchises already sold and the number proposed to be sold in the future;
- The responsibilities of the franchisor and the franchisee; and
- A statement whether the franchisee will receive an exclusive territory.

A franchisor that provides false information faces both civil and criminal penalties including compensation for damages, jail, and fines.

The required ten-day waiting period between disclosure and acceptance of money by the franchisor is intended to give the franchisee opportunity to review the information and discuss it with advisors such as a lawyer and an accountant.

Tying Arrangements as an Antitrust Issue

A franchisor often wants its franchisees to purchase supplies and equipment from the franchisor. This arrangement ensures the franchisor of both a market for its products and the uniformity that is so important to franchise operations. If its trademark is sufficiently in demand, franchisees may be willing to agree to buy from the franchisor in return for the right to use the name. From an antitrust point of view, this is a tying arrangement, that is, the obligation to purchase products from the franchisor is tied to the grant of the franchise. As a result, the franchisor is spared from competition from other suppliers and they in turn are denied access to the market for the tied product.

As we have seen, tying arrangements are not per se violations of the antitrust laws but rather are subject to the rule of reason. In determining whether a particular tying arrangement is legal or not, the court will examine several factors including the amount of commerce affected, and whether some special justification exists for the tying arrangement. The greater the impact on competition and the less special the justification is, the more likely the tying arrangement will be unenforceable. The desire by a franchisor to maintain uniformity and quality standards may not qualify as a special justification.

In the following case, franchisees of Domino's Pizza alleged that the franchisor violated antitrust laws by requiring that franchisees purchase ingredients and dough from the franchisor. The case clarifies the rule that a franchisor can require franchisees to purchase needed products exclusively from the franchisor without violating the antitrust laws.

CASE EXAMPLE 15–7

Queens City Pizza, Inc., v. Domino's Pizza, Inc.
124 F.3d 430 (3rd Cir., 1997)

Domino's Pizza, Inc. is a fast-food service company that sells pizza through a national network of over 4200 stores. Domino's Pizza owns and operates approximately 700 of these stores. Independent franchisees own and operate the remaining 3500. Domino's Pizza, Inc. is the second largest pizza company in the United States, with revenues in excess of $1.8 billion per year.

A franchisee joins the Domino's System by executing a standard franchise agreement with Domino's Pizza, Inc. Under the franchise agreement, the franchisee receives the right to sell pizza under the "Domino's" name and format. In return, Domino's Pizza receives franchise fees and royalties.

The essence of a successful nationwide fast-food chain is product uniformity and consistency. Uniformity benefits franchisees because customers can purchase pizza from any Domino's store and be certain the pizza will taste exactly like the Domino's Pizza with which they are familiar. This means that individual franchisees need not build up their own good will. Uniformity also benefits the franchisor. It ensures the brand name will continue to attract and hold customers, increasing franchise fees and royalties.

For these reasons, section 12.2 of the Domino's Pizza standard franchise agreement requires that all pizza ingredients, beverages, and packaging materials used by a Domino's franchisee conform to the standards set by Domino's Pizza Inc. Section 12.2 also provides that Domino's Pizza, Inc. may "in our sole discretion require that ingredients, supplies and materials used in the preparation, packaging and delivery of pizza be purchased exclusively from us or from approved suppliers or distributors." Domino's Pizza reserves the right to "impose reasonable limitations on the number of approved suppliers or distributors of any product." To enforce these rights, Domino's Pizza, Inc. retains the power to inspect franchisee stores and to test materials and ingredients. Section 12.2 is subject to a reasonableness clause

providing that Domino's Pizza, Inc. must "exercise reasonable judgment with respect to all determinations to be made by us under the terms of this Agreement." Under the standard franchise agreement, Domino's Pizza, Inc. sells approximately 90% of the $500 million in ingredients and supplies used by Domino's franchisees. These sales, worth some $450 million per year, form a significant part of Domino's Pizza, Inc.'s profits. Franchisees purchase only 10% of their ingredients and supplies from outside sources. With the exception of fresh dough, Domino's Pizza, Inc. does not manufacture the products it sells to franchisees. Instead, it purchases these products from approved suppliers and then resells them to the franchisees at a markup.

The plaintiffs in this case are eleven Domino's franchisees and the International Franchise Advisory Council, Inc. (IFAC), a Michigan corporation consisting of approximately 40% of the Domino's franchisees in the United States, formed to promote their common interests. The plaintiffs contend that Domino's Pizza, Inc. has a monopoly in "the $500 million aftermarket for sales of supplies to Domino's franchisees" and has used its monopoly power to unreasonably restrain trade, limit competition, and extract supra-competitive profits.

First, plaintiffs allege that Domino's Pizza, Inc. has restricted their ability to purchase competitively priced dough. Most franchisees purchase all of their fresh dough from Domino's Pizza, Inc. Plaintiffs here attempted to lower costs by making fresh pizza dough on site. They contend that in response, Domino's Pizza, Inc. increased processing fees and altered quality standards and inspection practices for store-produced dough, which eliminated all potential savings and financial incentives to make their own dough.

Plaintiffs also allege Domino's Pizza, Inc. prohibited stores that produce dough from selling their dough to other franchisees, even though the dough-producing stores were willing to sell dough at a price 25% to 40% below Domino's Pizza, Inc.'s price.

Next, plaintiffs object to efforts by Domino's Pizza, Inc. to block IFAC's attempt to buy less expensive ingredients and supplies from other sources. . . .

Plaintiffs also allege Domino's Pizza entered into exclusive dealing arrangements with several franchisees in order to deny [alternate purveyors] access to a pool of potential buyers sufficiently large to make an alternative purchasing scheme economically feasible. In addition, plaintiffs contend Domino's Pizza, Inc. commenced anti-competitive predatory pricing to shut other suppliers out of the market. For example, they maintain that Domino's Pizza, Inc. lowered prices on many ingredients and supplies to a level competitive with [others'] prices and then recouped lost profits by raising the price on fresh dough, which [competitors] could not supply.

As a result of these and other alleged practices, plaintiffs maintain that each franchisee store now pays between $3000 and $10,000 more per year for ingredients and supplies than it would in a competitive market. Plaintiffs allege these costs are passed on to consumers. . . .

Courts and legal commentators have long recognized that franchise tying contracts are an essential and important aspect of the franchise form of business organization because they reduce agency costs and prevent franchisees from freeriding—offering products of sub-standard quality insufficient to maintain the reputational value of the franchise product while benefitting from the quality control efforts of other actors in the franchise system. Franchising is a bedrock of the American economy. More than one-third of all dollars spent in retailing transactions in the United States are paid to franchise outlets. We do not believe the antitrust laws were designed to erect a serious barrier to this form of business organization. . . .

Here, plaintiffs' acceptance of a franchise package that included purchase requirements and contractual restrictions is consistent with the existence of a competitive market in which franchises are valued, in part, according to the terms of the proposed franchise agreement and the availability of alternative franchise opportunities. Plaintiffs need not have become Domino's franchisees. If the contractual restrictions in section 12.2. of the general franchise agreement were viewed as overly burdensome or risky at the time they were proposed, plaintiffs could have purchased a different form of restaurant, or made some alternative investment. They chose not to do so. Plaintiffs must purchase products from Domino's Pizza not because of Domino's market power . . . but because they are bound by contract to do so. If Domino's Pizza, Inc. acted unreasonably when, under the franchise agreement, it restricted plaintiffs' ability to purchase supplies from other sources, plaintiffs' remedy, if any, is in contract, not under antitrust laws. . . .

Termination of Franchise

Many abuses have occurred surrounding terminations of franchises. Once a franchisee has invested money, time, and energy in developing the franchise business, courts have been reluctant to allow the franchisor to terminate the franchise without good cause. Many states have passed statutes limiting the circumstances under which a franchisor can withdraw the franchise. Typical is the Indiana statute which bars a franchisor from terminating a franchise "without good cause or in bad faith." Ind. Code Sections 23-2-2.7-1(7) and(8). Sufficient grounds for termination include repeated failures by a franchise restaurant to pay weekly royalties, *Hacienda Mexican Restaurant of Kalamazoo Corp. v. Hacienda Franchise Group, Inc.*, 569 NE2d 661 (Ind.,1991); and fraudulent repackaging of outdated beer by a wholesale distributor franchisee in an attempt to resell the product as fresh, *Beermart, Inc. v. The Stroh Brewery Co.*, 804 F.2d 409 (7th Cir., 1986).

Once a franchise agreement expires or is terminated, the franchisee's right to use the franchisor's trademark terminates. Continued use of the name by the franchisee constitutes trademark infringement. Thus, where a Burger King franchise expired and was not renewed, and the franchisee continued to operate the business under the name Burger King, the franchisee was liable for trademark infringement. The franchisee's claim of wrongful termination was not a defense to the trademark infringement action. The remedy for the alleged wrongful termination was money damages for breach of contract. *Burger King Corp. v. Agad*, 911 F. Supp. 1499 (Fl., 1995). Similarly, where a Dunkin' Donuts franchisee failed to pay franchise and advertising fees, triggering a contractual termination of the franchise agreement, the continued use of the Dunkin' Donuts name constituted trademark infringement. *Dunkin' Donuts, Inc. v. Towns Family, Inc.*, 1996 WL 328018 (Ill., 1996).

Regulation of Internal Affairs

Numerous regulatory laws impact the operation of hospitality establishments. These laws apply to maintenance of guest registers, posting of rates, and recycling.

Guest Register

Most cities and states have passed ordinances that require motels and similar businesses to maintain a register containing guests' names and addresses. The government's interest in a guest register includes, for example, the register's use in criminal investigations and, for long term guests whose right to vote is challenged on residency grounds, verification of residence. In one case a defendant charged with a crime sought to use his signature in an out-of-town motel's guest register to substantiate his alibi defense. *Norris v. State*, 469 S.E.2d 214 (Ga., 1996). A guest registration statute requiring innkeepers to record on the hotel register the make and license number of guests' automobiles, the date and hour of arrival, and the guest's room number has been held valid by a court on the grounds that the register can aid authorities in locating lost or stolen automobiles and finding wanted persons.

Many states have regulations making it unlawful for a hotelkeeper to knowingly accept as a guest a person who has registered under a pseudonym. Falsification of a guest's name frustrates the use of the register as a law-enforcement aide. The innkeeper should not permit a guest to register under a name the innkeeper knows is not the guest's true name.

Innkeepers should familiarize themselves with the laws concerning guest registers in their state. In the case of *Commonwealth v. Blinn*, 503 N.E.2d 25 (Mass., 1987), a state trooper wanted to examine the guest register of a Howard Johnson Motor Lodge. The manager refused, believing such an examination constituted an illegal search. However, the applicable state statute clearly stated that law enforcement officers were allowed to examine motel registers to determine if someone who was the target of a criminal investigation had registered. The trooper charged the innkeeper with violation of the law and the manager was successfully prosecuted. If the manager had been more informed about the law, much time, money, and embarrassment would have been saved.

Many states require that the register be retained for a period of several years. The statutes usually specify that the register can be kept on microfilm, electronic imaging, or other like storage process.

Rates

Many states or localities have passed statutes requiring hotels to make known the price charged for each room by posting the rates at the hotel. The purpose of these statutes is to eliminate price gouging in the industry. As the court in *State v. Norval Hotel Co.*, 133 N.E. 75 (Ohio, 1921), observed,

> *It is a matter of common knowledge that at times when large numbers of the public meet in cities or towns for conventions, or similar gatherings, the capacity of hotels and places for public accommodation is overtaxed and opportunity is thereby given for the exaction of exorbitant or unfair charges.*

The prices are set by the hotel; legislatures do not attempt to fix the price of any room in a hotel, nor do they require that a hotel offer accommodations or services at any particular rate. But when a law has been duly passed requiring posting of rates, and the hotel has fixed its rate, the hotel must post and abide by the posted price. Such statutes do not prevent the hotel from raising its rates, but they do require that the hotel post the new rate schedule within the time stipulated by the law.

A hotel can charge different guests different rates provided the higher rates are not unreasonably high and provided the different rates are not the result of illegal discrimination. Varying rates would constitute illegal discrimination if based upon sex, race, color, religion, national origin, marital status, or disability. (For further discussion on illegal discrimination, see Chapter 3.) Issues associated with charging different rates were addressed in the following case.

CASE EXAMPLE 15–8

Archibald v. Cinerama Hotels
140 Cal. Rptr. 599 (1977)

[Plaintiff is a resident of California who stayed at the defendant's hotel in Hawaii.].

It is alleged in the first cause of action that the rates charged plaintiff and members of her class are higher than those charged to residents of the State of Hawaii. It is not alleged that the rates charged Californians are different than the rates charged any person or class of persons from anywhere else in the world, nor is it alleged that the rates charged plaintiff are unreasonable or excessive. While the complaint categorizes the rate charged her and other nonresidents as a "surcharge" which is "discriminatory," the "preferential treatment" described in the complaint consists of . . . an unspecified rate presumably lower than the regular rate paid by all nonresidents and is illustrated by advertisement in the yellow pages of the telephone book placed by certain hotels such as "Ask about our [local resident] rates or [local resident] discounts."

Plaintiff has based her case in large part on the common law pertaining to innkeepers. She asserts there was, and is, a duty to charge exactly the same rates to everyone. Reliance is placed by plaintiff principally on textbook authority that innkeepers must provide lodging for all at a reasonable price and that all should be served equally and without discrimination. However, looking at plaintiff's authorities, . . . we observe that the concern of the common law was and is limited to assuring each traveler freedom from unreasonably high rates. Since travel upon the highway at night was hazardous and there was little choice of lodging for the night, the common law approved restrictions upon innkeepers to insure a charge of "reasonable value" for services, to prevent them from extorting exorbitant rates.

We have found no authority holding that the offering of a discount to certain clients, patrons or customers based on an attempt to attract their business is unlawful under the common law, whether the discount be for salesmen, clergymen, armed services personnel, or local residents. In fact it has been indicated in court decisions that even the common law duty to charge reasonable value for services is inapplicable where the guest is not one who might be stranded on a road in the nighttime or might otherwise be at the mercy of a single innkeeper. . . .

We do not perceive that the common law is concerned with rates as such, except that they not be unreasonable; nor is it concerned with charges *lower* than reasonable charges, or discounts to induce patronage from certain groups or classes. . . .

Our research has disclosed no California statute, rule or policy which requires a hotel to charge a uniform rate to all its guests. . . . Insofar as policy or rules are concerned, an innkeeper has a duty to receive and accommodate all persons at a reasonable charge.

The judgment [dismissing the complaint] is affirmed.

CASE QUESTION

1. Can a motel that is the only inn within a twenty-five mile radius charge whatever rates it chooses? Why or why not?

Mandatory Recycling

Most states and localities have adopted laws requiring businesses and individuals to recycle some of their waste stream. The purpose of recycling is to save natural resources, reduce pollution, and decrease the amount of waste that goes into landfills. For example, up to 17 trees are needed to make a ton of paper; when paper is recycled, less new paper is needed and so fewer trees are harvested. To help appreciate the need for recycling, consider that the average American generates approximately five pounds of trash every day.

Recycling laws vary from state to state and locality to locality, but basically they require that businesses and individuals separate recyclable waste from the rest of the garbage, and waste haulers are required to deliver the recyclable waste to recycling centers. Food service businesses are typically required to separate certain food and beverage containers, such as wine bottles, metal and aluminum containers, and certain types of plastic containers. The law may require that the containers be cleaned, that the glass containers be separated from other recycleables, that each color of glass containers be separated from other colors, and that tops and caps be removed. All businesses are typically required to recycle office paper and corrugated cardboard. Penalties for noncompliance are usually fines ranging in amount from $50 to $1,000 per infraction.

Restaurants and hotels have found a variety of additional ways to further the environment. These include installing water-saving shower heads in guest rooms, offering guests the option of less than daily washing of towels, using reusable dishes and silverware, and donating used furniture and linens to charitable organizations.

Licensing and Zoning

Licensing

The state or municipality may require that the owner of an inn, hotel, apartment house, rooming house, restaurant, or similar establishment obtain a license before opening for business. The goal of licensing requirements is to prevent hospitality establishments from becoming menaces to the public welfare by requiring licensed businesses to maintain proper operation, sanitation, construction, and fire protection. The authority to license and regulate is based on the power of government to adopt laws that further public health, safety, and welfare. This power is referred to as the **police power**.

When a government licenses a business, it confers the right to do something that would otherwise be prohibited. A license is a special privilege rather than a right common to all. For example, you cannot drive a car without a license. Only people who have proven their ability to pilot a motor vehicle are entitled to a driver's license. The operation of hotels and restaurants is likewise subject to legislative authority to regulate and license because, like driving, those businesses affect the public welfare.

A considerable body of law has been developed concerning the granting and revoking of licenses, seeking to balance the concerns of the licensing body and the interest of the licensed party or party seeking a license.

Principles for Granting Licenses

Hotel and restaurant owners must obtain all necessary licenses and permits before opening their businesses. Those required vary from locality to locality and may include a hotel operator's license, a restaurant operator's license, a liquor license, health and fire code permits, and zoning permits. Determination of what licenses and permits are required and what is necessary to qualify for them usually requires considerable research and the aid of an attorney.

Compliance with Laws.   To qualify for a license, the applicant must prove that he will abide by all applicable laws. In the following case an applicant was denied a hotel license because the government entity charged with issuing the license believed the applicant would permit immoral activity there.

CASE EXAMPLE 15–9

Hertenberger v. City of Texarkana
272 S.W.2d 435 (Ark., 1954)

The applicant [E]velyn Hertenberger applied to the City of Texarkana for a license to operate a hotel. The [City] council, after considering the application, refused to issue the license. [She appealed the decision of the City Counsel.]

Ordinance B-439 of the City of Texarkana pertains to the licensing of rooming houses and hotels, and provides: "such license shall not be granted unless it shall appear probable to the Council that such applicant will not rent rooms for immoral purposes or allow prostitutes or pimps to remain on such premises or permit gambling or the sale, storage or keeping of intoxicating liquor on such premises." . . .

Without going into detail as to the evidence, suffice it to say that the council was justified in reaching the conclusion that if Mrs. Hertenberger was granted a license, in all probability the hotel rooms would be rented for immoral purposes; and Ordinance B-439 specifically provides that the license shall not be granted in such circumstances.

Although the right to operate a hotel is a property right, this fact does not preclude the city council from refusing to issue a license where the issuance of such license would be in violation of a valid ordinance. . . .

We have reached the conclusion that the ordinance is valid and none of the applicant's constitutional rights were violated in refusing her a license to operate a hotel in Texarkana.

CASE QUESTIONS

1. Why would the City of Texarkana want to ensure that a hotel or boarding house owner would not permit gambling, prostitution, and other similar illegal activities on the premises?

2. What evidence do you think was presented to convince the city council that Hertenberger would have permitted immoral activity at her hotel?

Fair Application of the Law.   To deny a license, the licensing body must have a reasonable basis; it cannot deny the license on arbitrary, capricious, or unreasonable grounds. In *Hertenberger*, the court held that the city council's concern about immoral activity was a reasonable basis for denying the license. Apparently the court felt immoral activity can create a nuisance and threaten the public welfare. The court further found that city council's conclusion that the applicant would permit such activity, probably based on prior incidents involving the applicant, was reasonable.

In a 1980 Massachusetts case, McDonald's, the fast-food hamburger company, was denied a victualer's (restaurateur's) license for a proposed restaurant in a shopping center. The reasons the town board gave for the denial were increased traffic that would endanger students in a nearby high school and inadequate parking. McDonald's appealed and the court ruled the denial of the license was arbitrary and capricious, and McDonald's was entitled to the license.

The court, rejecting the board's reasoning concerning the alleged traffic problem, noted the following: the proposed McDonald's location was in a relatively empty corner of the shopping center; peak hours at the restaurant did not coincide with the arrival and departure of school buses; and police were assigned to traffic duty at times the school buses operate. Further, the shopping center was not close to a major highway. Therefore the restaurant was not likely to attract new customers but rather would serve only those already in the immediate area on other business. The court also held the board had incorrectly interpreted a town parking ordinance that required businesses located on a separate lot, as the proposed McDonald's would be, to have adequate parking on that lot, which McDonald's did not. By lease, McDonald's was entitled to use the mall's common parking lot, which contained sufficient parking space. The court thus held that adequate parking was available. *McDonald's Corporation v. Board of Selectmen of Randolph*, 399 N.E.2d 38 (Mass., 1980). Do you agree with the court that the denial of the license was arbitrary and capricious? Why or why not?

In the following case, also involving McDonald's, the court held that the licensing body can consider, when deciding whether to grant a license, the number of similar licenses already granted, the need for another restaurant, and public sentiment. Note the interesting conflict of interest issue raised near the end of the decision.

CASE EXAMPLE 15–10

McDonald's Corp. v. Town of East Longmeadow
506 N.E.2d 172 (Mass., 1987)

[McDonald's Corp. appeals the denial of a victualler's license.] . . . In denying the license the board [of Selectmen, which is the equivalent of a Town Council] gave the reasons set forth in the margin.[1] McDonald's claims that the board considered factors which are not connected with the preparation and delivery of food, and that the reasons were not supported by evidence. It urges, for example, that the number of twenty-two licenses deemed sufficient was determined arbitrarily and without any studies. We agree with the trial judge that McDonald's has not shown the decision was arbitrary or capricious. . . .

The breadth of discretion which local authorities enjoy in granting or denying licenses varies. In the case of common victualler licenses . . . for example, town and city boards may exercise judgment about public convenience and public good

that is very broad indeed. . . . There is no question that the board may consider the number of licenses already granted in determining the public good. . . . The board was not required to make studies to determine the number of licenses to be issued. The board members, local residents of the town, were aware of local patron needs, took a view, and noted that there were fifteen restaurants along route 83. The board also properly considered the proximity of another McDonald's.

In particular, McDonald's challenges the board's consideration of public sentiment, traffic, and litter. There was widespread opposition to the grant of the license at the board's hearing. This was in large part because of the "traffic danger to children in the nearby park." . . .

While the board's decision appears to be based primarily on the lack of a need for an additional license, the board also took these other considerations into account . . . These "ancillary and contributing reasons," even if not sufficient in themselves to warrant a denial of license to McDonald's, did not vitiate the action of the [board]. . . .

The licensing authorities are not . . . required to grant any licenses to common victuallers. Whether any such licenses shall be granted and, if any, the number to be granted rest in the sound judgment of the licensing board as to the demands of the public welfare in the respective communities. . . . There was here no basis on the record to disturb the board's decision.

One of the selectmen disqualified himself from voting because he was employed by Friendly's Corporation. McDonald's, a competitor of Friendly's, asserts that the selectman's participation in speaking against the application and chairing the board's meetings was a [conflict of interest]. Although such participation may have been inappropriate, . . . the trial judge, on the basis of the testimony of the other two selectmen, concluded that the facts did not warrant a finding that the selectman's affiliation with Friendly Corporation constitutes a conflict of interest which tainted the . . . decision. That finding was not clearly erroneous and is consonant with applicable law. . . .

Judgment [denying the license] affirmed.

---

[1]The applicant has offered no evidence of the need for the new establishment on North Main Street, or that the good of the Town of East Longmeadow requires it, and the Board finds that the need does not exist, and the License and Permit would not be for the good of the town.

An expression of protest of the restaurant is reflected in the petition bearing 600 names, and delivered to the Selectmen. The Board finds that with regards to need, there are already 22 Common Victualler's Licenses in this small town. The Springfield McDonald's is but a short distance away.

In making its decision the Selectmen have also considered the potential for increased traffic particularly during peak hours on North Main Street which is the town's main thoroughfare, and the immediacy of the proposed location to the public park and the resulting negative concerns as to pedestrian safety and adequate disposal of waste.

Past Use of the Property.   Another factor the licensing body will consider is the prior use of the property. A junior college applied for a license to operate as dormitories certain buildings it owned. Although the buildings had previously been used as dorms by another college, the neighbors staged an intense protest to the proposed use based on fears of congestion, inadequate parking, and noise. The license was initially denied but granted on appeal. The court held the denial was not based on a reasonable basis and noted that the buildings had previously been used as dormitories with no complaints by neighbors. The court also noted that the junior college applicant was an accredited institution and no unfavorable evidence was presented about its capacity to operate the dorms or about the character of its officers. *Newberry Junior College v. Town of Brookline*, 472 N.E.2d 1373 (Mass., 1985).

Administrative Procedure.   Licenses are often issued by a government agency, that is, a government subdivision appointed by elected officials responsible for administering particular laws.

When a licensee fails to abide by the rules applicable to licensees, the agency is responsible for prosecuting the violation. Until now most of the cases we have discussed in the book have been pursued in court. When a government agency is involved, the initial forum for the case is usually the agency rather than a court. If the matter is appealed, the first appeal is often still within the agency. If it is appealed again it will be heard by a court.

Before a matter that is within the jurisdiction of a government agency can be heard in a court, the **administrative remedies must be exhausted**. This means all appeals available within the agency must have first been utilized.

License Fees

Licensees often complain that the cost of a license is high. A municipality can require a reasonable fee to be paid for a license intended to protect the public. If the fee is adequate to cover the municipality's costs to administer the license—including the cost to prepare and distribute applications, inspect licensed and would-be licensed premises, and pursue violators—the fee is reasonable and valid. Governments cannot use licensing fees as a revenue-raising device. If a license fee generates a significant profit above the costs of administration, the fee will be considered unreasonable and subject to modification. In a 100-year-old plus case that remains the law today a court said:

> *The amount the municipality has a right to demand for such fee depends upon the extent and expense of the municipal supervision made necessary by the business in the city or town where it is licensed. A fee sufficient to cover the expense of issuing the license, and to pay the expenses which may be incurred in the enforcement of such police inspection or superintendence as may be lawfully exercised over the business, may be required. It is obvious that the actual amount necessary to meet such expenses cannot, in all cases, be ascertained in advance, and that it would be futile to require anything of the kind. The result is, if the fee required is not plainly unreasonable, the courts ought not to interfere with the discretion exercised by the [legislature] in fixing it; and, unless the contrary appears on the face of the ordinance requiring it, or is established by proper evidence, they should presume it to be reasonable.* City of Fayetteville v. Carter, 12 S.W. 573 (Ark., 1889).

Consequences of Operating Without a License

Failure to obtain a required license can lead to unpleasant consequences, as can failure to obtain a renewal which is required at regular intervals, often annually.

Penalties and Fines.   The government can bar a business from opening or, in the case of an existing business that fails to obtain a renewal, force the business to close. In addition, fines may be imposed and, in Florida, the innkeeper or restaurateur may be required to attend, "at personal expense, an educational program sponsored by the Hospitality Education Program." Florida Statutes Section 509.261(a)(b).

Loss of Protection of Law.   Depending on the type of license involved, another consequence of operating without a license may be that the business is unable to enforce its contracts. If the purpose of the license is to protect the public, as is the case with a license to operate a restaurant, the absence of the license will bar the restaurant from enforcing its contracts. For example, if a restaurant is not properly licensed and a diner fails to pay, the restaurant may be unable to enforce the guest's contractual duty to pay. This should be motivation enough for restaurateurs and innkeepers to abide by the applicable licensing laws. Where, however, the purpose of the license is to raise revenue (income for the government) and is unrelated to protection of the public, the business' right to enforce its contracts will not be affected.

In *Randall v. Tuell*, 36 A. 910 (Me., 1897), a hotelkeeper who did not have a license was unable to recover from a guest who did not pay for lodging. Think of the case where a hotel fails to obtain a necessary license required to protect the public and a large group or convention fails to pay. The loss to the innkeeper could be substantial. Such was the circumstance in the following case. Fortunately for the innkeeper who failed to renew its license, the court allowed the hotel to recover the money owed to avoid unjust enrichment by the hotel guests. (**Unjust enrichment** is profit obtained unfairly at someone else's expense.)

CASE EXAMPLE 15–11

Hiram Ricker & Sons v. Students International Meditation Society
342 A.2d 262 (Me., 1975)

Hiram Ricker & Sons [hereinafter "Ricker"] and Students International Mediation Society [hereinafter "SIMS"] had entered into an agreement wherein Ricker agreed to furnish lodging and food to approximately 1,000 SIMS students at a one-month teacher training course to be held at Ricker's premises in Poland Spring, Maine, from June 26 to July 28, 1970.

The Poland Spring's complex, once a fashionable spa for those with the leisure and means to enjoy its amenities, was sold in 1962 to Ricker, which subsequently leased the premises to the federal government for a Job Corps residential installation.

. . . Ricker agreed with SIMS . . . to furnish both lodging and food to SIMS's students. The one-month course was held at the Poland Spring complex as scheduled, and at the conclusion of the course, SIMS had paid Ricker $185,000. A dispute arose between the parties as to the amount of the outstanding balance due Ricker on the contract, and this action followed. . . .

At trial, the evidence conclusively established that Ricker's victualer's license, (a license to serve food or alcohol) issued in December 1969, had expired in May 1970. Similarly, the record established that Ricker did not have sanitation licenses for all its premises during the entire period. . . . [T]he last time the Maine court had had occasion to decide whether failure to comply with licensing statutes precluded recovery on a contract was over three-quarters of a century ago in a case involving $28 due an innkeeper. . . . [The Court in that case, refusing to enforce the contract, said:]

[W]here a license is required for the protection of the public, and to prevent improper persons from engaging in a particular business, and the license is not for revenue merely, a contract made by an unlicensed person in violation of the act is void. . . .

Thus, the issue squarely presented by this [case] is whether or not this court's decision in [the prior case referenced above] is still viable, thus barring the right of [Ricker] to recover the value of the services and lodging it supplied [to SIMS].

The licensing statute construed in [the earlier case] was identical to the one now in force . . .

The present statute provides that: "No person shall be a common innkeeper, victualer or tavernkeeper without a license, under a penalty of not more than $50."

[In the previous case, the] court construed the language of the statute as demonstrating a legislative intent "to prevent improper persons from engaging in a particular business" in the interest of public protection. Had the statute been enacted for revenue purposes only . . . the court concluded, the innkeeper could properly recover on his contract even though he was in violation of the licensing requirement.

In the absence of any express legislative intention to declare contracts made and performed by unlicensed innkeepers void, we will not infer such intention.

The statute fixes its own penalties. The additional penalty of nonenforceability of agreements is a judicial engraftment we now expressly reject as unduly harsh and unsound.

Why should one party to a contract be allowed to avoid the payment of debts he has contracted to pay and thus gain an unconscionable advantage because the other party deliberately, or through inability or mere oversight, has failed to discharge an obligation to the city when there is available to the city a remedy for the wrong?.

Cases in other jurisdictions which have discussed the question of enforceability of contracts under similar licensing statutes demonstrate a reluctance to apply [the law] where such application would produce an unduly harsh result. In some cases, the decision turns on the same distinction viz., whether the purpose of the statute is the collection of revenue (in which case the express statutory penalties are held to be exclusive), or the protection of public health and safety (in which case non-enforceability of the bargain may be inferred as an additional penalty). . . . Other courts have eschewed such distinction, but have allowed recovery under circumstances where equitable considerations weighed heavily against the imposition of a forfeiture. . . .

In some instances, the courts have circumvented rigid application of the rule by determining that a license was not required because the transaction was an isolated one and the plaintiff not really practicing the profession or engaged in the business described in the licensing statute. . . .

Finally, a few unlicensed plaintiffs have been allowed to recover, where such recovery would avoid inequities and unjust enrichment. . . .

We are satisfied it would be unjust and inequitable for us to rule that Ricker's noncompliance with the licensing statute makes its contract with SIMS void. We will not so hold in any case unless the legislature has mandated such result by specific terms in the statute.

CASE QUESTIONS

1. Why did the court deviate from stare decisis?
2. Why does the decision distinguish between a situation where only one guest fails to pay, and a situation where many fail to pay?

In another case in which a court avoided unjust enrichment, a restaurant utilized the services of an employment agency to hire an employee. The restaurant refused to pay the agency's fee because the agency lacked a license to operate as an employment agency. The agency sued the restaurant for its fee and the trial court dismissed the case because the agency was unlicensed and the purpose of the licensing requirement was to protect job seekers and employers from unscrupulous agencies. The agency appealed and the appellate court reversed, ordering the hotel to pay. The reason for the reversal was a technical one. The licensing statute, by its terms, was applicable only to employment agencies "regularly doing business" in the state, and the agency had never done business in the state before this one transaction. The appellate court thus held that, under the particular circumstances of this case, the licensing statute did not apply to the plaintiff employment agency and so it could sue for its fee. *S.A.S. Personnel Consultants, Inc. v. Pat-Pan, Inc.*, 407 A.2d 1139 (Md., 1979). If the employment agency regularly did business in the state, the decision of the appellate court would likely have been that the employment agency was not entitled to collect its fee.

The lesson from these cases is that a hotel or restaurant that does not obtain the required licenses risks losing the ability to enforce its contracts. To avoid the various penalties that await the unlicensed, innkeepers and restaurateurs should obtain all the mandated licenses.

Revocation or Suspension of a License

A license is a privilege, not a right. A licensee must establish it is worthy of the license; there is no automatic entitlement to it. If a licensee fails to continuously meet the requirements of the license, it can be suspended or revoked by the licensing body, which is usually a government agency.

Cause for Revocation or Suspension.   The legislature empowers a licensing board to revoke a license when it is satisfied that the licensee is unfit to hold a license. Licensed innkeepers who allow illegal or objectionable activity on the premises, such as illicit gambling or drinking by minors, may be found unfit to keep the license. A license was suspended where a restaurant and hotel had been actively used for bootlegging activities. *Bailey v. Runyon*, 293 S.W.2d 631 (Ky., 1956).

In the following case a restaurant was found to have tolerated numerous safety violations resulting in a denial of its application for renewal of its liquor license. Take note of the breadth of reasons in the relevant statute for denying a liquor license.

CASE EXAMPLE 15–12

**Oronoka Restaurant, Inc. v.
Maine State Liquor Commission
532 A.2d 1043 (Maine, 1987)**

. . . On January 8, 1986, Oronoka Restaurant (Oronoka) applied for the renewal of its liquor license. On February 10, 1986, the municipal officers of the Town of Orono [in which the restaurant was located] conducted a public hearing on the application and voted unanimously to deny the application for renewal. The Town based its decision on sewage discharge violations, numerous fire code violations, and the failure of the applicant to allow the Town's code enforcement officer access to the premises to inspect for code or ordinance vi-

olations. Oronoka filed a timely appeal with the Maine State Liquor Commission (Commission). The Commission ruled that the fire code violations constituted health and safety hazards and thus were valid grounds to deny the application for renewal. . . .

Under the [applicable state statute] the Commission may consider all of the following as grounds to deny a liquor license:

A. Conviction of the applicant of any [of a specified level of crime];

B. Noncompliance of the licensed premise with any local zoning ordinance or other land use ordinance not directly related to liquor control;

C. Conditions of record such as waste disposal

violations, health or safety violations, or repeated parking or traffic violations on or in the vicinity of the licensed premises and caused by persons patronizing or employed by the licensed premises or other such conditions caused by persons patronizing or employed by the licensed premises which unreasonably disturb, interfere with or affect the ability of persons or businesses residing or located in the vicinity of the licensed premises to use their property in a reasonable manner;

D. Repeated incidents or record of breaches of the peace, disorderly conduct, vandalism or other violations of law on or in the vicinity of the licensed premises and caused by persons patronizing or employed by the licensed premises; and

E. A violation of any [of the liquor sales laws]. . . . The Commission heard extensive and very

specific testimony concerning the fire code violations from the Town's fire chief and its code enforcement officer. Of particular concern was an unlicensed, unapproved and illegally installed solid fuel unit or "wood burning boiler." Witnesses testified that the unit lacked appropriate safety systems and could possibly explode. Despite repeated warnings by Town officials that the boiler failed to meet applicable safety standards, Oronoka's owner, as of the time of the Town hearing, had not brought the unit into compliance and had not obtained the necessary approval for its use.

The hazards solid fuel unit and Oronoka's other fire code violations fall within the ground s specified [by the state statue] upon which a town may deny a liquor license renewal. . . . We affirm the judgment.

CASE QUESTION

1. Why are safety violations relevant to the renewal of a liquor license?

A license might also be suspended if the licensee provided false information on the application. Thus, where a restaurant obtained a license to operate a family style eatery but instead offered nude dancing and the "hottest adult entertainment to hit the Northeast," its license was suspended. *D.H.L. Associates, Inc. v. Krussel*, 1996 WL 754910 (1996).

A victualer's license cannot be revoked for mere failure by the proprietor to ask known prostitutes or other criminals to leave if they are not engaging in illegal activity at the restaurant. Thus, the license of a coffee shop owner which had been revoked because of the presence of known prostitutes was reinstated on appeal. *Saxon Coffee Shop v. Boston Licensing Board*, 407 N.E.2d 311 (Mass., 1980). A licensing body likewise acted beyond its authority in *Company-IHOP Restaurant v. Town of Saugus*, 1997 WL 339117 (Mass., 1997). The Town issued the International House of Pancakes (IHOP) a victualer's license that restricted the restaurant's hours to 6:00 A.M. through 1:00 A.M. IHOP sought to operate 24 hours per day and challenged the town's authority to limit its hours of business. After reviewing the legislative history of the licensing statute, the court concluded that the Town was not authorized to regulate IHOP's hours of operation. Commenting on this lack of authority, the court stated, "This count concedes that this interpretation promises some unfortunate consequences. It is perfectly understandable why the Board of Selectmen would wish to limit the hours of certain restaurants, particularly those such as IHOP that are near residential areas."

Due Process.   The licensee is entitled to **due process**, the right not to be deprived of life, liberty, or property (including a license) without a fair hearing. This means that, before a license can be revoked, the licensee is entitled to reasonable notice of the grounds for revocation, an opportunity to prepare a defense, and a hearing.

In the notice, the licensee is entitled to information identifying the specific conduct attributable to him that allegedly violates the rules relating to the license. The reason for this rule is to provide sufficient information to enable the licensee to address the allegations and prepare a defense. Clearly, a notice of revocation that does not state the grounds for the proposed revocation is not sufficiently specific. In *Manchester v. Selectmen of Nantucket*, 293 S.W.2d 631 (Ky., 1956), the licensee was charged with operating a hotel improperly. The licensing body gave Manchester the following notice:

> *You are herewith advised that . . . a hearing will be held at 10 AM Wednesday, August 24, 1955, at the Selectmen's Rooms, 17 Federal Street, on complaints received by the board as regards your operation of the premises known as "Nantucket New Ocean House."*

The court held this notice did not adequately inform the license holder of the charges she faced, and thus violated her due process rights.

To satisfy due process rights, not just the notice of the grounds for revocation but also the date of the hearing must be given far enough in advance of the hearing that the licensee has time to prepare a defense. In another case, a lounge was licensed to provide live entertainment including exotic dancing. One night it presented male dancers rather than the usual females. The crowd exceeded permissible building capacity. Two days later the town Board of Selectmen, the body that issues and revokes entertainment licenses, notified the owner of the lounge at 5:30 P.M. that a special meeting would be held that evening at 7:00 P.M. to consider the revocation of his license. This short notice was held to be violative of the owner's due process rights. *Konstantopoulos v. Town of Whately*, 424 N.E.2d 210 (Mass., 1981).

Where a licensee receives a notice to appear before the licensing board and believes the notice is inadequate, the licensee should request additional information concerning the charges or additional time to prepare a defense, as the case may be. Failure to object may result in a waiver of any due process defects in the notice.

Zoning

Zoning is a process by which local governments can restrict the ways property owners can use their land. For example, a zoning ordinance may restrict use of property to residential purposes and preclude commercial and industrial uses, or may provide a maximum height for a building—for example, five stories; or may restrict the size and type of sign a business can display on its property to advertise its services—for example, flashing neon signs may be prohibited.

For the would-be innkeeper or restaurateur, zoning laws may ban development of a planned business. For example, a commercial establishment will not be permitted in an area zoned residential. Before any resources are committed to a new hotel or restaurant, the owner should investigate the zoning restrictions.

The purpose of zoning laws is to achieve balanced development, preserve the residential quality of residential neighborhoods, and minimize adverse effects resulting from inappropriate location, use, or design of certain buildings or businesses. A 1991 Connecticut case further clarifies zoning's objectives. It involved a zoning district in the Town of Stratford in which only single-family residences were permitted. The owners of one of the homes operated a rooming house with ten boarders. The zoning enforcement officer ordered the owners to terminate the boarding house. The owners, wanting to continue to operate the boarding house, challenged the law. The court upheld it, stating,

> *[Local governments are empowered] to lay out zones where family values, youth values, and the blessings of quiet seclusion and clean air make the area of sanctuary for people . . . [b]oarding houses . . . present urban problems. More people occupy a given space; more cars rather continuously pass by; more cars are parked; noise travels with crowds.* **Dinan v. Board of Zoning Appeals of the Town of Stratford**, *595 A.2d 864 (Conn., 1991).*

In the following case a sports bar violated a local zoning ordinance and therefore was required to discontinue its business.

CASE EXAMPLE 15–13

Schleuter v. City of Fort Worth
947 SW.2d 920 (Tex., 1997)

. . . In an attempt to mitigate the negative secondary effects of sexually oriented businesses, the City of Fort Worth added sections to its Comprehensive Zoning Ordinance (CZO). A person violates the CZO if he or she operates a "sexually oriented business" within 1000 feet of residentially zoned property. "Sexually oriented business" is defined as any commercial venture whose operations include the 'providing, featuring or offering of employees or entertainment personnel who appear on the premises while in a state of nudity or simulated nudity.'" . . .

On May 11, 1995, Sports Fantasy opened for business in Fort Worth. Sports Fantasy is a "sports bar" . . . described by the owner as an "upscale sports bar . . . catered to gentlemen clientele." Sports Fantasy featured entertainment in the form of "state dancing" by female entertainers." While dancing, the female entertainers would strip their clothing off to the point where they would only be wearing "T-back" bottoms and latex pasties covering only the areola of their breasts. Sports Fantasy was located within 1000 feet of residentially zoned property.

After a bench trial the trial court entered a permanent injunction against Fantasy Sports [prohibiting it from carrying on a sexually oriented business].

[On appeal, the sports bar raised various arguments seeking to have the zoning ordinance declared invalid and unenforceable. The court rejected these arguments, determined the ordinance was valid and enforceable, and affirmed the injunction.]

In circumstances where zoning laws prohibit a desired use or development, the land owner can seek a **variance**, which is permission from the local government to deviate from the restrictions. Variances are given only when the deviation will not have a significant negative impact on the goals sought by the zoning law in issue.

In a 1991 New Jersey case, a hotel sought a variance from a zoning ordinance which limited hotels in a particular district to two stories and 35 feet in height. The hotel seeking the variance wanted to build a five-story, 45 foot high hotel. The local planning board granted the variance and the town appealed. The court upheld the variance for three reasons: (1) office buildings in the district were permitted to be six stories and 90 feet high; (2) the facade of the proposed hotel was designed to resemble the nearby offices; and (3) the hotel was targeted to commercial travelers and so would complement the surrounding commercial area. The court thus concluded that granting a variance for the hotel's height was consistent with commercial development in the area and had "positive relevance to the town's planned economic development." *Commercial Realty & Resources Corp. v. First Atlantic Properties Co.*, 585 A.2d 928 (N.J., 1991).

Summary

The business of operating a hotel or restaurant is highly regulated. The owner must be aware of applicable laws to avoid liability for their violation.

Businesses are prohibited from using another's trademark or service mark, as well as copyrighted works, without the permission of the owner. One arrangement where permission is granted to use a trademark or service mark is franchising. The relationship between a franchisor and franchisee is contractual. The parties should include in their agreement all terms important to them relevant to their relationship.

To encourage competition, the law prohibits certain practices that restrain competition. The laws that ban these practices are called antitrust laws.

A hotel is required to maintain a guest register including some or all of the following information, depending on the state: names; addresses; make and model of car; license number; room assignment; and date and hour of arrival. The innkeeper may also be required to post notices of the rates charged for rooms.

Concerns about protecting our environment have engendered laws mandating recycling. While the particular requirements vary from state to state, the purpose of these laws is to save natural resources, reduce pollution, and reduce the amount of waste that goes into landfills.

An innkeeper or restaurateur must obtain all necessary licenses. Operating a business without the required licenses can result in the business being closed, fines being imposed, and contracts being unenforceable. Zoning laws restrict the permissible uses of land. For example, a business cannot be built in an area which is zoned residential.

Preventive Law Tips for Managers

- *Do a trademark search before adopting a name for your hotel or restaurant.* Use of another's trademark or service mark can result in forced discontinuance of a name in which you have invested money to advertise and promote. This can be avoided by undertaking a trademark search prior to adopting the name. The search is customarily done by a trademark attorney who has the necessary computer program. It reveals the names of any other businesses that are using the same or similar name you propose to use. If someone else is already using it for a similar product, you can save promotion money and an infringement lawsuit by selecting another name.

- *Do not intercept and transmit copyrighted television programs without the permission of the copyright owner.* Use of a satellite dish to intercept copyrighted programming without the permission of the copyright owners constitutes copyright infringement and can lead to an expensive lawsuit. If you want to offer your guests the opportunity to watch cable television in their rooms or to view limited access sporting events in a bar or restaurant, make the necessary arrangements with the cable stations to receive cable programming through legal means.

- *Do not offer musical entertainment without first obtaining a license from ASCAP and BMI.* Providing music for the enjoyment of a hotel or restaurant's patrons without purchasing the required copyright licenses constitutes copyright infringement. To comply with the law and avoid a lawsuit, make the necessary arrangements with the organizations that represent the owners of copyrights in music compositions and recordings.

- *Review the operating practices of your hotel or restaurant to be sure you are not in violation of antitrust laws.* Failure to comply with antitrust laws results in criminal liability and steep damage awards (treble damages) in civil cases. You should initiate regular reviews of the practices of your hotel or restaurant—including pricing, purchasing, selling, advertising, and relationships with other hotels—to ensure the hotel is not engaging in antitrust violations. Use for this purpose the checklist of illegal activities contained in this chapter.

- *If you buy a franchise, review carefully the disclosure documents and discuss them with your attorney and accountant before making a decision to buy.* By law, a franchisor is required to disclose in writing detailed information about the franchise operation at least ten days prior to accepting any money from a franchisee. Review this information carefully and ask your lawyer and accountant to do the same. The purpose for the disclosure requirement is to give a potential franchisee time to absorb and evaluate all relevant information. Take advantage of the law.

- *If you buy a franchise, be sure all agreements are embodied in the contractual agreement.* The contract between the franchisor and franchisee should be embodied in a written document. The terms of the contract should accurately reflect the understanding of the parties. Read the contract carefully before signing to ensure the terms are as expected and all agreements are included.

- *As a manager, keep fully apprised of your employees' actions and practices.* As seen in *United States v. Hilton Hotels Corp.*, (p. 500), an employer may be liable for the acts of its employees even when the employee is violating the employer's policies. To avoid liability on this ground, keep close tabs on your employees. Inquire often about methods they are using to fulfill job responsibilities, watch them work, review their outgoing mail, meet with them frequently to discuss the job.

- *Keep a register of guests' names and other information required by law.* Laws in most states require an innkeeper to keep a record of information about all registered guests at the hotel and to preserve the record for a specified period of time. The type of information required varies from state to state but customarily includes the guest's name and address, make and model of any car parked at the hotel, the license number, date and time of arrival, and room number assigned. Failure to maintain the register or failure to show the register to an inquiring law enforcement officer violates the law and leads to penalties. Be sure to obtain the necessary information from your guests, preserve the register for the time period required, and provide it to those legally entitled to access.

- *File and post room rates.* Laws in many states require innkeepers to post the rates at the hotel in a place where they will be easily seen. Whenever the rates are changed, the new rates must likewise be posted.

- *Comply with recycling laws applicable in the locality where your business is located.* Laws requiring businesses to recycle parts of their waste have been adopted in most states and localities. Typically these laws require a restaurant to recycle glass, metal, aluminum, and some plastic containers. Failure to comply can result in fines, and damages the environment.

- *Determine the necessary licenses and permits needed for your business and take the necessary steps to obtain them.* Failure to obtain necessary licenses and permits can result in the government forcing you to close your business, fines, and inability to enforce your contracts. The types of licenses needed for a particular business vary from locality to locality. You should check with your lawyer to ensure you are aware of all the licenses and permits you will need. Thereafter you should contact the relevant government officials to determine what conditions must be met to qualify for the licenses, and then satisfy those conditions.

- *Determine whether and when your licenses must be renewed and take the necessary steps to renew them.* Failure to renew a license or permit within the allotted time can result in the same penalties as failing to obtain a license when you first open your business. Check with your lawyer or the governmental entity responsible for administering the license to determine when your licenses must be renewed and the process you must follow. Do the necessary to ensure your licenses do not expire without obtaining a renewal.

- *When planning to build or expand a hotel or restaurant, comply with the zoning laws or seek a variance.* Zoning laws restrict the ways in which land and buildings can be used. Planning a construction project without verifying that the proposed use and construction comply with applicable zoning laws can result in having to abandon or scale down a project. Advance research of the zoning laws will enable you to plan within zoning restrictions and avoid unwanted and costly surprises.

Review Questions

1. What interest does a city have in requiring a hotel to maintain a register containing guests' names, addresses, type of car and license plate numbers?
2. What is the objective of the antitrust laws?
3. Name and define three examples of per se violations of the antitrust laws.
4. Name and define three examples of antitrust violations subject to the rule of reason.
5. Must a business register its name to obtain trademark protection? If not, how else is protection obtained?
6. What constitutes a trademark infringement?
7. What is a franchise?
8. What information must a franchisor disclose to a franchisee?
9. What is a copyright? Give three examples of copyrighted works.
10. What are the objectives of recycling laws?
11. What is the purpose of zoning laws?
12. If zoning laws negatively impact you, what remedy can you seek?
13. What is the basis for the government's authority to require hotels and restaurants to obtain a license before opening their business?
14. What penalties can be imposed on a business that operates without the necessary licenses?
15. If the government wants to revoke a liquor license, what rights, if any, does the licensee have?

Discussion Questions

1. What is the policy reason behind the requirement that licensees must be given due process rights before a license can be revoked?

2. Why are some violations of the antitrust laws subject to the rule of reason and others are violations per se?

3. In the Holiday Inn trademark case, Findings of Fact, paragraph 3, the judge, while talking about the great sign, said that in some locals the Holiday Inn chain uses smaller versions to comply with local zoning laws. What objective would be fulfilled by limiting the size of business signs?

4. Buy a soda and look at the can. How many copyright and trademark notices do you see? What aspect of the soda can is copyrighted?

5. Xerox Corporation, known for its copiers and other office machines, has expressed concern that it may lose its trademark on the name Xerox. Indeed, it has advertised in various trade journals that Xerox has two "R's" in it. Why is the trademark in the name in jeopardy, and what is meant when the company says there are two "R's" in Xerox?

6. In what ways do the disclosure requirements imposed on franchisors help franchisees to avoid becoming victims of dishonest franchisors?

Application Questions

1. Sharina is a franchisee of Burger King. She has an exclusive territory with a five mile radius in which Burger King cannot authorize anyone else to open a Burger King restaurant. Does this agreement violate the antitrust laws? Why or why not?

2. You are licensed to operate a hotel in a summer tourist area. You receive a notice from the town council, which has the authority to issue and revoke licenses, that your license may be revoked because of illegal activity occurring at your hotel. What rights do you have concerning the revocation proceeding? What action should you take in response to this notice? What will happen if you take no action?

3. Tamika opened a restaurant in California and named it "The Best in the West." The nationwide hotel chain of Best Western brought a trademark action against Tamika for her choice of names. What factors will the judge consider in deciding whether or not Tamika has violated the Best Western trademark? How would you rule on the issue? Why?

4. Samantha bought a taco at a Mexican food franchise. When she took a bite of the food, she discovered a piece of glass in it. The glass injured her gums. What additional information would you need to know to determine if the franchisor is liable to Samantha for her injuries?

CHAPTER 16

The Developing Law of Casinos

CHAPTER OUTLINE

Introduction

Contracts and Gambling Debts

Torts Involving Casinos

Sexual Harassment at Casinos

Criminal Activity at Casinos

Casinos and the Dram Shop Act

Riverboat Casinos and the Jones Act

Casinos on Native American Reservations

INTRODUCTION

An exciting development in the hospitality industry is the increased numbers of casinos and casino resorts. Just as these facilities present unique management challenges, they create specialized legal issues and applications as well. This chapter will look at the developing law of casinos. In the chapter you will reacquaint yourself with some areas of law we have studied in other sections of this book but the application here will be limited to casinos. You will also learn about laws we have not yet studied that are applicable exclusively to casinos.

Contracts and Gambling Debts

Many casino patrons who bet large amounts of money will establish credit with the casino. The transaction is a contractual one, not unlike seeking credit on a Visa or Mastercharge card. See the discussion on contract law in chapter 4. In a credit transaction, the casino agrees to extend credit to the patron to enable her to gamble. In return, the customer agrees to repay the casino for the amount borrowed plus interest. The patron hopes to make money on gambling in which case reimbursement to the casino is easy. Unfortunately a gambler often loses. If the patron fails to repay the casino, it will likely pursue payment in court. The action is based on contract. As in any contract case, the gambler can assert any applicable contract defenses including incapacity (underage, mentally incompetent, or very intoxicated), duress (threats of harm) and unconscionability (grossly unfair resulting from unequal bargaining power).

One case addressing this issue involved a gambler who, in a 24 hour period, incurred over $165,000 in gambling debts at several casinos. He alleged he was a compulsive gambler and offered as evidence of this condition the following. At various casinos he was abusive, cursed the dealers, accused them of cheating him, threw cards, smashed an ashtray, and made a spectacle of himself. He asserted that because he was a compulsive gambler, it was unconscionable of the casino to have extended him credit. The casino defendants sought to have the case dismissed for failure of the plaintiff to state a cause of action. The court rejected plaintiff's defense of compulsive gambling, stating, "This court finds no support in legislation or case law that the disorder of compulsive gambling should, in and of itself, be recognized as a defense to capacity to contract which will render a contract void." *Lomonaco v. Sands Hotel Casino and Country Club*, 614 A.D.2d 634 (Superior Crt., 1992). Thus we learn that, the circumstance of being a compulsive gambler will not relieve the borrower from liability to repay a gambling debt.

Compulsive Gamblers

Unfortunately, some people suffer from a recognized disorder called pathological gambler, that is, an inability to refrain from gambling. It is a recognized illness in the field of psychology. The casino industry has addressed this problem in certain ways. For example, in Atlantic City, a person who knows s/he is a compulsive gambler can initiate placement of his name on a list of persons to whom the extension of credit by a casino is prohibited. The list is kept by the Casino Control Commission, an agency that regulates casinos, which is required to provide the list to the credit departments of each casino. N.J.S.A. 5:12-101(j).

Congress has created the National Gambling Impact and Policy Commission to conduct a study of the social and economic impact of gambling at all levels of our society. Among the issues the Commission will review is, "pathological or problem gambling and its impact on society." The resulting data will be used for the development of future legislation dealing with gaming. The commission's report is due in June, 1999.

Torts Involving Casinos

Negligence

The rules of negligence applicable to hotels and restaurants are also applicable to casinos. See the discussion of negligence in chapter 5. Like other hospitality facilities, casinos are not insurers of their guests' safety. They are however obligated to act reasonably to safeguard the wellbeing of their patrons.

A plaintiff was playing nickel poker in a slot machine at the Grand Casino in Golfport, Mississippi. She noticed a chair to her immediate right. While putting money in the machine she reached back to pull the chair to her and began to sit. Unfortunately, in the short interim the chair was moved. When she started to sit she lost her balance and fell to the floor. She sued the casino claiming it had provided an insufficient number of chairs to accommodate the players. The casino established that it provided one seat for each slot machine and that virtually all slot machines are designed to be played by only one patron at a time. The court, holding in favor of the casino, held plaintiff was negligent for attempting to sit on the chair before she made certain she had a place to sit. Said the court, "Plaintiff's inattentiveness resulted in her fall, not an unsafe condition of the casino." *Greco v. Grand Casinos of Mississippi*, 1996 WL 617401 (La., 1996). If the number of chairs in the slot machine area had been less than one per machine the casino would likely have been at least partially liable.

In another case the injured party was a change attendant on a riverboat casino. Her duties included selling customers slot machine tokens which she carried in a velcro change belt tied around her waist. Depending on the amount of tokens in the belt, it could weigh as much as 50 pounds. All change attendants had their own storage container known as a change bank, which was stocked with buckets of tokens delivered on a mobile change cart. When plaintiff's change bank ran low, she ordered additional tokens from a slot attendant who brought the token order to her in buckets on a mobile change cart. The buckets had handles and weighed approximately five to ten pounds. All change attendants were required to lift the buckets from the change cart to their individual change bank. They then replenished the change belt from the change bank. One day, while lifting the buckets, she suffered a back pain for which she sought treatment. It was diagnosed as a dorsal spine sprain resulting from her job and required physical therapy. She was permanently restricted from lifting more than 35–40 pounds.

Plaintiff sought damages from the casino claiming it was negligent for requiring her to carry such heavy loads in the course of her job. The casino moved to dismiss the case on the ground it had done nothing illegal. The court refused to dismiss the case holding that a reasonable jury could find that the employer failed to use reasonable care in providing plaintiff with safe equipment to perform the job. For example, the jury might conclude that the employer should have provided plaintiff with a mobile cart to carry the change rather than wearing a heavy change belt and lifting buckets of tokens. *Watson v. Hollywood Casino-Aurora, Inc.*, 1996 WL 559960 (Ill., 1996).

[Note: while in most states lawsuits by employees against employers are controlled by Workers' Compensation Laws, different rules may apply when the employer is at sea. See the discussion of the Jones Act later in this chapter.]

The following case addresses the liability of a casino to a guest having a medical emergency while gambling. Note the emergency response system in place by the casino.

CASE EXAMPLE 16–1

Lundy v.
Adamar of New Jersey, Inc. t/a Trop World
34 F.3d 1173 (3rd Cir., 1994).

Appellant Sidney Lundy suffered a heart attack while a patron at appellee's casino, TropWorld Casino ("TropWorld"), in Atlantic City, New Jersey. While he survived, Lundy was left with permanent disabilities. . . .

On August 3, 1989, Lundy, a 66 year old man with a history of coronary artery disease, was patronizing TropWorld Casino. While Lundy was gambling at a blackjack table, he suffered cardiac arrest and fell to the ground unconscious. Three other patrons [including a critical nurse, a surgeon and a Dr. Geenberg, a pulmonary specialist] quickly ran to Lundy and began to assist him. . . .

Meanwhile, the blackjack dealer at the table where Lundy had been gambling pushed an emergency "call" button at his table which alerted TropWorld's Security Command Post that a problem existed. The Security Command Post is electronically designed to designate the location from which such alarms are triggered and record the time that the alarm is sounded. The alarm was recorded as being received at 10:57 P.M. Noting that the source of the alarm was "Pit 3," a Security Command Post employee notified by phone the security post located on the casino floor near where Lundy had suffered his cardiac arrest. At

10:59 P.M., the Security Command Post employee sent radio directions to all of the guards on the casino floor requesting that they each go to Lundy's location.

A sergeant in Trop/world's security force and a tropWorld security guard arrived at the blackjack table apparently within fifteen seconds of their receiving the radio message from the Security Command Post. [The three patrons] were already assisting Lundy. Upon arriving, the security guard called the Security Command Post on her handheld radio and requested that someone contact the casino medical station, which was located one floor above the casino. Several witnesses agree that Nurse Margaret Slusher ("Nurse Slusher"), the nurse who was on duty at the casino medical station at the time, arrived on the scene within a minute or two of being summoned. As soon as Nurse Slusher arrived, she instructed the security guards to call for an ambulance. TropWorld's records indicate that an ambulance was summoned at 11:00 P.M.

Nurse Slusher brought with her an ambu-bag, oxygen, and an airway. She did not, however, bring an intubation kit [a tube inserted into one's trachea to help restore the ability to breath] to the scene. Dr. Greenberg testified that he asked Nurse Slusher for one and she told him that it was TropWorld's "policy" not to have an intubation kit on the premises. . . . Nurse Slusher testified that some of the equipment normally found in an intubation kit was stocked in TropWorld's medical center, but that she did not bring this equipment with her because she was not qualified to use it.

Nurse Slusher proceeded to assist the three patrons in performing CPR on Lundy. Specifically, Nurse Slusher placed the ambu-bag over Lundy's face while the others took turns doing chest compressions. . . . Dr. Greenberg testified that he was sure that air was entering Lundy's respiratory system and that Lundy was being adequately oxygenated during the period when he was receiving both CPR treatment and air through the ambu-bag. Dr. Greenberg went on to say that the only reason he had requested an intubation kit was "to establish an airway and subsequently provide oxygen in a more efficient manner."

. . . [A]n Emergency Medical Technician ("EMT") unit arrived at TropWorld by ambulance at approximately 11:03 P.M. A technician, with the help of the two doctor patrons, attempted to intubate Lundy using an intubation kit brought by the EMT unit. Dr. Greenberg claimed that, due to Lundy's stout physique and rigid muscle tone, it was a very difficult intubation, and that there were at least a half dozen failed attempts before the procedure was successfully completed. After intubation, Lundy regained a pulse and his color improved. According to EMT reports, the ambulance departed from TropWorld with Lundy at 11:27 P.M. . . .

TropWorld had a contract with Dr. Carlino providing that he would run an in-house medical station to supply medical services for TropWorld's employees, guests, and patrons in cases of work-related injuries and injuries or sicknesses occurring on the premises. The contract required that Dr. Carlino provide a licensed physician on the casino premises for five hours each day, and a physician "on-call" for the rest of the day. . . Furthermore, Dr. Carlino was obligated to have a registered nurse present in the medical station during the hours that the casino was open. . . . In August of 1989, Nurse Slusher was a registered, licensed nurse . . . .

The District Court held that TropWorld had fulfilled its duty to Lundy . . .

Generally, a bystander has no duty to provide affirmative aid to an injured person, even if the bystander has the ability to help. New Jersey courts have recognized, however, that the existence of a relationship between the victim and one in a position to render aid may create a duty to render assistance. . . . .

The Restatement of Torts [a compilation of rules used for guidance by courts] provides that an innkeeper is under a duty to its guests "to take reasonable action to protect them against unreasonable risk of physical harm and to give them first aid after it knows or has reason to know that they are ill or injured, and to care for them until they can be cared for by others. . . ". The duty does not extend to providing all medical care that the innkeeper could reasonably foresee might be needed by a patron.

Nurse Slusher was a registered, licensed nurse who had been trained in emergency care and who had fifteen years of nursing experience. Despite this training and experience, she was not competent to perform an intubation. The Lundys claim the casino was obligated to provide full-time on-site capability to perform intubations. Certainly, maintaining on a full-time basis the capability of performing an intubation goes far beyond any "first aid" contemplated by the Restatement of Torts. . .

We understand Lundy's contention to be that Nurse Slusher should have returned to the medical center and retrieved the intubation tube for Dr. Greenberg's use, and TropWorld is liable for her failure to do so. We reject the notion that TropWorld, by contracting with Dr. Carlino, voluntarily assumed a duty to Mr. Lundy it would not otherwise have had. . . .

The duty owed to Mr. Lundy was a duty limited to summoning aid and, in the interim, taking reasonable first aid measures. It did not include the duty to provide medical equipment and personnel necessary to perform an intubation. . . .

The judgment of the district court [granting summary judgment to the casino] will be affirmed.

CASE QUESTIONS

1. How big a role did the casino emergency alarm system play in the court's decision?

2. Why do the Restatement of Torts and the courts impose a duty on the casino to provide first aid to a patron in distress?

False Imprisonment

False imprisonment occurs when a person is restrained without justification against his will. See the discussion of false imprisonment in Chapter 11. Occasionally a facility believes a patron has engaged in illegal activity and wants to detain the person during an investigation. A potential problem exists. If the investigation reveals that the patron has done nothing illegal, the facility may be liable for false imprisonment. To save casinos from this liability, some states have adopted a defense for gambling establishments for this type of claim. The defense authorizes the casino to detain a person if it has probable cause to believe the patron is engaging in criminal activity. "Probable cause" means sufficient evidence to lead a reasonable person to conclude that the individual detained was committing a crime. Probable cause is to be distinguished from a whim or guess.

In the following case the casino lacked probable cause for the detention of a keno player and thus was liable for false imprisonment. This case also contains an insightful discussion of certain rules relating to this popular casino game.

CASE EXAMPLE 16–2

Hazelwood v. Harrah's
862 P.2d 1189 (Nev., 1993)

Phillip Hazelwood was a regular patron of Harrah's Club of Reno where he played keno with his friend Frank Ivaldi ("Ivaldi"). The two were acquainted with several Harrah's employees.

On June 9, 1990, Hazelwood and Ivaldi were at Harrah's Club as participants in a keno tournament. While waiting for a keno tournament dinner, Hazelwood noticed that a keno game being played was delayed, and from experience he knew that someone had won the game. Hazelwood confirmed this with keno supervisor James Eto ("Eto"), who told Hazelwood that a $20,000 ticket had not been presented for payment. Eto gave Hazelwood permission to search for the discarded ticket in the trash. Eto did not inform Hazelwood that what he was doing might be wrong. Hazelwood took the trash bag to his room, found the ticket, and re-

turned to the kino area to inform Eto and obtain payment of $20,000.

Eto began to follow Harrah's procedures for confirmation of the ticket and payment by calling the surveillance supervisor on duty. The surveillance supervisor refused to sign off on the ticket due to this unusual situation which apparently no one had previously encountered. Harrah's Club keno manager was informed that Hazelwood had found a ticket and presented it for payment. After considerable discussion, the Harrah's Club employees decided that the Gaming Control Board [a regulatory body for casinos] should be called. According to Nevada law, whenever a dispute occurs concerning a payment exceeding $500, the Gaming Control Board must be called.

Surveillance department employees asked Hazelwood to accompany them to the keno manager's office. Hazelwood asked if Ivaldi could come as well and was told he could. Hazelwood testified that on the way to the office, a Harrah's Club employee told him it was a crime for someone to cash a ticket for which he had not paid.

Hazelwood claimed that once inside the manager's office, he "knew" he could not leave. The Club employee told Hazelwood that he had been instructed by the Gaming Control Board to inform Hazelwood that he would not be paid for the ticket since he had not purchased it. The Club employee then made a phone call and shortly thereafter three agents from the Gaming Control Board arrived.

Hazelwood went to another room with the agents. They read Hazelwood his constitutional rights [the so-called Miranda Warnings]. One of the agents, John Dickenson ("Dickenson"), informed Hazelwood that in order to receive winnings from a gambling game, it was necessary to purchase a ticket. He also informed Hazelwood that in Nevada it is unlawful to claim, collect or attempt to collect a wager with the intent to commit fraud. . . .

The three agents decided to refer the matter to the district attorney. One of the agents testified that he was not informed of Eto's comments to Hazelwood about the lost ticket. However, another agent testified that had he been informed of Eto's actions, he still would have submitted a report to the district attorney.

Shortly thereafter, Hazelwood filed a complaint against Harrah's claiming false imprisonment, negligence and negligent misrepresentation.

On December 7, 1990, two police officers visited Hazelwood's home to inform him that they had a felony warrant for his arrest. Hazelwood turned himself in and was booked in Reno on December 11, 1990. The charges were dismissed over a year later.

On the tort claims, the jury returned a verdict for Hazelwood, awarding $425,000. Harrah's filed a motion for judgment notwithstanding the verdict or, in the alternative, a motion for a new trial on the grounds that Hazelwood had failed to prove essential elements of his claims.

The court granted Harrah's motion for a new trial on damages, finding that the verdict was apparently based on passion and prejudice. However, the court provided Hazelwood with the option of accepting $200,000. In so doing, the court noted that Hazelwood provided no evidence of physical injury. It also noted that Hazelwood, a retired California Highway Patrol Officer, facing Harrah's, a large corporation, must have incited feelings of passion and prejudice in the jury. . . .

Harrah's argues that it is immune from civil liability for false imprisonment under Nevada law NRS 465.101(1) which provides that any licensed casino or its officers may question any person in his establishment suspected of violating any of the gaming statutes without incurring civil liability. In addition, this statute also allows the licensee to detain the suspect provided the detention is for a reasonable time and the licensee has probable cause to believe a violation has occurred, again without incurring civil liability for false imprisonment.

The district court correctly points out that Harrah's employees failed to obtain more information concerning Hazelwood's possible violation of any statute. [Had they done so, they would have learned that Hazelwood acted with Eto's approval.] The failure to inquire caused the detention to be unreasonable and without probable cause. Therefore, we hold that the district court was correct in finding that Harrah's was not immune from civil liability under Nevada law.

As to negligence and negligent misrepresentation, we agree with the district court that the statements made by Eto created a false impression in the mind of Hazelwood; that is, that there was nothing improper about looking for the discarded ticket and that if he found it, he would be paid.

CASE QUESTIONS

1. Why was Harrah's not entitled to the benefit of the statutory defense for false imprisonment?

2. What rules about the game of keno do we learn from this game?

Trademark Infringement

A trademark is a name or logo that identifies the source of a product or service. See the discussion of trademarks in Chapter 15. A well-known trademark has considerable value in attracting customers. For example, if you decide to have a hamburger for lunch, you would be more apt to stop at McDonald's, Wendy's or Burger King than a place called Karen's Hamburgers. The reason is that you are familiar with the former but not the latter. Rather than take a chance on something new, many people will go where they know the product.

As a result, a trademark of a popular product can be very valuable. Occasionally competing companies will adopt a trademark similar to the leading company in the field. Their purpose may be to divert customers to their establishment. This is unfair to the owner of the popular trademark. To help prevent this, the law makes illegal the use of a trademark that is confusingly similar to another business' mark. An example of such a circumstance is provided in the following case.

CASE EXAMPLE 16–3

Resorts International, Inc. v. Greate Bay Hotel and Casino, Inc.
22 U.S.P.Q.2d 1740 (N.J., 1992)

. . . Resorts International, Inc. ("Resorts") owns and operates a casino on the boardwalk in Atlantic City, and owns and operates the resort and casino "Paradise Island," located on Paradise Island in the Bahamas. Greate Bay Hotel and Casino, Inc, otherwise referred to as the Sands Hotel Casino and Country Club ("the Sands") also owns and operates a casino on the boardwalk in Atlantic city. In May 1990, the Sands opened a new slot lounge which it called "Paradise Isle." Resorts brought suit against defendant Sands alleging trademark infringement, specifically that the Sands' use of "Paradise Isle" infringed on Resorts' "Paradise Island" mark;. . . .

There are two elements to recovery for trademark infringement. First, plaintiff's mark must be a valid, legally protectible mark. Second, there must be a "likelihood of confusion" between plaintiff's mark and defendant's mark.

[The parties did not dispute that Resorts' mark was valid and legally protectible.] Sands contests that there exists a likelihood of confusion.

The likelihood of consumer confusion between plaintiff's and defendant's marks is the test for infringement. Likelihood of confusion exists when consumers viewing the mark would probably assume that the product or service it represents is associated with the source of a different product or service identified with a similar mark. Likelihood of confusion should be determined by viewing the two marks from the perspective of an ordinary consumer of the goods or services.

In determining likelihood of confusion, the court should consider the following factors:

1. the degree of similarity between the plaintiff's mark and the alleged infringing mark;
2. the strength of the plaintiff's mark;
3. the price of the goods and other factors indicative of the care and attention expected of consumers when making a purchase;
4. the length of time the defendant has used the mark without evidence of actual confusion arising;
5. the defendant's intent in adopting the mark;
6. the evidence of actual confusion;
7. the extent to which the targets of the parties' sales efforts are the same.

A likelihood of confusion exists if parties offer competing services, such as the casinos now before us, and if the court determines that these factors are present in sufficient number or intensity.

First Resorts' "Paradise Island" and Sands' "Paradise Isle" are nearly identical as to their appearance, sound and meaning, as well as in the manner in which they are used. The degree of similarity is consequently very high. This dictates in favor of Resorts. . . .

Third, the price of services indicative of care and attention expected of consumers making a purchase did not in this case present a likelihood of confusion, because the cost of a trip to Paradise Island in the Bahamas was not comparable with the cost of gambling at the Sands in Atlantic City. This factor is thus neutral.

Fourth, we find clear evidence Sands intended to imitate Resorts' "Paradise Island". . . .

Fifth, we find no evidence of actual confusion among consumers. However, this does not dimin-ish the likelihood of confusion that a patron might encounter the name paradise Isle and believe there was some connection between the parties. Likelihood of confusion is the inquiry relevant to liability, not actual confusion. . .

We conclude that consumers viewing the Sands' Paradise Isle mark would probably assume that the product or service it represents is associated with the source of a different product or service identified with a similar mark, specifically Resorts' "Paradise Island" mark. We therefore hold that there is a likelihood of confusion between plaintiff's and defendant's marks, such that liability for trademark infringement is established. . . .

Judgment entered for plaintiff.

CASE QUESTION

1. Why did the court find that an infringement occurred in this case when there was not evidence of actual confusion among consumers of Resorts International and Sands Casino?

Copyright Infringement

A **copyright** is the exclusive right to reproduce creative work such as artwork and writings (books, poetry, essays, etc.). One who creates such works is entitled to the exclusive right to reproduce them. See discussion of copyrights in Chapter 15. If another party wishes to reproduce copyrighted work, such as a restaurant owner who would like to reproduce a painting onto paper placemats, the restaurateur must first obtain the permission of the artist. Customarily the artist will charge a fee for that permission. Copying without permission constitutes copyright infringement, a tort. A person whose copyrighted work has been infringed can sue to force the infringer to "cease and desist" from further copying and to compensate the copyright owner for any losses resulting from the unauthorized copying.

A copyright dispute over casino advertising led to a lawsuit in *Le Moine d/b/a Le Moine Studios v. Empress River Casino Corp.*, 1996 WL 332688 (Ill., 1996). Plaintiff was hired by defendant's advertising company to create concepts for billboard advertising for defendant riverboat gambling company. The concepts were rejected by Empress' senior director of marketing and public relations. Thereafter Empress developed an advertising campaign for outdoor billboards, radio and television. Plaintiff claimed the advertisements copied his compositions and therefore infringed his copyright. Empress conceded that both Le

Moine's work and the advertising campaign it adopted emphasize the excitement of the casinos but denied that the work was sufficiently similar to constitute copyright infringement. The court noted the following similarities: both incorporate the Empress logo; both express the idea of boredom (from which the casino can supposedly save the observer) with a front-loading washing machine; and both represent Empress Casinos with a slot machine.

The court found the works were not substantially similar and therefore awarded judgment to Empress. The court noted,

> "[T]here are only a few stereotyped means to represent the idea of a casino. Le Moine's use of a slot machine was more or less dictated by the idea of a casino, or at least standard to the treatment of casinos. . . the similar appearance of the two works stems only from the individual elements they share, not from a substantially similar total concept and feel arising from the creative arrangement and inter-action of common elements. Accordingly, as a matter of law, an ordinary observer could not conclude that Le Moine's compositions and Empress' advertising campaign evoke a substantially similar total concept and feel."

Sexual Harassment Occurring at Casinos

Sexual harassment laws protect employees from harassing conduct of a sexual nature in the workplace. For discussion on sexual harassment see Chapter 14. A good example of a hostile environment sexual harassment case in a casino setting is provided by the next case.

The facts of the case also provide insight into the practice of "comping," whereby gamblers who bet large sums of money may be offered free meals, rooms and even air transportation as an inducement to secure their patronage at a particular casino.

CASE EXAMPLE 16–4

Steiner v. Showboat Hotel & Casino
25 F.3d 1459 (9th Cir., 1994).

. . . Showboat hired Barbara Steiner to work as a blackjack dealer at Showboat Hotel and Casino in March of 1986. Two months later she was promoted to be the casino's first female "floorperson." Her supervisor was Jack Trenkle, a Showboat vice-president.

In 1987 Steiner complained to Showboat management that Trenkle was calling her offensive names based on her gender, such as "dumb fucking broad," "cunt," and "fucking cunt." Trenkle was not reprimanded; rather, Steiner was moved to a different shift so that she would not have to be in contact with him. After about one month, however, she decided the new shift was too inconvenient and moved back to her old shift.

On December 19, 1989, Trenkle learned that Steiner had "comped" (offered a free meal to players betting high stakes) a breakfast for two men who had been playing Blackjack at her table. He confronted Steiner in front of customers and other employees, expressing his disapproval of her decision in the following words: "You are not a fucking floor man [her job]. You are a fucking casino host. You comp every fucking fleabag that walks through the door." She claims he moved toward her in a threatening manner during this tirade. By his own admission, he then yelled, "Why don't you go in the restaurant and suck their dicks while you are at it if you want to comp them so bad?"

She claims he repeated this two or three times, laughed, and walked off with a grin on his face. Her version is corroborated by the deposition of a cocktail waitress who overheard the exchange.

Steiner complained to Showboat's manager the next day, and Trenkle was told to apologize. He did, although Steiner claims it was in a rude and sarcastic manner. Unsatisfied with this response, Steiner filed a complaint with the Nevada Equal Rights Commission. Once aware of her complaint, Showboat conducted a more serious investigation, in which numerous Showboat employees were questioned about Trenkle's treatment of Steiner and of women generally. Their statements establish that Trenkle was abusive to men and women alike; however, his abusive treatment and remarks to women were of a sexual or gender-specific nature.

As a result of its investigation, Showboat sent a written reprimand to Trenkle for "sexually harassing" Steiner. Trenkle was told that if he ever again used sexual or derogatory language to or about any employee, he would be fired. Trenkle's shift was changed so that he and Steiner would no longer be at work during the same hours. . . .

In November, Trenkle was fired because he broke the terms of his disciplinary letter. Specifically, he denied a female employee's request to leave early by saying, "I wouldn't want you to lose your job either because you have got big boobs. I'd hate to terminate someone with big boobs." . . .

Steiner's claim relies upon the hostile or offensive work environment theory of liability for sexual harassment. . . . while coworkers' occasional annoying or "merely offensive" comments do not constitute sexual harassment, [illegal conduct] comes into play before the harassing conduct leads to a nervous breakdown. It is enough, rather, if such hostile conduct pollutes the victim's workplace, making it more difficult for her to do her job, to take pride in her work, and to desire to stay on in her position.

Steiner has established without contradiction that Trenkle habitually referred to her and to other female employees in a derogatory fashion using sexually explicit and offensive terms. Moreover, Trenkle's ongoing comments and conduct were sexually explicit, offensive, highly derogatory, and publicly made. Steiner has made her case unless Showboat can demonstrate that it took adequate remedial and disciplinary action. . . .

Showboat claims in defense that Trenkle harassed everyone, male and female alike, and therefore his harassment of Steiner was not based on her gender. . . .

[While] Trenkle was indeed abusive to men, his abuse of women was different. It relied on sexual epithets, offensive, explicit references to women's bodies and sexual conduct. While Trenkle may have referred to men as "assholes," he referred to women as "dumb fucking broads" and "fucking cunts," and when angry at Steiner, suggested that she have sex with customers. And while his abuse of men in no way related to their gender, his abuse of female employees, especially Steiner, centered on the fact that they were females. It is one thing to call a woman "worthless," and another to call her a "worthless broad."

Furthermore, even if Trenkle used sexual epithets equal in intensity and in an equally degrading manner against male employees, he cannot thereby "cure" his conduct toward women. . . . We do not rule out the possibility that both men and women working at Showboat have viable claims against Trenkle for sexual harassment.

[Concerning whether Showboat took adequate remedial action], The evidence suggests that Showboat was consistently slow to react to Steiner's claims, and did not serious investigate them or strongly reprimand Trenkle until after Steiner had filed her complaint with the Nevada Equal Rights Commission. Moreover, Showboat [originally] changed Steiner's shift rather than changing his shift or work area within the casino or, indeed, firing him outright and early on. A victim of sexual harassment should not have to work in a less desirable location [or time] as a result of the employer's remedial plan.

We reverse the district court's grant of summary judgment in Showboat's favor . . . it would seem that on remand Steiner herself may be entitled to summary judgment on her claim of sexual harassment.

CASE QUESTIONS

1   Why did the court object to the casino changing Steiner's work schedule as a method to curb the sexual harassment?

2   To avoid liability for sexual harassment, what should an employer do when addressing a claim of sexual harassment?

An employer can avoid liability for sexual harassment if it takes appropriate remedial action. To be appropriate the response must be prompt and reasonably calculated to end the harassment. In *Klutch v. Grand Victoria Casino*, 1996 WL 465393 (Ill., 1996), a female coat check attendant at the casino filed a complaint against an employee in the engineering department alleging that the latter continually made inappropriate sexual remarks to her. The day after the complaint was filed, the general manager placed the alleged offender on a three-day investigative suspension. Plaintiff quit during the three-day period. The offender was allowed to return to work but a written warning was placed in his file directing him to refrain from sexually harassing conduct and advising him that any further complaints would result in immediate termination. The court determined this was an appropriate response by the casino and therefore dismissed plaintiff's case.

Criminal Activity at Casinos

The large sums of money that flow in casinos unfortunately attract criminal activity. See discussion of crimes in chapter 10. One vivid example is the kidnapping of the daughter of Stephen Wynn, the chief executive officer of Mirage Resorts, Inc. which owns several large, upscale casinos in Las Vegas and elsewhere. Mr. Wynn paid $1.45 million in ransom money after which Ms. Wynn was safely returned. One of the perpetrators was sentenced to 24 years in jail; the other to 19 years. *United States. v. Sherwood*, 98 F.3d 402 (9th Cir., 1996).

One scam involves manufacture and sale of fraudulent slot machine tokens. When discovered, casinos will alter the machines so that they reject the fraudulent tokens. *United States v. Joost*, 92 F.3d 7 (1st Cir., 1996). Another illegal scheme promoted by organized crime involved blackjack and consisted of "capping" - increasing the amount of winning bets after the cards were dealt. This requires the participation of the dealer in the fraudulent scheme. In one instance in Massachusetts the dealers were paid 25 percent of the proceeds. They regularly met their associates at a secret location to split the take. Before the conspiracy was caught on surveillance cameras, it went on for five months, five days a week, with an average nightly profit of $10,000.

Would-be robbers seeking a target with a lot of money can easily spot the ideal victim in a casino by watching for gamblers with many chips. In *State of Louisiana v. Timon*, 683 So.2d 315 (La., 1996), the robbers' target won $20,000 at a blackjack table. He was escorted to his car by casino security. The robbers followed him on an expressway and, in a remote area, shot his tires causing a flat and forcing him to stop, thus creating the opportunity for the robbery. Like hotels and restaurants, casinos must exercise reasonable care to protect the safety of their guests. In this case, in addition to the parking lot escort, the casino provided surveillance cameras at the gambling tables and cashier's stand. These reasonable efforts by the casino to protect its guests proved unavailing in this case to stop the criminal act. These precautions will, however, protect the casino from civil liability in the event a crime victim sues the casino for the loss.

Casinos and The Dram Shop Act

The Dram Shop Act is a statute that imposes on establishments that sell alcohol liability for certain injuries resulting from illegal sales (the patron was visibly intoxicated when served, underage or a known alcoholic). See the discussion on this topic in chapter 12. In most states the liability applies only to a third party injured by the illegally-served patron. Some states, including New Jersey, allow the illegally-served patron to recover for at least a portion of his own damages. An interesting attempt was made to extend Dram Shop liability to a uniquely-casino application. Most casinos offer their guests free drinks while they are gambling. The plaintiffs in several lawsuits were given free drinks by a casino after becoming intoxicated. They then incurred significant gambling debts. They sued the casino claiming that, since they had been served illegally, they should be relieved from their debt.

The complaint in one case described this practice as follows.

"The Casino [Taj Mahal in Atlantic City] continuously provided [plaintiff] with complementary 4-5 ounce gin martinis during the entire period he was gambling and the casino continued to provide this stream of alcohol to plaintiff beyond the point when he was visibly and substantially intoxicated. Because defendant allowed plaintiff to continue gambling while visibly intoxicated, including extending him additional credit by permitting him to draw markers against his credit account while intoxicated, he allegedly sustained gambling losses in excess of $2,000,000 while visibly intoxicated."

Hakimoglu v. Trum Taj Mahal, Inc., *876 F. Supp. 625, 625 (N.J., 1994), aff'd, 70 F.3d 291 (3rd Cir., 1995).*

The court rejected this argument and held for the casino. Among the reasons were the following.

1   Dram shop liability had not previously been extended beyond injuries related to drunken driving, barroom accidents and barroom brawls.

2   The casino industry is very highly regulated. Had New Jersey intended to impose liability on casinos for allowing intoxicated patrons to gamble, a statute to that effect would likely have been adopted. Said the court in *Hakimoglu*, "The State has regulated the minutiae of gaming rules and alcohol service and expressly permitted the serving of free drinks to patrons at the gambling tables. Surely it could not have been unaware that the cognitive functioning of many gamblers would be impaired by drinking or of the consequences of permitting persons so impaired to gamble."

3   Extension of dram shop liability to gambling debts would present difficult questions of proximate cause since sober gamblers can play well and nonetheless suffer significant losses, intoxicated gamblers can win big, and under the prevailing rules and house odds, the house will win and the gamblers will lose in the typical transaction.

4   Even if we assume that alcohol will affect the gambler's judgment, many casino games require no skill and instead, are determined by the draw of a card, the throw of the dice, or the random appearance of pictures on a slot machine.

5   Proof of intoxication could be more easily fabricated in a gambling case than in the typical dram shop situation which is a car accident. In the later case, the occurrence of the accident is a specific event marked by police and accident reports. Reliable evidence of alcohol in a person's body is usually obtained as part of the accident investigation. None of this occurs in the gambling scenario. A gambler's loss at the gambling table is not cause for investigation nor is a casino dealer likely to recall it at a later date.

For the above reasons, a gambler who is served alcohol by a casino after becoming visibly intoxicated and who continues to place bets and thereby incurs a gambling debt is not entitled to reimbursement of his loss from the casino.

Riverboat Casinos and the Jones Act

Many cities bordering on waterways have adopted riverboat casinos. The recent increase in the number of this type of casino is the result of laws that prohibit gambling on shore. These laws do not apply at sea. In some states, a riverboat located dockside but totally in a body of water can legally house gaming. In other states a boat must travel a ways off shore before it can legally permit gambling.

Numerous federal laws affect events occurring on boats on the waterways of the United States. These laws are referred to as **maritime laws**. Sometimes the outcome of a case can depend on whether maritime law or a state law applies. Litigation has resulted to determine which law applies to riverboat casinos. One issue that varies greatly depending on which law applies is the appropriate remedy when an employee on a riverboat casino is injured while on duty. According to state law, any monetary recovery from the employer will be limited by workers' compensation laws. Such laws produce a relatively prompt resolution of the case but restrict the amount of compensation an employee will receive. For example, under workers' compensation laws, an employee cannot recover damages for pain and suffering, a measure of damages that compensates an injured person for the physical pain and mental anguish that he may have endured because of an injury.

Contrasted with state workers' compensation laws is a federal maritime law known as the Jones Act which enables employees injured while on a boat to sue in court for the full value of their injury, including pain and suffering. For the Jones Act to apply, the boat on which the injury occurred must qualify as a "vessel".

The application of the Jones Act was at issue in *Pavone v. Mississippi Riverboat Amusement Corporation*, 52 F.3d 560 (5th Cir., 1995). A bartender stepped on a screw that penetrated his shoe and injured his foot while he was working on a dockside casino in Biloxi, Mississippi. The casino, named the Biloxi Belle, sat on a barge that was moored to shore by lines tied to sunken steel pylons that were filled with concrete. Shoreside utility lines were permanently connected. A continual stand-by towing contract existed for the barge and casino to tow them to sheltered waters in the event potentially damaging weather was forecast. The Biloxi Belle had no engine, no captain, no navigational aids, no crewquarters and no lifesaving equipment. For visual effects only, it had a decorative pilot house which contained no operating parts other than a single light switch. It also had a motorized but nonfunctional paddle wheel which rested permanently above the water level and so served no propulsion function.

The barge had not been built to transport passengers, cargo or equipment and had never been used for that purpose. The Biloxi Belle did not employ a crew for navigation or nautical purposes. All employees were engaged solely in connection with the casino business.

The court determined that the casino and barge were not seagoing vessels for purposes of the Jones Act. Therefore the employee's remedy for his injuries was limited by workers' compensation laws.

In the following case, the court similarly analyzed whether another floating casino qualified as a vessel under the Jones Act.

CASE EXAMPLE 16–5

McAdow v. Harrah's Shreveport Casino
926 F. Supp. 93 (La., 1996).

Brian McAdow instituted this action seeking damages under the Jones Act for an injury arising from an accident that allegedly occurred while he was working on the Shreveport Rose, then the home of Harrah's Shreveport casino. . . .

The dimensions of the Shreveport Rose are 210 feet by 78 feet. The craft was constructed in Morgan City, Louisiana. Upon completion, it travelled to Shreveport, through navigable waters, with the assist of tugs. Upon reaching Shreveport in March, 1994, it was docked for use as a dockside floating casino. Until the time of its departure from Shreveport in February of 1995, it was moored in a coffer cell in the Red River and connected to the shore through the use of four one-inch diameter steel cables. It was accessed from the shore by steel ramps, and connected to shore-side utility lines (telephone, electric, sewer, water and computer).

It has a pilothouse but not a galley and crew quarters. It has a radar unit which, while the vessel is moored, is used solely to monitor weather conditions. Except on the two occasions when it arrived in and departed from Shrevesport, it has not been used by defendant to transport cargo and/or passengers over navigable waters. Upon its departure in February, 1995, the craft did not move on its own power but was towed and pushed by tug boats. . . .

The Shreveport Rose was removed from navigation before, during and after McAdow's alleged injury. The structure was for all intents and purposes, a land-based casino. There is a striking degree of permanent connection between the Shreveport Rose and the shore; only by removing steel pins from the ramps, letting loose all lines and cables and lifting the gate of the coffer cell by means of a crane barge could the Shreveport Rose be freed from its retaining walls. Moreover, the casino was not at all self-sufficient. All utilities, including telephone, electric, sewer, water and computer connections were permanently accessed from the shore. These too would have to be removed for the casino to break free from the concrete barriers separating it from the flow of the Red River.

Indeed the Shreveport Rose was always used as a casino and a work platform. Gaming tables, slot machines, and cocktails could all be found in abundance, along with the attending personnel.

There also was full, continuous access to the Shreveport Rose from the shore. The floating casino was never moved, except when it arrived in and departed from its spot on the Shreveport riverfront. While in Shreveport it was never used to transport passengers or cargo. . . .

Because of increasing business, it became necessary for Harrah's to bring in a larger casino. This is why the Shreveport Rose was extracted from its position on the riverfront. The New Orleans Times-Picayune reported in its March 12, 1996 issue that, based upon Louisiana State Police sources, the top three revenue producing floating casinos in the state were from the Shreveport/ Bossier City area for the month of February 1996. In that month Harrah's gross revenue was $12,057,340, Isle of Capri's gross revenue was $12,745,882, and Horseshoe's gross revenue was $14,246,989. No other area in the state rivaled these astonishing numbers.

The court simply cannot fathom that the Shreveport Rose can be deemed a vessel for Jones Act purposes with the above considerations in mind. . . . Since being moved to Shreveport it was in its own right a creature of the land. The Shreveport Rose was not intended to be used for transporting freight or passengers. Therefore the Shreveport Rose is not a vessel for Jones Act purposes. It follows that there is no possibility that McAdow has a cause of action for a Jones Act claim.

Casinos on Native American Reservations

Many casinos are located on Indian reservations. This phenomenon was a natural outgrowth of two circumstances. First, the laws in most states prohibit gambling. Second, the law accords to Indian reservations sovereign authority which means the governing bodies of the Indian tribes have the supreme authority to govern the reservation and its inhabitants independent of state and federal laws. Therefore, although the law of the state in which the reservation is located may outlaw gambling, that fact does not preclude the reservation's governing body from determining that gambling will be permissible on the reservation. However, as the following discussion reveals, some limitations do apply.

Sovereign Authority

Native American tribes exercise **sovereign authority** over their members and territories. This means tribes are separate from our federal and state governments and have the power to regulate their internal affairs by making their own substantive law. The power to enforce that law rests with their own tribal courts and not federal courts. Tribal sovereignty is subordinate only to the federal government. As sovereigns, tribes are immune from lawsuits unless they specifically waive that immunity. These concepts are illustrated in the following cases.

A decisive application of the tribal sovereignty rule occurred in a California case. Two Native American tribes in that state were engaging in various forms of gambling. The state sought to force the tribes to comply with state gambling regulations. Resistance by the tribes led to a lawsuit that ultimately was decided by the United States Supreme Court. That court held the state did not have authority to enforce its gambling laws on the Indian reservation. *California v. Cabazon Band of Mission Indians*, 480 U.S. 202, 107 S.Ct. 1083 (1987). That case led Congress to pass the Indian Gaming Regulatory Act (hereinafter "IGRA") in 1988 which restricts to some extent a tribe's ability to conduct gambling activities. Before gaming can legally occur on a reservation, the tribe must comply with IGRA. One of IGRA's goals was to balance the states' interest in regulating high stakes gambling within their borders and the Indians' resistance to state intrusions on their sovereignty. IGRA is discussed in more detail in the next section of this chapter.

In another case, a table game operator who had been employed at an Indian casino claimed he was wrongfully terminated. He commenced a lawsuit in federal district court. The tribe moved to dismiss the case claiming the proper forum was the Tribal Court. The federal court held that, as a sovereign power, the tribe was entitled to sovereign immunity and it had not waived that entitlement. Accordingly, the court dismissed the case. *Barker v. Menominee Nation Casino*, 897 F. Supp. 389 (Wis., 1995).

In *Romanella v. The Mashantucket Pequoz Tribal Nation*, 993 F. Supp. 163 (Conn., 1996), a pit cashier at Foxwoods Resort & Casino fell in a nearby parking lot used by casino patrons. Her fall resulted from an accumulation of snow and ice. The lot was not on the reservation but was owned and maintained by the tribe. The cashier sued in federal court the Indian tribe that operates Foxwoods. The court, noting that Native American tribes are independent domestic nations, held that the defendant tribe was immune from lawsuits in federal court that involved events occurring on tribal territory, including land it controlled for its commercial activities such as the parking lot.

A limitation on Native American sovereignty is provided by *Reich v. Mashantucket Sand & Gravel*, 95 F.3d 174 (2nd Cir., 1996). The issue in this case was whether a construction company maintained by an Indian tribe and used to construct additions to a casino was subject to the federal Occupational Safety and Health Act ("OSHA"). That Act imposes many requirements in workplace situations to help ensure the safety of workers. Federal OSHA inspectors entered the casino and found four safety violations that threatened the wellbeing of the construction workers. For these violations, the construction company was fined $4000. The tribe challenged the imposition of the fine claiming OSHA did not apply to it due to the tribe's sovereignty.

The federal court ruled that the sovereignty of a tribe is limited, not unlike the sovereignty of a state. A tribe's sovereignty applies only to the power needed to control internal matters of the reservation. The construction work, although it occurred entirely on the reservation, has a much broader impact than just within the reservation. The company employed non-Indians, and it involved a resort and casino that serves a multi-state clientele much broader than just residents of the reservation. For these reasons the court held that the tribe was bound by OSHA.

Indian Gaming Regulatory Act

The Federal government has maintained some oversight of gaming conducted on reservations. Its authority is embodied in the Indian Gaming Regulatory Act (hereinafter "IGRA"), 25 U.S.C. Section 2701 et seq, which was adopted by Congress in 1988. IGRA provides a comprehensive design for regulating gaming activities on Indian lands.

One of IGRA's objectives is, "to provide a statutory basis for the operation of gaming by Indian tribes as a means of promoting tribal economic development, self-sufficiency, and strong tribal governments."

IGRA divides gaming into three classes, each subject to differing degrees of tribal, state and federal jurisdiction and regulation. The class most highly regulated is known as Class III and includes black jack, craps and related dice games, wheel games, roulette, electronic games of chance, slot machines, card games in which the players play against the house, and keno. For a casino on a reservation to host these types of games, IGRA mandates the following four requirements: 1) the gaming must be authorized by an ordinance or resolution adopted by the governing body of the Indian tribe having jurisdiction over the land; 2) the type of gaming involved must be permitted by the state for some purpose by some person or organization (such as for charitable purposes); 3) the gaming must be approved by the chairperson of the National Indian Gaming Commission which was established by Congress; and 4) the gaming must be conducted consistent with a Tribal-State treaty entered into by the Indian tribe and the state. Such a treaty is initiated by the tribe requesting the state in which the lands are located to negotiate for the purpose of entering into an agreement governing such gaming.

Where tribes have undertaken gaming operations without satisfying these prerequisites, the federal government is authorized to obtain search warrants and seize slot machines and related gambling devices and paraphernalia from the casinos. The managers and operators of the casino are subject to federal prosecution for the violation. In *United States v. E.C. Investments, Inc.*, 77 F.3d 327 (9th Cir., 1996), the managers of a California Indian casino were prosecuted for providing slot machines without first entering a compact with the state. Further, the United States government can seek injunctive relief to prevent the casino from operating. *U.S. v. Santee Sioux Tribe of Nebraska*, 135 F.3d 558 (8th Cir., 1998). However, parts of IGRA have recently been held to be unconstitutional. *Seminole Tribe of Florida v. Florida*, 517 U.S.609, 116 S.Ct. 1114 (1996). As a result, at least one court has refused to uphold a preliminary injunction that had forced a tribe to close a casino that was not in compliance with IGRA. *U.S. v. Spokane Tribe of Indians*, 139 F.3d 1297 (9th Cir., 1998). Legislative remedies have been proposed and are currently being considered by Congress. See for example Senate bill S.1870, called The Indian Gaming Regulatory Improvement Act of 1998.

Summary

Casinos are rapidly growing in popularity, and their numbers are growing fast in response. This phenomenon offers new opportunities for workers in the hospitality field. The legal challenges associated with this relatively new entity include some known to other hospitality facilities and others unique to casinos.

Just as hotels and restaurants need to take appropriate precautions to protect the safety and wellbeing of their guests, casinos must do the same. Laws dealing with negligence, false imprisonment, trademarks, and copyrights are equally applicable to gaming facilities. The Dram Shop Act and the law of contracts are likewise binding on casinos.

Casinos have new venues not normally associated with hotels and restaurants. These include riverboats and Native American reservations. Both of these sites are the subject of laws that are not applicable elsewhere. A thorough study of the law of casinos requires exposure to maritime law and Native American law.

Preventive Law Tips for Managers

- *Anticipate circumstances that may cause injury to patrons and take the necessary action to eliminate the risks.* Casinos are obligated to use reasonable care to protect their patrons from injury. Failure to do so will result in liability. Managers and employees should also be alert to conditions on the premises that may present risks. Upon discovery of any such conditions, take the necessary action to eliminate them.

- *Aid patrons who evidence signs of physical distress.* While the law does not generally require that people come to the aid of someone in danger, where a special relationship exists - such as a casino and the people it invites to its premises - a duty does exist to exercise reasonable care to provide first aid to an ill or injured patron. The casino should develop an emergency response system and thoroughly train its employees concerning the system.

- *Do not detain a patron without probable cause to believe the customer has engaged in illegal conduct.* Detaining a patron without probable cause can lead to liability for false imprisonment. Casinos can be victims of criminal conduct that can cause considerable loss to the casino or its clientele. The casino must balance its interest in preventing crime against the interest of its customers who have a right not to be detained unless the casino has probable cause to believe a patron has engaged in illegal activity.

- *Do not adopt a trademark that is confusingly similar to another mark used in the gaming industry.* If a casino uses a name that is confusingly similar to a competitor's, the casino may be forced to discontinue use of that name regardless of money spent to advertise and promote it. To avoid this, adopt marks that are unique and not likely to be confused with other trademarks already in use.

- *Use only original material in advertising.* If your advertising or promotional materials are copied from another marketing campaign or other source, you may be liable for copyright infringement. When designing advertising, use original ideas and elements. If you decide to utilize someone's else's materials, obtain their authorization first.

- *Take precautions to protect your customers from criminal activity.* Successful gamblers are attractive targets for criminals. Adopt procedures to protect your customers. Such procedures might include providing a security escort to patrons' cars; surveillance cameras; well-trained security force; training all employees to detect and prevent criminal activity; maintaining contact with security personnel in other nearby casinos to learn of the latest schemes in your area; and maintaining a close relationship with the local police for ongoing security assistance.

- *Do not sell alcohol illegally.* Dram Shop acts render a casino liable when a person is injured by someone who was illegally served alcohol. To avoid this type of liability, do not sell alcohol to prohibited classes of people; train employees on how to detect if a customer is intoxicated or underage; and reinforce the training regularly.

- *For casinos on Native American reservations, comply fully with the Indian Gaming Regulatory Act.* The Indian Gaming Regulatory Act (IGRA) contains the prerequisites a casino on a reservation must meet to legally provide gambling on its premises. Failure to comply can result in government seizure of gaming devices and criminal prosecution of the casino's officers and managers. To ensure compliance with this specialized area of law, consult with an attorney knowledgeable about the IGRA.

Review Questions

1. What defenses are available to a gambler who has incurred a sizeable loss while betting on credit?

2. What is a pathological gambler?

3. What duty of care is owed by a casino to its patrons?

4. What is the Jones Act and what is its relevance to casinos?

5. What is "probable cause" and how does it apply to the tort of false imprisonment?

6. What led to the proliferation of riverboat casinos?

7. What led to the proliferation of casinos on Native American reservations?

8. What is the Indian Gaming Regulatory Act?

9. What is the meaning of the term Indian sovereignty?

Discussion Questions

1. Describe several criminal schemes to which casinos may be vulnerable. How can casinos protect themselves?

2. What determines whether the Jones Act applies to a water-based casino? What attributes of the casino will be considered by a court in determining whether the Jones Act applies to a riverboat casino?

3. What factors will a court consider when deciding whether a name constitutes trademark infringement?

4. In *Le Moine v. Empress River Casino, Corp.*, concerning an allegation of copyright infringement relating to advertising adopted by the Empress Riverboat Casino, both plaintiff's proposed advertising campaign and the one adopted by Empress represented the casino pictorially with a slot machine. Why was this not significant evidence of copyright infringement?

5. Why have the courts not applied Dram Shop Act liability to gambling debts?

6. Explain the hostile work environment theory of sexual harassment and identify why it is illegal.

7. What must a reservation do to comply with the Indian Gaming Regulatory Act? What are the consequences if it offers gaming without complying with the Act?

Application Questions

1. Latasha was a security employee at a casino. Her boss, who was male, often made demeaning comments to her related to her gender. She felt humiliated and distressed as a result. Latasha filed a complaint with the Personnel Office of the casino.

   a) What legal wrong did Latasha's boss commit?

b) What action can the casino take to limit its liability?

2. Eduardo was gambling at a casino. Luck was with him and he won almost $10,000. What security precautions should the casino have in operation to protect Eduardo and other customers from criminal activity?

3. Barry was a security guard at a casino. He took a 15 minute break in the middle of his shift. When he returned he noticed a player at a blackjack table who had not been there when he left. Barry also noticed the player had a large number of betting chips. Barry suspected foul play and detained the player. While Barry undertook further investigation he later learned that the player had done nothing wrong. The player then sued the casino for false imprisonment, would the casino be able to utilize the defense of probable cause? Why or why not?

APPENDIX A

Limiting Liability Statutes

All fifty states, Washington, D.C., Puerto Rico, the Virgin Islands, and Guam place statutory limits on the liability of hotels for loss or damage to guests' property. To qualify for this protection in any of these jurisdictions, hotels must provide a safe for guests' valuables and post notice of its availability and the hotel's limited liability in strict accord with the state law. The statutes and liability limitations are as follows. The statute references are to the particular title within each state's statutory scheme that addresses hotels. That title is variously referred to as Hotels, Commerce, Business Regulations, or General Business Law.

State	Statutory Limitation	Statute Section
Alabama	$300	34-15-13
Alaska	$1,000	08.56.050
Arizona	$500	33-302
Arkansas	$300	20-26-302
California	$500	1860
Colorado	value declared by guest	12-44-105
Connecticut	$500	44-1
Delaware	none given	24-1502
Florida	$1,000	509.111
Georgia	$750	43-21-10
Guam	$250	41402
Hawaii	$500	486K-4

State	Statutory Limitation	Statute Section
Idaho	$1,000	39-1804
Illinois	$500	90/1
Indiana	$600	32-8-28-1
Iowa	$100	671.1
Kansas	$250	36-402
Kentucky	$300	306.020
Louisiana	$500	2971
Maine	$300	3851
Maryland	$300	15-103
Massachusetts	$1,000	140-10
Michigan	$250	427.102
Minnesota	$1,000	327.71
Mississippi	$500	75-73-5
Missouri	$0	419.020
Montana	$0	70-6-504
Nebraska	$500	41-208
Nevada	$750	651.010
New Hampshire	$1,000	353:1
New Jersey	$5,000	29:2-2
New Mexico	$1,000	57-6-1
New York	$1,500	12-10
North Carolina	$500	72-3
North Dakota	$300	60-01-29
Ohio	$500	4721.02
Oklahoma	$250	15-503b
Oregon	$300	699.010
Pennsylvania	$300	37-61
Puerto Rico	$1,000	10-712
Rhode Island	$500	5-14-1
South Carolina	$2,000	45-1-40
South Dakota	$300	43-40-1
Tennessee	$300	62-7-104
Texas	$50	73-4592
Utah	$250	29-1-2
Vermont	$0	9-3141
Virginia	$500	35.1-28
Virgin Islands	$200	27-402
Washington	$1,000	19.48.030
Washington, D.C.	$1,000	34-106
West Virginia	$250	16-6-22
Wisconsin	$300	254.80
Wyoming	$0	33-17-101

APPENDIX B

Guidelines on Discrimination Because of Sex

(From the Federal Register, Vol. 29, § 1604.11

Sexual Harassment

(a) Harassment on the basis of sex is a violation of Sec. 703 of Title VII. Unwelcome sexual advances, requests for sexual favors, and other verbal or physical conduct of a sexual nature constitute sexual harassment when (1) submission to such conduct is made either explicitly or implicitly a term or condition of an individual's employment, (2) submission to or rejection of such conduct by an individual is used as a basis for employment decisions affecting such individual, or (3) such conduct has the purpose or effect of unreasonably interfering with an individual's work performance or creating an intimidating, hostile or offensive working environment.

(b) In determining whether alleged conduct constitutes sexual harassment, the Commission will look at the record as a whole and at the totality of the circumstances, such as the nature of the sexual advances and the context in which the alleged incidents occurred. The determination of the legality of a particular action will be made from the facts, on a case by case basis.

(c) Applying general Title VII principles, an employer, employment agency, joint apprenticeship committee, or labor organization (hereinafter collectively referred to as "employer") is responsible for its acts and those of its agents and supervisory employees with respect to sexual harassment regardless of whether the specific acts complained of were authorized or even forbidden by the employer and regardless of whether the employer knew or should have known of their occurrence. The Commission will examine the circumstances of the particular employment relationship and the job functions performed by the individual in determining whether an individual acts in either a supervisory or agency capacity.

(**d**) With respect to conduct between fellow employees, an employer is responsible for acts of sexual harassment in the workplace where the employer (or its agents or supervisory employees) knows or should have known of the conduct, unless it can show that it took immediate and appropriate corrective action.

(**e**) An employer may also be responsible for the acts of nonemployees, with respect to sexual harassment of employees in the workplace, where the employer (or its agents or supervisory employees) knows or should have known of the conduct and fails to take immediate and appropriate corrective action. In reviewing these cases the Commission will consider the extent of the employer's control and any other legal responsibility which the employer may have with respect to the conduct of such nonemployees.

(**f**) Prevention is the best tool for the elimination of sexual harassment. An employer should take all steps necessary to prevent sexual harassment from occurring, such as affirmatively raising the subject, expressing strong disapproval, developing appropriate sanctions, informing employees of their right to raise and how to raise the issue of harassment under Title VII, and developing methods to sensitize all concerned.

(**g**) Other related practices: Where employment opportunities or benefits are granted because of an individual's submission to the employer's sexual advances or requests for sexual favors, the employer may be held liable for unlawful sex discrimination against other persons who were qualified for but denied that employment opportunity or benefit.

Model Program Dealing with Sexual Harassment

(Excerpted from the National Labor Relations Board Policy)

Sexual harassment is a form of employee misconduct that undermines the integrity of the employment relationship. All employees must be allowed to work in an environment free from unsolicited and unwelcome sexual overtures. Sexual harassment does not refer to occasional compliments. It refers to behavior that is not welcome, that is personally offensive, that debilitates morale and that therefore interferes with the work effectiveness of its victims and their co-workers. Sexual harassment may include actions such as: sex-oriented verbal "kidding" or abuse; subtle pressure for sexual activity; physical contact such as patting, pinching or constant brushing against another's body; demands for sexual favors, accompanied by implied or overt promises of preferential treatment or threats concerning an individual's employment status.

Sexual harassment is a prohibited personnel practice when it results in discrimination for or against an employee on the basis of conduct not related to work performance, such as the taking or refusal to take a personnel action, including promotion of employees who submit to sexual advances or refusal to promote employees who resist or protest sexual overtures.

Complaints of sexual harassment involving misuse of one's official position should be made orally or in writing to a higher-level supervisor, to an appropriate personnel official, or to anyone authorized to deal with discrimination complaints (EEO counselor a union official, for example).

Because of differences in employees' values and backgrounds, some individuals may find it difficult to recognize their own behavior as sexual harassment. To create an awareness of office conduct that may be construed as sexual harassment, we will incorporate sexual harassment awareness training in future managerial, supervisory, EEO, employee orientation, and other appropriate training courses. Additionally, a copy of this policy will be placed in each new employee orientation kit.

APPENDIX C

The Americans With Disabilities Act

Title I—Employment

§ 101. DEFINITIONS. As used in this title:

(1) COMMISSION.—The term "Commission" means the Equal Employment Opportunity Commission. . . .

(2) COVERED ENTITY.—The term "covered entity" means an employer, . . .

(3) DIRECT THREAT.—The term "direct threat" means a significant risk to the health or safety of others that cannot be eliminated by reasonable accommodation.

(4) EMPLOYEE.—The term "employee" means an individual employed by an employer.

(5) EMPLOYER.—

(A) IN GENERAL.—The term "employer" means a person engaged in an industry affecting commerce who has 15 or more employees for each working day in each of 20 or more calendar weeks in the current or preceding calendar year, . . .

(8) QUALIFIED INDIVIDUAL WITH A DISABILITY.—The term "qualified individual with a disability" means an individual with a disability who, with or without reasonable accommodation, can perform the essential functions of the employment position that such individual holds or desires. For the purposes of this title, consideration shall be given to the employer's judgment as to what functions of a job are essential, and if an employer has prepared a written de-

scription before advertising or interviewing applicants for the job, this description shall be considered evidence of the essential functions of the job.

(9) REASONABLE ACCOMMODATION.—The term "reasonable accommodation" may include—

(A) making existing facilities used by employees readily accessible to and usable by individuals with disabilities; and

(B) job restructuring, part-time or modified work schedules, reassignment to a vacant position, acquisition or modification of equipment or devices, appropriate adjustment or modifications of examinations, training materials or policies, the provision of qualified readers or interpreters, and other similar accommodations for individuals with disabilities.

(10) UNDUE HARDSHIP.—

(A) IN GENERAL.—The term "undue hardship" means an action requiring significant difficulty or expense, when considered in light of the factors set forth in subparagraph (B).

(B) FACTORS TO BE CONSIDERED.—In determining whether an accommodation would impose an undue hardship on a covered entity, factors to be considered include—

(i) the nature and cost of the accommodation needed under this Act;

(ii) the overall financial resources of the facility or facilities involved in the provision of the reasonable accommodation; the number of persons employed at such facility; the effect on expenses and resources, or the impact otherwise of such accommodation upon the operation of the facility;

(iii) the overall financial resources of the covered entity; the overall size of the business of a covered entity with respect to the number of its employees; the number, type, and location of its facilities; and

(iv) the type of operation or operations of the covered entity, including the composition, structure, and functions of the workforce of such entity; the geographic separateness, administrative, or fiscal relationship of the facility or facilities in question to the covered entity.

§ 102. DISCRIMINATION

(a) GENERAL RULE.—No covered entity shall discriminate against a qualified individual with a disability because of the disability of such individual in regard to job application procedures, the hiring, advancement, or discharge of employees, employee compensation, job training, and other terms, conditions, and privileges of employment.

(b) CONSTRUCTION.—As used in subsection (a), the term "discriminate" includes—

(1) limiting, segregating, or classifying a job applicant or employee in a way that adversely affects the opportunities or status of such applicant or employee because of the disability of such applicant or employee;

(2) participating in a contractual or other arrangement or relationship that has the effect of subjecting a covered entity's qualified applicant or employee with a disability to the discrimination prohibited by this title (such relationship includes

a relationship with an employment or referral agency, labor union, . . . an organization providing fringe benefits to an employee of the covered entity, or an organization providing training and apprenticeship programs);

(3) utilizing standards, criteria, or methods of administration—

(A) that have the effect of discrimination on the basis of disability; or

(B) that perpetuate the discrimination of others who are subject to common administrative control;

(4) excluding or otherwise denying equal jobs or benefits to a qualified individual because of the known disability of an individual with whom the qualified individual is known to have a relationship or association;

(5) (A) not making reasonable accommodations to the known physical or mental limitations of an otherwise qualified individual with a disability who is an applicant or employee, unless such covered entity can demonstrate that the accommodation would impose an undue hardship on the operation of the business of such covered entity; or

(B) denying employment opportunities to a job applicant or employee who is an otherwise qualified individual with a disability, if such denial is based on the need of such covered entity to make reasonable accommodation to the physical and mental impairments of the employee or applicant;

(6) using qualification standards, employment tests or other selection criteria that screen out or tend to screen out an individual with a disability or a class of individuals with disabilities unless the standard, test or other selection criteria, as used by the covered entity, is shown to be job-related for the position in question and is consistent with business necessity; and

(7) failing to select and administer tests concerning employment in the most effective manner to ensure that, when such test is administered to a job applicant or employee who has a disability that impairs sensory, manual, or speaking skills, such test results accurately reflect the skills, aptitude, or whatever other factors of such applicant or employee that such test purports to measure, rather than reflecting the impaired sensory, manual or speaking skills of such employee or applicant (except where such skills are the factors that the test purports to measure).

(c) MEDICAL EXAMINATIONS AND INQUIRIES.—. . .

(A) PROHIBITED EXAMINATIONS OR INQUIRY.—. . . [A] covered entity shall not conduct a medical examination or make inquiries of a job applicant as to whether such applicant is an individual with a disability or as to the nature or severity of such disability.

(B) ACCEPTABLE INQUIRY.—A covered entity may make preemployment inquiries into the ability of an applicant to perform job-related functions. . . .

(4) EXAMINATION AND INQUIRY—

(A) PROHIBITED EXAMINATIONS AND INQUIRIES.—A covered entity shall not . . . make inquiries of an employee as to whether such employee is an individual with a disability or as to the nature or severity of the disability, unless such examination or inquiry is shown to be job-related and consistent with business necessity.

(B) ACCEPTABLE EXAMINATIONS AND INQUIRIES.—. . .A covered entity may make inquiries into the ability of an employee to perform job-related functions. . . .

§ 103 DEFENSES.

(a) IN GENERAL.—It may be a defense to a charge of discrimination under this Act that an alleged application of qualification standards, tests, or selection criteria that screen out or tend to screen out or otherwise deny a job or benefit to an individual with a disability has been shown to be job-related and consistent with business necessity, and such performance cannot be accomplished by reasonable accommodation, as required under this title.

(b) QUALIFICATION STANDARDS.—The term "qualification standards" may include a requirement that an individual shall not pose a direct threat to the health or safety of other individuals in the workplace. . . .

(d) LIST OF INFECTIOUS AND COMMUNICABLE DISEASES.-

(1) IN GENERAL.—The Secretary of Health and Human Services, shall . . .

(B) publish a list of infectious and communicable diseases which are transmitted through handling the food supply; . . .

Such list shall be updated annually.

(2) APPLICATIONS.—In any case in which an individual has an infectious or communicable disease that is transmitted to others through the handling of food, that is included on the list developed by the Secretary of Health and Human Services . . . and which cannot be eliminated by reasonable accommodation, a covered entity may refuse to assign or continue to assign such individual to a job involving food handling. . . .

§ 104. ILLEGAL USE OF DRUGS AND ALCOHOL

(a) QUALIFIED INDIVIDUAL WITH A DISABILITY.—For purposes of this title, the term "qualified individual with a disability" shall not include any employee or applicant who is currently engaging in the illegal use of drugs, when the covered entity acts on the basis of such use.

(b) RULES OF CONSTRUCTION.—Nothing in subsection (a) shall be construed to exclude as a qualified individual with a disability an individual who—

(1) has successfully completed a supervised drug rehabilitation program and is no longer engaging in the illegal use of drugs, or has otherwise been rehabilitated successfully and is no longer engaging in such use;

(2) is participating in a supervised rehabilitation program and is no longer engaging in such use; or

(3) is erroneously regarded as engaging in such use, but is not engaging in such use; except that it shall not be a violation of this Act for a covered entity to adopt or administer reasonable policies or procedures, including but not limited to drug testing, designed to ensure that an individual described in paragraph (1) or (2) is no longer engaging in the illegal use of drugs.

(c) AUTHORITY OF COVERED ENTITY.—A covered entity—

(1) may prohibit the illegal use of drugs and the use of alcohol at the workplace by all employees;

(2) may require that employees shall not be under the influence of alcohol or be engaging in the illegal use of drugs at the workplace; . . .

§ 105. POSTING NOTICES.

Every employer, employment agency, labor organization, or joint labor-management committee covered under this title shall post notices in an accessible format to applicants, employees, and members describing the applicable provisions of this Act, . . .

TITLE III—PUBLIC ACCOMMODATIONS AND SERVICES OPERATED BY PRIVATE ENTITIES

§ 301. DEFINITIONS.

As used in this title: . . .

(7) PUBLIC ACCOMMODATION.—The following private entities are considered public accommodations for purposes of this title, if the operations of such entities affect commerce—

(A) an inn, hotel, motel, or other place of lodging, except for an establishment located within a building that contains not more than five rooms for rent or hire and that is actually occupied by the proprietor of such establishment as the residence of such proprietor;

(B) a restaurant, bar, or other establishment serving food or drink;

(C) a motion picture house, theater, concert hall, stadium, or other place of exhibition or entertainment;

(D) an auditorium, convention center, lecture hall, or other place of public gathering; . . .

(I) a park, zoo, amusement park, or other place of recreation; . . .

(L) a gymnasium, health spa, bowling alley, golf course, or other place of exercise or recreation.

(9) READILY ACHIEVABLE.—The term "readily achievable" means easily accomplishable and able to be carried out without much difficulty or expense. In determining whether an action is readily achievable, factors to be considered include—

(A) the nature and cost of the action needed under this Act;

(B) the overall financial resources of the facility or facilities involved in the action; the number of persons employed at such facility; the effect on expenses and resources, or the impact otherwise of such action upon the operation of the facility;

(C) the overall financial resources of the covered entity; the overall size of the business of a covered entity with respect to the number of its employees; the number, type, and location of its facilities; and

(D) the type of operation or operations of the covered entity, including the composition, structure, and functions of the work force of such entity; the geographic separateness, administrative or fiscal relationship of the facility or facilities in question to the covered entity. . . .

§ 302. PROHIBITION OF DISCRIMINATION BY PUBLIC ACCOMMODATIONS.

(a) GENERAL RULE.—No individual shall be discriminated on the basis of disability in the full and equal enjoyment of the goods, services, facilities, privileges, advantages, or accommodations of any place of public accommodation by any person who owns, leases (or leases to), or operates a place of public accommodation.

(b) CONSTRUCTION. . .

(i) DENIAL OF PARTICIPATION.—It shall be discriminatory to subject an individual or class of individuals on the basis of a disability or disabilities of such individual or class, directly, or through contractual, licensing, or other arrangements, to a denial of the opportunity of the individual or class to participate in or benefit from the goods, services, facilities, privileges, advantages, or accommodations of an entity.

(ii) PARTICIPATION IN UNEQUAL BENEFIT.—It shall be discriminatory to afford an individual or class of individuals, on the basis of a disability or disabilities of such individual or class, directly, or through contractual, licensing, or other arrangements with the opportunity to participate in or benefit from a good, service, facility, privilege, advantage, or accommodation that is not equal to that afforded to other individuals.

(iii) SEPARATE BENEFIT.—It shall be discriminatory to provide an individual or class of individuals, on the basis of a disability or disabilities of such individual or class, directly or through contractual, licensing, or other arrangements with a good, service, facility, privilege, advantage, or accommodation that is different or separate from that provided to other individuals, unless such action is necessary to provide the individual or class of individuals with a good, service, facility, privilege, advantage, or accommodation, or other opportunity that is as effective as that provided to others. . . .

(B) INTEGRATED SETTINGS.—Goods, services, facilities, privileges, advantages, and accommodations shall be afforded to an individual with a disability in the most integrated setting appropriate to the needs of the individual. . . .

(D) ADMINISTRATIVE METHODS.—An individual or entity shall not, directly or through contractual or other arrangements, utilize standards, or criteria or methods of administration—

(i) that have the effect of discriminating on the basis of disability; or

(ii) that perpetuate the discrimination of others who are subject to common administrative control.

(E) ASSOCIATION.—It shall be discriminatory to exclude or otherwise deny equal goods, services, facilities, privileges, advantages, accommodations, or other opportunities to an individual or entity because of the known disability of an individual with whom the individual or entity is known to have a relationship or association.

(2) SPECIFIC PROHIBITIONS.

(A) DISCRIMINATION.—For purposes of subsection (a), discrimination includes—

(i) the imposition or application of eligibility criteria that screen out or tend to screen out an individual with a disability or any class of individuals with disabilities from fully and equally enjoying any goods, services, facilities, privileges, advantages, or accommodations, unless such criteria can be shown to be necessary for the provision of the goods, services, facilities, privileges, advantages, or accommodations being offered;

(ii) a failure to make reasonable modifications in policies, practices, or procedures, when such modifications are necessary to afford such goods, services, facilities, privileges, advantages, or accommodations to individuals with disabilities, unless the entity can demonstrate that making such modifications would fundamentally alter the nature of such goods, services, facilities, privileges, advantages, or accommodations;

(iii) a failure to take such steps as may be necessary to ensure that no individual with a disability is excluded, denied services, segregated or otherwise treated differently than other individuals because of the absence of auxiliary aids and services, unless the entity can demonstrate that taking such steps would fundamentally alter the nature of the good, service, facility, privilege, advantage, or accommodation being offered or would result in an undue burden;

(iv) a failure to remove architectural barriers, and communication barriers that are structural in nature, in existing facilities, and transportation barriers in existing vehicles and rail passenger cars used by an establishment for transporting individuals (not including barriers that can only be removed through the retrofitting of vehicles or rail passenger cars by the installation of a hydraulic or other lift), where such removal is readily achievable; and

(v) where an entity can demonstrate that the removal of a barrier under clause (iv) is not readily achievable, a failure to make such goods, service, facilities, privileges, advantages, or accommodations available through alternative methods if such methods are readily achievable. . . .

(C) DEMAND RESPONSIVE SYSTEM.—For purposes of subsection (a), discrimination includes . . .

(ii) the purchase or lease by [a private entity] that provides transportation on an as-needed basis and not along a prescribed route with a fixed schedule for use on such system of a vehicle with a seating capacity in excess of 16 passengers (including the driver), . . . that is not readily accessible to and usable by individuals with disabilities (including individuals who use wheelchairs) unless such entity can demonstrate that such system, when viewed in its entirety, provides a level of service to individuals with disabilities equivalent to that provided to individuals without disabilities.

§ 303. NEW CONSTRUCTION AND ALTERATIONS IN PUBLIC ACCOMMODATIONS AND COMMERCIAL FACILITIES.

(a) APPLICATION OF TERM.—. . .[D]iscrimination for purposes of section 302(a) includes—

(1) a failure to design and construct [new] facilities . . . that are readily accessible to and usable by individuals with disabilities, except where an entity can demonstrate that it is structurally impracticable to meet the requirements of

such subsection in accordance with standards set forth or incorporated by reference in regulations issued under this title; and

(2) with respect to a facility or part thereof that is altered by, on behalf of, or for the use of an establishment in a manner that affects or could affect the usability of the facility or part thereof, a failure to make alterations in such a manner that, to the maximum extent feasible, the altered portions of the facility are readily accessible to and usable by individuals with disabilities, including individuals who use wheelchairs. Where the entity is undertaking an alteration that affects or could affect usability of or access to an area of the facility containing a primary function, the entity shall also make the alterations in such a manner that, to the maximum extent feasible, the path of travel to the altered area and the bathrooms, telephones, and drinking fountains serving the altered area, are readily accessible to and usable by individuals with disabilities where such alterations to the path of travel or the bathrooms, telephones, and drinking fountains serving the altered area are not disproportionate to the overall alterations in terms of cost and scope (as determined under criteria established by the Attorney General).

(b) ELEVATOR.—Subsection (a) shall not be construed to require the installation of an elevator for facilities that are less than three stories or have less than 3,000 square feet per story unless the building is a shopping center, a shopping mall, or the professional office of a health care provider or unless the Attorney General determines that a particular category of such facilities requires the installation of elevators based on the usage of such facilities. . . .

§. 307. EXEMPTIONS FOR PRIVATE CLUBS AND RELIGIOUS ORGANIZATIONS

The provisions of this title shall not apply to private clubs or establishments exempted from coverage under. . .the Civil Rights Act of 1964 or to religious organizations or entities controlled by religious organizations, including places of worship.

§ 308. ENFORCEMENT.

(a) IN GENERAL.—. . .

(2) INJUNCTIVE RELIEF.—In the case of violations of sections 302(b)(2)(A)(iv) and section 303(a), injunctive relief shall include an order to alter facilities to make such facilities readily accessible to and usable by individuals with disabilities to the extent required by this title. Where appropriate, injunctive relief shall also include requiring the provision of an auxiliary aid or service, modification of a policy, or provision of alternative methods, to the extent required by this title.

(b) ENFORCEMENT BY THE ATTORNEY GENERAL.—

(i) IN GENERAL.—The Attorney General shall investigate alleged violations of this title, and shall undertake periodic reviews of compliance of covered entities under this title.

(B) POTENTIAL VIOLATION.—If the Attorney General has reasonable cause to believe that

(i) any person or group of persons is engaged in a pattern or practice of discrimination under this title; or

(ii) any person or group of persons has been discriminated against under this title and such discrimination raises an issue of general public importance, the Attorney General may commence a civil action in any appropriate United States district court.

(2) AUTHORITY OF COURT.—In a civil action under paragraph (1)(B), the court—

(A) may grant any equitable relief that such court considers to be appropriate, including to the extent required by this title—

(i) granting temporary, preliminary, or permanent relief—

(ii) providing an auxiliary aid or service, modification of policy, practice, or procedure, or alternative method; and

(iii) making facilities readily accessible to and usable by individuals with disabilities.

(B) may award such other relief as the court considers to be appropriate, including monetary damages to persons aggrieved when requested by the Attorney General; and

(C) may, to vindicate the public interest, assess a civil penalty against the entity in an amount—

(i) not exceeding $50,000 for a first violation; and

(ii) not exceeding $100,000 for any subsequent violation. . .

(4) PUNITIVE DAMAGES.—For purposes of subsection (b)(2)(B), the term "monetary damages" and "such other relief" does not include punitive damages.

(5) JUDICIAL CONSIDERATION.—In a civil action under paragraph (1)(B), the court, when considering what amount of civil penalty, if any, is appropriate, shall give consideration to any good faith effort or attempt to comply with this Act by the entity. In evaluating good faith, the court shall consider, among other factors it deems relevant, whether the entity could have reasonably anticipated the need for an appropriate type of auxiliary aid needed to accommodate the unique needs of a particular individual with a disability. . . .

GLOSSARY

ab initio   "From the beginning" (Latin)

abrogate   The destruction, ending, or annulling of a former law.

absolute liability   See strict liability.

acceptance   An expression of agreement by the offeree to the terms of an offer.

accessory   A person who had some part in a crime without being present.

accessory before the fact   A person who, without being present, encourages or helps someone commit a crime.

accessory after the fact   A person who condones a crime by concealing it or the criminal.

accord and satisfaction   Agreement to settle or compromise a claim and satisfactory payment of the amount agreed upon.

action   A lawsuit.

action ex delicto   "Action arising out of a tort" (Latin)

act of God   A happening not controlled by the power of humans but rather from the direct, immediate, and exclusive operations of the forces of nature.

actual notice   Notice expressly given to a person directly.

additur   An increase provided by the courts to an award of damages to the plaintiff.

adduce   To offer an example or a reason.

adjudication   The legal process of resolving a dispute.

administrative agency   A governmental subdivision charged with administering legislation that applies to a particular industry.

administrative law   Laws that impact administrative agencies.

admissible evidence   Evidence that is allowed to be used by the triers of fact in a court proceeding.

adversary system   Any system similar to that of the United States, Canada, or England where the judge makes the decisions between opposing parties.

adverse   Opposed to or against one's position or interest.

affidavit   A written statement that has been sworn to before an officer who is permitted by law to administer such an oath.

affirmative defense   A defense that introduces new matters which, even if the plaintiff's contentions are true, constitutes a defense to the complaint.

a fortiori   With a greater force; said of a conclusion which, as compared with some other, is even more certain or necessary.

agency   A relationship in which one person (the agent) acts for another (the principal) based on authority voluntarily given.

agent   A person authorized by a principal to act on the principal's behalf under the principal's direction.

allegation   In pleading, that which a person will attempt to prove; an unproven assertion.

allege   To assert before proving.

alternative pleading   Alleges claims that constitute conflicting courses of action.

amicus curiae   "Friends of the court" (Latin); usually one who is not a party to the lawsuit but is permitted to give to the court information that is in doubt or would not otherwise be considered by the court, or to advise the court in respect to some matter of law that directly affects the case in question.

annul   To cancel a relationship as if it never was.

anticipatory breach   A breach committed before the arrival of the actual time of required performance.

antitrust laws   Laws that attempt to ensure that open competition is preserved.

appeal   A review by one court of the decision of another court, initiated by the party who lost in the prior court; a complaint made by a litigant to a superior court that a trial judge committed an error, and a request that the superior court correct the error.

appearance   The coming into court as a party plaintiff or defendant to a lawsuit.

appellant   The party involved in an appeal who initiated the appeal.

appellate court   A court with the authority to review the handling and decisions of a case tried in a lower court.

appellee   The party involved in an appeal who did not initiate the appeal.

appreciation   An increase in value.

appurtenance   Attached to something else.

arbitration   The process of dispute resolution by an arbitrator chosen by the parties who decides the case.

arbitrator   An objective third party chosen by litigants to decide their dispute out of court.

arguendo   Purely for the sake of argument; the parties assume something as true, whether false or true.

arraigned   Brought before the court to hear and assume the charges and to plead guilty or not guilty.

arrest   Deprive a person of liberty because of criminal charges; or detain a person for some reason that may involve force.

arrogate   Claim or take something without having any right to it; to usurp or appropriate as one's own.

assault   The tort of intentionally putting someone in fear of harmful physical contact, such as making a fist in a way suggestive of an imminent punch. (Compare battery.) Also, the crime of intentionally causing physical injury to another person.

assumpsit   An action of equitable character founded upon contract.

attachment   A writ to seize (take and hold) by legal procedure.

attempt to commit   An intent to commit an act combined with some action that moves beyond mere preparation.

attractive nuisance   A potentially dangerous object or condition of exceptional interest to young people.

aver   To allege, assert, verify or justify as in a formal complaint.

averment   A statement of the allegations.

baggage   That which a person travels with while on a journey, of short or long duration.

bail   Valuables, usually money or property, that are put up for release of a person in jail.

bailee   The person receiving possession of goods or personal property.

bailment   A transfer of possession of goods or personal property from a person in possession of the property to another, with the understanding that the property will be returned.

bailor   The owner of goods or personal property transferred to a bailee.

battery   The tort of causing harmful physical contact to a person, such as punching someone. (Compare assault.)

beneficiary   The receiver of some benefit or advantage.

best evidence rule   A rule of evidence that requires the most persuasive evidence be used; original documents, not copies must be made.

bill of exceptions   A written statement submitted to the trial court stating all objections made to the rulings of the trial judge, as well as any instructions given by the trial judge.

blue laws   A law that forbids certain activities, such as selling of certain goods on Sunday.

boiler plate forms   A preprinted form for a document that is usually sold commercially and that is standardized without tailoring to individual legal problems.

bona fide   In good faith (Latin)

bone fide occupational qualification (BFOQ)   A job qualification that legally discriminates on the basis of race, religion, national origin, or sex because: (1) excluded classes cannot perform the job effectively, and (2) such inability is factually supported, and (3) the job classification is reasonably necessary for the normal operation of the business.

breach   The failure of performance by a party of some contracted-for or agreed-upon act.

brief   A written statement of a person's case to be submitted to a court, usually including a summary of the law involved in the case; a condensed statement of facts, and arguments of how the law applies to the facts.

burden of proof   The required amount of evidence for the plaintiff to win a lawsuit. In civil cases, the proof required is a preponderance of the evidence; in criminal cases, the proof must be beyond a reasonable doubt.

burglary   Entering a building unlawfully with the intent to commit a crime therein.

business judgment rule   The principle that bad results—if made in an honest, careful manner by corporate powers—will not be interfered with by the courts.

"but for" rule   Primarily refers to the question, Would the accident or happening have occurred "but for" the negligence involved?

capacity to contract   The ability to understand the terms of a contract and to understand also that failure to perform its terms can lead to legal liability.

case books   Books in which decisions are published.

case decision   An interpretation of the law applied by a judge to a set of facts in a given case.

case method or system   The study of actual cases (opinion of the court) and the drawing of a general legal principal based on other similar cases.

cases   Written decisions by judges.

cashier check   A prepaid check issued by a bank that authorizes payment to the payee of the stipulated sum of the check on demand.

cause of action   The legal basis on which to bring a lawsuit.

caveat   "Let him beware" (Latin); usually used with another word such as emptor ("buyer") expresses the general idea that the buyer purchased at his or her peril, and no warranties (expressed or implied) are included by the seller.

certified check   A check containing a certification that funds are available for the amount of the check.

certiorari   An appeal to a higher court but one that the court need not accept.

chattels   Any property other than land; includes personal property and animals.

check   A draft upon a bank and payable on demand, signed by the maker as an unconditional promise to pay a stated amount to the order of the payee.

citation   A reference to a legal authority such as a court decision, a statute, or a treatise.

citator   A set of books (such as Shepard's Citator) that traces the history of a statute or case since it was passed or ruled on.

civil action   A lawsuit brought by one person against another, usually seeking monetary damages.

civil contempt   Usually the failure to do something that the court orders done for the benefit of another party.

civil rights   Personal rights that derive primarily from the constitution such as equal protection, free speech, freedom of contract, privacy, and due process.

claim   A demand for a remedy, usually money, to compensate for a perceived wrong.

class action   A lawsuit brought by a group of persons who are similarly situated.

clean hands doctrine   A doctrine that will not allow equitable relief to a person bringing a lawsuit who has been guilty of impropriety in the case.

code   A compilation of laws such as the Uniform Commercial Code.

cognizance   Right of a court to take action.

cohabitation   Living together; often refers to an unmarried couple living together and having sexual intercourse.

collusion   Action by two or more persons together for the purpose of committing a fraud.

common carrier   One who transports for hire.

common law   Legal rules that evolved in England from decisions of judges and from customs and practices, intended to be common or uniform for the entire English kingdom, and obtaining their authority from the test of time. Also refers to judges' decisions as opposed to statutory law.

common law marriage   A marriage created by a couple publicly living together as married for a time period sufficient to create a legal marriage.

common victualler   A keeper of a restaurant.

comparable worth   The concept that two jobs requiring different skills and responsibilities have equal value to the employer. Courts have rejected the concept that comparable worth requires equal pay.

comparative negligence   The rule followed in some states that apportions damages according to the comparative contribution of the negligence of the parties. A jury will allocate the liability between the plaintiff and the defendant depending on their degree of culpability based on a total of 100 percent.

compensatory damages   Out-of-pocket expenses including doctor bills and lost wages, and compensation for pain and suffering, loss of enjoyment of life, loss of consortium, and loss of services.

complainant   The originator of a lawsuit; the plaintiff.

complaint   The initial pleading filed in court in a civil lawsuit consisting of a statement of the wrong or harm allegedly done to the plaintiff by the defendant and a request for specific help from the court.

conclusion of law   Application of a rule of law to a set of facts.

condition precedent   A right or obligation created if a certain future event happens.

condition subsequent   A right or obligation ended if a certain future event happens.

condominium   A form of separate ownership of individual units in a nultiunit development where parts of the development are owned as tenants in common.

confession of judgment   A method of permitting a judgment to be entered by consent against a person in advance of his default on his debt, for a stipulated sum, without the formality, time, or expense of an ordinary legal proceeding.

conflicts of law   Variations that exists between different laws of the same state or sovereignty upon the same subject matter; or when a choice exists between laws of more than one state, in which case the judge makes the decision as to applicable law.

Congress   The primary law-making body of the federal government.

consanguinity   Blood relationship, kinship.

consent   To agree.

consideration   Something of value exchanged for something else of value.

consortium   The right of a married couple to each other's love and services.

conspicuous   Out in the open; easily seen.

constitutional law   The law embodied in the federal constitution, prescribing the organization and powers of the federal government, and defining rights of the people..

constructive   The opposite of actual wherein a law is accepted as a substitute for what is otherwise required.

constructive bailment   bailment created by law rather than by the parties agreeing.

constructive notice   Information or knowledge of a fact imputed to a person by law because he or she could have discovered the fact by proper diligence or because the situation was such as to put upon such person the duty of inquiry.

contempt   Any action by a person or persons to obstruct a court's work or lessen the dignity of the court—for example, disobeying a court order or an official of the court.

contract   An agreement between two or more people that is enforceable in court.

contract (voidable)   A contract which may be canceled at the option of one party.

contributory negligence   The rule followed in some states that prevents plaintiff from collecting damages if plaintiff's negligence contributed to the injury.

conversion   Action that deprives owners of the property that legally belongs to them.

copyright   The exclusive right of a creator or other copyright owner to reproduce and license (authorize) the reproduction of the following: literature, art, music, drama, sculpture, choreography, motion pictures, computer software, and other audiovisual works including broadcasts of sporting events.

corporate veil   An assumption that all action by the corporation is not that of the owners and therefore not impugned to the corporate officers.

corporation   An organization that is formed under state or federal law and exists, for legal purposes, as a separate being or an "artificial person."

corpus delicti   "Body of the crime" (Latin); facts that prove a crime has been committed.

counteroffer   A response to an offer that modifies one or more of its provisions.

court   The place where judges work; also refers to the judge.

criminal contempt   Acts of disrespect of the courts or its processes.

damages   The remedy sought by the injured party in a civil case.

declaratory relief   Establishes the rights of the parties or expresses the opinion of the court on a question of law without ordering anything to be done.

decree   A judgment by a court as to its decision on the facts of the case; the power of the court derived from its equity jurisdiction.

defamation   The tort of making false written statements about a person to a third person, when those statements subject the former to ridicule or scorn.

defendant   The party who is sued in a lawsuit by the plaintiff.

defraud   To cheat or trick, intentionally misrepresenting an important fact intending for someone to rely on the misrepresentation and thereby suffer damages.

delegated powers   Those powers expressly allocated to the federal government in the constitution.

demeanor   Physical appearance and behavior.

de minimus   Insignificant, minute, or frivolous.

demise   A term used to describe a conveyance of an estate in real property.

demurrer   A method of pleading that asserts that the allegations in the complaint are insufficient to constitute a cause of action.

derogation   Partial taking away of the effectiveness of a law; to repeal partially or abolish a law.

disability (as defined by the Americans with Disabilities Act)   A physical or mental impairment that substantially limits a person's ability to walk, see, hear, perform manual tasks, learn, work, or care for him/herself.

disclaimer   A term in a contract that attempts to avoid all liability on the part of one party.

discrimination   Failing to treat all people equally.

disparate impact   Neutral employment practices that unintentionally results in unequal treatment.

disparate treatment   Intentional discrimination based on race, color, religion, sex, or national origin.

discovery   The process by which each side obtains evidence known to the other side.

dissolution   The termination of business operations, sometimes applied as a penalty for antitrust violations.

diversity of citizenship   Takes place in a federal court when the plaintiff is a resident of one state and the defendant is a resident of another.

divestiture   The act of giving up part of a business operation, sometimes imposed as a penalty for antitrust violations.

doctrine of apparent authority   Authority granted by legal principals to agents to act in their behalf.

due process   The right not to be deprived of life liberty or property without a fair hearing. With respect to licenses and regulations this means that proprietors are entitled to reasonable notice of the grounds for any proposed legal action, an opportunity to prepare a defense, and a hearing.

duty   A responsibility imposed by law, the disregard for which can lead to liability.

effects   Personal property; in hotel law usually refers to a traveler's baggage.

enjoin   Require or command; a court's issuing of an injunction directing a person or persons to do, or more likely, to refrain from doing certain acts; to restrain.

entity   A real being; a separate existence.

equitable estoppel   A legal principle that precludes a person from claiming a right or benefit that might otherwise have existed because that person made a false representation to a person who relied on it to his/her detriment.

equitable relief   A remedy in a court of equity that is just, fair, and right for a particular situation.

equity court   A court having authority over cases involving various rights or matters of equity rather than matters of the written laws or statutes.

eschew   To abstain from or shun as something wrong or distasteful.

escrow   A written instrument deposited with a neutral third party.

essential job functions (as defined by the Americans with Disabilities Act)   The core responsibilities of a job as distinguished from marginal or incidental assignments.

estoppel   A bar to alleging or denying a fact because of one's previous actions or words to the contrary.

estray   Anything out of its normal place.

exclusionary rule   The rule that holds evidence obtained in consequence of a warrantless search is not admissible in court.

ex contractu   "From" or "out of a contract" (Latin).

exemplary damages   The terms exemplary, punitive, and vindictive damages are synonymous and are awarded when the wrong done to plaintiff is aggravated by circumstances of violence, oppression, malice, fraud, or wanton conduct.

ex parte   "With only one side present" (Latin).

feasance   Performing a duty; doing an act.

felony   A crime that has a sentence of more than one year; a serious crime.

forbearance   Refraining from doing something you have a legal right to do.

foreign/natural substance test   A test which holds that the presence of an object natural to a food product does not breach the warranty implied in its sale. (The presence of a foreign object is a breach of warranty.)

forum   "Court" (Latin).

forum non conveniens   "Inconvenient court" (Latin).

franchise   An arrangement in which the owner of a trademark, service mark or copyright licenses others, under specified conditions, to use the mark or copyright in the sale of goods or services.

franchisee   The party who receives the right to use a trademark, service mark, or copyright in connection with the sale of goods or services.

franchisor   The owner of a trademark, service mark, or copyright who has licensed another to use it in connection with the sale of goods or services.

fraud   An intentional untruthful statement made to induce reliance by another person or for the purpose of misleading someone, usually for the other's gain.

full faith and credit   The constitutional requirement that each state must treat as valid, and enforce where appropriate, the laws and court decisions of other states.

goodwill   A favorable reputation producing an expectation of future business.

government agency   A government subdivision, usually appointed by elected officials, responsible for administering particular laws.

gratuities   Something given voluntarily or without obligation.

gravamen   The essence of a complaint.

guest room   The rooms in a hotel assigned to guests for overnight stays.

guest   A person who contracts for an overnight room at a hotel.

hospitality law   Law applicable to hotels, restaurants, travel agents, airlines and places of entertainment.

hotel, inn, motel   Terms used interchangeably to refer to places that provide overnight accommodations to transients.

hung jury   A jury so irreconcilably divided that it cannot reach a verdict.

illegal alien   One who enters this country without the necessary authorization.

impute   To assign to a person or other entity the legal responsibility for the act of another, because of the relationship between the person so made liable and the actor, rather than because of actual participation in or knowledge of the act.

in accordance with   In agreement with or following a specific rule or act.

independent contractor   One who contracts to do work for another, but who maintains control of the method of accomplishing the work. Also, someone hired by another to perform a given task according to methods and procedures that are independent from the control of the hiring party.

infra   "Below," "beneath" (Latin); refers to something appearing subsequently in a text.

infra hospitium   Meaning "within the inn." This doctrine states that under common law hotels were liable as insurers for guests' property on the hotel premises.

injunction A court order forbidding a party to a lawsuit from engaging in specified acts.

innkeepers, hoteliers, hotelkeepers Terms used interchangeably to refer to the operator or manager of a hotel.

innocent misrepresentation An untruthful statement that the speaker believes is accurate.

insurer One who is generally obligated to compensate another for losses.

inter alia "Among other things" (Latin).

interstate commerce Business affecting more than one state, as opposed to business done between two parties in the same state.

in toto "In entirety," "in total" (Latin).

invitee One who comes to an establishment for its business purpose; that is, for a purpose directly or indirectly connected with that business.

ipso facto "By the fact itself," "in and of itself" (Latin).

jurisdiction The authority of a court to hear a case as determined by the legislature.

landmark A court decision that sets a precedent marking a turning point in the interpretation of law.

larceny Stealing of any kind; petit larceny is usually under $1000; grand larceny over $1000.

law Rules enforceable in court requiring people to meet certain standards of conduct.

law court A court that administers justice according to the rules and practice of the common law and statutes but that has no powers dealing with equitable problems.

legislative process The process by which the federal government as well as other units of government adopt laws.

legislators The elected members of the legislature.

legislature A law-making body whose members are elected to office by the citizenry.

lessee A person who leases or rents something from someone; a tenant.

lessor Person who leases or rents land or a building to another person.

liability Culpability; responsibility for a legal wrong obligating the wrongdoer to compensate an injured party for the consequences of the wrongful conduct.

libel Written defamation.

licensee In cases of negligence, one who does not qualify as an invitee but who has been given permission by the owner or occupier to enter or remain on the property. Also, a person who has been granted a license to engage in certain conduct, such as the sale of alcohol.

lien A charge or obligation due or owing against real or personal property for the satisfaction of a debt.

limiting liability statutes Laws that restrict an innkeepers' liability for property loss in exchange for strict statutory compliance by the innkeeper. Also called limiting statutes.

litigants   The parties to a lawsuit.

long-arm statute   A state law that allows the courts of that state to claim jurisdiction over persons or property outside the state.

magistrate   A judge with limited power.

malfeasance   Wrongdoing; sometimes doing an illegal act by a public official.

mediation   The process in which litigants settle their dispute out of court by mutual agreement with the aid of a mediator.

mediator   An objective third party chosen by litigants to facilitate discussion and negotiations between the parties toward settlement of the dispute out of court.

minor   A person under the legal age (usually under 18).

misdemeanor   A criminal offense less than a felony that is usually punishable by less than a year in jail.

misfeasance   Doing something wrong.

Mrs. Murphy's boarding house clause   A stipulation that an establishment that has five or fewer rooms for rent and that is actually occupied by the proprietor is excluded from the Civil Rights Act of 1964.

mutuality of contract   A principle of law that says each side must do something or promise to do something to make a contract binding and valid.

mutual mistake   A mistake made by both parties.

negligence   Breach of a legal duty to act reasonably which is the direct (or proximate) cause of injury to another.

negligence per se   When a defendant has violated a law or ordinance designed to protect the safety of the public.

negligent entrustment   Providing a product for use by another, knowing that person is likely to use the product in a dangerous manner.

nondelegable duty   A duty that cannot be assigned (or delegated) to another.

nonfeasance   Failure to perform a required duty.

novation   The substitution of another party for one of the original parties to a contract with the consent of the remaining party.

nuisance   Anything that annoys or disturbs unreasonably one's right to enjoy one's property, or violates the public health, safety, or decency of others.

offer   A proposal to do or give something in exchange for something else.

offeree   The person to whom the offer is made.

offeror   The person who makes an offer.

ordinance   A law adopted by a local governmental body.

parol   Oral or spoken.

parol evidence rule   What prevents the parties from successfully modifying a complete written contract with evidence of oral agreements made prior to signing the writing.

parties   The individuals in conflict in a lawsuit; also referred to as litigants. A party may be a person, a business or other private organization, or a governmental body.

patron   A customer of a hotel or restaurant, including but not limited to a guest.

per se   "In and of itself," "by itself" (Latin).

per se violations (of antitrust laws)   Activities that are always considered illegal under antitrust legislation.

personal service of process   The direct hand-to-hand delivery of a summons to the person being summoned.

persona non grata   A person not acceptable.

petitioner   One who starts an equity procedure or appeals a case.

plain view doctrine   The observation of objects in plain view, as opposed to a search to find those objects, does not constitute an illegal search.

plaintiff   The party who commences a lawsuit seeking a remedy for an injury or loss that is the responsibility of another party, the defendant.

pleadings   The complaint, the answer and the reply.

preamble   Usually introductory comments explaining why a document was written.

precedent   A court decision that becomes a basis for deciding future cases.

preventive law   An approach to the study of law that has as its objective the prevention of lawsuits.

prima facie   Such evidence as will suffice to establish a cause of action until contradicted and overcome by other evidence.

prima facie liability rule   A rule that states that hotelkeepers are liable for property loss only if the loss occurs through their negligence; if the loss results from some other cause, the innkeeper is not liable.

principal   A person who authorizes an agent to act on his or her behalf, and controls or directs the method used by the agent in performing authorized tasks.

privity   Private or inside knowledge or a close, direct financial relationship.

privity of contract   A contractual relationship that exists between two parties.

probable cause   A reasonable ground for belief in certain alleged facts; facts sufficient for a reasonably intelligent and prudent person to believe the defendant committed a crime or that evidence of a crime is located in the place the police want to search.

probation   A system whereby criminal offenders remain out of jail but are supervised by a probation officer.

procedural law   Rules for carrying out the lawsuit; the way to enforce rights in court such as laws of pleading, evidence, and jurisdiction.

promulgate   publish; to announce officially.

proximate cause   The direct and immediate foreseeable connection between a breach of duty and a resulting injury.

public domain   Belonging to the general public and not subject to patent or trademark protection.

punitive damages   Also called exemplary damages, money awarded to a plaintiff over and above compensatory damages, to punish or make an example of the defendant. They are awarded only in cases where the defendant's wrongful acts are aggravated by violence, malice, or fraud.

pursuant   In accordance with.

rape   Forceful sexual intercourse against the victim's will.

ratification   Confirmation of a previous act.

readily achievable   Easily accomplishable without great difficulty or expense.

reasonable   Not excessive or extreme.

reasonable expectation test   A test which examines whether an object found in food ought to have been anticipated by the consumer. If so, its presence in the food does not constitute a breach of the warranty.

rebuttal presumption   A conclusion that will be drawn unless facts or arguments are raised to counter it.

register   In a hotel, to make oneself known by putting down one's name; book or cards used to keep track of guests.

regulations   Laws adopted by administrative agencies.

res ipsa loquitur   The doctrine (meaning "the thing speaks for itself") which frees the plaintiff from the burden of proving the specific breach of duty committed by the defendant. It applies where an accident would not normally happen without negligence and the instrumentality causing the injury was in defendant's exclusive control.

reinstate   To put a case back on the calendar.

remand   To send back; a higher court might remand a case back to a lower court for action.

remedial statute   A law, the purpose of which is to correct an existing law that is not working or that has caused harm instead of good.

remuneration   To pay for; to be recompensed.

replevin   An action in law to get back personal property in the hands of another person.

reprisal   To take action against.

res judicata   "A thing decided," (Latin); when a case is decided by the courts, the subject of that case is finally decided between the persons involved in the suit. Therefore no further lawsuit on the same subject may be brought by the persons involved.

respondeat superior   The liability of the employer for the acts of its employees. The term means "let the master (employer) answer".

restaurateur   The operator, owner, or manager of a restaurant.

revocation   To end; to withdraw power or authority.

riparian rights   Rights of a person owning land bordering on a body of water.

rule of reason (applied to antitrust laws)   The balancing by the court of the economic benefits and drawbacks in determining the legality of a particular business practice as it affects open competition.

search warrant   An order from a judge commanding a police officer to search a designated place for evidence of criminal activity.

secular day   A nonreligious day.

service mark Any word, name, symbol, or device adopted and used by an organization to identify its services and distinguish them from services provided by others. Compare trademark.

service of process Formally notifying the defendant of the impending lawsuit by the plaintiff.

sexual harassment 1) Quid pro quo sexual harassment: unwelcome sexual advances or requests for sexual favors in return for job benefits. 2) hostile environment sexual harassment: verbal or physical conduct of a sexual nature that creates an intimidating, hostile or offensive work environment.

shepardization A method by which statutes or legal cases are updated to see whether they have been modified or overruled by court decisions or legislature; discovering the present status of a statutory law, court decisions, or administrative decisions.

slander The tort of making defamatory statements orally, as opposed to in writing.

stare decisis Latin for "the matter stands decided;" the principle that courts will follow precedents when they are applicable.

statute A law adopted by the federal or state legislature.

statutory law Law passed by legislatures.

strict liability Also called "absolute liability," the doctrine that imposes all the risks of an ultra-hazardous activity upon those who engage in it.

strict products liability The doctrine that imposes liability on the seller of a defective product without regard to negligence.

subpoena An order by a court for a person to appear in court to testify in a case.

substantive law The basic law of rights and duties as opposed to procedural law; for example, contract law, criminal law, negligence, and liquor liability.

subterfuge Deception; to evade.

summary judgment A procedural device available for prompt and expeditious disposition of a case where there is no genuine issue of fact and the moving party is entitled to win as a matter of law.

summary jury trial Sometimes used in federal courts to save time and money, a trial heard by a jury without witnesses. The jury renders a nonbinding decision and the law requires the parties to negotiate their dispute after the jury rules.

supra "Above" (Latin); in a written work, refers readers to a previous section.

surety One who undertakes or guarantees to pay the debut of another in the event the debt is not paid.

surrogate A judicial officer of limited jurisdiction in probate and in some adoptions; one who acts for another.

tariff A rule or condition of air travel that binds the airline and passengers. Tariffs are developed by airlines and approved by the federal Department of Transportation.

tavern A place where alcoholic beverages are sold to be consumed on the premises.

tenancy A person's right to possess or hold an estate whether by lease or by title.

joint tenancy A single estate in property, real or personal, owned by two or more persons, under one legal paper and having equal rights in everything to share during their lives.

tenancy at suffrage A tenancy whereby one is originally in lawful possession of a lease and subsequently holds over beyond the end of one's expired lease without lawful authority.

tenancy at will A right of possession that arises by an express contract or by implication for an indefinite time.

tenancy by the entirety Ownership by husband and wife.

tenancy in common The possession of property by two or more people wherein each party possesses an undivided interest in the entire property.

time sharing A joint ownership of property that unites in unity of interest or liability; participated in or used by two or more; held or shared in common.

theft of services A crime consisting of the use of services, such as a hotel room or a restaurant meal, with the intent of avoiding payment, and the act of failing to pay.

tort A violation of a legal duty (a wrongful act) by one person that injures another. (Breaches of contractual duties are not considered torts, however.)

tortious Wrongful.

trade usage Practices or modes of dealing generally adhered to in a particular industry, such that an expectation arises that they will be honored in a given transaction.

trademark Any word, name, symbol, or device adopted and used by a manufacturer or merchant to identify its goods and distinguish them from goods sold or manufactured by others (such as McDonald's yellow arches).

trademark infringement Use of another company's business name or logo without permission.

transient A person who seeks a room at an inn, not as a permanent living place, but on a temporary basis.

treble damages The award of three times the loss suffered by an injured plaintiff.

trespasser One who enters a place without permission of the owner or occupier.

under seal A signed document that attests it was made in a most formal manner by a particular insignia attached that imports consideration as a necessary part of a valid contract.

Uniform Commercial Code (UCC) A set of rules designed to simplify and modernize the law governing the sale of goods.

uniform standards Regular; even; applying generally to all equally.

unilateral mistake An error made by one party to a contract as to the terms or performance expected.

unitary rule The rule enforcing the Civil Rights Act when a covered facility is located within a noncovered business: both the covered and noncovered businesses are subject to the Act.

unjust enrichment   An inequitable profit at someone else's expense.

variance   Permission from the local government to deviate from a zoning restriction.

victualler   A keeper of a restaurant.

violation   Not in accordance with.

vitiate   Destroy the legal effect or binding force of something.

void contract   A contract which is unenforceable in court.

will   The expression of a person's wishes concerning disposition of property after death.

withhold   To hold back; refrain.

writ of attachment   The act of taking or seizing property of persons in order to bring them under the control of the court.

zoning   The process by which local governments can restrict the ways property owners can use their land.

INDEX